Adjustment Policies, Poverty, and Unemployment

Adjustment Policies, Poverty, and Unemployment

The IMMPA Framework

Edited by

Pierre-Richard Agénor, Alejandro Izquierdo, and Henning Tarp Jensen

Blackwell
Publishing

© 2007 by Blackwell Publishing Ltd
except for editorial material and organization © 2007 by Pierre-Richard Agénor

BLACKWELL PUBLISHING
350 Main Street, Malden, MA 02148-5020, USA
9600 Garsington Road, Oxford OX4 2DQ, UK
550 Swanston Street, Carlton, Victoria 3053, Australia

The right of Pierre-Richard Agénor, Alejandro Izquierdo, and Henning Tarp Jensen to be identified as
the Authors of the Editorial Material in this Work has been asserted in accordance with the UK
Copyright, Designs, and Patents Act 1988.

First published 2007 by Blackwell Publishing Ltd

1   2007

Library of Congress Cataloging-in-Publication Data

Adjustment policies, poverty, and unemployment: the IMMPA framework/edited by
Pierre-Richard Agénor, Alejandro Izquierdo, and Henning Tarp Jensen.
    p. cm.
  Includes bibliographical references and index.
  ISBN-13: 978-1-4051-3633-4 (hardcover: alk. paper)
  ISBN-10: 1-4051-3633-2 (hardcover: alk. paper)
    1. Developing countries — Economic policy — Econometric models. 2. Structural adjustment
(Economic policy) — Developing countries — Econometric models. 3. Poverty Econometric models —
Developing countries. 4. Unemployment — Developing countries — Econometric models.
5. Macroeconomics — Econometric models. I. Agénor, Pierre — Richard. II. Izquierdo, Alejandro,
1964– III. Jensen, Henning Tarp.

  HC59.7.A735 2006
  331.12'042091724—dc22

                                                                                2006006935

A catalogue record for this title is available from the British Library.

Set in 10/11.5 ACaslon
by Newgen Imaging Systems (P) Ltd, Chennai, India
Printed and bound in the United Kingdom
by TJ International Ltd, Padstow, Cornwall

The publisher's policy is to use permanent paper from mills that operate a sustainable forestry policy, and
which has been manufactured from pulp processed using acid-free and elementary chlorine-free
practices. Furthermore, the publisher ensures that the text paper and cover board used have met
acceptable environmental accreditation standards.

For further information on
Blackwell Publishing, visit our website:
www.blackwellpublishing.com

To those whose daily concern is the plight of
the poor and the unemployed

Contents

6   Stabilization Policy, Poverty, and Unemployment in Brazil   329
Pierre-Richard Agénor, Reynaldo Fernandes,
Eduardo Haddad, and Henning Tarp Jensen

7   Disinflation, Fiscal Sustainability, and Labor Market Adjustment in Turkey   383
Pierre-Richard Agénor, Henning Tarp Jensen,
Mathew Verghis, and Erinç Yeldan

8 Linking Representative Household Models with Household Surveys for Poverty Analysis: A Comparison of Alternative Methodologies 465

Pierre-Richard Agénor, Derek H. C. Chen, and
Michael Grimm

Acknowledgments

This book is the product of several years of research conducted initially at the World Bank. Much of this research was initiated and led by Pierre-Richard Agénor while he was at the World Bank, in very close collaboration with Alejandro Izquierdo. A great deal of thinking continued subsequently in other institutions with which the editors became affiliated (Pierre-Richard Agénor with the University of Manchester and the Centre for Growth and Business Cycle Research, Henning Tarp Jensen with the University of Copenhagen, and Alejandro Izquierdo with the Inter-American Bank).

In addition to our co-authors in this volume, many others contributed to the research agenda on IMMPA. Peter Montiel's insightful comments on preliminary formulations of the IMMPA framework led to many important improvements. Koray Alper, Nihal Bayraktar, Mongi Boughzala, Mamadou Dansokho, Christian Emini, Toussaint Houeninvo, Ousmane Samba Mamadou, Essama Nssah, Emmanuel Pinto Moreira, Issouf Samake, Abdelhalek Touhami, all provided much needed help and feedback at various stages. Without the commitment and involvement of so many capable economists, we would not have been able to produce a volume as dense as this one. But our most important debt is to Zia Qureshi at the World Bank. Without his support, this work would never have come to light. At a time when most of the discussion at the World Bank was about rehashing or recycling existing macroeconomic models and approaches, he encouraged us to take the "hard road" and develop fresh thinking on macroeconomic policy tools for poverty and unemployment analysis. His constant encouragement was an important source of motivation for all of us.

Finally, we dedicate this volume to all the men and women who have chosen to devote their lives to improving the plight of the poor and the unemployed in the developing world. Our hope is that this volume will contribute, if only in a small way, to addressing this most important challenge of our times.

About the Editors

Pierre-Richard Agénor is Hallsworth Professor of International Macroeconomics and Development Economics at the University of Manchester, and co-director of the Centre for Growth and Business Cycle Research. His research interests include international macroeconomics, development economics, and growth theory. He has published widely in leading professional journals and is the author of several best-selling books, including *Development Macroeconomics* (with Peter Montiel) and *The Economics of Adjustment and Growth*.

Alejandro Izquierdo is Senior Economist in the Research Department of the Inter-American Development Bank and a former economist at the World Bank. His current research focuses on international finance and open-economy macroeconomics, with a particular interest in the analysis of sudden stops in capital flows.

Henning Tarp Jensen is Assistant Professor and member of the Development Economics Research Group (DERG) at the Institute of Economics, University of Copenhagen. He has a well-established publication record within the area of computable general equilibrium modeling and a long-standing research interest in low- and middle-income countries, including Mozambique and Vietnam, as well as Argentina, Brazil, Bolivia, Colombia, and Turkey.

Introduction and Overview

Pierre-Richard Agénor, Alejandro Izquierdo, and Henning Tarp Jensen

Unemployment reduction and poverty alleviation remain key objectives of adjustment programs in developing countries. Yet, in many of them progress in achieving these objectives has remained elusive. Part of the problem has no doubt been faulty diagnostic and policy failures, but part of it has been also the lack of quantitative models that are detailed enough to inform policy decisions. Indeed, it is only in recent years that economists in academia and international development institutions have begun to develop new policy tools aimed at better understanding the channels through which adjustment policies affect the poor and the unemployed. These tools have been useful as well for analyzing the dynamic trade-offs that poverty-reduction strategies may entail regarding the sequencing of policy reforms – particularly between short-term stabilization policies and structural measures.

For instance, large budgetary cuts aimed at cutting the budget deficit and reducing inflationary pressures may well fall to a significant extent on transfers to households and other types of social expenditure, thereby worsening the plight of lower-income groups in the short term. At the same time, these groups tend also to be the ones most adversely affected by rapid inflation, credit rationing, and high interest rates. To the extent that fiscal austerity leads to a durable reduction in inflation, greater access to credit by private firms, and lower borrowing rates, the poor may benefit from government spending cuts in the longer run. In designing poverty reduction strategies, it is therefore important to carefully evaluate the net benefits that such trade-offs entail.

Some of the recent attempts to develop applied macro models for poverty and unemployment analysis have met with little success. A key reason is that some of these attempts entailed "recycling" models that were built for a very different purpose. Under the false pretense of "simplicity," some of the fundamental characteristics of developing countries (especially with respect to the labor and credit markets) were ignored, and some of the most important channels through which macroeconomic and structural policies may affect the poor and the unemployed were left out. As a result, they are also unable to address some of the key policy issues (and trade-offs) that policymakers in these countries are faced with – including, as discussed in subsequent chapters, those related to the allocation of public investment. Although simplicity can be a virtue in an environment where technical capacity is limited, it may entail significant costs. Factoring in too much "simplicity" into the transmission process may render policy analysis meaningless and lead to serious and costly mistakes in policy decisions.

This book presents our own line of investigation in this area. In contrast to some, we used what we believe is the correct strategy in building macroeconomic models (whether applied or theoretical in nature), which is to start from a set of questions to address and build a tractable structural framework that does justice to the complexity of the issues involved. Specifically, the book presents a quantitative macroeconomic framework that we and others have developed in recent years for analyzing the impact of policy and exogenous shocks on the labor market, poverty and income distribution in low- and middle-income developing economies. This framework (baptized IMMPA, for Integrated Macroeconomic Model for Poverty Analysis) dwells on the extensive analytical and applied research conducted in academic and policy circles over the past two decades on macroeconomic and structural adjustment issues in these economies.

The approach underlying IMMPA, as discussed in detail in subsequent chapters, differs from existing approaches in several dimensions. It emphasizes, first and foremost, the role of labor market structure in the transmission of shocks to the poor and the unemployed. At the same time, it accounts for the impact of different components of government investment (on infrastructure, education, and health) on the production process and the accumulation of physical and human capital by the private sector. In the complete version of the model, which provides an integrated treatment of the real and financial sides, firms' borrowing needs (for both working capital and physical capital formation) are related to bank lending – often the major external source of finance for firms, in low- and middle-income countries alike. IMMPA therefore allows policy analysts to study not only the impact of structural reforms (such as changes in tariffs or the composition of public expenditure) on poverty and unemployment, but also the effect of short-term stabilization policies (such as a cut in domestic credit or a rise in policy interest rates) and exogenous financial shocks (such as an outflow of private capital or a rise in world interest rates). The detailed treatment of the labor market is particularly important to assess the poverty reduction effects of adjustment programs, because the poor often generate their main source of income from wages, and the latter depend on available employment opportunities. By distinguishing between rural and urban sectors (and accounting for migration dynamics driven by relative wages), the evolution of poverty and unemployment in urban and rural areas can be studied separately. At the same time, the degree of disaggregation is kept to a minimum, thereby avoiding the "black box" nature of large-scale models.

Within the range of tools used by development economists to provide quantitative policy assessments, IMMPA is closer in spirit to dynamic, financial computable general equilibrium (FCGE) models. However, the IMMPA approach differs from existing models in that class in important ways. As indicated earlier, our point of departure is the need to construct a framework that allows analysts to provide appropriate answers to a series of specific policy questions that developing countries are currently facing in designing pro-poor, pro-employment development strategies. For instance, how does resource reallocation induced by structural policy shocks affect the composition of employment and poverty rates? To maximize the impact of debt relief on the poor, should governments increase lump-sum transfers to the poor, or invest in health, education, or infrastructure capital? If so, by how much? Are there trade-offs between stabilization and structural adjustment policies with respect to their impact on employment levels and poverty, and if so within what time frame? What are the implications of these potential trade-offs for the sequencing of policy reforms? Our fundamental premise is that these questions can be addressed in a meaningful manner only if *a*) the complexity of the labor market structure that often prevails in developing countries is properly represented; *b*) linkages between the financial and the real sides that often condition the transmission process of macroeconomic (and structural) policy shocks are properly accounted for; and *c*) the channels through which government expenditure affects the economy are adequately captured.

Thus, the first important distinguishing feature of IMMPA is its detailed specification of the labor market. Although it has long been recognized that the structure of the labor market can have a major impact on the transmission of macroeconomic shocks and adjustment policies to economic activity, employment, and relative prices (see Agénor (1996, 2004c), Bigsten and Horton (1998), and the World Bank (1995)), the treatment of this market in *applied* policy models has focused on only a narrow set of its documented features – such as an economy-wide rigid minimum wage. With a few exceptions (see for instance Maechler and Roland-Host (1995, 1997), and Bodart and Le Dem (1996)), modelers have paid little attention to the macroeconomic implications of alternative sources of labor market segmentation, differences in wage formation across various labor categories, inter-sectoral wage rigidity (as opposed to aggregate wage rigidity), and feedback effects between relative prices and wage decisions by price-setting firms or trade unions. All of these features have important implications for understanding the impact of policy and exogenous shocks on employment and poverty in low- and middle-income developing countries. Labor market segmentation, in particular, tends to restrict labor mobility and can be associated with persistent wage differentials; these, in turn, may prevent the reallocation of resources necessary to cope with external and policy-induced shocks. Because, again, the poor in many countries generate a significant fraction of their income from labor services, modeling these features of the labor market is crucial for understanding the impact of pretty much any type of shocks on poverty and employment in the short, medium, and long run.

The second important feature of IMMPA (in its most complete incarnation) is the treatment of the financial system. In the "archetype" poor economy considered in Chapter 5, for instance, savers have access to only a limited range of financial assets (essentially money and bank deposits, held both at home and abroad) and commercial banks play a predominant role in the financial intermediation process. Specifically, firms are assumed to be unable to issue tradable claims on their assets or future output. IMMPA also dwells on some of the existing literature on FCGE models and the various channels that they have embedded: a portfolio structure that accounts for the impact of interest rates on asset allocation decisions and capital flows (see for instance Robinson (1991), Adam and Bevan (1998), Rosensweig and Taylor (1990), Thissen (1999, 2000), and Thissen and Lensink (2001)), real balance effects on expenditure (as in Easterly (1990)), and linkages between bank credit and the supply side through working capital needs – as in Taylor (1983), Bourguignon, de Melo, and Suwa (1991), Bourguignon, Branson, and de Melo (1992), Lewis (1992), and Fargeix and Sadoulet (1994). In particular, existing full-blown IMMPA models explicitly incorporate the bank lending rate into the effective price of labor faced by urban sector firms, given the need to finance working capital requirements prior to the sale of output. This link turns out to be an important channel through which the real and financial sectors interact. But IMMPA models depart from the specification adopted in many existing studies in two important ways. First, a full *stock* treatment of portfolio decisions is provided, as opposed to the *flow* approach used in several studies. Second, the role of balance sheet (or net worth) effects in the determination of bank lending rates is captured, in addition to funding costs, by explicitly modeling the "finance premium" along the lines of recent research on credit market imperfections and especially collateral requirements, as discussed by Agénor and Aizenman (1998, 1999b), Bernanke, Gertler, and Gilchrist (2000), Kiyotaki and Moore (1997), and Izquierdo (2000). In the application of the framework to Turkey (Chapter 7), liability dollarization (a typical feature of the financial system in many developing countries, as documented for instance by Nicoló, Honohan, and Ize (2005)) is explicitly accounted for, together with the effects of exchange rate depreciation on balance sheets, lending interest rates, and thus the effective price of labor.

Finally, the IMMPA approach differs from existing studies by accounting explicitly for the channels through which various types of public investment outlays affect the economy. Economists and policymakers have long known that different components of public investment can have different effects on output and employment, but the channels through which alternative components operate have seldom been incorporated explicitly in applied macroeconomic models used for development policy analysis. In most IMMPA models, investment in infrastructure (or, rather, the stock of public capital in infrastructure) affects directly the level of production in the private sector – and thus the marginal productivity of primary factors employed in that sector – whereas public investment in education has a direct impact on unskilled workers' decision to acquire skills. In addition, public capital in infrastructure exerts a complementarity effect on private investment, a feature that has been well documented in the empirical literature on private capital formation in developing countries (see Agénor and Montiel (1999) and Agénor (2004b)).

The book is organized as follows. Chapter 1 begins with an analytical overview of models of segmented labor markets in developing countries. After reviewing some of the salient characteristics of the labor market, including institutions and regulations (such as minimum wages and firing costs) that may lead to segmentation, a variety of models of wage formation in the formal, urban sector are discussed. This chapter therefore sets the stage for understanding why the labor market receives so much attention in IMMPA. It also serves to introduce, and provide the analytical foundations of, several of the labor market specifications used in the applied models presented later in the book.

Chapter 2 provides an overview of some of the recent research on the macroeconomics of poverty reduction. It discusses some of the reasons why research on the macroeconomic aspects of poverty may have been "distorted" by either a relative neglect of the issue by macroeconomists (in industrial and developing countries alike), or an excessive focus on the micro/measurement aspects (a key problem for an institution like the World Bank). It then provides a review of the transmission channels of macroeconomic policies to the poor, with a particular focus on the role of the labor market. After presenting a two-household theoretical macro model aimed at analyzing the poverty and employment effects of macroeconomic policies, it identifies various directions for future research. This chapter is thus also important for understanding the motivation for proceeding with full-blown empirical models like IMMPA: because of the complexity of the interactions between poverty, unemployment and other macroeconomic variables, small analytical models quickly reach their limit and recourse to numerical techniques becomes essential for applied policy analysis.

Chapter 3 presents the "real only" version of IMMPA, dubbed Mini-IMMPA, which excludes the financial side. As discussed earlier, at the very core of IMMPA is an emphasis between the real and financial sectors. However, "real only" applications have proved fruitful in countries where the policy focus was limited to labor market issues, or where the data requirements for building a complete IMMPA model were not fully met. Chapter 4 presents an application of Mini-IMMPA to labor market policies in Morocco – a country where unemployment has remained very high and poverty has increased in recent years. The policy issues discussed include a cut in the minimum wage and a reduction in the payroll tax on unskilled labor. This last experiment helps to illustrate the link between labor market policies and tax reform. An important feature of this application is the explicit account of international migration of labor and its implications for labor market adjustment.

Chapter 5 presents a prototype IMMPA model for low-income economies, with the type of financial structure described earlier. In addition, the prototype incorporates an adverse effect of external debt on private investment – the so-called "debt-overhang" effect, which can result from various channels, such as disincentive effects associated with a large external debt.

Chapters 6 and 7 develop IMMPA models for two large middle-income countries, Brazil and Turkey. The Turkey model is the most sophisticated IMMPA framework to date, given notably its detailed treatment of dollarization, and its explicit account of the link between default risk on public debt, credibility, and expectations. Both models are used to analyze the impact of a change in official interest rates, in the case of Turkey with a focus on labor market outcomes, and in the case of Brazil with a focus on both poverty and unemployment. In the Turkey case, we also examine the labor market effects of fiscal adjustment.

Chapter 8 is a methodological contribution. IMMPA models are typically based on a parsimonious production structure (rural, urban informal, urban private formal, and urban public formal) and distinguish between a fairly small number of representative households. As discussed in Chapters 3 and 5, for poverty analysis data from a household survey are classified according to the categories of households identified in the structural component of the model. Following a policy or exogenous shock, real growth rates in per capita consumption and disposable income for all these categories are obtained from the structural model, up to the end of the simulation horizon. These growth rates are applied separately to (disposable) income and consumption expenditure for each household in the survey, giving therefore a new vector of absolute income and consumption levels for each individual in each category or group of households. Poverty and income distribution indicators are then calculated with these new data, after updating the initial poverty lines using the price indexes generated by the structural component of the model, to reflect changes in the price of the consumption basket and the purchasing power of income. Because changes in within-group distribution are ignored, these indicators reflect essentially changes *across* groups. But this approach is open to the criticism that it does not account for heterogeneity among agents *within* groups and introduces only in a partial manner the relevant changes that occur at the macro level as a result of shocks (most importantly, changes in employment) to the micro component of the analysis. At the same time, however, the nature of the practical gains entailed by dropping the assumption of a stable within-group distribution and accounting fully for heterogeneity at the micro level remain a matter of debate. Chapter 8 contributes to this debate by comparing three approaches aimed at linking macro and micro levels to analyze the poverty and distributional effects of policy and exogenous shocks in applied general equilibrium models.

Although IMMPA models have already helped researchers and policymakers address a number of important issues associated with adjustment policies in low- and middle-income countries, a number of methodological issues remain to be addressed. Chapter 9 provides some directions for further research on IMMPA models. Our list is far from exhaustive and dictated in part by our own research interests and involvement in policy analysis. Areas that are identified include the analysis of labor market structure and policies, the macroeconomics of foreign aid, public investment allocation and growth, and methods for linking macroeconomic models and household surveys. We conclude with an emphasis on data collection (particularly on the composition of financial flows) and econometric estimation of key behavioral parameters.

All the chapters that constitute this book were published and circulated as individual papers at different times during the past few years.[1] The first two chapters take a broader view of issues related to labor markets and poverty and were written partly to put in perspective the various IMMPA studies that had been completed. Mini-IMMPA (described in Chapter 3) was developed after the low-income IMMPA prototype was built, and came in large part as a result of the realization that a "real" version of IMMPA could be a useful intermediate step before developing a fully integrated real-financial application. The country applications reflected the special concerns of the authors at the time of their writing – labor market reforms in Morocco, the impact of high interest rates on unemployment and poverty in Brazil, and disinflation, unemployment, and fiscal reform in Turkey.

Inevitably, those reading this book cover to cover will find many elements of repetition across chapters. But our intention was not to produce a "textbook" introduction to general equilibrium modeling for poverty and unemployment analysis. The fact

---

[1] These individual papers (all of which are available on Pierre-Richard Agénor's website at the University of Manchester) also contain detailed listings of equations, variables, and parameters.

that the chapters are very much self-contained is, in our view, a benefit. By allowing different groups of readers to focus on different subsets of chapters, the book's appeal is enhanced. The reader interested only in labor market issues, for instance, should read Chapters 1, 3, and 4; those who want to focus on the poverty effects of fiscal reform should study Chapters 2, 3, and 7. Readers concerned about the impact of monetary policy on the labor market in middle-income countries should focus on Chapters 6 and 7. Finally, readers interested in the methodology of linking macroeconomic models and household surveys (an important research issue in its own right) should focus on Chapters 3 and 8. We have no doubt that other combinations will find their way into the reading lists of teachers and trainers.

Chapter 1

The Analytics of Segmented Labor Markets

Pierre-Richard Agénor

A pervasive feature of urban labor markets in developing countries is segmentation, that is, a situation where observationally identical workers (or workers with similar apparent productive abilities) receive different wages depending on their sector of employment. Workers in one segment of the market may be prevented from having access to jobs in another segment where similar qualifications are required, even if wages are fully flexible. As a result, equilibrium of the labor market is often characterized by job rationing in one segment of the market, despite the fact that workers able and willing to take these jobs at the going wage are unemployed (or underemployed) in another segment. In such conditions, the distinction between voluntary and involuntary unemployment (a much debated issue in the past by economists in industrial countries) lacks analytical meaning.

There is an extensive literature in development economics focusing on labor market segmentation, with early observers (most notably Mazumdar (1983)) emphasizing restrictions on occupational mobility induced by institutional barriers. However, much of this literature is descriptive in nature, and only recently have macroeconomists begun to systematically incorporate various sources of segmentation into formal models, both theoretical and applied. This chapter contributes to this agenda by providing an analytical overview of models of segmented labor markets in developing countries. Section 1.1 reviews some of the salient characteristics of the labor market in these countries, including institutions and regulations (such as minimum wages and firing costs) that may lead to segmentation.[1] Section 1.2 argues that the

---

[1] I do not address in this chapter what determines labor market regulations themselves, in particular the role of political economy considerations. See Saint-Paul (2002) for a discussion of some of the issues involved, albeit in a different context.

Harris-Todaro model, initially developed to explain rural–urban migration, is a useful framework for analyzing the employment and wage implications of imperfect labor mobility between the formal and informal sectors in urban areas. A partial equilibrium analysis of the impact of a demand shock in the formal economy is used to illustrate the predictions of the model, compared to the benchmark case of perfect mobility and full wage flexibility in both sectors. Section 1.3 discusses a variety of formal models of wage formation in the urban sector, including those based on efficiency wages, trade union behavior, bilateral bargaining, job search, and adverse selection. Throughout the discussion, the emphasis is on the determination of skilled wages, although some of these models could be equally relevant to understanding wage formation for the unskilled. Section 1.4 presents a two-sector model with segmented labor markets that emphasizes shirking behavior and the role of unemployment as a "discipline device," as emphasized early on by Shapiro and Stiglitz (1984). The model is used to examine the impact of an increase in the minimum wage on open unemployment. Section 1.5 offers concluding remarks and identifies some perspectives for future research on the economics of segmented labor markets.

1.1   Overview of Labor Markets

In order to set the stage for the rest of the analysis, this section provides an overview of the economic, institutional, and regulatory features of labor markets in developing countries. This review is not exhaustive; rather, it focuses on those characteristics that are most relevant for understanding the sources of labor market segmentation in these countries. The discussion begins by describing some of the most salient structural characteristics of the labor market in a developing-country setting and the composition of employment. Attention then turns to labor market institutions and regulations, in particular minimum wage laws, hiring and firing regulations, nonwage labor costs and unemployment benefit schemes, indexation practices, and wage bargaining mechanisms. Recent evidence on unemployment is also discussed. A key aspect of the analysis is the attention paid to the influence of government regulations regarding pay and other employment conditions – such as regulations related to job security and nonwage labor costs – on different segments of the labor market.

1.1.1   Basic Structure

Labor markets in developing countries differ in important ways from those in industrial countries. Key structural differences are the importance of the agricultural sector in economic activity (which tends to impart a marked seasonal pattern to employment), the importance of self-employment, and irregular work activities. These differences imply that standard labor market concepts used in the industrial world (such as employment and unemployment) do not necessarily have the same meaning and must be interpreted with care.

Development economists typically distinguish three sectors in the labor market in developing countries (see Rosenzweig (1988)). The first is the rural sector, which is often characterized by a large share of self-employed persons and unpaid family workers. The second is the informal urban sector, which emerged largely as a result of accelerated rural–urban migration and the labor surplus that it generated in the cities. This sector is characterized by self-employed individuals with limited skill levels (such as small traders, street vendors, taxi drivers, tailors, carpenters, and bricklayers) or small privately-owned enterprises with limited access to credit markets and producing mainly services and other nontradables. Activities in this sector rely mostly on the provision of labor services by owners and their families, but occasionally also on paid labor without formal employment contracts. Job insecurity is pervasive, underemployment (as a result of low labor productivity) is high, wages are highly flexible, and workers get very few benefits from their employers. Legal minimum wage laws do not apply or are not enforced, and labor unions play a very limited role. Wages are typically much lower than those offered in the formal sector, often below legislated minimum wage levels. In Turkey, for instance, according to calculations made by Tansel (2000, pp. 15–16) on the basis of household survey data, male workers in the formal sector earn on average 35 percent more than their counterparts in the informal sector; for women, the differential is about 80 percent. Similar figures are suggested by Tunali (2003). However, surveys conducted in several other countries also suggest that earnings of some categories of self-employed workers in the informal sector compare favorably with wage earners in the formal sector, often being significantly higher than the minimum wage (see below).

The third segment of the labor market is the formal urban sector, consisting of medium and large enterprises (including state-owned firms) producing both tradable and nontradable goods, and using workers with a wide range of skills. Firms tend to hire workers (at least the more qualified ones) on the basis of formal contracts. Workers and employers are subject to various labor market regulations; employers, in particular, must provide a variety of benefits (such as pension, health insurance, and relative job security) to their workers.[2] Labor unions and productivity considerations often play an important role in the determination of wages, and legal minimum wage laws exist – albeit enforced with varying intensity across professional occupations and across countries.

Since the concept of the informal sector first appeared in the literature (apparently in a report on Kenya prepared by the International Labor Organization in the early 1970s), a variety of criteria have been employed in the development literature to measure it. These criteria include establishment size, type of employment (notably the ratio of self-employed workers to the labor force as a whole), technological or capital level of firms, income level and legal status (or the degree of coverage under existing labor regulations). In practice, some of these criteria have tended to overlap. Nowadays, the notion of informality is being used to refer to conditions under which

---

[2]In some countries, the formal sector is not entirely confined to urban areas; wage earners bound by explicit contracts may also be employed in agriculture.

transactions are carried out, that is, to the fact that the activities being encompassed are unregulated.[3]

Recent estimates suggest that the size of the informal sector in developing countries is about 40 percent of official GDP on average (see Schneider (2005)). Across countries, the relative size of the informal sector varies as a result of differences in the costs of formality, which can be divided into costs of accessing the formal sector (such as those incurred to register a small firm) and costs of remaining in the formal sector, such as taxes, compliance with labor regulations – nonwage benefits, social security, and firing compensation – and bureaucratic requirements (see Braun and Loayza (1994), Loayza (1994), Dessy and Pallage (2003), and Ihrig and Moe (2004)). A further distinction between an "easy-entry" informal sector and an "upper-tier" informal sector was proposed by Fields (1990) to account for the heterogeneity of informal activities. Earnings in some of the upper-tier activities (which involve small-scale enterprises with a higher degree of capital intensity and a greater use of educated labor) can be significantly higher than in the lower-tier sector and may compare very favorably with some occupations in the formal sector.[4] Earnings and employment may also be more pro-cyclical. Workers may, however, face barriers to entry in the upper-tier segment of the informal sector, as a result, for instance, of financial capital requirements.

1.1.2   Composition of Employment

In a large number of developing countries, agriculture still employs a large share of the labor force in rural areas, whereas the "modern" (or urban) sector – despite a sharp expansion in some cases – continues to provide limited employment opportunities. The share of informal sector employment in total urban employment is sizable in many developing countries – particularly in Latin America, the Middle East, Sub-Saharan Africa, and some parts of Asia – and may vary from anywhere between 30 and 70 percent (see International Labor Organization (2005)). Most estimates are derived from labor force surveys and, less frequently, general censuses of population. The definition of the informal sector used in arriving at these estimates is generally based on firm size; firms employing five or fewer workers are often classified as informal. Workers in certain occupational categories – typically, self-employed workers (excluding professionals or those with higher levels of education) and unpaid family workers – are also generally classified as informal.[5] Indeed, a large proportion of employment in nonagricultural sectors is found in micro enterprises and small firms.

---

[3] See Charmes (1990), Schneider and Enste (2000), and Blunch et al. (2001) for a discussion of changes over time in the definition of the informal sector. The role of labor market legislation in the distinction between formal and informal labor markets was emphasized in early contributions by Mazumdar (1983) and Kannappan (1985).

[4] See for instance Yamada (1996) for the case of Peru. Blunch et al. (2001) also proposed a disaggregation of the informal sector between nonwage employment (which comprises the self-employed and those working in family businesses) and wage employment (which includes both regular and casual workers).

[5] For instance, PREALC (the International Labor Organization's regional program for employment for Latin America) has adopted the following definition: "The informal labor market consists of those

As a result, formal sector firms account for only a small fraction of all enterprises in manufacturing, and formal sector employment is often limited to the public sector. Even in upper middle-income developing countries, the informal sector continues to account for a sizable part of total urban employment.

Because of the importance of the rural and urban informal sectors, the proportion of wage earners in total employment in developing countries tends to be much lower than in the industrial world, although large variations exist across countries and regions. Formal wage employment tends to be particularly low in Sub-Saharan Africa. In many developing countries, public sector employment accounts for a large share of wage employment and the formal sector workforce.

1.1.3   Public Sector Pay and Employment

The public sector (including both employment in parastatal enterprises and regular government services) is often the dominant employer of educated labor. At the same time, the distribution of public sector employment across different levels of government (central and local) and public enterprises varies substantially across countries and regions. In part, this is related to the degree of centralization of power and the degree of government involvement in "strategic" industries. Employment in the public sector tends to increase not only in response to growing demand for public services (such as education and health) but also partly in response to adverse conditions in private labor markets – sometimes giving governments the role of "employer of last resort." This counter-cyclical role, however, may lead to fiscal instability, because recessions also hamper the ability of the government to raise resources.

Public sector employment may provide a variety of benefits that help attract workers: relative job security and sometimes less than complete enforcement of performance standards, nonwage entitlements (such as subsidized or free housing), enhanced social status, and opportunities for moonlighting and rent-earning offered by some government positions (see Gelb, Knight, and Sabot (1991)). However, a high level of government employment may be the result of the need to provide (partial) insurance against undiversifiable external risk faced by the domestic economy, rather than the need to generate and redistribute rents. There is indeed some evidence suggesting that countries that are greatly exposed to external risk have also higher levels of public employment (see Rodrik (2000)). "Overemployment" in government, however, often translates into low public sector wages and salaries; to the extent that these wages and salaries are low in comparison with private sector salaries, attracting and retaining qualified workers may prove difficult.

In principle, relatively high public sector wages can be justified in the presence of adverse selection and moral hazard problems. They may help attract more qualified or more productive workers, thereby mitigating some of the potentially adverse effects associated with public sector employment (such as the incentive to engage in rent-seeking activities) noted earlier. At the same time, however, the

---

persons who develop activities for self-employment, those who work in small firms and those who provide low-productivity personal services."

combination of attractive public sector jobs and government hiring policies may be an important source of "wait" unemployment, particularly among the skilled. Public sector employment may also be inefficient and unproductive, and the cost in terms of forgone income may be high.

Government wage and employment decisions are often determined more by political considerations than conventional economic considerations (see Nelson (1994)). When faced with budgetary pressures, it is easier politically for governments to cut investment outlays or maintenance expenditure than to fire public sector workers. An unstable political climate may lead to increases in employment or higher wages to attract followers (prior to elections, in participatory democracies) or to retain them (by rewarding key followers). Because the government's primary constituency is often the urban labor force (of which it employs a large share), it tends to legislate in its favor – for instance, by raising the minimum wage at a faster rate than food prices or the overall cost-of-living index.

Government pay and employment policies affect private labor markets through a variety of channels. Public sector employment may have a limited effect on market wages when labor is hired at wages below market rates (possibly in exchange for job security). At the same time, however, wage increases in the public sector may exert a "leadership effect" on wage setting in the private sector. In countries like Morocco and Turkey, for instance, this signaling role seems to be quite pronounced; wage increases in the regulated manufacturing sector appear to be highly correlated with wage movements in the public sector (see Chapter 4 and Tunali (2003)).

In practice, data on public–private pay differentials are often difficult to interpret, for a variety of reasons (see Stevenson (1992)). In addition to base pay, compensation packages often include bonuses and nonwage compensation (such as subsidized or free housing, insurance, and other benefits, as noted earlier), which are normally not captured by the wage data. Because of the difficulties involved in controlling for differences in education and the composition of skills, most studies do not weight wages by skill categories – making comparisons of average wages difficult to interpret. In some countries, there are also important differences between the compensation packages of government employees and those of workers in state enterprises or local government.

1.1.4   Labor Market Institutions and Regulations

Allocation of the work force and wage formation depend critically on labor market institutions and government regulations. As indicated earlier, trade union activity and minimum wage laws may represent important sources of labor market segmentation. These and other institutional features of the labor market – such as wage indexation and labor tenure laws – have been blamed for pushing labor costs above market-determined levels, for contributing to large differentials between wages and the marginal product of labor (particularly in urban areas), and for limiting the ability of firms to adjust production patterns to changes in relative prices, factor supply, and aggregate demand conditions.

In what follows the main features of labor market institutions and regulations in developing countries are briefly described. I begin by examining minimum wage laws, and then consider hiring and firing regulations, nonwage labor costs and unemployment benefits, indexation practices, and bargaining structures. The next sections will analyze in the context of formal models the implications of several of these features for the functioning of the labor market and the degree of segmentation.

Minimum Wage Laws

The effects of minimum wages on the labor market depend on both the degree to which the legislation is enforced and the frequency at which they are adjusted (the latter often at the government's discretion). In most developing countries, enforcement of minimum wage laws is typically lax, often more so in public sector enterprises (compared to private enterprises), as a result of "soft" budget constraints or implicit government guarantees. In an inflationary environment, the real minimum wage can fall to very low levels if it is adjusted only infrequently. In such conditions, the minimum wage may not operate as a binding constraint. In the presence of lax enforcement, excessively high minimum wages (relative to the marginal product of labor) provide incentives to evade the law and operate partly illegally, or to shift activities entirely to the informal economy – in a manner very similar to a tightening of job security provisions, as discussed later. They may also lead firms to rely more on casual labor, with possibly adverse effects on productivity.

The lack of effectiveness of minimum wage policies can be inferred from data on real minimum wages (compared to average wages) and the actual proportion of workers earning the minimum wage or above. In many countries, a substantial number of workers (even in large-scale enterprises) still earn less than the minimum wage, and minimum wages can be up to less than half the average wage. One reason for this in some cases is that high unemployment has led governments to allow employers some flexibility in hiring workers on a temporary and apprenticeship basis at wages below the minimum rate. Nevertheless, there is some evidence suggesting that the role of minimum wages can be significant. In several countries, private firms in the regulated sector pay wages near or above the minimum, suggesting that the minimum wage may play the role of a "wage floor" in the formal sector labor market. There is also evidence suggesting that wages of unskilled workers in the formal sector tend to shift concomitantly with changes in the minimum wage. Thus, although minimum wages are not binding in a strict sense, changes in minimum wages may still have a significant causal effect on average wages.

Declines in real minimum wages may be large enough to erode over time the distortions created by excessively high nominal wage levels in the first place. However, despite an erosion in its real value, the minimum wage measured in proportion to the average unskilled labor wage – a more relevant indicator of the effect of minimum wages on the labor market – may not change to a significant degree. Bell (1997), for instance, estimated the impact of minimum wages on the demand for skilled and unskilled labor in the formal manufacturing sector in Mexico and Colombia. At the end of the 1980s, the minimum wage stood at just 31 percent of the average unskilled manufacturing wage in Mexico, and roughly 53 percent of the average unskilled wage in Colombia. Bell found substantial adverse employment effects of minimum wages in Colombia, with significantly larger effects on unskilled employment. She attributed the lack of evidence on negative employment effects in the case of Mexico to the relationship between the legally imposed minimum wage and the distribution of average unskilled wages across firms. She found that the minimum wage is very far to the left in the Mexico distribution and much closer to the mean in the Colombia distribution. Thus, minimum wages appeared ineffective in the formal manufacturing sector in Mexico and effective in Colombia.[6]

Other evidence on the impact of minimum wages on unemployment is also mixed. Lustig and McLeod (1997) examined (using cross-section regression techniques) the effect of changes in statutory minimum wages on unemployment in a group of 22 developing countries, controlling at the same time for various other variables – such as per capita income growth, inflation, changes in the terms of trade, and the share of the labor force in agriculture.[7] They found that high minimum wages tend to be associated with high unemployment: a 10 percent increase in real minimum wages raises unemployment by 0.5 to 1 percentage point. They attribute this effect to the negative impact of the wage increase on the demand for unskilled labor. In one of the few studies (in addition to Bell (1997)) that uses micro-level data to examine the impact of minimum wages on employment in developing countries, Alatas and Cameron (2003) examined the experience of the Philippines during the period 1990–6. They found some evidence of a negative employment effect of higher minimum wages for small domestic firms, but no effect for large firms, either domestic or foreign. One reason for this outcome may be that small firms tend to be more labor intensive, and therefore tend to adjust faster to changes in labor costs.

Hiring and Firing Regulations

Legislation on hiring, firing and regulation of working time is aimed at providing protection to workers engaged in a contractual employment relationship. Although the exact nature of regulations varies considerably across countries, many developing nations provide extensive employment protection to workers in the formal sector, such as restrictions on firms' ability to lay off workers without "proper" justification or reason (the definition of "proper" sometimes being very narrow and subject to false claims), the requirement of long notification periods prior to dismissal, generous severance arrangements that must be borne by firms, and administrative procedures that delay or prevent layoffs and plant closures. In some countries, employers must pay several months' wages as a minimum severance pay to workers dismissed with "just cause" (major misconduct). In the absence of "just cause," the severance payment often rises (by a multiple of the daily or monthly wage) for each year on the job. In others, if a worker quits voluntarily or is dismissed with "just cause," the employer

---

[6] Of course, it is also possible that in Mexico changes in the minimum wage affected other sectors.

[7] The sample includes 5 Asian (India, Indonesia, the Philippines, Sri Lanka, and Thailand), 13 Latin American (Argentina, Bolivia, Brazil, Colombia, Costa Rica, Guatemala, Honduras, Mexico, Panama, Paraguay, Peru, Uruguay, and Venezuela), and 4 African (Ghana, Mauritius, Morocco, and Tunisia) countries.

must pay compensation equivalent to a fraction of the worker's monthly salary per year of service. If dismissal is deemed "without just cause," there can be an additional severance payment of several months' salary if the employee has less than a certain number of years of service, or one month's salary per year of service (up to a maximum) if the employee has more than the minimum number of years of service.[8]

Empirical studies of the impact of job security regulations on employment in developing countries are scarce. Restrictions on layoffs in the formal sector often make firing redundant (or unproductive) workers difficult. Although in practice enforcement is not uniform across sectors and skill categories, regulating the workplace with severe restrictions on firing and generous severance pay may have a perverse effect on hiring: more stringent job security provisions may reduce hiring rates (by increasing the fear of incurring expensive dismissal costs in the future) and raise the duration of unemployment. Job protection may therefore reduce both job destruction and creation, as argued by Bertola (1990). By implication, the net impact of firing costs on unemployment is (in theory at least) ambiguous. For instance, Hopenhayn and Rogerson (1993) examined the consequences of job protection in a general equilibrium framework in which firms are subject to idiosyncratic productivity shocks, and a continuum of identical consumers choose their labor supply and consumption. In their model, a rise in firing costs (which are redistributed to consumers in the form of lump-sum transfers) corresponds to a distortion that decreases the returns of labor, leading to a fall in labor supply and eventually to a drop in employment. The model predicts that more stringent employment protection has an ambiguous impact on the level of overall employment, because it reduces both job creation and destruction.

Recent evidence on the impact of job security provisions on employment in developing countries is rather mixed.[9] In Latin America, for instance, job turnover rates (that is, the sum of job creation and destruction rates) appear to be quite high in the manufacturing sector, ranging from 15 to 30 percent depending on the country (Inter-American Development Bank (2003, p. 48)). Put differently, up to about one in every three jobs is created or destroyed in any given year. However, at the same time, changes in the net employment rate (the difference between job creation and destruction rates) tend to be significantly smaller than total job turnover.[10] This evidence is thus partly consistent with the theoretical predictions highlighted earlier. Nevertheless, Heckman and Pagés (2000) estimated that, in Latin America,

---

[8] See Cox Edwards (1997) and Heckman and Pagés (2000) for data on redundancy payments (measured in terms of days' salary for each year worked) that employers are required to make in Latin America, and Betcherman and Ogawa (2001) for some broader evidence.

[9] Addison and Teixeira (2001) surveyed the literature on the effects of job security provisions on employment and unemployment rates in industrial countries and found it to be largely inconclusive. In their own research on severance pay (see Addison and Teixeira (2003)), they found some evidence supporting the view that severance pay tends to increase overall unemployment, but much weaker support for other possible effects on long-term unemployment, the employment–population ratio, or the labor force participation rate.

[10] High turnover rates appear to characterize only workers with low human capital and low wages.

a 10-percentage-point increase in social security contributions reduces the overall employment-to-population rate by 1.7 percentage points.

The evidence also suggests that, in some countries, high firing costs for permanent employees increased firms' incentives to hire workers on temporary contracts. In India, for instance, legislation was passed in the mid-1970s making it illegal for a firm with more than 100 employees to lay off workers without the authorization of the state governor. Regulations such as these encouraged the use of casual labor and subcontracting (see Besley and Burgess (2004)). In Zimbabwe, job security regulations had an equally adverse effect on the demand for labor in the manufacturing sector (Fallon and Lucas (1993)). Montenegro and Pagés (2004) also found that in Chile job security provisions are nonneutral across age and skill groups. They argued that these provisions reduced youth and unskilled employment rates in total employment. Kugler (2004) studied the impact on open unemployment of the Colombian labor market reform of 1990, which reduced severance payments, widened the definition of "just cause" for dismissals, extended the use of temporary contracts, and eased advance notice requirements for mass layoffs. The reform thus substantially lowered firing costs for firms in the formal sector, although it had little effect on informal sector firms (which did not comply with the legislation in the first place). Using household survey data, and informal sector firms as a "control" group, she estimated that the reform contributed to 10 percent of the subsequent reduction in unemployment.

Botero et al. (2004) found that Latin America and the Caribbean is the region with the highest job security index in the world. The index that they compiled is a normalized sum of the following four dimensions of protection: *a*) whether employment at will is allowed and whether termination for economic reasons is considered a fair cause for dismissal; *b*) procedures that an employer must follow and approvals it must seek prior to individual or collective dismissals; *c*) advance notice and severance payments; and *d*) whether job security is explicitly recognized in a country's constitution. Heckman and Pagés (2000) provide an alternative measure of job security that takes into account the monetary transfer that by law a firm has to pay to a worker on dismissal. Their measure includes advance notice, severance pay, and mandatory contributions to individual savings accounts. In line with Botero et al. (2004), they found that the average cost of job security in Latin America is significantly higher (by a factor of three) than in developed countries. Both studies also find that the degree of job security is inversely related to income levels, which is itself related to the presence of a state-run unemployment insurance system. Thus, in poorer countries where a public unemployment insurance scheme does not exist, mandatory job security provisions appear to be used to provide a form of partial insurance against adverse conditions in the job market.

Other studies, however, did not prove conclusive. In a study on Brazil, for instance, Paes de Barros and Corseuil (2001) found no evidence of a statistically significant effect of job security provisions on employment. Downes et al. (2003) found that labor market regulations in English-speaking Caribbean countries had only a limited impact on employment creation; output growth was the key factor. Thus, whether or not reducing firing costs would help to reduce unemployment by enhancing labor market flexibility (through increased worker turnover into and out of the pool of the unemployed), as advocated by some, is an open question.

Nonwage Labor Costs and Unemployment Benefits

Nonwage labor costs include social security contributions and nonwage benefits, such as housing, health care, pensions, subsidized transportation and meals, and family allowances. Their importance varies substantially across countries and there is little systematic evidence of their effect on labor market outcomes in developing countries. In one of the few studies available, Heckman and Pagés (2000) found that, in Latin America, part of the cost of nonwage benefits (namely, social security contributions, and mandatory benefits such as paid vacation, maternity leave, health benefits, pensions, and work insurance) is passed on to workers in the form of lower wages.

Unemployment benefit schemes exist in only a small number of developing countries.[11] Financing of these schemes is usually shared between employers and employees.[12] The relative contribution of employers is often in the form of a flat payroll tax and is usually substantially higher than employees' contributions. Although net replacement rates (benefits after taxes as a percentage of previous net earnings) are often the same between industrial and developing countries, there are several important differences in the design of these schemes. In particular, the potential duration of benefits is generally shorter in schemes implemented in developing countries, waiting periods are more likely, and government workers are rarely covered.

It has been argued that unemployment insurance may act as a disincentive to search for (or accept) employment, and that they may encourage individuals to enter the labor force for the sole purpose of collecting unemployment benefits. By raising incentives to extend job search (or equivalently by reducing the intensity of job search effort), an overly generous unemployment insurance may therefore increase both the level and duration of unemployment. In addition, unemployment insurance schemes, to the extent that they benefit low-skilled workers more, may serve as an income insurance substitute for human capital acquisition (see Dellas (1997)). By reducing incentives to accumulate human capital, they may lead to an increased supply of low-skilled workers and to higher unemployment among them. Moreover, by reducing precautionary savings, an adverse and possibly permanent growth effect may also result.

However, unemployment insurance may also have positive effects by encouraging long-term labor force participation and favoring regular, as opposed to marginal or casual, employment (Atkinson and Micklewright (1991)). There is consequently an "optimal" level of unemployment insurance, as argued by Hopenhayn and Nicolini (1997) and Acemoglu and Shimer (1999), which balances positive and negative effects.[13] Because of limited data on variables such as the duration of unemployment benefits in developing countries, it has proved difficult to test alternative views on

---

[11] As noted earlier, the absence of an unemployment benefit scheme is often viewed as a key reason why severance pay upon dismissal can be quite generous.

[12] See Inter-American Development Bank (2003, Chapter 8) for a review of current features of unemployment benefit systems in Latin America and the Caribbean.

[13] In contrast to Hopenhayn and Nicolini (1997) and Acemoglu and Shimer (1999), Young (2004) found that unemployment insurance may have unambiguously negative output and welfare effects. The key reason in his model (which treats both interest rates and capital accumulation as endogenous, unlike

these issues. The elasticity of unemployment with respect to replacement rates may be relatively low; but whether high unemployment benefits tend to increase open unemployment remains a largely unresolved issue.

Indexation Practices

The traditional economic rationale for indexation of wages to prices is that a high degree of real wage rigidity helps to insulate output and employment from monetary (aggregate demand) shocks, although not from real (supply) shocks.[14] However, a high degree of wage indexing in specific production sectors (such as the nontradables sector) may also distort the signaling effect of policy-induced changes in relative prices (such as a nominal devaluation) and may hamper the reallocation of resources. In addition, wage contracts indexed on *past* inflation have been blamed for creating sticky inflationary expectations and causing inflation persistence and, by reducing the welfare losses caused by price instability, for weakening the will of governments to fight inflation (Simonsen (1983)). However, as discussed by Agénor (1996, 1998), *forward-looking* wage contracts, based on (expected) *future* inflation, may speed up disinflation instead of hampering it.

Indexation clauses usually aim at allowing for the adjustment of wages not only for inflation but also productivity changes. In practice, indexation procedures differ among countries and over time in three main respects: the interval between wage adjustments; the degree of indexation to past or future inflation; and the nature of adjustments for productivity changes. In some countries, the law permits productivity adjustments to be negotiated freely between workers and employers; in others, adjustments are specified by the government. In some high-inflation countries in the 1980s, the frequency of wage adjustments tended to increase with the rate of inflation; the frequency itself was viewed as one of the structural elements in the inflationary process.[15] Indeed, in chronic-inflation countries, inflationary shocks tended to increase the frequency of adjustment in nominal wages, as workers attempted to prevent an erosion in their real wages – thereby leading to a shortening of wage contracts and/or periods over which adjustments to past inflation are specified. In some cases, the degree of indexation to inflation was a function of the wage level, with overindexation at certain levels and underindexation at others.

In practice, real wage rigidity induced by indexation in some sectors often coexists with full wage flexibility in others. The consequence is thus labor market segmentation – in a manner consistent with the "stylized" description of the labor market provided earlier, if differences in wage formation occur along the lines of the formal–informal sector dichotomy. In recent years, many developing countries

---

the previous studies) is that by affecting labor supply, unemployment insurance also affects the marginal productivity of capital and the precautionary demand for savings.

[14]Carmichael, Fahrer, and Hawkins (1985) provided a detailed discussion of wage indexation rules in an open-economy context; see also van Gompel (1994). Most of the analytical literature focuses on the role of *ex ante* indexation. In practice, wage indexation is often *ex post*, with current wages adjusting to past changes in prices. Fischer (1988) examined the role of *ex post* wage indexation in the conduct of disinflation programs. See Agénor (1996) for a further discussion.

[15]See Dornbusch, Sturzenegger, and Wolf (1990), and Parkin (1991).

have enacted legislation aimed at either curbing wage indexation or at changing the mechanisms through which wages are indexed. Some countries (particularly in Latin America) have prohibited all types of indexation, including wage and pension indexation. This measure has helped to reduce inflation both directly and indirectly (by lowering pressure on public finances) and increase the degree of wage flexibility.

Bargaining Structures and Trade Unions

Wage bargaining mechanisms vary considerably across developing countries. In some cases, collective bargaining is fairly centralized and involves substantial government intervention at both the sectoral and national levels. Such intervention thus has a direct effect on the structure of wages in the formal sector and may be a key source of segmentation.

Another source of labor market segmentation is related to the presence of trade unions, which play an essential role in collective bargaining mechanisms in many developing countries. A common strategy of unions – in Latin America in particular, but also in other regions – has been to seek ties with the state and political parties to obtain legislated protections (for instance, regarding employment conditions) and redistributive policies (such as severance payments, or high minimum wages). Rent-seeking behavior by overly politicized trade unions implies that bargaining systems may be subject to heavy government involvement (see O'Connell (1999) for Latin America). Another implication is that the degree of unionization is not a good indicator for assessing the potential influence of trade unions in the bargaining process and wage formation.[16] At the same time, if trade union movements are not very centralized, organizing collective labor action becomes more difficult (see Nelson (1994)).

Much research has aimed at understanding the implications of centralization in bargaining mechanisms on wage formation. Studies by Calmfors (1993), Moene, Wallenstein, and Hoel (1993), and Flanagan (1999) have argued that the relationship between the degree of centralization in wage bargaining – defined as the extent to which unions and employers cooperate in wage negotiations – and wage pressures may actually have an inverted U-shape, rather than being monotonic. Wage push is limited when bargaining is highly centralized (conducted at the union level) and highly decentralized – when it takes place at the level of individual firms. The highest degree of influence on wage formation would thus tend to occur in countries where centralization is in the intermediate range, that is, at the industry level.

Various types of externalities can explain why centralized bargaining is likely to produce lower aggregate real wages and higher employment. The basic idea is that a high degree of cooperation between unions and employers implies that the effects on others of a wage increase in one part of the economy is internalized, thereby lowering the marginal benefit of an increase in wages. In particular, if unions are averse to inflation, they will tend to moderate their wage demands in order to induce the central bank to stick to a low inflation target.

---

[16] A low degree of unionization is often viewed as an indication that trade unions may be more relevant in affecting working conditions and enforcing labor regulations than in influencing wage negotiations.

Decentralized bargaining systems, for their part, produce real wage moderation because of the restraint imposed by competitive forces – although moderation may occur at the cost of increased wage dispersion. Indeed, Pencavel (1997) argued that decentralized bargaining tempers the union's ability to impose across-the-board increases in wages, thereby keeping labor compensation more in line with productivity of workers in a competitive market.

Thus, decentralizing collective bargaining may increase labor market flexibility (and reduce the degree of segmentation) by more closely linking contract provisions to the conditions of the firm. Similarly, increasing collective autonomy may increase flexibility if it facilitates direct negotiations and helps the parties to internalize the costs and benefits of their negotiations. With intermediate centralization, neither internalization effects nor competitive forces are sufficiently strong to restrain unions' incentives to demand higher wages.

However, a higher degree of centralization may not always reduce wage pressures. Cukierman and Lippi (1999), in particular, argued that an increase in the degree of centralization of wage bargaining (as measured by a fall in the number of trade unions in the economy) triggers two opposite effects on real wages. On the one hand, the reduction in the number of unions tends to reduce the degree of effective competition among unions; this competition effect tends to raise real wages. On the other, the fall in the number of unions strengthens the moderating influence of inflationary fears on the real wage demands of each union. This strategic effect tends to lower wages. Consequently, the net effect is ambiguous.[17]

In practice, it is not always easy to classify wage bargaining systems into completely centralized or decentralized systems. In addition, as noted earlier, the degree of unionization is a highly imperfect measure of the influence of trade unions on wage formation and the labor market. Trade unions in certain "strategic" sectors or industries may exert considerable influence on wage formation and working conditions at the national level, even if overall union membership is a low proportion of the work force. Indeed, although union density is low in some countries, collective bargaining agreements may be extended to the nonunionized workers within individual firms.

Empirical evidence suggests that there is great diversity in the impact of unions on real wages in developing countries. Nelson (1994) argued that in Latin America unions have caused wages to rise above the opportunity cost of labor through a combination of union pressure, minimum wage legislation, and wage policies in the public sector. Other studies have attempted to estimate directly the bargaining strength of organized labor, as reflected in the union–nonunion wage differential. Park (1991), for instance, estimated that blue-collar workers in the unionized manufacturing sector in Korea are paid on average only 4 percent more than their counterparts in the nonunionized sector. By contrast, Panagides and Patrinos (1994) estimated the union–nonunion wage differential in Mexico to be about 10.4 percent, which would suggest significant bargaining strength on their part.

---

[17] As noted by Groth and Johansson (2004), the degree of centralization in wage bargaining may also affect contract negotiation costs, which may in turn lead to temporary wage rigidity. However, this argument explains nominal, not real, wage rigidity.

However, a significant premium is not necessarily a direct reflection of the ability of unions to impose rent sharing on firms through their bargaining power (rents that workers could not obtain on their own). If union workers are more productive than their nonunion counterparts (as a result of reduced shirking prompted by greater job security, for instance), the productivity differential between the two categories of labor may be large enough to offset the union–nonunion wage differential. Unions may also extract rents that are distributed to members through higher wages by either reducing turnover and negotiation costs. As noted by Booth and Chatterji (1998), for instance, unions can also have an indirect effect on the wage premium if they promote training. Indeed, Blunch and Verner (2004) found evidence of a union premium related to training in Ghana. In general, however, given the paucity of reliable panel data sets in developing countries, it is difficult to test rigorously these different effects – particularly the view that union workers may be significantly more productive than nonunion workers.

1.1.5   Unemployment

Published data on unemployment in developing countries are not very reliable and often incomplete. They usually include unemployed workers looking for jobs in the formal sector, but not underemployed workers in the informal and rural sectors (what is known as "disguised" unemployment), thereby understating the effective excess supply of labor. They also do not account for the fact that job seekers may be employed part of the time in the informal sector. Very few countries provide information on the duration of unemployment. Nevertheless, available data suggest that open unemployment is often concentrated in urban areas and is mostly associated with wage employment, and that underemployment is far more pervasive than open unemployment. In some countries, open and disguised unemployment combined amount to as much as 70 percent in proportion of the labor force.

In recent years several regions have experienced a sharp increase in open unemployment, most particularly the Middle East and North Africa (MENA), and Latin America. In MENA the population nearly quadrupled during the second half of the past century. At the same time, as noted by the World Bank (2004), although output grew at healthy rates during the 1970s, it slowed down (particularly in the oil-exporting countries) during the 1980s and the 1990s. Employment growth therefore failed to keep pace with the expansion of the labor force, and the region recorded some of the highest unemployment rates among developing regions. In Latin America, during the 1990s, unemployment rates increased in most countries. In some countries, as noted by Saavedra (2003) and Duryea, Jaramillo, and Pagés-Serra (2003), higher unemployment was caused by falling employment rates. In others, the increase in unemployment resulted from a substantial rise in participation rates that were not fully absorbed by increases in employment. Duryea and Székely (2000) also emphasized changes in labor supply (which began in the 1960s and will persist well into the next decades for some countries) as a factor underlying the increase in unemployment, particularly among the young, in Latin America. At the same time, improvements in educational attainments in the region have been slow (at about one year per decade during the past 30 years), which translated into an increase in wage inequality.[18]

The composition of unemployment by skill categories varies considerably across countries. In many cases the openly unemployed tend to be skilled workers. Hirata and Humphrey (1991) found that skilled workers in Brazil, upon losing their job, are more likely than other labor categories to remain in open unemployment, rather than working in the informal sector. This is also the case in several other Latin American countries (see Inter-American Development Bank (2003)). Similarly, Banerjee and Bucci (1995) found that the open unemployment rate in India is higher among the educated. Hollister and Goldstein (1994), Said (2001), and the World Bank (2004) provide evidence of high levels of skilled unemployment in MENA; in several countries of the region, a large majority of individuals in open unemployment have secondary or postsecondary degrees.

Given that the informal sector is characterized by free entry, skilled workers who choose to remain unemployed are, in a sense, "quasi-voluntarily" unemployed. This may be because their reservation wage (that is, the wage that makes workers indifferent between taking a job or remaining unemployed) is higher than the going wage in the informal sector. Alternatively, it may be because job search in the formal sector is more efficient while unemployed, or because the higher family income of the educated allows them to remain openly unemployed while searching for a job. Unskilled workers, by contrast, often cannot afford to remain unemployed for long and are often "forced" to enter the informal sector. Unskilled unemployment may nevertheless emerge if (as in the modified Harris-Todaro framework discussed later) workers who expect to be hired at the higher formal sector wage are willing and able to wait for the good jobs. The shirking model discussed in Section 1.4 will integrate both "quasi-voluntary" or "luxury" unemployment of skilled workers and "wait" unemployment of unskilled workers.

A common observation in developing countries is that the correlation between the rate of output growth and the open unemployment rate tends to be unstable and weak (unlike what Okun's law would predict). In the long term, open unemployment may show a rising trend despite strong output and employment growth, as industrialization combined with migration from rural to urban sectors frequently means that previously underemployed workers are registered as openly unemployed while they are looking for modern sector jobs. In the short term, the absence of a stable output–unemployment relationship may be the result of spillover effects across different segments of the labor market and shifts in production activities, which are not properly accounted for in published employment and output data. Following a recession for instance, the loss of jobs in the formal or modern sector may lead to a sharp increase in self employment. Thus, employment in the informal sector tends to evolve counter-cyclically.[19] The partial equilibrium setup of the next

---

[18]They recommended a reduction in hiring and firing costs for young workers as an essential step to facilitate their insertion in the labor market. In light of the foregoing discussion, however, the likely impact of this measure is open to question.

[19]Blunch et al. (2001, p. 10) noted that there is much evidence supporting the counter-cyclical role of the informal sector.

section and the model developed in Section 1.4 capture these interactions between the formal and informal sectors. They help to illustrate how the adverse output and employment effects of macroeconomic shocks can be mitigated by a shift to informal production activities.

1.2   Urban Labor Mobility and the Harris-Todaro Framework

An early model of labor market segmentation in developing countries is the migration model of Harris and Todaro (1970). The main objective of the model was to explain the persistence of rural-to-urban migration, despite the existence of widespread urban unemployment in developing countries. The starting point of the analysis is that migrants from rural areas are attracted to the urban formal sector by the *expectation* of higher wages, even if they are unlikely to find jobs in the formal sector immediately. A key element of the model is thus the equality of expected (rather than actual) wages as the basic equilibrium condition across the different segments of the labor market.

Specifically, Harris and Todaro assumed that rural workers, in deciding to migrate, compare (in present value terms) wages in agriculture, w_A, to the expected urban wage, w_U^e, which is calculated by multiplying the prevailing wage, w_U – assumed fixed as a result of the existence of, say, a minimum wage law or trade union activity, as discussed earlier – by the urban employment ratio, which measures the probability of being hired. In equilibrium, the Harris-Todaro hypothesis yields

$$w_A = w_U^a = \left(\frac{L_U}{L_U + N_U} \right) w_U, \tag{1}$$

where L_U is urban employment and N_U the number of unemployed workers in urban areas.

The Harris-Todaro model has been extended in a variety of directions over the years; these extensions have been reviewed in a number of contributions.[20] Given the focus here on segmentation in urban labor markets, the key issue is whether an equation similar to (1) can be used to explain movements of labor between the formal and informal sectors in *urban* areas, as opposed to rural-to-urban migration. I have argued elsewhere that this is indeed a reasonable assumption (see Agénor (1996, 2005)), given the typical informational inefficiencies that prevail in labor markets in developing countries. These markets are indeed characterized by the absence (or poor functioning) of institutions capable of processing and providing in a timely manner relevant information on job opportunities to potential applicants – particularly

---

[20]See Djajic (1985), Rozensweig (1988), Fields (1989, 2005), Bhattacharya (1993), Ghatak, Levine, and Price (1996), and Lucas (1997). Stark (1991) provides a more critical view. Fields (2005), for instance, analyzed the welfare effect of various types of labor market reforms in a basic version of the Harris-Todaro framework. His results, however, should be viewed with some caution, given that general equilibrium effects are not fully accounted for.

those with low levels of qualifications. As a result, low-skilled workers employed in the informal sector are unable to engage in on-the-job search; looking for a job in the formal sector for that category of workers often requires, literally speaking, waiting for employment offers at factory gates. Evidence of queuing by informal sector workers for formal sector jobs as hypothesized here has been provided by several authors. Gong, van Soest, and Villagomez (2004), for instance, found evidence of significant entry barriers into the formal sector for workers with low levels of education in Mexico.[21]

I will discuss later, in the context of a formal model with two categories of labor, how the assumption of imperfect labor mobility between the formal and informal sectors may lead to unskilled unemployment. For the moment, the implications of this assumption for the response of urban wages and employment to shocks can be illustrated with a simple, partial equilibrium graphical analysis with homogeneous labor, adapted from Agénor and Montiel (1999, Chapter 2). Consider a small open economy producing formal and informal goods using only labor, the supply of which is given. Prices of both goods are also taken as given. The determination of wages and employment under four different assumptions regarding labor market adjustment is shown in Figure 1.1. In all four panels the horizontal axis measures total labor available to the economy, $O_F O_I$. The vertical axis on both sides measures the wage rate, which is either uniform across sectors or sector specific. The demand for labor in the formal (informal) sector is represented by the downward-sloping curve L_F^d (L_I^d).

Consider first panel A, which is based on the assumption that wages are perfectly flexible and labor perfectly mobile across sectors. Segmentation of any kind is therefore absent. The initial equilibrium position of the labor market obtains at point E, where the economy-wide wage rate is equal to w^*, labor employed in the formal sector is $O_F L_F^*$, and labor used in the informal sector is $L_F^* O_I$.

In panels B, C, and D the wage rate in the formal sector is fixed at w_F^c (above the economy-wide, market-clearing wage) whereas wages in the informal sector remain flexible.[22] The panels differ in the underlying assumptions regarding the degree of intersectoral labor mobility. In panel B, labor can move freely across sectors, as in panel A. Perfect labor mobility, together with wage flexibility in the informal sector, prevents the emergence of unemployment. The initial equilibrium obtains at point A in the formal sector, corresponding to an employment level of $O_F L_F^c$, and at point E_I in the informal sector, with a wage rate equal to w_I and employment equal to $L_F^c O_I$. In panel C, labor is completely immobile within the time frame of the analysis. The labor force in the formal sector is equal to $O_F \bar{L}_F$, whereas the supply of labor in the informal sector is measured by $\bar{L}_F O_I$. Because sectoral labor supply is completely inelastic and wages cannot adjust in the formal sector, unemployment will typically emerge there. The situation depicted in panel C indicates

---

[21]There is also evidence, however, of a relatively high degree of mobility between the informal and formal sectors; see, for instance, Funkhouser (1997) for El Salvador and Inter-American Development Bank (2003) for some Latin American countries.

[22]The source of wage rigidity in the formal sector is left unspecified at this stage. It is discussed more formally in the next section.

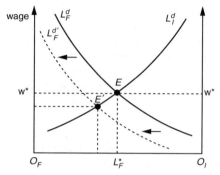
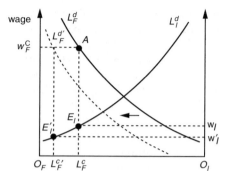

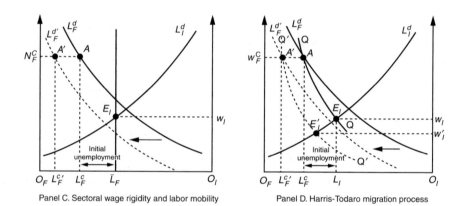

Figure 1.1 Labor mobility, sectoral wage rigidity, and adjustment. *Source*: Adapted from Agénor and Montiel (1999, p. 73).

that employment in the formal sector is equal to $O_F L_F^c$ and unemployment to $L_F^c \bar{L}_F$. Finally, panel D is an adaptation of the Harris-Todaro labor allocation mechanism (1), which assumes that equilibrium obtains when the wage rate in the informal sector is equal to the expected wage in the formal sector. The downward-sloping locus QQ is a rectangular hyperbola along which this equality holds (see Corden and Findlay (1975)). As indicated above, the expected wage in the formal sector is defined as the product of the actual wage in that sector times the probability of being hired, which is measured by the employment ratio: $w_F(L_F^d/O_F L_F^c)$. The equilibrium condition of the Harris-Todaro model implies, therefore, that $w_I(O_F L_F^c) = w_F L_F^d$. Because L_F^d is normally a decreasing function of w_F, the preceding condition defines the rectangular hyperbola QQ. The requirement that the wage rate be equal to the marginal product of labor for $w_F = w_F^c$ is met only at points A and E_I on the QQ curve. The intersection of the L_I^d curve with QQ determines the wage rate and the employment level in the informal sector, whereas the intersection of the L_F^d curve with the horizontal line drawn at w_F^c determines employment in the formal sector. The initial equilibrium is therefore also characterized by sectoral unemployment, which is equal to $L_F^c L_I$.

Suppose that, as a result of an exogenous shock, the demand for labor in the formal sector falls, shifting the curve L_F^d to the left while leaving the demand curve for labor in the informal sector unchanged. With constant relative prices, if wages are perfectly flexible and labor perfectly mobile across sectors, adjustment of the labor market entails a fall in the overall wage rate in the economy and a reallocation of labor across sectors, leading the economy to a new equilibrium (point E' in panel A) with full employment.

Consider now what happens in the presence of a sector-specific wage rigidity. If labor is perfectly mobile across sectors, the demand shock leads only to a reallocation of the labor force toward the informal sector and a fall in wages in that sector (panel B). However, if workers cannot move across sectors, the adverse labor demand shock leads to an increase in unemployment in the formal sector, with no effect on wages and employment in the informal sector (panel C). With a labor allocation mechanism of the Harris-Todaro type, the demand shock reduces employment in the formal sector, as in the preceding case (panel D). However, the effect on the unemployment rate is now ambiguous. This is due to the fact that QQ shifts to the left following the shift in L_F^d; the fall in employment reduces the likelihood of being hired and, therefore, the expected wage in the formal sector. This implies that more workers would elect to seek employment in the informal sector, bidding wages there down. Employment therefore increases in the informal sector, whereas wages fall. However, despite the reallocation of labor across sectors, in equilibrium unemployment may well increase in the formal sector.

The foregoing discussion provides a good illustratation of the importance of accounting for labor market segmentation (as well as the degree of labor mobility) for understanding the response of wages and employment to shocks. However, while the hypothesis of a high degree of wage flexibility in the informal sector conforms well with the evidence alluded to earlier, wage rigidity in the formal sector was simply postulated. I now examine various approaches that have been proposed to explain rigidity in that sector.

1.3   Wage Formation in the Formal Sector

In explaining wage rigidity in the urban formal sector, I will consider an economy with a heterogeneous labor force, consisting of skilled and unskilled workers, and will focus on the determinants of skilled wages only. One reason for doing so is that wages of the unskilled are often set in relation to a minimum wage (as discussed earlier); such wages are generally set by government fiat – although in practice trade unions can exert significant influence on the timing and magnitude of wage increases. A second reason is that some of the underlying explanations for departure from market-clearing that I will examine below relate to observability of effort, which is likely to be more difficult for skilled workers. Indeed, for workers engaged in nonmanual activities, firms may be able to monitor directly the level of effort only at a substantial cost. In addition, bargaining (either through a trade union or on a bilateral basis) may be more relevant for skilled workers, compared to low-skilled workers engaged in more routine work.[23]

In general, rigidity of skilled wages can result from a variety of factors. In what follows I consider five alternative approaches and examine their implications for the degree of rigidity of skilled wages in the urban formal sector. These approaches dwell on efficiency wages (motivated by shirking or turnover costs), trade union behavior, bilateral bargaining between firms and workers, job search, and adverse selection.[24]

1.3.1   Efficiency Wages

The basic idea of efficiency wages is that firms set wages so as to minimize labor costs per efficiency unit, rather than direct labor costs per worker (see Stiglitz (1982)). The difference is crucial if, for instance, the level of effort expended by skilled workers depends positively on the wage paid in the current sector of employment, relative to the wage paid in other production sectors.[25] The outcome of the firms' wage-setting decisions would then take the form of a markup of wages over the opportunity cost of effort, which is such that the efficiency wage exceeds the market-clearing wage. Other models of efficiency wages lead to a similar prediction: wages in equilibrium end up being higher than the competitive wage because firms try to motivate their employees by offering them a premium over the market average. But because the premium may result in a wage that is too high compared with the market-clearing wage, involuntary unemployment may prevail in equilibrium.

Despite this common prediction of efficiency wage models, the specific mechanism through which efficiency considerations are introduced does have a bearing on the outcomes of policy shocks and the effect of structural parameters. In what follows I examine two types of efficiency-wage formulations; the first dwells on the link between effort (or productivity) and wages, and the second on quits and turnovers. In both cases I consider several alternative specifications and illustrate the different predictions of these models.[26]

---

[23]Some of these arguments should not be pushed too far, however. Labor unions may also play an important role as bargaining agents for unskilled workers, either directly, or (as noted earlier) indirectly, as collective agreements are extended to nonunionized workers.

[24]I do not consider insider–outsider models (see Lindbeck and Snower (2001)), for which there has been more limited research in developing countries.

[25]The fact that a higher wage raises productivity suggests that the term proposed by Phelps (1994), "incentive wages," is a more accurate description of the role of wages in these models than the standard heading "efficiency wages."

[26]I will consider in detail in the next section another form of efficiency wage model, based on shirking behavior, along the lines of Shapiro and Stiglitz (1984).

The Wage–Productivity Link

As a benchmark case, I will focus first on exogenous effort. Consider an economy producing one traded good (whose price is fixed on world markets) using only skilled labor, S. The economy consists of a large (arbitrary) number of identical firms. The production function is Cobb-Douglas:

$$Y = (eS)^{\alpha}, \tag{2}$$

where Y is output, $\alpha \in (0, 1)$, and $e \in (0, 1)$ is the level of effort, taken as given for the moment. eS is thus the effective supply of skilled labor. If the labor market is competitive, the skilled wage, w_S, is given by

$$w_S = \partial Y / \partial S = \alpha e^{\alpha} S^{\alpha-1}, \tag{3}$$

from which the demand function for skilled labor can be written as

$$S = \left(\frac{w_S}{\alpha e^{\alpha}}\right)^{-1/(1-\alpha)}. \tag{4}$$

A higher level of effort (for a given wage) therefore raises the demand for skilled labor. If the supply of skilled labor is constant at L_S, the equilibrium wage is given by

$$w_S = \alpha e^{\alpha} / L_S^{1-\alpha},$$

which implies that higher productivity raises the skilled wage.

Suppose now that there are two types of imperfectly substitutable workers, skilled and unskilled, in quantities U and S. Both are combined with a CES function in production:

$$Y = [U^{\rho} + (eS)^{\rho}]^{1/\rho}, \tag{5}$$

where $\rho \leq 1$. The elasticity of substitution is $\sigma = 1/(1 - \rho)$. Skilled and unskilled labor are gross substitutes if $\sigma > 1$ (that is, $\rho > 0$), and gross complements when $\sigma < 1$ (or $\rho < 0$).[27]

Let $x = S/U$. If the labor market is competitive, skilled and unskilled wages (w_U and w_S, respectively) are given by

$$w_U = \partial Y / \partial U = [1 + e^{\rho} x^{\rho}]^{(1-\rho)/\rho}, \tag{6}$$

$$w_S = \partial Y / \partial S = e^{\rho} [x^{-\rho} + e^{\rho}]^{(1-\rho)/\rho}, \tag{7}$$

which imply that $\partial w_U / \partial x > 0$ and $\partial w_S / \partial x < 0$. Equivalently, combining these two equations yields the wage ratio as

$$\omega = \frac{w_S}{w_U} = e^{\rho} x^{-(1-\rho)} = e^{(\sigma-1)/\sigma} x^{-1/\sigma}, \tag{8}$$

---

[27] If $\sigma \to \infty$, skilled and unskilled labor are perfect substitutes. If $\sigma \to 0$ (or $\rho \to -\infty$), the production function takes the Leontief form, and output can be produced only by using skilled and unskilled labor in fixed proportions. If $\sigma \to 1$ (or $\rho \to 0$), the production function tends to the Cobb-Douglas case.

which is greater than unity as long as $e > x^{1/(\sigma-1)}$. Equation (8) implies that $\partial \ln \omega / [\partial \ln x] = -\sigma^{-1} < 0$, so that the wage ratio falls as the relative supply of skilled labor increases.[28] Most importantly for the purpose at hand, equation (8) also implies that

$$\frac{\partial \ln \omega}{\partial \ln e} = (\sigma - 1)/\sigma,$$

so that if $\sigma > 1$ (that is, $\rho \in (0, 1)$ and labor categories are gross substitutes) then an increase in skilled labor's effort increases the wage ratio. Conversely, when $\sigma < 1$, and labor categories are gross complements, a rise in the effort level of skilled labor reduces the wage gap. Improved effort, in a sense, creates an excess supply of skilled labor, driving down the return to that category of labor.[29] Note also that if the unskilled wage is set at a binding minimum, the behavior of ω will reflect only the behavior of w_S; as can be seen in (7), an increase in e then always increases the wage ratio.

I now endogenize the level of effort, e, under the assumption that wages affect the productivity of skilled workers. Following Agénor and Aizenman (1999a), a simple form of the effort function e can be specified as

$$e = 1 - (1 - e_m)\left(\frac{\Omega}{w_S}\right)^{\theta}, \qquad e_m \in (0, 1), \tag{9}$$

where Ω denotes workers' reservation wage or an alternative wage, e_m a "minimal" level of effort, and $\theta \geq 0$. This equation indicates that an increase in the skilled wage relative to the reservation wage raises the level of effort, so that $e_{w_S} > 0$. Effort is also concave in w_S, so that $\partial^2 e / \partial w_S^2 < 0$. If effort is independent of relative wages ($\theta = 0$), or if w_S is continuously equal to the reservation wage, then $e = e_m$.[30]

The micro foundations of this function can be derived as follows (see Agénor and Aizenman (1999a, pp. 280–1)). Suppose that consumption and effort decisions are separable and that the decision to provide effort depends only on the wage earned, w_S, and the disutility of effort. All workers share the same instantaneous utility function $V(w_S, e)$, which, after appropriate normalization, is defined as

$$V(w_S, e) = \ln w_S^{\delta}(1 - e)^{1-\delta}, \tag{10}$$

where $\delta \in (0, 1)$.[31] Let π denote the probability (per unit time) that the worker is caught shirking, in which case he is fired and must seek employment in another sector, where efficiency considerations are absent and the going wage is Ω. The level of effort provided is either e (when employed and not shirking) or e_m (when shirking while

---

[28]The average wage, given by $(w_S S + w_U U)/(S + U)$, is also increasing in x as long as the wage gap is positive, that is, $\omega > 1$.

[29]Bernal and Cárdenas (2003) found an average value of σ of 0.9 for Colombia during the period 1976–96. However, a number of other studies suggest that $\sigma > 1$. See, for instance, Hamermesh (1993).

[30]An alternative, common specification is $e = [(w_S - \Omega)/\Omega]^{\theta}$, where $\theta > 0$.

[31]The quantity $1 - e$ can be viewed as measuring leisure, although the supply of hours is assumed fixed.

employed, or when working elsewhere). The optimal level of effort is determined so that the expected utility derived from working is at least equal to the expected utility of shirking:

$$V(w_S, e) \geq \pi [\ln \Omega^\delta (1 - e_m)^{1-\delta}] + (1 - \pi) \ln[w_S^\delta (1 - e_m)^{1-\delta}]. \qquad (11)$$

The left-hand side in this expression measures the expected utility derived by a worker who is not shirking and provides a level of effort equal to e, whereas the right-hand side measures the expected utility of a shirking worker as a weighted average of the wage earned if caught shirking and fired (with probability π) but working at the alternative wage Ω, and if not caught (with probability $1 - \pi$) and earning w_S, with a level of effort equal to e_m in both cases.

In equilibrium, workers are indifferent between shirking and not shirking; condition (11) therefore holds with equality. Thus,

$$w_S^\delta (1 - e)^{1-\delta} = [\Omega^\pi w_S^{1-\pi}]^\delta (1 - e_m)^{1-\delta},$$

or equivalently,

$$\left(\frac{1 - e}{1 - e_m}\right)^{1-\delta} = \left(\frac{\Omega}{w_S}\right)^{\pi\delta}.$$

Solving this equation for the level of effort yields (9), with

$$\theta \equiv \frac{\pi\delta}{1 - \delta},$$

which implies that an increase in the probability of getting caught shirking (a rise in π) raises the level of effort at any given level of the wage ratio. An increase in the alternative wage Ω (which measures the opportunity cost of effort) lowers productivity.

Suppose that the production function is given by (2). Profits can thus be written as $(eS)^\alpha - w_S S$. Maximization with respect to both S and w_S yields the first-order conditions

$$\frac{\partial (eS)^\alpha}{\partial S} - w_S = 0, \qquad \frac{\partial (eS)^\alpha}{\partial w_S} - S = 0,$$

or equivalently,

$$w_S = \alpha S^{\alpha-1} e^\alpha, \qquad S = \alpha e^{\alpha-1} S^\alpha e', \qquad (12)$$

where $e' = de/dw_S$.[32] Combining these equations gives $w_S = e/e'$, or equivalently

$$\eta_{e/w_S} \equiv w_S e'/e = 1. \qquad (13)$$

Thus, in equilibrium, the effort–wage elasticity, η_{e/w_S}, is equal to unity. This result is known as the Solow condition.

---

[32] The second-order conditions imply that the second derivative of the effort function, e'', must be negative. This is ensured with the present specification (which implies that e is concave with respect to w_S).

Using (9), expressions (12) can be rewritten as

$$w_S = \alpha S^{\alpha-1} \left[1 - (1 - e_m) \left(\frac{\Omega}{w_S} \right)^{\theta} \right]^{\alpha}, \tag{14}$$

$$S = \alpha e^{\alpha-1} S^{\alpha} \theta (1 - e_m) w_S^{-1} \left(\frac{\Omega}{w_S} \right)^{\theta}. \tag{15}$$

These equations can be combined to give

$$w_S = \kappa \Omega, \tag{16}$$

where $\kappa \equiv [(1 + \theta)(1 - e_m)]^{1/\theta} > 1$. Thus, the efficiency wage is proportional to, and higher than, the opportunity cost Ω. Figure 1.2 illustrates the determination of the efficiency wage. The concavity of the relationship between e and w_S guarantees a unique solution. When $w_S/\Omega = 1$, the level of effort is e_m. At the optimal wage, given in (16), the equilibrium level of effort is constant at $e^* = 1 - (1 - e_m)\kappa^{-\theta} > 0$ (see point E).

Given the Cobb-Douglas form of the production function, the optimal values of w_S and e do not depend on the technology parameters but only on the worker's preferences and the detection technology, as summarized by δ and π.

The Solow condition given earlier (equation (13)) has been criticized as implying too high an elasticity of labor supply. As shown by Schmidt-Sorensen (1990), however, accounting for fixed employment costs is sufficient to obtain an elasticity lower than unity. Suppose indeed that there are fixed employment costs per worker, χ, resulting for instance from mandated employer-provided insurance, or from a tax levied on the number of employees to support an unemployment benefit scheme. Profits are now given by $(eS)^{\alpha} - (w_S + \chi)S$. The first-order conditions become

$$w_S + \chi = \alpha S^{\alpha-1} e^{\alpha}, \qquad S = \alpha e^{\alpha-1} S^{\alpha} e',$$

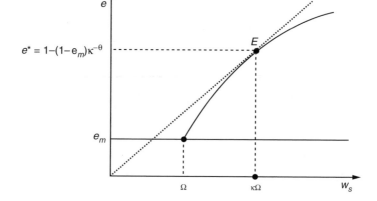

Figure 1.2   Productivity and the efficiency wage. *Source*: Adapted from Agénor and Santaella (1998, p. 272).

so that

$$\eta_{e/w_S} = \frac{1}{1 + \chi/w_S} < 1.$$

This condition shows that the (equilibrium) effort–wage elasticity, η_{e/w_S} is now lower than unity (with the standard case corresponding to $\chi = 0$). It can also be shown that $dw_S/d\chi > 0$ and $dS/d\chi < 0$, so that an increase in fixed employment costs results in a rise in the wage and a reduction in employment. By reducing employment, the firm can counteract an increase in total labor costs stemming from higher employment costs. As a result, output falls; to counteract this effect, the firm increases the wage in order to raise the level of effort, which tends to increase output. The net effect on output is, nevertheless, negative ($dY/d\chi < 0$). Thus, the positive effect on output from higher wages via increased work effort is outweighed by the adverse effect operating through the reduction in labor demand.

An alternative approach is to assume, as in Esfahani and Salehi-Esfahani (1989), that firms face a recurrent cost c (measured in effort units) to organize and manage each worker. The production function therefore takes the form

$$Y = [(e - c)S]^{\alpha}.$$

Maximizing profits with respect to w_S and S yields now

$$w_S = \alpha S^{\alpha-1}(e - c)^{\alpha}, \quad S = \alpha[(e - c)]^{\alpha-1}S^{\alpha}e',$$

which can be combined to give

$$\eta_{e/w_S} = (e - c)/e < 1.$$

Thus, higher recurrent costs lower the elasticity of effort. The Solow condition holds only if $c = 0$.

Several extensions to the specification of the effort function have been considered. For instance, instead of considering the gross wage in (10), the after-tax wage, $(1 - \tau)w_S$, could be introduced, where $\tau \in (0, 1)$ is the tax rate. Taxation would therefore drive a wedge between the consumption wage (which affects workers' behavior) and the product wage (which is what producers are concerned about), in addition to differences in price deflators, as discussed later. Pisauro (1991) for instance, in his derivation of an effort function based on expected utility maximization, accounts explicitly for taxes on labor. In his analysis, the representative worker's utility function is additively separable in effort and consumption, linear in effort, and concave in income. These restrictions lead to an effort function that depends on the unemployment rate and is not homogeneous of degree zero in the wage ratio. The unemployment rate, in a sense, acts as a "worker discipline" device, in a manner similar to its role in the model of Shapiro and Stiglitz (1984) discussed below: the higher the unemployment rate, the stronger are the incentives to put forth more effort, as the fear of being unemployed increases or, more generally, the outside options of the worker become worse.[33] This effect may increase with the level of unemployment, in which

---

[33]Brecher (1992) also developed an efficiency-wage model in which effort is positively related to unemployment.

case effort can be specified as a convex function of unemployment. By introducing unemployment in the effort function, a feedback effect is also introduced in the behavior of wages: an increase in unemployment would tend to lower wages. Thus, in contrast to the Phillips curve, efficiency-wage models explain a relationship between the *level* of real wages and unemployment, as opposed to a relationship between the *growth rate* of wages and unemployment.

Quits, Turnover Costs, and Wages

An alternative model of efficiency wages emphasizes the impact of quits and turnover costs on wages. To illustrate the model's implications, suppose that effort is now constant and normalized to unity. The production function is thus given by

$$Y = S^{\alpha}. \tag{17}$$

In addition to normal labor costs, firms incur a total cost of cqS in hiring and training new skilled workers, where $q \in (0, 1)$ is the quit rate, and $c > 0$ the cost incurred in recruiting and training each worker. Suppose that the quit rate takes the form

$$q = \frac{1}{1 + \delta w_S / \Omega}, \qquad \delta > 0, \tag{18}$$

where Ω is an alternative (or reservation) wage. This specification implies that $q_{\omega} < 0$ and $q_{\omega\omega} > 0$, where $\omega = w_S / \Omega$ is the wage ratio.

As shown by Agénor and Aizenman (1996), specification (18) can be derived from fairly general conditions. Suppose that the net compensation of worker h when employed in sectors i and j are given by, respectively, the following equations:

$$V_i^h = b + \ln w_S + \varepsilon_i^h, \tag{19}$$

$$V_j^h = \ln \Omega + \varepsilon_j^h, \tag{20}$$

where b measures the nonpecuniary benefits of working in sector i, such as proximity to family and friends, and physical location of activities. ε^h is a personal taste (or idiosyncratic) variable.

Suppose that worker h is currently employed in sector i. The worker decides to quit when the net compensation in sector j is likely to be higher than the current one, that is:

$$V_j^h > V_i^h. \tag{21}$$

Using equations (20) and (19), equation (21) implies

$$\varepsilon_i^h < -b + \varepsilon_j^h - \ln \omega. \tag{22}$$

Under the assumption that ε^h follows a standard Weibull (or extreme value) distribution across agents, Agénor and Aizenman (1996) showed that the probability that an individual drawn randomly from the population of employed workers in the formal sector will opt to quit yields equation (18), with $\delta = \exp(b)$.[34]

Profits are given by $S^{\alpha} - w_S S - cqS$. Maximization with respect to w_S and S (for Ω given) yields the first-order conditions

$$-cq_{w_S} = 1, \tag{23}$$

$$\alpha S^{\alpha-1} - w_S - cq = 0. \tag{24}$$

From (18), $q_{w_S} = -\delta q^2/\Omega = -\delta/\Omega(1+\delta\omega)^2$. Substituting this result in equation (23) yields

$$\frac{c\delta}{\Omega} = \left(1 + \frac{\delta w_S}{\Omega}\right)^2, \tag{25}$$

that is

$$w_S = \sqrt{c\delta^{-1}\Omega} - \delta^{-1}\Omega, \tag{26}$$

which indicates that an increase in the unit cost of hiring and training, c, raises the efficiency wage, whereas an increase in the alternative wage has in general an ambiguous effect. To understand the latter result, note that equation (23) can be written in the form $1 = -cq_\omega/\Omega$, given that $q_{w_S} = q_\omega/\Omega$. This equation can be interpreted as equating the marginal cost of a unit of labor (which is unity) to the marginal benefit of that unit, which results from a reduction in labor turnover costs.[35] It also indicates that an increase in the alternative wage has an ambiguous effect on the marginal benefit. On the one hand, it drives the quit rate up, thereby raising the marginal benefit resulting from an increase in the efficiency wage. On the other, it reduces the marginal benefit associated with a rise in the efficiency wage because a unit increase in that wage represents now a smaller percentage improvement in the relative wage (this is captured by $1/\Omega$). For low values of the alternative wage the first effect dominates, whereas for large values of Ω the second effect dominates. If the net nonpecuniary benefit associated with employment, given by δ, is sufficiently high (a condition that implies that the elasticity of the quit rate with respect to relative wages is also high), the net effect will be positive.[36] From (26), the elasticity of the efficiency wage with respect to the alternative wage would then be less than unity.

Combining (23) with $q_{w_S} = -\delta q^2/\Omega$ yields $cq = \Omega\delta^{-1}/q$, that is, using (18) to substitute for q on the right-hand side, $cq = w_S + \delta^{-1}\Omega$. Unit labor costs, defined

---

[34]The density function of the standard Weibull distribution is $f(x) = \gamma x^{\gamma-1}\exp(-x^\gamma)$, with $x \geq 0$ and $\gamma > 0$ is the shape parameter. The cumulative distribution function is $1 - \exp(-x^\gamma)$. The exponential distribution corresponds to $\gamma = 1$.

[35]Given that $q_\omega = \Omega q_{w_S} = -\delta q^2$, (24) implies that the marginal benefit curve is $c\delta q^2/\Omega$. Using (18) shows that this curve is a decreasing function of w_S, for Ω given.

[36]Formally, the condition for an increase in Ω on w_S to be positive is that $\delta\omega > 1$, or (see equation (18)) that the quit rate be less than one half, as assumed below.

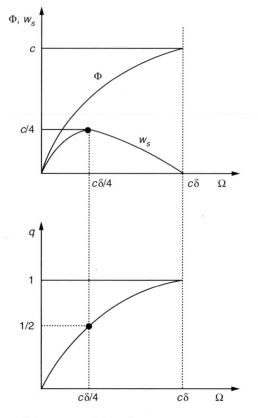

Figure 1.3 Wages, unit labor costs and the quit rate.

as $\Phi = w_S + cq$, can therefore be written as, using (26),

$$\Phi = 2w_S + \delta^{-1}\Omega = 2\sqrt{c\delta^{-1}\Omega} - \delta^{-1}\Omega.$$

As can be inferred from (26), for an internal solution to obtain (that is, for the skilled wage to be positive) the restriction $\Omega < c\delta$ must be imposed. By implication, therefore, $\Phi > 0$.

The behavior of wages, unit labor costs and the quit rate are shown in Figure 1.3. Equation (26) implies that w_S is concave in Ω. For $\Omega = c\delta$, $w_S = 0$ and $\Phi = c$. For the restriction given earlier ($\Omega < c\delta$) to hold, the economy must operate along the upward-sloping portion of the wage curve shown in the upper panel of the figure. As indicated in the lower panel, this assumption is equivalent to restricting the quit rate to be less than one half. The main implication of this specification, in contrast to (16), is that the skilled wage is not a constant markup over the alternative wage.

The foregoing derivation of a wage-setting equation based on turnover costs was based on a static optimization problem. Campbell and Orszag (1998) provided an alternative derivation, based on a dynamic optimization problem. Suppose that the production function is again given by (17). Suppose also that now the objective of each firm is to maximize discounted profits at time $t_0 = 0$:

$$V_0 = \int_0^\infty [S^\alpha - w_S(1 + \tau)S - (1 - \theta)T(H)S]e^{-\beta t}\,dt, \tag{27}$$

where S and w_S are as defined before, H is the hiring rate, and $T(H)$ represents training costs, measured in terms of time existing skilled workers need to devote to training new employees. $\beta > 0$ denotes the discount rate, $\tau \in (0, 1)$ is a payroll tax paid by employers, and θ a training subsidy. Maximization is subject to a dynamic constraint on employment adjustment,

$$\dot{S}/S = H - q(w_S, w_A, L_A), \tag{28}$$

where $q(\cdot)$ is the quit rate, which depends now on the firm's specific wage, w_S, the economy-wide average wage, w_A, and the economy-wide average level of employment, L_A. Whereas an increase in the firm's specific wage, as before, lowers the propensity to quit ($q_{w_S} < 0$), higher economy-wide averages for wages and employment tend now to increase quits ($q_{w_A} > 0$, $q_{L_A} > 0$). The economy-wide average wage plays therefore the role of the "alternative" wage defined earlier, whereas the economy-wide average employment level (relative to an exogenous supply of labor) may be viewed as measuring the probability of finding a job elsewhere – in a manner similar to the Harris-Todaro mechanism discussed in the previous section.

Each individual firm treats economy-wide averages as given in solving its maximization problem, but in equilibrium, wages and employment levels are the same across firms.

Suppose that the quit rate has the following constant elasticity form:

$$q(w_S, w_A, L_A) = q_0\left(\frac{w_S N}{w_A L_A}\right)^{-\eta} = q_0\left[\frac{w_S}{(1 - u)w_A}\right]^{-\eta}, \tag{29}$$

where $q_0, \eta > 0$, N is the total labor force, and u the unemployment rate. The quantity $(1 - u)w_A$ can be interpreted as the *expected* wage available outside the firm, with $1 - u$ measuring the probability of finding a job (equal to one minus the unemployment rate, u).

Suppose also that the training cost function is quadratic, that is

$$T(H) = \frac{A}{2}H^2, \tag{30}$$

where $A > 0$.

From (27), (28), (29), and (30), the current-value Hamiltonian for the firm is

$$\Lambda = S^\alpha - w_S(1 + \tau)S - (1 - \theta)\left(\frac{A}{2}H^2\right)S$$

$$+ \lambda\left[H - q_0\left[\frac{w_S}{(1 - u)w_A}\right]^{-\eta}\right]S, \tag{31}$$

where λ is the shadow price associated with constraint (28). The first-order conditions for maximization are given by

$$A(1 - \theta)H = \lambda, \tag{32}$$

$$1 + \tau = \lambda q_0 \eta w_S^{-\eta-1}[(1 - u)w_A]^{\eta}, \tag{33}$$

$$-\frac{\partial \Lambda}{\partial S} = \dot{\lambda} - \beta\lambda. \tag{34}$$

In equilibrium, $w_S = w_A$. Equation (33) therefore yields

$$w_S = \frac{q_0}{1 + \tau}\eta(1 - u)^{\eta}\lambda. \tag{35}$$

Substituting (32) into (35) and imposing the steady-state condition $H = q$ yields

$$w_S = \kappa \left(\frac{1 - \theta}{1 + \tau}\right)(1 - u)^{2\eta},$$

where $\kappa \equiv q_0^2 A\eta$. Thus, a rise in the unemployment rate u, an increase in the subsidy rate θ, or a reduction in the payroll tax rate τ, lower the equilibrium skilled wage.[37] In a sense, the effect of unemployment on the skilled wage comes about because the alternative wage (Ω in the previous model) is endogenized and specified as an expected value, equal to $(1 - u)w_A$.

An alternative dynamic approach to wage determination in the job turnover model is that of Amano (1983), which also emphasizes the impact of employment adjustment costs in hiring and firing decisions. Suppose again that the production function takes the form (17), and that adjustment of the number of skilled workers entails costs to the firm, which can be training costs (as before) or simply "settling in" costs (as in Stiglitz (1974)).

Let H denote now the flow of newly-employed workers (or of discharged and quitting workers, when $H < 0$), and $x = H/S$. Costs associated with $H > 0$ consist of training expenses and forgone output in the form of lower productivity, whereas those arising when $H < 0$ are compensation to workers who leave the firm voluntarily or involuntarily (in which case they correspond indeed to firing costs).

Adjustment costs for the new flow of workers, C, are defined as

$$C = C(x), \quad C(0) = 0, \quad C' \gtrless 0 \leftrightarrow x \gtrless 0, \quad C'' > 0.$$

Total adjustment costs are therefore $C(x)S$. The assumption $C'' > 0$ reflects scale effects in the sense that firms with larger S find it cheaper to adjust their labor force, for a given number of workers.

---

[37]Moreover, the elasticity with respect to unemployment is 2η, which is independent of τ and θ and thus of public policies. However, this result is not general; the model can readily be extended to restore a role for labor market policies.

The new flow of workers consists of net changes in employment and quits:

$$H = \dot{S} + q\left(\frac{w_S}{\Omega}, v\right)S, \quad \frac{\partial q}{\partial (w_S/\Omega)} < 0, \quad \frac{\partial q}{\partial v} > 0, \tag{36}$$

where q is the quit rate, w_S the (real) wage paid by the firm, Ω the average wage expected by workers, over all firms in the sector, and v the skilled employment rate in the urban formal sector, with $v \in (0, 1)$. The quit rate depends negatively on the firm's relative wage position and positively on the employment rate, which captures labor market tightness. When the employment rate is high, job opportunities are also assumed to improve.

Assume further that the expected alternative wage Ω is an increasing function of the actual wage w_S in the sector under consideration and that the elasticity of Ω with respect to w_S is less than unity. Then Ω can be suppressed in (36), so that

$$H = \dot{S} + q(w_S, v)S. \tag{37}$$

Assume, as before, that $q_{w_S} < 0$, $q_{w_S w_S} > 0$, and that now $q_v > 0$, $q_{w_S v} = 0$. Given the definition of x, (37) can also be written as

$$\dot{S} = [x - q(w_S, v)]S. \tag{38}$$

The firm's profits are now $S^\alpha - w_S S - C(x)S$. With $\beta > 0$ denoting again the discount rate, the firm's problem is thus

$$\max_{w_S, x} \int_0^\infty [S^\alpha - w_S S - C(x)S]e^{-\beta t} dt,$$

subject to (38), which determines the dynamics of the state variable S. The firm treats the skilled employment rate, v, as a parameter. The current-value Hamiltonian can be written as

$$\Lambda = S^\alpha - w_S S - C(x)S + \lambda[x - q(w_S, v)]S,$$

where λ is the imputed price of an additional unit of labor employed. Necessary conditions are[38]

$$1 + \lambda q_{w_S}(w_S, v) = 0, \tag{39}$$

$$\lambda - C'(x) = 0, \tag{40}$$

$$\dot{\lambda} = [\beta + q(w_S, v) - x]\lambda + w_S + C(x) - \alpha S^{\alpha-1}, \tag{41}$$

together with the transversality condition

$$\lim_{t \to \infty} \lambda S \exp(-\beta t) = 0.$$

Eliminating λ from (39) and (40) yields

$$1 + C'(x)q_{w_S}(w_S, v) = 0,$$

---

[38] Sufficiency is ensured by the assumptions that $\partial^2 Y/\partial S^2 < 0$ and $q_{w_S w_S} > 0$.

which, given that $q_{w_S v} = 0$, can be solved for x to give

$$x = x(w_S), \quad x' \equiv \frac{-q_{w_S w_S} C'}{q_{w_S} C''} > 0. \tag{42}$$

Substituting this result in (38) yields

$$\dot{S} = [x(w_S) - q(w_S, v)]S. \tag{43}$$

Equation (39) implies that $\lambda = -1/q_{w_S}$, which can be differentiated with respect to time to give

$$\dot{\lambda} = \left(\frac{q_{w_S w_S}}{q_{w_S}^2}\right) \dot{w}_S. \tag{44}$$

Substituting (40) for λ, as well as (41) and (42) in (44), therefore yields

$$\dot{w}_S = \frac{q_{w_S}}{q_{w_S w_S}}\{-\beta - q(w_S, v) + x(w_S) + q_{w_S}[w_S + C[x(w_S)] - \alpha S^{\alpha-1}]\}. \tag{45}$$

Equations (43) and (45) define a dynamic system in w_S and S, which can be written as

$$\begin{bmatrix} \dot{w}_S \\ \dot{S} \end{bmatrix} = \begin{bmatrix} a_{11} & a_{12} \\ a_{21} & 0 \end{bmatrix} \begin{bmatrix} w_S - \tilde{w}_S \\ S - \tilde{S} \end{bmatrix},$$

where

$$a_{11} = \frac{q_{w_S}}{q_{w_S w_S}}\{x' - q_{w_S} + q_{w_S w_S}[\tilde{w}_S + C[x(\tilde{w}_S)] - \alpha \tilde{S}^{\alpha-1}] + q_{w_S}(1 + C'x')\},$$

$$a_{12} = \frac{\alpha(1-\alpha)\tilde{S}^{\alpha-2}q_{w_S}^2}{q_{w_S w_S}} > 0, \quad a_{21} = \tilde{S}(x' - q_{w_S}) > 0.$$

Given that $1 + C'q_{w_S} = 0$, the expression for a_{11} is actually

$$a_{11} = q_{w_S}[\tilde{w}_S + C[x(\tilde{w}_S)] - \alpha \tilde{S}^{\alpha-1}],$$

which is positive given that $\tilde{w}_S + C[x(\tilde{w}_S)] - \alpha \tilde{S}^{\alpha-1} < 0$ in the neighborhood of the steady state.

The steady-state solution of this system is obtained by setting $\dot{w}_S = \dot{S} = 0$, so that

$$-\beta - q(\tilde{w}_S, v) + x(\tilde{w}_S) + q_{w_S}(\tilde{w}_S, v)[\tilde{w}_S + C[x(\tilde{w}_S)]] = \alpha \tilde{S}^{\alpha-1},$$

$$x(\tilde{w}_S) = q(\tilde{w}_S, v).$$

Substituting the second equation in the first and rearranging yields

$$\tilde{S} = \left\{\frac{q_{w_S}(\tilde{w}_S, v)[\tilde{w}_S + C[x(\tilde{w}_S)]] - \beta}{\alpha}\right\}^{-1/(1-\alpha)}.$$

The phase diagram of this system is shown in Figure 1.4 Curve *WW* (respectively *LL*) corresponds to values of wages and employment for which $\dot{w}_S = 0$ (respectively

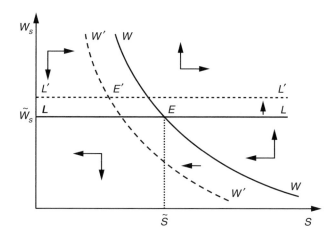

Figure 1.4 Dynamics of wages and employment in the urban sector. *Source*: Adapted from Amano (1983, p. 314).

$\dot{S} = 0$) are constant over time. Curve LL is horizontal, whereas WW is downward sloping, with a slope given by

$$\left.\frac{dw_S}{dS}\right|_{\dot{w}_S=0} = -\frac{\alpha(1-\alpha)\tilde{S}^{\alpha-2}q_{w_S}}{q_{w_S w_S}\{\tilde{w}_S + C[x(\tilde{w}_S)] - \alpha S^{\alpha-1}\}} < 0.$$

The initial equilibrium is at point E. Local stability, as implied by the Routh-Hurwitz conditions, requires that $\operatorname{tr} A < 0$ and $\det A > 0$, to ensure the existence of two negative roots.

Figure 1.4 can be used to illustrate the impact of various shocks on skilled wages and employment. Consider, for instance, an increase in the economy-wide employment rate, υ. It can readily be shown that

$$\left.\frac{dw_S}{d\upsilon}\right|_{\dot{S}=0} = \frac{q_\upsilon}{x_{w_S} - q_{w_S}} > 0, \quad \left.\frac{dw_S}{d\upsilon}\right|_{\dot{w}_S=0} = \frac{q_\upsilon}{q_{w_S w_S}(w_S + C - \alpha\tilde{S}^{\alpha-1})} < 0,$$

which imply that curve LL shifts upward (to $L'L'$) whereas curve WW shifts downward (to $W'W'$).

The new equilibrium point is E', which shows that in the long run wages are higher and employment lower. Thus, firms respond to an increase in the economy-wide employment rate by raising wages, to reduce incentives to quit. Equivalently, an increase in the unemployment rate (a drop in υ), reduces the skilled wage, just as in the Campbell-Orszag model discussed earlier.

Efficiency-wage models with a wage–productivity link and turnover costs can be combined into "hybrid" specifications, to highlight their complementarity (see, for instance, Marti (1997)). In such specifications, it has been shown that the elasticity of effort with respect to wages is a function of recruiting and training costs, which depend on quit behavior. Beyond that, however, hybrid models do not add much to the main result regarding the impact of unemployment on wage formation – which is that, regardless of the source of efficiency considerations, these models generate a relationship between real wages and the *level* of unemployment. Moreover, because unemployment is only one of the determinants of real wages, they may also lead to a significant degree of wage rigidity.

There is significant evidence supporting the view that efficiency wage considerations matter in explaining wage formation in the urban formal sector in developing countries. For instance, Schaffner (1998) and Velenchik (1997), in studies on Peru and Zimbabwe, respectively, found that larger establishments in manufacturing, where the level of effort may be more difficult to observe, pay higher wages, even after controlling for other (individual and firm) characteristics. Other relevant evidence is provided by Hoddinot (1996) and Kristensen and Verner (2005) for Côte d'Ivoire, with more general reviews for Sub-Saharan Africa discussed by Bigsten and Horton (1998) and Dabalen (2000).

Finally, it should be noted that, in the above analysis, wages in the effort and quit functions were measured in terms of the same price; there is no relative price effect, as one would expect in multi-sector models. This distinction is actually critical for understanding the transmission of policy and exogenous shocks in an open-economy general equilibrium setting, as shown by Agénor (2004*b*, 2005*a*).

1.3.2   Trade Unions

As discussed earlier, trade unions play a pervasive role in wage formation in many developing countries. Calvo (1978) developed one of the first models of urban wage determination based on bargaining between formal sector firms and a utility-maximizing trade union.[39]

Suppose that production is as in (5), with effort normalized to unity:

$$Y = (U^\rho + S^\rho)^{1/\rho}, \tag{46}$$

With profits given by $Y - w_U U - w_S S$, and letting again $\sigma = 1/(1-\rho)$, the demand for skilled labor is

$$S^d = Y w_S^{-\sigma}. \tag{47}$$

The simplest way of capturing union behavior is based on the "monopoly union" framework, which is derived as follows (see, for instance, Agénor (2005*a*), Devarajan, Ghanem, and Thierfelder (1997), and Thierfelder and Shiells (1997)). Let w_S^T and S^T denote the union's wage and employment targets, respectively. A centralized labor union sets w_S with the objective of maximizing a utility function that depends on deviations of both employment and the real wage from their target levels, subject to the firm's labor demand schedule. Specifically, suppose that the union's utility function is given by

$$V = (w_S - w_S^T)^\nu (S - S^T)^{1-\nu}, \quad \nu \in (0,1), \tag{48}$$

---

[39]Calvo's model was subsequently reexamined by Quibria (1988), who showed that the properties of the model depend crucially on the specification of the objective function of the trade union.

where the parameter ν reflects the relative importance that the union attaches to wage deviations from target, as opposed to employment deviations.[40] The union's problem is thus to maximize (48) with respect to w_S, subject to (47). The first-order condition is given by

$$\nu \left\{ \frac{S^d - S^T}{w_S - w_S^T} \right\}^{1-\nu} - (1-\nu) \left\{ \frac{S^d - S^T}{w_S - w_S^T} \right\}^{-\nu} \sigma \left(\frac{S^d}{w_S} \right) = 0,$$

or equivalently

$$\nu \left\{ \frac{S^d - S^T}{w_S - w_S^T} \right\} - \frac{(1-\nu)\sigma S^d}{w_S} = 0.$$

Solving this condition yields

$$\frac{w_S - w_S^T}{w_S} = \frac{\nu}{(1-\nu)\sigma} \left(\frac{S^d - S^T}{S^d} \right),$$

which indicates that percentage deviations of the optimal wage from its target value are linearly related to percentage differences of employment from its target level.

The union's target wage, w_S^T, can be assumed to be related positively to wages elsewhere (for instance, in the public sector, w_{SG}) and negatively to the skilled unemployment rate, z_S, and the real firing cost per skilled worker, f_S.[41] In developing countries, as noted earlier, wage-setting in the public sector can play a signaling or "leadership" role for wage setters in the rest of the economy. When unemployment is high, the probability of finding a job (at any given wage) is low. Consequently, the higher the unemployment rate, the greater the incentive for the union to moderate its wage demands in order to induce firms to increase employment. As also noted earlier, firing costs do prevent excessive job losses in bad times (thereby preventing the loss of firm-specific human capital if downturns are temporary) but they also discourage new hires – namely because reversing mismatches is costly if workers prove to be inadequate matches with their job requirements. It is therefore natural to assume that the union internalizes the disincentive effect of severance payments on labor demand. As a result, the higher the firing cost, the greater the incentive for the union to reduce its wage demands, in order to encourage firms to hire.

---

[40]If skilled workers can work in a sector other than the one where the union operates, an alternative assumption would be to assume, as in Agénor and Santaella (1998, Appendix A), that it is the wage differential, rather than deviations from the target wage, that appears in the union's utility function.

[41]The target wage could also be specified as increasing in the income tax rate, implying that the union would demand higher wages to compensate for a decrease in after-tax income.

Normalizing the target level of employment to zero ($S^T = 0$), the above expression can thus be rewritten as

$$w_S = \frac{z_S^{-\phi_1} f_S^{-\phi_2} w_{SG}^{\phi_3}}{1 - \nu/(1-\nu)\sigma}, \tag{49}$$

where the ϕ_i coefficients are all positive. This equation implies, in particular, that a higher level of unemployment lowers the *level* of the skilled wage, as predicted by the various efficiency wage theories reviewed earlier.[42]

As an alternative to the "monopoly union" framework, it could be assumed that firms and the union bargain over wages (through a generalized Nash bargaining process), with either firms determining employment (the so-called "right to manage" approach) or firms and the union bargaining over *both* wages and employment (see McDonald and Solow (1985)). In the former case, the firm and the union would determine ω_S by maximizing the product of each party's gains from reaching a bargain, weighted by their respective bargaining strengths, and once wages are set, employment would be determined by the firm. As shown for instance by Creedy and McDonald (1991), for wage determination, it does not make much difference whether bargaining is over wages only, or over wages and employment. However, in the case of bargaining over both wages and employment, the equilibrium outcome is typically such that firms are not in general on their labor demand schedule (see for instance Booth (1995)).

1.3.3   Bilateral Bargaining

In the real world, individual wage bargaining is common among higher-paid (skilled) workers. Another approach to wage determination is thus to assume direct bilateral bargaining, in each period, between producers and workers over compensation. If a bargain is reached, each worker receives w_S, whereas the producer receives $m_S - w_S$, where m_S is the marginal product of the worker, given by, from (46):

$$m_S = \frac{\partial Y}{\partial S} = \left(\frac{Y}{S}\right)^{1-\rho}. \tag{50}$$

The worker's bargaining surplus is $\omega_S - \Omega$, where Ω represents an alternative wage, an unemployment benefit (if one exists), or the value of a non-market activity. The firm's bargaining surplus is normally $m_S - w_S$, but this expression must be modified in the presence of firing costs (see Coe and Snower (1997)). Suppose that, in case of disagreement in the bargaining process, the worker engages in industrial action that is costly to the firm (but not to himself). The greater the cost of industrial action is, the lower will be the producer's fallback position and thus the higher will be the wage that the worker can achieve – up to a limit, beyond which the firm has an incentive to fire him. Suppose that producers face a firing cost of f_S per worker, and assume for simplicity that all workers become eligible for severance payments immediately upon

---

[42]Note that, in general, the optimal wage would also be an increasing function of union density. Here, it is implicitly assumed that all skilled workers are members of the union.

hiring.[43] If the cost of the industrial action to the firm exceeds the firing cost f_S, the worker will be replaced by another one. Consequently, the worker will set the level of industrial action so that its cost to the firm is exactly f_S, making the firm indifferent between retaining him and replacing him. Thus, the firm's bargaining surplus is $m_S - (w_S + f_S)$.

The Nash bargaining problem can be formulated as

$$\max_{w_S} N = (w_S - \Omega)^{\nu} [m_S - (w_S + f_S)]^{1-\nu}, \quad \nu \in (0, 1),$$

where ν measures now the bargaining strength of the worker relative to the firm. The first-order condition is given by

$$\frac{d \ln N}{dw_S} = \frac{\nu}{\omega_S - \Omega} - \frac{1 - \nu}{m_S - (w_S + f_S)} = 0,$$

from which the equilibrium wage can be derived as

$$w_S = \nu(m_S - f_S) + (1 - \nu)\Omega.$$

Suppose that $\Omega = 0$, and that the bargaining strength of a skilled worker, ν, varies inversely with the rate of unemployment, u, with an elasticity ϕ. The wage-setting equation can thus be written as

$$w_S = u^{-\phi}(m_S - f_S), \tag{51}$$

which implies again that the *level* of wages and the rate of unemployment are inversely related, as in some efficiency wage models and the trade union formulation described previously. In addition, an increase in the firing cost now reduces the skilled wage.

In the above framework, all firms in the economy behave identically, whereas all workers have the same bargaining strength. This is a useful analytical abstraction when studying the general equilibrium implications of homogeneous behavior among workers and firms, but it may not a realistic description of an actual economy. For instance, the ability to bargain over the wage may vary considerably across sectors (or across jobs in any given sector). Thus, wage determination may follow different patterns in different sectors, thereby complicating significantly the task of identifying the causes of labor market segmentation.

1.3.4 Job Search

In the formal sector in developing countries, just as in industrial countries, a large number of workers move between activity, unemployment, and inactivity at any given point in time. These movements occur regardless of whether the economy is in a boom or a recession. For instance, the Inter-American Development Bank (2003, Chapter 2) found that in Brazil and Mexico, for each job created or destroyed every year, three workers change jobs or employment status. The evidence also suggests that those

---

[43]In practice, as noted earlier, redundancy payments are only made to workers with some minimum period of continuous service with the firm.

who change jobs have generally higher skills. This is consistent with the evidence, alluded to earlier, suggesting that the poorest workers (generally among the unskilled) cannot afford long periods of job search (and therefore enter or leave the informal economy quite rapidly), whereas richer workers (often among the skilled) are better able to undergo a period of open unemployment and wait for a proper match.[44] Understanding the determinants of workers' search decisions is thus important to explain wage formation, open unemployment, labor mobility, and therefore labor market segmentation in the formal sector.

Models of job search make explicit the role of frictions in the decision to look for employment and accept a job offer, such as the existence of unemployment insurance or hiring subsidies.[45] One branch of the literature, which is particularly relevant here, focuses on the effects of market frictions on the determination of wages, under the assumption that wage offers are set and posted by employers, and workers search for the best offer among them. Search frictions, in this context, relate essentially to the fact that workers must allocate some time to gather information about wage offers – a particularly relevant consideration in developing countries where (as noted earlier) centralized employment agencies do not exist or do not perform very well. A key feature of this literature is that it helps to explain, in an equilibrium setting, differences in wages paid across employers that are not associated with observed differences in productivity among workers. One reason for this is the existence of differential costs of search among workers.

The ability of this class of job search models to explain wage dispersion across observably identical workers provides therefore an explanation for (urban, formal) labor market segmentation in developing countries. However, models along these lines have seldom been applied in the context of these countries.[46] As a result, the relevance for these countries of the policy implications discussed by Mortensen and Pissarides (1999), for instance, is difficult to ascertain. This is an important area of investigation for improving our understanding of the dynamics of labor markets in developing countries. In that regard, job search models in which only firms incur a cost to match workers with their opened vacancies (with workers passively waiting for a match, comparing their prospective income with the opportunity cost of being unemployed) are unlikely to be useful. As in King and Welling (1995), for instance, a more judicious specification would be to assume that workers bear a direct cost when they decide to actively search for a job. This assumption would be more appropriate for developing countries, where the lack of adequate institutions in the labor market may create severe informational frictions. Indeed, as noted earlier, centralized employment agencies do not exist or do not perform very well in these countries. Search costs may

---

[44]Workers in rural areas typically have more limited opportunities to engage in job search than those in urban areas.

[45]For recent reviews of the equilibrium job search literature (whose focus has been mostly on industrial countries), see Mortensen and Pissarides (1999) and Rogerson, Shimer, and Wright (2004).

[46]Davidson, Martin, and Matusz (1999), for instance, developed a model with search-generated unemployment, but it dwells on the matching approach, as opposed to the approach based on wage offers. See Mortensen and Pissarides (1999) for an attempt to integrate the two approaches.

therefore be prohibitive for some categories of workers – thereby contributing to persistence in unemployment.

1.3.5 Adverse Selection Models

Adverse selection models of the labor market dwell on the fact that workers differ in terms of their abilities and that information about these abilities is private. Key contributions to this approach are those of Weiss (1980, 1991), whose work was subsequently expanded in several directions (see, for instance, Cahuc and Zylberberg (2004)).

There are relatively few studies focusing on adverse selection as a source of labor market segmentation and unemployment in developing countries. But the assumption that workers are generally better informed than alternative potential employers about their true abilities has important implications for a number of labor market issues of great importance for these countries. For instance, Bencivenga and Smith (1997) showed how an adverse selection problem in the formal economy can give rise to open urban unemployment in equilibrium and wage dispersion. Thus, adverse selection may provide an alternative explanation of labor market segmentation in the urban formal sector. Furthermore, as shown by Weiss (1991), adverse selection may also provide a rationale for efficiency wages. A higher than market-clearing wage induces workers to self select and, in a sense, "reveal" their true characteristics. In addition, if current employers are better informed about the abilities of their workers than alternative employers, they may concentrate their effort on preventing rapid turnover of their better workers.[47] Because this may induce fewer quits among better workers, unemployment (or more generally the stream of individuals changing jobs) may consist disproportionately of the less capable ones. Without lower wages, firms may be unwilling to hire, and unemployment may display strong persistence. Moreover, workers who do change jobs may send adverse signals about their abilities, thereby lowering their future bargaining power and wages. In turn, this perceived loss of future income may represent a major impediment to mobility. Thus, these models may not only explain high unemployment rates among the unskilled, but also low quit rates among the skilled.

1.4   A Shirking Model with Segmented Markets

This section presents a two-sector, partial equilibrium model of a closed economy with segmented urban labor markets. It distinguishes between the formal and informal sectors and accounts for two categories of labor, skilled and unskilled. Unskilled wages in the formal sector are assumed set by government fiat, whereas informal sector wages are flexible. In addition, the model also assumes imperfect mobility of the unskilled

---

[47] As argued by Kugler and Saint-Paul (2000), this tendency may be exacerbated by the existence of high hiring and firing costs.

labor force between the formal and informal sectors, in line with the Harris-Todaro mechanism described earlier.

Following Shapiro and Stiglitz (1984), firms set skilled wages in order to avoid shirking. Models of segmented labor markets in which wages are determined along these lines have been developed by a variety of authors, including Bulow and Summers (1986), Jones (1987), and Fukushima (1998).[48] Jones (1987) showed that a large enough differential between the primary- and secondary-sector wages removes the need for (involuntary) unemployment as a discipline device – a key feature of the Shapiro-Stiglitz contribution. Fukushima (1998) also developed a two-sector version of the Shapiro-Stiglitz model (with efficiency wage-setting in both sectors), and studied the impact of active labor market policies on employment and wages. However, all of these papers consider only the case of homogeneous labor. Here, as in Agénor and Aizenman (1997), I consider explicitly two categories of workers and highlight differences in wage formation between them.

The basic setup, in which only skilled workers may face unemployment, is presented first. It is then extended to account for unskilled unemployment by introducing a Harris-Todaro migration mechanism, which generates wait unemployment as a result of workers' decisions to queue for jobs in the formal sector. To illustrate the functioning of the model, the effects of an increase in the minimum wage are examined.

1.4.1   The Economy

Consider an economy producing two nonstorable goods. Both goods are tradables; their domestic prices are given on world markets and normalized to unity. The first good is produced in the formal sector, using skilled and unskilled labor. Unskilled workers earn a legally-binding minimum wage, whereas skilled workers' wages (together with the employment level of both categories of labor) are determined by firms' optimization decisions. The second good is produced in the informal sector using only unskilled labor. In the informal sector, wages adjust instantaneously to clear the labor market.

There are no physical or institutional impediments to mobility across sectors for either category of workers. As a result, skilled workers who are unable to find employment in the formal sector may work (as unskilled labor) in the informal economy if they so decide. Both categories of workers have infinite lives, and discount future earnings at a constant rate. Capital markets do not exist, so neither group may lend or borrow.

Endowments of skilled and unskilled workers – and thus the economy's total labor force – are assumed fixed throughout. The number of firms operating in each production sector is also assumed fixed, and is normalized to unity.

---

[48] In addition, Strand (2003) proposed a synthesis of the Shapiro-Stiglitz model with an individual wage bargaining framework.

Production

The representative firm in the informal sector produces output, Y_I, using labor in quantity L. Supervision and monitoring of workers' activities are costless, so that employed workers always provide the constant level of effort (normalized to unity, for simplicity) required by their employers (possibly themselves). The production technology is characterized by diminishing returns:

$$Y_I = Y_I(L), \quad Y_I' > 0, \ Y_I'' < 0. \tag{52}$$

The firm takes wages as given and hires labor up to the point where the cost of the marginal unit of labor just offsets its product. The demand for labor in the informal sector is therefore given by

$$L^d = L^d(w_I), \quad L^{d'} = Y_I''^{-1} < 0, \tag{53}$$

where w_I denotes the market-clearing informal wage.

Production in the formal sector, Y_F, is a function of both skilled and unskilled labor, U and S:

$$Y_F = Y_F(S, U), \tag{54}$$

The production function exhibits positive but decreasing marginal productivity to each labor category. Using a quadratic approximation and dropping constant terms yields

$$Y_F = b_1 S + b_2 U - b_{11} S^2/2 - b_{22} U^2/2 + b_{12} S \cdot U,$$

where all coefficients are positive. Thus, labor inputs are assumed to be Edgeworth complements, that is, $b_{12} > 0$.[49]

The minimum wage for unskilled labor in the formal sector is set by the government at the level w_m, and firms comply fully with the legislation. In equilibrium, the minimum wage is assumed to be strictly greater than the informal sector market-clearing wage ($w_m > w_I$). This assumption ensures that unskilled workers will look for job opportunities in the formal sector first, thereby avoiding corner solutions.[50]

From the first-order conditions for profit maximization, and normalizing constant terms to zero, the demand functions for unskilled and skilled labor in the formal sector are, respectively,

$$U^d = -(b_{11} w_m + b_{12} w_S)/\Delta, \tag{55}$$

$$S^d = -(b_{22} w_S + b_{12} w_m)/\Delta, \tag{56}$$

---

[49] Evidence on the degree of substitutability between skilled and unskilled labor in developing countries was briefly discussed earlier. It suggests that skilled and unskilled workers in the modern sector tend to be Hicks-Allen substitutes, that is, that the output-constant cross elasticities of demand for each category of labor are positive. This, of course, does not preclude the possibility that these two groups of workers be gross complements at the same time.

[50] More generally, it could be assumed that employment in the formal sector provides also a nonpecuniary benefit, such as enhanced social status. As a result of this assumption, in equilibrium the informal sector wage could be either higher or lower than the legal minimum wage – but the wage differential would still need to be less than the nonpecuniary benefit.

where w_S denotes the skilled wage and

$$\Delta = b_{22}b_{11} - b_{12}^2,$$

which is positive as a result of the second-order conditions for profit maximization. Equations (55) and (56) indicate that increases in either wage reduces the demand for both categories of labor.

Effort and Utility

Both categories of workers are risk neutral and dislike effort. The instantaneous utility function is taken to be additively separable and linear in w and e:

$$u(w, e) = w - e,$$

where w is the wage earned in the sector of employment and e the level of effort. The effort level provided by unskilled workers in the formal sector and those employed in the informal sector is the same, e_U, and corresponds to the level of effort required by employers. Skilled workers, however, have the possibility to shirk because firms in the formal sector cannot monitor perfectly their on-the-job effort. They supply either the level of effort required from them ($e = e_S$) or zero effort when shirking ($e = 0$). Effort is thus dichotomous.[51] Firms, in equilibrium, set the wage of skilled workers so as to deter them from shirking and induce them to provide the required level of effort, e_S.

Effort Monitoring and the Skilled Wage

The monitoring technology is such that there exists a constant probability (per unit time), υ, that a skilled worker engaged in shirking is caught. If detected, the worker is fired and faces two options: remain unemployed in the formal sector, or seek employment in the informal economy.[52] In general, the choice between these two options depends on a variety of factors, both noneconomic (such as the perceived loss of social status) and economic – for instance, whether informal sector employment has an adverse signaling effect, or whether it is easier to seek a job in the formal sector while being unemployed instead of working in the informal sector. Here the choice is assumed to depend solely on whether the worker's reservation wage is higher or lower than the going wage in the informal sector, adjusted for the disutility of effort.

Let τ denote the exogenous turnover rate per unit of time for skilled workers. Following Shapiro and Stiglitz (1984), arbitrage equations can be used to derive the wage of skilled workers. Let V_{Fs}^S denote the expected lifetime utility of a skilled worker currently employed in the formal sector who chooses to shirk, and let V_{Fn}^S be

---

[51]The assumption that shirking involves a zero level of effort is made for simplicity only.

[52]In principle, a skilled worker who attaches a nonpecuniary benefit to formal sector employment may also be willing to accept an unskilled position in that sector. This case can be excluded by assuming that an employer whose aim is to minimize frictions among its employees would refrain from hiring skilled workers to fulfill unskilled tasks, while at the same time other skilled workers occupy positions consistent with their qualifications.

the expected utility stream if the employed worker is not shirking. The steady-state arbitrage equations are

$$\beta V_{Fs}^S = w_S + (\tau + \upsilon)(V_n^S - V_{Fs}^S), \tag{57}$$

$$\beta V_{Fn}^S = w_S - e_S + \tau(V_n^S - V_{Fn}^S), \tag{58}$$

where $\beta > 0$ is the rate at which future earnings are discounted and V_n^S is the expected lifetime utility of a skilled worker who is not employed in the formal sector.

To see how these expressions are derived, consider for instance (58). Following Shapiro and Stiglitz (1984), the expected utility stream derived within an infinitesimally small time interval $(t, t + dt)$ can be defined as

$$V_{Fn}^S = (w_S - e_S)dt + \exp(-\beta dt)[(1 - \tau dt)V_{Fn}^S + \tau dt V_n^S],$$

because τdt measures the probability of a skilled worker leaving the job during the interval $(t, t + dt)$. Approximating the discount factor by $\exp(-\beta dt) \simeq 1 - \beta dt$ and solving for V_{Fn}^S yields

$$V_{Fn}^S = \frac{dt}{1 - (1 - \beta dt)}(w_S - e_S) + \frac{(1 - \beta dt)dt}{1 - (1 - \beta dt)}\tau(V_n^S - V_{Fn}^S).$$

Taking limits as $dt \to 0$ therefore yields equation (58). Equation (57) can be derived in a similar manner.

Equations (57) and (58) can be interpreted as indicating that the interest rate times the asset value equals the flow benefits (dividends) plus the expected capital gain (or loss). For instance, if a skilled worker shirks, he or she obtains the wage w_S without providing any effort but faces a probability $\tau + \upsilon$ of losing his or her job, thus incurring a loss in utility equal to $(V_{Fs}^S - V_n^S)$.

To elicit the appropriate level of effort requires that $V_{Fn}^S \geq V_{Fs}^S$, so that, using equations (57) and (58):

$$w_S \geq \beta V_n^S + \frac{\Lambda e_S}{\upsilon}, \quad \Lambda \equiv \upsilon + \beta + \tau. \tag{59}$$

Equation (59) is the no-shirking condition (NSC) originally derived by Shapiro and Stiglitz (1984). In equilibrium this condition holds as an equality, and a rational worker will be indifferent between working and not working.

1.4.2   Equilibrium with Skilled Unemployment

The equilibrium solution of the model requires solving for the informal sector wage and calculating V_n^S, the expected lifetime utility of a skilled worker not employed in the formal sector, to determine w_S. As indicated before, whether a skilled worker who is not hired in the formal sector takes up employment in the informal economy or enters the unemployment pool depends on whether utility while employed in the informal sector, $w_I - e_U$, is greater or lower than Ω, the reservation wage – which can be viewed here as the imputed value (in wage units) of leisure.

In the spirit of Shapiro and Stiglitz (1984), suppose that skilled workers perceive the transition probabilities into a formal sector job out of informal employment or unemployment as identical and equal to the exogenous hiring rate (or employment probability), a. The steady-state arbitrage equations for a skilled worker who is not employed in the formal sector are therefore equal to

$$\beta V_n^S = \Omega + a(V_F^S - V_n^S), \quad w_I - e_U \leq \Omega, \tag{60}$$

$$\beta V_n^S = w_I - e_U + a(V_F^S - V_n^S), \quad w_I - e_U > \Omega, \tag{61}$$

where it is assumed that, in equilibrium, the no-shirking condition (59) holds with equality so that

$$V_{Fn}^S = V_{Fs}^S = V_F^S.$$

The quantity $a(V_F^S - V_n^S)$ in equations (60) and (61) is equal to the net expected utility gain of being employed in the formal sector, times the probability (per unit time) of being hired in that sector.

Solving equations (58), (60), and (61) simultaneously yields the expected discounted utility of a skilled worker not employed in the formal sector:

$$\beta V_n^S = \frac{\Omega(\beta + \tau)}{\Gamma} + \frac{a}{\Gamma}(w_S - e_S), \quad w_I - e_U \leq \Omega, \tag{62}$$

$$\beta V_n^S = w_I - e_U + \frac{a}{\Gamma}[(w_S - e_S) - (w_I - e_U)], \quad w_I - e_U > \Omega, \tag{63}$$

where $\Gamma = a + \beta + \tau$.

Substituting these results in (59) yields

$$w_S = \Gamma^{-1}[\Omega(\beta + \tau) + a(w_S - e_S)] + \frac{\Lambda e_S}{\upsilon}, \quad w_I - e_U \leq \Omega, \tag{64}$$

$$w_S = w_I - e_U + \frac{a}{\Gamma}[(w_S - e_S) - (w_I - e_U)] + \frac{\Lambda e_S}{\upsilon}, \quad w_I - e_U > \Omega. \tag{65}$$

In a steady-state equilibrium, flows of skilled workers in and out of employment in the formal sector must be equal. Because all skilled workers who are not currently employed in the formal sector can be hired by firms in that sector, it must be that

$$\tau S^d = a(N_S - S^d), \tag{66}$$

where N_S denotes the total number of skilled workers available.

Substituting equation (66) for a in equations (64) and (65) yields the steady-state NSC:

$$w_S = \Omega + \frac{e_S}{\upsilon}\left\{\Lambda + \frac{\tau S^d}{N_S - S^d}\right\}, \quad w_I - e_U \leq \Omega, \tag{67}$$

$$w_S - e_S = w_I - e_U + \frac{e_S}{\upsilon}\left\{\Lambda + \frac{\tau S^d}{N_S - S^d}\right\}, \quad w_I - e_U > \Omega. \tag{68}$$

Equations (67) and (68) indicate that to deter skilled workers from shirking, firms must pay a going wage sufficiently high relative to the opportunity cost of effort. The difference between equations (67) and (68) is that in the first case an increase in the informal sector wage – which is such that the condition $w_I - e_U \leq \Omega$ continues to hold – has no effect on the efficiency wage, whereas in the second case it raises the efficiency wage in the exact same proportion. The wage differential between skilled and unskilled workers (adjusted for the disutility of effort) for $w_I - e_U > \Omega$, and the wage level itself for $w_I - e_U \leq \Omega$, depend positively on the required level of effort in the formal sector, the turnover rate, and the discount rate (because future losses incurred if caught shirking are valued less), and negatively on the probability υ of being caught shirking.

The market-clearing wage in the informal sector depends on whether skilled workers seek employment in the informal economy or not, that is, on whether $w_I - e_U \lessgtr \Omega$. If skilled workers choose to remain unemployed, the equilibrium wage is determined by

$$N_U - U^d = L^d, \quad w_I - e_U \leq \Omega, \tag{69}$$

where $N_U = N - N_S$ denotes the total number of unskilled workers, and N the overall size of the labor force. By contrast, if skilled workers decide to take up employment in the informal sector, the equilibrium condition of the informal sector labor market is

$$N - (S^d + U^d) = L^d, \quad w_I - e_U > \Omega. \tag{70}$$

Equations (69) and (70) can be solved for w_I as a function of the efficiency wage and the minimum wage, as shown below.

Thus, depending on whether $w_I - e_U \lessgtr \Omega$, two equilibria may emerge in the above framework. In both cases, wages and actual employment are determined at the intersection of a wage-setting curve and an employment schedule.

Consider first the case where the informal sector wage – net of the disutility of effort – exceeds the reservation wage ($w_I - e_U > \Omega$), so that skilled workers subject to job rationing opt to take unskilled positions in the informal sector. The equilibrium is consequently characterized by full employment, and is depicted in Figure 1.5. In panel A, the demand curves for both skilled and unskilled workers in the formal sector are inversely related to the efficiency wage. Panel B gives the supply constraint imposed by the given size of the labor force. Using the 45-degree line shown in that quadrant, the demand for unskilled labor in the formal sector can be reported from panel A to panel C. The overall labor supply constraint determines, given the level of employment of skilled workers, the residual supply of labor in both sectors, $N - S^d$. This quantity is also equal to total demand for unskilled workers, the demand curve of which is shown in panel C as $L^d + U^d$. By subtracting vertically from the total demand curve the level of employment of unskilled workers in the formal sector, the demand curve for unskilled labor in the informal sector and the market-clearing wage are obtained. The equilibrium wage for unskilled workers is determined at point C, with total employment in the informal sector measured by the distance CC'. The NSC condition, which is shown in panel D as a positive and concave relation between w_S and w_I, is derived by substituting the demand function for skilled workers, equation (56), in equation (68). Given the informal sector wage (determined at point C),

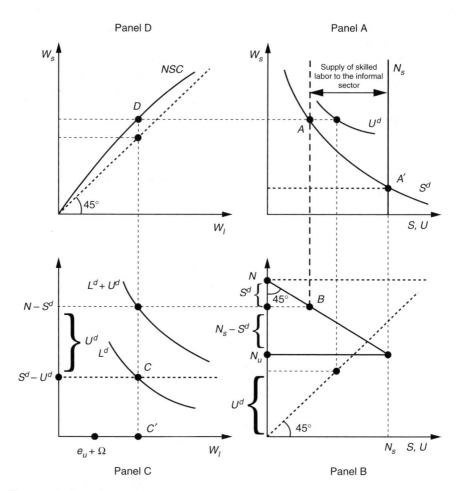

Figure 1.5   Equilibrium with full employment.

the efficiency wage is determined through the NSC curve at point D.[53] Finally, given the NSC, the demand for skilled labor is determined at point A. Because the efficiency wage exceeds the market-clearing wage for skilled labor (which is obtained at point A'), the horizontal distance between A and A' gives the supply of skilled labor in the informal sector.

In the second case, where the informal sector wage (adjusted for the disutility of effort) is too low relative to the reservation wage ($w_I - e_U \leq \Omega$), rationed workers prefer to remain unemployed rather than work in the informal sector.

---

[53] Note that when skilled workers elect to seek employment in the informal sector the no-shirking efficiency wage will depend, through w_I, on the level of employment of both categories of workers in the formal economy. Note also that from equation (68), the informal sector wage is always lower than the efficiency wage.

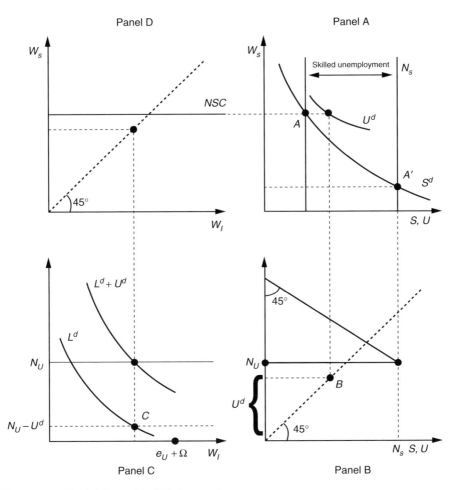

Figure 1.6 Equilibrium with skilled unemployment.

The luxury unemployment equilibrium is illustrated in Figure 1.6, which is constructed essentially in the same manner as Figure 1.5. The NSC, however, is now horizontal – because w_S does not depend on w_I – as shown in panel D of the diagram. The demand for skilled workers is again determined at point A, but skilled unemployment prevails, at the rate $(N_S - S^d)/N_S$.[54]

Thus, in this basic framework, unemployment affects only skilled workers, and can be deemed quasi-voluntary. It is involuntary in the sense that employment opportunities requiring highly qualified workers are demand constrained, and all

---

[54]Because there is no unemployment benefit scheme in the present framework, unemployed workers are implicitly assumed to either turn to a subsistence activity (home production) or to rely on other members of their household for their survival.

skilled workers (given the required level of effort) would prefer to earn the efficiency wage. It is also voluntary, however, in the sense that skilled workers could find employment in the informal sector but opt not to work there – because their reservation wage (or, equivalently, the opportunity cost of effort) is too high relative to the going wage.

1.4.3   Labor Mobility and Unskilled Unemployment

The assumption of wage flexibility and the absence of barriers to entry in the informal sector in the basic framework developed above implies that unemployment of unskilled workers cannot emerge in equilibrium. A worker who is unable to find employment in the formal economy can always be hired in the informal sector at the going wage. These features of the model, as discussed by Agénor (1996), and as noted the first part of this chapter, are well supported by the evidence. In many developing countries, open unemployment tends to affect mostly skilled workers, because unskilled workers (in the absence of unemployment benefits) often cannot afford to remain unemployed for long. Nevertheless, even if it does not exist on a massive scale, open unskilled unemployment can also be observed in a number of developing countries, as documented earlier.

Accordingly, the basic framework is now extended to account for the possibility of unskilled unemployment. The analysis essentially applies the Harris-Todaro mechanism to labor movements within the urban sector, as proposed earlier. This extension allows the model to provide an explanation for wait unemployment, that is, a situation where (high) wage expectations by informal sector workers induce them to remain unemployed and queue up for job opportunities in the formal sector.

Suppose that, as before, on-the-job search is excluded and that employers in the formal sector can hire only out of the pool of unemployed workers. Unskilled workers may opt not to take a job in the informal sector and instead remain unemployed if the perceived benefit of doing so is higher than the opportunity cost of waiting. To determine these benefits and costs, suppose that unskilled workers' reservation wage, denoted Ω_U, is lower than the legal minimum wage adjusted for the disutility of effort, so that $w_I - e_U > \Omega_U$. Thus, unskilled workers are always willing to work in the formal sector, if given the opportunity to do so.[55]

Let π denote the perceived employment probability (that is, the perceived hiring rate) for unskilled workers in the formal sector. In analogy with equations (60) and (61), the arbitrage equation for an unskilled worker who decides to remain unemployed is given by

$$\beta V_H = \pi (V_F^U - V_H), \tag{71}$$

---

[55] With an informal sector wage (adjusted for the disutility of effort) lower than the reservation wage ($w_I - e_U \le \Omega_U$), all unskilled workers who are unable to find a job in the formal economy would opt to remain unemployed. This situation would yield an unemployment equilibrium similar to the one described in the previous section. I therefore exclude it and focus instead on the case where $w_I - e_U > \Omega_U$. As shown later, however, this condition is not sufficient to prevent the emergence of wait unemployment of unskilled workers.

where V_F^U measures the discounted utility stream derived by an unskilled worker employed in the formal sector, and V_H the discounted utility stream derived by an unskilled worker who is unemployed. V_F^U is obtained from the arbitrage condition

$$\beta V_F^U = w_m - e_U + \tau_U(V_H - V_F^U), \tag{72}$$

where τ_U denotes the turnover rate for unskilled workers in the formal sector.

Solving equations (71) and (72) implies

$$\beta V_H = \frac{\pi(w_m - e_U)}{\Phi}, \quad \Phi \equiv \tau_U + \beta + \pi. \tag{73}$$

Unskilled workers opt to wait for employment in the formal sector as long as the net expected utility stream of queuing is positive. In equilibrium, the expected utility stream associated with queueing (that is, being openly unemployed), V_H, must be equal to the discounted utility stream associated with employment in the informal sector, V_I. Because employers in the formal sector hire only out of the pool of unemployed workers, the turnover rate in the informal sector is zero in equilibrium. As a result, $V_I = (w_I - e_U)/\beta$. Using equation (73), the migration equilibrium condition, $V_H = V_I$, can be solved to yield

$$w_I = e_U + \beta V_H = \left(\frac{\tau_U + \beta}{\Phi}\right) e_U + \frac{\pi}{\Phi} w_m,$$

which can be rewritten as

$$w_I = e_U + \frac{\pi}{\tau_U + \beta + \pi}(w_m - e_U). \tag{74}$$

Equation (74) shows that in equilibrium, for a given turnover rate, an increase in the minimum wage leads to a less-than-proportional increase in wages in the informal sector.

In a stationary equilibrium, flows of unskilled workers in and out of employment in the formal sector must be equal. Thus, because formal sector firms hire only unemployed workers, an equilibrium condition similar to equation (66) holds:

$$\tau_U U^d = \pi(N_U - U^d - L^d), \tag{75}$$

where $N_U - U^d - L^d$ denotes the total number of unskilled workers openly unemployed in the formal sector.

This condition can be solved for π to give

$$\pi = \frac{\tau_U U^d}{N_U - U^d - L^d}. \tag{76}$$

The effect of w_S on w_I is given by

$$\frac{dw_I}{dw_S} = \frac{(w_m - e_U)(\tau_U + \beta)}{(\tau_U + \beta + \pi)^2} \left(\frac{d\pi}{dw_S} \right).$$

By definition, from (76), (53), and (55), $\pi = \pi(w_S, w_I; w_m)$. Thus, $d\pi_I/dw_S = (\partial\pi/\partial w_S) + (\partial\pi/\partial w_I)(dw_I/dw_S)$. Substituting this result in the previous equation yields

$$\frac{dw_I}{dw_S} = \frac{\Gamma(\partial\pi/\partial w_S)}{1 - \Gamma(\partial\pi/\partial w_I)}, \quad \Gamma \equiv \frac{(w_m - e_U)(\tau_U + \beta)}{(\tau_U + \beta + \pi)^2}.$$

Using (76), as well as (53) and (55), it can be shown that

$$\mathrm{sg}\left(\frac{\partial\pi}{\partial w_I} \right) = \mathrm{sg}(L^{d\prime}) < 0, \quad \mathrm{sg}\left(\frac{\partial\pi}{\partial w_S} \right) = \mathrm{sg}\left(\frac{\partial U^d}{\partial w_S} \right) = -b_{12} < 0,$$

Thus, the equilibrium wage in the informal sector is given by

$$w_I = G(w_S; w_m), \quad G_{w_S} < 0. \tag{77}$$

Equation (77) shows that the skilled wage in the formal sector and wages in the informal economy are negatively related.

Given the assumed flexibility of wages in the informal sector, firms in that sector must be on their labor demand curve. Combining equations (53) and (77) yields the equilibrium level of employment in the informal sector:

$$L^d = L^d(w_S; w_m), \quad L^d_{w_S} < 0. \tag{78}$$

Aggregate unskilled unemployment is thus given by[56]

$$N_U - U^d(w_S; w_m) - L^d(w_S; w_m). \tag{79}$$

The case of generalized unemployment is illustrated in Figure 1.7, using a similar construction process as the one used before. It assumes that $w_I - e_U \leq \Omega$, so that, as discussed in the previous section, skilled workers who are unable to find a job in the formal sector choose to remain unemployed. The NSC curve in panel D is thus horizontal, as in Figure 1.6. The relation between the efficiency wage and the informal sector wage, obtained by inverting (77), is denoted ILC in panel D. The equilibrium wage in the informal sector is thus determined at the intersection of the NSC and ILC curves, at point D in that panel. Employment in the informal economy is determined at the intersection between the equilibrium wage, and the labor demand curve in the informal sector (point C). Given the total demand for unskilled labor (in the formal and informal sectors), unskilled unemployment, $N_U - (U^d + L^d)$, is given by the distance $C'C''$ in panel C.

---

[56]When skilled workers opt to seek employment in the informal sector, equation (79) holds only if it is assumed that unskilled workers are hired first. This assumption is needed to equate the demand for labor in the informal sector with actual employment of unskilled workers in that sector. In practice, of course, it is not necessarily appropriate.

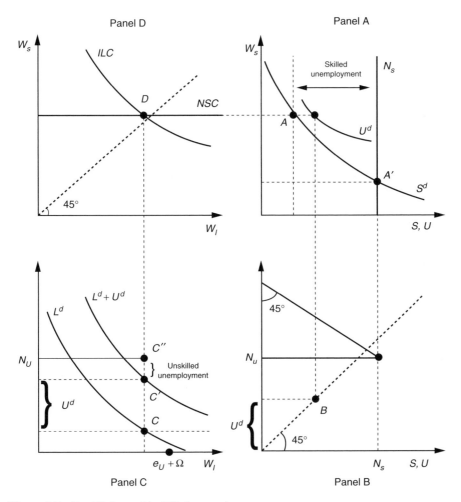

Figure 1.7 Equilibrium with skilled unemployment.

1.4.4 Increase in the Minimum Wage

As discussed in the first part of this chapter, the impact of changes in minimum wages on employment (as well as relative wages) in developing countries remains controversial. In what follows, the effects of an increase in the minimum wage on wage dispersion and employment allocation are examined. This is done first under the assumption that in the initial position of the economy skilled workers who are unable to find a job in the formal sector choose to work in the informal sector – an outcome that requires, as shown earlier, $w_I - e_U > \Omega$.

The Appendix shows that an increase in the minimum wage lowers the informal sector wage, because it reduces the demand for unskilled workers in the formal sector and raises labor supply in the informal economy. The efficiency wage also falls, thereby dampening the direct effect of the increase in the minimum wage on the demand for unskilled labor in the formal sector. The net effect on the demand for skilled labor is ambiguous; the direct effect is to reduce the demand for that category of labor, but the indirect effect (associated with the reduction in the efficiency wage) is to increase it. The demand for labor in the informal economy tends to increase, offsetting job losses in the formal sector.[57] Wage dispersion in the formal sector (that is, the skilled wage–minimum wage differential) tends to fall.

However, because $w_m > w_I$ in the initial equilibrium, the differential between wages earned by unskilled workers in the formal and informal sectors rises. In addition, because both the skilled workers' wage and the informal sector wage fall, the net effect on the differential between these two wages is ambiguous.

An important implication of the above analysis is that it is possible for the informal sector wage to fall so much that the inequality $w_I - e_U > \Omega$ is reversed. In that case, skilled workers who were initially employed in the *informal sector* will opt to quit and choose instead to remain openly unemployed. As can be inferred from the results presented in the Appendix, the lower the elasticity of labor demand in the informal sector, the larger will be the reduction in the market-clearing wage, and thus the more likely it is that skilled unemployment will emerge.

Suppose now that in the initial equilibrium position skilled workers who are unable to find a job in the formal sector choose to remain unemployed (that is, $w_I - e_U \leq \Omega$). Similar conclusions to those obtained in the preceding case can be derived (see the Appendix): the increase in the legal minimum wage shifts unskilled employment toward the informal sector and has an ambiguous effect on skilled employment. Again, the skilled wage–minimum wage differential falls, but wage disparity between unskilled workers in the formal economy and those in the informal sector rises.

Consider now the extended framework in which unemployment of unskilled workers may emerge in equilibrium and suppose that $w_I - e_U > \Omega$ initially. From equations (77), (78), and (68), written as $w_S = w_S(w_m)$ with $w_S' < 0$, it can readily be established that

$$dw_I/dw_m \lessgtr 0, \quad dL^d/dw_m \lessgtr 0, \tag{80}$$

which shows that an increase in the minimum wage has, in general, an ambiguous effect on the equilibrium levels of employment and wages in the informal sector. On the one hand, the increase in the minimum wage raises the supply of labor in the informal sector, thus exerting downward pressure on wages there and stimulating the demand for labor. On the other, the minimum wage hike (at a given employment rate in the formal sector) leads more workers to queue up for employment in the formal economy. That is, for a given turnover rate in the formal sector, the increase in the minimum wage raises the expected utility stream associated with waiting for a

---

[57]Graphically, as can be inferred from Figure 1.5, the labor demand curves for both skilled and unskilled workers shift to the left in panel A. The labor demand curves in panel C also shift to the right. The *NSC* curve in panel D – which depends on the minimum wage as a result of the labor demand curve – shifts downward.

job in the formal economy. But because the higher legislated wage also lowers labor demand in the formal sector, the employment probability (the hiring rate) falls.

Whether the indirect wage effect is large enough to compensate for the direct effect cannot be determined a priori. If the elasticity of unskilled labor demand in the formal sector with respect to a change in the minimum wage is less than unity in absolute value (that is, if $\eta \equiv |w_m h'_U / h_U| < 1$, where the function h_U is defined in the Appendix, equation (A6)), the wage effect will dominate and the overall impact of an increase in the minimum wage on employment in the informal sector will be negative. By contrast, if the elasticity η is sufficiently large, employment in the informal sector will increase.

From these results, it can be inferred that an increase in the minimum wage has also an ambiguous effect on unskilled unemployment. If the elasticity of the demand for unskilled labor in the formal sector with respect to a change in the minimum wage is sufficiently low, unemployment will unambiguously increase.

Alternatively, consider the case where the initial situation is characterized by generalized unemployment (that is, $w_I - e_U \leq \Omega$), so that the skilled workers' wage is independent of w_I. As shown in the Appendix, for the formal sector, the results are

$$\frac{dw_S}{dw_m} < 0, \quad \frac{dS^d}{dw_m} < 0, \quad \frac{dU^d}{dw_m} < 0, \tag{81}$$

together with

$$\frac{d(w_S - w_m)}{dw_m} < 0, \quad \frac{d(S^d + U^d)}{dw_m} < 0. \tag{82}$$

Thus, an increase in the minimum wage lowers skilled wages and labor demand, as well as unskilled employment in the formal sector. Wage dispersion in the formal sector (given that $w_S > w_m$ initially) therefore unambiguously falls. Also, aggregate employment in the formal sector $S^d + U^d$ falls, as the increase in skilled employment is not large enough to offset the reduction in unskilled employment. As also shown in the Appendix, the effect of an increase in the minimum wage on employment and wages in the informal sector remains ambiguous; if the minimum wage (adjusted for the disutility of effort) is initially very low, the effect is likely to be positive.

To conclude, it should be noted that there are other (longer-run) effects of minimum wages that are not captured in the above setting. To the extent that these effects are favorable and significant, they could overturn some of the results derived above. For instance, high minimum wages may have positive nutritional effects on workers in poor countries – as emphasized in the efficiency wage models of Bliss and Stern (1978) and Dasgupta and Ray (1986), for instance – and result in strong increases in productivity in the formal sector. High minimum wages may help to raise productivity also by enticing workers in the formal sector to work harder, as in De Fraja (1999), and to change jobs less frequently.[58] Furthermore, in a longer-run perspective, they may enhance growth prospects and increase welfare if the positive

---

[58] A long literature, going back at least to the mid-1940s, has argued that (reasonably) high minimum wages may have a direct *positive* effect on employment in the presence of monopsony factors. See Boal and Ransom (1997) for a discussion.

externality associated with human capital accumulation and the incentive to acquire skills has a sufficiently large impact on overall productivity, as noted by Agell and Lommerud (1997), Cahuc and Michel (1996), and Cubitt and Heap (1999).

1.5   Concluding Remarks

Labor market segmentation, which can be defined as a situation where observationally identical workers receive different wages depending on their sector of employment, is a pervasive feature of developing economies. The purpose of this chapter has been to provide an analytical overview of models aimed at explaining this phenomenon. The first part reviewed some of the salient characteristics of the labor market in developing countries, including institutions and regulations that may lead, directly or indirectly, to segmentation – such as minimum wages, hiring and firing regulations, nonwage labor costs and unemployment benefits, wage indexation provisions, and bargaining structures.

The second part argued that the Harris-Todaro model of rural–urban migration is also a useful device to examine labor mobility between the formal and informal sectors in urban areas. The implications of this assumption were illustrated by examining the wage and employment effects of an adverse labor demand shock in the formal sector. The third part discussed alternative models of wage formation in the urban sector and examined their implications for labor market segmentation. These models include those focusing on efficiency wages, trade union behavior, bilateral bargaining, search behavior, and adverse selection. Efficiency wage theories, in particular, postulate that real wage cuts lower productivity because they may reduce incentives to provide effort, as well as increase incentives to shirk or quit. Thus, efficiency wage theories help explain why firms in the urban formal sector may pay some workers (particularly among the skilled) more than the market-clearing wage. They also predict noncompetitive wage differentials across segments of the labor market, even in the absence of institutional impediments to wage flexibility. If, for instance, efficiency wage considerations apply differentially across sectors (owing to, say, differences in specific training costs), then intersectoral wage gaps that cannot be eliminated by market forces will emerge. Finally, they help explain a relationship between the level of wages and unemployment, in contrast to the relationship between the growth rate of wages and unemployment implied by the Phillips curve.

The fourth part presented a two-sector model with segmented labor markets and shirking behavior by the skilled, dwelling on the work of Shapiro and Stiglitz (1984). Using a Harris-Todaro migration mechanism, the model explains the emergence of both skilled and unskilled unemployment. The impact of an increase in the minimum wage on open unemployment was examined in this setting. The analysis highlighted the importance of accounting for interactions in the process of wage formation across different segments of the labor market and the role of imperfect labor mobility in assessing the employment and wage effects of minimum wage regulations. In particular, once impefect mobility of unskilled labor between the formal and informal sectors is accounted form, the effect of an increase in the minimum wage on earnings and employment in the informal sector become ambiguous.

Two important areas for future research on wage formation and labor market segmentation in developing countries are the role of informational frictions in the search process and the determinants of reservation wages. Regarding the latter, little empirical work exists (even in industrial countries), despite the importance of this concept for various theories of the labor market and more generally for modeling labor supply decisions. For instance, under the assumption of a stationary reservation wage, optimal search theory predicts a positive correlation between the duration of unemployment and the reservation wage; that is, workers with higher reservation wages would tend to have longer unemployment spells (see Mortensen and Pissarides (1999)). In one of the few studies available, Prasad (2003) used longitudinal micro data to examine the determination of the reservation wage of unemployed workers in Germany. He found that the availability of unemployment benefits raises the reservation wage and has a strong disincentive effect on the decision of the unemployed to seek employment. By contrast, Hogan (2004), in a study of the United Kingdom, found that previous wages (which may impart inertia in perceived standards of living) have a significant but relatively small effect on reservation wages. He also found no significant effect of unemployment benefits, and a small impact of the local unemployment rate. Studies along these lines are important to examine the determinants of job search in developing countries. As noted earlier, many workers (especially the poorest) cannot afford long periods of job search in these countries, and therefore are forced to accept the first job opportunity that comes their way, even if waiting would have meant finding a better alternative and earning a higher wage.

Appendix
The Impact of a Change in the Minimum Wage

This Appendix begins by establishing the sign of dw_I/dw_m under alternative assumptions about $w_I - e_U$ and perfect and imperfect mobility of the unskilled labor force in the model with shirking.

Consider first the case of perfect mobility, and suppose that initially $w_I - e_U > \Omega$. From equation (70), we have

$$dU^d + dS^d + dL^d = 0. \tag{A1}$$

From equation (53), $dL^d = L^{d'}dw_I$, whereas from equations (55) and (56):

$$dU^d = -\Delta^{-1}(b_{11}dw_m + b_{12}dw_S), \tag{A2}$$

$$dS^d = -\Delta^{-1}(b_{22}dw_S + b_{12}dw_m), \tag{A3}$$

where Δ, as defined in the text, is positive. Substituting the above results in (A1) yields

$$-\Delta^{-1}[(b_{11} + b_{12})dw_m + (b_{22} + b_{12})dw_S] + L^{d'}dw_I = 0. \tag{A4}$$

From equation (68), we have[59]

$$dw_S = dw_I + \gamma \, dS^d, \quad \gamma \equiv \frac{e_S \tau N_S}{\upsilon(N_S - \tilde{S}^d)^2} > 0,$$

or, using equation (A3),

$$dw_S = dw_I - \gamma \Delta^{-1}(b_{22}dw_S + b_{12}dw_m). \tag{A5}$$

Equations (A4) and (A5) can be written as

$$\begin{bmatrix} L^{d\prime} & -\Delta^{-1}(b_{22} + b_{12}) \\ 1 & -\gamma\Delta^{-1}b_{22} - 1 \end{bmatrix} \begin{bmatrix} dw_I \\ dw_S \end{bmatrix} = \begin{bmatrix} \Delta^{-1}(b_{11} + b_{12}) \\ \gamma\Delta^{-1}b_{12} \end{bmatrix} dw_m,$$

from which it can be shown that

$$dw_I/dw_m < 0, \quad dw_S/dw_m < 0.$$

Substituting these results in (53), (A2), and (A3), yields

$$dL^d/dw_m > 0, \quad dU^d/dw_m < 0, \quad dS^d/dw_m = -(dU^d + dL^d)/dw_m \lessgtr 0.$$

Suppose now that initially $w_I - e_U \leq \Omega$. From equation (67), the efficiency wage w_S is thus independent of w_I. Using the implicit function theorem, it can be shown that the minimum wage lowers again the efficiency wage; thus, $w_S = w_S(w_m)$, with $w_S' < 0$. Substituting this result in equation (55) yields

$$U^d = -\Delta^{-1}[b_{11}w_m + b_{12}w_S(w_m)] \equiv h_U(w_m). \tag{A6}$$

I assume in what follows that $h_U' < 0$, so that the net effect of an increase in the minimum wage on the demand for unskilled workers in the formal sector is negative.

Solving equation (69) using (53) and (A6) yields

$$w_I = \frac{N_U - h_U(w_m)}{L^{d\prime}} \equiv w_I(w_m), \quad w_I' < 0,$$

which shows that an increase in the minimum wage lowers the market-clearing wage in the informal sector. Thus, the results obtained are similar to those derived with $w_I - e_U > \Omega$.

Consider now the model with the Harris-Todaro migration mechanism and suppose that initially $w_I - e_U \leq \Omega$. From equations (56) and (67),

$$w_S = \Omega + \frac{e_S}{\upsilon}\left\{\Lambda + \frac{\tau S^d}{N_S - S^d}\right\},$$

which implies that

$$dw_S = -\phi(b_{22}dw_S + b_{12}dw_m),$$

---

[59]In evaluating γ as well as ϕ and the C coefficients later, labor demand functions are valued at initial steady-state levels, which are denoted by "‑".

where $\phi \equiv e_S \tau N_S / \upsilon (N_S - \tilde{S}^d)^2 \Delta > 0$. Thus

$$\frac{dw_S}{dw_m} = -\frac{\phi b_{12}}{1 + \phi b_{22}} < 0. \tag{A7}$$

Using equation (55) yields

$$\frac{dU^d}{dw_m} = -\Delta^{-1}\left[b_{11} + b_{12}\left(\frac{dw_S}{dw_m}\right)\right],$$

that is, using equation (A7), and given that $\Delta = b_{22}b_{11} - b_{12}^2$,

$$\frac{dU^d}{dw_m} = -\frac{(\phi + \Delta^{-1}b_{11})}{1 + \phi b_{22}} < 0. \tag{A8}$$

Equation (A7) also implies that

$$\frac{d(w_S - w_m)}{dw_m} = -\frac{[1 + \phi(b_{22} + b_{12})]}{1 + \phi b_{22}} < 0.$$

Equation (56) or (A3) yields

$$\frac{dS^d}{dw_m} = -\Delta^{-1}\left[b_{22}\left(\frac{dw_S}{dw_m}\right) + b_{12}\right],$$

that is, using equation (A7):

$$\frac{dS^d}{dw_m} = -\frac{\Delta^{-1}b_{12}}{1 + \phi b_{22}} < 0. \tag{A9}$$

Combining equations (A8) and (A9) yields

$$\frac{d(S^d + U^d)}{dw_m} = -\frac{\Delta^{-1}(b_{12} + b_{11}) + \phi}{1 + \phi b_{22}} < 0.$$

To calculate dw_I/dw_m, begin by differentiating (74) with respect to w_m. This yields

$$\frac{dw_I}{dw_m} = \frac{\pi}{\tau_U + \beta + \pi} + \Gamma\frac{d\pi}{dw_m}, \tag{A10}$$

where $\Gamma \equiv (w_m - e_U)(\tau_U + \beta)/(\tau_U + \beta + \pi)^2$, as defined previously.
From equation (76), it can also be shown that

$$\frac{d\pi}{dw_m} = -C_1\frac{dw_I}{dw_m} + C_2\frac{dw_S}{dw_m} - C_3, \tag{A11}$$

where

$$C_1 = -\frac{\pi L^{d'}}{(N_U - \tilde{U}^d - \tilde{L}^d)} > 0, \quad C_2 = -\frac{b_{12}(N_U - \tilde{L}^d)\pi}{\Delta \tilde{U}^d(N_U - \tilde{U}^d - \tilde{L}^d)} > 0,$$

$$C_3 = -\frac{b_{11}(N_U - \tilde{L}^d)\pi}{\Delta \tilde{U}^d(N_U - \tilde{U}^d - \tilde{L}^d)} > 0.$$

Equations (A10) and (A11) imply

$$\frac{dw_I}{dw_m} = (1 + \Gamma C_1)^{-1} \left\{ \frac{\pi}{\tau_U + \beta + \pi} + \Gamma C_2 \frac{dw_S}{dw_m} - \Gamma C_3 \right\},$$

from which it can be shown that, in the general case, dw_I/dw_m (and thus dL^d/dw_m) is ambiguous in sign. For $w_m - e_U \simeq 0$ initially, then $\Gamma \simeq 0$ and therefore $dw_I/dw_m > 0$.

Chapter 2

The Macroeconomics of Poverty Reduction

Pierre-Richard Agénor

Poverty remains a widespread phenomenon in the developing world, despite significant progress in raising living standards in many countries in recent years. According to World Bank estimates, the headcount ratio (which measures the incidence of poverty; that is, the proportion of individuals or households earning less than a given level of income), based on an international poverty line of $1.08 per day, dropped from 40.4 percent in 1981 to 21.1 percent in 2001 when China is included.[1] But the drop is only from 31.7 percent to 22.5 percent without China, where poverty dropped from 63.8 percent to 16.6 percent during the same period. In Sub-Saharan Africa alone, the incidence of poverty increased from 41.6 percent in 1981 to 46.4 percent in 2001 with a $1.08 per day poverty line, and from 73.3 percent to 76.6 percent with a $2.15 per day poverty line. Moreover, as a result of sustained population growth, the absolute number of poor doubled during the period, from 164 million in 1981 to 313 million in 2001 with a $1.08 per day poverty line, and from 288 million to 516 million with a $2.15 per day poverty line. As a result, the share of the world's poor living in Sub-Saharan Africa rose from 11 percent in 1981 to 29 percent in 2001. The depth of poverty, as measured by the poverty gap (defined as the average shortfall of the income of the poor with respect to the poverty line, multiplied by the headcount ratio) remains also the highest in Sub-Saharan Africa, having increased from 17 percent in 1981 to 21 percent in 2001.

---

[1] See Chen and Ravallion (2004). The poverty line is measured at 1993 purchasing power parity exchange rates.

"Getting the facts right" on world poverty has proved to be difficult and remains a matter of controversy between the World Bank and some academic researchers.[2] Nevertheless, most observers would agree that millions of individuals around the world continue to endure lives of deprivation, and that prospects for reducing poverty remain bleak in some regions. Based on current trends, Sub-Saharan Africa as a whole will not be able to reduce poverty by half between 1990 and 2015, as called for under the Millennium Development Goals proclaimed in 1999 by the United Nations (see World Bank (2005)).

Bringing relief to the world's poorest remains therefore one of the central policy issues of the new millennium. In that context, much effort has been devoted in recent years to understanding how macroeconomic policy affects poverty and how aggregate shocks (whether policy-induced or otherwise) are transmitted to the poor. A key reason for this has been the growing recognition that economic crises hurt the poor the most, because the latter often lack the means to protect themselves from adverse income and employment shocks. The poor lack assets, such as land and bank deposits, and often have no direct access to credit markets (or face prohibitive borrowing costs when they do), to smooth the impact of these shocks. For the very poor, unfavorable shocks may be large enough to result in actual declines in consumption, with adverse effects on their longer-term nutrition and health prospects. Moreover, due to the lack of education and marketable skills, the poor tend to be less mobile than workers with better education. Another reason has been the need to develop quantitative macroeconomic models to help countries conduct systematic policy analysis and examine the trade-offs that are inherent to the formulation of medium- and long-term poverty reduction strategies.

The purpose of this chapter is to provide an overview of some of the recent research on the macroeconomics of poverty reduction, as well as my own perspective on what may constitute fruitful research directions.[3] In doing so, I will focus on income poverty. It is now well recognized that poverty is a multi-dimensional phenomenon, which is not only evident in low levels of income, but also in poor people's vulnerability to ill health, personal violence, and natural disasters. The focus on income is, however, justified to some extent because the impact of macroeconomic policy on the poor operates essentially through changes in earnings, and because changes in income tend to be highly correlated in the medium and long term with other social and demographic indicators, such as life expectancy, infant mortality, fertility, and the literacy rate (the direction of causality remaining, of course, a matter of debate).

Section 2.1 discusses some of the reasons why research on the macroeconomic aspects of poverty may have been "distorted" by either a relative neglect of the issue by macroeconomists, or an excessive focus on micro/measurement aspects. The lack of a macro perspective is well illustrated by the recent debate on "pro-poor growth," which is also discussed in that section. Section 2.2 provides a brief

---

[2] A key issue in this context has been the discrepancies between national accounts data and household survey data. See Deaton (2005) and Bhalla (2004) for a detailed discussion, including a criticism of World Bank estimates.

[3] This chapter is an updated, and somewhat condensed, version of Agénor (2005c).

analytical review of the transmission channels of macroeconomic policies to the poor, with a particular focus on the role of the labor market. Section 2.3 illustrates how the type of labor market distortions that are typically observed in developing countries can be integrated in a two-household theoretical macro model to analyze the poverty effects of macroeconomic policies – in particular, the impact of a cut in government spending on the urban poor. Section 2.4 identifies various directions for future research, including the sources of, and evidence on, poverty traps; the causes of asymmetric effects of output shocks on the poor; potential trade-offs between unemployment reduction and poverty alleviation; the allocation of public investment and its implications for long-run growth; and channels through which redistribution can actually hurt the poor. The final section offers some concluding remarks.

2.1   A Distorted Agenda

My initial contention is that macroeconomists have for a long time ignored the issue of poverty and consequently disregarded the question of how macroeconomic policy shocks are transmitted to the poor. This has been the case in both academic circles and in international development institutions (IDIs). These institutions have a special mandate for conducting policy-oriented research on low-income countries; but their agenda, for most of the past decades, has been largely biased – in some cases because of the failure to consider poverty reduction in itself as a legitimate target for macroeconomic policy, and in others because of an excessive focus on microeconomic and measurement issues. I illustrate the implications of these distortions by reviewing the rather confusing state of the debate on "pro-poor growth."

2.1.1   A Topic Neglected by Macroeconomists

The collapse of the Keynesian-Neoclassical "synthesis" and the subsequent shift in paradigm in macroeconomics toward the homogeneous, representative agent framework led macroeconomists away from considering distributional issues. This shift, which occurred despite well-known conceptual obstacles (such as the aggregation problems discussed by Kirman (1992)) also led, in my view, away from the consideration of poverty issues. The state of the literature on this subject is very telling in that regard: until recently, papers focusing on the macro aspects of poverty were relatively rare, regardless of whether one is focusing on developing or industrial countries.[4] Moreover, many of the papers that attempted to focus on the transmission mechanism of macro shocks to the poor in developing countries were deficient in several dimensions – most notably, as discussed later, in their failure to capture the complex nature of the labor market in these countries.

---

[4]For industrial countries, two of the few papers that I am aware of are those of Romer (2000) and DeFina (2004). For developing countries, among the few examples are studies by Dorosh and Sahn (2000) and Akinbobola and Saibu (2004).

Of course, since early contributions by Nurkse (1953) and others, growth theorists have spent considerable time and effort formulating and analyzing models of underdevelopment traps; much of this literature is aptly surveyed by Azariadis (2001) and Azariadis and Stachurski (2004). However, too often the focus in this literature has been on the "intrinsic" properties of these models, and less on their policy implications. As it turns out, in some cases these implications are either far from obvious, or lack operational content. For instance, in some of these models, the role of government policy is to coordinate expectations into self-fulfilling growth beliefs, so as to move the economy from a "bad" equilibrium (a low-growth poverty trap) to a "good" (high-growth) equilibrium. Put differently, public policy acts as a "selection device" among different convergent paths. But how, in practical terms, public policy must be implemented to achieve such a shift in expectations is not specified. As another example, Boldrin (1992), in an important contribution, showed how accounting for human capital accumulation can lead in an endogenous growth framework to multiple equilibria – one of which being a low-income (locally stable) stationary state.[5] He went on to show that a nonlinear tax scheme may eliminate the multiplicity of equilibria. In practice, however, such schemes are notoriously difficult to implement – even more so in the context of low-income countries with limited administrative capacity. Moreover, as discussed subsequently, a number of important issues have not yet been addressed in the analytical literature on poverty traps.

One would have hoped that international institutions like the IMF, whose job it is to provide advice on macroeconomic policy to poor countries, would have developed a strong research agenda in this area. But until very recently (or so I would like to believe), the issue was essentially swept under the rug. Part of the reason was surely the Fund's relatively narrow mandate (or, more accurately perhaps, the narrow interpretation of it), which appeared to exclude direct consideration of poverty reduction as a legitimate policy goal in its programs. Instead, poverty was viewed as something to be "left to the World Bank." The lack of direct interest on poverty, and the focus on price stability, was occasionally justified by IMF economists by what still remains one of the Fund's favorite dictums: "inflation is a tax on the poor" (just as it is, of course, on everybody else with nonindexed income or nominally-fixed assets). But as discussed later, inflation can affect the poor in many ways, and understanding (and quantifying) these different channels is critical for good policy advice. Another common belief among IMF economists is that growth will, in a sense, "take care" of the poverty problem. Again, this may well be true in many cases, but it may turn out to be wrong in many others also. The danger is that, without careful analysis, strong priors can lead to erroneous (and socially costly) policy recommendations. Moreover, these priors may have encouraged a "benign neglect" attitude at the IMF regarding the need to study carefully and thoroughly the transmission process of macro shocks to the poor. Some analytical research on the macro implications of labor market distortions in low-income countries (an important first step in poverty analysis, as I argue later) was indeed initiated in the mid-1990s; however, by the

---

[5]Put differently, in this type of model the set of initial conditions for which positive growth is an equilibrium is not disjoint from the set of initial conditions for which permanent stagnation is also an equilibrium.

IMF's own account, little has happened since then (see International Monetary Fund (2003)). Sporadic contributions do not, in any case, amount to a coherent research agenda.

At a more policy-oriented level, recent attempts to bring poverty issues to the forefront of IMF programs have not been met with much greater success. There are a number of reasons as to why this has happened, and going through them at any length is beyond the scope of this chapter. However, I suspect that high on the list would be the lack of a clear conceptual macro framework with an explicit account of *a*) the transmission channels of macro shocks to the poor; *b*) the interactions between poverty, growth, and inequality; and *c*) the role of public investment and public capital in fostering growth.

In a sense, the relative lack of interest in the issue by mainstream macroeconomists and institutions like the IMF involved in research and policy advice on macroeconomic management in low-income countries paved the way for a control (I am refraining from saying "hijacking") of the research agenda on poverty by economists primarily concerned with purely microeconomic aspects and measurement issues.

Let me be clear. By calling for greater attention to the macroeconomic dimension of poverty reduction strategies, I do not mean to revive sterile controversies between micro and macro approaches to economic analysis, or draw too sharp a divide between the practical importance of micro and macro factors in affecting poverty. Countless examples of failed attempts at structural adjustment in the past decades have taught us a lot (unfortunately the hard way) about how microeconomic rigidities and institutional constraints can condition the outcome of macroeconomic policies and their impact on poverty. Policy economists understand well now that a currency devaluation aimed at improving external accounts may have a limited impact on the trade balance if farmers in rural areas cannot respond to improved price incentives because of a lack of access to credit, at the micro level, to finance production inputs. And if urban and rural households suffer from the rise in the domestic-currency price of imported goods, overall poverty rates may well increase. Likewise, policies aimed at promoting human capital accumulation and growth may have little effect on the aggregate stock of skilled labor if individual choices are distorted by labor market regulations – despite a strong signaling effect provided by large skilled-unskilled wage differentials. And it is certainly true to argue that more needs to be learned about the macro implications of micro and institutional factors, particularly with respect to risk-coping strategies, the gender dimension of vulnerability, the decentralization of public services, and the relationship between crime and poverty (see Dercon (2002), Sahn and Younger (2004), and Huang, Laing, and Wang (2004)).

My argument, rather, is that there are still important gaps in our understanding of issues that are fundamentally "macro" in nature, and that investigators (or the institutions sponsoring them) should strike a better balance between research on the role of micro and macro factors in poverty analysis. At the same time, it is also important to recognize and account for the complementarity or interaction between these factors – what one may call "micro–macro" linkages – in determining poverty outcomes.

2.1.2   An Excessive Focus on Micro Aspects and Measurement Issues

As noted earlier, poverty is a complex and multi-dimensional phenomenon, and there is considerable controversy in the literature about how it should be defined and measured. Indeed, there are many alternative (and perhaps equally legitimate) approaches to the measurement of poverty.[6]

Measurement is obviously important, given the need for an *ex ante* analysis of the quantitative impact of policies (both macroeconomic and structural) on poverty. Through the development of comprehensive household and income surveys, we have learned a great deal on household behavior and the characteristics of poverty. However, in my view, there has been too much focus on measurement, particularly in IDIs like the World Bank, and not enough on the substantive macro issues. In part, this has been the result of a relative lack of interest on the part of macroeconomists, as noted earlier. But at another level, this has been also the result of undue influence exerted by economists preoccupied with little else than measurement aspects.

Let me illustrate my argument with a more precise example. As I argue later, understanding the nature of poverty and low-growth traps and how to escape from them, as well as the interaction between micro decisions and macro outcomes, is crucial for the design of poverty-reduction strategies in low-income countries. This also involves developing new empirical methods to determine whether such traps are present or not. Yet, IDIs have conducted surprisingly little research in these areas, despite being in a unique position to do so. A recent search of the IMF's "Publications" website for the word "poverty trap" yielded no result. The term is mentioned once in the IMF's own review of its research on macroeconomic issues in low-income countries (International Monetary Fund (2003)), in connection with the conceptual contribution of Masson (2001). Thus, the IMF, in part because of its narrow focus on the financial aspects of macroeconomic adjustment, and in part because of insufficient work on the functioning of labor markets in developing countries, has made limited contributions to the topic. A search of the World Bank's site yielded two publications with a deliberate analytical focus, Hoff (2000) and Jalan and Ravallion (2002)). The first paper, however, focuses mainly on coordination failures as a source of multiple equilibria and underdevelopment traps, whereas the second is an empirical exercise (on China) whose broader implications are far from clear.

A search of the United Nations Development Program (UNDP) website yielded more results, with one of the most important documents being the 2002 report on poverty traps (United Nations (2002)). However, the report contains too many assertions, with little attempt to discriminate rigorously among alternative potential causes of these traps. A search of the African and Asian Development Banks for the same term yielded no result. On both the UNDP and World Bank websites, the search produced also several country reports (for instance, on Haiti and Madagascar) where the word "poverty trap" is mentioned; but in most of these publications, the existence of a trap is postulated, not demonstrated with rigorous empirical analysis.

---

[6] See Duclos (2002) for an overview of the theory of poverty measurement.

As discussed later, establishing empirically the existence of poverty traps is a crucial step for sensible policy design, given the multiplicity of potential causes.

Of course, checking the number of publications on "poverty traps" is by no means a scientific test. It reveals, nevertheless, a lack of systematic discussion of an issue of crucial importance for low-income countries. Referring to the term "poverty trap" in a policy paper without systematic and rigorous analysis is problematic, because the term is often used as a substitute for "constraints," and because we know so little about how to test for the existence of these traps. And this is not an isolated problem; many aspects of the transmission of macro shocks to the poor have also been neglected, and the lack of a macro perspective has led to much confusion about the extent to which growth affects the poor.

2.1.3   The Confusion over "Pro-Poor Growth"

Indeed, a good illustration of what is wrong with an excessive "micro" perspective on poverty issues (and also perhaps with fads and fashion with catchy terms) is provided by the debate on "pro-poor growth." The term is now widely used in both academic and international policy circles, but a perusal of the literature reveals that it means very different things for different people.[7]

A common view is that growth is pro-poor if it reduces poverty "significantly." The issue then boils down to how "significant" the reduction in poverty must be, for growth to be deemed pro-poor. A first definition then is that growth is pro-poor if the poor benefit equally (that is, relative to other groups) from income growth. Thus, growth is pro-poor if it has a one-to-one (inverse) relationship with poverty. A second definition is that growth is pro-poor if the poor benefit more than proportionately from income growth – or, equivalently, if the poor benefit more than the nonpoor. This requires that the income growth rate of the poor be larger than the income growth rate of the nonpoor. The pro-poor growth index of Kakwani and Pernia (2000), defined as the ratio between total poverty reduction and poverty reduction in the case of distribution-neutral growth, is consistent with this definition. So is Bhalla's (2004) definition, which considers growth to be pro-poor if the growth rate of consumption of the poor is (on average) higher than the growth rate of consumption of the nonpoor. Thus, according to this definition, a one-to-one relationship between growth and poverty (as in the first definition) would imply that growth, on average, is not pro-poor, because it is not associated with a reduction in inequality among the two groups. A third and broader definition is to define growth as pro-poor as long as poverty falls as a result of growth. From that perspective, then, the Kakwani-Pernia index and Bhalla's definition are too restrictive, because they imply that even if growth reduces poverty (as measured by either higher income or consumption), it is not pro-poor as long as the poor do not gain relatively more than the nonpoor. A final definition, which is quite orthogonal to the previous ones, is that growth is pro-poor if it is labor intensive – the reason being that labor is the production factor that the poor possess in greater quantity.

---

[7] Ravallion's (2004) "primer" on the issue does little, in my view, to clear up the confusion.

There are several problems with all these definitions, both at the conceptual and empirical levels. Let me start with the last definition (growth is pro-poor if it is labor intensive), because it is easy to dismiss. The fact that the poor generate most of their earned income from the sale of labor by no means implies that pro-poor growth should be understood as (unskilled) labor-intensive growth. The reason is clear enough – high levels of employment may not reduce poverty if the increase in jobs is brought about through a reduction in real wages. Instead, the consequence may be an increase in the so-called "working poor" and potential trade-offs between unemployment reduction and poverty alleviation, as discussed later.

The other definitions are also problematic. First, changes in mean income are not what most macroeconomists would consider to be "growth." What matters from a growth perspective is long-run changes in standards of living. However, many of the studies on growth and poverty are based on changes in mean income derived from relatively small samples of household surveys, conducted at different times across countries and irregular intervals within countries – with adjacent observations in some cases, but sometimes gaps of several years in others. Several studies, for instance, have used the survey data compiled by the World Bank, which cover mostly the 1990s and (for some countries) the 1980s.[8] Gaps between consecutive surveys vary considerably over time and across countries, exceeding ten years in several cases. Most importantly, changes in observed mean income should not be confused with growth effects; business cycle effects are likely to dominate income fluctuations, particularly in surveys that are conducted frequently. These changes are therefore poor proxies for capturing the long-run changes in income that are due to growth effects. The implication is that it should not be at all surprising to find, as Kraay (2004) does, that growth in average household survey incomes is poorly correlated with some of the most common determinants of long-run growth identified in cross-country regressions, such as trade openness and quality of institutions. This may have nothing to do with limited coverage or measurement errors (which led the author to arbitrarily remove from his final sample of poverty spells what he considered "implausibly large" changes) with the household survey data, as Kraay asserts, but rather to the failure to identify short- and long-run components of income changes.[9] Indeed, this failure, coupled with the use of different samples, may be one reason why results on the growth–poverty link differ so much across studies.

Making a proper distinction between short-run fluctuations in income and longer-run changes due to "fundamental" forces related to growth is obviously hampered by the lack of sufficiently long time series (that is, sequences of surveys) in many countries. Time intervals used to measure poverty changes from household surveys are determined by the availability of these surveys, which (as noted earlier) varies significantly across countries. Some of these intervals are short, so changes in poverty are likely to reflect short-term fluctuations in consumption and income, rather than longer-run trends. But the problem does not only arise with high-frequency

---

[8]These data are available at http://www.worldbank.org/research/povmonitor/.

[9]Kraay's regressions also fail to account for possible nonlinearities – a common problem in this literature, as discussed later.

data: regardless of the frequency of the surveys, it is always possible for changes in income to reflect cyclical factors. What this implies, first, is that it is incorrect, in most of this literature, to talk about the effect of "growth" on poverty; "changes in income" is more appropriate. But there is more than just semantics at stake here; it also means that one cannot tell whether an increase, say, in mean income is due to "luck" (in the sense of positive, but temporary, shocks) or changes in fundamentals (related to idiosyncratic changes in private behavior, or induced by deep policy reforms). Such a distinction is of course crucial from a policy perspective.

Second, studies based on mean incomes of the poor are often subject to large reporting errors. The use, by some researchers, of the average income of the bottom quintile to analyze the "growth" effect of poverty may thus provide unreliable results. In addition, it is also an arbitrary indicator. Foster and Székely (2001) proposed instead to use changes in the generalized mean, instead of setting arbitrarily (as in some studies) the poverty threshold at 20 percent to define who is poor.[10] The advantage of doing so is that it gives elasticities of poverty with respect to income changes that capture features of the distributional process. They found that when the change in income is weighted for all individuals similarly, the elasticity is close to one. But as more weight is given to the income of the poorest, the elasticity declines substantially.

Third, studies based on an *ex post*, additive decomposition of poverty between "growth" and inequality components (such as Kakwani and Pernia (2000)), which are often used to determine if a particular episode was characterized by pro-poor growth, essentially treat growth and inequality as independent. However, inequality, poverty, and growth are interrelated, and causality can run in different directions. For instance, in the "circular relationship" emphasized by Nurkse (1953), while growth may be necessary to reduce poverty, high poverty can also be an impediment to growth: in a subsistence economy, saving and investment (in both physical and human capital) may be insufficient to promote growth, because income is used solely to acquire basic necessities and avoid starvation. High poverty rates may also depress private capital formation and impose constraints on the ability of the government to raise resources to finance lumpy investment in infrastructure, thereby inhibiting growth. From a macroeconomic perspective, all three variables are endogenously determined, and respond to *policies*.[11] By implication, it is meaningless to talk about "growth" being pro-poor or not: policies are pro-poor, not growth *per se*.

The thrust of the foregoing discussion is thus that *ex post* decompositions, of the type described by Kakwani and Pernia (2000), are essentially useless for *ex ante* policy analysis. The elasticities that are derived from them do not differentiate between policies and shocks. They say nothing about the interactions, and transmission

---

[10]The generalized mean can be defined as $\bar{y}_\alpha = [\sum_{i=1}^{n} y_i^\alpha / n]^{1/\alpha}$, for $\alpha \neq 0$, and $\bar{y}_\alpha = (\Pi_{i=1}^{n} y_i)^{1/n}$, when $\alpha = 0$. The parameter α defines the weighting of income y_i of individual i. When $\alpha = 1$, the generalized mean is the standard arithmetic average. When $\alpha = 0$, $\bar{y}_\alpha$ is the geometric mean. When $\alpha < 0$, the income weighting is inverse to income ($\alpha = -1$ gives the harmonic mean); put differently, individuals with lower incomes receive greater weights in the calculation of the generalized mean.

[11]This endogeneity explains in part why the empirical evidence on the relationship between growth and inequality is, by and large, ambiguous. See Banerjee and Duflo (2003) for a recent survey, as well as Barro (2000) and the discussion below.

channels, between growth and inequality. In addition, their additive nature means that they cannot account for the fact that the elasticity of poverty with respect to the change in mean income depends also on income inequality. For *ex ante* policy assessment, growth and distribution need to be considered jointly, in the context of a fully specified macroeconomic framework.

Indeed, once one realizes that it is policies that must be defined as pro-poor or not, not growth itself, the nature of the "measurement problem" changes radically. To determine whether a policy is pro-poor requires the use of a structural macro model – of the type discussed later in this book – in which growth, inequality and poverty are all determined endogenously. The outcome of numerical simulations can then be used to derive an *ex ante* measure of the "pro-poorness" of these policies. What matters, therefore, is the net effect of a given policy on poverty, not its decomposition between "growth" and "redistribution" components, which is shock-dependent. This is important because some policies may entail a trade-off between these components, whereas others may not; focusing only on (aggregate) *ex post* decompositions cannot tell us anything about these trade-offs at the level of individual policies.

To illustrate the measurement issue in this context, let μ_P (μ_R) denote mean consumption of the poor (nonpoor) in real terms, and let x denote a policy instrument (say, government spending or the tax rate); a pro-poor policy index can be defined as

$$I_x = \frac{d\mu_P/dx}{d\mu_R/dx} - 1, \tag{1}$$

where $d\mu_h/dx$ measures the numerical (or multiplier) effect of a change in x on μ_h, with $h = P, R$. Assuming that these effects are positive, the index I_x is negative (positive) if the impact of x on mean consumption of the poor is lower (higher) than on mean consumption of the nonpoor. It is zero if the impact of x on mean consumption of the poor and nonpoor is the same. More generally, the following definition holds:

Definition 1. *Let $d\mu_h/dx > 0$, for $h = P, R$. Policy x is strongly pro-poor if the model-based index defined in (1) $I_x > 0$, nonpro-poor if $I_x < 0$, and poverty-neutral if $I_x = 0$. If $d\mu_h/dx < 0$, policy x is weakly pro-poor if $I_x < 0$ and nonpro-poor if $I_x > 0$.*

If $d\mu_P/dx$ and $d\mu_R/dx$ are of opposite sign, I_x is always negative, and the above definition (based on relative effects and the sign of I_x) is no longer meaningful. It can be replaced by a direct evaluation of the sign of each absolute effect:

Definition 2. *If $d\mu_P/dx > 0$ and $d\mu_R/dx < 0$, policy x is strictly pro-poor, whereas if $d\mu_P/dx < 0$ and $d\mu_R/dx > 0$, policy x is strictly nonpro-poor.*

Thus, according to Definition 1, a policy can still be considered pro-poor (albeit in a weak sense), even if it entails a fall in mean consumption of the poor – as long as this fall is less than the reduction in consumption of the nonpoor. Put differently, when a policy operates in the same direction on consumption of the poor and the nonpoor, it is the relative magnitude that matters. But, as indicated in Definition 2, if mean consumption of the poor falls, whereas mean consumption of the nonpoor increases, policy x can never be deemed pro-poor – even if the fall in consumption of the poor is small relative to the increase in consumption of the nonpoor. In addition, Definition 1 above differs from the broad definition adopted by some in the literature: in the present setting, a policy that leads to higher consumption of the poor but at the same time increases consumption of the nonpoor by the exact same magnitude is defined as poverty-neutral, not as pro-poor.

The index defined in (1) can be easily generalized to the case of a combination of policies x_h, with $h = 1, \ldots, n$,

$$I_{x_1 \ldots x_n} = \left[\frac{d\mu_R}{dx_1 \ldots dx_n} \right]^{-1} \left[\frac{d\mu_P}{dx_1 \ldots dx_n} \right] - 1,$$

with obvious modifications to Definitions 1 and 2.

The proposed definitions (which depend, of course, on how mean consumption of the poor and nonpoor is measured in the structural macro model) are simple and quite appealing empirically. Their "macro" nature is evident in the fact that they do not account explicitly for changes in the distribution among the poor and the nonpoor, thereby assuming implicitly that within-group distributions are homogeneous. Moreover, mean consumption could be replaced by a poverty index specific to the poor and the nonpoor. The advantage of doing so is that changes in the poverty line would be explicitly accounted for, as in some of the applied macro models discussed later where the purchasing power of the consumption basket of various household groups are determined endogenously. The previous definitions, by contrast, assume that the poverty line is fixed in real terms. But given uncertainties associated with the exact location of the poverty line, focusing directly on changes in real consumption also has advantages.

Model-based measures of the pro-poorness of policies can also incorporate a temporal dimension. With a static model, I_x can be viewed as measuring long-term effects; but with a dynamic macro framework, I_x can be calculated for different time horizons – say, the short term (within two years after a shock), the medium term and the long term. Specifically, let $d\mu_h/dx|_j$ denote, for $h = P, R$, the numerical effect of a change in x on μ_h at horizon j, where $j = s, l$ (for short and long term) and define I_x^j, using (1), accordingly. The following definition therefore complements Definition 1:

Definition 3. *Let $d\mu_h/dx|_j > 0$ (respectively < 0), $\forall h = P, R$ and $j = s, l$. Policy x is dynamically strongly (respectively, weakly) pro-poor if, $\forall j$, $I_x^j > 0$ (respectively, < 0), dynamically nonpro-poor if $I_x^j < 0$ (respectively, > 0), and uniformly poverty-neutral if $I_x^j = 0$. If $d\mu_h/dx|_j$ changes sign for $j = s, l$, policy x entails a dynamic trade-off with respect to group h.*

Similarly, in a dynamic setting Definition 2 can be complemented with the following definition, which involves comparing the sign of each absolute effect at the same horizon:

Definition 4.   *If $d\mu_P/dx|_j > 0$ and $d\mu_R/dx|_j < 0$, policy x is strictly pro-poor at horizon j, whereas if $d\mu_P/dx|_j < 0$ and $d\mu_R/dx|_j > 0$, policy x is strictly nonpro-poor at horizon j.*

Thus, a policy can be pro-poor in the long run but nonpro-poor in the short run, or vice versa. The reason is, of course, that policies may affect income and consumption differently in the short and the longer term, perhaps because demand-side effects tend to predominate initially, whereas supply-side factors tend to develop more gradually. If the structural macro model is sufficiently disaggregated, the policy index (1) can also be given a regional dimension – by distinguishing, for instance, between urban and rural areas.

The key question to ask, then, is not whether growth itself is pro-poor, but rather what are the policies needed for growth to be pro-poor. Such policies, to have lasting effects on poverty, should focus on fostering long-run growth, not short-run increases in income. Here, there are of course many lessons to keep in mind. There is ample evidence suggesting that one of the key engines of growth in the long run is human capital accumulation.[12] In turn, this requires a growth process that raises the demand for skilled labor – in part through greater public and private investment in physical capital, due to complementarity effects. By raising skilled wages, the increase in labor demand acts as a "signal" for investment in human capital. For many low-income countries, the key is thus to reduce barriers to access to education (possibly through credit market reforms), not to promote labor-intensive growth. Of course, the need to increase the skills composition of the labor force does not create a *prima facie* case for government intervention; incentives could also be provided through higher subsidies to private education.

In addition, the composition of growth matters, and this must be reflected in the design of growth-enhancing adjustment programs. In particular, the allocation of public investment matters, not only between functional components (namely, infrastructure, education, and health, as discussed later), but also across regions. If the poor are concentrated in rural areas, as is the case in many of the poorest countries, pro-poor growth policies must be designed accordingly. The key then is to improve productivity in the rural sector – through higher and "strategic" public investment in irrigation, roads, and so on. Such growth would not only improve standards of living in rural areas, but also (by reducing rural-to-urban migration flows) raise income levels in the informal urban sector. Through these linkages, therefore, the benefits of these policies can spread out to the rest of the economy. But because these are supply-side effects, such strategy requires taking a longer-term view of what pro-poor policies can achieve. In other words, one should refrain from using changes in income calculated over relatively short periods of time to make statements about the "pro-poorness" of particular policies. To do so with some degree of confidence, it is crucial to use a macro framework that is dynamic in nature.

---

[12] See Agénor (2004*b*, Chapter 13) for an overview of the evidence for developing countries, and the study by Coulombe, Tremblay, and Marchand (2004) for industrial countries.

The foregoing discussion has important implications for the research program of many institutions, including the IDIs. For the World Bank, the challenge is to broaden its research agenda to go beyond the current goals of improving current household survey data and (micro) methods of poverty and inequality analysis. The focus on measurement and microeconomic issues has to give way to a more balanced agenda involving deeper analytical research on some of the key macroeconomic issues facing low-income countries, and greater focus on micro-macro linkages for poverty analysis. Other institutions like the IMF and regional multilateral banks (particularly the African Development Bank, whose role in this agenda has so far been largely marginal) face similar challenges.

2.2 Transmission of Macro Shocks to the Poor

In the short run, macroeconomic shocks are transmitted to the poor through changes in output, employment, wages, and prices. After a general discussion of the role played by the labor market in the transmission process, this section identifies how these various channels operate. Specifically, it focuses on changes in aggregate demand; changes in inflation and expenditure deflators; changes in the real exchange rate; and macroeconomic volatility. In addition, longer-run effects of macroeconomic policy through growth and distribution, and possible asymmetric effects of negative output shocks on the poverty rate, are also discussed.

2.2.1 The Central Role of the Labor Market

Labor markets play an important role in the transmission process of macroeconomic and structural adjustment policies. In developing countries, a typical labor market consists of three segments (see Agénor (1996), and Chapter 1): the rural sector, which continues to employ a sizable proportion of the labor force in some countries, particularly in Sub-Saharan Africa; the informal urban sector, which is characterized by self-employment, a limited proportion of hired labor, a high degree of wage flexibility, a low degree of employment security, and a lack of enforcement of labor regulations; and the formal (public and private) urban sector, where workers are hired on the basis of explicit contracts and the degree of compliance with labor market regulations is higher. The share of informal sector employment in total urban employment is sizable in many developing countries, as indicated in estimates provided by Blunch, Canagarajah, and Raju (2001), Saavedra (2003), and the International Labor Organization in its *Global Employment Trends* reports. One reason, as discussed in Chapter 1, is that unemployment insurance or compensation schemes are not well developed in these countries; as a result, workers cannot afford to remain openly unemployed for long. Underemployment (or disguised unemployment) in the informal sector tends therefore to be far more pervasive than open unemployment – at least for some categories of workers.

As discussed at length in Chapter 1, segmentation of the urban labor market may result from government-imposed regulations (such as minimum wage laws, firing restrictions, and severance payments); the existence of trade unions, which may prevent wages from being equalized across sectors by imposing a premium for their members; or wage-setting behavior by firms leading to efficiency wages. Frictions in bilateral bargaining and job search, as well as adverse selection considerations, may also result in segmentation. In all of these cases, wage determination will typically depart from market-clearing mechanisms. For instance, the basic idea of efficiency wages (whether they are due to nutritional factors, large turnover costs, or productivity considerations) is that firms set wages so as to minimize labor costs per efficiency unit, rather than labor costs per worker. Workers' level of effort, in particular, may depend positively on the wage paid in the current sector of employment (say, the urban formal sector), relative to the wage paid in other production sectors (say the informal economy). The outcome of the firms' wage-setting decision may be a markup of formal sector wages over informal sector wages. Because the efficiency wage may exceed the market-clearing wage, such models also help to explain the existence of involuntary unemployment.

The complex structure of the labor market in developing countries implies that macroeconomic models, theoretical or applied, designed to study the transmission of macroeconomic shocks and adjustment policies to economic activity, employment, and poverty, must be carefully specified to avoid incorrect inference in assessing how a given policy measure affects the poor. As I illustrate later, accounting for these distortions has been one of the key features of the recent literature on the macroeconomics of poverty reduction.

2.2.2   Changes in Aggregate Demand

In most circumstances, aggregate demand tends to respond fairly rapidly, and often significantly, to monetary, fiscal, and exchange rate policies. Changes in aggregate demand, in turn, may have a sizable effect on poverty through changes in employment and wages. Fiscal shocks, in the form of layoffs and wage cuts in the public sector, may raise directly the poverty rate, particularly in the absence of a safety net or if they occur during periods when economic activity is subdued to begin with (such as during downswings or crises). Other shocks, such as reductions in government transfers, and cuts in current spending on goods and services or capital spending (which have longer-run supply-side effects as well, as discussed later), may also increase poverty, by reducing aggregate demand and the demand for labor. In addition, if fiscal adjustment lowers overall government expenditure and reduces pressures for monetization of the budget deficit, it may lower inflation and generate an indirect benefit for the poor (see below). The net welfare effect in present value terms, therefore, is ambiguous because of conflicting effects on current and future income.

In addition to the level effect associated with reductions in public expenditure, there may be a compositional effect. For instance, the impact of a cut in social expenditure (including spending on education and health) on the poor often depends on who benefits from these expenditures in the first place. If upper-income households benefit disproportionately, large cuts in social expenditure may have little impact on the poorest among the poor. Castro-Leal, Dayton, Demery, and Mehra (1999) found that in Africa public spending on education and health tend to benefit the richest income quintile, not the poorest households. More generally, the share of social spending in total government expenditure may actually increase at the same time that overall spending is being cut.[13] Transfers, in particular, may fall as a percentage of both GDP and total government expenditure without any adverse effect on poverty if, at the same time, improved targeting of social spending takes place – thereby improving the flow of resources actually reaching the poor. Thus, even in cases where fiscal consolidation requires a reduction in the overall level of public expenditure, it may still benefit the poor; the composition of spending cuts is crucial in that regard.

Macroeconomic policy also affects aggregate demand through changes in private spending. Fiscal adjustment, for instance, can lead to a reduction in private expenditure if public capital and private sector investment are complementary (particularly with regard to public capital in infrastructure, as discussed later) or if an increase in tax rates on wages or profits reduces private expenditure on consumption and investment, by lowering expected income and the net rate of return on capital. Restrictive credit and monetary policies may lower private expenditure as well, either directly (by increasing the incidence of credit rationing) or by raising interest rates. However, cuts in public expenditure may also lead to *higher* private expenditure, for instance, if the reduction in financing requirements by the public sector reduces the cost, or increases the availability, of bank credit to the private sector. Thus, although there are various channels through which macroeconomic policies may reduce aggregate demand and worsen the plight of the poor, there are also channels through which they may stimulate spending, lower unemployment, and reduce in poverty.

2.2.3 Expenditure Deflators and Inflation

Because the poor allocate a large share of their income (or own production, if they are self-employed in agriculture or the urban informal sector) to subsistence, the impact of macroeconomic shocks on the behavior of the prices of the goods and services that they consume matters significantly. If, for instance, basic staple foods account for a large share of expenditure of low-income households, and if the prices of these commodities are kept under control, a positive shock to inflation may have little impact on the poor. Conversely, increases in prices of goods and services produced by the public sector (such as electricity and other utilities) may reduce sharply the purchasing power of the poor's income; a reduction in subsidies on goods and services (such as basic food items) that are consumed by the poor would have a similar effect. In general, the net effect of this type of measures on the poor will depend on their expenditure pattern and their ability to dissave (or borrow) to offset a negative, and persistent, income shock.

But the behavior of overall inflation matters also. The poor are more vulnerable to inflation than higher-income groups because their earnings (wages or income from

---

[13]Conversely, of course, social spending may fall more than proportionately during periods of fiscal consolidation.

self-employment) are generally not indexed. They also have limited access to inflation hedges – few real assets, such as land, and usually no indexed financial assets – with which to insulate themselves from the effect of price increases, and their holdings of cash balances are subject to the inflation tax.[14] Lower inflation also contributes indirectly to growth – as shown in various empirical studies (see Agénor (2004*b*, Chapter 13)) – by increasing the level and efficiency of private investment.

Thus, by lowering the level of inflation (and possibly the variability of inflation, as discussed below), macroeconomic policy may provide substantial benefits to the poor. Recent empirical evidence has indeed corroborated this assertion (see Agénor (2004*a*, 2004*c*)). However, other factors must also be taken into account. To the extent that disinflation is accompanied by a contraction in aggregate demand and employment (as discussed earlier), the excess supply of labor may lead to downward pressure on wages and higher poverty. And even if reducing inflation has desirable effects in the longer run, the short-run effect of disinflation may be to worsen poverty if (as also noted earlier) fiscal adjustment takes the form of extensive cuts in social programs. Thus, a dynamic trade-off may emerge between short-term costs and longer-run benefits.

2.2.4   The Real Exchange Rate and the Supply Side

A sustained depreciation of the real exchange rate – brought about either through a nominal depreciation or, less commonly, a fall in the price of nontradable goods – is the key channel through which macroeconomic policy aims to foster a reallocation of resources toward the tradables sector and correct external imbalances. In turn, a real depreciation may affect poverty in at least two ways. First, if it is implemented through a nominal depreciation, the domestic price of imported goods will typically rise. Whether this increase hurts the poor depends on how large the resulting adverse income effect is; this, in turn, depends on whether the poor consume these goods relatively more than nontradables. In general, the urban poor tend to be affected more than the rural poor, because imported goods represent a larger share of their consumption basket. Second, a real depreciation tends to foster a reallocation of resources toward agricultural exports, raising the income of export-crop farmers and rural households. Thus, in countries where the poor are predominantly located in rural areas (as is the case in Sub-Saharan Africa), a depreciation of the real exchange rate will normally tend to reduce poverty.

A more competitive exchange rate may have other supply-side effects as well. Because resources are reallocated toward the tradable sector, the demand for labor in the nontradable sector may fall; lower employment and nominal wages (in the presence of downward rigidity of prices) may translate into a fall in real wages and a higher incidence of poverty. In particular, if the urban poor are also producers of nontraded goods (because they operate in the informal sector, for instance), urban poverty may increase, at the same time that rural poverty is falling. Alternatively, a

---

[14]In principle, revenue from the inflation tax could be used to finance a higher level of public expenditure that benefits the poor directly – thereby mitigating the adverse, partial equilibrium effect of the tax. In practice, however, it is seldom possible to make that direct connection.

real depreciation can lead to an increase in the user cost of capital in the tradable sector, because capital goods (machinery and equipment) are imported. This may lower investment in fixed capital and, as a result of complementarity, reduce the demand for skilled workers. To the extent that skilled and unskilled labor are net substitutes (as the evidence suggests for many countries), the demand for unskilled labor may increase, raising employment and average income of the poor, thereby reducing the incidence of poverty. However, if the real depreciation is accompanied by (or results from) a cut in tariffs, the cost of imported capital goods may actually fall – thereby leading to an increase in the demand for skilled labor, a fall in unskilled employment, and an increase in poverty. Finally, as discussed at length in Agénor and Montiel (1999, Chapter 8), if the real exchange rate depreciation is brought about by a nominal devaluation, but the economy is a net importer of intermediate inputs (such as oil), the real depreciation will also represent a negative supply-side shock which may reduce the demand for labor in all production sectors – so much so that the net effect may be a contraction in output, an increase in unemployment of all labor categories, and a higher incidence of poverty.

2.2.5 Macroeconomic Volatility

A high degree of macroeconomic volatility, as measured by large and erratic movements in inflation and real exchange rates, is a well-documented feature of the economic environment in developing countries (see Agénor, McDermott, and Prasad (2000), and Agénor and Montiel (1999, Chapter 4)). Such volatility very often results from external factors (such as changes in a country's terms of trade or fluctuations in world interest rates) but it is also sometimes policy-induced, in part as a result of "stop-and-go" policies.

Macroeconomic volatility can affect the poor in various ways. First, volatility tends to distort price signals and the expected rate of return for investors; in the presence of irreversibility effects, the decision to postpone capital outlays may lower the growth rates of output and employment. Second, increased macroeconomic volatility may heighten the perceived risk of default, and either increase the incidence of credit rationing or lead to a higher risk premium and borrowing rates for private firms (see Agénor and Aizenman (1998)). This may have an adverse effect on labor demand and possibly on poverty, by depriving small and labor-intensive firms of the loans needed to finance their working capital needs. Third, the propensity to save (of rich and poor households alike) may increase if macroeconomic volatility translates into higher income uncertainty (see, for instance, Agénor, 2004*b*, Appendix to Chapter 2) or an increased probability of facing borrowing constraints in "bad times," as in Agénor and Aizenman (2004). For instance, Soto (2004) found that in Chile, during the period 1990–2002, unemployment had an adverse, short-term impact on consumption of nondurable goods. A possible explanation of this inverse correlation is that unemployment is positively related to income volatility. In turn, increased uncertainty regarding future income may lower consumption by enhancing the precautionary motive for saving. It is also important to note, however, that an increase in saving induced by higher volatility may actually lead to higher growth rates, despite adverse short-term effects on employment and poverty; the issue, then, becomes one of evaluation of benefits and costs that accrue at different periods of time.

2.2.6   Growth and Distributional Effects

Macroeconomic policy affects the poor not only through its impact on the level of output or short-run changes in income, but also its growth rate over time. There are several channels through which this can occur. For instance, if cuts in public sector investment (particularly in infrastructure) lead to lower private investment through a "reverse" complementarity effect, they may reduce also the rate of economic growth. Tax increases in the formal sector may encourage evasion and the shifting of activities to the informal economy – so much so that the net impact may be a fall in revenue. In turn, the loss in resources may reduce the government's capacity to invest in infrastructure, thereby reducing the rate of economic growth. At the same time, a reduction in inflation associated with a tightening of macroeconomic policy may increase growth rates through its effect on the level and efficiency of investment, as noted earlier.

The impact of growth on poverty depends also on changes in income distribution, as noted in the previous section. In general, large differences may exist between countries regarding the extent to which growth (even when it is distribution-neutral) will affect poverty. Initial distribution may affect subsequent growth through credit market imperfections, which often translate into collateralized lending requirements. If the poor lack assets, their ability to borrow and invest in acquiring skills will therefore be limited, and poverty may perpetuate itself (see, for instance, Galor and Zeira (1993) and the discussion of poverty traps below). Inequality may also have an adverse effect on growth through changes in macroeconomic volatility, as a result for instance of greater political instability.[15]

An important question is, then, what accounts for changes in income distribution? Recent formal econometric studies, such as Barro (2000) and Bleaney and Nishiyama (2004), have been unable to find a robust relation between per capita income and inequality. In particular, the Kuznets curve hypothesis (an inverted U-shape relation between income levels and inequality) appears to be fragile. Bleaney and Nishiyama (2004), for instance, found that the estimated parameter on the initial Gini coefficient in various cross-country growth regressions does not seem to vary with the level of per capita GDP. At the same time, these parameters are never significantly negative. There is stronger evidence that changes in income distribution are related to human capital inequality – and thus to borrowing constraints, as noted earlier (see Castelló and Doménech (2002) and Iradian (2005)). A worsening in income distribution may therefore be the result of growing inequalities in educational opportunities and inadequate access to credit markets. Inflation may also explain changes in distribution; by lowering the values of both nominal assets and liabilities, it favors debtors and

---

[15] See Aghion, Caroli, and García-Peñalosa (1999) for a more detailed discussion of alternative channels. Conversely, macroeconomic volatility may lead to greater inequality, as documented empirically by Breen and García-Peñalosa (2005).

holders of real equity over lenders and owners of nominal assets. The net distributional effects will depend on access to hedging instruments and the distribution of nominal assets and liabilities across income groups. Indeed, Bulir (2001) found that inflation has an adverse effect on income distribution; this effect is highly significant at high inflation levels.

2.2.7   Recessions and Crises: Asymmetric Effects

That large output contractions can have a significant impact on the poor in developing countries is well recognized. Economic downturns, by reducing the demand for labor, tend to put downward pressure on wages and raise unemployment in the formal sector. The greater the degree of downward rigidity in wages, the larger the increase in the number of unemployed. Both effects tend to increase poverty in the formal economy.

In addition, in the absence of well-functioning credit markets (and thus limited ability to borrow in bad times) and often with no insurance benefits available for the unemployed, workers (particularly the unskilled ones) cannot remain unemployed for long. In some countries they migrate back to the rural sector; in others they move into the informal sector, where the poorest among the urban poor are usually concentrated. The resulting increase in labor supply in the informal urban economy tends to depress wages there. Thus, recessions and crises raise poverty in two related ways: directly by lowering wages and increasing the rate of job losses and the number of poor in the formal sector; and indirectly, by lowering the going wage of those who are already employed (or quasi-unemployed) in the informal economy.

These labor market effects are compounded by a number of factors, which tend to exacerbate the impact of adverse economic shocks on the poor. As noted earlier, the poor lack assets and often have no direct access to credit markets to smooth the impact of these shocks. In addition, there is growing evidence that cyclical downturns and economic crises may have an asymmetric effect on poverty: recessions and/or sharp output contractions tend to increase poverty rates significantly (through some of the channels identified above), whereas expansions tend to have a more limited effect. Understanding the sources of asymmetric effects of economic cycles and crises on poverty, and assessing with quantitative techniques the strength of these effects, is thus essential for the design of effective policy interventions.

I have reviewed elsewhere (see Agénor (2002a)) some of the evidence related to the effect of crises on the poor; Appendix A summarizes five main classes of explanations.[16] The first dwells on parents' decisions regarding their children attending school; the second is based on asymmetric changes in expectations and confidence factors; the third relies on a "credit crunch" faced by employers, with rationing resulting from either adverse selection problems or negative shocks to net worth; the fourth emphasizes the impact of borrowing constraints on household consumption behavior; and the fifth dwells on "labor hoarding" by firms facing high turnover costs for more educated labor.

---

[16]For evidence related to the effect of crises on the poor, see also Fallon and Lucas (2002). However, they did not elaborate on the possible sources of asymmetric effects.

In particular, in a recession or crisis-induced contraction, unskilled workers (among which the poor tend to be concentrated) are often the first to lose their jobs as firms "hoard" their highly-trained workers. The incentive to hoard results from the existence of high hiring and training costs associated with the use of skilled labor, and is higher the more the shock is perceived to be temporary, regardless of its size. Legally-mandated severance payments (which often serve as a substitute for unemployment benefit payments in developing countries) may also tend to limit layoffs of skilled workers. When the "good times" come back, however, firms have incentives to recoup, in priority, the productivity losses incurred during the downturn. Given the greater degree of complementarity between skilled labor and physical capital, they may be inclined to increase fixed investment instead of increasing their demand for unskilled labor. Unemployment and poverty may therefore persist for that category of workers.

In sum, the channels through which macroeconomic policy affects poverty are complex and often operate in opposite directions in the short and the longer run. It is thus hard to generalize or make blanket statements about the poverty effects of specific policies, given the fact that many of them entail dynamic trade-offs. In fact, it is tempting to repeat the conclusion of Winters, McCulloch, and McKay (2004, p. 73), following their review of the impact of trade liberalization on poverty, which highlights the importance of careful empirical analysis:

> ... there are no general comparative static results about whether trade liberalization will increase or reduce poverty. Simple statements about "the poor" will lose information, at best, and simple generalizations about all countries will just be wrong.

2.3   Theoretical Models for Poverty Analysis

As noted earlier, although it is well recognized that the poor in developing countries often generate a sizable share of their income from wage employment, the role of the labor market in the transmission of macroeconomic policy shocks to lower-income groups has not (until recently) been explored in its full complexity in analytical and empirical models. Understanding this role is all the more important given the peculiarities and imperfections that often characterize labor markets in these countries.

My contention is that macroeconomic models (both theoretical and applied) designed for poverty analysis must incorporate a specification of the labor market that reflects the characteristics highlighted earlier. This section illustrates how this can be done in a simplified version of an open-economy analytical framework that I have developed elsewhere (see Agénor (2005*f*)) and examines the impact of a "typical" macro shock, a cut in government spending, on the urban poor.

2.3.1   A Two-Household Framework

Consider a small open economy in which there are two segments: a formal sector, which produces an exportable good and whose output is entirely sold abroad, and an informal sector, which produces a nontraded good used only for domestic consumption. There are three categories of agents: producers, households, and the government. There is a single producer in each sector, and two households: a rich household, which consists of all workers employed in the formal economy, and a poor household, consisting of those workers employed in the informal sector. The rich household optimizes consumption, pays taxes, saves and borrows abroad. The poor household pays no taxes and spends all of its income.[17] Both rich and poor households supply labor inelastically and consume, in addition to the nontraded good produced in the informal sector, an imported good which is imperfectly substitutable for the home good.

Production and Labor Demand

Production of exportables in the formal economy, Y_E, requires capital as well as both labor categories, in quantities n_S and n_U. The capital stock is constant and normalized to unity. Thus,

$$Y_E = n_S^\alpha n_U^\beta, \tag{2}$$

where $\alpha, \beta \in (0, 1)$ and $\alpha + \beta < 1$. The world price of exportables is exogenous and normalized to unity. The domestic price of exportables is thus equal to the nominal exchange rate, E, which is assumed fixed.

Unskilled workers are paid a government-mandated minimum wage, ω_m, which is fixed in terms of the price of exportables. The skilled real wage, ω_S, measured also in terms of the price of exportables, is given by

$$\omega_S = \theta(z) > \omega_m, \tag{3}$$

where $z = E/P_N$ denotes the relative price of imports in terms of nontradables (referred to in what follows as the real exchange rate), and $\theta' < 0$. Equation (3) indicates that the skilled wage is related negatively to the real exchange rate. It can be derived from an efficiency wage setting in which effort is a function of the *consumption* wage, whereas firms determine the *product* wage (see Agénor (2004c)). A similar result could be obtained if instead firms face high turnover costs associated with skilled labor and if the quit rate is a function of the consumption wage as well (see Agénor (2001)). Alternatively, (3) could be derived by assuming that the skilled wage is determined by a centralized labor union whose objective is to minimize a quadratic loss function that depends on deviations of employment and the consumption wage from their target levels, subject to the firm's labor demand schedule (see Agénor (2005a)).

Profit maximization requires equating the marginal product of each category of labor to the relevant product wage:

$$\alpha n_U^\beta / n_S^{1-\alpha} = \omega_S, \quad \beta n_S^\alpha / n_U^{1-\beta} = \omega_m,$$

---

[17]Dynan, Skinner, and Zeldes (2004) provide evidence that the rich tend to save more, or more generally that saving rates tend to increase with the level of income. They identify various reasons for this pattern, including differences in rates of time preference. Ogaki and Atkeson (1997) also provide evidence that the poor save proportionately less than the rich.

which can be combined to give the skilled-unskilled wage ratio:

$$\frac{\omega_S}{\omega_m} = \frac{\alpha n_U}{\beta n_S}. \tag{4}$$

The demand functions for labor can be derived as

$$n_S^d = n_S^d(\bar{\omega}_S; \bar{\omega}_m), \quad n_U^d = n_U^d(\bar{\omega}_S; \bar{\omega}_m). \tag{5}$$

Equations (5) indicate that, as a result of gross complementarity, an increase in the product wage for either category of workers reduces the demand for both categories of labor.

Substituting these results in equation (2) and using (3) yields

$$Y_E^s = Y_E^s(\overset{+}{z}), \quad Y_E^{s\prime} > 0, \tag{6}$$

which shows that a depreciation raises output of exportables.

In the informal sector, production of the nontraded good, Y_N, requires only unskilled labor, in quantity n_N:

$$Y_N = A_N n_N^\eta, \tag{7}$$

where $A_N > 0$ is a shift parameter and $\eta \in (0, 1)$. Profit maximization yields equality between marginal revenue and marginal cost, $\omega_N = Y_N'/z$, where ω_N denotes the real wage in the informal sector, measured in terms of the price of exportables. The condition $\omega_N < \omega_m$ is assumed, in order to prevent a corner solution in which unskilled workers have no incentive to seek employment in the formal economy.

Setting for simplicity $A_N = 1/\eta$, labor demand is given by

$$n_N^d = (\omega_N z)^{1/(\eta-1)}, \tag{8}$$

where $\omega_N z$ measures the product wage in the informal sector and $n_N^{d\prime} < 0$. Substituting (8) in (7) yields the supply function of informal sector goods:

$$Y_N^s = (\omega_N z)^{\eta/(\eta-1)}, \quad Y_N^{s\prime} < 0. \tag{9}$$

Informal Labor Market

The informal labor market absorbs all unskilled workers who do not queue up for employment in the formal sector.[18] Suppose that N_U, the total number of unskilled workers in the labor force, is constant. The supply of unskilled workers in the informal sector is thus $N_U - n_U^d$. Using (5) and (8), the equilibrium condition of the informal labor market is thus given by

$$N_U - n_U^d(\omega_S; \omega_m) = n_N^d(\omega_N z).$$

---

[18]See Chapter 1 for a discussion of this assumption. Agénor (2004c, 2005a) considers the case where labor mobility between the formal and informal sectors is imperfect.

Wages adjust continuously to equilibrate supply and demand. Using (3) to solve this condition for ω_N therefore yields

$$\omega_N = \upsilon(z), \tag{10}$$

where[19]

$$\upsilon' = -\left[1 + \theta'(n_N^{d'})^{-1}\left(\frac{\partial n_U^d}{\partial \omega_S}\right)\right].$$

A real exchange rate depreciation (a rise in z) has, in general, an ambiguous effect on the market-clearing wage. On the one hand, a real depreciation lowers the demand for labor in the informal sector, because the product wage in the informal sector, $\omega_N z$, tends to increase. To eliminate the excess supply of labor, the informal sector wage must fall. On the other, the rise in z lowers the skilled wage in the formal sector, which tends to increase the demand for unskilled labor in the formal sector. This reduces labor supply in the informal economy and puts upward pressure on wages there. The net effect on ω_N therefore depends on the relative strength of the direct and indirect effects. I will assume in what follows that the direct effect dominates (or, equivalently, that θ' is sufficiently small), to ensure that $\upsilon' < 0$.

Moreover, given that $\theta' < 0$, $|\upsilon'| < 1$ and the product wage increases as a result of a real depreciation ($\partial(\omega_N z)/\partial z = 1 + \upsilon' > 0$). Thus, a real depreciation lowers employment and output in the informal sector, even if the informal sector wage (measured in terms of the price of exportables) falls. These results are important to understand the impact of policy shocks on poverty, as discussed later in this chapter.

Household Consumption

The rich household's consumption decisions follow a two-step process. First, the level of total spending is determined, based on intertemporal optimization and subject to a flow budget constraint. Second, total spending is allocated between consumption of the home good and the imported good, based on relative prices.

The rich household's discounted lifetime utility is given by

$$\int_0^\infty \ln c_R e^{-\rho t} dt, \tag{11}$$

where c_R is total consumption (measured in terms of the price of exportables) and $\rho > 0$ the rate of time preference, assumed constant.

Let D_R denote the rich household's stock of foreign debt, measured in foreign-currency terms. Its flow budget constraint can thus be written as

$$\dot{D}_R = i^* D_R + c_R + T - Y_E^s, \tag{12}$$

where i^* is the cost of borrowing on the world capital market and T lump-sum taxes, also measured in terms of the price of exportables.

---

[19]In what follows a "~" over a variable is used to denote a steady-state value. Derivatives are all evaluated at steady-state values of z and ω_N equal to unity.

The world capital market is imperfect. Specifically, the interest rate facing domestic borrowers is the sum of a risk-free rate, i_f^*, and a country-risk premium, which varies positively with the economy's foreign debt:

$$i^* = i_f^* + \kappa(D), \tag{13}$$

where $\kappa' > 0$, and $\kappa'' > 0$ and $D = D_R + D_G$ is the economy's total stock of external debt, defined as the sum of the rich household's debt, D_R, and government debt, D_G.

The rich household treats Y_E^s, i^*, and T as given, and maximizes (11) subject to (12), by choosing a sequence $\{c_R, D_R\}_{t=0}^{\infty}$. The optimality condition is the standard Euler equation:

$$\dot{c}_R/c_R = i_f^* + \kappa(D) - \rho. \tag{14}$$

Ruling out Ponzi games also requires imposing a transversality condition on D.

The rich household allocates total consumption spending between purchases of the informal sector (respectively, imported) good, c_R^N (respectively, c_R^M):

$$c_R^N = \delta z c_R, \quad c_R^M = (1 - \delta)c_R, \tag{15}$$

where $0 < \delta < 1$.

Income of the poor household (measured in terms of exportables) consists of informal sector output, $z^{-1}Y_N^s$. All income is spent on consumption, c_P:

$$c_P = z^{-1}Y_N^s. \tag{16}$$

Assuming for simplicity an allocation rule across consumption goods that is similar to the rich household's yields

$$c_P^N = \delta z c_P, \quad c_P^M = (1 - \delta)c_P. \tag{17}$$

Government

The government derives revenue by levying lump-sum taxes on the rich household. It spends on imported goods, G, and services its foreign debt, D_G, also at the (premium-inclusive) rate i^*. It finances its deficit by borrowing on world capital markets:

$$\dot{D}_G = i^* D_G + G - T. \tag{18}$$

Market for Informal Sector Goods

The equilibrium condition of the market for informal sector goods can be written as

$$Y_N^s = c_R^N + c_P^N. \tag{19}$$

Using equations (9), (15) and (17), this condition becomes

$$Y_N^s(\omega_N z) = \delta z(c_R + c_P),$$

which can be rewritten as, using (16):

$$Y_N^s(\omega_N z) = \frac{\delta}{1-\delta} z c_R. \tag{20}$$

The price of the nontraded good is flexible and adjusts to eliminate excess demand. Condition (20) can therefore be solved for the equilibrium real exchange rate:

$$z = z(c_R, \omega_N), \tag{21}$$

where

$$z_{c_R} = \left[Y_N^{s\prime} - \frac{\delta \tilde{c}_R}{1-\delta} \right]^{-1} \frac{\delta}{1-\delta} < 0,$$

$$z_{\omega_N} = -\left[Y_N^{s\prime} - \frac{\delta \tilde{c}_R}{1-\delta} \right]^{-1} Y_N^{s\prime} < 0,$$

so that $|z_{\omega_N}| < 1$. This equation shows that an increase for instance in ω_N (for c_R given), by raising the product wage and lowering the supply of goods in the informal sector, requires an appreciation of the real exchange rate (a fall in z) to eliminate excess demand. This effect is less than proportional because the appreciation mitigates the initial adverse effect of the rise in ω_N on the product wage. An increase in expenditure by the rich household raises demand for informal sector goods and also leads to a real appreciation.

Substituting (10) for ω_N in (21) yields

$$z = \chi'(c_R), \tag{22}$$

where $\chi' = z_{c_R}/(1 - z_{\omega_N} v') < 0.$[20]

Informal Employment, Consumption, and Poverty

Suppose that the legal minimum wage corresponds to the official poverty line, and that average income in the informal sector, $P_N Y_N^s / n_N^d$, is less than $E\omega_m$ at all times; given (8) and (9), this implies that $\omega_N < \omega_m$, as assumed earlier. In the present setting, two approaches can be used to measure poverty. The first is to define a headcount poverty index, H, as the number of workers employed in the informal sector, plus unemployed skilled workers in the formal economy, divided by the total size of the labor force, N:

$$H = \frac{1}{N}\{n_N^d + (N_S - n_S^d)\},$$

or equivalently, given that $N_S = N - (n_U^d + n_N^d)$:

$$H = 1 - \left(\frac{n_S^d + n_U^d}{N} \right). \tag{23}$$

---

[20]Note that, because $|v'|$ and $|z_{\omega_N}|$ are both less than unity from equation (10) and equation (21), $1 - z_{\omega_N} v' > 0.$

The headcount poverty index is thus given by the number of workers who are not employed in the formal sector, in proportion of the labor force.

Alternatively, if unemployed skilled workers are assumed to benefit from a nonmarket source of income that keeps them above the poverty line, the poverty index can be defined simply as

$$H = \frac{n_N^d}{N} = 1 - \left(\frac{N_S + n_U^d}{N} \right). \tag{24}$$

The second approach is to use formula (1) provided earlier. In the present case, assuming that G (government spending on imported goods) is the policy instrument yieldsh

$$I_G = \frac{d[(n_N^d)^{-1}c_P]/dG}{d[(n_S^d + n_U^d)^{-1}c_R]/dG} - 1.$$

Given that from (16) $c_P = z^{-1}Y_N^s$, and that $Y_N^s/n_N^d = \omega_N z$, this expression is equivalent to

$$I_G = \frac{d\omega_N/dG}{d[(n_S^d + n_U^d)^{-1}c_R]/dG} - 1, \tag{25}$$

which can be used to determine whether a change in G is pro-poor. Unemployed skilled workers are excluded from the calculation of mean income of the rich, $c_R/(n_S^d + n_U^d)$, but this can easily be modified.

2.3.2   Equilibrium

Figure 2.1 depicts the partial equilibrium of the labor market, under the assumption that skilled workers who are unable to obtain a job in the formal sector opt to remain openly unemployed rather than seek employment in the informal economy.[21]

Panel A depicts the demand functions for labor in the formal sector. Both demand curves for skilled labor, n_S^d, and unskilled labor, n_U^d, are downward-sloping, because they are negatively related to ω_S, the skilled wage (see (5)). Panel B determines the supply of labor (and thus actual employment) in the informal economy, $N_U - n_U^d$, given unskilled employment in the formal sector (point B). Given the labor demand curve in the informal sector n_N^d, the market-clearing wage is determined at point C in Panel C.[22] Curve WW in Panel D depicts the positive relationship between the skilled wage and the informal sector wage (for c_R given), which is obtained by substituting z from (21) into (3). Skilled unemployment (which can be deemed "quasi-voluntary") is given in Panel A by the distance between the supply of skilled labor, N_S, and

---

[21] See Agénor (1996) and Chapter 1 for a further discussion of this hypothesis and a review of the evidence on skilled unemployment in developing countries.

[22] From equation (8), n_N^d is negatively related to $\omega_N z$. From (21), with c_R given, z is inversely related to ω_N, with $|z_{\omega_N}| < 1$. Thus, $n_N^{d\prime}(1 + z_{\omega_N}) < 0$ is the derivative of n_N^d with respect to ω_N, so that the demand curve is indeed downward-sloping.

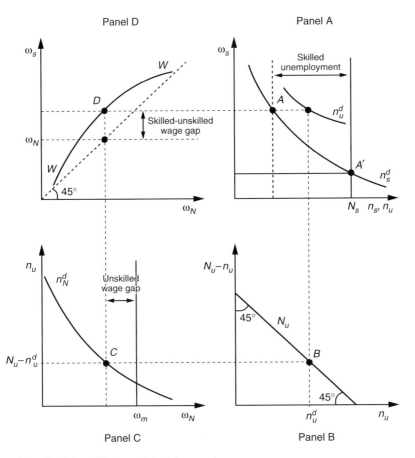

Figure 2.1   Partial equilibrium of the labor market.

the equilibrium point on the demand curve n_S^d (point A).[23] At point A, the skilled wage is too high (relative to the market-clearing wage, corresponding to point A') to eliminate the excess supply of labor and skilled unemployment prevails. Both the skilled-unskilled wage gap (which can be derived from (4)), and the unskilled wage gap (that is, the difference $\omega_m - \omega_N$) are also shown in the figure.

Appendix B shows how the complete model can be reduced into a dynamic system in c_R, consumption of the rich household, and D, the economy's total stock of debt. The phase diagram of the system is depicted in the upper northeast quadrant of Figure 2.2. The phase curve CC represents the combinations of c_R and D for which consumption of the rich is constant ($\dot{c}_R = 0$), whereas the phase curve DD represents the combinations of c_R and D for which the current account is in equilibrium

---

[23] Because there is no unemployment benefit scheme in the present framework, unemployed workers are implicitly assumed to either turn to a subsistence activity (home production) or to rely on other members of the household for their survival.

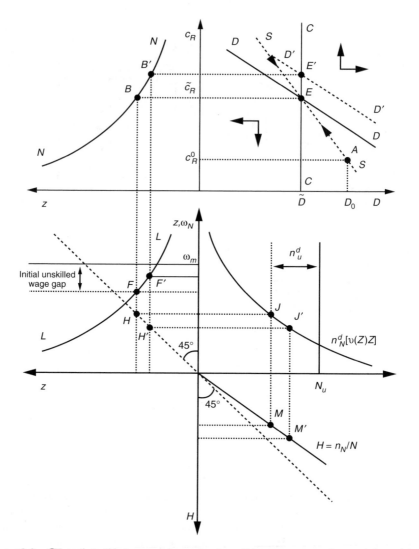

Figure 2.2   General equilibrium and determination of the poverty rate. *Source*: Adapted from Agénor (2005*f*).

($\dot{D} = 0$). Curve CC is vertical, whereas curve DD is downward-sloping. As shown in Appendix B, saddlepath stability is always ensured. The saddlepath itself, denoted SS, has a negative slope, which is steeper than DD. Thus, starting from a position (c_R^0, D_0), transition to the long-run equilibrium (which is reached at point E) requires consumption of the rich and external borrowing to evolve in opposite directions. In the upper northwest panel, the curve NN shows the relationship between c_R and z given by (22), whereas curve LL in the lower northwest panel displays the relationship between z and ω_N given in (10). The equilibrium real exchange rate is determined at point B, which is translated to point H, whereas the equilibrium informal sector wage is determined at F. The demand curve for labor in the informal sector, obtained solely as a function of z by combining equations (8) and (10), is shown as $n_N^d[\upsilon(z)z]$ in the lower northeast panel. Equilibrium informal employment is determined at point J. Finally, the lower southeast panel shows the determination of the poverty headcount index solely as a function of informal sector employment, as defined in (24). The poverty rate is determined at point M.

2.3.3 Cut in Government Spending

The above framework can be used to study the impact and steady-state effects of a variety of macroeconomic policy shocks. Given the illustrative nature of the exercise, I will confine my analysis here to a permanent (and unanticipated) cut in government spending on imported goods, G.

As can be inferred from (14) with $\dot{c}_R = 0$, and as formally established in Appendix B, a cut in G has no effect on the economy's stock of debt in the long run (see equation (A10)). Given that the current account must be in balance in the steady state (that is, $\dot{D} = 0$), the reduction in G must be offset by an increase in private consumption of the rich or a reduction in domestic supply of exportables. This requires an appreciation of the real exchange rate to either dampen demand for informal sector goods or reduce incentives for producing exportables.

In turn, the appreciation leads to an increase in the informal sector wage, but to a fall in the product wage in that sector (recall that $\partial(\omega_N z)/\partial z > 0$). The demand for labor and output in the informal sector therefore increase, and so does the poverty index. At the same time, the real appreciation raises the skilled wage (as implied by (3)), which tends to reduce output and employment of both categories of labor in the formal sector. Skilled unemployment rises, whereas the reduction in demand for unskilled labor increases supply in the informal sector, thereby mitigating the upward movement in wages in that sector. Consumption of the poor increases, as implied by (16), given that z falls and Y_N^s rises.

Because the stock of foreign debt D cannot change on impact, and does not change across steady states either, a permanent increase in G entails no transitional dynamics. Graphically, curve CC (which does not depend on G) does not change; curve DD, on the contrary, shifts upward to $D'D'$. The economy jumps immediately from point E to a point like E' located on CC. Consumption of the rich increases, the real exchange rate appreciates from B to B' or from H to H', the informal sector wage rises from F to F', informal employment rises from J to J', and the headcount poverty index increases from M to M'. The unskilled wage gap (the difference between the minimum wage and the informal sector wage, both measured in terms of the price of exports) falls, reducing inequality among unskilled workers.[24]

As shown in Appendix B, $d\tilde{c}_R/dG < 0$, whereas $d(\tilde{n}_S^d + \tilde{n}_U^d)/dG > 0$. Thus, the net effect of the cut in G on average consumption of the rich, $\tilde{c}_R/(\tilde{n}_S^d + \tilde{n}_U^d)$,

---

[24]Of course, a temporary shock to G would entail transitional dynamics, as would any shock that leads to a shift in DD, such as a change in the world risk-free interest rate; see Agénor (2005f).

is unambiguously positive. Moreover, given that $d\tilde{\omega}_N/dG < 0$, the net effect of a reduction in G on mean consumption of the poor, $\tilde{c}_P/\tilde{n}_N^d$, is positive.

Given these results, and the index defined in (25), a reduction in G is pro-poor (that is, $I_G > 0$) if

$$\frac{d\tilde{\omega}_N/dG}{d[(n_S^d + n_U^d)^{-1}\tilde{c}_R]/dG} > 1,$$

a condition that depends, in particular, on the elasticity of output with respect to labor in the informal sector. Indeed, because spending by the poor is based on their current resources, the higher η is, the higher will be the wage elasticity of labor demand, $-(1 - \eta)^{-1}$ (see (8)). As a result, the lower will be the increase in the informal sector wage needed to absorb the inflow of labor in that sector induced by the cut in government spending, and the more likely it is that the policy will not be pro-poor. Put differently, whether a cut in government spending reduces poverty depends on how the "pro-poorness" effect is measured. Because employment shifts to the informal sector, where workers earn a wage that is lower than the poverty line, poverty (as measured by the number of workers employed in that sector) increases. At the same time, however, because the increase in output in the informal economy leads to higher income, it is possible for consumption of the poor to rise by more than consumption of the rich.

More generally, the model helps to illustrate that the poverty effects of macroeconomic policies in a typical developing-country context operate through complex channels involving changes in aggregate demand and supply in the formal and informal sectors, as well as changes in relative prices and wages. In the foregoing analysis, a key issue is the impact of the shock on the demand for unskilled labor in the formal sector. The contraction in the demand for that category of labor in the formal economy requires the product wage in the informal sector to fall to stimulate demand there and generate an increase in output. Accounting for these general equilibrium effects is crucial to determine whether macroeconomic policy benefits or hurts the poor.[25]

2.4   Some Research Directions

The foregoing discussion suggests that much has been learned in recent years on how macroeconomic policy affects the poor. However, there are still important gaps in our knowledge, and the scope for further research remains considerable. In what follows I provide my own perspective on what could be fruitful areas of investigation. The suggested list of topics is by no means exhaustive and reflects heavily my own research

---

[25]Note that the foregoing analysis assumes that the poverty line is fixed at the level of the minimum wage. In general, of course, the poverty effects of government spending shocks will depend not only on changes in employment levels but also on where the different after-tax wages (formal and informal) lie relative to the poverty line.

interests. Some of these topics are motivated by the recognition that although much research is needed on issues that are essentially "macro" in nature, there are many questions that involve understanding interactions between micro and macro factors.

Specifically, issues that I identify as important areas for research include poverty traps, the sources of asymmetric effects of output shocks, the effect of macroeconomic volatility on the poor, trade-offs between unemployment reduction and poverty alleviation, and the extent to which redistribution can hurt the poor.

2.4.1 Poverty Traps

Why do poor countries remain poor? This issue has long been the subject of intense scrutiny by economists. As noted earlier, the "circular relationship" between growth and poverty emphasized by Nurkse (1953) suggests that at low levels of per capita income (and thus low saving and investment rates), countries may be caught in a low-growth trap from which it is difficult to escape. Put succinctly, a country may be poor because it is poor to begin with.

This view, and much of the early literature on low-growth traps, focused on settings in which the equilibrium is unique, in the sense that, given the economy's characteristics, and the policy environment, there is only one possible growth outcome – stagnation. By contrast, much of the subsequent literature on poverty traps is based on models with multiple equilibria, in which a low-income or low-growth trap is but one of possible outcomes or steady-state properties of the economy. A key feature of these models is that whether the economy settles on a low- or high-growth equilibrium depends either on some inherent nonlinearity in the economy, such as threshold externalities associated with human capital or nonconvexities associated with the production technology.

Externalities associated with human capital formation provide a good illustration of how multiple steady-state growth rates can emerge. Various models have shown indeed that countries that are identical in their structural characteristics, but differ in their initial level (or distribution) of human capital, may cluster around different steady-state growth equilibria, as a result of either social increasing returns to scale from human capital accumulation (as in Azariadis and Drazen (1990)) or credit market imperfections (coupled with a fixed cost in the production of human capital, as in Galor and Zeira (1993)).

For instance, an economy with a low stock of human capital to begin with will also offer low returns to education, and consequently be trapped in a stage of underdevelopment. Conversely, growth perpetuates itself when an economy starts with a high level of human capital. Alternatively, by preventing the poor from making productive, but indivisible, investments in human capital, credit constraints (due either to imperfect information about individual abilities or the inability to enforce the terms of loan contracts) can perpetuate a low-growth, high poverty process. Inequality in the initial wealth distribution, which determines how many agents can save and invest in the acquisition of human capital, can therefore have a significant negative impact on poverty. Furthermore, the more inequitable the initial distribution is (or equivalently, the greater the number of poor households that are credit-constrained to begin with), the more severe this effect will be.

Threshold externalities associated with public capital in infrastructure (such as roads, electricity, and telecommunications) may also lead to a low-growth, poverty trap. Indeed, as indicated earlier, public capital in infrastructure may have not only a positive effect on the marginal productivity of private inputs (as emphasized in various growth models in the tradition of Barro (1990)) but also a complementarity effect on private investment. But this complementarity effect may be subject to a threshold – the productivity effect of public capital on the private rate of return must be sufficiently high, to begin with, to stimulate private capital formation. If this effect is too low (perhaps because of indivisibilities, due to the fact that some types of investment in infrastructure are lumpy in nature), the economy may be stuck in a low-growth, high poverty trap, in which small increases in public capital outlays in infrastructure bring few benefits.

A "big push," that is, a large increase in public investment, may raise the public capital stock sufficiently for the complementarity effect to "kick in," unleashing "animal spirits" and eventually lifting the economy to a higher growth path (see Agénor and Aizenman (2006)). This increase in public capital formation, in turn, may result from a large inflow of foreign aid, or alternatively an increase in available domestic resources triggered by generous debt relief. By implication, countries with a large external public debt may be "trapped" in poverty, because debt servicing absorbs an excessive fraction of the resources that could be available to finance public investment in infrastructure.

As documented by Azariadis (2001) and Azariadis and Starchuski (2004), various other sources of poverty traps have been identified in the recent literature. They relate to malnutrition and ill health (resulting for instance from exposure to tropical diseases), gender inequality and high fertility rates (which affect both women's labor supply and decisions to invest in human capital), extreme geographical limitations (for instance, landlocked countries), coordination failures among private agents, and weak political institutions (leading, for instance, to a highly corrupt government bureaucracy).

Kremer and Chen (1999) provide a good illustration of how the interaction between wages, fertility, and the cost of education can lead to a poverty trap. Their model is based on three major assumptions: higher wages reduce fertility; children of the unskilled are more likely to be unskilled; and skilled and unskilled workers are complements in production. Fertility and incentives to acquire education depend on the wage structure, and thus on the fraction of skilled labor in the workforce, whereas the fraction of skilled labor depends itself on fertility and the decision to invest in the acquisition of skills. Thus, the positive feedback between fertility differentials and wage inequality may lead to multiple steady states. If the initial proportion of skilled workers is high enough, wage and fertility differentials between skilled and unskilled workers will be small, allowing the economy to converge to a steady state with low inequality. However, if the initial proportion of skilled workers is too low, inequality will be self-reinforcing, and the economy may approach a steady state with a low proportion of skilled labor and a high degree of inequality between skilled and unskilled workers.

I have reviewed elsewhere other sources of poverty traps and their policy implications (see Agénor (2005*h*)). This is important because, as noted earlier, the policy message that one can take from analytical models is sometime difficult to put in practice. And because poverty traps can result from multiple causes, the issue of how best to sequence public policies to escape from them arises also. Much depends therefore on what causes the trap to emerge in the first place.

For instance, what role should the state play in "solving" coordination failures, if one takes the view that these failures are a key reason that prevents countries from growing out of a poverty trap? History suggests that too much optimism about the success of centralized coordination mechanisms would be misplaced. Yet, it is possible for even a *temporary* change in government policies to alter private beliefs sufficiently to lead to a switch from a "bad" equilibrium to a "good" equilibrium. As a matter of fact, Tirole (1996) showed that a government anticorruption program of sufficient duration and depth can lead to a switch from an equilibrium with high corruption (sustained by expectations of high corruption) to one with low corruption (sustained by the belief of a less corrupt bureaucracy).

Another important policy issue for low-income countries is the role of foreign aid. Indeed, for many of the poorest countries, a large increase in aid may be crucial to provide the "big push" to public investment alluded to earlier, given that the ability to mobilize domestic resources through taxation is limited.

Key issues in this context are what type of conditionality should foreign assistance be subject to without hampering its catalytic role (see Mosley, Hudson, and Verschoor (2004)), and whether aid entails diminishing returns, as a result of country-specific absorption constraints (see Clemens and Radelet (2003)). Analytical research on these issues remains, however, limited. For instance, in their analysis of the macroeconomic effects of aid, Dalgaard, Hansen, and Tarp (2004) focus on the impact of foreign assistance on productivity. But they do not account for a possible link between aid (or at least some components of it) and public investment.[26]

In addition, there is a crucial need to develop rigorous empirical tests of the existence of poverty traps and, equally important, tests that would allow the investigator to identify the most important factors, or causes, leading to these traps. Most of the available evidence on poverty traps is indirect and relies on conditional convergence tests. By and large, these tests have shown that per capita incomes in poor countries appear not to be catching up with developed economies. Instead of "global" convergence, economies appear to gravitate around "convergence clubs," whereby wealthy economies converge to common high-level income growth paths while poor countries converge to common low-level income growth paths (see Agénor (2004*b*) and Islam (2003)).

However, as emphasized in an early contribution by Durlauf and Johnson (1995), standard regression models used for testing for cross-country convergence are based on linear specifications and do not provide great insight as to the sources of multiple steady states. The reason is that poverty trap models are fundamentally nonlinear in

---

[26] By affecting the terms of trade, aid may also have an impact on private investment. See Djajic, Lahiri, and Raimondos-Moller (1999).

nature, and in standard applications of panel data methods individual heterogeneities are not explicitly accounted for (Durlauf and Quah (1999, p. 286)).

Using regression tree analysis, Durlauf and Johnson (1995) found evidence that different countries indeed follow different growth paths when grouped according to initial conditions. More recent research is also encouraging; Canova (2004) for instance presented an approach that dwells on the econometric literature on testing for the existence of an unknown break point in time series. Although Canova provides empirical results only on industrial countries, his approach shows some promise for addressing the broader issue of poverty traps. At this stage, however, the lack of direct empirical tests remains problematic from a policy standpoint. Given the large number of competing hypotheses, it is crucial for researchers to devise more elaborate tests that would allow one to discriminate among these hypotheses and determine which factors matter the most from a policy perspective.

2.4.2   Asymmetric Effects of Output Shocks

As noted earlier, business cycles and economic crises may have an asymmetric effect on poverty. Accounting for these effects is important for evaluating the welfare costs of recessions and crises, and for judging the correlation between growth and poverty: observing a negative correlation between these two variables can be misleading in the presence of asymmetry. Indeed, if it results essentially from associations that pertain to recessions rather than expansions, it may lead to erroneous predictions about the potential of growth-oriented policies to reduce poverty.

As discussed in Appendix A, there are several potential sources of asymmetric effects, and discriminating among them is important for policy design. Yet, the techniques that have been used so far to assess the scope of asymmetric effects are silent in that respect. Depending on the exact source of asymmetry, an appropriate policy response may involve the implementation of a social safety net focusing on subsidies to keep children in school, measures to help the poor access credit markets, or incentives for firms to restrain from firing unskilled workers during downturns.

Some of these policies may have unintended longer-run consequences for poverty; for instance, raising firing costs may increase labor market rigidities and may reduce firms' incentives to hire unskilled workers in the first place – thereby affecting the poor by constraining employment growth.

2.4.3   Welfare Costs of Macroeconomic Volatility

As noted earlier, macroeconomic volatility can affect growth and poverty through a number of channels. Some of these channels have been explicitly accounted for and quantified in cross-country empirical regressions. However, there has been relatively little quantitative research on the cost of macroeconomic fluctuations for the welfare of the poor – despite the well-documented fact that developing countries tend to be more exposed to volatility than industrial countries (see Agénor and Montiel (1999)). Suppose that the poor are risk averse, and that the lack of access to effective risk-coping mechanisms (such as well-functioning credit markets) forces them to engage in "risk avoidance" strategies, which involve allocating resources to low-risk, low-return activities to reduce their vulnerability to idiosyncratic shocks. Intuition suggests that, in such conditions, macroeconomic volatility may entail large welfare losses. The simulation results of Pallage and Robe (2003), albeit based on archetype economies with a single representative consumer, suggest that this is indeed likely. They also found that even if consumers are only moderately risk averse, eliminating these fluctuations altogether may be preferable to a permanent increase in consumption growth.

An important direction of investigation would thus be to extend the Pallage-Robe analysis to a multi-agent setting to analyze the implications of differences in the degree of risk aversion for measuring the welfare effects of macroeconomic fluctuations. To the extent that their results hold in this more general setting, they would have an important policy implication: if the focus is on the welfare of the poor, as opposed to consumption growth *per se*, policies aimed at reducing volatility in consumption may be equally, or even more, beneficial to the poor than policies aimed at stimulating growth. Such policies may include not only greater and better access to credit markets, to allow the poor to smooth the impact of income shocks, but also policies aimed at reducing the economy's vulnerability to adverse external shocks – through, for instance, greater diversification of production and foreign trade. Arrangements designed to limit price fluctuations on world commodity markets could also be desirable from that perspective. Moreover, some of these policies may be useful to limit the impact of microeconomic volatility as well. Indeed, the poor typically face a multitude of risks at the micro level – such as the risks of crop failure faced by farmers due to area-specific drought or floods, and livestock disease – which can also translate into high consumption volatility. Greater access to credit markets would allow the poor to cope better with these shocks.

2.4.4 Unemployment–Poverty Trade-offs

The focus on reducing poverty in low-income countries has, to some extent, overshadowed another key policy goal – the reduction in unemployment. Indeed, progress has remained elusive on that front as well. During the 1990s, many developing counties (particularly in Latin America and in the Middle East), experienced major increases in unemployment.

In some of my recent work, I have argued that unemployment reduction and poverty alleviation may entail trade-offs (see Agénor (2004*d*)). An obvious reason is that the higher growth rates of output and job creation that are needed to absorb an increase in the supply of labor and reduce unemployment may require a significant drop in real wages. In turn, the deterioration in living standards may lead to higher poverty. Thus, the share of the "working poor" in total employment may increase, as observed in several countries in recent years (see International Labor Organization (2003)).

A trade-off between unemployment and poverty may also result from the implementation of specific policies. An increase in employment subsidies, for instance, may have a direct, beneficial impact on unskilled employment; at the same time, if it is financed by an increase in the sales tax on domestic goods, it may increase poverty, because of the adverse effect that the tax hike may have on the cost of living and the consumption wage. Depending on the exact nature of the tax that is used to offset the impact of the increase in spending on the budget (whether it is indeed an increase in the sales tax, or on the contrary a rise in income tax on individuals or firms), as well as the composition of household spending, the impact may be significant for the poorest households in urban areas. It is possible for poverty to rise in the informal sector (because workers in that sector bear the brunt of the increase in consumer prices, for instance), while at the same time unskilled unemployment falls in the formal economy. A reduction in the payroll tax on unskilled labor (a policy that has often been advocated to reduce unemployment) may have similar results. If the reduction in the payroll tax is financed by a mixture of higher taxes on domestic goods and corporate income, and the reduction in the net rate of return on physical capital accumulation lowers investment incentives, the net effect on employment may be mitigated. As a result of gross complementarity between capital and labor, the demand for labor may not increase over time as much as it would otherwise. Unemployment may thus fall to a limited extent, whereas poverty among the most vulnerable urban groups can increase significantly – again, because higher taxes on domestic goods have a large impact on the cost of living faced by that category of households.

The existence of trade-offs between unemployment and poverty reduction – either at the aggregate, economy-wide level or at the level of individual household groups (for instance, urban households) – must receive greater attention. To determine whether these trade-offs exist is not straightforward, because unemployment and poverty are jointly endogenous; the correlation between them are driven by factors that vary over time, depending on the nature of shocks that affect the economy. Nevertheless, to the extent that they do exist, these trade-offs imply that to assess the welfare effects of adjustment policies a composite index may be needed to gauge performance with respect to both objectives, that is, the degree to which policies are "pro-poor, pro-employment." An interesting issue, then, is how to generalize the index proposed in (1), given that poverty and unemployment may receive different weights in social welfare.

2.4.5   Can Redistribution Hurt the Poor?

A fashionable idea in some policy circles is that redistribution is essential to reduce poverty rapidly in some countries, because changes in income are unlikely to be sufficient. Clearly, the more pronounced the degree of inequality in a country, the smaller will be the impact of economic growth on the poor. More equal distribution is desirable for a number of reasons, but whether it is so because of its impact on poverty reduction is not clear. First, in theory the relation between growth and income distribution can go both ways (see Aghion, Caroli, and García-Peñalosa (1999)). At the empirical level, results are also mixed. Knowles (2001), for instance, showed that the relationship between inequality and growth can change once one distinguishes between data based on income measures of inequality and those based on consumption, instead of mixing the two datasets. Bleaney and Nishiyama (2004), as noted earlier, report fragile results as well. Deininger and Olinto (2000) found that it is asset (land) inequality that is negatively correlated with growth, not income inequality. Thus, if anything, policymakers should be more concerned about poor households' access to assets and their ability to accumulate them, than about the distribution of income. But policies aimed at reallocating assets have proved to be awfully difficult to implement in practice, and the experience shows that it is often not the poorest among the poor who benefit from them. Indeed, market-based land reforms, where the poor receive subsidies to purchase land from willing sellers, are often too limited in scope to have much of an impact on income distribution – in part because the poorest among the poor are often excluded (Bardhan (1996)).

Second, changes in income distribution typically have feedback effects on growth. In models of poverty traps that emphasize the role of initial inequality, redistributing wealth from the rich to the poor may help individuals with no assets to escape from poverty. In the model of Galor and Zeira (1993), for instance, redistribution would allow the poor to invest in human capital. Thus, a policy-initiated shift in the distribution of income might shift the economy to a "good" equilibrium. But asset and income redistribution may mitigate the impact of growth on poverty by adversely affecting growth itself. For instance, imposing greater equality through higher taxation of income may lower the propensity to save of capitalists and their ability to invest. Redistribution policies can therefore push the economy into a new form of poverty trap, if it leads over time to a large reduction in saving and investment by the rich, which "helps" the poor through its effect on growth.[27] Alternatively, higher statutory tax rates may increase incentives to evade taxes and induce workers and firms to move into the informal sector. The loss in revenue and may constrain the government's capacity to invest in infrastructure, thereby hampering the expansion of private activity.

More generally, much of the literature fails to recognize that what can be achieved through the redistributive measures that are often suggested is likely to be quite limited. The reality is that governments in poor countries have limited ways to alter inequality. Taxing the very rich is often unfeasible due to their political connections. Forced redistribution of assets (through government-mandated reallocation of land, for instance) is politically difficult and often a recipe for disaster, as noted earlier. Progressive taxation (in the form of inheritance taxes, for instance) is either not feasible (due to administrative constraints) or ineffective (due to evasion). Transfer payments through social safety nets are temporary, not permanent measures to reduce poverty, to a large extent because they create moral hazard problems. They do not foster self-reliance and may reduce incentives to invest in skills.

Other theoretical studies that have pointed out the possibility of a positive association between inequality and growth include early contributions by Lewis (1954) and Kaldor (1957), and studies by Perotti (1993) and Li and Zou (1998). In Lewis

---

[27] General equilibrium interactions could mitigate the adverse effect on growth, to the extent that some of the increased tax revenue is used to finance higher public investment in infrastructure.

(1954), for instance, entrepreneurs save a larger fraction of their profit income than the other groups in the economy; income inequality may therefore lead to more savings overall and faster growth for the economy as a whole. A similar idea is developed in Kaldor (1957), where the saving rate of the working class is taken to be zero. Perotti (1993) found that a very egalitarian but poor economy may be unable to kick off a growth process, whereas an economy with a very unequal income distribution may be in the best position to do so. Li and Zou (1998) found that when government revenues collected through income taxation are used to finance public consumption instead of production, a more equal distribution of income may lead to a higher income tax rate and lower economic growth – even though welfare effects can be positive (as one would expect if public consumption spending enters in households' utility functions).

In sum, although there are plausible economic arguments to suggest that high levels of inequality may hurt growth and the poor, there are equally plausible reasons (at least on analytical grounds) to suggest that greater equality may have the very same effects. A fair conclusion therefore is that, given the state of the empirical literature, the emphasis on redistributive policies (as, for instance, in Klasen (2003)) as a way to lower poverty may be misplaced, particularly in low-income countries.

2.5   Concluding Remarks

The purpose of this chapter has been to provide an overview of some of the recent literature on the macroeconomics of poverty reduction and to offer some perspectives (mostly my own, actually) on future research. The first part of the chapter argued that the research agenda on poverty, in the profession at large and in international development institutions in particular, was biased toward an excessive focus on measurement and micro issues, partly as a result of a lack of interest by macroeconomists.

My contention is that the bias in the agenda has done a lot of good, but also much harm. The lack of rigorous analytical and empirical research on poverty traps (a critical issue for low-income countries) at the IMF, the World Bank, and other international development institutions illustrates the problem well. I emphasized that growth and inequality are both endogenous; it is policies, not growth *per se*, that have to be considered pro-poor or not. The implication is that much of the recent debate on measuring pro-poor growth is misguided. *Ex post* additive decompositions of changes in poverty into growth and inequality components are useless to inform policy design; the elasticities that are derived from these decompositions do not differentiate between policies and shocks, and they say nothing about the interactions, and transmission channels, between growth and inequality. Recognizing the fact that only policies can be deemed pro-poor has an important methodological implication – measuring the degree of "pro-poorness" of policies requires using a structural macroeconomic model, where poverty, growth, and income distribution are simultaneously determined. I proposed a simple, model-based index that accounts for changes in consumption of the poor and the nonpoor. With a dynamic macro framework, the index can also be given a temporal dimension and, if the model is sufficiently disaggregated, a regional dimension as well. It can therefore provide a guide to the potential trade-offs (temporal and spatial) that policymakers may face in designing poverty reduction strategies.

The second part reviewed various channels through which macroeconomic policy can affect the poor in in a typical developing-country setting. The essential role played by the labor market was emphasized at the outset, although distortions in goods and credit markets may also play an important role. I then examined how macroeconomic policies affect the poor through changes in aggregate demand, inflation and relative prices, the real exchange rate and the supply side, aggregate volatility, and growth and redistribution effects. It was noted that in periods of fiscal consolidation, the tendency has been to cut public capital outlays more than current expenditure. Although this strategy may protect social spending in the short run, and prevent an increase in poverty, the longer-run effects may be much worse because the lack of new investment may hamper growth. Conversely, sharp cuts in social expenditure in the short run may be beneficial to the poor in the long run if they bring lower inflation and interest rates, as a result of smaller public sector deficits. This argument is particularly relevant if social expenditures are not well targeted to the poor, to begin with. It was also noted that a growing body of evidence suggests that cyclical downturns and economic crises may have an asymmetric effect on poverty: recessions or sharp output contractions may increase poverty rates significantly, whereas expansions tend to have a more limited effect. Various reasons as to why such effects may occur were explored.

The third part of the chapter examined analytical macro models designed for poverty analysis. The importance of a proper modeling of the labor market was illustrated in a two-household framework, and the response of poverty to a government spending shock was analyzed. The analysis provided useful insights regarding the transmission process of macroeconomic policy on on the poor. Nevertheless, more elaborate applied models (of the type discussed in the rest of this book), are important to measure quantitatively how different policies contribute to poverty reduction (in both the short and the long run), and to study policy complementarities in the context of a comprehensive strategy aimed at reducing poverty.

The fifth part of the chapter focused on directions for future research. I identified the following areas: causes of, and empirical evidence on, poverty traps; the identification of the sources of asymmetric effects of output shocks; the welfare effects of macroeconomic volatility; trade-offs between unemployment reduction and poverty alleviation; the allocation of public investment and growth; and the extent to which redistribution can hurt the poor. I argued, in particular, that a lot more empirical research is needed on poverty traps. There are many competing explanations regarding the causes of these traps, but given how limited the existing evidence is, it is difficult to conclude in favor of one or another. In turn, the lack of reliable evidence hampers the ability to design policies to escape from poverty traps.

I also argued that the possible existence of trade-offs between unemployment and poverty reduction has received scant attention in the analytical literature focusing on labor market reforms and poverty reduction. Many economists regard labor market rigidities as being a major obstacle to an expansion of employment in the formal economy and a reduction of urban poverty, which tends to be concentrated in the informal sector. But if unemployment is also a source of concern, and trade-offs exist between unemployment reduction and poverty alleviation, then a question arises regarding the relative importance of each policy goal in the social welfare function. I also urged caution in adopting the view that redistribution can help to alleviate poverty. Theory and facts suggest that the relationship between growth and inequality is ambiguous, and reducing inequality may have adverse effects on growth. For instance, lower inequality may reduce the propensity to save and invest of capitalists, thereby reducing growth rates and hurting the poor indirectly. This implies that the emphasis on redistributive policies as an attempt to reduce poverty may be misplaced, particularly in low-income countries. In the long run, growth is essential for alleviating poverty. It tends to reduce poverty through rising employment, increased labor productivity, and higher real wages. It creates the resources to raise incomes, increase public investment, and even if "trickle down" is insufficient to bring the benefits of growth to the poor, governments will have scope for stronger redistributive measures when income is higher and growing faster.

A great deal has been learned about the macroeconomics of poverty reduction in the past few years. But, in my view, a lot more remains to be done. Policy research on poverty traps, in particular, is in its infancy. International development institutions have a particular responsibility to foster research on this topic, as well as others identified earlier, given their mandate to assist low-income countries in the pursuit of their development goals. To do so they must redesign the research agenda that they have followed in the past and give the macro dimension the place that it deserves. For macroeconomists in general, this is also a call to arms and a plea for greater focus on one of the most pressing challenges of the new millennium.

Appendix A
Asymmetric Effects of Output Shocks

There are at least five main sources of asymmetry in the impact of output shocks on poverty (see Agénor (2002*a*)). First, the fall in real income associated with economic downturns may have an irreversible impact on the human capital of the poor. Children in poor families are sometimes taken out of school and put to work in response to large adverse shocks (thereby mitigating the fall in the household's income) but do not return to school in upswings.

Second, confidence in the economy's prospects may change over the course of the business cycle and during crises. The degree of pessimism of consumers and firms may be higher during recessions and crises than the degree of optimism during expansions. If so, a positive output shock – induced by, say, a cut in interest rates – may have a smaller impact (and thus be less effective) on private spending decisions during recessions. Output and labor demand may thus be less sensitive to positive shocks, implying that the initial increase in poverty induced by higher unemployment or lower wages may be more persistent.

Third, recessions and crises may be accompanied by high or increasing interest rates. An economic slowdown may raise the risk of default and may lead banks to increase the premium that they charge over and above the cost of funds; or the need to defend the domestic currency on foreign exchange markets may force the central bank to raise interest rates. High borrowing costs may have an adverse effect on output – particularly if, as is often the case in developing countries, firms rely significantly on bank lending to finance their short-term working capital needs (see Agénor and Montiel (1999)). An initial increase in policy interest rates may also lead to a tightening of credit constraints if banks are unwilling to lend more, because higher loan rates are perceived to increase the debt burden of borrowers and may raise the risk of default, leaving only riskier borrowers willing to take on loans, in Stiglitz-Weiss fashion. To avoid the deterioration in the quality of their loan portfolio, banks may opt to ration credit.[28] The tightening of credit constraints magnifies the impact of the initial recession or output contraction on borrowing and spending, through a direct supply-side effect. The resulting fall in labor demand, and thus the effect on poverty, may also be (all else equal) compounded. Thus, if credit constraints bind only (or become more binding) in periods when output is below capacity, they may impart an asymmetric bias to output shocks. If small and medium-size firms (particularly in the manufacturing sector) tend to be more dependent on bank credit than large firms, they may suffer the most from a credit crunch induced by a perceived increase in the risk of default in a downturn.[29] And because small and medium-size enterprises tend to use more labor-intensive production technologies, the reduction in output and employment induced by the drop in the availability of credit may be particularly large, implying a potentially severe adverse effect on poverty.

Credit constraints may also affect the ability of low-income households to smooth consumption and thereby impart an asymmetric bias to the response of poverty to output shocks. Of course, the possibility of binding borrowing constraints in adverse states of nature does not, by itself, result in an asymmetric effect: households may well be able to achieve some level of consumption smoothing by depleting their assets (selling land, for instance) or using nonmarket mechanisms (such as increased own production) when faced with unfavorable shocks. It is also possible that households may decide, in response to income risk, to accumulate more assets or engage in precautionary savings in "good" times in order to shelter consumption in "bad" times. There is indeed some evidence that this is the case in Sub-Saharan Africa (see Agénor and Aizenman (2004)). Nevertheless, for the poor specifically, the bulk of the evidence suggests that risk sharing and consumption smoothing remain imperfect (see Alderman and Paxson (1994) and Dercon (2002)). Households may thus respond to a sharp drop in income, associated with a crisis, by changing not the level of expenditure (as a result of liquidity constraints), but instead the composition of expenditure, reducing spending on durables and items deemed nonessential (including primary health care), in order to maintain spending on basic food items. McKenzie (2003),

---

[28] An alternative argument that may explain a credit crunch in an economic downturn is based on net worth effects; see Agénor (2002*a*).

[29] See for instance Arbeláez and Echavarría (2003) for evidence on the impact of of financing constraints on small firms in Colombia.

using survey data, found evidence of this mechanism in Mexico, in the aftermath of the peso crisis of December 1994. He also finds that households postponed having children. He found no evidence of an increase in child labor; actually, school attendance rates improved for children aged 15–18 years. Transfers from abroad also increased. Despite these coping strategies, consumption fell dramatically, indicating that households were unable to completely smooth adverse shocks to income.

A final source of asymmetry relates to "labor hoarding" by firms facing high turnover costs for skilled labor. In a recession or crisis-induced contraction, unskilled workers (among which the poor tend to be concentrated) are often the first to lose their jobs as firms "hoard" their highly-trained workers. The incentive to hoard may be related to high turnover costs (or high severance payments) associated with the use of skilled labor, and is greater the more temporary the shock is perceived to be, regardless of its size. When the "good times" come back, firms may want, in priority, to recoup the productivity losses incurred during the downturn. Given the greater degree of complementarity (or lower degree of substitutability) between skilled labor and physical capital, they may therefore increase fixed investment instead of increasing their demand for unskilled labor. As a result, unskilled unemployment and poverty may display a strong degree of persistence in the aftermath of a negative output shock.

Appendix B
Dynamic Structure and Stability Conditions

The model consists of equations (6), (12), (13), (14), (18), and (22), which are repeated here (in compact form) for convenience:

$$\dot{D}_R = i^* D_R + c_R + T - Y_E^s[\chi(c_R)], \tag{A1}$$

$$i^* = i_f^* + \kappa(D), \tag{A2}$$

$$\dot{c}_R / c_R = i_f^* + \kappa(D) - \rho, \tag{A3}$$

$$\dot{D}_G = i^* D_G + G - T. \tag{A4}$$

To derive the dynamic form of the model, the first step is to combine the rich household and government budget constraints, equations (A1) and (A4). Together with (A2), this yields

$$\dot{D} = [i_f^* + \kappa(D)]D + G + c_R - Y_E^s[\chi(c_R)], \tag{A5}$$

where $D = D_R + D_G$. Note that in (A5), c_R corresponds also to total imports by the rich and the poor (see Agénor (2005f)).

The model therefore boils down to (A3) and (A5). These equations form a dynamic system in c_R and D^* that can be linearized around the steady state to give

$$\begin{bmatrix} \dot{c}_R \\ \dot{D} \end{bmatrix} = \begin{bmatrix} 0 & \kappa' \tilde{c}_R \\ 1 - Y_E^{s'} \chi_{c_R} & i_f^* + \kappa(\tilde{D}) + \kappa' \tilde{D} \end{bmatrix} \begin{bmatrix} c_R - \tilde{c}_R \\ D - \tilde{D} \end{bmatrix}, \tag{A6}$$

where $1 - Y_E^{s'} \chi_{c_R} > 0$, given that $Y_E^{s'} > 0$ and $\chi_{c_R} < 0$.

Saddlepath stability requires one unstable (positive) root. A necessary and sufficient condition is thus that the determinant of the matrix of coefficients $\mathbf{A}$ in (A6) be negative:

$$\det \mathbf{A} = -\kappa' \tilde{c}_R (1 - Y_E^{s\prime} \chi_{c_R}) < 0, \tag{A7}$$

a condition that always holds.

From the linearization given above, the stable manifold is given by

$$c_R = \tilde{c}_R + (D_0 - \tilde{D}) \exp(\nu t), \tag{A8}$$

or equivalently

$$c_R = \tilde{c}_R + \beta (D - \tilde{D}), \tag{A9}$$

where β is the slope of the saddlepath (denoted SS in Figure 2.2), defined as

$$\beta \equiv \frac{\nu - [i_f^* + \kappa(\tilde{D}) + \kappa' \tilde{D}]}{1 - Y_E^{s\prime} \chi_{c_R}} = \nu^{-1} \kappa' \tilde{c}_R < 0,$$

with ν denoting the negative root of (A6). With $\nu < 0$, $|\beta|$ is greater than the absolute value of the slope of DD, which is given by $-[i_f^* + \kappa(\tilde{D}) + \kappa' \tilde{D}]/(1 - Y_E^{s\prime} \chi_{c_R})$. Thus, SS is steeper than DD, as shown in Figure 2.2.

In the long-run equilibrium, with $\dot{c}_R = 0$, (A3) yields

$$\tilde{D} = \kappa^{-1}(\rho - i_f^*), \tag{A10}$$

which indicates that the more impatient domestic agents are (the higher ρ is), the higher the foreign debt will be. Setting $\dot{D} = 0$ in (A5) implies that in the steady state the current account must be in equilibrium:

$$[i_f^* + \kappa(\tilde{D})]\tilde{D} + G + \tilde{c}_R - \tilde{Y}_E^s = 0. \tag{A11}$$

The long-run effect of an increase in G on $\tilde{c}_R$ and $\tilde{D}$ is determined by setting $\dot{c}_R = \dot{D} = 0$ and calculating $d\tilde{D}/dG$ and $d\tilde{c}_R/dG$. From (A10), $d\tilde{D}/dG = 0$; using this result, (A11) implies that $d\tilde{c}_R/dG = -1/(1 - Y_E^{s\prime} \chi_{c_R}) < 0$. Thus, $d\tilde{z}/dG > 0$, $d\tilde{\omega}_N/dG < 0$, $d(\tilde{\omega}_N \tilde{z})/dG > 0$, $d\tilde{n}_N^d/dG < 0$, and $d\tilde{Y}_N^s/dG < 0$.

From (A9), the impact effect of a rise in G on consumption of the rich, given that D cannot change instantaneously (so that $dD_0/dG = 0$), is

$$\frac{dc_R(0)}{dG} = \frac{d\tilde{c}_R}{dG} - \beta \left(\frac{d\tilde{D}}{dG} \right) = \frac{d\tilde{c}_R}{dG}, \tag{A12}$$

given that $d\tilde{D}/dG = 0$. Thus, impact and long-run effects are the same, and the economy jumps instantaneously to the new equilibrium.

Chapter 3

The Mini Integrated Macroeconomic Model for Poverty Analysis

Pierre-Richard Agénor

Fiscal and labor market reforms are at the forefront of the policy agenda in many developing countries, and assessing their effects on unemployment and poverty is a key issue in the design and sequencing of adjustment programs. In turn, assessing these effects requires understanding not only how the labor market operates, but also how fiscal variables (taxes and expenditure) interact with the labor market. Because most taxes have an effect on the functioning of the economy, they also affect the labor market, both directly and indirectly, through changes in the level and distribution of wages, labor supply decisions, and the level and composition of employment. For instance, taxing the profits of small firms (which tend to be more labor intensive) may affect their ability to create jobs, whereas income taxation and the existence of an unemployment benefit system may affect the propensity of the unemployed to seek employment (see Chapter 1). Payroll taxes (such as employers' social security contributions) raise the effective cost of labor over and above the wage paid, thereby affecting the demand for labor, whereas income taxes and employees' social security contributions reduce the return to being employed, thereby influencing the decision to enter (or remain in) the labor force and possibly to invest in the acquisition of knowledge and skills.[1]

---

[1] As is well known, changes in income taxes affect labor supply and leisure choices through both substitution and income effects. Because these effects tend generally to operate in opposite direction, the net effect of a change in the income tax on the supply of labor is *a priori* ambiguous.

In addition to influencing the decision to enter into (or exit from) the labor force, changes in taxation may also affect the decision to engage in part-time work. Similarly, taxes on goods and services may affect the purchasing power of wages, and thus the decision to seek formal employment. High tax rates on income and activities in the formal economy may also drive firms underground, thereby impeding an efficient allocation of resources, with adverse effects on employment and poverty. Indeed, as shown in Figure 3.1, in developing economies the overall tax ratio (as a proportion of GDP), as well as the direct income tax ratio, seem to be positively correlated with the size of the informal economy, and thus with "disguised" unemployment.[2]

To the extent that the urban poor tend to be concentrated in the informal sector (as illustrated in Figure 3.2), taxation could be positively correlated with poverty. But of course, the taxation–poverty correlation could also be weak or non-existent, because it also depends on the use of tax proceeds – namely, whether taxes serve to finance expenditure on the poor, public spending on infrastructure (which indirectly affect the poor through a complementarity effect on private investment and thus labor demand), or are simply wasted on inefficient projects. Labor market distortions, and the links between taxation and the labor market, have received limited attention in quantitative, general equilibrium models that have often been used for development policy analysis.

The purpose of this chapter is to present a quantitative framework that account for many of these distortions and linkages, and that modelers and policy economists in developing countries can use to assess the effects of fiscal and labor market reforms on unemployment and poverty. This framework, called Mini-IMMPA, is a specialized, and less data intensive, version of the Integrated Macroeconomic Model for Poverty Analysis (IMMPA) presented in Chapters 5 and 6. Although Mini-IMMPA focuses only on the "real" side, it offers a more detailed treatment of the labor market (by accounting for features such as bilateral wage bargaining, public education, employment subsidies, and job security provisions) and the tax structure than IMMPA. The resulting framework allows the user to analyze a variety of important policy issues, such as the trade-offs involved in shifting the tax burden away from unskilled labor in the formal sector and toward other tax bases.

The remainder of the chapter is organized as follows. The next section describes in detail the structure of Mini-IMMPA, considering in turn the production structure, the labor market, supply and demand of commodities, external trade, prices, profits and income, private consumption and savings, private investment, the public sector, and the balance of payments. The description of the labor market is particularly detailed, given the type of distortions discussed in Chapter 1. I account, in particular, for the existence of firing costs in the formal sector. Such costs tend to benefit the employed (or "insiders") by lowering their probability of losing their job and increasing their bargaining power in wage determination. They also make firms reluctant to both hire and fire workers, thereby raising the duration (if not the level) of unemployment

---

[2]At a more formal level, Loayza (1996), Johnson, Kaufman, and Zoido-Lobaton (1998), Schneider and Enste (2000), Ihrig and Moe (2000), and Dessy and Pallage (2003), have also found that a higher tax burden tends to be correlated with a larger informal sector. By contrast, there does not appear to be a simple correlation between the overall tax ratio and open unemployment.

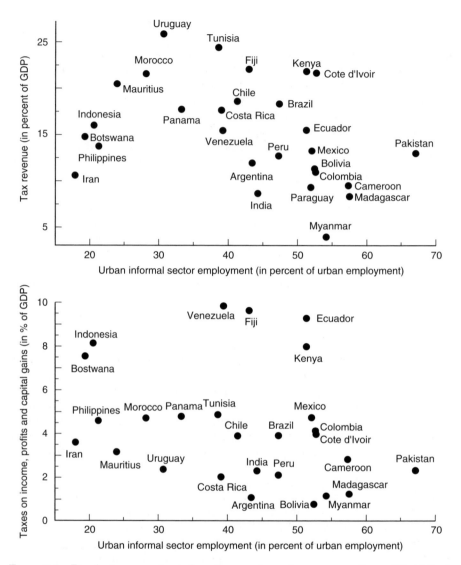

Figure 3.1   Developing countries: informal sector size and tax revenue. *Source*: World Bank and International Labor Organization.

(Lindbeck and Snower (2001)). Section 3.2 presents and discusses the results of two policy simulations: a cut in the minimum wage and a reduction in payroll taxes on unskilled labor (assuming both neutral and nonneutral revenue effects). The payroll tax experiment is of particular interest in light of the previous discussion emphasizing the links between fiscal and labor market reforms. Naturally enough, the unemployment and poverty effects of this policy change depend on whether or

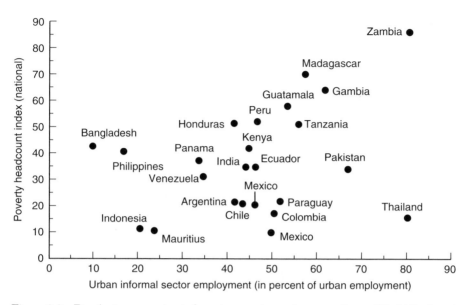

Figure 3.2 Developing countries: informal sector size and poverty. *Source*: World Bank and International Labor Organization.

not it is offset by other changes in sources of revenue, and on the precise nature of these alternative sources. The last section summarizes the main results of the analysis and suggests various extensions.

3.1 Structure of Mini-IMMPA

The building blocks of the "structural" component of mini-IMMPA consist of the production structure, the labor market, the supply and demand for goods and services, external trade, sectoral and aggregate prices, profits and income formation, private consumption and savings, private investment, the public sector, and the balance of payments. The link between the structural component and a (fictitious) household income and expenditure survey, which is necessary for poverty and distributional analysis, is also explained later on.

3.1.1 Production

The basic distinction on the production side is that between rural and urban sectors. In the rural economy (or agriculture, for short) firms produce one good (referred to as good 1), which is sold domestically or exported. The urban economy consists of two components, formal and informal. The informal economy produces nontraded services (referred to as good 2). In the formal urban economy, production consists of a private good (referred to as good 3) and a nontraded public good (referred to as good 4).

Rural Production

Land available for rural activities is assumed to be nonmarketed and in fixed supply. Gross output of the agricultural good, X_1, is the sum of value added, V_1, and intermediate consumption:

$$X_1 = V_1 + \sum_{i=1}^{4} a_{i1}X_1, \tag{1}$$

where the a_{ij} are input–output coefficients measuring relative sales from sector i to sector j.

Value added is produced with a Cobb-Douglas function of land and a composite factor, defined as a constant elasticity of substitution (CES) function of the number of unskilled workers employed in the sector, U_1, and the economy-wide stock of public physical capital, K_G. Normalizing the area of land allocated to production to unity yields

$$V_1 = [\alpha_{X_1}\{\beta_{X_1}U_1^{-\rho_{X_1}} + (1 - \beta_{X_1})K_G^{-\rho_{X_1}}\}^{-1/\rho_{X_1}}]^{1-\eta_{X_1}}, \tag{2}$$

where $0 < \eta_{X_1} < 1$ and the other parameters have the standard interpretation (namely, α_{X_1} is a shift parameter and $0 < \beta_{X_1} < 1$ a distribution parameter). Given the Cobb-Douglas specification, agricultural production exhibits decreasing returns to scale in the composite input. The presence of K_G in (2) is based on the view (discussed in more detail in Chapter 5) that a greater availability of public physical capital in the economy – roads, power plants, and the like – improves the productivity of all production units in the rural sector, because it facilitates not only trade but also production itself.

Firms in the rural sector allocate their output to exports, E_1, or the domestic market, D_1, according to a constant elasticity of transformation (CET) function:

$$X_1 = \alpha_{ED_1}[\beta_{ED_1}E_1^{\rho_{ED_1}} + (1 - \beta_{ED_1})D_1^{\rho_{ED_1}}]^{1/\rho_{ED_1}}, \tag{3}$$

where $\alpha_{ED_1} > 0$ is a shift parameter and $0 < \beta_{ED_1} < 1$. As noted below, profit maximization yields a relationship between the ratio E_1/D_1 and the prices of exported and domestic goods.

Urban Informal Production

Gross production in the urban informal sector, X_2, is given also as the sum of value added, V_2, and intermediate consumption:

$$X_2 = V_2 + \sum_{i=1}^{4} a_{i2}X_2. \tag{4}$$

There is no physical capital in the informal sector, and production requires (as in the shirking model of Chapter 1) only unskilled labor. Assuming decreasing returns to scale, value added can thus be written solely as a function of the number of unskilled workers employed in the informal economy, U_2:

$$V_2 = U_2^{\eta_{X_2}}, \qquad 0 < \eta_{X_2} < 1. \tag{5}$$

From (5), the demand for labor in the informal sector is given by

$$U_2^d = \eta_{X_2}(V_2/\omega_2), \tag{6}$$

where $\omega_2 = W_2/PV_2$ is the product wage, with W_2 the nominal wage and PV_2 the price of value added in the informal sector.

Urban Formal Private Production

Gross production of the private formal urban sector, X_3, is once again given by the sum of value added, V_3, and intermediate consumption:

$$X_3 = V_3 + \sum_i^4 a_{i3}X_3. \tag{7}$$

Private formal production uses as inputs both skilled and unskilled labor, as well as physical capital. Skilled labor and private physical capital are assumed, in line with the evidence discussed in Chapter 1, to have a higher degree of complementarity – that is, a lower degree of substitution – than physical capital and unskilled labor. In order to account for these differences in the degree of substitutability among inputs, a nested CES production structure is adopted. Specifically, at the lowest level of factor combination, skilled labor, S_3, and private physical capital, K_3, are combined to form the composite input J_L, with a relatively low elasticity of substitution (as measured by $\sigma_{X_3L} = 1/(1 + \rho_{X_3L})$) between them:

$$J_L(S_3, K_3) = \alpha_{X_3L}[\beta_{X_3L}S_3^{-\rho_{X_3L}} + (1 - \beta_{X_3L})K_3^{-\rho_{X_3L}}]^{-1/\rho_{X_3L}}. \tag{8}$$

At the second level, this composite input is used together with unskilled labor, U_3, to form the composite input J_H:

$$J_H(J_L, U_3) = \alpha_{X_3H}\{\beta_{X_3H}J_L^{-\rho_{X_3H}} + (1 - \beta_{X_3H})U_3^{-\rho_{X_3H}}\}^{-1/\rho_{X_3H}}. \tag{9}$$

The elasticity of substitution between J_L and unskilled labor, measured by $\sigma_{X_3H} = 1/(1 + \rho_{X_3H})$, is taken to be higher than between S_3 and K_3, to reflect the ease with which workers with no qualifications can be replaced:

$$\sigma_{X_3H} > \sigma_{X_3H}.$$

The final layer combines J_H and K_G (the stock of government capital) as production inputs, with public capital subject to congestion effects:

$$V_3(J_H, K_G) = \alpha_{X_3}\left[\beta_{X_3}J_H^{-\rho_{X_3}} + (1 - \beta_{X_3})\left\{\frac{K_G}{URB^{dc_3}}\right\}^{-\rho_{X_3}}\right]^{-1/\rho_{X_3}}, \tag{10}$$

where URB is the size of the urban population, and $dc_3 \geq 0$. The presence of the term K_G/URB in this equation can be explained as follows. As in agriculture, public physical capital has a positive impact on the productivity of production factors in the urban private sector. However, this positive effect is now subject to congestion: As long as $dc_3 > 0$, the positive externality of public capital decreases as its usage by the urban population increases. Put differently, the larger the size of the urban population, the lower is the contribution of the public capital stock to private urban production.

Private firms in the urban formal sector allocate their output to exports, E_3, or the domestic market, D_3, according to a production possibility frontier, again defined by a CET function:

$$X_3 = \alpha_{ED_3}[\beta_{ED_3}E_3^{\rho_{ED_3}} + (1 - \beta_{ED_3})D_3^{\rho_{ED_3}}]^{1/\rho_{ED_3}}. \tag{11}$$

As shown later, the ratio E_3/D_3 depends on the relative prices of exported and domestic goods.

Production of the Public Good

Gross production of the public good, X_4, is given by the sum of value added, V_4, and intermediate consumption:

$$X_4 = V_4 + \sum_{i=1}^{4} a_{i4}X_4. \tag{12}$$

Value added in the public sector is measured by the government wage bill, as in national accounts:

$$V_4 = (W_{UG}U_4 + W_{SG}S_4)/PV_4. \tag{13}$$

where S_4 and U_4 (respectively W_{SG} and W_{UG}) denote employment levels (respectively wages) of skilled and unskilled workers in government. Employment levels are treated as predetermined policy variables, whereas wage formation is discussed later.

3.1.2   The Labor Market

As noted earlier, there are two categories of workers in the economy, skilled and unskilled. Unskilled workers may be employed either in the rural economy or in the urban economy, whereas skilled workers are employed only in the urban sector. In line with the discussion of "luxury" unemployment in Chapter 1, skilled workers are assumed to have a high reservation wage and therefore do not seek employment in the informal economy, even when they are unable to find a job in the formal sector.

As discussed in Chapter 1, in many developing countries severance payments tend to be a partial substitute to unemployment insurance benefits. An important issue is whether these costs contribute to a high level of unemployment and to its degree of persistence – perhaps by reducing employment variation over the business cycle, as argued by Bertola (1990).[3] A general conclusion of the literature is that firing costs affect employment dynamics more than the average level of employment; unemployment tends to be more persistent in countries characterized by high job security provisions, because mandatory firing costs play a stabilizing effect on aggregate employment. On the one hand, firing costs prevent workers from losing their jobs (thereby preventing the loss of firm-specific human capital if downturns are temporary); but on the other, they discourage new hires.[4] They also tend to increase the incidence of temporary employment contracts, as noted by Betcherman, Luinstra, and Ogawa (2001), Heckman and Pagés (2000), and Lindauer (1999).

Mini-IMMPA accounts explicitly for the existence of state-mandated firing costs. Specifically, the effect of firing costs on both employment and wage formation is captured under the assumption that workers (or the trade union that represents them) internalize, while bargaining with employers, the value of the severance payment that they would receive in the event of dismissal.

Rural Wages and Employment

The demand for (unskilled) labor in agriculture, U_1^d, is derived in standard fashion from the first-order condition for profit maximization and, using (2), is given by

$$
U_1^d = \left\{ V_1^{1+\rho_{X_1}/(1-\eta_{X_1})} \frac{1-\eta_{X_1}}{\omega_1} \cdot \frac{\beta_{X_1}}{\alpha_{X_1}^{\rho_{X_1}}} \right\}^{1/(1+\rho_{X_1})}, \tag{14}
$$

where $\omega_1 = W_1/PV_1$ is the product wage in agriculture, with W_1 denoting the nominal wage and PV_1 the net output price.

The nominal wage in agriculture, W_1, adjusts to clear the labor market. With U_R^s representing labor supply in agriculture, the equilibrium condition of the labor market is thus given by

$$
U_R^s = U_1^d \left(V_1, \frac{W_1}{PV_1} \right). \tag{15}
$$

Equation (15) can be solved for W_1.

The supply of labor in the rural sector rises over time as a result of the increase in the rural population, which grows at the exogenous rate g_R, taking into account worker migration to urban areas, MIG:

$$
U_R^s = U_{R,-1}^s (1 + g_R) - MIG. \tag{16}
$$

---

[3] Bertola's analysis assumes that workers are risk-neutral. But as noted by Booth (1997), typically most workers derive their income from employment, and it is difficult for most of them to diversify across jobs; it seems therefore more plausible to assume that workers are risk averse. She also considers the case in which firms and workers bargain about both wages and the size of redundancy payments. However, these modifications do not change Bertola's main insight, which is that firing costs tend to stabilize employment over the business cycle.

[4] As shown by Gavin (1986), the impact of firing costs on labor demand depends not only on the size of the required severance payments and the wage elasticity of labor demand, but also on the variability and persistence of shocks to labor demand, and the firm's discount rate.

Following Harris and Todaro (1970), the incentives to migrate are taken to depend negatively on the ratio of the average expected *consumption* wage in rural areas to that prevailing in urban areas. Unskilled workers in the urban economy may be employed either in the private formal sector, in which case they are paid a minimum wage, W_M, or they can enter the informal economy and receive the average income in that sector (before transfers), y_2^m.[5] When rural workers make the decision to migrate to urban areas, they are uncertain as to which type of job they will be able to get, and therefore weigh wages in each sector by the probability of finding a job in that sector. These probabilities are approximated by prevailing employment ratios. Finally, potential migrants also consider what their expected purchasing power in rural and urban areas is likely to be, depending on whether they stay in the rural sector and consume the "typical" basket of goods of rural households, or migrate and consume the "typical" urban basket of goods.

The expected unskilled urban real wage, w_U^e, is thus a weighted average of the minimum wage in the formal sector and the going wage in the informal sector, deflated by the urban consumption price index for unskilled workers, P_{UU}:

$$w_U^e = \frac{\theta_U W_{M,-1} + (1 - \theta_U) y_{2,-1}^m}{P_{UU,-1}}, \qquad (17)$$

where $0 < \theta_U < 1$ is the probability of finding a job in the urban formal sector, measured by the proportion of unskilled workers in the private formal sector, relative to the total number of unskilled urban workers (net of government employment) looking for a job, $U_F^s - U_4$, both in the previous period:

$$\theta_U = \frac{U_{3,-1}}{U_{F,-1}^s - U_{4,-1}}. \qquad (18)$$

A similar reasoning is used to calculate the expected rural consumption real wage, w_A^e. Here the employment probability is equal to unity, because workers can always find a job at the going wage. Assuming again a one-period lag yields

$$w_A^e = \frac{W_{1,-1}}{P_{R,-1}},$$

where P_R is the rural consumption price index.

The migration function is therefore specified as

$$\frac{MIG}{U_{R,-1}} = \left\{ \frac{w_U^e}{w_A^e} \right\}^{\sigma_M}, \qquad (19)$$

where $\sigma_M > 0$ measures the elasticity of (relative) migration flows with respect to expected wages.

The migration function (19) provides only a partial account of the evidence, which suggests that there are several factors (in addition to wage differentials) that affect

---

[5] As discussed below, there is no job turnover for either category of workers in the public sector. Given that, as made clear later, households in the informal sector receive all profits from production, average income is a better measure of expected earnings in that sector than the going wage.

rural-to-urban migration. The family, in particular, appears to play a particularly important role in explaining migration by individuals (Lucas (1997)) as well as cash-seeking behavior, which translates into a positive impact of the *composition* or rural income, in addition to its level (Velenchik (1993)). Moreover, if workers are risk averse, they may require a premium to compensate them for the risk of being unemployed; the urban–rural wage differential would then have to be quite large to induce them to migrate. However, some of these considerations are difficult to integrate in the type of models considered here.

Urban Unskilled Wages, Employment, and Unemployment

Both the government and private firms in the formal and informal urban sectors use unskilled labor in production. The public sector hires an exogenous level of unskilled workers, U_4, at the nominal wage W_{UG}, whereas the demand for unskilled labor by the formal private sector is determined by firms' profit maximization subject to the given minimum wage, W_M.[6] Both W_{UG} and W_M are assumed to be indexed on the price of the consumption basket for urban unskilled households:

$$W_i = \omega_i P_{UU}^{idx_i}, \quad i = UG, M, \tag{20}$$

where ω_i is the real wage and $0 \le idx_i \le 1$ the indexation parameter. To avoid a corner solution in which no unskilled individual would want to seek employment for the government, public sector jobs are assumed to provide a nonpecuniary benefit, such as enhanced job security, less volatile earnings, or greater opportunity to shirk (see the discussion in Chapter 1). This benefit is measured as a proportion $b_{UG} > 0$ of the wage. Thus, as long as $(1 + b_{UG})W_{UG} > W_M$, unskilled workers in the urban area will always seek employment in the private formal sector first.

Firms also pay a payroll tax, at the rate $0 < ptx_U < 1$, on the wage bill that they incur for employing unskilled workers, $W_M U_3$. They also receive an employment subsidy of $ES_U \le W_M$ per unskilled worker. Using (9), unskilled labor demand by the private sector is thus given by

$$U_3^d = J_H \left\{ \frac{P_H^J}{(1 + ptx_U)W_M - ES_U} \cdot \frac{\beta_{X_3H}}{\alpha_{X_3H}^{\rho_{X_3H}}} \right\}^{\sigma_{X_3H}}. \tag{21}$$

In line with the discussion in Chapter 1, mobility of the unskilled labor force between the formal and informal sectors is assumed to be imperfect and determined by expected income opportunities. Specifically, the total supply of unskilled workers in the formal sector (including public sector workers), U_F^s, is taken to change over time as a function of the expected wage differential across sectors. Wage and employment prospects are formed on the basis of prevailing conditions in the labor market. Because there is no job turnover in the public sector, the expected real wage in the formal

---

[6]The assumption that the minimum wage is binding in the formal sector is actually a source of debate; see Chapter 1 and Dabalen (2000) for a review of the evidence for Sub-Saharan Africa. However, what is assumed here essentially is that the distribution of unskilled wages shifts as a result of a change in the minimum wage.

economy, w_F^e, is equal to the real minimum wage (measured in terms of the price of the consumption basket for unskilled workers) weighted by the probability of being hired in the private sector. Assuming that hiring in that sector is random, this probability can be approximated again by the ratio of employed workers to those seeking employment, as in (18). Assuming a one-period lag,

$$w_F^e = \frac{U_{3,-1}^d}{U_{F,-1}^s - U_{4,-1}} \left(\frac{W_{M,-1}}{P_{UU,-1}} \right).$$

The expected real wage in the informal economy is simply the average real income in that sector (measured in terms of the relevant consumption price index), because there are no barriers to entry. Assuming again a one-period lag,

$$w_I^e = \frac{y_{2,-1}^m}{P_{UU,-1}}.$$

Thus, the flow supply of unskilled workers in the formal sector evolves over time according to

$$\frac{U_F^s}{U_{F,-1}^s} = \left\{ \frac{w_F^e}{P_{UU,-1}^{-1} y_{2,-1}^m} \right\}^{\sigma_F} = \left\{ \frac{U_{3,-1}^d W_{M,-1}}{(U_{F,-1}^s - U_{4,-1}) y_{2,-1}^m} \right\}^{\sigma_F}, \quad \sigma_F > 0, \quad (22)$$

where σ_F denotes the elasticity of labor flows with respect to the (expected) wage ratio. The rate of unskilled unemployment in the formal sector, UNE_U, is thus given by

$$UNE_U = 1 - \frac{(U_3^d + U_4)}{U_F^s}, \quad (23)$$

where $U_3^d + U_4$ is total unskilled formal employment.

The supply of labor in the informal economy, U_2^s, is given by

$$U_2^s = U_U^s - U_F^s. \quad (24)$$

The informal labor market clears continuously, so that $U_2^d = U_2^s$. From this condition and equation (6), the equilibrium nominal wage is thus given by

$$W_2 = \eta_{X_2} \left(\frac{PV_2 V_2}{U_U^s - U_F^s} \right) = \eta_{X_2} y_2^m. \quad (25)$$

The supply of unskilled labor in the urban sector, U_U^s, grows in part as a result of "natural" urban population growth and migration of unskilled labor from the rural economy, as discussed earlier. Moreover, some urban unskilled workers, in quantity *SKL*, acquire skills and leave the unskilled labor force to augment the supply of qualified labor. All individuals are born unskilled, and thus natural urban population growth (not resulting from migration or skills acquisition factors) is represented by urban unskilled population growth only, at the exogenous rate g_U. Thus, the urban unskilled labor supply evolves according to

$$U_U^s = U_{U,-1}^s (1 + g_U) + MIG - SKL. \quad (26)$$

Urban Skilled Wages and Employment

As noted earlier, the employment levels of both skilled and unskilled workers in the public (urban) sector are taken as exogenous. The lack of turnover may in part due to the fact that (as discussed in Chapter 1) working for the government provides a nonpecuniary benefit, which takes the form of greater job security. The real wage rate that skilled workers receive in the public sector, ω_{SG}, is also taken as given. With W_{SG} denoting the nominal wage, and P_{US} the consumption price index for urban skilled workers, full indexation therefore implies that

$$W_{SG} = \omega_{SG} P_{US}. \tag{27}$$

Again, to avoid corner solutions requires imposing $(1 + b_{SG})W_{SG} > W_S$, where $b_{UG} > 0$ measures the monetary value of the nonpecuniary benefit associated with working for the public sector; this benefit is assumed proportional to the going wage. From (8), the demand for skilled labor is, noting that $\rho_{X_3L}\sigma_{X_3L} = 1 - \sigma_{X_3L}$:

$$S_3^d = \left\{ \frac{P_L^J J_L}{W_S} \beta_{X_3L} \right\}^{\sigma_{X_3L}} \left\{ \frac{J_L}{\alpha_{X_3L}} \right\}^{1-\sigma_{X_3L}} = J_L \left\{ \frac{P_L^J}{W_S} \cdot \frac{\beta_{X_3L}}{\alpha_{X_3L}^{\rho_{X_3L}}} \right\}^{\sigma_{X_3L}}. \tag{28}$$

Two alternative specifications are used for determining skilled workers' wages in the private sector, W_S. The first approach is based on the "monopoly union" framework, and is derived as follows (see Chapter 1). Let ω_S^c denote the *consumption* real wage, that is, the nominal wage earned by skilled workers deflated by the cost-of-living index that these workers face in the urban sector, P_{US}. A centralized labor union sets ω_S^c with the objective to maximize a utility function that depends on deviations of both employment and the consumption wage from their target levels, subject to the firm's labor demand schedule. Specifically, the union's utility function is given by

$$U = (\omega_S^c - \omega_S^{cT})^\nu (S_3^d - S_3^T)^{1-\nu}, \qquad 0 < \nu < 1,$$

where S_3^d is given by equation (28). The quantities ω_S^{cT} and S_3^T measure the union's wage and employment targets, respectively, and are both assumed predetermined with respect to ω_S^c. The parameter ν reflects the relative importance that the union attaches to wage deviations from target, as opposed to employment deviations. The union's problem is thus

$$\max_{\omega_S^c} U = (\omega_S^c - \omega_S^{cT})^\nu (S_3^d - S_3^T)^{1-\nu}.$$

Using (28), the first-order condition is given by

$$\nu \left\{ \frac{S_3^d - S_3^T}{\omega_S^c - \omega_S^{cT}} \right\}^{1-\nu} - (1-\nu) \left\{ \frac{S_3^d - S_3^T}{\omega_S^c - \omega_S^{cT}} \right\}^{-\nu} \sigma_{X_3L} \left(\frac{S_3^d}{\omega_S^c} \right) = 0,$$

or equivalently

$$\nu \left\{ \frac{S_3^d - S_3^T}{\omega_S^c - \omega_S^{cT}} \right\} - \frac{(1-\nu)\sigma_{X_3L}S_3^d}{\omega_S^c} = 0.$$

Solving this condition yields

$$\frac{\omega_S^c - \omega_S^{cT}}{\omega_S^c} = \frac{\nu}{(1-\nu)\sigma_{X3L}}\left(\frac{S_3^d - S_3^T}{S_3^d}\right),$$

which indicates that percentage deviations of the optimal wage from its target value are linearly related to percentage differences of employment from its target level.

The union's target real wage, ω_S^{cT}, is assumed to be related positively to skilled wages in the public sector (measured in terms of the relevant price index), ω_{SG}, and negatively to the skilled unemployment rate, UNE_S, and the real firing cost per skilled worker, f_S, measured in terms of the price of valued added in the private formal sector, PV_3. Wage-setting in the public sector is assumed to play a signaling role for wage setters in the rest of the economy (see Chapters 1 and 7). When unemployment is high, the probability of finding a job (at any given wage) is low. Consequently, the higher the unemployment rate, the greater the incentive for the union to moderate its wage demands in order to induce firms to increase employment. As noted earlier, firing costs do prevent excessive job losses in bad times (thereby preventing the loss of firm-specific human capital if downturns are temporary) but they also discourage new hires – namely because reversing mismatches is costly if workers prove to be inadequate matches with their job requirements. The union internalizes the disincentive effect of severance payments on labor demand. As a result, the higher the firing cost, the greater the incentive for the union to reduce its wage demands, in order to encourage firms to hire. Normalizing the target level of employment to zero ($S_3^T = 0$) the above expression can thus be rewritten as

$$W_S = P_{US}\frac{UNE_S^{-\phi_1}f_S^{-\phi_2}\omega_{SG}^{\phi_3}}{1 - \nu/(1-\nu)\sigma_{X3L}}, \tag{29}$$

where the ϕ_i coefficients are all positive. This equation implies, in particular, that a higher level of unemployment lowers the *level* of wages, as predicted by the various efficiency-wage theories reviewed in Chapter 1.[7]

The second approach to determining skilled wages assumes direct bargaining, in each period, between producers and workers over the product wage, $\omega_S = W_S/P_L^J$. If a bargain is reached, each worker receives $\omega_S = W_S/PJ_L$, whereas the producer receives $m_S - \omega_S$, where $m_S = \partial J_L(S_3, K_3)/\partial S_3$ is the marginal product of the worker. Using equation (8), this expression is given by

$$m_S = \left(\frac{\beta_{X3L}}{\alpha_{X3L}^{\rho_{X3L}}}\right)\left(\frac{J_L}{S_3}\right)^{1+\rho_{X3L}}. \tag{30}$$

The worker's "fallback" position is denoted Ω_S, which may represent an unemployment benefit (if one exists). The firm's fallback position is assumed to

---

[7]Note that, in general, on would expect the optimal wage to be also an increasing function of union density. Here, it is implicitly assumed that all skilled workers are members of the union. In addition, note that the target wage could also be specified as increasing in the income tax rate, itx_S, implying that the union would demand higher wages to compensate for a decrease in after-tax income.

depend on firing costs in the following way (see Coe and Snower (1997)). In case of bargaining disagreement, the worker engages in industrial action that is costly to the firm (but not to himself). The greater is the level of industrial action, the lower will be the producer's fallback position and thus the higher will be the wage that the worker can achieve, up to a limit, beyond which the firm has an incentive to fire him. Producers face a firing cost of fs per worker (measured now in terms of the price of the composite output J_L, that is, P_L^J), and for simplicity all workers become eligible for severance payments immediately upon hiring.[8] If the cost of the industrial action to the firm exceeds the firing cost fs, the worker will be replaced by another one. Consequently, the worker will set the level of industrial action so that its cost to the firm is exactly fs, making the firm indifferent between retaining him and replacing him.

Thus, the worker's bargaining surplus is $\omega_S - \Omega_S$, whereas the firm's bargaining surplus is $m_S - (\omega_S + fs)$. The Nash bargaining problem can be formulated as

$$\max_{\omega_S}(\omega_S - \Omega_S)^\nu [m_S - (\omega_S + fs)]^{1-\nu}, \quad 0 < \nu < 1,$$

where ν measures the bargaining strength of the worker relative to the firm. The first-order condition is given by

$$\nu \left\{ \frac{m_S - (\omega_S + fs)}{\omega_S - \Omega_S} \right\}^{1-\nu} - (1 - \nu) \left\{ \frac{m_S - (\omega_S + fs)}{\omega_S - \Omega_S} \right\}^{-\nu} = 0,$$

that is,

$$\nu \frac{m_S - (\omega_S + fs)}{\omega_S - \Omega_S} - (1 - \nu) = 0.$$

From this equation, the equilibrium wage can be derived as

$$\omega_S = \nu(m_S - fs) + (1 - \nu)\Omega_S.$$

Suppose that there is no unemployment benefit, so that $\Omega_S = 0$, and that the bargaining strength of a skilled worker, ν, varies inversely with the rate of skilled unemployment, UNE_S. The wage-setting equation can thus be written as[9]

$$W_S = P_L^J UNE_S^{-\phi_1}(m_S - fs), \tag{31}$$

which implies again that the level of wages and the rate of unemployment are inversely related, and that an increase in the firing cost reduces the skilled wage.

Skilled workers who are unable to find a job in the formal economy opt to remain openly unemployed, instead of entering the informal economy (in contrast to unskilled workers), as a result of either a reservation wage that systematically exceeds the informal sector wage, or concerns about adverse signaling effects to potential future

---

[8]In practice, as noted in Chapter 1, redundancy payments are only made to workers with some minimum period of continuous service with the firm.

[9]With an unemployment benefit proportional to the wage, so that $\Omega_S = \iota\omega_S$, the coefficient ν in the negotiated wage should be replaced by $\nu/[1 - (1 - \mu)\iota]$.

employers, as argued in a different setting by McCormick (1990) and Gottfries and McCormick (1995). Accordingly, the skilled open unemployment rate, UNE_S, is given by the ratio of skilled workers who are not employed either by the private or the public sector, divided by the total population of skilled workers:

$$UNE_S = 1 - \frac{(S_3^d + S_G)}{S}, \qquad (32)$$

where S_G is the *total* number of skilled workers in the public sector, engaged in both the production of public services, S_4, and education, S_G^E:

$$S_G = S_4 + S_G^E. \qquad (33)$$

The evolution of the skilled labor force depends on the rate at which unskilled workers acquire skills:

$$S = (1 - \delta_S)S_{-1} + SKL, \qquad (34)$$

where $0 < \delta_S < 1$ is the rate of depreciation, or "de-skilling", of the skilled labor force. The size of the urban population, URB, is thus

$$URB = U_U^s + S,$$

that is, using (26) and (34):

$$URB = (1 + g_U)U_{U,-1}^s + MIG + (1 - \delta_S)S_{-1}. \qquad (35)$$

Skills Formation

The acquisition of skills by unskilled workers takes place through an education system operated (free of charge) by the public sector. Specifically, the flow of unskilled workers who become skilled, SKL, is taken to be a CES function of the "effective" number of teachers in the public sector, S_G^E, and the government stock of capital in education, K_E:

$$SKL = [\beta_E(\varphi S_G^E)^{-\rho_E} + (1 - \beta_E)K_E^{-\rho_E}]^{-1/\rho_E}, \qquad (36)$$

where φ measures the productivity of public workers engaged in providing education. The function φ is assumed to depend on the relative wage of skilled workers in the public sector, W_{SG}, relative to the expected wage for that same category of labor in the private sector, which (in the absence of unemployment benefits) is given by one minus the unemployment rate, $1 - UNE_S$, times the going wage, W_S. Assuming a simple logistic form (as for instance in Maechler and Roland-Holst (1997, p. 492)), and a one-period lag, this function can be written as[10]

$$\varphi = \left\{1 + \kappa \exp\left[-\frac{(1 - UNE_{S,-1})W_{S,-1}}{W_{SG,-1}}\right]\right\}^{-1}, \quad \kappa > 0. \qquad (37)$$

---

[10]Wages in equations (37) and (38) are specified in nominal terms, because they are assumed to be both deflated by the same price index – the price of the consumption basket for skilled workers in the urban sector.

This equation shows that the higher the public sector wage relative to its opportunity cost, the greater the level of effort by teachers, and thus the greater the number of skilled workers produced by the system. Alternatively, the effort function derived by Agénor and Aizenman (1999) and discussed in Chapter 1 could also be used:

$$\varphi = 1 - \varphi_m \left\{ \frac{(1 - UNE_{S,-1})W_{S,-1}}{W_{SG,-1}} \right\}^{\kappa}, \quad \kappa > 0, \tag{38}$$

where $0 < \varphi_m < 1$ denotes the "minimum" level of effort.

3.1.3 Supply and Demand

Both the informal and public sector goods are nontradables, and both markets clear continuously. In each sector, total supply, Q^s, is thus equal to gross production, that is,

$$Q_i^s = X_i, \quad i = 2, 4.$$

Goods produced in the rural and private formal urban, by contrast, compete with imported goods. Supply of the composite good in each sector consists of a CES combination of imports and domestically produced goods:

$$Q_i^s = \alpha_{Q_i} \{\beta_{Q_i} M_i^{-\rho_{Q_i}} + (1 - \beta_{Q_i})D_i^{-\rho_{Q_i}}\}^{-1/\rho_{Q_i}}, \quad i = 1, 3. \tag{39}$$

For the agricultural, public and informal sector goods, aggregate demand consists of intermediate consumption and private final consumption (C_1, C_2, and C_4). Aggregate demand for the private formal good consists of intermediate consumption, final consumption by households and the public sector, C_3 and G_3, and private investment, Z_3:

$$Q_i^d = C_i + INT_i, \quad i = 1, 2, 4 \tag{40}$$

$$Q_3^d = C_3 + G_3 + Z_3 + INT_3, \tag{41}$$

where INT_j is defined as total demand (by all productions sectors) for intermediate consumption of good j:

$$INT_j = \sum_i a_{ji} X_i \quad j = 1, \ldots 4. \tag{42}$$

Government spending on the private formal good, G_3, is the sum of public investment expenditure, Z_G, and other current government spending, G_C (excluding salaries, transfers to households, and employment subsidies):

$$G_3 = Z_G + G_C. \tag{43}$$

Each category of household h determines final consumption for each type of good i, C_{ih}, so as to maximize a Stone-Geary utility function, U_h, which takes the form

$$U_h = \sum_{i=1}^{4} (C_{ih} - PC_i x_{ih})^{cc_{ih}},$$

where x_{ih} is real autonomous consumption of good i by household h, the coefficients cc_{ih} are the marginal budget shares of good i in total consumption expenditure by household h, C_h, and PC_i is the sales price of good i. These shares satisfy the standard restrictions

$$0 \leq cc_{ih} \leq 1, \; \forall i, h \quad \text{and} \quad \sum_{i=1}^{4} cc_{ih} = 1, \; \forall h.$$

Maximization of the utility function U_h subject to household h's budget constraint $\sum_{i=1}^{4} PC_i C_{ih} - CO_h = 0$, where CO_h is total consumption expenditure at current prices, yields the familiar demand functions

$$C_{ih} = x_{ih} + \frac{cc_{ih}(CO_h - \sum_{i=1}^{4} PC_i x_{ih})}{PC_i}. \tag{44}$$

Total final private consumption for each production sector i, C_i, is the summation across all categories of households of consumption of good i:

$$C_i = \sum_{h=1}^{n} C_{ih}. \tag{45}$$

Total private investment, Z_P, consists of purchases of urban private sector goods:

$$Z_3 = \frac{P_K Z_P}{PC_3}, \tag{46}$$

where P_K is the price of capital goods.

3.1.4   External Trade

As indicated earlier, firms in agriculture allocate their output to exports or the domestic market according to the PPF specified in equation (3). Standard efficiency conditions require that firms equate the relative price of exports, PE_1, vis-à-vis domestic goods, PD_1, to the opportunity cost in production. This yields:

$$\frac{E_1}{D_1} = \left\{ \frac{PE_1}{PD_1} \cdot \frac{1 - \beta_{ED_1}}{\beta_{ED_1}} \right\}^{\sigma_{ED_1}}. \tag{47}$$

Similarly, using the PPF specified in equation (11), the allocation of output between exports and domestic sales by firms in the private formal sector is given by

$$\frac{E_3}{D_3} = \left\{ \frac{PE_3}{PD_3} \cdot \frac{1 - \beta_{ED_3}}{\beta_{ED_3}} \right\}^{\sigma_{ED_3}}. \tag{48}$$

Imports compete with domestic goods in agriculture as well as in the urban formal private sector. Making use of Armington functions for the demand for imported vs. domestic goods and relative prices, import demand for both sectors (M_1 and M_3) can be written as:

$$M_i = D_i \left\{ \frac{PD_i}{PM_i} \cdot \frac{\beta_{Q_i}}{1 - \beta_{Q_i}} \right\}^{\sigma_{Q_i}}, \quad i = 1, 3, \tag{49}$$

where $\sigma_{Q_i} = 1/(1 + \rho_{Q_i})$, which measures the elasticity of M_i/D_i with respect to changes in relative prices, is also the elasticity of substitution between these goods, as derived from (39).

3.1.5 Prices

By definition, the net value of output (that is, gross output adjusted for indirect taxes) in sector i must be equal to value added plus spending on intermediate inputs (purchased at composite prices):

$$(1 - atx_i)PX_iX_i = PV_iV_i + \sum_{j=1}^{4} a_{ji}PC_jX_i,$$

where PX_i is the gross price of output, and atx_i the indirect tax rate (or a subsidy rate, if negative) on output in sector i, with $atx_2 = 0$ (there is no indirect taxation of informal sector production). From this equation, the net or value added price of output can be derived as

$$PV_i = V_i^{-1} \left\{ (1 - atx_i)PX_i - \sum_{j=1}^{4} a_{ji}PC_j \right\} X_i. \tag{50}$$

The world prices of imported and exported goods are taken to be exogenously given. The domestic currency price of these goods is obtained by adjusting the world price by the exchange rate, with import prices also adjusted by the tariff rate, itm:

$$PE_i = wpe_iER, \quad i = 1, 3, \tag{51}$$

$$PM_i = wpm_i(1 + itm_i)ER, \quad i = 1, 3, \tag{52}$$

where ER denotes the nominal exchange rate.

Because the transformation function between exports and domestic sales of agricultural goods is linear homogeneous, the gross output price, PX_1, can be derived from the expenditure identity:

$$PX_1 = \frac{PD_1D_1 + PE_1E_1}{X_1}. \tag{53}$$

Similarly, the gross output price in the urban formal private sector, PX_3, is given by

$$PX_3 = \frac{PD_3D_3 + PE_3E_3}{X_3}. \tag{54}$$

The price of domestic sales in agriculture, PD_1, adjusts to equilibrate supply and demand.[11] For the price of domestic sales by firms in the urban formal private sector,

---

[11]In solving the model, equation (49) is used to solve for PD_1, and, because $Q_1^s = Q_1^d$, (40) is used to solve for the equilibrium value of Q_1. The composite good CES equation (39) is then inverted to solve for M_1 and the CET function (3) is inverted to solve for D_1. This procedure ensures that the composite price (and thus indirectly the price of domestic sales) adjusts to equilibrate supply and demand.

PD_3, two alternatives can be considered. In the first case, PD_3 is assumed to be fully flexible and determined in a manner similar to PD_1. In the second, PD_3 is assumed to be set as a markup over variable costs. Because both private and public stocks of physical capital are taken as given, total variable costs (involving labor and intermediate consumption) associated with private urban production, TVC_3, are given by

$$TVC_3 = [(1 + ptx_U)W_M - ES_U]U_3^d + W_S S_3^d + X_3 \sum_i a_{i3} PC_i. \qquad (55)$$

The average variable cost, AVC_3, is thus

$$AVC_3 = TVC_3/PX_3X_3, \qquad (56)$$

The price of domestic sales, PD_3, can therefore be written as

$$PD_3 = (1 + mk)AVC_3, \qquad (57)$$

where mk is the constant markup rate. Given this specification, and to maintain market equilibrium, it must be assumed that the actual quantity of domestic goods is determined by the demand side. The production function can then be inverted to solve for the demand of one of the labor categories. Firms would thus typically be off their optimal labor demand curve.

For the agricultural sector and the urban formal private sector, the substitution function between imports and domestic goods is also linearly homogeneous, and the composite price for each sector, PQ_i, is determined accordingly by the expenditure identity:

$$PQ_i = \frac{M_i PM_i + D_i PD_i}{Q_i^d}, \quad i = 1, 3. \qquad (58)$$

The actual sales price for the agricultural and formal private sector goods, PC_i, differs from the composite price as a result of a sales tax, levied at the rate stx_i:

$$PC_i = (1 + stx_i)PQ_i, \quad i = 1, 3.$$

For the informal and public sectors (both of which do not export and are not subject to taxes on sales), the composite price is equal to the domestic market price. In turn, because these sectors produce a good that does not compete with imports, the domestic price, PD_i, is simply equal to the gross output price, PX_i:

$$PQ_i = PD_i = PX_i = PC_i, \quad i = 2, 4. \qquad (59)$$

The nested CES production function of private formal urban goods is also linearly homogeneous; prices of the composite inputs are therefore derived in similar fashion:

$$J_H P_H^J = J_L P_L^J + [(1 + ptx_U)W_M - ES_U]U_3. \qquad (60)$$

$$J_L P_L^J = PR_3 + W_S S_3. \qquad (61)$$

where PR_3 is (before tax) profits by private firms in the formal urban sector, which measures here the (gross) return to physical capital.

Investment involves only the urban private sector good. Because, as a result, $Z_3 = Z_P$, equation (46) implies that the price of capital is simply equal to the sales price of that good:

$$PK = \frac{PC_3 Z_3}{Z_P} = PC_3, \tag{62}$$

The consumption price index for the rural sector is given by

$$PR = \sum_i \theta_i^R PC_i,$$

where $0 < \theta_i^R < 1$ denotes the relative weight of good i in the index, with $\sum_i \theta_i^R = 1$. Similarly, the consumption price indexes for urban unskilled and skilled workers are given by

$$P_{UU} = \sum_i \theta_i^U PC_i, \quad P_{US} = \sum_i \theta_i^S PC_i, \tag{63}$$

where the θ_i^U and θ_i^S are relative weights that reflect the composition of spending by each group in a base period, with $\sum_i \theta_i^U = \sum_i \theta_i^S = 1$. As discussed later, these indexes are used to update systematically the rural and urban poverty lines in the simulation experiments.

3.1.6 Profits and Income

Firms' profits are defined as revenue minus total labor costs. In the rural and urban informal sectors, profits are simply given by the difference between net output and the wage bill:

$$PR_i = PV_i V_i - W_i U_i, \quad i = 1, 2. \tag{64}$$

Profits of urban private sector firms account for both working capital costs and salaries paid to both categories of workers, as well as payroll taxes and firing costs, FC:[12]

$$PR_3 = PV_3(V_3 - FC) - [(1 + ptx_U)W_M - ES_U]U_3 - W_S S_3, \tag{65}$$

where total firing costs are given by

$$FC = f_U \max(0, U_{3,-1} - U_3) + f_S \max(0, S_{3,-1} - S_3), \tag{66}$$

with f_S, f_U denoting the fixed firing cost per worker (skilled and unskilled, respectively). Note that firing costs are taken to be related to the total reduction in the number of workers, thereby neglecting "natural" attrition (retirement) and voluntary quits.

Household income is based on the return to labor (salaries), distributed profits, and government transfers. Households are defined according to the level of skills of its members and their sector of employment. There is one rural household (indexed

---

[12]Note that payroll taxes are assumed to be levied on the total wage bill excluding interest payments, that is, $W_M U_3$ instead of $(1 + i_L)W_M U_3$.

by *a*), comprising all workers employed in agriculture. In the urban sector there are two types of unskilled households (denoted by *b* and *c*), those working in the informal sector and those employed in the formal sector (both public and private). The fourth household (denoted by *d*) consists of skilled workers employed in the formal urban economy (in both the private and public sectors). Finally, there is a capitalist-rentier household (denoted by *e*) whose income derives mainly from firms' net earnings in the urban private sector. Households in both agriculture and the informal urban economy own the firms in which they are employed.

Income of agricultural and informal sector households is given by, with $h = a, b$ and $i = 1, 2$:

$$YH_h = (PR_i + W_i U_i) + \gamma_h TR = PV_i V_i + \gamma_h TR, \tag{67}$$

where γ_h is the portion of total government transfers (TR) group h receives, so that $\sum_h \gamma_h = 1$, for $h = a, \ldots e$.

Income of the urban formal unskilled, and skilled households, depends on government transfers, salaries, and possibly redundancy payments; firms provide no source of income, because those groups do not own the production units in which they are employed:

$$YH_c = W_M U_3 + W_{UG} U_4 + PV_3 f_U \max(0, U_{3,-1} - U_3) + \gamma_c TR, \tag{68}$$

$$YH_d = W_S S_P + W_{SG} S_G + PV_3 f_S \max(0, S_{3,-1} - S_3) + \gamma_d TR, \tag{69}$$

where S_G is the total number of skilled workers in the public sector, engaged in both the production of services and training (see (33)).

Firms in the private urban sector pay income taxes, and interest on their foreign borrowing, FL_3. Their net (after-tax) profits, NPR_3, are thus

$$NPR_3 = (1 - itx_f)PR_3 - i^* ER \cdot FL_{3,-1}, \tag{70}$$

where itx_f is the corporate income tax rate and i^* is the interest rate paid on foreign loans, taken to be exogenous. A portion of these net profits, χ, are retained for the purpose of financing investment; the remainder is transferred to the capitalist-rentier household. Thus, total income of that group is given by

$$YH_e = (1 - \chi)NPR_3 + \gamma_e TR. \tag{71}$$

3.1.7   Private Consumption and Savings

Each category of household $h = a, \ldots e$ saves a fixed fraction, $0 < sr_h < 1$, of its disposable income:

$$SAV_h = sr_h(1 - itx_h)YH_h, \tag{72}$$

where $0 < itx_h < 1$ is the income tax rate applicable to household h. Income in the informal sector is not taxed, so that $itx_I = 0$.

The portion of disposable income that is not saved is allocated to consumption:

$$CO_h = (1 - sr_h)(1 - itx_h)YH_h. \tag{73}$$

3.1.8 Private Investment

Capital accumulation occurs only in the urban formal private sector. To examine the decision to invest, define first the after-tax rate of return on private physical capital, IK, as the ratio of after-tax profits to the stock of capital:

$$IK = \frac{(1 - itx_f)PR_3}{P_K K_3}. \tag{74}$$

The desired capital stock by firms in the private formal urban sector is determined so as to equate the after-tax rate of return on capital, plus the rate of capital gains due to changes in the price of capital, and minus depreciation (at the rate δ_3), to the opportunity cost of investment, which (assuming the absence of "effective" restrictions to capital mobility) is here taken to be the world interest rate, adjusted for the rate of depreciation of the nominal exchange rate, ε:

$$IK - \delta_3 + \frac{\Delta P_K}{P_{K,-1}} = i^* + \varepsilon, \tag{75}$$

where $0 < \delta_3 < 1$. One could also add to the marginal cost of foreign capital on the right-hand side of this equation a risk premium, to reflect the type of imperfections that developing countries face on world capital markets (see Chapter 7). Such a premium could be specified, for instance, as a convex function of the ratio of, or difference between, the value of the private capital stock, $P_K K_3$, relative to firms' foreign borrowing, $ER \cdot FL_3$, which in the present setting represents a measure of firms' net worth.

Using equation (74), and setting $\varepsilon = 0$, the arbitrage condition (75) yields[13]

$$K_3^* = \frac{PR_3}{P_K} \cdot \frac{(1 - itx_f)}{i^* + \delta_3 - \Delta P_K / P_{K,-1}}. \tag{76}$$

Actual investment in each period is determined by a partial adjustment process, and is given as a function of the ratio between the desired capital stock and last period's capital stock:

$$\frac{Z_P}{K_{3,-1}} = z_0 \left\{ \frac{K_{3,}^*}{K_{3,-1}} \right\}^{\sigma_Z}, \tag{77}$$

where $z_0, \sigma_Z > 0$. This investment function is, of course, very simple and does not account for a variety of other factors that have been shown to be important for developing countries – such as inflation, macroeconomic volatility, public capital in infrastructure, and possibly foreign borrowing.[14] Some of these modifications can be introduced without too much difficulty. Note also that, although there is no direct,

---

[13]When checking for homogeneity of degree zero in prices (including the exchange rate, which is the numéraire here), the rate of depreciation must indeed be accounted for in (76).

[14]See Agénor (2004*b*, Chapter 2), Agénor and Montiel (1999, Chapter 3), Jimenez (1995), and recent studies by Sanchez-Robles (1998), Ahmed and Miller (2000), Ghura and Goodwin (2000), Hendricks (2000), and Wang (2002).

explicit effect of the public capital stock in infrastructure, K_R, on private investment, K_R does affect the overall stock of public capital, K_G, which in turn affects the production process – and thus indirectly the desired capital stock, through profits.

The capital stock evolves as a function of the flow level of investment and the depreciation rate:

$$K_3 = (1 - \delta_3)K_{3,-1} + Z_{P-1}, \qquad (78)$$

where $0 < \delta_3 < 1$.

The net worth of private urban firms in nominal terms, NW_3, is defined as the value of physical capital, net of foreign borrowing, FL_3:

$$NW_3 = P_K K_3 - ER \cdot FL_3,$$

which changes over time according to

$$NW_3 = NW_{3,-1} + P_K \Delta K_3 - ER \cdot \Delta FL_3 + \Delta P_K K_{3,-1}.$$

The last term on the right-hand side of this expression represents capital gains associated with changes in the price of capital. Note that changes in NW_3 have no feedback effects on the economy, unlike what happens in the "full" IMMPA model of Chapter 5 and subsequent chapters. In those models, banks charge a risk premium on their loans that is inversely related to the borrower's net worth. In the present setting, a feedback effect could be introduced by adding a risk premium to the marginal cost of *foreign* capital, as noted earlier.

The *ex post* aggregate identity (or *ex ante* equilibrium condition) between savings and investment is specified as follows. Total gross investment in physical capital measured in nominal terms, which is equal to $P_K(Z_P + Z_G)$, is financed by firms' retained earnings, household savings, "primary" government savings (that is, before investment), and foreign borrowing by firms and the government. Given the definition of the *overall* government fiscal balance given below in (81), $GBAL$, this identity can therefore be written with private investment only on the left-hand side:

$$P_K Z_P = \chi NPR_3 + \sum_b SAV_b + GBAL + ER(\Delta FL_3 + \Delta FL_G), \qquad (79)$$

where FL_G is foreign borrowing by the government. In the simulations reported below this equation is solved residually for the savings rate of rentiers and capitalists, sr_e. In that sense, then, the basic model is "investment driven," although of course other closure rules are possible. For instance, the government budget balance could be solved "backward" to determine the level of current public expenditure that is consistent with (79). Alternatively, the investment equation (77) could be dropped and (79) could be solved instead for Z_P, as in the application to Morocco described in Chapter 4. In that case, then, the model would be "savings driven" (see Dewatripont and Michel (1987)).

3.1.9   Public Sector

Government spending consists of final consumption, which only has demand-side effects, and public investment, which has both demand- and supply-side effects. Total public investment, Z_G, consists of investment in infrastructure, I_R, education, I_E, and health, I_H,which are all considered exogenous policy variables:[15]

$$Z_G = I_R + I_E + I_H. \tag{80}$$

Investment in infrastructure consists of the accumulation of public capital such as roads, power plants and railroads. Investment in education consists of the accumulation of assets such as school buildings and other infrastructure affecting the acquisition of skills (for instance, research institutions), but does not represent human capital. In a similar fashion, investment in health comprises public assets such as hospitals.

From (13), $PV_4 V_4 - (W_{UG} U_4 + W_{SG} S_4) = 0$, that is, all value added generated by the production of public services is distributed as wages. The government fiscal balance, $GBAL$, is thus defined as

$$GBAL = TAX - TR - W_{SG} S_G^E - ES_U U_3^d$$
$$- PC_3 (G_C + Z_G) - i_G^* ER \cdot FL_{G,-1}. \tag{81}$$

where TAX denotes tax revenues, TR transfers to households, $W_{SG} S_G^E$ the wage bill on school teachers, $ES_U U_3^d$ employment subsidies to firms in the private formal sector, G_C other real current expenditures on goods and services, Z_G real investment spending, and $i_G^* ER \cdot FL_{G,-1}$ is interest payments on foreign borrowing.

Tax revenues consist of revenue generated by import tariffs, sales taxes, income taxes, and payroll taxes on unskilled labor:

$$TAX = \sum_{i=1,3} itm_i (ER \cdot wpm_i M_i) + ptx_U W_M U_3$$

$$+ itx_f PR_3 + \sum_{i=1}^{4} atx_i PX_i X_i + \sum_h itx_h YH_h + \sum_{i=1,3} stx_i PQ_i Q_i, \tag{82}$$

with $atx_2 = 0$.

Public investment in infrastructure, health, and education, determines the rate at which the stock of each type of public capital, K_j, grows over time. Accumulation of each type of capital is defined as:

$$K_j = K_{j,-1}(1 - \delta_j) + e_G^j I_{j,-1}, \quad j = E, H, R. \tag{83}$$

where $0 < \delta_j < 1$ is a depreciation rate and $0 < e_G^j \leq 1$ a coefficient measuring the efficiency of public investment. This specification, which follows Arestoff and Hurlin (2005), is motivated by the evidence suggesting that in developing countries a large fraction of the resources invested in investment projects may not have a positive

---

[15] See Jimenez (1995), Tanzi and Zee (1997), Sanz and Velázquez (2001), and Webber (2002), for a discussion of the links between the composition of public investment and growth. It should be noted that this treatment of public investment differs from standard data classification reported in national accounts; in many instances these investments are classified as current expenditures.

impact on the public capital stock (see Prichett (1996)). The case of full efficiency (where a unit of investment translates one to one into an increase in the capital stock) corresponds therefore to $e'_G = 1$.

Infrastructure and health capital are combined through a CES function to produce the stock of public capital, K_G:

$$K_G = \alpha_G\{\beta_G K_R^{-\rho_G} + (1 - \beta_G)K_H^{-\rho_G}\}^{-1/\rho_G}. \qquad (84)$$

3.1.10   Balance of Payments

The external constraint implies that any current account surplus (or deficit) must be compensated by a net outflow (or inflow) of foreign capital, given by the sum of changes in net foreign borrowing by the government, ΔFL_G, and private firms, ΔFL_3:

$$\sum_{i=1,3}(wpe_i E_i - wpm_i M_i) + i^*(FL_{G,-1} + FL_{3,-1}) + \Delta FL_G + \Delta FL_3 = 0. \qquad (85)$$

In the simulations reported below, public foreign borrowing is taken to be exogenous whereas private borrowing adjusts to equilibrate the balance of payments.

Figure 3.3 summarizes the structure of the labor market in mini-IMMPA, whereas Figure 3.4 captures overall linkages. The Appendix to this chapter discusses calibration and solution procedures, as well as parameter values.

As implied by Walras' Law, one equilibrium condition may be dropped because it can be deducted from the other equilibrium conditions. If the savings–investment balance (79) is used to solve for private investment, the balance of payments identity (85) for instance could be dropped. Alternatively, instead of dropping one equation, the computer program could be used to check numerically for continuous equality between savings and investment, or that the sum of the current and capital accounts sum to zero, by ensuring that a residual variable is continuously equal to zero. In the experiments reported in this chapter the savings-investment balance is solved residually for the savings rate of rentiers and capitalists (as noted earlier) and equation (85) is solved for private capital flows.

3.1.11   Poverty and Distributional Effects

The procedure followed in mini-IMMPA to assess the poverty and distributional effects of exogenous and policy shocks is similar to the one in IMMPA, which is described at length in Chapter 5 and evaluated against some alternatives in Chapter 8. This procedure assumes that initial rural and urban poverty lines are exogenously set in real terms and involves linking the "structural" component described earlier to a household income and expenditure survey, organized along the household structure described earlier.

Specifically, the calculation of poverty indices – the poverty headcount index (the proportion of individuals earning less than the poverty line) and the poverty gap (the average shortfall of the income of the poor with respect to the poverty line, multiplied by the headcount index) – as well as distributional indicators (the Gini

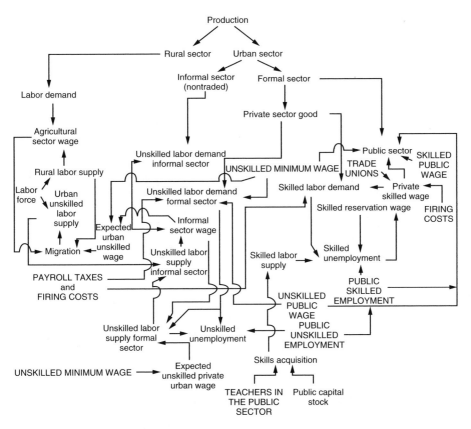

Figure 3.3   Mini-IMMPA: production structure and the labor market.

coefficient and the Theil inequality index) involves the following steps:

- **Step 1**. Classify the data in the household survey into the five categories of households defined in the structural component of the model, namely, workers in the rural sector, those in the urban (unskilled) informal economy, urban unskilled workers in the formal sector, urban skilled workers in the formal sector, and capitalists-rentiers.
- **Step 2**. Following a policy or exogenous shock, generate growth rates in per capita consumption and disposable income for all household categories, up to the end of the simulation horizon (say, T periods).
- **Step 3**. Apply these growth rates separately to the per capita (disposable) income and consumption expenditure for each household in the survey. This gives a new vector of absolute income and consumption levels for each group, for periods $1, \ldots T$.
- **Step 4**. Calculate poverty and income distribution indicators, using the new absolute nominal levels of income and consumption for each individual and

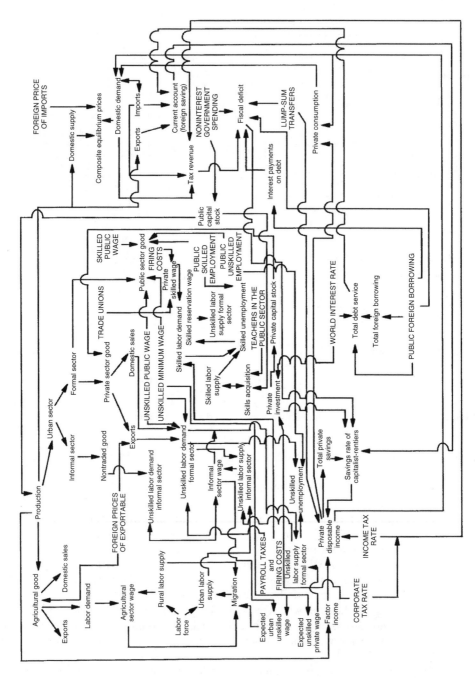

Figure 3.4 Mini-IMMPA: analytical structure.

each group, and after updating the initial rural and urban poverty lines, using the prices indexes generated by the structural component of the model, to reflect changes in the price of the consumption basket and purchasing power of income.

- **Step 5**. Compare the postshock poverty and income distribution indicators with the baseline values to assess the impact of the shock on the poor and the degree of inequality for periods $1, \ldots T$.

The household survey that I use to perform the policy experiments reported below is an artificial survey, constructed as follows. First, a sample of 5,000 observations was produced, with the share of each household group corresponding exactly to that in the structural component of the model.[16] Each observation was considered to represent one household. Second, using a random number generator and a lognormal distribution, values for disposable income and consumption expenditure were drawn for each household. As parameters for each group, the initial values for average disposable income and average consumption expenditure (which are taken from the calibrated database) are imposed as mean and as standard deviation. For skilled workers in the formal urban sector and for capitalist and rentiers, a standard deviation of 0.8 times the mean is assumed.

Figure 3.5 shows the distribution of consumption in each group. Third, the income poverty line for the rural sector is set (somewhat arbitrarily) such that the percentage of rural households in poverty is 50 percent. The poverty line in urban areas is then assumed to be 15 percent higher. The rural and urban poverty lines for consumption expenditure are calculated in the same manner. This procedure produces an economy-wide, income-based headcount poverty index of 38.6 percent and an economy-wide consumption-based headcount index of 41.1 percent. For income distribution, the overall Gini index is 0.48 (consumption based) and 0.49 (income based).[17] The within-group Theil inequality decomposition is 78 percent (consumption based) and 73 percent (income based). Thus, the economy considered is ont characterized by both substantial poverty and a relatively high degree of inequality.

3.2 Policy Experiments

Mini-IMMPA can be used to analyze a variety of policy and exogenous shocks. For illustrative purposes, the growth, unemployment and poverty effects of two types of labor market policies are examined in this section: a cut in the minimum wage and a reduction in the payroll tax rate on unskilled labor.[18] Both experiments relate to

---

[16]These shares are 28.2 percent of workers in the rural sector, 45.3 percent of workers in the informal urban sector, 13.7 percent of unskilled workers in the formal urban sector, 9.9 percent of skilled workers in the formal urban sector, and 3 percent of capitalists and rentiers.

[17]The income-based Gini coefficients are 0.45 for the rural sector, 0.48 for the urban sector, 0.44 for the informal sector households, 0.43 for urban unskilled households, 0.38 for urban skilled households, and 0.39 for capitalists and rentiers.

[18]In these simulations, PD_3 is assumed to be fully flexible, the skilled wage-setting equation (29) and the effort function (38) are used, and both the unskilled public sector wage and the minimum wage are

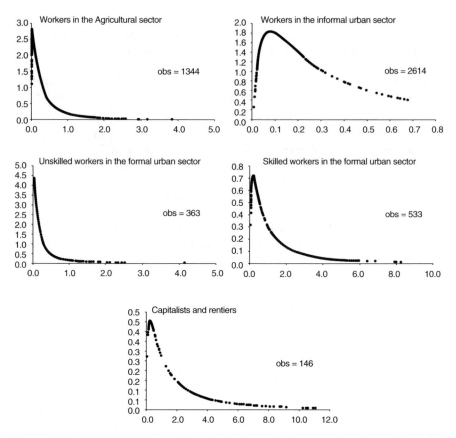

Figure 3.5 Mini-IMMPA: initial distribution of income, based on log-normal approximation.

critical policy issues in developing countries. As discussed in Chapter 1, economists have long debated the role of minimum wage legislation in labor market adjustment. Advocates have often viewed minimum wages as being beneficial in various ways – through their positive effect on nutrition or productivity, or as an instrument of income redistribution and social justice. By contrast, opponents argue that high minimum wages, by preventing the cost of labor from adjusting downward to excess supply, imposes an implicit tax on employers in the formal economy. As a result, they often lead to misallocation of labor and create unemployment, particularly for unskilled workers. In addition to reducing employment, a government-mandated increase in the minimum wage may also raise poverty, if the unemployed are forced

---

taken to be fixed in nominal terms ($idx_U = idx_M = 0$). Full efficiency of public investment is also assumed (that is, $\mathcal{E}'_G = 1$ in equation (83)).

to enter the informal sector – thereby depressing wages there.[19] Thus, changes in the minimum wage are likely to have important distributional effects among (unskilled) workers, notably between those employed in the formal sector and those in the informal sector. Finally, by increasing the relative cost of employing unskilled workers, a high minimum wage may also accelerate the substitution of capital for unskilled labor. Because physical capital and skilled labor tend to have a high degree of complementarity, high minimum wages may restrain the expansion of unskilled labor demand over time.

Similarly, in both industrial and developing countries, a flat payroll tax is often imposed on employers to finance general government expenditure, or more specifically the pension system or the unemployment benefit scheme.[20] The conventional, partial equilibrium view suggests that the incidence of such a tax – its actual burden – depends on the elasticity of labor supply and the degree of wage rigidity. But it is also important to account for general equilibrium effects. The effect on wages depends on the structure of the labor market. For instance, an increase in employers' social security contributions may cause labor costs to rise and employment to fall initially; but the ensuing increase in unemployment may drive wages down over time, thereby offsetting the increase in nonwage costs. In addition, the effect of a reduction in payroll taxation depends to a very significant extent on how the cut is financed; with a binding budget constraint, reducing the payroll tax requires shifting the tax burden to some other tax base. Thus, it is important to consider alternative financing rules in evaluating the effect of a cut in the payroll tax.

3.2.1 Reduction in the Minimum Wage

The simulation results associated with a permanent, 5-percent reduction in the minimum wage are illustrated in Tables 3.1 and 3.2, which display relative and absolute percentage changes from the baseline solution, respectively, for the first 10 periods (or years) after the shock. This time period is referred to below as the "adjustment period." The experiment assumes that the government borrows domestically to finance its deficit – implying therefore (as discussed earlier) an offsetting adjustment in the savings rate of capitalists and rentiers, in order to maintain the aggregate balance between savings and investment (equation (79)).[21] Table 3.1 provides data on national accounts, fiscal accounts, and the labor market,

---

[19] If a binding minimum wage does not reduce employment among the poor, it will also reduce poverty if a large number of poor households consist of low-wage workers. However, in many poor households, no one may be employed in a formal sector job. If indeed low-paid workers are not in poor households, much of an income gain that may come from an increase in the minimum wage would benefit those who are not poor to begin with.

[20] Financing of unemployment benefit schemes is in general shared between employers and employees, but employers' contributions are usually substantially higher than employees' contributions. In Chapter 7, the latter are explicity accounted for.

[21] How this transfer of private savings to the government takes place is not explicitly specified; one can think of a "pure" financial intermediary operating in the background. A more elaborate approach would involve accounting explicitly for the issuance of government bonds (as in Chapters 6 and 7), and thus portfolio decisions on the part of savers.

Table 3.1 Mini-IMMPA: simulation results 5-percent cut in minimum wage (Percentage deviations from baseline, unless otherwise indicated)

	Periods									
	1	2	3	4	5	6	7	8	9	10
Real Sector										
Total resources	0.2	0.0	0.3	0.4	0.2	0.1	0.2	0.2	0.2	0.1
Gross domestic product	0.3	0.3	0.5	0.5	0.3	0.3	0.3	0.4	0.3	0.3
Imports of goods and NFS	−0.7	−1.3	−0.5	0.0	−0.5	−0.9	−0.7	−0.5	−0.6	−0.8
Total expenditure	0.2	0.0	0.3	0.4	0.2	0.1	0.2	0.2	0.2	0.1
Total consumption	0.0	0.7	0.5	0.0	−0.1	0.2	0.2	0.0	−0.1	0.0
Private consumption	0.0	0.8	0.6	0.0	−0.1	0.2	0.3	0.0	−0.1	0.0
Public consumption	0.0	0.0	0.0	0.0	0.0	0.0	0.0	0.0	0.0	0.0
Total investment	−0.9	−4.1	−1.6	0.9	−0.1	−1.9	−1.6	−0.5	−0.5	−1.2
Private investment	−1.0	−5.5	−2.1	1.5	0.1	−2.4	−2.1	−0.5	−0.4	−1.4
Public investment	−0.7	−0.9	−0.6	−0.4	−0.6	−0.7	−0.7	−0.6	−0.6	−0.7
Exports of goods and NFS	1.7	1.8	1.5	1.4	1.6	1.7	1.7	1.6	1.7	1.8
External Sector (% of GDP)[1]										
Current account	0.5	0.6	0.4	0.4	0.5	0.6	0.6	0.6	0.6	0.7
Exports of goods and NFS	0.3	0.3	0.2	0.2	0.3	0.3	0.3	0.3	0.3	0.3
Imports of goods and NFS	−0.2	−0.3	−0.2	−0.1	−0.1	−0.2	−0.2	−0.1	−0.2	−0.2
Factor services	0.0	0.0	−0.1	−0.1	−0.1	−0.1	−0.1	−0.1	−0.2	−0.2
Capital account	−0.5	−0.6	−0.4	−0.4	−0.5	−0.6	−0.6	−0.6	−0.6	−0.7
Private borrowing	−0.5	−0.6	−0.4	−0.4	−0.5	−0.6	−0.6	−0.6	−0.6	−0.7
Public borrowing	0.0	0.0	0.0	0.0	0.0	0.0	0.0	0.0	0.0	0.0

Government Sector (% of GDP)[1]

Total revenue	−0.2	−0.3	−0.2	−0.1	−0.2	−0.2	−0.2	−0.2	−0.2	−0.2
Direct taxes	−0.1	−0.1	0.0	0.0	−0.1	0.0	0.0	0.0	0.0	0.0
Indirect taxes	−0.2	−0.3	−0.2	−0.1	−0.2	−0.1	−0.1	−0.1	−0.1	−0.2
Total expenditure	−0.1	−0.1	−0.2	−0.2	−0.1	−0.1	−0.1	−0.1	−0.1	−0.1
Consumption	0.0	0.0	0.0	−0.1	0.0	0.0	0.0	0.0	0.0	0.0
Investment	−0.1	−0.1	−0.1	−0.1	−0.1	−0.1	−0.1	−0.1	−0.1	−0.1
Transfers to households	0.0	0.0	0.0	0.0	0.0	0.0	0.0	0.0	0.0	0.0
Foreign interest payments	0.0	0.0	0.0	0.0	0.0	0.0	0.0	0.0	0.0	0.0
Total financing	0.1	0.2	0.0	−0.1	0.1	0.1	0.0	0.0	0.1	0.1
Foreign financing	0.0	0.0	0.0	0.0	0.0	0.0	0.0	0.0	0.0	0.0
Domestic borrowing	0.1	0.2	0.0	−0.1	0.1	0.1	0.0	0.0	0.1	0.1

Labor Market

Nominal wages

Agricultural sector	1.8	2.0	1.4	0.3	−0.3	−0.4	−0.6	−1.2	−1.6	−1.8
Informal sector	2.0	2.6	1.6	1.3	2.2	2.7	2.5	2.3	2.6	2.9
Private formal sector										
Unskilled	−5.0	−5.0	−5.0	−5.0	−5.0	−5.0	−5.0	−5.0	−5.0	−5.0
Skilled	−1.6	−2.4	−1.4	−0.7	−1.2	−1.7	−1.5	−1.2	−1.2	−1.4
Public sector										
Unskilled	0.0	0.0	0.0	0.0	0.0	0.0	0.0	0.0	0.0	0.0
Skilled	0.1	0.1	0.1	0.0	0.1	0.1	0.1	0.1	0.1	0.1

Employment

Agricultural sector	0.0	0.2	0.4	0.5	0.7	0.8	0.9	1.1	1.2	1.3
Informal sector	0.0	0.2	0.4	0.2	−0.1	−0.1	0.0	0.0	−0.2	−0.2
Private formal sector										
Unskilled	4.3	3.2	4.7	5.8	5.0	4.2	4.5	5.1	5.0	4.7
Skilled	−0.1	−0.2	−0.1	−0.1	−0.1	−0.2	−0.1	−0.1	−0.1	−0.1
Public sector										
Unskilled	0.0	0.0	0.0	0.0	0.0	0.0	0.0	0.0	0.0	0.0
Skilled	0.0	0.0	0.0	0.0	0.0	0.0	0.0	0.0	0.0	0.0

Continued

Table 3.1 Continued

					Periods					
	1	2	3	4	5	6	7	8	9	10
Labor supply (urban formal sector)										
Unskilled	0.0	−1.2	−2.3	−1.9	−1.2	−1.5	−2.2	−2.3	−2.0	−2.1
Skilled	0.0	0.0	0.0	0.0	0.0	0.0	0.0	0.0	0.0	0.0
Unemployment rate (urban formal sector)[1]										
Unskilled	−2.8	−3.3	−5.4	−5.7	−4.5	−4.3	−5.2	−5.6	−5.4	−5.2
Skilled	0.1	0.1	0.1	0.0	0.1	0.1	0.1	0.1	0.1	0.1
Real wage differentials[1]										
Expected urban-rural (% of rural wage)	0.0	−8.7	−8.9	−8.8	−7.6	−6.5	−6.3	−6.2	−5.6	−5.0
Expected formal-informal (% of informal wage)	0.0	−3.1	−3.2	1.2	1.9	−0.8	−1.7	−0.3	0.6	−0.1
Migration[1]										
Rural-urban (% of urban labor supply)	0.00	−0.08	−0.09	−0.08	−0.07	−0.06	−0.06	−0.05	−0.05	−0.04
Formal-informal (% of formal urban labor supply)	0.00	−1.16	−1.20	0.44	0.71	−0.32	−0.65	−0.10	0.23	−0.02
Memorandum items[2]										
GDP at market prices	0.3	0.2	0.4	0.5	0.3	0.3	0.3	0.4	0.4	0.3
Value added at factor cost	0.3	0.3	0.4	0.5	0.4	0.3	0.4	0.4	0.4	0.4
Value added in rural sector	0.0	0.1	0.3	0.4	0.5	0.7	0.8	0.9	0.9	1.0
Value added in urban informal sector	0.0	0.2	0.3	0.2	−0.1	−0.1	0.0	0.0	−0.1	−0.2
Value added in urban formal sector	0.8	0.6	0.8	0.9	0.8	0.7	0.7	0.8	0.8	0.7
Private Consumption	−0.4	0.3	0.3	−0.2	−0.4	−0.1	0.0	−0.2	−0.3	−0.3
Private Investment	−0.3	−4.6	−1.6	1.9	0.6	−1.7	−1.4	0.1	0.2	−0.7
Disposable income	0.3	0.4	0.5	0.5	0.4	0.5	0.5	0.6	0.6	0.6
Capitalists and rentiers savings rate[1]	5.8	0.8	1.9	5.9	6.6	4.7	4.3	5.8	6.6	6.2

[1] Absolute deviations from baseline. [2] In real terms.

Table 3.2 Mini-IMMPA: price, poverty and distributional indicators 5-percent cut in minimum wage (Percentage deviations from baseline, unless otherwise indicated)

	Periods									
	1	2	3	4	5	6	7	8	9	10
Consumer Prices and the Real Exchange Rate										
Rural CPI	0.6	0.7	0.5	0.3	0.3	0.3	0.3	0.2	0.1	0.1
Urban CPI	0.3	0.4	0.3	0.2	0.2	0.3	0.3	0.2	0.2	0.2
Unskilled	0.2	0.3	0.2	0.1	0.2	0.2	0.2	0.2	0.2	0.2
Skilled	0.1	0.1	0.1	0.0	0.1	0.1	0.1	0.1	0.1	0.1
Real exchange rate	-0.2	-0.2	-0.2	-0.1	-0.1	-0.1	-0.1	-0.1	-0.1	-0.1
Value Added Prices										
Rural agriculture	1.8	2.0	1.5	0.4	-0.1	-0.2	-0.4	-0.9	-1.4	-1.6
Urban private informal	2.0	2.7	1.7	1.3	2.1	2.7	2.5	2.3	2.6	2.9
Urban private formal	-2.4	-3.1	-2.0	-1.4	-1.9	-2.4	-2.1	-1.8	-1.8	-2.0
Urban public	0.0	0.0	0.0	0.0	0.0	0.1	0.0	0.0	0.0	0.1
Real Disposable Income[1]										
Rural households	1.1	1.3	1.2	0.6	0.1	0.1	0.0	-0.3	-0.5	-0.7
Urban households	0.1	0.2	0.3	0.5	0.5	0.6	0.7	0.8	0.8	0.9
Informal	1.5	2.1	1.5	1.2	1.7	2.1	2.1	1.9	2.1	2.3
Formal unskilled	-0.7	-1.3	-0.5	0.1	-0.3	-0.7	-0.6	-0.3	-0.3	-0.5
Formal skilled	-0.8	-1.2	-0.7	-0.4	-0.6	-0.9	-0.8	-0.6	-0.6	-0.7
Capitalists and rentiers	-1.9	-2.6	-1.2	-0.2	-0.7	-1.2	-0.7	-0.1	0.0	-0.1
Real Consumption[1]										
Rural households	1.1	1.3	1.2	0.6	0.1	0.1	0.0	-0.3	-0.5	-0.7
Urban households	-0.7	0.1	0.1	-0.4	-0.5	-0.1	0.0	-0.1	-0.2	-0.1
Informal	1.5	2.1	1.5	1.2	1.7	2.1	2.1	1.9	2.1	2.3
Formal unskilled	-0.7	-1.3	-0.5	0.1	-0.3	-0.7	-0.6	-0.3	-0.3	-0.5
Formal skilled	-0.8	-1.2	-0.7	-0.4	-0.6	-0.9	-0.8	-0.6	-0.6	-0.7
Capitalists and rentiers	-9.5	-3.7	-3.6	-7.9	-9.0	-7.0	-6.1	-7.1	-7.9	-7.4

Continued

Table 3.2 Continued

					Periods					
	1	2	3	4	5	6	7	8	9	10
Household Size[1]										
Rural households	0.0	0.2	0.4	0.5	0.7	0.8	0.9	1.1	1.2	1.3
Urban households	0.0	−0.1	−0.1	−0.2	−0.3	−0.3	−0.4	−0.4	−0.4	−0.5
Informal	0.0	0.2	0.4	0.2	−0.1	−0.1	0.0	0.0	−0.2	−0.2
Formal unskilled	0.0	−1.2	−2.3	−1.9	−1.2	−1.5	−2.2	−2.3	−2.0	−2.1
Formal skilled	0.0	0.0	0.0	0.0	0.0	0.0	0.0	0.0	0.0	0.0
Capitalists and rentiers	0.0	0.0	0.0	0.0	0.0	0.0	0.0	0.0	0.0	0.0
Poverty and Distributional Indicators										
Consumption-based										
Poverty Line[1]										
Rural	0.6	0.7	0.5	0.3	0.3	0.3	0.3	0.2	0.1	0.1
Urban	0.3	0.4	0.3	0.2	0.2	0.3	0.3	0.2	0.2	0.2
Poverty headcount										
Rural households	−0.7	−0.8	−0.6	0.0	0.4	0.4	0.6	1.0	1.0	1.0
Urban households	−0.4	−0.6	−0.5	−0.5	−0.5	−0.7	−0.7	−0.7	−0.7	−0.7
Informal	−0.8	−0.9	−0.5	−0.5	−0.8	−1.0	−1.0	−0.8	−1.0	−1.1
Formal unskilled	0.1	0.1	−1.5	−1.2	−0.3	−0.1	−0.7	−1.0	−0.4	−0.4
Formal skilled	0.0	0.0	0.6	0.2	0.2	0.0	0.2	0.0	0.2	0.4
Capitalists and rentiers	0.7	0.0	0.0	0.7	0.7	0.0	0.0	0.0	0.0	0.0
Economy	−0.5	−0.6	−0.6	−0.3	−0.3	−0.4	−0.3	−0.2	−0.2	−0.2
Poverty Gap										
Rural households	−0.3	−0.3	−0.2	0.0	0.2	0.2	0.3	0.4	0.5	0.6
Urban households	−0.2	−0.3	−0.3	−0.3	−0.3	−0.4	−0.4	−0.4	−0.5	−0.5
Informal	−0.5	−0.6	−0.4	−0.3	−0.5	−0.6	−0.6	−0.6	−0.6	−0.7
Formal unskilled	0.2	0.1	−0.4	−0.5	−0.2	−0.2	−0.4	−0.5	−0.4	−0.4
Formal skilled	0.1	0.1	0.1	0.0	0.1	0.1	0.1	0.1	0.1	0.1
Capitalists and rentiers	0.1	0.0	0.0	0.1	0.1	0.1	0.1	0.1	0.1	0.1
Economy	−0.3	−0.3	−0.3	−0.2	−0.2	−0.2	−0.2	−0.2	−0.2	−0.2

Distributional Indicators[2]										
Gini coefficient	−1.3	−1.3	−1.2	−1.1	−1.2	−1.5	−1.4	−0.8	−0.9	−1.7
Theil index	−0.9	−0.9	−0.8	−0.7	−0.8	−1.0	−0.8	−0.5	−0.5	−0.9
Poverty and Distributional Indicators										
Income-based										
Poverty Line[1]										
Rural	0.1	0.1	0.2	0.3	0.3	0.3	0.3	0.5	0.7	0.6
Urban	0.2	0.2	0.2	0.3	0.3	0.2	0.2	0.3	0.4	0.3
Poverty Headcount										
Rural households	1.0	1.1	0.8	0.5	0.4	0.4	0.0	−0.4	−0.5	−0.6
Urban households	−1.1	−1.0	−0.9	−1.0	−1.0	−0.9	−0.6	−0.6	−0.8	−0.7
Informal	−1.7	−1.5	−1.4	−1.5	−1.5	−1.3	−0.8	−0.9	−1.4	−1.2
Formal unskilled	−0.3	−0.3	−0.4	−0.4	−0.1	−0.1	−0.6	−0.4	0.0	0.1
Formal skilled	0.2	0.0	0.4	0.2	0.0	0.0	0.2	0.0	0.6	0.2
Capitalists and rentiers	0.0	0.0	0.0	0.7	0.7	0.0	0.0	0.7	0.7	0.0
Economy	−0.5	−0.4	−0.4	−0.6	−0.6	−0.5	−0.4	−0.6	−0.7	−0.7
Poverty Gap										
Rural households	0.6	0.5	0.4	0.3	0.2	0.2	0.0	−0.2	−0.3	−0.3
Urban households	−0.5	−0.4	−0.4	−0.4	−0.4	−0.3	−0.2	−0.3	−0.3	−0.2
Informal	−0.7	−0.6	−0.5	−0.6	−0.6	−0.5	−0.3	−0.3	−0.6	−0.4
Formal unskilled	−0.3	−0.3	−0.4	−0.3	−0.1	−0.2	−0.4	−0.4	0.0	0.2
Formal skilled	0.1	0.1	0.1	0.1	0.1	0.0	0.0	0.1	0.1	0.0
Capitalists and rentiers	0.0	0.0	0.0	0.0	0.1	0.0	0.0	0.0	0.1	0.1
Economy	−0.2	−0.2	−0.2	−0.2	−0.2	−0.2	−0.2	−0.3	−0.3	−0.3
Distributional Indicators[2]										
Gini Coefficient	−0.1	−0.1	−0.1	−0.3	−0.3	−0.2	−0.2	−0.4	−0.7	−0.5
Theil Index	−0.1	−0.1	−0.1	−0.2	−0.2	−0.2	−0.1	−0.3	−0.4	−0.3

[1] Percentage deviations from baseline. [2] Gini Coefficients and Theil Indices measure between group inequality.

whereas Table 3.2 shows changes in prices, consumption and income for each household group, as well as poverty and distributional indicators, both income- and consumption-based. Also shown in Table 3.2 is the "trade-weighted" real exchange rate, defined as a weighted average of the domestic-currency price of exports and imports (with weights based on initial volumes of trade), divided by a weighted average of the price of domestic sales of agricultural and private sector goods (the only two sectors involved in trade with the rest of the world).

The impact effect of the reduction in the minimum wage is an increase in the demand for unskilled labor in the private sector of the order of 4.3 percent in the first year. The increase in demand is met by the existing pool of unskilled workers seeking employment in the urban sector. As a result, the unskilled unemployment rate drops significantly, by 2.8 percentage points in the first year. The cut in the minimum wage, by reducing the relative cost of unskilled labor, leads to substitution among production factors not only on impact but also over time. Because unskilled labor has a relatively high elasticity of substitution with respect to the composite factor consisting of skilled labor and physical capital, the lower cost of that category of labor gives private firms in the formal sector an incentive to substitute away from both skilled labor and physical capital. In turn, the fall in the demand for skilled labor puts downward pressure on wages for that category of labor, which drop by 1.6 percent in the first period.

On impact, labor supply is fixed in agriculture and the informal economy, so the level of employment does not change in either sector – and neither does the level of activity (real value added in both sectors is constant). The rise in real disposable income (by 1.1 percent and 1.5 percent, respectively) and real consumption of rural and informal sector households leads to higher value added prices and higher wages in both sectors. But value added prices go up by slightly more than wages in the second and subsequent periods, implying a fall in the product wage in both sectors and a rise in employment.

Over time, changes in wage differentials affect both rural–urban and formal–informal migration flows, and therefore labor supply in the various production sectors. The expected unskilled wage in the formal sector is constant on impact, as implied by equations (17) and (18).

Despite the rise in private unskilled employment in the first period (and thus the rise in the probability of finding a job), the fall in the minimum wage is such that the urban expected wage falls. Moreover, because agricultural sector wages rise, the expected urban–rural wage differential (measured in proportion of the rural wage) falls by 8.7 percentage points in the second period, with this differential narrowing over time. As a result, migration flows from rural to urban areas (measured in proportion of urban labor supply) operate in reverse. The concomitant outflow of labor from the informal sector tends to push wages upward in that sector, by 2.6 percent in period 2, 1.6 percent in period 3, and so on. This increase in the informal sector wage, coupled with the reduction in the minimum wage (as well as the expected wage in the urban formal private sector, despite the higher employment probability) leads to a sharp fall in period 2 in the expected formal–informal wage differential (measured in proportion of the informal sector wage). This tends therefore to reduce (by 1.2 percent in period 2, and about 2 percent over the entire adjustment period) the number of workers willing to queue for employment in the urban private sector. This, coupled with the sustained effect of the cut in the minimum wage on labor demand, explains the large effect on unemployment, which averages about 5 percent in the long run. Note also that throughout the adjustment period, despite significant fluctuations in the expected formal–informal wage differential and formal–informal migration flows, the supply of unskilled labor in the formal private sector remains systematically lower than its baseline value.

On impact, the behavior of nominal wages in agriculture reflects essentially changes in value added prices (as noted earlier), hwereas over time it is also affected by changes in labor demand and migration flows. After an initial increase in nominal wages, lower migration flows to urban areas begin to put downward pressure on rural wages, which end up falling (in nominal terms) by 1.6 percent in period 9 and 1.8 percent in the last period. As also indicated earlier, the reduction in the cost of unskilled labor induces a substitution away from skilled labor, which brings a sustained fall in skilled wages in nominal terms (by about 1.3 percent in the longer run). Moreover, the direct substitution effect associated with the reduction in the minimum wage is magnified by an increase in the skilled product wage, resulting from general equilibrium effects. Indeed, the drop in the nominal skilled wage is less than the fall in the value added price of the urban private formal sector, implying a rise in the product wage, and thus dampening further the demand for skilled labor. For instance, the nominal skilled wage drops by 1.6 percent in period 1, 2.4 percent in period 2, 1.4 percent in period 3, and 0.7 percent in period 4; at the same time, the price of value added in the private formal sector drops by 2.4 percent in period 1, 3.1 percent in period 2, 2.0 percent in period 3, and 1.4 percent in period 4. Nevertheless, the overall effect is not large; skilled employment in the private formal sector falls in the long run by only about 0.1 percent. And because the supply of skilled labor remains roughly constant throughout (public investment in education and the number of school teachers are held constant at their baseline values), the skilled unemployment rate rises by about the same amount (in percentage points).[22]

The long-run effect on aggregate output (or real GDP) is slightly positive, at about 0.3 percent.[23] Changes in real output (as measured by real value added) are also positive and small in the urban informal sector, but between 0.7 to 1 percent in agriculture and the urban formal sector, which reflects here essentially changes in private activity. The impact on agricultural output tends to grow slightly over time, as a result of the gradual fall in agricultural wages, as noted earlier.

On the fiscal side, tax revenue falls by about 0.2 percentage points as a share of GDP during the adjustment period, mostly as a result of indirect taxes changing at a slower pace than nominal GDP. Because public investment falls by about 0.1 percentage points of GDP (reflecting a lower price of capital, that is, because $P_K = PV_3$, a fall

---

[22]As implied by equation (38), the level of effort of skilled workers changes as a result of variations in the skilled unemployment rate. However, given the magnitude of these variations, and the elasticity of the effort function with respect to relative wages, the impact on the (effective) supply of skilled labor is negligible relative to the baseline.

[23]Note that this analysis of the growth effects of a cut in the minimum wage does not account for the possible negative externality that may arise if such a cut reduces incentives for human capital accumulation, as emphasized by Cahuc and Michel (1996).

in the value added price in the urban private formal sector), the increase in the overall deficit is about 0.1 percent of GDP. This deficit is financed by domestic borrowing. From the aggregate balance between investment and savings, and given the closure rule discussed earlier, this means that the savings rate of capitalists and rentiers has to increase to maintain equilibrium. Given the small size of that group (about 3 percent of the total number of households), this increase turns out to be quite large – between 5.8 and 6.6 percentage points in the long run.[24]

Despite relatively large changes in real consumption and disposable income (mostly in urban areas), overall poverty indicators for the rural and urban sectors change relatively little during the adjustment period. This is, of course, related to the fact that the aggregate growth and income effects of the shock are fairly limited and involve essentially a reallocation of resources across sectors.

In addition, however, there are large differences among household groups within the urban sector. In particular, although consumption of the capitalists-rentiers group drops significantly in real terms, and the incidence of poverty (as measured by the consumption-based headcount index) rises somewhat during the first part of the adjustment period, the *depth* of poverty (as measured by the poverty gap) is barely affected. Similar results obtain with income-based poverty indicators. For unskilled workers engaged in the informal and formal sectors, both measures of poverty indicate a slight improvement in the longer run, regardless of whether the consumption- or income-based measure is used. This is also the case in the short run for informal sector workers. However, for unskilled workers in the formal sector, poverty increases slightly on impact – by about 0.1 percentage points when the income-based headcount index is used – and so does the skilled poverty rate in the longer run.

There is therefore a potential *trade-off* emerging between unemployment and poverty: although the reduction in the minimum wage raises unskilled employment in the formal sector, it also increases poverty (albeit slightly) in the short term for that category of households, whereas the poverty rate for skilled workers in the formal sector rises in both the short and the long run.[25]

Changes in the consumption-based Gini coefficient indicate that income distribution is affected quite significantly by a cut in the minimum wage; the degree of inequality falls by more than one percentage point in the long run. This effect is directly related to the sharp reduction in consumption experienced by capitalists and rentiers, relative to other household groups.

3.2.2   Cut in Payroll Taxes on Unskilled Labor

The simulation results associated with a permanent, 5-percentage-point reduction in the payroll tax rate on unskilled labor are illustrated in Tables 3.3 to 3.8. The results

---

[24]It is worth noting that, if instead a "classical closure" rule had been chosen (with private investment determined now residually), the government budget deficit would have had a direct crowding out effect on private capital formation. See the discussion of the case of Morocco in Chapter 4.

[25]See Agénor (2004*d*) for a more detailed discussion of unemployment–poverty trade-offs, together with some cross-country econometric evidence.

correspond to three alternative budget financing rules: domestic borrowing (that is, an endogenous adjustment in the capitalists-rentiers savings rate, as in the previous case) with no offsetting tax change; an offsetting, revenue-neutral increase in sales taxes on private formal sector goods only; and a revenue-neutral increase in income taxes.[26]

Domestic Borrowing

Consider first the case of domestic borrowing (Tables 3.3 and 3.4). The impact effect of a reduction in the payroll tax rate is qualitatively similar to a cut in the minimum wage, as discussed earlier: by reducing the effective cost of unskilled labor, it tends to increase immediately the demand for that category of labor – in the present case by 3.4 percent in the first year, and by about 3.2 percent on average during the rest of the adjustment period. The unskilled unemployment rate drops by 2.2 percentage points in the first year as well, and in the longer run by an average of 1.4 percent. At the same time, the reduction in the "effective" cost of unskilled labor leads firms in the private formal urban sector to substitute away from skilled labor and physical capital, leading to a reduction in skilled wages in nominal terms (by 1.4 percent in period 1, 2.5 percent in period 2, 1.9 percent in period 3, and so on) and a reduction in the price of capital (that is, the net price of the private formal good).

In the present case, however, the skilled nominal wage falls by more than the price of value added in the private formal sector (which drops by 1.2 percent in period 1, 2.1 percent in period 2, 1.4 percent in period 3, and so on), implying a fall in the skilled product wage and higher demand for that category of labor. Thus, the adverse impact of the substitution effect induced by the reduction in the cost of unskilled labor on the demand for skilled labor is dampened, unlike what happened with the previous experiment. Nevertheless, skilled employment falls by about 0.1 percent on impact and 0.2 percent in the longer run, bringing with it a concomitant increase in the skilled unemployment rate.

The behavior of the (expected) urban–rural wage differential follows a pattern qualitatively similar to the one described in the previous experiment, although the magnitude of the initial effects are not as large.

The expected formal–informal wage differential, however, *increases* now in the second period. The reason is that the minimum wage does not change this time around, and the increase in unskilled employment raises the probability of finding a job in the private sector, which in turn raises the expected formal sector wage for unskilled workers. As a result, therefore, there is an *increase* in the number of unskilled job seekers in the formal economy in period 2 (by 0.6 percent), which mitigates the initial reduction in unemployment.

---

[26] A potential problem with these simulations, as in other studies along the same line – such as Drèze, Malinvaud, and others (1994) – is the failure to distinguish between changes in *average* tax rates, and changes in *marginal* tax rates. The effects could be very different. For instance, a reduction in the average payroll tax rate might reduce "wage-push" pressures, whereas a cut in marginal rates might reduce the unemployment cost of achieving a higher net income, thereby influencing trade unions' bargaining strategies.

Table 3.3 Mini-IMMPA: simulation results 5-percent cut in unskilled payroll tax rate, nonrevenue neutral (Percentage deviations from baseline, unless otherwise indicated)

	Periods									
	1	2	3	4	5	6	7	8	9	10
Real Sector										
Total resources	0.1	−0.2	0.0	0.1	0.0	−0.2	−0.1	0.0	0.0	−0.1
Gross domestic product	0.2	0.0	0.1	0.2	0.1	0.0	0.1	0.1	0.1	0.0
Imports of goods and NFS	−0.6	−1.5	−1.0	−0.4	−0.7	−1.1	−1.0	−0.7	−0.7	−0.9
Total expenditure	0.1	−0.2	0.0	0.1	0.0	−0.2	−0.1	0.0	0.0	−0.1
Total consumption	0.0	0.3	0.2	−0.3	−0.4	−0.2	−0.1	−0.2	−0.3	−0.3
Private consumption	0.0	0.3	0.2	−0.3	−0.5	−0.2	−0.1	−0.2	−0.4	−0.3
Public consumption	0.0	0.0	0.0	0.0	0.0	0.0	0.0	0.0	0.0	0.0
Total investment	−0.8	−3.7	−2.2	0.4	0.0	−1.6	−1.7	−0.7	−0.5	−1.0
Private investment	−0.9	−5.0	−2.9	0.7	0.2	−2.0	−2.1	−0.8	−0.5	−1.2
Public investment	−0.6	−0.9	−0.7	−0.4	−0.6	−0.7	−0.7	−0.6	−0.6	−0.6
Exports of goods and NFS	1.4	1.5	1.3	1.1	1.3	1.3	1.3	1.2	1.2	1.3
External Sector (% of GDP)[1]										
Current account	0.4	0.6	0.5	0.4	0.5	0.6	0.6	0.5	0.5	0.6
Exports of goods and NFS	0.3	0.3	0.3	0.2	0.3	0.3	0.3	0.3	0.3	0.3
Imports of goods and NFS	−0.2	−0.3	−0.2	−0.1	−0.1	−0.2	−0.2	−0.1	−0.1	−0.2
Factor services	0.0	0.0	0.0	−0.1	−0.1	−0.1	−0.1	−0.1	−0.1	−0.2
Capital account	−0.4	−0.6	−0.5	−0.4	−0.5	−0.6	−0.6	−0.5	−0.5	−0.6
Private borrowing	−0.4	−0.6	−0.5	−0.4	−0.5	−0.6	−0.6	−0.5	−0.5	−0.6
Public borrowing	0.0	0.0	0.0	0.0	0.0	0.0	0.0	0.0	0.0	0.0
Government Sector (% of GDP)[1]										
Total revenue	−0.4	−0.5	−0.4	−0.3	−0.4	−0.4	−0.4	−0.4	−0.4	−0.4
Direct taxes	0.0	−0.1	0.0	0.0	0.0	0.0	0.0	0.0	0.0	0.0
Indirect taxes	−0.4	−0.5	−0.4	−0.3	−0.3	−0.4	−0.4	−0.3	−0.3	−0.4

Total expenditure	−0.1	−0.1	−0.1	−0.1	−0.1	0.0	−0.1	−0.1	−0.1	0.0
Consumption	0.0	0.0	0.0	0.0	0.0	0.0	0.0	0.0	0.0	0.0
Investment	−0.1	−0.1	−0.1	0.0	0.0	0.0	0.0	0.0	0.0	0.0
Transfers to households	0.0	0.0	0.0	0.0	0.0	0.0	0.0	0.0	0.0	0.0
Foreign interest payments	0.0	0.0	0.0	0.0	0.0	0.0	0.0	0.0	0.0	0.0
Total financing	0.3	0.5	0.4	0.3	0.3	0.4	0.4	0.3	0.3	0.3
Foreign financing	0.0	0.0	0.0	0.0	0.0	0.0	0.0	0.0	0.0	0.0
Domestic borrowing	0.3	0.5	0.4	0.3	0.3	0.4	0.4	0.3	0.3	0.3
Labor Market										
Nominal wages										
Agricultural sector	1.5	1.4	1.3	0.7	0.4	0.6	0.7	0.6	0.4	0.4
Informal sector	1.7	2.8	2.0	1.4	1.9	2.3	2.1	1.8	1.8	2.0
Private formal sector										
Unskilled	0.0	0.0	0.0	0.0	0.0	0.0	0.0	0.0	0.0	0.0
Skilled	−1.4	−2.5	−1.9	−1.1	−1.4	−1.9	−1.8	−1.5	−1.5	−1.7
Public sector										
Unskilled	0.0	0.0	0.0	0.0	0.0	0.0	0.0	0.0	0.0	0.0
Skilled	0.0	0.1	0.1	0.0	0.0	0.1	0.1	0.0	0.0	0.1
Employment										
Agricultural sector	0.0	0.0	0.1	0.1	0.1	0.1	0.1	0.1	0.1	0.1
Informal sector	0.0	−0.2	0.0	−0.2	−0.4	−0.4	−0.3	−0.2	−0.3	−0.4
Private formal sector										
Unskilled	3.4	2.0	3.0	4.0	3.6	2.8	3.0	3.5	3.5	3.2
Skilled	−0.1	−0.2	−0.2	−0.1	−0.1	−0.2	−0.2	−0.1	−0.1	−0.2
Public sector										
Unskilled	0.0	0.0	0.0	0.0	0.0	0.0	0.0	0.0	0.0	0.0
Skilled	0.0	0.0	0.0	0.0	0.0	0.0	0.0	0.0	0.0	0.0
Labor supply (urban formal sector)										
Unskilled	0.0	0.6	0.0	0.4	1.2	1.2	0.8	0.7	1.0	1.1
Skilled	0.0	0.0	0.0	0.0	0.0	0.0	0.0	0.0	0.0	0.0

Continued

Table 3.3 Continued

	Periods									
	1	2	3	4	5	6	7	8	9	10
Unemployment rate (urban formal sector)[1]										
Unskilled	-2.2	-0.7	-2.0	-2.3	-1.3	-0.8	-1.3	-1.7	-1.4	-1.1
Skilled	0.1	0.1	0.1	0.1	0.1	0.1	0.1	0.1	0.1	0.1
Real wage differentials[1]										
Expected urban-rural (% of rural wage)	0.0	-1.7	-1.2	-1.3	-0.7	-0.2	-0.2	-0.5	-0.4	-0.2
Expected formal-informal (% of informal wage)	0.0	1.7	-1.8	1.1	2.2	0.1	-1.2	-0.2	0.8	0.3
Migration[1]										
Rural-urban (% of urban labor supply)	0.00	-0.02	-0.01	-0.01	-0.01	0.00	0.00	0.00	0.00	0.00
Formal-informal (% of formal urban labor supply)	0.00	0.65	-0.68	0.41	0.83	0.02	-0.45	-0.08	0.28	0.13
Memorandum items[2]										
GDP at market prices	0.2	-0.1	0.1	0.2	0.1	0.0	0.0	0.1	0.1	0.0
Value added at factor cost	0.2	0.1	0.1	0.2	0.1	0.0	0.1	0.1	0.1	0.1
Value added in rural sector	0.0	0.0	0.0	0.1	0.1	0.1	0.1	0.1	0.1	0.1
Value added in urban informal sector	0.0	-0.2	0.0	-0.1	-0.3	-0.3	-0.2	-0.2	-0.3	-0.3
Value added in urban formal sector	0.6	0.3	0.4	0.6	0.5	0.4	0.4	0.5	0.5	0.4
Private Consumption	-0.3	-0.1	-0.1	-0.6	-0.8	-0.6	-0.4	-0.5	-0.6	-0.6
Private Investment	-0.3	-4.1	-2.2	1.2	0.8	-1.3	-1.5	-0.2	0.1	-0.6
Disposable income	0.5	0.4	0.5	0.5	0.5	0.5	0.5	0.5	0.5	0.5
Capitalists and rentiers savings rate[1]	7.5	5.1	5.4	8.7	9.8	8.2	7.3	8.2	8.9	8.5

[1] Absolute deviations from baseline. [2] In real terms.

Table 3.4 Mini-IMMPA: price, poverty, and distributional indicators 5-percent cut in unskilled payroll tax rate, nonrevenue neutral (Percentage deviations from baseline, unless otherwise indicated)

	Periods									
	1	2	3	4	5	6	7	8	9	10
Consumer Prices and the Real Exchange Rate										
Rural CPI	0.5	0.6	0.5	0.3	0.3	0.4	0.4	0.3	0.3	0.3
Urban CPI	0.3	0.4	0.3	0.2	0.2	0.3	0.3	0.2	0.2	0.2
Unskilled	0.2	0.3	0.2	0.1	0.2	0.2	0.2	0.2	0.2	0.2
Skilled	0.0	0.1	0.1	0.0	0.0	0.1	0.1	0.0	0.0	0.1
Real exchange rate	-0.2	-0.2	-0.2	-0.1	-0.1	-0.1	-0.1	-0.1	-0.1	-0.1
Value Added Prices										
Rural agriculture	1.5	1.4	1.3	0.7	0.4	0.6	0.7	0.6	0.4	0.4
Urban private informal	1.7	2.8	2.0	1.4	1.8	2.3	2.1	1.8	1.8	2.0
Urban private formal	-1.2	-2.1	-1.4	-0.7	-1.0	-1.5	-1.4	-1.0	-1.0	-1.2
Urban public	0.0	0.0	0.0	0.0	0.0	0.0	0.0	0.0	0.0	0.0
Real Disposable Income[1]										
Rural households	0.9	0.7	0.8	0.4	0.1	0.2	0.4	0.3	0.2	0.2
Urban households	0.4	0.4	0.5	0.5	0.5	0.5	0.5	0.6	0.6	0.6
Informal	1.3	1.9	1.5	0.9	1.1	1.5	1.4	1.2	1.1	1.3
Formal unskilled	1.6	0.8	1.4	2.0	1.7	1.3	1.4	1.7	1.7	1.5
Formal skilled	-0.7	-1.2	-0.9	-0.6	-0.7	-0.9	-0.9	-0.7	-0.7	-0.8
Capitalists and rentiers	-1.7	-2.8	-1.7	-0.7	-0.9	-1.4	-1.1	-0.5	-0.4	-0.4
Real Consumption[1]										
Rural households	0.9	0.7	0.8	0.4	0.1	0.2	0.4	0.3	0.2	0.2
Urban households	-0.6	-0.3	-0.3	-0.8	-1.0	-0.7	-0.6	-0.7	-0.8	-0.8
Informal	1.3	1.9	1.5	0.9	1.1	1.5	1.4	1.2	1.1	1.3
Formal unskilled	1.6	0.8	1.4	2.0	1.7	1.3	1.4	1.7	1.7	1.5
Formal skilled	-0.7	-1.2	-0.9	-0.6	-0.7	-0.9	-0.9	-0.7	-0.7	-0.8
Capitalists and rentiers	-11.5	-9.4	-8.8	-12.0	-13.3	-11.5	-10.1	-10.5	-11.0	-10.5

Continued

Table 3.4 Continued

					Periods					
	1	2	3	4	5	6	7	8	9	10
Household Size[1]										
Rural households	0.0	0.0	0.1	0.1	0.1	0.1	0.1	0.1	0.1	0.1
Urban households	0.0	0.0	0.0	0.0	0.0	0.0	0.0	0.0	0.0	0.0
Informal	0.0	−0.2	0.0	−0.2	−0.4	−0.4	−0.3	−0.2	−0.3	−0.4
Formal unskilled	0.0	0.6	0.0	0.4	1.2	1.2	0.8	0.7	1.0	1.1
Formal skilled	0.0	0.0	0.0	0.0	0.0	0.0	0.0	0.0	0.0	0.0
Capitalists and rentiers	0.0	0.0	0.0	0.0	0.0	0.0	0.0	0.0	0.0	0.0
Poverty and Distributional Indicators										
Consumption-based										
Poverty Line[1]										
Rural	0.5	0.6	0.5	0.3	0.3	0.4	0.4	0.3	0.3	0.3
Urban	0.3	0.4	0.3	0.2	0.2	0.3	0.3	0.2	0.2	0.2
Poverty Headcount										
Rural households	−0.5	−0.4	−0.6	−0.3	0.0	−0.1	−0.2	−0.1	−0.1	0.0
Urban households	−0.6	−0.6	−0.5	−0.4	−0.4	−0.5	−0.4	−0.5	−0.4	−0.3
Informal	−0.6	−0.9	−0.7	−0.5	−0.7	−0.9	−0.7	−0.6	−0.7	−0.7
Formal unskilled	−1.2	0.0	−1.0	−0.7	−0.1	0.0	−0.1	−0.4	−0.1	0.0
Formal skilled	0.0	0.0	0.6	0.4	0.2	0.0	0.2	0.0	0.2	0.0
Capitalists and rentiers	0.7	0.7	0.7	0.7	0.7	0.7	0.0	0.0	0.0	1.0
Economy	−0.6	−0.5	−0.5	−0.3	−0.3	−0.4	−0.4	−0.4	−0.3	−0.2
Poverty Gap										
Rural households	−0.3	−0.2	−0.2	−0.1	0.0	0.0	−0.1	−0.1	0.0	0.0
Urban households	−0.3	−0.4	−0.3	−0.3	−0.3	−0.3	−0.3	−0.3	−0.3	−0.3
Informal	−0.4	−0.6	−0.5	−0.3	−0.4	−0.5	−0.5	−0.4	−0.4	−0.5
Formal unskilled	−0.4	0.0	−0.3	−0.4	−0.1	0.0	−0.1	−0.2	−0.2	−0.1
Formal skilled	0.1	0.1	0.1	0.1	0.1	0.1	0.1	0.1	0.1	0.1
Capitalists and rentiers	0.2	0.1	0.1	0.2	0.2	0.1	0.1	0.1	0.1	0.1
Economy	−0.3	−0.3	−0.3	−0.2	−0.2	−0.2	−0.2	−0.2	−0.2	−0.2

Distributional Indicators²										
Gini coefficient	−1.9	−1.9	−1.9	−1.8	−2.0	−2.3	−2.1	−1.6	−1.7	−2.0
Theil index	−1.3	−1.3	−1.2	−1.1	−1.2	−1.4	−1.2	−0.9	−1.0	−1.1
Poverty and Distributional Indicators										
Income-based										
Poverty Line¹										
Rural	0.3	0.3	0.3	0.4	0.4	0.3	0.3	0.5	0.6	0.5
Urban	0.2	0.2	0.2	0.3	0.3	0.2	0.2	0.3	0.4	0.3
Poverty Headcount										
Rural households	−0.1	−0.1	−0.1	−0.1	−0.1	−0.1	−0.2	−0.4	−0.4	−0.5
Urban households	−0.8	−0.7	−0.6	−0.7	−0.8	−0.7	−0.6	−0.7	−0.9	−0.7
Informal	−1.2	−1.1	−1.1	−1.2	−1.3	−1.1	−0.8	−1.1	−1.6	−1.0
Formal unskilled	−0.3	−0.1	0.0	0.0	0.0	0.0	−0.4	−0.4	0.0	−0.4
Formal skilled	0.4	0.0	0.4	0.2	0.0	0.0	0.2	0.2	0.6	0.2
Capitalists and rentiers	0.0	0.0	0.7	0.7	0.7	0.0	0.0	0.7	0.7	0.0
Economy	−0.6	−0.5	−0.5	−0.5	−0.6	−0.5	−0.5	−0.6	−0.7	−0.6
Poverty Gap										
Rural households	0.0	0.0	−0.1	−0.1	0.0	0.0	−0.1	−0.2	−0.2	−0.3
Urban households	−0.3	−0.3	−0.3	−0.3	−0.3	−0.3	−0.2	−0.3	−0.4	−0.3
Informal	−0.5	−0.4	−0.4	−0.5	−0.5	−0.4	−0.3	−0.4	−0.6	−0.4
Formal unskilled	−0.1	−0.1	−0.2	−0.1	0.0	−0.1	−0.3	−0.2	0.0	−0.3
Formal skilled	0.1	0.1	0.1	0.1	0.1	0.1	0.0	0.1	0.1	0.0
Capitalists and rentiers	0.0	0.0	0.0	0.0	0.1	0.0	0.0	0.1	0.1	0.1
Economy	−0.2	−0.2	−0.2	−0.2	−0.2	−0.2	−0.2	−0.3	−0.3	−0.3
Distributional Indicators²										
Gini coefficient	−0.2	−0.2	−0.3	−0.4	−0.4	−0.3	−0.3	−0.5	−0.7	−0.5
Theil index	−0.1	−0.1	−0.2	−0.2	−0.2	−0.2	−0.2	−0.3	−0.4	−0.3

¹ Percentage deviations from baseline. ² Gini Coefficients and Theil Indices measure between-group inequality.

In the subsequent period, however, because of the sharp increase in the informal sector wage in period 2 (itself due to the reduction in labor supply in the informal economy), the formal–informal wage differential moves in the opposite direction and by about the same amount (1.8 percentage points) – thereby reducing the number of unskilled job seekers in the formal sector.

But this in turn puts downward pressure on informal sector wages, pushing the expected formal–informal sector wage differential in the opposite direction. These fluctuations in wage differentials, migration flows, and labor supply in the formal and informal sectors continue throughout the adjustment period.

The overall effect on aggregate real output is, again, fairly small – given that this is also a shock that fundamentally entails a change in relative prices as the initial impulse. An important feature of the long-run adjustment process, however, is a reduction in the size of the informal sector and an expansion of the private formal urban sector, which essentially results from the transfer of unskilled labor across these two sectors.

This result is therefore consistent with the widely-held view (discussed in the introduction to this chapter) that reducing the tax burden on the formal sector is essential to limit the growth of the informal sector, although in the present case the "disincentive" effects of taxation are indirect and captured at the level of firms, as opposed to individuals and their propensity to evade income taxes.

The government budget is of course more significantly affected, with indirect tax revenue falling by about 0.4 percentage points of GDP. Despite the drop in the price of capital (which tends to raise the desired capital stock, as implied by (76)), the drop in profits – resulting from the reduction in private consumption by capitalists and rentiers, and to a lesser extent by skilled households in the formal sector – translates into a significant drop in private investment in the first three periods, followed by a partial recovery thereafter. Because the current account improves (by about 0.6 percentage points of GDP on average), private capital inflows fall. Despite the initially large reduction in private investment, borrowing by the government and the reduction in foreign savings lead to a significant increase in the savings rate of capitalists-rentiers relative to its baseline value (about 8 percentage points on average).

Poverty and distributional indicators are affected in the same direction as before. In particular, after increasing during the first part of the adjustment period, the consumption-based headcount index for capitalists and rentiers shows a slight increase toward the end of the adjustment period, whereas the poverty gap barely changes. And because the drop in consumption for that category of households is larger than in the case of a cut in the minimum wage, the degree of inequality (as measured by the consumption-based Gini coefficient or the Theil index) falls by a larger amount. In addition, in the present case, the poverty rate for unskilled households in the formal sector drops on impact, with no significant long-run effect, whereas skilled poverty rates increase throughout the adjustment period.

Revenue-Neutral Change

Consider now the case where the revenue effect of the cut in payroll taxes is offset by either an increase in sales taxes on private formal sector goods (Tables 3.5 and 3.6) or an increase in income taxes (Tables 3.7 and 3.8). In the latter case, the increase in the tax rate is assumed to be proportional across households – except of course for informal sector households, who are not subject to direct taxation to begin with.

In both cases, the impact and longer-run effects of the shock are qualitatively similar to those described earlier, although their magnitude differs. In particular, movements in the informal sector wage are less pronounced, in part because changes in rural–urban migration flows are not as large. By contrast (or, rather, by implication), movements in the expected formal–informal wage differential during the first part of the adjustment period are larger, implying more pronounced and more persistent movements in the number of unskilled job seekers in the formal sector.

Compared to the case of private sector borrowing, the reduction in the unskilled unemployment rate is less significant with an offsetting change in the sales tax, and of about the same magnitude when the income tax is adjusted.

Effects on overall real GDP and private investment are quite similar. When the sales tax is adjusted, the fall in total private consumption is more pronounced than in the case of domestic borrowing or with an offsetting adjustment in the income tax (see Table 3.5). The reason, of course, is that the increase in the sales price reduces the purchasing power of income (everything else equal) and tends to reduce demand, particularly in urban areas (see Table 3.6).

In both cases, the offsetting changes in the budget imply that domestic borrowing by the government does not change as a result of the reduction in the payroll tax; thus, the increase in the savings rate of capitalists and rentiers is much less pronounced than in the case where the government finances its deficit through private sector savings.

Changes in the poverty and distributional effects (as measured by the indicators based on consumption) are also less pronounced initially than in the case of a nonneutral shock, although the income-based poverty gap for formal skilled workers displays slightly larger and more persistent fluctuations in the case of an offsetting income tax change. This is obviously what one would expect given that disposable income for this particular group falls by a much larger amount compared to the nonneutral case – by about 2 percent for skilled workers in the formal sector between periods 6 and 10 (see Table 3.8), compared to about 0.8 percent with a nonneutral policy shock (see Table 3.4). As a result, the income-based Gini coefficient falls by more (by 0.4 percentage points in the long run, compared to 0.2 in the non-neutral case), despite the fact that changes in the consumption-based measures of inequality are less pronounced.

Overall, the results indicate that there are some significant differences in economic and poverty outcomes, depending on the offsetting change in the budget that accompanies the reduction in the payroll tax.

3.3   Conclusions

This chapter presented the structure, and illustrated the functioning, of Mini-IMMPA, a specialized version of IMMPA that is particularly suitable for users interested mainly in assessing the quantitative effects of fiscal and labor market reforms on unemployment and poverty. Although Mini-IMMPA focuses only on the "real" side, it offers a more detailed treatment of the labor market than typical IMMPA applications (by accounting for features such as employment subsidies and firing costs) and the tax structure. It is also less data intensive and may represent a convenient intermediate step on the road to building a full IMMPA application.

Table 3.5 Mini-IMMPA: simulation results 5-percent cut in unskilled payroll tax rate, sales tax revenue neutral (Percentage deviations from baseline, unless otherwise indicated)

	Periods									
	1	2	3	4	5	6	7	8	9	10
Real Sector										
Total resources	0.0	−0.3	−0.2	−0.2	−0.2	−0.2	−0.2	−0.2	−0.2	−0.2
Gross domestic product	0.2	−0.1	0.0	0.0	−0.1	−0.1	−0.1	−0.1	−0.1	−0.1
Imports of goods and NFS	−0.8	−1.5	−1.1	−1.0	−1.1	−1.2	−1.1	−1.1	−1.1	−1.1
Total expenditure	0.0	−0.3	−0.2	−0.2	−0.2	−0.2	−0.2	−0.2	−0.2	−0.2
Total consumption	−0.2	−0.3	−0.4	−0.5	−0.6	−0.5	−0.5	−0.5	−0.5	−0.5
Private consumption	−0.3	−0.4	−0.5	−0.6	−0.7	−0.6	−0.6	−0.6	−0.6	−0.6
Public consumption	0.0	0.0	0.0	0.0	0.0	0.0	0.0	0.0	0.0	0.0
Total investment	−0.6	−2.0	−0.9	−0.4	−0.7	−0.8	−0.8	−0.7	−0.8	−0.8
Private investment	−0.8	−2.7	−1.2	−0.5	−0.9	−1.1	−1.0	−1.0	−1.0	−1.0
Public investment	−0.3	−0.3	−0.3	−0.3	−0.3	−0.3	−0.3	−0.2	−0.2	−0.2
Exports of goods and NFS	1.4	1.5	1.4	1.3	1.3	1.3	1.3	1.3	1.3	1.2
External Sector (% of GDP)[1]										
Current account	0.5	0.6	0.5	0.5	0.6	0.6	0.6	0.6	0.6	0.7
Exports of goods and NFS	0.3	0.4	0.3	0.3	0.3	0.3	0.3	0.3	0.3	0.3
Imports of goods and NFS	−0.2	−0.2	−0.2	−0.2	−0.2	−0.2	−0.2	−0.2	−0.2	−0.2
Factor services	0.0	0.0	0.0	−0.1	−0.1	−0.1	−0.1	−0.1	−0.2	−0.2
Capital account	−0.5	−0.6	−0.5	−0.5	−0.6	−0.6	−0.6	−0.6	−0.6	−0.7
Private borrowing	−0.5	−0.6	−0.5	−0.5	−0.6	−0.6	−0.6	−0.6	−0.6	−0.7
Public borrowing	0.0	0.0	0.0	0.0	0.0	0.0	0.0	0.0	0.0	0.0

Continued

Table 3.5 Continued

	Periods									
	1	2	3	4	5	6	7	8	9	10
Government Sector (% of GDP)[1]										
Total revenue	0.0	0.0	0.0	0.0	0.0	0.0	0.0	0.0	0.0	0.0
Direct taxes	−0.1	−0.1	−0.1	0.0	0.0	0.0	0.0	0.0	0.0	0.0
Indirect taxes	0.0	0.1	0.1	0.0	0.1	0.1	0.1	0.1	0.1	0.1
Total expenditure	−0.1	0.0	0.0	0.0	0.0	0.0	0.0	0.0	0.0	0.0
Consumption	0.0	0.0	0.0	0.0	0.0	0.0	0.0	0.0	0.0	0.0
Investment	0.0	0.0	0.0	0.0	0.0	0.0	0.0	0.0	0.0	0.0
Transfers to households	0.0	0.0	0.0	0.0	0.0	0.0	0.0	0.0	0.0	0.0
Foreign interest payments	0.0	0.0	0.0	0.0	0.0	0.0	0.0	0.0	0.0	0.0
Total financing	0.0	0.0	0.0	0.0	0.0	0.0	0.0	0.0	0.0	0.0
Foreign financing	0.0	0.0	0.0	0.0	0.0	0.0	0.0	0.0	0.0	0.0
Domestic borrowing	0.0	0.0	0.0	0.0	0.0	0.0	0.0	0.0	0.0	0.0
Labor Market										
Nominal wages										
Agricultural sector	0.9	0.3	0.3	0.1	0.0	0.0	0.0	0.0	0.0	0.0
Informal sector	0.7	1.1	0.9	0.9	1.0	1.0	0.9	0.9	0.9	0.9
Private formal sector										
Unskilled	0.0	0.0	0.0	0.0	0.0	0.0	0.0	0.0	0.0	0.0
Skilled	−1.7	−2.4	−2.0	−1.8	−2.0	−2.0	−2.0	−2.0	−2.0	−2.0
Public sector										
Unskilled	0.0	0.0	0.0	0.0	0.0	0.0	0.0	0.0	0.0	0.0
Skilled	0.0	0.0	0.0	0.0	0.0	0.0	0.0	0.0	0.0	0.0
Employment										
Agricultural sector	0.0	0.0	0.0	0.0	0.0	0.0	0.0	0.0	0.0	0.0
Informal sector	0.0	−0.3	−0.2	−0.3	−0.4	−0.4	−0.4	−0.4	−0.4	−0.4

Private formal sector									
Unskilled	3.1	2.1	2.7	2.9	2.7	2.7	2.8	2.8	2.8	2.8
Skilled	-0.1	-0.2	-0.2	-0.2	-0.2	-0.2	-0.2	-0.2	-0.2	-0.2
Public sector									
Unskilled	0.0	0.0	0.0	0.0	0.0	0.0	0.0	0.0	0.0	0.0
Skilled	0.0	0.0	0.0	0.0	0.0	0.0	0.0	0.0	0.0	0.0
Labor supply (urban formal sector)									
Unskilled	0.0	0.9	0.8	1.1	1.3	1.3	1.3	1.3	1.4	1.4
Skilled	0.0	0.0	0.0	0.0	0.0	0.0	0.0	0.0	0.0	0.0
Unemployment rate (urban formal sector)[1]									
Unskilled	-2.0	-0.5	-1.1	-0.9	-0.6	-0.6	-0.7	-0.6	-0.6	-0.6
Skilled	0.1	0.1	0.1	0.1	0.1	0.1	0.1	0.1	0.1	0.1
Real wage differentials[1]									
Expected urban-rural (% of rural wage)	0.0	-1.1	-0.2	-0.2	0.0	0.2	0.2	0.1	0.2	0.2
Expected formal-informal (% of informal wage)	0.0	2.5	-0.3	0.8	0.6	0.0	0.0	0.1	0.1	0.1
Migration[1]									
Rural-urban (% of urban labor supply)	0.00	-0.01	0.00	0.00	0.00	0.00	0.00	0.00	0.00	0.00
Formal-informal (% of formal urban labor supply)	0.00	0.91	-0.12	0.30	0.22	-0.01	-0.02	0.03	0.04	0.02
Memorandum items[2]									
GDP at market prices	0.1	-0.1	0.0	0.0	0.0	-0.1	0.0	-0.1	-0.1	-0.1
Value added at factor cost	0.2	0.0	0.1	0.1	0.0	0.0	0.0	0.0	0.0	0.0
Value added in rural sector	0.0	0.0	0.0	0.0	0.0	0.0	0.0	0.0	0.0	0.0
Value added in urban informal sector	0.0	-0.2	-0.2	-0.3	-0.3	-0.3	-0.3	-0.3	-0.3	-0.3
Value added in urban formal sector	0.6	0.3	0.4	0.4	0.4	0.4	0.4	0.4	0.3	0.3
Private Consumption	-0.4	-0.5	-0.6	-0.8	-0.8	-0.7	-0.7	-0.7	-0.7	-0.7
Private Investment	-0.5	-2.4	-0.9	-0.2	-0.6	-0.8	-0.7	-0.7	-0.8	-0.8
Disposable income	0.1	-0.1	0.0	0.0	0.0	0.0	0.0	0.0	0.0	0.1
Capitalists and rentiers savings rate[1]	5.0	3.8	5.2	6.3	6.1	5.9	6.0	6.1	6.1	6.1

[1] Absolute deviations from baseline. [2] In real terms.

Table 3.6 Mini-IMMPA: price, poverty and distributional indicators 5-percent cut in unskilled payroll tax rate, sales tax revenue neutral (Percentage deviations from baseline, unless otherwise indicated)

	Periods									
	1	2	3	4	5	6	7	8	9	10
Consumer Prices and the Real Exchange Rate										
Rural CPI	0.2	0.2	0.2	0.1	0.1	0.1	0.1	0.1	0.1	0.1
Urban CPI	0.1	0.1	0.1	0.1	0.1	0.1	0.1	0.1	0.1	0.1
Unskilled	0.1	0.1	0.1	0.1	0.1	0.1	0.1	0.1	0.1	0.1
Skilled	0.0	0.0	0.0	0.0	0.0	0.0	0.0	0.0	0.0	0.0
Real exchange rate	0.1	0.2	0.2	0.2	0.2	0.2	0.2	0.2	0.2	0.2
Value Added Prices										
Rural agriculture	0.9	0.3	0.3	0.1	0.0	0.0	0.0	0.0	0.0	0.0
Urban private informal	0.7	1.1	0.9	0.8	0.9	0.9	0.9	0.9	0.8	0.8
Urban private formal	-1.4	-2.0	-1.6	-1.4	-1.5	-1.6	-1.5	-1.5	-1.5	-1.5
Urban public	0.0	0.0	0.0	0.0	0.0	0.0	0.0	0.0	0.0	0.0
Real Disposable Income[1]										
Rural households	0.6	0.1	0.1	0.0	-0.1	-0.1	-0.1	-0.1	-0.1	-0.1
Urban households	0.0	-0.2	0.0	0.0	0.0	0.0	0.0	0.1	0.1	0.1
Informal	0.5	0.6	0.5	0.4	0.4	0.4	0.4	0.4	0.4	0.4
Formal unskilled	1.5	1.0	1.4	1.5	1.4	1.4	1.4	1.4	1.4	1.4
Formal skilled	-0.8	-1.1	-0.9	-0.9	-0.9	-1.0	-0.9	-0.9	-0.9	-0.9
Capitalists and rentiers	-2.0	-2.7	-1.9	-1.5	-1.6	-1.4	-1.2	-1.0	-0.8	-0.6
Real Consumption[1]										
Rural households	0.6	0.1	0.1	0.0	-0.1	-0.1	-0.1	-0.1	-0.1	-0.1
Urban households	-0.7	-0.7	-0.8	-0.9	-0.9	-0.9	-0.9	-0.9	-0.9	-0.9
Informal	0.5	0.6	0.5	0.4	0.4	0.4	0.4	0.4	0.4	0.4
Formal unskilled	1.5	1.0	1.4	1.5	1.4	1.4	1.4	1.4	1.4	1.4
Formal skilled	-0.8	-1.1	-0.9	-0.9	-0.9	-1.0	-0.9	-0.9	-0.9	-0.9
Capitalists and rentiers	-8.6	-7.6	-8.7	-9.7	-9.2	-8.7	-8.5	-8.3	-8.0	-7.7

Household Size [1]

Rural households	0.0	0.0	0.0	0.0	0.0	0.0	0.0	0.0	0.0	0.0
Urban households	0.0	0.0	0.0	0.0	0.0	0.0	0.0	0.0	0.0	0.0
Informal	-0.3	-0.3	-0.2	-0.3	-0.4	-0.4	-0.4	-0.4	-0.4	-0.4
Formal unskilled	0.9	0.8	1.1	1.3	1.3	1.3	1.3	1.3	1.4	1.4
Formal skilled	0.0	0.0	0.0	0.0	0.0	0.0	0.0	0.0	0.0	0.0
Capitalists and rentiers	0.0	0.0	0.0	0.0	0.0	0.0	0.0	0.0	0.0	0.0

Poverty and Distributional Indicators

Consumption-based

Poverty Line[1]

Rural	0.2	0.2	0.1	0.1	0.1	0.1	0.1	0.1	0.1	0.1
Urban	0.1	0.1	0.1	0.1	0.1	0.1	0.1	0.1	0.1	0.1

Poverty Headcount

Rural households	-0.3	-0.1	-0.1	0.0	0.1	0.1	0.1	0.1	0.0	0.1
Urban households	-0.4	-0.3	-0.2	-0.2	-0.2	-0.2	-0.2	-0.3	-0.2	0.0
Informal	-0.3	-0.4	-0.3	-0.4	-0.4	-0.4	-0.3	-0.3	-0.3	-0.2
Formal unskilled	-1.2	0.0	-0.4	0.0	0.0	0.0	0.0	0.0	0.0	0.0
Formal skilled	0.0	0.0	0.6	0.4	0.2	0.2	0.2	0.2	0.2	0.0
Capitalists and rentiers	0.7	0.7	0.7	0.7	0.7	0.0	0.0	0.0	0.0	1.0
Economy	-0.3	-0.2	-0.1	-0.1	-0.1	-0.1	-0.1	-0.1	-0.1	0.0

Poverty Gap

Rural households	-0.2	0.0	0.0	0.0	0.0	0.0	0.0	0.0	0.0	0.0
Urban households	-0.2	-0.2	-0.1	-0.1	-0.1	-0.1	-0.1	-0.1	-0.1	-0.1
Informal	-0.2	-0.3	-0.2	-0.2	-0.2	-0.2	-0.2	-0.2	-0.2	-0.2
Formal unskilled	-0.3	0.0	-0.1	0.0	0.0	0.0	0.0	0.0	0.0	0.0
Formal skilled	0.1	0.1	0.1	0.1	0.1	0.1	0.1	0.1	0.1	0.1
Capitalists and rentiers	0.1	0.1	0.1	0.1	0.1	0.1	0.1	0.0	0.1	0.1
Economy	-0.2	-0.1	-0.1	-0.1	-0.1	-0.1	-0.1	-0.1	-0.1	-0.1

Distributional Indicators[2]

Gini coefficient	-1.4	-1.2	-1.4	-1.6	-1.5	-1.4	-1.4	-1.4	-1.3	-1.3
Theil index	-0.8	-0.7	-0.8	-0.9	-0.9	-0.9	-0.9	-0.9	-0.9	-0.9

Continued

Table 3.6 Continued

					Periods					
	1	2	3	4	5	6	7	8	9	10
Poverty and Distributional Indicators										
Income-based										
Poverty Line[1]										
Rural	0.2	0.2	0.2	0.1	0.1	0.1	0.1	0.1	0.1	0.1
Urban	0.1	0.1	0.1	0.1	0.1	0.1	0.1	0.1	0.1	0.1
Poverty Headcount										
Rural households	−0.4	0.0	−0.1	0.0	0.1	0.1	0.1	0.1	0.1	0.1
Urban households	−0.4	−0.3	−0.4	−0.4	−0.4	−0.4	−0.4	−0.3	−0.3	−0.2
Informal	−0.6	−0.7	−0.6	−0.7	−0.7	−0.6	−0.7	−0.7	−0.4	−0.4
Formal unskilled	−0.4	0.0	−0.3	0.0	0.0	0.0	0.0	0.0	0.0	−0.1
Formal skilled	0.2	0.6	0.0	0.2	0.0	0.0	0.2	0.6	0.0	0.4
Capitalists and rentiers	0.0	0.7	0.7	0.0	0.0	0.7	0.7	0.7	0.7	0.0
Economy	−0.4	−0.2	−0.3	−0.3	−0.3	−0.2	−0.2	−0.2	−0.2	−0.1
Poverty Gap										
Rural households	−0.2	0.0	0.0	0.0	0.0	0.0	0.0	0.0	0.0	0.0
Urban households	−0.1	−0.2	−0.1	−0.1	−0.1	−0.1	−0.1	−0.1	−0.1	−0.1
Informal	−0.2	−0.3	−0.2	−0.2	−0.2	−0.2	−0.2	−0.2	−0.2	−0.2
Formal unskilled	−0.3	0.0	−0.1	−0.1	0.0	0.0	0.0	0.0	0.0	0.0
Formal skilled	0.0	0.1	0.1	0.1	0.1	0.1	0.1	0.1	0.1	0.1
Capitalists and rentiers	0.1	0.1	0.1	0.1	0.1	0.1	0.0	0.0	0.0	0.0
Economy	−0.2	−0.1	−0.1	−0.1	−0.1	−0.1	−0.1	−0.1	−0.1	−0.1
Distributional Indicators[2]										
Gini coefficient	−0.4	−0.5	−0.4	−0.3	−0.3	−0.3	−0.2	−0.2	−0.2	−0.2
Theil index	−0.3	−0.3	−0.2	−0.2	−0.2	−0.2	−0.2	−0.1	−0.1	−0.1

[1] Percentage deviations from baseline. [2] Gini Coefficients and Theil Indices measure between group inequality.

Table 3.7 Mini-IMMPA: simulation results 5-percent cut in unskilled payroll tax rate, income tax revenue neutral (Percentage deviations from baseline, unless otherwise indicated)

					Periods					
	1	2	3	4	5	6	7	8	9	10
Real Sector										
Total resources	0.1	-0.2	0.0	0.1	0.0	-0.1	-0.1	0.0	0.0	-0.1
Gross domestic product	0.3	0.0	0.1	0.2	0.1	0.0	0.1	0.1	0.1	0.0
Imports of goods and NFS	-0.6	-1.4	-0.9	-0.4	-0.7	-1.0	-0.9	-0.7	-0.7	-0.8
Total expenditure	0.1	-0.2	0.0	0.1	0.0	-0.1	-0.1	0.0	0.0	-0.1
Total consumption	0.0	0.3	0.2	-0.3	-0.4	-0.2	-0.1	-0.2	-0.3	-0.2
Private consumption	0.0	0.3	0.2	-0.3	-0.5	-0.2	-0.1	-0.2	-0.3	-0.3
Public consumption	0.0	0.0	0.0	0.0	0.0	0.0	0.0	0.0	0.0	0.0
Total investment	-0.8	-3.6	-2.1	0.3	-0.1	-1.5	-1.6	-0.7	-0.5	-1.0
Private investment	-0.9	-4.8	-2.7	0.6	0.1	-1.9	-2.0	-0.8	-0.5	-1.2
Public investment	-0.6	-0.9	-0.6	-0.4	-0.5	-0.7	-0.6	-0.5	-0.5	-0.6
Exports of goods and NFS	1.4	1.5	1.3	1.2	1.3	1.3	1.3	1.2	1.2	1.3
External Sector (% of GDP)[1]										
Current account	0.4	0.6	0.5	0.4	0.5	0.6	0.6	0.5	0.5	0.6
Exports of goods and NFS	0.3	0.3	0.3	0.2	0.3	0.3	0.3	0.3	0.3	0.3
Imports of goods and NFS	-0.1	-0.3	-0.2	-0.1	-0.1	-0.2	-0.2	-0.1	-0.1	-0.2
Factor services	0.0	0.0	0.0	-0.1	-0.1	-0.1	-0.1	-0.1	-0.1	-0.2
Capital account	-0.4	-0.6	-0.5	-0.4	-0.5	-0.6	-0.6	-0.5	-0.5	-0.6
Private borrowing	-0.4	-0.6	-0.5	-0.4	-0.5	-0.6	-0.6	-0.5	-0.5	-0.6
Public borrowing	0.0	0.0	0.0	0.0	0.0	0.0	0.0	0.0	0.0	0.0
Government Sector (% of GDP)[1]										
Total revenue	-0.1	0.0	0.0	0.0	0.0	0.0	0.0	0.0	0.0	0.0
Direct taxes	0.3	0.4	0.3	0.3	0.3	0.4	0.4	0.3	0.3	0.3
Indirect taxes	-0.4	-0.5	-0.4	-0.3	-0.3	-0.4	-0.4	-0.3	-0.3	-0.3

Continued

Table 3.7 Continued

	Periods									
	1	2	3	4	5	6	7	8	9	10
Total expenditure	-0.1	-0.1	-0.1	-0.1	-0.1	0.0	-0.1	-0.1	-0.1	0.0
Consumption	0.0	0.0	0.0	0.0	0.0	0.0	0.0	0.0	0.0	0.0
Investment	-0.1	-0.1	-0.1	0.0	0.0	0.0	0.0	0.0	0.0	0.0
Transfers to households	0.0	0.0	0.0	0.0	0.0	0.0	0.0	0.0	0.0	0.0
Foreign interest payments	0.0	0.0	0.0	0.0	0.0	0.0	0.0	0.0	0.0	0.0
Total financing	0.0	-0.1	0.0	0.0	0.0	0.0	0.0	0.0	0.0	0.0
Foreign financing	0.0	0.0	0.0	0.0	0.0	0.0	0.0	0.0	0.0	0.0
Domestic borrowing	0.0	-0.1	0.0	0.0	0.0	0.0	0.0	0.0	0.0	0.0
Labor Market										
Nominal wages										
Agricultural sector	1.4	1.2	1.1	0.6	0.3	0.4	0.6	0.5	0.3	0.3
Informal sector	1.7	2.7	2.0	1.4	1.9	2.3	2.1	1.8	1.8	2.0
Private formal sector										
Unskilled	0.0	0.0	0.0	0.0	0.0	0.0	0.0	0.0	0.0	0.0
Skilled	-1.4	-2.3	-1.8	-1.1	-1.4	-1.8	-1.7	-1.5	-1.5	-1.6
Public sector										
Unskilled	0.0	0.0	0.0	0.0	0.0	0.0	0.0	0.0	0.0	0.0
Skilled	0.0	0.1	0.1	0.0	0.0	0.1	0.1	0.0	0.0	0.0
Employment										
Agricultural sector	0.0	0.0	0.0	0.1	0.1	0.1	0.1	0.1	0.1	0.1
Informal sector	0.0	-0.2	-0.1	-0.2	-0.4	-0.4	-0.3	-0.3	-0.3	-0.4
Private formal sector										
Unskilled	3.5	2.2	3.1	4.1	3.6	3.0	3.1	3.5	3.6	3.3
Skilled	-0.1	-0.2	-0.2	-0.1	-0.1	-0.2	-0.2	-0.1	-0.1	-0.2
Public sector										
Unskilled	0.0	0.0	0.0	0.0	0.0	0.0	0.0	0.0	0.0	0.0
Skilled	0.0	0.0	0.0	0.0	0.0	0.0	0.0	0.0	0.0	0.0

Labor supply (urban formal sector)									
Unskilled	0.0	0.7	0.1	0.5	1.3	1.3	0.9	0.8	1.1	1.2
Skilled	0.0	0.0	0.0	0.0	0.0	0.0	0.0	0.0	0.0	0.0
Unemployment rate (urban formal sector)[1]									
Unskilled	-2.3	-0.8	-2.0	-2.2	-1.3	-0.8	-1.3	-1.6	-1.4	-1.1
Skilled	0.1	0.1	0.1	0.1	0.1	0.1	0.1	0.1	0.1	0.1
Real wage differentials[1]									
Expected urban-rural (% of rural wage)	0.0	-1.5	-0.9	-1.1	-0.6	-0.1	-0.1	-0.3	-0.3	-0.1
Expected formal-informal (% of informal wage)	0.0	1.9	-1.6	1.1	2.1	0.1	-1.1	-0.2	0.7	0.3
Migration[1]									
Rural-urban (% of urban labor supply)	0.00	-0.01	-0.01	-0.01	-0.01	0.00	0.00	0.00	0.00	0.00
Formal-informal (% of formal urban labor supply)	0.00	0.71	-0.61	0.39	0.77	0.02	-0.39	-0.06	0.24	0.11
Memorandum Items[2]									
GDP at market prices	0.2	0.0	0.1	0.2	0.1	0.0	0.0	0.1	0.1	0.0
Value added at factor cost	0.2	0.1	0.1	0.2	0.1	0.1	0.1	0.1	0.1	0.1
Value added in rural sector	0.0	0.0	0.0	0.1	0.1	0.1	0.1	0.1	0.1	0.1
Value added in urban informal sector	0.0	-0.2	0.0	-0.1	-0.3	-0.3	-0.2	-0.2	-0.3	-0.3
Value added in urban formal sector	0.7	0.4	0.4	0.6	0.5	0.4	0.4	0.5	0.5	0.5
Private Consumption	-0.3	-0.1	-0.1	-0.6	-0.7	-0.5	-0.4	-0.5	-0.6	-0.6
Private Investment	-0.3	-4.0	-2.1	1.1	0.7	-1.2	-1.3	-0.3	0.0	-0.6
Disposable income	0.1	-0.2	0.0	0.1	0.0	-0.1	0.0	0.1	0.1	0.0
Capitalists and rentiers savings rate[1]	3.9	-0.5	1.3	5.8	6.1	3.8	3.3	4.7	5.3	4.7

[1] Absolute deviations from baseline. [2] In real terms.

Table 3.8 Mini-IMMPA: price, poverty and distributional indicators 5-percent cut in unskilled payroll tax rate, income tax revenue neutral (Percentage deviations from baseline, unless otherwise indicated)

					Periods					
	1	2	3	4	5	6	7	8	9	10
Consumer Prices and the Real Exchange Rate										
Rural CPI	0.5	0.6	0.4	0.3	0.3	0.4	0.4	0.3	0.3	0.3
Urban CPI	0.2	0.3	0.3	0.2	0.2	0.3	0.2	0.2	0.2	0.2
Unskilled	0.2	0.2	0.2	0.1	0.2	0.2	0.2	0.2	0.2	0.2
Skilled	0.0	0.1	0.1	0.0	0.0	0.1	0.1	0.0	0.0	0.0
Real exchange rate	-0.1	-0.2	-0.2	-0.1	-0.1	-0.1	-0.1	-0.1	-0.1	-0.1
Value Added Prices										
Rural agriculture	1.4	1.2	1.1	0.6	0.3	0.5	0.6	0.5	0.4	0.4
Urban private informal	1.7	2.7	1.9	1.4	1.8	2.2	2.0	1.7	1.8	1.9
Urban private formal	-1.1	-2.0	-1.3	-0.7	-0.9	-1.4	-1.3	-1.0	-1.0	-1.1
Urban public	0.0	0.0	0.0	0.0	0.0	0.0	0.0	0.0	0.0	0.0
Real Disposable Income[1]										
Rural households	0.4	0.0	0.2	0.0	-0.3	-0.4	-0.2	-0.2	-0.3	-0.3
Urban households	0.0	-0.3	-0.1	0.2	0.1	0.0	0.0	0.1	0.2	0.1
Informal	1.2	1.9	1.4	0.9	1.1	1.4	1.4	1.2	1.1	1.2
Formal unskilled	1.4	0.5	1.2	1.8	1.5	1.1	1.2	1.5	1.5	1.4
Formal skilled	-1.7	-2.7	-2.1	-1.4	-1.7	-2.1	-2.0	-1.8	-1.7	-1.9
Capitalists and rentiers	-2.9	-4.7	-3.2	-1.8	-2.2	-2.9	-2.6	-1.9	-1.7	-1.9
Real Consumption[1]										
Rural households	0.4	0.0	0.2	0.0	-0.3	-0.4	-0.2	-0.2	-0.3	-0.3
Urban households	-0.5	-0.1	-0.2	-0.7	-0.8	-0.5	-0.4	-0.6	-0.6	-0.6
Informal	1.2	1.9	1.4	0.9	1.1	1.4	1.4	1.2	1.1	1.2
Formal unskilled	1.4	0.5	1.2	1.8	1.5	1.1	1.2	1.5	1.5	1.4
Formal skilled	-1.7	-2.7	-2.1	-1.4	-1.7	-2.1	-2.0	-1.8	-1.7	-1.9
Capitalists and rentiers	-8.0	-4.1	-4.9	-9.2	-9.9	-7.6	-6.6	-7.5	-8.0	-7.3

Household Size[1]

Rural households	0.1	0.1	0.1	0.1	0.1	0.1	0.1	0.0	0.0	0.0
Urban households	0.0	0.0	0.0	0.0	0.0	0.0	0.0	0.0	0.0	0.0
Informal	−0.4	−0.3	−0.3	−0.3	−0.4	−0.4	−0.2	−0.1	−0.2	0.0
Formal unskilled	1.2	1.1	0.8	0.9	1.3	1.3	0.5	0.1	0.7	0.0
Formal skilled	0.0	0.0	0.0	0.0	0.0	0.0	0.0	0.0	0.0	0.0
Capitalists and rentiers	0.0	0.0	0.0	0.0	0.0	0.0	0.0	0.0	0.0	0.0

Poverty and Distributional Indicators

Consumption-based

Poverty Line[1]

Rural	0.3	0.3	0.3	0.4	0.4	0.3	0.3	0.4	0.6	0.5
Urban	0.2	0.2	0.2	0.2	0.3	0.2	0.2	0.3	0.3	0.2

Poverty headcount

Rural households	0.2	0.1	0.1	0.1	0.2	0.2	0.0	−0.1	0.0	−0.2
Urban households	−0.3	−0.4	−0.3	−0.4	−0.4	−0.4	−0.3	−0.4	−0.4	−0.5
Informal	−0.7	−0.7	−0.6	−0.7	−0.8	−0.7	−0.5	−0.7	−0.9	−0.6
Formal unskilled	0.0	0.0	−0.3	−0.1	0.1	−0.1	−0.6	−0.7	0.1	−1.0
Formal skilled	1.2	0.4	0.8	0.2	0.2	0.2	0.6	0.6	1.0	0.4
Capitalists and rentiers	0.0	0.0	0.0	0.0	0.0	0.7	0.7	0.7	0.7	0.7
Economy	−0.1	−0.2	−0.2	−0.3	−0.3	−0.2	−0.2	−0.3	−0.3	−0.4

Poverty Gap

Rural households	0.1	0.1	0.1	0.1	0.1	0.1	0.0	0.0	0.0	−0.1
Urban households	−0.3	−0.3	−0.3	−0.3	−0.3	−0.3	−0.2	−0.3	−0.4	−0.3
Informal	−0.5	−0.4	−0.4	−0.5	−0.5	−0.4	−0.3	−0.5	−0.6	−0.4
Formal unskilled	0.0	−0.1	−0.1	−0.1	0.1	−0.1	−0.3	−0.2	0.1	−0.3
Formal skilled	0.2	0.2	0.2	0.2	0.2	0.2	0.1	0.2	0.2	0.1
Capitalists and rentiers	0.1	0.1	0.1	0.1	0.1	0.1	0.1	0.1	0.0	0.1
Economy	−0.2	−0.2	−0.2	−0.2	−0.2	−0.2	−0.2	−0.2	−0.2	−0.2

Distributional Indicators[2]

Gini coefficient	−1.3	−1.4	−1.3	−1.2	−1.3	−1.7	−1.6	−1.0	−0.8	−1.4
Theil index	−0.9	−0.9	−0.9	−0.7	−0.8	−1.0	−0.9	−0.5	−0.5	−0.8

Continued

Table 3.8 Continued

		Periods								
	1	2	3	4	5	6	7	8	9	10
Poverty and Distributional Indicators										
Income-based										
Poverty Line[1]										
Rural	0.5	0.6	0.4	0.3	0.3	0.4	0.4	0.3	0.3	0.3
Urban	0.2	0.3	0.3	0.2	0.2	0.3	0.2	0.2	0.2	0.2
Poverty Headcount										
Rural households	−0.3	0.1	−0.1	0.1	0.3	0.3	0.2	0.1	0.2	0.2
Urban households	−0.6	−0.9	−0.6	−0.6	−0.6	−0.7	−0.6	−0.5	−0.7	−0.6
Informal	−1.0	−1.6	−1.1	−0.8	−1.1	−1.3	−1.2	−1.1	−1.1	−1.2
Formal unskilled	−0.4	0.0	−0.3	−0.4	0.0	0.0	0.0	0.0	−0.1	−0.1
Formal skilled	0.8	0.8	0.4	0.2	0.6	0.8	1.0	1.0	0.0	1.0
Capitalists and rentiers	0.0	0.7	0.7	0.0	0.0	0.7	0.7	0.7	0.7	0.7
Economy	−0.5	−0.6	−0.5	−0.4	−0.3	−0.4	−0.4	−0.3	−0.4	−0.4
Poverty Gap										
Rural households	−0.1	0.0	0.0	0.0	0.1	0.1	0.1	0.1	0.1	0.1
Urban households	−0.3	−0.3	−0.3	−0.2	−0.3	−0.3	−0.3	−0.3	−0.2	−0.3
Informal	−0.4	−0.6	−0.4	−0.3	−0.4	−0.5	−0.5	−0.4	−0.4	−0.5
Formal unskilled	−0.3	0.0	−0.2	−0.2	0.0	0.0	0.0	−0.1	−0.1	0.0
Formal skilled	0.1	0.2	0.1	0.1	0.1	0.2	0.2	0.2	0.2	0.2
Capitalists and rentiers	0.1	0.2	0.1	0.1	0.1	0.1	0.1	0.1	0.1	0.1
Economy	−0.2	−0.2	−0.2	−0.2	−0.1	−0.2	−0.2	−0.2	−0.1	−0.2
Distributional Indicators[2]										
Gini coefficient	−0.6	−0.9	−0.7	−0.4	−0.5	−0.6	−0.5	−0.4	−0.4	−0.4
Theil index	−0.4	−0.6	−0.4	−0.3	−0.3	−0.4	−0.3	−0.3	−0.2	−0.3

[1] Percentage deviations from baseline. [2] Gini Coefficients and Theil Indices measure between-group inequality.

The first part of the chapter described in detail the structure of Mini-IMMPA. In the second part the model was used to analyze the growth, unemployment, and poverty effects of two types of labor market policies: a cut in the minimum wage and a reduction in the payroll tax rate on unskilled labor.

The results (which are obviously dependent on the selected closure rule) showed that a reduction in the minimum wage may have a sizable impact on unskilled unemployment, and that the extent to which a reduction in payroll taxes on unskilled labor lower unemployment for that category of labor depends on how it is financed. More generally, the foregoing analysis suggests that the fiscal implications of labor market reforms have to be carefully analyzed in order to assess the potential impact of these reforms on unemployment and poverty.

Another important implication of the foregoing analysis (which is discussed in more detail in Chapter 2) is that labor market reforms aimed at reducing unemployment may end up increasing poverty, if they are implemented in a context in which fiscal constraints impose offsetting changes in financing. Consider, again, a reduction in payroll taxation on unskilled labor. Despite stimulating employment for that category of labor, this policy measure may also lead to higher poverty, depending on how it is financed. An offsetting, across-the-board reduction in transfers, for instance, would have an immediate adverse effect on the poor. Financing through an increase in consumption taxes may raise the price of the consumption basket of low-income groups and reduce their real expenditure to a level below the poverty line. Financing through higher income taxes may reduce disposable income and the ability to spend; it may also drive activity underground over time, leading to a fall in the overall tax ratio, which in turn could force cuts in expenditure (including transfers to the most needy). Financing through a tax on capital (usually a limited option for governments in developing countries, due to concerns about capital flight) may deter private capital formation; as noted earlier, this may reduce skilled employment because of the complementarity relationship between human capital and physical capital and mitigate the overall, positive effect on total employment. Finally, financing through a cut in government spending on infrastructure may adversely affect the productivity of private inputs (including labor) and lead to a reduction in wage income; it may also have a negative impact on private investment. This, in turn, will have an adverse overall effect on the demand for labor (due to the negative effect of investment on growth) as well as an adverse effect on the demand for skilled labor as a result of complementarity. Thus, although the direct effect of the reduction in the payroll tax rate on the demand for unskilled labor may be positive (both in the short and medium run), overall employment (and thus unemployment) may not change much, as an increase in the number of unskilled jobs is offset by lower employment of skilled labor. In all of those cases, again, unemployment may fall, but poverty may increase – because of adverse effects on income, due either to lower after-tax wages or lower public transfers. There may therefore be a trade-off between unemployment and poverty goals, as discussed by Agénor (2004*d*).

In addition, of course, labor market reforms may be complementary, if labor market institutions are themselves complementary. As emphasized by Coe and Snower (1997), this implies that partial or piecemeal labor market reforms are unlikely to achieve significant and persistent reductions in unemployment rates or poverty. For instance, active labor market policies (such as retraining schemes) may not be very effective in the presence of substantial passive policies (such as stringent job security provisions). Reform programs must be sufficiently broad (in the sense of covering a wide range of complementary policies) and deep (of substantial magnitude) to have much of an effect. In addition, these reforms may also need to be combined with measures that address more efficiently the distributional objectives of the prereform policies, such as the imposition of high minimum wages.

Appendix
Calibration and Parameter Values

This appendix presents the characteristics of the data underlying the calibration procedure for the Mini-IMMPA prototype described in the text. The basic data set consists of a Social Accounting Matrix (SAM) and a set of initial levels and lagged variables.

The mapping between Mini-IMMPA variables and the SAM data framework is set out in Table A3.1. The SAM encompasses 27 accounts comprising production and retail sectors (4 accounts), labor production factors and profits (3 accounts), firms (1 account), households (5 accounts), government current expenditures and taxes (9 accounts), government investment expenditures (3 accounts), private investment spending (1 account), and the rest of the world (1 account). The actual SAM data are presented in Table A3.2. The data satisfy the double-entry accounting principle and can therefore be used to initialize model variables and calibrate level parameters, such as effective tax rates.

The characteristics of the SAM data and other data (including initial labor market quantities and debt and capital stocks) are summarized in the following. On the output side, agriculture and the informal sector account for respectively 12 and 35 percent of total output. On the demand side, private current and capital expenditures account for whereas overall government expenditure accounts for 18 percent of GDP.

The economy has a balanced current account but runs a trade surplus, amounting to 4 percent of GDP, to finance foreign interest payments. This structure of production and final demand characterize fairly well a poor or lower middle-income economy with moderate potential for agricultural production.

Total investment expenditure amounts to 22 percent of GDP, and the private sector account for two-thirds of these outlays. This implies that investment spending accounts for 19 percent of private expenditure, and 40 percent of public expenditure. The public sector investment budget allocates 30 percent of expenditure to investment in the health sector, 30 percent to investment in the education sector, and 40 percent to investment in infrastructure. Furthermore, the public sector wage bill makes up 30 percent of overall public sector expenditures.

In the base period the government is assumed to run a balanced budget, and therefore does not resort to domestic or foreign borrowing. Sales taxes and import tariffs make up for more than 70 percent of total government revenues, whereas private income and corporate taxes account for less than 20 percent of revenues. This structure of tax revenue is a common feature of many developing economies, low- and middle-income.

The trade balance is dominated by nonagricultural imports and exports. Agricultural exports account for only 8 percent of total export earnings, whereas nonagricultural imports account for 92 percent of total imports. The level of trade openness, measured by the ratio of the sum of imports and exports to GDP, amounts to a moderate 40 percent.

Because the economy runs a balanced current account in the base period, there is no foreign borrowing, neither private nor public. Nevertheless, the stock of external debt in the base period amounts to 51 percent of GDP (or 233 percent of export earnings), whereas foreign interest payments amount to 4 percent of GDP (or 18 percent of exports earnings). The hypothetical country considered therefore has a significant debt burden initially.

Looking at the labor market, 29 percent of the total labor force is living in rural areas, whereas the rest is concentrated in urban areas. Altogether, 47 percent of the workers are employed in some kind of urban informal occupation, whereas only 22 percent of the labor force is employed in the urban formal sector. Open unemployment among formal urban workers amounts to 2 percent of the total labor force. The formal labor force consists of 58 percent of unskilled workers and 42 percent of skilled workers, and unemployment rates are 10 percent among formal unskilled labor and 8 percent among skilled labor. Migration from rural to urban areas amounts to 1.3 percent of the rural population, and the urban–rural wage differential amounts to 54 percent of the rural wage. In comparison, unskilled labor migration from the informal to the formal sector amounts to 0.8 percent of the informal sector labor force, whereas the formal–informal wage differential amounts to 106 percent of the informal wage.

A set of 17 elasticity parameters has to be estimated (or "guesstimated"), as they cannot be derived from the calibration procedure. These parameters include CES substitution elasticities in the rural sector and urban private formal production (4 parameters); CES Armington elasticities and CET transformation elasticities for aggregating domestic composite goods and transforming domestic production (4 parameters); elasticities related to rural–urban, and formal–informal sector migration (2 parameters); elasticities related to the computation of ordinary and congested government capital (2 parameters), the elasticity of effort by teachers and the elasticity of substitution between labor and capital in skill upgrading (2 parameters); the elasticities related to determination of skilled labor wages (2 parameters); and the elasticity of investment with respect to the desired private capital stock (1 parameter). In addition, a set of minimum consumption levels (15 parameters) has to be determined, because they cannot be derived from the calibration procedure either.

The substitution elasticity between labor and government capital in rural production is set at 0.7, whereas elasticities in the nested private formal sector production structure ranges from 0.7 between skilled labor and capital to 1.2 between the skilled labor–capital bundle and unskilled labor. Import and export elasticities are uniformly set at 0.7 for agriculture and 1.5 for the urban private formal sector. This is again meant to reflect a poor or lower middle-income economy with limited agricultural potential. The elasticity of rural–urban migration with respect

Table A3.1[1] Mini-IMMPA: variables in SAM framework

		1	2	3	4	5	6	7	8	9	10	11	12	13	14
Rural Agricultural Sector[1]	1		$PC * (a_{j,i} * X)$									$PC * C$			$PC * G$
Urban Informal Sector	2														
Urban Formal Sector	3														
Urban Public Sector	4														
Urban Unskilled Labor	5			$W * U$											
Urban Skilled Labor	6			$W * S$											
Profits	7			PR											
Enterprises	8							PR_3							
Rural Agricultural Households	9							PR_1							
Urban Informal Households	10							PR_2							
Urban Formal Unskilled Households	11					$W * U$									$gamma * TR$
Urban Formal Skilled Households	12						$W * S$								
Capitalist Households	13								$(1 - chi) * NPR_3$						
Current Government	14														
Payroll Taxes	15		$ptx * W * U$												
Employment Subsidies	16		$es * U$												
Production Taxes	17			$atx * PX * X$											
Value Added Taxes	18			$vtx * PV * V$											
Sales Taxes	19			$stx * PQ * Q$											
Import Tariffs	20			$itm * ER * wpm * M$											
Enterprise Taxes	21								$etx * PR_3$						
Income Taxes	22											$itx * YH$			
Education Capital	23														
Health Capital	24														
Infrastructure Capital	25														
Private Capital	26								$chi * NPR_3$			$sr * (1 - itx) * YH$			$PK * Z_G$
Rest of the World	27			$ER * wpm * M$					$I_3 * ER * FL_3$						$GBAL + ER * (FL_G - FL_{G,-1})$ $i_G * ER * FL_G$

Table A3.1[1] Continued

		15	16	17	18	19	20	21	22	23	24	25	26	27
									Accounts					
Rural Agricultural Sector[1]	1										PK^*Z_G		PK^*Z_P	ER^*wpe^*E
Urban Informal Sector	2													
Urban Formal Sector	3													
Urban Public Sector	4													
Urban Unskilled Labor	5													
Urban Skilled Labor	6													
Profits	7													
Enterprises	8													
Rural Agricultural Households	9													
Urban Informal Households	10													
Urban Formal Unskilled Households	11													
Urban Formal Skilled Households	12													
Capitalist Households	13													
Current Government	14				TXR									$ER^*(FL_G - FL_{G,-1})$
Payroll Taxes	15													
Employment Subsidies	16													
Production Taxes	17													
Value Added Taxes	18													
Sales Taxes	19													
Import Tariffs	20													
Enterprise Taxes	21													
Income Taxes	22													
Education Capital	23													
Health Capital	24													
Infrastructure Capital	25													
Private Capital	26													
Rest of the World	27													$ER^*(FL_3 - FL_{3,-1})$

[1] See Appendix A for a definition of the variables used in this table.

Table A3.2 Mini-IMMPA: social accounting matrix (In millions of currency units)

		1	2	3	4	5	6	7	8	9	10	11	12	13	14
Rural Agricultural Sector	1	18.0	7.0	46.0	0.8					20.5	24.2	6.0	5.6	2.8	
Urban Informal Sector	2	20.4	105.0	82.8	3.2					25.1	63.1	18.5	22.9	9.1	
Urban Formal Sector	3	14.4	91.0	202.4	8.4					15.7	30.7	18.9	32.1	15.5	53.8
Urban Public Sector	4	1.2													
Urban Unskilled Labor	5	52.8	109.2	26.5	9.8										
Urban Skilled Labor	6			37.0	32.8										
Profits	7	13.2	27.3	66.1											
Enterprises	8							66.1							
Rural Households	9					52.8		13.2							5.1
Urban Informal Households	10					109.2		27.3							0.0
Urban Formal Unskilled Households	11					36.3									14.9
Urban Formal Skilled Households	12						69.8								13.7
Capitalist Households	13								41.1						3.2
Current Government	14														
Payroll Taxes	15			5.3											
Employment Subsidies	16			-0.9											
Production Taxes	17		10.5												
Value Added Taxes	18			4.8											
Sales Taxes	19			58.0											
Import Tariffs	20	12.0		27.2											
Enterprise Taxes	21								5.0						
Income Taxes	22									2.8	0.0	1.1	8.0	5.5	
Education Capital	23														10.8
Health Capital	24														10.8
Infrastructure Capital	25														14.7
Private Capital	26								12.5	7.1	18.5	6.8	15.0	11.5	0
Rest of the World	27	7.2	80.3						7.5						12.2
TOTAL	28	139.2	350.0	635.5	55.0	198.3	69.8	106.6	66.1	71.1	136.5	51.2	83.5	44.3	139.3

Accounts

Table A3.2 Continued

							Accounts							
		15	16	17	18	19	20	21	22	23	24	25	26	27	28
Rural Agricultural Sector	1													8.4	139.2
Urban Informal Sector	2														350.0
Urban Formal Sector	3									10.8	10.8	14.7	71.3	98.8	635.5
Urban Public Sector	4														55.0
Urban Unskilled Labor	5														198.3
Urban Skilled Labor	6														69.8
Profits	7														106.6
Enterprises	8														66.1
Rural Households	9														71.1
Urban Informal Households	10														136.5
Urban Formal Unskilled Households	11														51.2
Urban Formal Skilled Households	12														83.5
Capitalist Households	13														44.3
Current Government	14	5.3	-0.9	10.5	4.8	58.0	39.2	5.0	17.4					0	139.3
Payroll Taxes	15														5.3
Employment Subsidies	16														-0.9
Production Taxes	17														10.5
Value Added Taxes	18														4.8
Sales Taxes	19														58.0
Import Tariffs	20														39.2
Enterprise Taxes	21														5.0
Income Taxes	22														17.4
Education Capital	23														10.8
Health Capital	24														10.8
Infrastructure Capital	25														14.7
Private Capital	26													0	71.3
Rest of the World	27												0		107.2
TOTAL	28	5.3	-0.9	10.5	4.8	58.0	39.2	5.0	17.4	10.8	10.8	14.7	71.3	107.2	107.2

to the relative rural–urban wage-differential is set at 0.4, whereas the elasticity of formal–informal migration with respect to the formal–informal wage ratio is set at 0.8.

In relation to the computation of public sector capital, the substitution parameter between infrastructure and health capital stocks are set at 0.5, whereas congestion is assumed to be absent by setting the elasticity to zero. The substitution elasticity between teachers and public capital in education in the production of skilled labor is set to 0.3, whereas the effort elasticity with respect to the relative wage ratio (using the specification in Agénor and Aizenman (1999)) is set to 0.8. Furthermore, skilled labor wages in the urban private formal sector is only assumed to be affected by the skilled unemployment rate. Accordingly, the private skilled wage elasticity with respect to unemployment is set at −2.0, whereas the elasticity with respect to the skilled labor–capital bundle is assumed to be zero.

Turning to the specification of private capital formation, the investment elasticity with respect to the desired growth rate of the private capital stock is set at 0.3. This reflects an economy facing structural difficulties in the process of capital accumulation. Minimum household consumption levels were uniformly assumed to amount to 10 percent of initial good-specific consumption levels.

Among the remaining set of parameters, the foreign interest rate on private borrowing is calibrated to 3.8 percent, whereas the public foreign interest rate is calibrated to 4.9 percent. In addition, the initial depreciation rates are calibrated to 6.4 percent for private capital and 3.9–5.8 percent for public capital (depending on whether investment is in education, health, or infrastructure). Turning to the government budget, output and value added tax rates range from 3.0–3.7 percent, whereas the tax rate on sales of the urban private formal sector and the payroll tax rate paid by firms in that sector are calibrated to respectively 12.1 and 20.1 percent. Import tariffs range from 34 percent on private formal sector goods to 167 percent on agricultural goods, reflecting a country with significant protection on agriculture. Finally, the corporate income tax rate is set at 7.6 percent, whereas income tax rates on households range from 2.2–3.9 percent for rural agricultural and urban unskilled households, to 9.6–12.5 percent for the urban skilled household and capitalists-rentiers. As noted in the text, workers in the urban informal sector do not pay income taxes.

Chapter 4

Unemployment and Labor Market Policies in Morocco

Pierre-Richard Agénor and Karim El Aynaoui

The Moroccan economy grew at a yearly average rate of 3.5 percent during the period 1983–92 and 3.1 percent during 1993–2001, despite a high degree of output volatility (particularly in the agricultural sector). However, rapid population growth limited income gains in per capita terms to yearly averages of only 1.4 percent during the 1980s and to negligible rates during the 1990s. Moreover, the sharp increase in the labor force induced by greater participation rates (at about 2.5 percent per annum during the past two decades), combined with low output growth rates, led to high rates of unemployment in urban areas and underemployment in the rural sector (see Figure 4.1).

Concerns over the insufficient pace of job creation has led many observers to recommend the implementation of a series of structural reforms aimed at accelerating the rate of economic growth. Of particular interest in this context has been the potential impact of various kinds of labor market reforms on employment and resource allocation. The purpose of this chapter is to apply the Mini-IMMPA framework described in the previous chapter to analyze the impact of various types of labor market policies on employment, wages, and economic growth in Morocco.[1] This framework is particularly adequate to understand the functioning of the labor market in a country like Morocco, where segmentation (particularly in the urban sector) is pervasive. As can be inferred from the discussion in Chapter 1 and the simulations reported in Chapter 3, such segmentation is likely to play a key role in shaping the effects of labor market reforms on resource allocation.

---

[1]Various computable general equilibrium (CGE) models have been built for Morocco in the recent past; these include Cogneau and Tapinos (1995), Lofgren (1999), and Rutherford, Rustrom, and Tarr (1994). None of these models, however, addresses the set of issues discussed in this chapter.

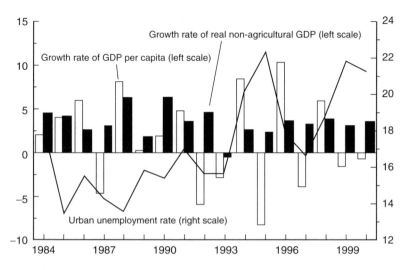

Figure 4.1 Morocco: urban unemployment and GDP growth, 1984–2000. *Source*: Direction de la statistique (Morocco) and World Bank.

Indeed, in the presence of a low degree of worker mobility, a segmented labor market contributes to persistent wage differentials that may hinder the resource allocation indispensable to cope with external and policy-induced shocks.

The remainder of the chapter is organized as follows. Section 4.1 provides an overview of the Moroccan labor market. It also explains the main constraints affecting the labor market, and identifies some of the challenges that Morocco will continue to face in the coming years. Section 4.2 describes the variant of Mini-IMMPA that we use to analyze the effects of labor market policies on growth, employment, and wages. In particular, open unskilled urban unemployment emerges as a consequence of modeling formal–informal migration flows through a Harris-Todaro type mechanism. This feature is very important for Morocco, where unskilled unemployment accounts for a large fraction of total open unemployment. Also as in Mini-IMMPA, wages in the public sector are treated as exogenous and we assume that there exists a nonpecuniary benefit (in terms of, say, increased job security) that leads to zero turnover for that category of workers – even in the presence of higher wages for that category of labor in the private sector. In order to analyze the impact of changes in the taxation of firms' wage bill on employment, we explicitly account for payroll taxation on the use of both skilled and unskilled labor in the private urban formal sector. The extent to which high payroll taxes have tended to discourage the demand for labor (particularly unskilled labor) has been an important policy issue in Morocco.

However, the version developed here differs in some ways from the Mini-IMMPA "prototype" described in Chapter 3, in order to reflect the country's economic and institutional specificities. First, in line with the full IMMPA prototype described in Chapter 5, the production structure in the rural sector explicitly distinguishes between production of tradables and nontradables. Nominal wages are taken to be fully flexible in both sectors and to adjust continuously to equilibrate supply and demand for labor in the rural labor market. Second, we use a monopoly union approach to determine skilled workers' wage in the private formal sector; in doing so, we account for the effect of firing costs, open unemployment, and a signaling role of public sector wages on the union's target wage. Third, we explicitly account for international migration of unskilled labor, and assess its implications for labor market adjustment.

Section 4.3 presents simulation experiments focusing on a cut in the minimum wage and a reduction in payroll taxation on unskilled labor, as in the previous chapter. Section 4.4 summarizes the main results of the analysis. We highlight, in particular, the need to extend the set of policy simulations to consider the impact of various "closure rules" for the government budget (that is, offsetting changes in taxes, as in Chapter 3), reductions in firing costs, public sector layoffs (possibly coupled with an increase in employment subsidies to private, formal sector firms), and changes in bargaining strength between unions and employers, as in Agénor, Nabli, Yousef, and Jensen (2004).

4.1   The Labor Market in Morocco

This section presents an overview of the labor market in Morocco. First, we present its basic structural features and discuss the degree of segmentation, with a focus on the role of the informal sector. Second, we examine the composition of the labor force (including public employment), the structure of unemployment, and the returns to education. Third, we review regulatory and institutional characteristics of the labor market, including (as in Chapter 1) minimum wage legislation, hiring and firing restrictions, nonwage labor costs, and the role of trade unions. Fourth, we examine the evidence on wage flexibility in the formal sector. Fifth, we discuss factors affecting domestic and international labor migration. Finally, we highlight some of the constraints and challenges that the labor market poses to policymakers in Morocco.

4.1.1   Basic Structure

As discussed in Chapter 1, the urban labor market in developing economies is generally well described as consisting of two sectors, formal and informal, with distinct functioning modes. The segmentation hypothesis has important implications for the functioning of the labor market. For instance, high-pay formal sector jobs are often rationed and, despite an excess supply of labor in the low-pay informal sector, wages do not adjust. Many studies have also suggested that the two segments are highly heterogeneous – in the nature of occupations, the production mode, the sources of income, and so on. The view that the informal sector is competitive has received mixed support from the empirical evidence. In fact, in some countries many activities classified in the informal sector present barriers to entry. For instance, access can be conditioned by customs practices and relatively strict unwritten rules. This appears to be the case for many crafting activities in Morocco. However, this does not imply that, from a modeling perspective, the assumption of perfect flexibility in the informal sector as a whole is inadequate.

Despite the absence of comprehensive micro-level data on enterprises at the national level, the common view of Morocco's urban labor market is that of a dual segmented market. Within this framework, there have been attempts to measure the respective size of the two segments. In some studies, civil servants (central government and local governments), workers in public enterprises, and those covered by the social security scheme (CNSS) are viewed as constituting the formal sector. The informal sector corresponds then to the residual.[2] Moreover, other studies have found that the functioning of the Moroccan urban labor market is far from competitive.[3] Noncompensating wage differentials between workers with similar productive endowments are pervasive: higher earnings are frequently observed when workers (even unskilled ones) are located in particular segments. In fact, despite the existence of excess labor supply, wages in the formal sector do not adjust, and the informal sector does not absorb all job seekers. Within this context of restricted labor mobility and specific participation dynamics, the sector of occupation is a key determinant of an individual's remuneration and standard of living. In addition, surveys have shown that private firms are willing to pay a premium – as suggested by efficiency wage theories – to secure workers' commitment.

4.1.2 Employment, Unemployment, and the Returns to Education

The first part of our review of the characteristics of the labor market in Morocco focuses on the sectoral distribution of the workforce, the structure of public employment, the composition of unemployment, and the returns to education.

Sectoral Distribution of the Workforce

In Morocco, a sizable share of the workforce (around 55 percent in 2000) remains employed in the agricultural sector. This proportion is quite high compared to around 35 percent for lower middle-income countries. At the same time, women still account for only 22 percent of the total urban workforce. Data on the occupational distribution of the workforce in urban areas show that wage employment is dominant, followed by self-employment. Panel 4 in Figure 4.2 displays the distribution of the workforce by occupational status in 2000. It shows that wage earners accounted for about 61 percent of total employment, and self employment for about 24 percent. Most of the wage earners are employed in the private urban sector, though public sector employment (central government, local communities, public enterprises) also accounts for a large proportion (around 19.5 percent).

---

[2] See, for instance, Belghazi (1998) and Touhami (2003).

[3] Empirical tests by El Aynaoui (1998) confirm the prevalence of the segmentation hypothesis.

182   *Chapter 4*

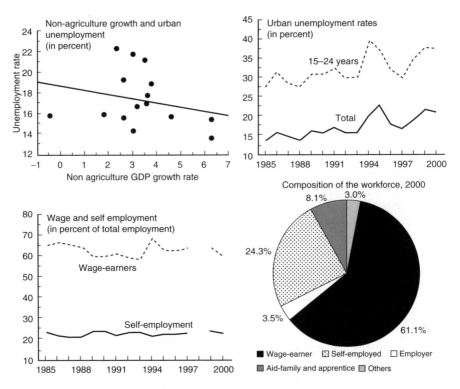

Figure 4.2 Morocco: labor market indicators, 1982–2000. *Source*: Direction de la statistique, Morocco.

The rest of the workers are non remunerated aid-families, apprentices, employers or home workers. The average educational level of the work force is rather low, with 55 percent not holding any degree in 2000.

The evidence for developing countries in general suggests that contractions of available opportunities in salaried occupations tend to drive workers toward self employment. In Morocco, the data seem also to suggest that the share of self employment in total urban employment tends to rise when wage employment decreases. However, during the 1990s (a decade marked by a weak growth performance, as noted earlier), self employment did not significantly increase, remaining at around 24 percent of total employment. Although some observers have argued that the urban labor market in Morocco has undergone a process of "informalization", this argument is debatable. If we simply define "informalization" as a reduction in the share of wage employment in total employment, it is not obvious that there has been a growing informalization of the urban labor market. Indeed, even if there are marked fluctuations on a yearly basis, wage employment is by far the major type of occupation in Morocco. Its share did not decrease significantly during the 1990s. The lowest value is 59.3 percent of the total workforce in 1993 (see Panel 3, Figure 4.2).

Public Sector Employment

The public sector (central government, municipalities, and public enterprises) plays an important role in Morocco. It represented about 18 percent of the country's GDP in 2000. With about 635,000 employees (central government excluding the military, and employees of municipalities), equivalent to 15 percent of total urban employment – or 19.5 percent if we add public enterprises. As a result, wage policy in the public sector has important consequences on the functioning of the labor market. A recent study by the World Bank (2002) found that monetary compensation is 8 percent higher in the public sector than in the private sector. If we were to include nonpecuniary compensation (such as job security, a generous pensions fund, and a higher shirking rate), then the divergence between private and public sector wages would be even larger. Calculations based on the Living Standard Measurement Survey for 1998–9 show that non-pecuniary compensation may vary between 60 to 100 percent of the monetary remuneration received by public sector workers. This implies that for a corresponding nominal remuneration, a civil servant would get an all-inclusive (or effective) wage between 1.6 and two times higher than what he would obtain in the private sector. This outcome may explain why queues for employment in the public sector are so long, particularly by skilled workers.

Unemployment

As in many developing countries, in Morocco open unemployment is essentially an urban phenomenon (see Panels 4 and 5, Figure 4.3). In 2000, the urban unemployment rate stood at 21.4 percent, against 15.8 percent in 1990. This is equivalent, in 2000, to 1.1 million unemployed out of an active population of 5.4 million. Several facts reveal important tensions on the domestic labor market. The youth (15–24 years old) are particularly vulnerable to unemployment in urban areas, with a rate often well above 30 percent since the early 1990s (see Panel 4, Figure 4.2). Whereas the unemployment rate for individuals with no instruction is somewhat low (12.2 percent in 2000) and fluctuates significantly in conjunction with economic activity, the unemployment rate is persistently high for individuals with a higher level of education. In 2000, their unemployment rate was 30.7 percent. Gender differences are also quite striking: in 2000, 26.7 percent of active urban women were unemployed, compared to only 19.9 percent of the men.

Turning now to the composition of unemployment, the data reveal that the 15–24 year old group and individuals with a higher level of education account for around 37 percent and more than 18 percent of the number of job seekers, respectively, in 2000. Individuals with no education represented 8 percent of the unemployed population that year.

Underemployment is pervasive, indicating that the "true" rate of unemployment may well be much worse than the data suggest: in 1991, it affected 20 percent of the urban workforce, and, for the under-25 group, the rate of underemployment was 34.5 percent. In 1995 this rate was 24.2 percent and 23.3 percent for the 15–24 and the 25–34 year old groups, respectively. Overall, movements in the unemployment rate are highly correlated with fluctuations in GDP. For instance, in 1995, a year

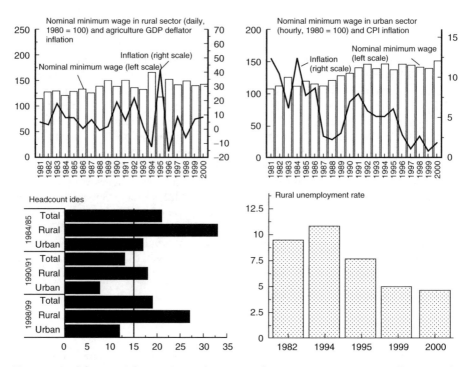

Figure 4.3   Morocco: labor market and poverty indicators, 1981–2000. *Source*: Direction de la statistique, Morocco.

marked by a severe drought, urban unemployment reached 22.9 percent, and the strong subsequent recovery in 1996, in which GDP grew by 12 percent, allowed to reduce it by about 5 percentage points.

Additional elements reveal several features of urban unemployment in Morocco. As in many developing countries, the majority (about 54.5 percent) of the unemployed are first-time job seekers. Among the unemployed, the impact of long-term unemployment is pervasive: in 2000, around 75 percent of job seekers were searching for a job for more than 12 months. Moreover, the educational level does not appear to reduce significantly the probability of staying unemployed. Indeed, if we only consider individuals with a higher level of education, around 85 percent had been searching for a job for over a year. More generally, in 2000, the average duration of unemployment was 41 months.

An analysis of the job search patterns of the unemployed reveals specific characteristics. A great majority of the unemployed (about two-thirds) searches through personal contacts. A targeted study on cohorts of students from vocational institutes also found that personal relations play a crucial role in finding a job in the private sector (see Montmarquette et al. (1996)). Only 9 percent of the unemployed are using formal strategies (such as written inquiries or responses to job openings). Hence, personal relations appears to be the most efficient way to find a job in Morocco. Within a context of tight hiring and firing regulations (as discussed below), the reliance on personal relations may also be a way for the employers to minimize, through maximum information on the candidate, the risks associated with hiring.

What type of jobs are the unemployed favoring? According to available surveys, more than 80 percent of the unemployed are searching for a salaried occupation. In fact, only a marginal portion of them is willing to start an independent activity. Skilled workers usually prefer to remain unemployed rather than accept a job in the informal sector (mostly due to the impact of the family environment on luxury unemployment, in line with the discussion in Chapters 1 and 2) or go into self-employment. Thus, the fact that around 36 percent of the urban poor job seekers are ready to accept any occupation, against less than 15 percent of their nonpoor counterparts, is a sign of their vulnerability.

In urban areas, the rate of unemployment for the poor is about 50 percent higher than the overall rate of unemployment. Overall, insertion in the labor market is a key determinant of the living standards. The dependency ratio – calculated as the ratio of the unemployed to the employed members of a household – is 50 percent higher for poor families. Along the same line, econometric estimates indicate that, ceteris paribus, unemployment significantly increases the probability of being poor (see El Aynaoui (1998)). The link between labor market functioning and poverty is an argument in favor of labor market reform to address segmentation and unemployment – although, as noted in Chapter 2, some policies may create trade-offs between reducing unemployment and alleviating poverty.

Returns to Education

Globally, the few available studies assessing the impact of educational attainments on earnings in Morocco show the usual positive influence. Experience also affects educational returns – albeit in a nonlinear manner. Estimations of earning functions for wage earners at the national and regional levels indicate that private marginal returns of investment in education are around 10 percent per each additional year of education (see Touhami (2003), and Cherkaoui et al. (2002)). Returns to education are higher for females, and in urban areas. However, estimates of the returns to education are rather different when controlling for segmentation (see El Aynaoui (1998)). In fact, an actual effect is observed only in the formal sector, whereas the private returns to education are not significant in the informal sector. This outcome might preclude investment incentives in human capital, specifically within particular categories of individuals who, as pointed out earlier, may not have access to the formal sector.

4.1.3   Regulatory and Institutional Features

Regulatory and institutional features of the labor market in Morocco that are important for understanding wage and employment formation include the minimum wage, hiring and firing regulations, the matching process between supply and demand for labor, the structure of nonwage labor costs, and the role of trade unions.

Minimum Wage Regulation

Morocco adopted as early as 1936 a minimum wage legislation that sets different wage floors for urban and rural labor markets, and for different age categories. Minimum wages are revised according to a formal price indexation mechanism, triggered as soon as the consumer price index increases by 5 percent at an annual rate.

In practice, however, revisions are irregular and rather independent of the indexation rule. They are usually the outcome of political and discretionary decisions, following overwhelming pressure from trade unions. The few available studies reveal that regulations regarding the urban minimum wage (which concerns mostly unskilled workers) is pretty well enforced in the private formal sector, through an active role of the administration and the trade unions. According to Benhayoun et al. (2001), only 13 percent of wage earners in the private formal sector are paid a wage lower than the minimum.

During the period 1970–2000, the nominal urban minimum wage has increased by an average of 6 percent a year (see Panels 1 and 4, Figure 4.3). In real terms, the urban minimum wage fluctuates, albeit slightly, due to the *ad hoc* nature of the revision process. Over the period 1970–2000, the real urban minimum wage rose on average by about 1.1 percent every year. Over the 1990s only, it increased by about 1.3 percent – a rate faster than the rate of growth of labor productivity in the industrial formal private sector. Many observers have argued that these increases adversely affected the demand for unskilled labor, and contributed to a rise in Morocco's unit labor costs, thereby affecting Morocco's external competitiveness.

The urban minimum wage represented 50 percent of the average wage in the formal private sector and 178 percent of GDP per capita in 2000 – a fairly high level in comparison to other developing countries. Benhayoun et al. (2001) found that minimum wage legislation influences, albeit weakly, the overall structure of wages in the private formal sector. Their study also found that increases in the minimum wage tend to reduce wage inequality in the short term, but that this effect is rather limited in the long term due to a diffusion effect through the wage structure.

These results are consistent with the evidence for Latin America reported in Chapter 1. Other estimates at the firm level in the formal private sector (Mouime (2001)) found that an increase in the minimum wage raises the average wage over time. More specifically, the short- and long-term elasticities are lower than one and superior to one, respectively. Azam (1995) found no evidence that the urban minimum wage had a direct effect on the level of employment, but concluded that it affects the level of employment via the wedge between the minimum wage and the average wage paid in the private formal sector.

Benhayoun et al. (2001) also found that the urban minimum wage has a tendency to deter job creation in the formal sector. Here, a major source of concern for policymakers is to assess whether the minimum wage deters formal job creation (particularly for low-skilled workers) by introducing downward rigidity in real wages. As discussed more formally later, this is an important issue in assessing the impact of labor market reforms in Morocco.

Hiring and Firing Regulations

Morocco has comprehensive and rather restrictive labor market regulations, particularly regarding firing procedures for the private sector workforce. These regulations are well enforced, through an active role of the administration and trade unions. For instance, individual layoffs for economic reasons are prohibited. Moreover, large-scale downsizing for economic reasons is subject to prior approval by the regional authorities. The only way for an employer to dismiss a worker is for disciplinary matters. Even then, the law opens the possibility for a dismissed worker to lodge an appeal before the court. Judicial procedures are so complicated that firms often seek to avoid them by engaging in (possibly costly) direct agreements with the laid-off worker. In fact, more than in its rigidity, the main flaw of the current legal framework resides in the unpredictability and inconsistency of the jurisprudence over time and across space that stem from the broad powers that the law grants to the courts in imposing settlements.

This constraining legal environment hinders the expansion of labor demand. The judicial practice further strengthens permanent workers' job security, giving insiders a substantial bargaining power, and leaving outsiders clearly disadvantaged. Also, the difficulties involved in firing workers, and the potential financial costs that such decisions can entail, partly explain why employers are usually reluctant to hire new workers and why they often rely on personal relationships to do so, as shown by some available studies (CNJA (1995), Montmarquette et al. (1996)) and as noted earlier. Through personal contacts, employers minimize the risk related to hiring by gathering detailed information on the worker. Knowing the candidate also increases the likelihood that they will be able to exercise social pressures to negotiate better terms for his/her eventual firing. Globally, nonetheless, the existing legal framework unduly constrains the capacity of enterprises to adapt to change and respond to relative price incentives, while at the same time encouraging temporary contracts. The very nature of these contracts prevents significant gains in productivity, because they dissuade firms from investing in the human capital of their workforce.

Institutional Job Matching Processes

Formally, the job matching process is a public monopoly. The country has recently adopted a set of active labor market policies aimed at improving this process for young skilled workers. These policies consist mainly in providing an enhanced role to regional public institutions, and specific labor tax deductions favoring the employment of young workers. A study by Ibourk and Perelman (1999) shows that these institutions tend to improve the efficiency of the job matching process, but that they are limited in their action by the gap between labor demand and labor supply.

Nonwage Labor Costs

In addition to minimum wage regulation and firing legislation, there are numerous compulsory social contributions that also affect the private labor demand function.

In the private formal industrial sector, besides income taxes,[4] nonwage labor costs represent about 24 percent of total labor costs. Hence, for a worker in the private formal sector, there is a substantial wedge between the gross wage and net income. According to the current regulatory framework, employers pay about 18.6 percent of the gross wage to the Social Security (CNSS) for pension contributions and other social coverages. There is also a 1.6 percent compulsory tax on the overall wage bill of every enterprise, exclusively to contribute to the budget of the public vocational training system. Besides, the employer is responsible for the security of his workers – work-related accidents and illness – and has to subscribe to a specific insurance to cover those risks. The cost ranges between 1 and 3 percent of the worker's total wage. In addition, the formal private sector often provides medical coverage to its labor force, because it is not provided by the Social Security scheme. The cost of such private health care schemes ranges from 2 to 4 percent of the total wage. Finally, the compulsory retirement plan provided by the Social Security scheme has led many firms to subscribe to additional pension plans for their workers. In general, the cost of these complementary plans is about 12 percent of the wage. In general, the cost of health care and retirement plans are shared on an equal basis by the employer and the worker.

It should be noted that CNSS does not provide any unemployment compensation. As in most developing countries (see Chapter 1), no unemployment benefit scheme exists in Morocco. Replacing the coercive firing regulations and the expensive severance pay upon dismissal by a well-targeted unemployment benefit scheme could be a way to improve significantly the functioning of the urban labor market.

Trade Unions

Morocco has three trade unions with nationwide representations. They derive most of their power from their tight relationship with some political parties, an heritage of their intense involvement in the fight for the country's independence. Trade unions are very active and their bargaining power is quite strong in the public sector and the private formal sector. In particular, they play an active role in enforcing the collective conventions existing in specific sectors (banking, transport), as well as the corpus of labor rules in the administration and in public enterprises. This collective action creates a dual situation where workers in any of the unionized sectors are protected whereas those in other sectors are subject to market forces. Trade unions also contribute to the enforcement of firing and minimum wage regulations, as noted earlier. For instance, in 2001, trade unions were able to negotiate a 10 percent increase in the minimum wage and a significant boost in remunerations in the public sector, despite low inflation and tight budget constraints. They have also for many years impeded the adoption of a new labor code, due to diverging views with private employers on the flexibility of labor contracts.

---

[4]Income tax rates range from 13 percent to 44 percent. Social contributions are deductible from the tax base.

4.1.4 Wage Flexibility

Many of the institutional factors reviewed earlier (most importantly, minimum wage regulation, firing regulations, and trade unions with strong bargaining power) may hinder real wage flexibility in Morocco. Comprehensive and accurate data on the evolution of real wages across sectors and skill categories over time are not available. Nevertheless, several sectoral surveys indicate that real wages are somewhat flexible in the urban labor market. For instance, between 1980 and 1987, data from CNSS show that the real average wage in the private formal sector decreased by 10 percent. Using various statistical sources, Morrisson (1991) found that real wages in the industry and the public sector fell substantially between 1980 and 1986. Over the period 1985–9, due to a rapid growth of temporary contracts with low remunerations, real wages fell by 2.5 percent per year in the manufacturing sector, thereby fueling rapid job creation. During the 1990s, real average wages increased in the public and formal private industrial sectors, by around 1.2 percent and 3.1 percent a year, respectively, driven by several revisions in the minimum wage and sweeping wage increases in the civil service.

In Morocco, nominal wages tend to be partially indexed to prices. According to the econometric calculations performed by Mouime (2001), the short-term elasticity of the average nominal wage to the consumer price index is 0.85 in the formal sector.[5] He also found that in the industrial sector the wage–productivity link is explained by an efficiency wage relationship. Although this analysis is not differentiated by levels of skills (due to data limitations), one would expect the relationship to be particularly relevant for skilled workers, thus introducing a significant degree of downward wage rigidity for that category of labor in the formal private sector.

The evidence presented here does not imply that there is no *relative* wage rigidity across skill categories and/or sectors of employment. This is important because as discussed below, in the presence of labor market segmentation – an important feature of the Moroccan urban labor market – relative wage rigidity across segments and skill categories may explain the persistence of widespread unemployment.

4.1.5 Domestic and International Labor Migration

Rural–Urban Migration

Significant rural–urban migration flows heightens the high pressures on the urban labor market. Available estimates indicate that, every year, around 200.000 migrants (in net terms) are entering urban areas, equivalent to around 40 percent of the change in the urban population.

These flows underly important movements from and to cities, as well as international migrations. Among other factors, a low level of productivity and weak growth outcomes in the agriculture sector over the last decade is deemed to contribute to these dynamics. Overall, the rural population is roughly stable (in absolute numbers), whereas its natural growth rate is around 2.6 percent. In fact,

---

[5]The Centre Marocain de Conjoncture (2001) obtains similar results for the industrial sector.

the urban population, expanding at around 3 percent a year, absorbs most of this expansion.

International Migration

Immigrants from Morocco represent an important share of the foreigners residing in the European Union. Due to adverse domestic economic conditions and numerous

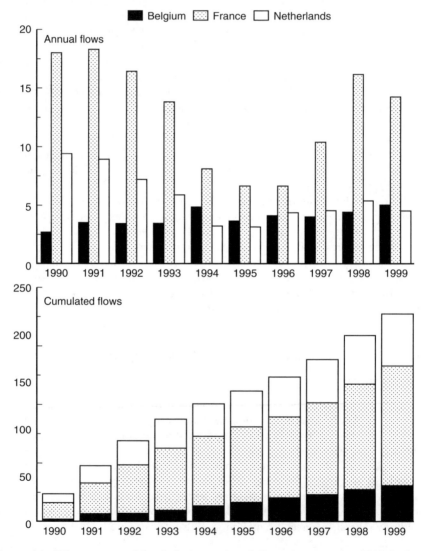

Figure 4.4   Morocco: gross labor inflows to selected European countries, 1990–9. *Source:* OECD.

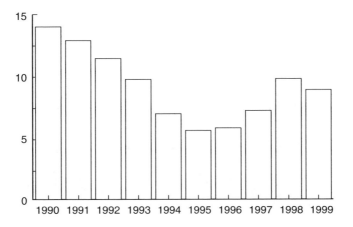

Figure 4.5 Morocco: gross labor outflows to selected European countries, 1990–99. *Source*: World Bank and OECD.

family and community links, migration flows (legal and illegal) continue to be important as shown in recent OECD data.

Data are available only for official flows and selected countries, namely Belgium, France, and Netherlands, which are traditional destinations for Moroccan international migrants. Over the period 1990–9, about 222,000 persons have migrated to these countries, equivalent to about 25,000 on average every year (see Figure 4.4). Hence, with between 6 and 13 percent of the change in the total domestic labor force (see Figure 4.5), yearly outflows to the three selected countries somewhat relieved pressure on the domestic labor market. In addition, the large number of workers abroad translates into a large amount of remittances, which represent a significant fraction of GDP and income (see Figure 4.6) and provide an important source of foreign exchange.

4.1.6 Constraints and Challenges

The main constraints operating on the labor market in Morocco, and by implication the challenges that policymakers would have to take up to substantially lessen unemployment, can be summarized as follows. First, human capital is weak. The average quality of the Moroccan active population, measured by educational attainments, remains low compared to similar countries. The national illiteracy rate stands at 57.7 percent (70 percent for women and 44 percent for men), although the overall figure drops to 48.5 percent in urban areas.

Second, the population is still growing rapidly. Between 1982 and 1994 (two census years), the Moroccan population grew by about 2 percent on average per year, compared to 2.6 percent during the period 1971–82. This reduction is essentially imputable to a decrease in the fertility rate (3.3 children per female in 1994). Nevertheless, the population growth rate remains 40 percent higher than the average for middle-income countries. As a result of the joint effect of the natural growth

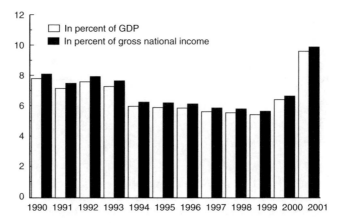

Figure 4.6   Morocco: worker remittances from abroad, 1990–2001. *Source*: World Bank and OECD.

rate and migration from rural areas, the urban population expanded by 27.7 percent between 1982 and 1994. In 2001, 56 percent of the population was living in urban areas.

Third, and related to the previous point, labor supply is growing at a sustained rate. Given the trend toward urbanization, and considering the demographic structure of the Moroccan population, one of the main challenge in the coming years will be the absorption by the urban labor market of a sustained flow of workers. The pressure to do so becomes more intense when the situation in the agricultural sector, strongly linked to the climatic situation, deteriorates – causing an acceleration in the pace of rural migration. Years of weak agricultural production are therefore associated with a significant growth in the urban labor force. In the course of the last century, Morocco has experienced, on average, a year of dryness every three years. This implies that reducing labor market imbalances must be viewed in a broader macroeconomic perspective (in addition to demographic measures), involving changes in the structure of production over time.

Finally, more active participation by women in the labor market could lead to a considerable increase in the labor force. Indeed, if for specific reasons – education, social status, opportunity cost associated with domestic activities, and so on – their involvement has remained weak so far, participation levels are likely to increase in the future. In addition, sustained economic growth could amplify their entry into the labor market by improving individual perceptions regarding employment conditions.

As a result of these developments, the active population is expected to grow more rapidly than the overall population. For the period 1996–2010, projections show that the active population should increase by 1.6 percent on average per year, against a conservative estimate of 2.4 percent for the total (urban and rural) labor force. In addition, during the last decade, job creation concerned essentially temporary occupations with a low productivity, and self-employment activities. Trends in the urban work force require creating such a significant number of job creations that, in the absence of sustained growth, the persistence of a substantial rate of urban unemployment is highly probable in the future.

Similarly, weaknesses in educational attainments are worrying, given the importance of human capital for growth.[6] To boost productivity and achieve higher growth rates, educational levels of the Moroccan work force would need to be raised significantly. Nevertheless, as suggested by a recent contribution, the positive influence of human capital accumulation on growth seems to be closely linked to the degree of external openness of a country; an open economy stimulates a more efficient factor allocation positively affecting the returns of human capital.

A continued effort to increase human capital is essential for trade driven growth. Indeed, within a context of greater trade openness, increased capital mobility, and higher rates of technology diffusion, the quality of the human capital stock is a crucial determinant of comparative advantage. In turn, the degree of external openness stimulates a more efficient factor allocation, positively affecting the returns to human capital. Both effects should speed up growth through a rise in productivity, and allow the country to attract more foreign direct investment. This is a key issue because, as a consequence of the progressive implementation by the European Union (EU) of the Uruguay Round agreement (which implies an erosion of the preferential access of Moroccan goods to the EU market), national firms will face increasing competition from low-wage countries on their essential export markets. Similarly, in the perspective of the free trade zone with the EU (by 2010), internal competition will stiffen.

In the short term, the structural factors highlighted in this section jeopardize a substantial improvement of the situation. Indeed, considering the demographic trends, the pace of rural–urban migration, and the volatile nature of growth, it is highly probable that tensions will persist on the urban labor market.

It is therefore necessary to implement appropriate policy actions to cope with this situation. The framework developed in the next section provide a useful tool to quantify the growth and labor market effects of some of these actions.

4.2   A Quantitative Framework

We now present a quantitative framework to analyze the effects of various labor market reforms on growth, employment, and wages in Morocco. As noted earlier, our framework is based in part on the Mini-IMMPA presented in Chapter 3, suitably modified to reflect the most salient structural characteristics of the labor market in Morocco.

We review the various building blocks of the model, the structure of which is summarized in Figure 4.7. We consider in turn the production side, employment, the demand side, external trade, sectoral and aggregate prices, income formation, and the public sector. Throughout the discussion, we often use "generic" forms to specify

---

[6]See Agénor (2004*b*, Chapter 13) for a review of the empirical evidence.

functional relationships; explicit functional forms can readily be matched with the corresponding equations in Chapter 3.

4.2.1   Production

We begin our description of the production side of the model with a distinction between rural and urban sectors.

As in the IMMPA prototype for low-income countries developed in Chapter 5, the rural economy (or agriculture, for short) is itself divided between a tradable sector, which consists of a homogeneous good sold abroad and on domestic markets, and a nontraded goods sector, which produces a good sold only domestically. Urban production includes both formal and informal components; in addition, the formal urban economy is separated between production of a private good (which can be sold either domestically or abroad) and a public good (which is sold only domestically).

Rural Sector

Land available for each rural activity is assumed to be in fixed supply and there is no market to trade property claims on it. Gross output of nontraded goods, X_{AN}, and exported agricultural goods, X_{AT}, are given by the sum of value added (V_{AN} and V_{AT}, respectively) and intermediate consumption:

$$X_{AN} = V_{AN} + X_{AN} \sum_i a_{iAN}, \tag{1}$$

$$X_{AT} = V_{AT} + X_{AT} \sum_i a_{iAT}, \tag{2}$$

where the a_{ij} are conventionally-defined input–output coefficients (sales from sector i to sector j) and subscripts AN, AT, I, P, G are used in what follows to refer, respectively, to the nontraded agricultural sector, the traded agricultural sector, the informal sector, the private urban sector, and the public sector. To simplify notations, and if not indicated otherwise, the index i or j will refer to all five sectors.

Value added in each sector is assumed to be produced with a Cobb-Douglas (CD) function of land, $LAND$, and a composite factor, defined as a constant elasticity of substitution (CES) function that depends on the number of unskilled rural workers employed (U_{AN} in the nontraded good sector and U_{AT} in the traded-good sector) and the economy-wide stock of public physical capital, K_G:

$$V_{AN} = CD[LAND_{AN}, CES(U_{AN}, K_G)], \tag{3}$$

$$V_{AT} = CD[LAN_{AT}, CES(U_{AT}, K_G)]. \tag{4}$$

Land allocated to production is constant and, for simplicity, is normalized to unity in what follows. Thus, given the CD specification, production in each agricultural sector exhibits decreasing returns to scale in the remaining (composite) input.

The nontraded agricultural good is exclusively produced for the domestic market,

$$X_{AN} = D_{AN}, \tag{5}$$

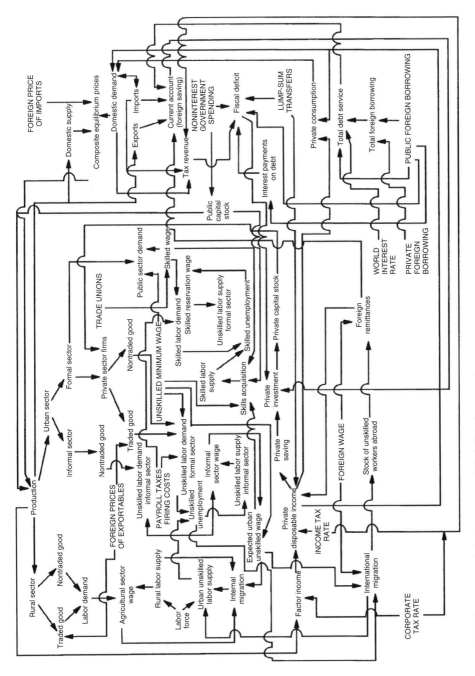

Figure 4.7 Morocco: analytical structure of IMMPA framework.

where D_{AN} denotes domestic demand for that good. By contrast, as discussed later, production of the rural traded good is allocated to both domestic consumption and exports.

Urban Informal Sector

Gross production in the urban informal sector, X_I, is the sum of value added, V_I, and intermediate consumption:

$$X_I = V_I + \sum_i a_{iI} X_I. \tag{6}$$

Value added is a function of the number of unskilled workers employed in the informal economy, U_I, with decreasing returns to scale:

$$V_I = \alpha_{XI} U_I^{\beta_{XI}}, \qquad \alpha_{XI} > 0, \; 0 < \beta_{XI} < 1. \tag{7}$$

From (7), the demand for labor in the informal sector can be derived as

$$U_I^d = \beta_{XI}(V_I/w_I), \tag{8}$$

where w_I is the product wage, given by $w_I = W_I/PV_I$, with PV_I denoting the price of value added in the informal sector.

Public Sector

Gross production of public goods and services (or public good, for short), X_G, is the sum of value added, V_G, and intermediate consumption:

$$X_G = V_G + \sum_i a_{iG} X_G. \tag{9}$$

Value added in the public sector is measured by the government wage bill:

$$V_G = (W_{UG} U_G + W_{SG} S_G)/PV_G. \tag{10}$$

Employment levels of both categories of workers are treated as exogenous.

Urban Formal Private Sector

Private formal production uses as inputs both skilled and unskilled labor, as well as physical capital. Skilled labor and private physical capital have a higher degree of complementarity (lower degree of substitution) than physical capital and unskilled workers. In order to account explicitly for these differences in the degree of substitutability among inputs, we adopt a nested CES production structure.

Specifically gross production of the private formal-urban sector, X_P, is given by the sum of value added, V_P, and intermediate consumption:

$$X_P = V_P + \sum_i a_{iP} X_P, \tag{11}$$

whereas value added is

$$V_P = CES\left\{ CES[CES(S_P, K_P), U_P], \frac{K_G}{(U_U + S)^{dcop}} \right\},$$ (12)

where $dcop \geq 0$. At the lowest level of equation (12), skilled labor, S_P, and private capital, K_P, are combined to form the composite input T_2, with a low elasticity of substitution between them. At the second level, this composite input is used together with unskilled labor, U_P, to form the composite input T_1.

The elasticity of substitution between T_2 and unskilled workers, U_P, is assumed to be higher than between S_P and K_P. The final layer combines T_1 and $K_G/(U_U + S)$, the ratio of the stock of government capital to the total size of the labor force in the urban sector, as production inputs.

When $dcop = 0$, there are no congestion effects. By contrast, when $dcop > 0$, the larger the urban population is, the more congested public capital is, and the lower will be its contribution to private urban production.

Private firms in the urban formal sector allocate their output to exports, E_P, or the domestic market, D_P, according to a production possibility frontier, defined as in Chapter 3 by a constant elasticity of transformation (CET) function:

$$X_P = CET(E_P, D_P).$$ (13)

4.2.2 Wages, Employment, Migration, and Skills Acquisition

Unskilled workers in the economy may be employed either in the rural economy, U_R, or in the urban economy, U_U, whereas skilled workers are employed only in the urban sector. We also assume that skilled workers are not employed in the informal economy either – perhaps as a result of signaling considerations, as discussed in Chapters 1 and 2.

Rural Wages, Employment, and Internal Migration

Profit maximization in the tradable rural sector yields the demand for (unskilled) labor, U_{AT}^d, as

$$U_{AT}^d = \left\{ V_{AT}^{1+\rho_{XAT}/(1-\eta_{XAT})} \frac{1-\eta_{XAT}}{w_{AT}} \cdot \frac{\beta_{XAT}}{\alpha_{XAT}^{\rho_{XAT}}} \right\}^{1/(1+\rho_{XAT})}, \quad \text{where } w_{AT} = \frac{W_A}{PV_{AT}},$$ (14)

with W_A denoting the nominal wage in agriculture and PV_{AT} the net output price in the traded agricultural sector. Equation (14) indicates that labor demand in the rural export sector is related positively to the level of net output, V_{AT}, and negatively to the product wage in that sector, w_{AT}.

The demand for (unskilled) labor in the nontraded agricultural sector is given by an equation similar to (14):

$$U_{AN}^d = \left\{ V_{AN}^{1+\rho_{XAN}/(1-\eta_{XAN})} \frac{1-\eta_{XAN}}{w_{AN}} \cdot \frac{\beta_{XAN}}{\alpha_{XAN}^{\rho_{XAN}}} \right\}^{1/(1+\rho_{XAN})}, \quad \text{where } w_{AN} = \frac{W_A}{PV_{AN}},$$

(15)

with again w_{AN} denoting the product wage in that sector.

Nominal wages in agriculture, W_A, adjust to clear the labor market. With U_R representing labor supply in agriculture, the equilibrium condition is thus given by

$$U_R = U_{AN}^d \left(V_{AN}, \frac{W_A}{PV_{AN}} \right) + U_{AT}^d \left(V_{AT}, \frac{W_A}{PV_{AT}} \right).$$

(16)

The size of the labor force in the rural sector, U_R, grows over time at the exogenous population growth rate, g_R, net of worker migration to urban areas, MIG:

$$U_R = (1 + g_R)U_{R,-1} - MIG.$$

(17)

As in Harris and Todaro (1970), incentives to migrate are taken to depend negatively on the ratio of the average expected *consumption* wage in rural areas to that prevailing in urban areas. Unskilled workers in the urban economy may be employed either in the formal sector, in which case they are paid a minimum wage, W_M, or they can enter the informal economy and receive the market-determined wage in that sector, W_I. When rural workers make the decision to migrate to urban areas, they are uncertain as to which type of job they will be able to get, and therefore weigh wages in each sector by the probability of finding a job in that sector. These probabilities are approximated by prevailing employment ratios. Potential migrants also consider what their expected purchasing power in rural and urban areas will be, depending on whether they stay in the rural sector and consume the "typical" basket of goods of rural households, or migrate and consume the "typical" urban basket of goods.

The expected unskilled urban real wage, Ew_U, is thus a weighted average of the minimum wage in the formal sector and the going wage in the informal sector, deflated by an urban consumption price index, P_{UU}:

$$Ew_U = \frac{\theta_U W_{M,-1} + (1 - \theta_U)W_{I,-1}}{P_{UU,-1}},$$

(18)

where θ_U is the probability of finding a job in the urban formal sector, measured by the number of unskilled workers employed in the private formal sector, relative to the total number of unskilled urban workers looking for a job in the urban formal sector (net of government employment), in the previous period:

$$\theta_U = \frac{U_{P,-1}}{U_{F,-1}^s - U_{G,-1}}.$$

(19)

A similar reasoning is used to calculate the expected rural consumption real wage, Ew_A. Here the employment probability is equal to unity, because workers can always find a job at the going wage. Assuming a one-period lag, we thus have

$$Ew_A = \frac{W_{A,-1}}{P_{R,-1}},$$

where P_R is the composite, rural consumption price index.

The migration function can therefore be specified as

$$MIG = U_{R,-1}\lambda_m \left\{ \sigma_M \ln \left[\frac{\mathrm{E}w_U}{\mathrm{E}w_A} \right] \right\} + (1 - \lambda_m) \frac{U_{R,-1}}{U_{R,-2}} MIG_{-1}, \qquad (20)$$

where $0 < \lambda_m < 1$ measures the speed of adjustment and $\sigma_M > 0$ the elasticity of migration flows with respect to expected wages. This specification implies that migration flows may display persistence, perhaps as a result of relocation costs.

Urban Unskilled Wages, Employment, and Unemployment

The public sector employs an exogenous number of unskilled workers, U_G, at the nominal wage rate $W_{UG} \geq W_M$, whereas the demand for unskilled labor by the formal private sector is determined by firms' profit maximization subject to the given minimum wage, W_M. Both wages are indexed to the overall consumer price index, $PLEV$:

$$W_{UG} = \omega_{UG} \cdot PLEV^{ind_{UG}}, \quad W_M = \omega_M \cdot PLEV^{ind_M}, \qquad (21)$$

where ω_M and ω_{UG} measure real wages in constant terms, and $0 < ind_{UG}, ind_M \leq 1$. In the simulation exercises reported later, we assume that both wages are fully indexed ($ind_{UG} = ind_M = 1$).

Labor demand by the formal private sector is determined by firms' profit maximization. We assume also that firms pay a payroll tax, at the rate $0 < ptax_U < 1$ for unskilled workers, which is proportional to the wage bill, $W_M U_P$. Unskilled labor demand by the private sector is thus given by

$$U_P^d = T_1 \left\{ \frac{1}{(1 + ptax_U)w_M} \frac{\beta_{XP1}}{\alpha_{XP1}^{\rho_{XP1}}} \right\}^{\sigma_{XP1}}, \quad \text{where } w_M = \frac{W_M}{PT_1}. \qquad (22)$$

In order to avoid corner solutions, we assume that the real minimum wage exceeds the real wage in the informal sector. Consequently, unskilled urban workers will first seek employment in the private formal sector first, implying that the actual level of unskilled employment in that sector is determined according to equation (22).

As in Chapters 1 and 3, we also assume that, as a result of relocation and congestion costs, mobility of the unskilled labor force between the formal and the informal sectors is imperfect. In Harris-Todaro fashion, migration flows are determined by expected income opportunities. Specifically, the supply of unskilled workers in the formal sector (including public sector workers), U_F^s, is assumed to change gradually over time as a function of the expected wage differential across sectors, measured in real terms. Wage and employment prospects are formed on the basis of prevailing conditions in the labor market. Because there is no job turnover in the public sector, the expected nominal wage in the formal economy is equal to the minimum wage weighted by the probability of being hired in the private sector. Assuming that hiring in that sector is random, this probability can be approximated by the ratio of employed workers to those seeking employment, $U_P^d/(U_F^s - U_G)$. The expected nominal wage in the informal economy, W_I, is simply the going wage, because there are no barriers to entry in that sector.

Assuming a one-period lag, changes in the supply of unskilled workers in the formal sector (measured in proportion of the total urban unskilled labor force) thus evolves over time according to

$$\frac{\Delta U_F^s}{U_{U,-1}} = \beta_F \left\{ \sigma_F \ln \left[\frac{U_{P,-1}^d}{U_{F,-1}^s - U_{G,-1}} \frac{W_{M,-1}}{W_{I,-1}} \right] \right\} + (1 - \beta_F) \frac{\Delta U_{F-1}^s}{U_{U,-2}}, \quad (23)$$

where $\beta_F > 0$ denotes the speed of adjustment.[7] The unskilled unemployment rate in the formal sector, $UNEMP_U$, is thus given by

$$UNEMP_U = 1 - \frac{(U_G + U_P^d)}{U_F^s}. \quad (24)$$

The supply of labor in the informal economy, U_I^s, is obtained by subtracting from the urban unskilled labor force, U_U, the quantity U_F^s:

$$U_I^s = U_U - U_F^s. \quad (25)$$

The informal labor market clears continuously, so that $U_I^d = U_I^s$. From equations (8) and (25), the equilibrium nominal wage is thus given by

$$W_I = \beta_{XI} \left(\frac{PV_I V_I}{U_U - U_F^s} \right). \quad (26)$$

The urban unskilled labor supply, U_U, grows as a result of natural urban population growth and migration of unskilled labor from the rural sector, as discussed earlier. Moreover, some urban unskilled workers, SKL, acquire skills and leave the unskilled labor force. We make the additional assumption that individuals are born unskilled. Thus, natural urban population growth (not resulting from migration or skills acquisition) results from urban unskilled population growth only, at the exogenous rate g_U. Finally, there are international migrations, the flow of which is measured by $IMIG$. Thus, the size of the urban unskilled labor supply evolves according to

$$U_U = (1 + g_U)U_{U,-1} + MIG - SKL - IMIG. \quad (27)$$

Urban Skilled Wages and Employment

As noted earlier, employment levels of both skilled and unskilled workers in the public (urban) sector are taken as exogenous. The nominal wage that skilled workers earn,

---

[7] As noted in Chapter 1, the absence of on-the-job search in the informal sector can be justified by the existence of informational inefficiencies, which may result from the absence of institutions capable of processing and providing in a timely manner relevant information on job opportunities to potential applicants. As a result, search activities for the unskilled in the formal sector may require, almost literally, waiting for job offers at the doors of potential employers.

W_{SG}, is indexed on the relevant consumption price index:

$$W_{SG} = \omega_{SG} P_{US}^{ind_{SG}}, \tag{28}$$

where ω_{SG} is an exogenous real wage level, and $0 < ind_{SG} \leq 1$. To avoid a corner solution in which no worker would want to seek employment in the public sector, we assume that working for the government provides a nonpecuniary benefit (related perhaps to higher job security, as noted in Chapter 1), valued at B_G, which is such that $W_{SG} + B_G > W_S$.

Private urban firms pay a payroll tax on their skilled wage bill, $W_S S_P$, at the proportional rate $0 < ptax_S < 1$. From (12), the demand for skilled labor is given by

$$S_P^d = T_2 \kappa_S \left\{ \frac{1}{(1 + ptax_S)\omega_S} \cdot \frac{\beta_{XP2}}{\alpha_{XP2}^{\rho_{XP2}}} \right\}^{\sigma_{XP2}}, \quad \text{where } \omega_S = \frac{W_S}{PT_2}. \tag{29}$$

The nominal wage for skilled labor in the private sector, W_S, is determined on the basis of a "monopoly union" approach, as follows.[8] Let ω_S^c denote the *consumption* real wage, that is, the nominal wage earned by skilled workers deflated by the cost-of-living index that these workers face in the urban sector, P_{US}. ω_S^c is assumed set by a centralized labor union whose objective is to maximize a utility function that depends on deviations of both employment and the consumption wage from their target levels, subject to the firm's labor demand schedule. Specifically, the union's utility function is given by

$$U = (\omega_S^c - \omega_S^{cT})^\nu (S_P^d - S_P^T)^{1-\nu}, \quad 0 < \nu < 1, \tag{30}$$

where S_P^d is given by equation (29). The quantities ω_S^{cT} and S_P^T measure the union's wage and employment targets, respectively, and are both assumed predetermined with respect to ω_S^c. The parameter ν reflects the relative importance that the union attaches to wage deviations, as opposed to employment deviations.

Substituting the labor demand curve (29) in the utility function above, the union's problem is thus

$$\max_{\omega_S^c} (\omega_S^c - \omega_S^{cT})^\nu \left\{ T_2 \kappa_S \left(\frac{PT_2}{P_{US}(1 + ptax_S)\omega_S^c} \cdot \frac{\beta_{XP2}}{\alpha_{XP2}^{\rho_{XP2}}} \right)^{\sigma_{XP2}} - S_P^T \right\}^{1-\nu}.$$

The first-order condition is given by

$$\nu \left\{ \frac{S_P^d - S_P^T}{\omega_S^c - \omega_S^{cT}} \right\}^{1-\nu} - (1-\nu) \left\{ \frac{S_P^d - S_P^T}{\omega_S^c - \omega_S^{cT}} \right\}^{-\nu} \sigma_{XP2} \left(\frac{S_P^d}{\omega_S^c} \right) = 0,$$

or equivalently, normalizing the target level of employment S_P^T to zero:

$$\frac{\nu S_P^d}{\omega_S^c - \omega_S^{cT}} - \frac{(1-\nu)\sigma_{XP2} S_P^d}{\omega_S^c} = 0.$$

---

[8] See Chapter 1 for a more detailed discussion. Alternatively, one could assume that firms and the union bargain over wages, with firms determining employment. As shown formally by Creedy and McDonald (1991), from the point of view of wage determination this approach would not lead to a specification that differs much from the one derived below.

This expression can be solved for the optimal wage:

$$\omega_S^c = \frac{\omega_S^{cT}}{1 - \nu/(1-\nu)\sigma_{XP2}}, \tag{31}$$

where we assume that $1 - \nu/(1-\nu)\sigma_{XP2} > 0$.

As discussed in the previous chapter, the union's target wage, ω_S^{cT}, is assumed to be related positively to skilled wages in the public sector (measured in terms of the relevant price index), ω_{SG}, and negatively to the skilled unemployment rate, $UNEMP_S$, and the firing cost per skilled worker, f_S. Wage-setting in the public sector is assumed to play a signaling role to wage setters in the rest of the economy. When unemployment is high, the probability of finding a job (at any given wage) is low. Consequently, the higher the unemployment rate, the greater the incentive for the union to moderate its wage demands and boost employment. Firing costs do prevent excessive job losses in bad times (thereby preventing the loss of firm-specific human capital if downturns are temporary), but they also discourage new hires – for instance because if workers prove to be inadequate matches with their job requirements, reversing mismatches is costly. As discussed in the previous section, cautious behavior among potential employers explains why informal job search activities appear to play such an important role in Morocco. Here, however, we assume that the union internalizes the disincentive effect of severance payments on labor demand. As a result, the higher the firing cost, the greater the incentive for the union to reduce its wage demands, in order to encourage firms to hire.

Equation (31) can thus be rewritten as

$$W_S = P_{US} \frac{UNEMP_S^{-\phi_1}(f_S/P_{US})^{-\phi_2}\omega_{SG}^{\phi_3}}{1 - \nu/(1-\nu)\sigma_{XP2}}. \tag{32}$$

This equation implies, in particular, that a higher level of unemployment lowers the *level* of wages, as implied by various types of efficiency-wage models.

Given that unions set nominal wages and firms are on their labor demand curve, open skilled unemployment may emerge. We assume that skilled workers who are unable to find a job in the formal economy opt to remain open unemployed, instead of entering the informal economy (in contrast to unskilled workers), perhaps because of adverse signaling effects. The skilled unemployment rate is thus given by the number of skilled workers who are not employed either by the private or the public sector, divided by the total population of skilled workers:

$$UNEMP_S = \frac{S - S_G - S_P^d}{S}. \tag{33}$$

The evolution of the skilled labor force depends on the rate at which unskilled workers acquire skills:

$$S = (1 - \delta_S)S_{-1} + SKL, \tag{34}$$

where $0 < \delta_S < 1$ is the rate of "depreciation" or "deskilling" of the skilled labor force.

Skills Acquisition

The acquisition of skills by unskilled workers depends on two factors: *a*) relative expected consumption wages of skilled to unskilled urban workers (as a proxy for the future stream of earnings associated with higher levels of education); and *b*) the government stock of education capital, K_E, which limits the ability to invest in skills.

Consider first the effect of wages. In case they acquire skills, current unskilled workers expect to earn wage W_S if they are employed (with probability θ_S) and nothing if they are unemployed. The purchasing power of this wage is obtained by deflating it by a skilled consumption price index, P_{US}. With a one-period lag,

$$\mathrm{E}w_S = \theta_S \frac{W_{S,-1}}{P_{US,-1}},$$

where θ_S (assuming again a one-period lag) is approximated by the initial ratio of the number of skilled workers employed in the private sector, over the total number of skilled workers who are not employed in the public sector:

$$\theta_S = \frac{S_{P,-1}}{S_{-1} - S_{G,-1}}. \tag{35}$$

If they remain unskilled, workers expect to get the average unskilled wage, which is a weighted average of the minimum wage and the informal wage rate. Assuming, again, that there is no job turnover in the public sector, the average expected real wage is given by (18), which is repeated here for convenience:

$$\mathrm{E}w_U = \frac{\theta_U W_{M,-1} + (1 - \theta_U) W_{I,-1}}{P_{UU,-1}},$$

with θ_U as defined in (19).

Given these effects, the flow increase in the supply of skilled labor can be written as:

$$SKL = \lambda_S \left\{ \kappa_e \left[\frac{\mathrm{E}w_S}{\mathrm{E}w_U} \right]^{\sigma_W} (K_{E,-1})^{\sigma_E} \right\} + (1 - \lambda_S) SKL_{-1},$$

where $0 < \lambda_S < 1$, and $\kappa_e > 0$ is a shift parameter.[9]

International Labor Migration

As noted in the previous section, international migration is an important feature of the labor market in Morocco. We assume here that migration involves only unskilled workers, and that potential migrants are in the urban sector (as captured in (27)). Moreover, international migration flows are taken to be determined by two factors: the prevailing unskilled unemployment rate in the formal urban sector, and the expected

---

[9]Note that we abstract from the cost of acquiring skills (as measured by the average number of years during which schooling is attended multiplied by the average cost of education per year, all in present-value terms), which should also affect the propensity to invest in skills acquisition. This may not be warranted if credit constraints prevent borrowing for human capital accumulation.

urban real wage for unskilled labor, Ew_U, given by (18), relative to the expected foreign wage measured in terms of the domestic urban price index, Ew_F. Assuming a one-period lag, this wage is defined as

$$Ew_F = \frac{ER \cdot W_{F,-1}}{P_{UU,-1}},$$

with W_F denoting the foreign wage measured in foreign-currency terms (assumed exogenous) and ER the nominal exchange rate. Adopting a specification similar to (20), the migration function is specified as

$$IMIG = U_{U,-1} \lambda_{im} \left\{ \sigma_{IM} \ln \left[\frac{Ew_F}{Ew_U} \right] \right\} + (1 - \lambda_{im}) \frac{U_{U,-1}}{U_{U,-2}} IMIG_{-1},$$

where $0 < \lambda_{im} < 1$ measures the speed of adjustment, and $\sigma_{IM} > 0$ the elasticity of migration flows with respect to expected wages. Again, costs associated with migration across countries are assumed to introduce some degree of persistence (see Lopez and Schiff (1998) for a further discussion). As discussed below, remittances associated with international migration flows of unskilled labor are assumed to benefit mainly unskilled households in the urban formal and informal sectors.

4.2.3   Supply and Demand

Both the informal and public sector goods are nontraded. Total supply in each sector is thus equal to gross production, that is

$$Q_I^s = X_I, \quad Q_G^s = X_G. \tag{36}$$

Similarly, there are no imports of tradable agricultural goods, and part of it is exported. Total domestic supply is thus equal to gross production minus exports, E_{AT}:

$$Q_{AT}^s = X_{AT} - E_{AT}. \tag{37}$$

Agricultural nontraded and private formal urban goods, by contrast, compete with imported goods. The supply of the composite good for each of these sectors consists of a CES combination of imports and domestically produced goods:

$$Q_{AN}^s = CES(M_{AN}, D_{AN}), \tag{38}$$

$$Q_P^s = CES(M_P, D_P), \tag{39}$$

where $D_{AN} = X_{AN}$, as noted earlier.

Aggregate demand for each of these sectors consists of intermediate and final consumption, government spending, and investment demand. For the traded and nontraded agricultural sectors, demand (Q_{AN}^d and Q_{AT}^d) consists of demand for final consumption by the private sector (C_{AN} and C_I) and the government (G_{AN} and G_{AT}) and intermediate consumption (INT_{AN} and INT_{AT}):

$$Q_{AN}^d = C_{AN} + G_{AN} + INT_{AN}, \tag{40}$$

$$Q_{AT}^d = C_{AT} + G_{AT} + INT_{AT}, \tag{41}$$

For the informal sector, aggregate demand (Q_I^d) consists of demand for intermediate and final consumption only:

$$Q_I^d = C_I + INT_I, \qquad (42)$$

Aggregate demand for the public good and the private formal good, Q_G^d and Q_P^d, consists of demand for intermediate and final consumption by households and the government, and investment demand, Z_P^G and Z_P^P, by the formal private sector, and Z_G by the government (which requires only private urban goods):

$$Q_G^d = C_G + G_G + Z_P^G + INT_G, \qquad (43)$$

$$Q_P^d = C_P + G_P + (Z_P^P + Z_G) + INT_P. \qquad (44)$$

In the above expressions, INT_j is defined as total demand (by all productions sectors) for intermediate consumption of good j:

$$INT_j = \sum_i a_{ji} X_i. \qquad (45)$$

Government expenditure on good j, G_j, is expressed in real terms as:

$$G_j = gg_j \frac{NG}{PQ_j} \quad j = AN, AT, G, P, \qquad (46)$$

where NG represents total current expenditure on goods and services (which is fixed in nominal terms), PQ_h is the market price of goods purchased by the government, and $\sum gg_j = 1$. Note that the government is assumed not to spend on informal sector goods.

Final consumption for each production sector i, C_i, is the summation across all categories of households of nominal consumption of good i, deflated by the demand price of good i:

$$C_i = \sum_h C_{ih} = \sum_h x_{ih} + \frac{\sum_h cc_{ih}(CON_h - \sum_i PQ_i x_{ih})}{PQ_i}, \quad \forall i, \qquad (47)$$

where C_{ih} is consumption of good i by household h, x_{ih} is the subsistence (or autonomous) level of consumption of good i by household h, CON_h total nominal consumption expenditure by household h, and PQ_i the composite sales price of good i. Equations (47) are based on the linear expenditure system, as discussed in Chapter 3. Coefficients cc_{ih} indicate how total nominal consumption expenditure by household h, CON_h, is allocated to each type of good. They satisfy the following restrictions:

$$0 < cc_{ih} < 1, \ \forall i, h, \quad \sum_i cc_{ih} = 1, \ \forall h.$$

Private investment by private urban firms, Z_P, consists of purchases of both public and urban formal private goods and services (Z_P^G and Z_P^P, respectively):

$$Z_P^i = zz_i \frac{PK \cdot Z_P}{PQ_i}, \quad \text{where } zz_G + zz_P = 1.$$

Coefficients zz_i measure the allocation of total investment demand to public and urban private goods.

4.2.4   External Trade

Exports of the tradable agricultural good are determined as a residual, once domestic demand is satisfied. From (37) and (41), and setting $Q_{AT}^s = Q_{AT}^d$, exports are thus determined by

$$E_{AT} = X_{AT} - (C_{AT} + G_{AT} + INT_{AT}). \tag{48}$$

As indicated earlier, firms in the private formal sector allocate their output to exports or the domestic market according to the production possibility frontier (PPF) specified in equation (13). Efficiency conditions yield:

$$E_P = D_P \left\{ \frac{PE_P}{PD_P} \cdot \frac{1 - \beta_{TP}}{\beta_{TP}} \right\}^{\sigma_{TP}}, \tag{49}$$

where PE_P is the price of exports and PD_P the price of domestic sales.

We assume that imports compete with domestic goods in the agricultural nontraded sector as well as in the private formal sector. Making use of Armington functions for the demand for imported vs. domestic goods and relative prices, import demand for both sectors (M_{AN} and M_P) can be written as:

$$M_i = D_i \left\{ \frac{PD_i}{PM_i} \cdot \frac{\beta_{Qi}}{1 - \beta_{Qi}} \right\}^{\sigma_{Qi}}, \quad i = AN, P. \tag{50}$$

These equations show that the ratio of imports to both categories of domestic goods depends on the relative prices of these goods and the elasticity of substitution between these goods.

4.2.5   Prices

The net or value added price of output is given by the gross price, PX_i, net of indirect taxes, less the cost of intermediate inputs (purchased at composite prices):

$$PV_i = V_i^{-1} \left\{ PX_i(1 - indtax_i) - \sum_j a_{ji} PQ_j \right\} X_i, \tag{51}$$

where $indtax_i$ is the rate of indirect taxation of output in sector i (with $indtax_I = 0$ because there is no indirect taxation of informal sector output).

The world prices of imported and exported goods are exogenously given. The domestic-currency price of these goods is obtained by multiplying the world price by the exchange rate, with import prices also adjusted by the tariff rate, tm:

$$PE_i = wpe_i ER, \quad i = AT, P, \tag{52}$$

$$PM_i = wpm_i(1 + tm_i) ER, \quad i = AN, P. \tag{53}$$

Because the transformation function between exports and domestic sales of the urban private good is linearly homogeneous, the sales price, PX_P, is derived from the expenditure identity:

$$PX_P X_P = PD_P D_P + PE_P E_P,$$

that is,

$$PX_P = \frac{PD_P D_P + PE_P E_P}{X_P},\qquad(54)$$

with PD_P determined from the equality between the supply of composite goods (39) and the demand for these goods (44).

For the informal and public sectors (both of which do not export and do not compete with imports), the sales price is equal to the domestic market price. In the agricultural sector, the sales price of the traded agricultural good, PX_{AT}, is simply the domestic-currency price of agricultural exports, PE_{AT}, whereas the sales price of the nontraded good, PX_{AN}, is equal to the domestic price of agricultural goods, PD_{AN}. In turn, these prices are equal to gross output prices. Thus,

$$PX_{AT} = PE_{AT},\quad PX_{AN} = PD_{AN},$$

For the nontraded agricultural sector and private urban production, the substitution function between imports and domestic goods is also linearly homogeneous, and the (composite) market price is determined accordingly by the expenditure identity:

$$PQ_i Q_i^d = PD_i D_i + PM_i M_i,\quad i = AN, P,$$

that is

$$PQ_i = \frac{PD_i D_i + PM_i M_i}{Q_i^d},\quad i = AN, P,\qquad(55)$$

with $Q_i^d = Q_i^s$.

For those sectors that do not compete with imports (informal and public goods), the domestic price, PD_i, is simply equal to the gross output (or market) price, PX_i:

$$PD_i = PX_i,\quad i = I, G.\qquad(56)$$

The nested CES production function of private formal urban goods is also linearly homogeneous; prices of the composite inputs are therefore derived in similar fashion:

$$T_1 PT_1 = T_2 PT_2 + (1 + ptax_U) W_M U_P.\qquad(57)$$

$$T_2 PT_2 = PROF_P + (1 + ptax_S) W_S S_P,\qquad(58)$$

where $PROF_P$ is profits by private sector firms in the urban formal sector.

The price of (private) capital is constructed by using the investment expenditure identity for private firms, which involves those goods for which there is investment demand, namely, the public good and private-formal urban good (see equations (43) and (44)):

$$PK = \frac{PQ_G Z_P^G + PQ_P Z_P^P}{Z_P}.\qquad(59)$$

In solving the model, we use equations (36) to determine the equilibrium quantities Q_I and Q_G, that is, equations (6) and (9), respectively. We use the demand equations (42) and (43) to solve residually for C_I and C_G, that is:

$$X_I - INT_I = C_I, \tag{60}$$

$$X_G - G_G - Z_G - INT_G = C_G. \tag{61}$$

Equation (47) for $i = I, G$, is then solved for $PQ_I = PX_I$ and $PQ_G = PX_G$, respectively. Define discretionary consumption expenditure of household h, $COND_h$, as

$$COND_h = CON_h - \sum_i PQ_i x_{ih}, \tag{62}$$

and define the share of autonomous consumption of good i in total consumption of good i, ac_i, as

$$ac_i = \frac{\sum_h PQ_i x_{ih}}{PQ_i C_i} = \frac{\sum_h x_{ih}}{C_i}. \tag{63}$$

Then, from (47), we have

$$PX_i = (1 - ac_i)^{-1} \cdot \left\{ \frac{\sum_h cc_{ih} COND_h}{C_i} \right\}, \quad i = I, G. \tag{64}$$

The consumption price index for the rural sector is given by

$$P_R = \sum_i wr_i PQ_i,$$

whereas the consumption price indexes for urban unskilled and skilled workers are given by

$$P_{UU} = \sum_i wu_i PQ_i, \quad P_{US} = \sum_i ws_i PQ_i, \tag{65}$$

where the wr_i, wu_i and ws_i are relative weights, which are such that

$$\sum_i wr_i = \sum_i wu_i = \sum_i ws_i = 1.$$

4.2.6 Profits and Income

Firms' profits are defined as revenue minus total labor costs. In the case of agricultural traded and nontraded sector firms, profits are given by

$$PROF_i = PV_i V_i - W_A U_i, \quad i = AT, AN, \tag{66}$$

whereas in the case of the urban informal sector firms, we have

$$PROF_I = PV_I V_I - W_I U_I. \tag{67}$$

Profits of private urban sector firms account for salaries paid to both categories of workers:

$$PROF_P = PV_P V_P - (1 + ptax_U) U_P W_M - (1 + ptax_S) S_P W_S - FC, \tag{68}$$

where total firing costs, as in Chapter 3, are given by

$$FC = f_U \max(0, U_{P,-1} - U_P) + f_S \max(0, S_{P,-1} - S_P), \tag{69}$$

with f_S, f_U denoting the fixed firing cost per worker (skilled and unskilled, respectively).

Firms' income is equal to profits minus corporate taxes and interest payments on foreign loans. Assuming that only firms in the formal urban economy accumulate capital and pay income taxes yields:

$$YF_i = PROF_i, \quad i = AN, AT, I, \tag{70}$$

$$YF_P = (1 - inctax_F)PROF_P - IF \cdot ER \cdot FL_{P,-1}, \tag{71}$$

where $inctax_F$ is the corporate income tax rate, IF is the foreign interest rate (taken to be exogenous), and FL_P is the level of foreign borrowing by private urban firms. The path of FL_P is set exogenously, to account for ceilings that Moroccan firms may face in their access to foreign markets.

Household income is based on the return to labor (salaries), distributed profits, remittances from abroad, and government transfers. Households are defined according to both labor categories and their sector of location. There are two types of rural households, one comprising workers employed in the traded sector, and the other workers in the nontraded sector. There are also two types of unskilled households in the urban sector, those working in the informal sector and those employed in the formal sector. The fifth type of household consists of skilled workers employed in the formal urban economy (in both the private and public sectors). The final group consists of capitalists and rentiers, whose income comes from firms' earnings in the formal private sector, the agricultural traded sector and commercial banks.

We further assume that households in both the nontraded agricultural sector and in the informal urban economy own the firms in which they are employed – an assumption that captures the fact that in Morocco firms in these sectors tend indeed to be small, family-owned enterprises.

Income of the agricultural nontraded household is given by

$$YH_{AN} = YF_{AN} + W_A U_{AN} + \gamma_{AN} TRH, \tag{72}$$

where $0 < \gamma_{AN} < 1$ is the portion of total government transfers (TRH) that the group receives, so that $\sum_h \gamma_h = 1$, $W_A U_{AN}$ denote wage earnings, and YF_{AN} firms' income in these sectors.

Income of the urban informal household is given by

$$YH_I = YF_I + W_I U_I + \gamma_I TRH + \tau_I ER \cdot REMIT, \tag{73}$$

where $0 < \gamma_I < 1$, $W_I U_I$, and YF_I have the same interpretation as above. *REMIT* measures the foreign-currency value of the flow of remittances from (unskilled) workers employed abroad, and $0 < \tau_I < 1$ the fraction of these remittances that are allocated to households in the informal economy.

Income of the agricultural traded sector household, as well as that of the urban formal skilled household, depends on government transfers and salaries, and possibly redundancy payments. Firms provide no source of income, because those groups do not own the production units in which they are employed:

$$YH_{AT} = W_A U_{AT} + \gamma_{AT} TRH, \tag{74}$$

$$YH_S = (W_S S_P + W_{SG} S_G) + f_S \max(0, S_{P,-1} - S_P) + \gamma_S TRH, \tag{75}$$

where $0 < \gamma_{AT}, \gamma_S < 1$.

Similarly, in the absence of any transfer of resources from firms, income of the urban formal unskilled household depends on government transfers, salaries (from both private and the public sectors), remittances from abroad, and possibly redundancy payments:

$$YH_{UF} = \gamma_{UF} TRH + W_M U_P + W_{UG} U_G$$
$$+ f_U \max(0, U_{P,-1} - U_P) + (1 - \tau_I) ER \cdot REMIT, \tag{76}$$

where $0 < \gamma_{UF} < 1$. As noted earlier, foreign remittances are allocated either to informal sector households or unskilled urban households.

Firms' income in the traded agricultural and private urban sectors goes to the capitalist-rentier household. Because there is no capital accumulation in the traded agricultural sector to be financed, the entire amount of firms' profits from that sector are transferred to the capitalist-rentier household. By contrast, firms in the private urban sector retain a portion of their after-tax earnings, $0 < re < 1$, to finance investment, and transfer only the remainder to the capitalist-rentier household. The latter's income is thus:

$$YH_{KAP} = YF_{AT} + (1 - re)YF_P + \gamma_{KAP} TRH, \tag{77}$$

where $0 < \gamma_{KAP} < 1$.

4.2.7   Consumption, Savings, and Investment

Each category of household h saves a constant fraction, $0 < savrate_h < 1$, of its disposable income:

$$SAV_h = savrate_h(1 - inctax_h)YH_h, \tag{78}$$

where $0 < inctax_h < 1$ is the income tax rate applicable to household h, with $inctax_I = 0$ (households located in the informal sector are not subject to direct taxation).

The portion of disposable income that is not saved is allocated to consumption:

$$CON_h = (1 - inctax_h)YH_h - SAV_h.$$

The accumulation of capital over time depends on the flow level of investment, Z_P, and the depreciation rate of capital from the previous period, δ_P:[10]

$$K_P = (1 - \delta_P)K_{P,-1} + Z_{P,-1}, \tag{79}$$

where $0 < \delta_P < 1$ is a constant depreciation rate.

---

[10]Capital gains or losses associated with changes in the price of capital are assumed to affect changes of firms' net worth (given by $PK \cdot K - ER \cdot FL_P$) over time, without any direct feedback on the economy. This would not be the case if the model had a financial sector, as discussed in the next three chapters.

The aggregate identity between savings and investment implies that total domestic investment, given by $PK \cdot Z_P + PQ_P Z_G$, must be equal to total savings, which in turn is equal to firms' after-tax retained earnings, total after-tax household savings, government savings, and foreign borrowing by firms and the government:

$$PK \cdot Z_P + PQ_P Z_G = re \cdot YF_P + \sum_h SAV_h + CBAL + ER(\Delta FL_P + \Delta FL_G),$$

(80)

where FL_G is foreign borrowing by the government (net of changes in reserves, and assumed exogenous in foreign-currency terms) and $CBAL$ the current public budget balance (with a negative value denoting a deficit). In the simulations reported below, this equation is solved residually for the level of private investment, Z.

Thus, the model is "savings driven" (corresponding to the "classical" closure rule discussed by Dewatripont and Michel (1987)) – a reasonable assumption in our view for Morocco, in light of the behavior of net saving during the second part of the 1990s. Indeed, during the period 1996–9, net government dissaving was accompanied by an increase in net private saving, which may have resulted from private investment being lower than otherwise. In addition, as noted by Schmidt-Hebbel and Muller (1992) in their review of the behavior of private investment during the period 1970–88, public sector deficits had a strong negative impact on private capital formation in Morocco. Of course, alternative closure rules are possible. For instance, with private investment treated as exogenous, equation (80) could be solved for the savings rate of capitalists-rentiers, as in Chapter 3. This closure rule would make the model "investment driven."

4.2.8 Government

Government expenditures consist of government consumption, which only has demand-side effects, and public investment, which has both demand- and supply-side effects. In line with all IMMPA models, public investment consists of investment in infrastructure, education, and health. We define investment in infrastructure as the expenditure affecting the accumulation of public infrastructure capital, which includes public assets such as roads, power plants and railroads. Investment in education affects the stock of public education capital, which consists of assets such as school buildings and other infrastructure affecting skills acquisition, but does not represent human capital. In a similar fashion, investment in health adds to the stock of public assets such as hospitals and other health facilities.

From (10), $PV_G V_G - (W_{UG} U_G + W_{SG} S_G) = 0$, that is, all value added in the production of public goods is distributed as wages. Thus, the current fiscal balance, $CBAL$, is defined as

$$CBAL = TXREV - TRH - NG - IF_G ER \cdot FL_{G,-1},$$ (81)

where $TXREV$ denotes total tax revenues, TRH total government transfers to households, NG total current expenditure on goods and services, and IF_G the interest rate on net foreign borrowing. The last term on the right-hand side measures interest payments on foreign public debt.

Net government saving is equal to the overall government budget balance, *OBAL*, and is obtained by subtracting public investment expenditure to the current fiscal balance:

$$OBAL = CBAL - PQ_P Z_G, \tag{82}$$

where, given our assumption that only the private urban good is used for capital accumulation, we calculate nominal investment outlays by multiplying Z_G by the composite price, PQ_P.

Total tax revenues, *TXREV*, consist of revenues generated by import tariffs, sales taxes, income taxes (on both households and firms in the urban private sector), and payroll taxes:

$$\begin{aligned} TXREV = {}& (wpm_{AN} tm_{AN} M_{AN} ER) + (wpm_P tm_P M_P ER) \\ & + \sum_i indtax_i PX_i X_i + inctax_{KAP} YH_{KAP} \\ & + inctax_r (YH_{AT} + YH_{AN}) + inctax_{UU}(YH_{UF} + YH_S) \\ & + ptax_U W_M U_P + ptax_S W_S S_P + inctax_F PROF_P. \end{aligned} \tag{83}$$

Government investment is the sum of investment in infrastructure, I_{INF}, investment in health, I_H, and investment in education, I_E, which are all considered exogenous policy variables:

$$Z_G = I_{INF} + I_E + I_H. \tag{84}$$

Government investment increases the stock of public capital in either infrastructure, education or health. The stock of public capital in education includes items such as school buildings, whereas the stock of health capital includes hospitals and the like. Infrastructure capital includes all other stocks of public property, such as roads, railroads, and power plants. Accumulation of each type of capital is defined as:

$$K_i = K_{i,-1}(1 - \delta_i) + I_{i,-1}, \quad i = INF, H, E, \tag{85}$$

and where $0 < \delta_i < 1$ is a depreciation rate.

Infrastructure and health capital affect the production process in the private sector as they both combine to produce the composite stock of government capital, K_G:

$$K_G = CES(K_{INF}, K_H). \tag{86}$$

Given the aggregate saving-investment balance defined earlier (see equation (80)), fiscal balance ($OBAL = 0$) does not need to be imposed period by period; all else equal, a higher public deficit would translate into lower private investment. Alternatively, it could be assumed that the budget is kept continuously in balance ($OBAL = 0$) through an adjustment in spending. In that case, equations (81) and (82) would be solved residually for *NG*.

4.2.9   Balance of Payments

The external constraint implies that any current account surplus (or deficit) must be compensated by a net flow of foreign capital, given by the sum of changes in net foreign loans made to the government, ΔFL_G, and to private firms, ΔFL_P:

$$0 = \sum_i (wpe_i E_i - wpm_i M_i)$$

$$+ REMIT - IF \cdot FL_{P,-1} - IF_G FL_{G,-1} + \Delta FL_G + \Delta FL_P, \qquad (87)$$

where the flow of remittances is given by

$$REMIT = W_F FORL_{-1}, \qquad (88)$$

with W_F denoting again the foreign wage measured in foreign-currency terms, and $FORL$ the stock of domestic workers abroad, given by

$$FORL = (1 - \delta_{IMIG})FORL_{-1} + IMIG, \qquad (89)$$

where $0 < \delta_{IMIG} < 1$ is the rate of "attrition" of the stock of migrants living abroad. Equation (88) indicates that there is a one-period lag between changes in the number of migrants abroad and the flow of remittances.[11]

The Appendix to this chapter discusses briefly the calibration of the model and our choice of parameter values. Essentially, the model is calibrated using a social accounting matrix, which is described at length in Touhami (2003). Estimates of the various stock variables appearing in the model (such as the stock of private capital, and the stock of public capital in infrastructure, health and education), were obtained by using conventional perpetual inventory methods, assuming for public capital, full efficiency of investment outlays (see Chapter 3).

The parameter values that we have selected are taken as much as possible from the existing literature on Morocco (such as export and import elasticities) but are also in part "educated guesses," regarding most notably the relative importance of skilled wages, as opposed to skilled employment, in the trade union's utility function (equation (30)), and the leadership effect of public sector wages in the union's target wage (equation (32)). These parameters are obviously important in assessing the labor market effects of a variety of policy shocks. Although we limit ourselves below to presenting a small set of illustrative experiments, assessing the sensitivity of the results to alternative values of these parameters, as well as various others for which guesses needed to be made, is essential to assess the robustness of the policy conclusions that one should draw from the model.

---

[11]Walras' Law implies that one equilibrium condition may be dropped (say, the balance of payments or the savings–investment identity), because it will be automatically satisfied if all the other equilibrium conditions hold. However, as noted earlier, in the experiments reported below we use the savings–investment identity to solve for private investment.

4.3   Policy Experiments

As noted earlier, the constraints and challenges that Morocco faces in reforming its labor market are the result of a variety of structural factors, including the demographic structure of the population, the lack of sustained rates of economic growth (which translates into weak growth in labor demand), the high degree of vulnerability of the economy to exogenous shocks (such as droughts), and the distortions introduced by existing labor market regulations. In a context of high and persistent unemployment, we argued that labor market reforms should be at the forefront of the policy agenda in Morocco. Indeed, a number of development economists have taken the view that reducing hiring and firing regulations, restricting the scope of minimum wages (particularly among the young and unskilled), reducing nonwage labor costs and payroll taxes, and moderating the influence of trade unions in the collective bargaining process would improve flexibility and reduce unemployment.[12]

The IMMPA framework described earlier can be used to provide quantitative estimates of the effects of a variety of labor market policies on resource allocation, the rate of economic growth, and unemployment in Morocco. Specifically, we focus here on the impact of a reduction in the minimum wage (which is binding only for unskilled workers in the urban informal economy), and a reduction in payroll taxes on unskilled labor paid by urban private sector firms.

Unlike the experiment considered in Chapter 3, we consider here only a nonneutral shock in the second case, that is, with no offsetting change in revenue. The government must therefore borrow domestically to balance its budget, implying – in the absence of offsetting changes in private and foreign savings – full crowding out of private investment, as implied by the savings–investment balance (equation (80)). As noted later, this allows us to highlight the important general equilibrium links that relate labor market reforms and fiscal adjustment in Morocco.

4.3.1   Cut in the Minimum Wage

The simulation results associated with a permanent, 5-percent reduction in the minimum wage are illustrated in Tables 4.1 and 4.2, which display percentage or absolute changes from the baseline solution for a variety of sectoral, macroeconomic, and structural variables. Included in Table 4.2 is the real exchange rate, defined as a weighted average of the domestic-currency price of exports and imports (with weights based on initial trade flows), divided by a weighted average of the price of tradable agricultural goods and private sector goods (the only two sectors engaged in external trade).

---

[12]For instance, in a study of 19 Latin American countries, Rama (1995) found that economies with more flexible labor regimes experience higher productivity and faster growth, compared to those with a rigid labor code. Others have argued that the fairly limited impact of trade unions and other distortions on the labor market was an essential contributing factor to the sustained growth rates achieved in East Asia prior to the 1997–8 crisis.

Table 4.1 Morocco: simulation results. 5-percent reduction in minimum wage. (Percentage deviations from baseline, unless otherwise indicated)

					Periods					
	1	2	3	4	5	6	7	8	9	10
Real Sector										
Total resources	0.04	0.05	0.06	0.08	0.10	0.12	0.13	0.14	0.15	0.15
Gross domestic product	0.04	0.05	0.06	0.08	0.10	0.12	0.13	0.14	0.15	0.15
Imports of goods and NFS	0.04	0.05	0.07	0.09	0.11	0.13	0.14	0.15	0.16	0.16
Total expenditure	0.04	0.05	0.06	0.08	0.10	0.12	0.13	0.15	0.15	0.15
Total consumption	0.02	0.03	0.04	0.06	0.08	0.09	0.11	0.11	0.12	0.12
Private consumption	0.03	0.04	0.05	0.07	0.09	0.11	0.13	0.14	0.14	0.14
Public consumption	0.00	0.00	0.00	0.00	0.00	0.00	0.00	0.00	0.00	0.00
Total investment	0.06	0.07	0.09	0.12	0.15	0.17	0.19	0.20	0.20	0.20
Private investment	0.17	0.20	0.23	0.28	0.32	0.36	0.38	0.40	0.41	0.41
Public investment	−0.02	−0.02	−0.01	0.00	0.01	0.01	0.02	0.02	0.01	0.00
Exports of goods and NFS	0.06	0.07	0.10	0.12	0.14	0.17	0.19	0.21	0.22	0.23
External Sector (% of GDP)[1]										
Current account	0.00	0.00	0.00	0.00	0.00	0.00	0.00	0.00	0.00	0.00
Exports of goods and NFS	0.00	0.01	0.01	0.01	0.01	0.01	0.01	0.01	0.01	0.01
Imports of goods and NFS	0.00	0.00	0.00	0.00	0.00	0.00	0.00	0.00	0.00	0.00
Factor services	0.00	0.00	0.00	0.01	0.01	0.01	0.01	0.01	0.01	0.01
Capital account	0.00	−0.01	−0.01	−0.01	−0.01	−0.02	−0.02	−0.02	−0.02	−0.02
Private borrowing	0.00	0.00	0.00	0.00	0.00	0.00	0.00	0.00	0.00	0.00
Public borrowing	0.00	0.00	−0.01	−0.01	−0.01	−0.01	−0.02	−0.02	−0.02	−0.02
Government Sector (% of GDP)[1]										
Total revenue	0.00	0.00	0.00	0.00	0.00	0.00	0.00	0.00	0.00	0.00
Direct taxes	0.00	0.00	0.00	0.00	0.00	0.00	0.00	0.00	0.00	0.00
Indirect taxes	0.00	0.00	0.00	0.00	0.00	0.00	0.00	0.00	0.00	0.00

Continued

Table 4.1 Continued

					Periods					
	1	2	3	4	5	6	7	8	9	10
Total expenditure	-0.02	-0.02	-0.02	-0.03	-0.03	-0.04	-0.04	-0.05	-0.05	-0.05
Consumption	-0.01	-0.01	-0.01	-0.01	-0.02	-0.02	-0.02	-0.02	-0.02	-0.02
Investment	-0.01	-0.01	-0.01	-0.01	-0.02	-0.02	-0.02	-0.02	-0.02	-0.02
Transfers to households	0.00	0.00	0.00	0.00	0.00	0.00	0.00	0.00	0.00	0.00
Foreign interest payments	0.00	0.00	0.00	0.00	0.00	0.00	0.00	0.00	0.00	0.00
Total financing	-0.02	-0.02	-0.03	-0.04	-0.04	-0.05	-0.05	-0.06	-0.06	-0.06
Foreign financing	0.00	0.00	-0.01	-0.01	-0.01	-0.01	-0.02	-0.02	-0.02	-0.02
Domestic borrowing	-0.02	-0.02	-0.02	-0.03	-0.03	-0.04	-0.04	-0.04	-0.04	-0.04
Labor Market										
Nominal wages										
Agricultural sector	0.06	0.03	-0.01	-0.08	-0.14	-0.19	-0.23	-0.25	-0.25	-0.23
Informal sector	0.04	0.24	0.57	0.95	1.33	1.66	1.91	2.04	2.06	1.97
Private formal sector										
Unskilled	-5.01	-5.00	-5.00	-4.99	-4.98	-4.98	-4.97	-4.97	-4.97	-4.97
Skilled	0.01	0.02	0.04	0.06	0.08	0.10	0.13	0.15	0.18	0.21
Public sector										
Unskilled	-0.01	0.00	0.00	0.01	0.02	0.02	0.03	0.03	0.03	0.03
Skilled	-0.01	-0.01	0.00	0.01	0.01	0.02	0.02	0.03	0.03	0.02
Employment										
Agricultural sector										
Traded	-0.02	0.00	0.05	0.10	0.15	0.20	0.24	0.26	0.27	0.26
Non-traded	0.07	0.10	0.14	0.20	0.26	0.32	0.37	0.41	0.43	0.45
Informal sector	0.00	-0.18	-0.46	-0.79	-1.12	-1.41	-1.61	-1.72	-1.73	-1.65
Private formal sector										
Unskilled	3.71	3.72	3.73	3.75	3.76	3.78	3.79	3.80	3.80	3.81
Skilled	0.02	0.03	0.04	0.05	0.06	0.08	0.08	0.09	0.09	0.09

Public sector									
Unskilled	0.00	0.00	0.00	0.00	0.00	0.00	0.00	0.00	0.00
Skilled	0.00	0.00	0.00	0.00	0.00	0.00	0.00	0.00	0.00
Labor supply (urban formal)									
Unskilled	0.00	−0.01	−0.01	−0.03	−0.05	−0.07	−0.09	−0.12	−0.15	−0.17
Skilled	0.00	0.00	0.00	0.00	0.00	0.00	0.00	0.01	0.01	0.01
Workers abroad	0.00	0.02	0.06	0.09	0.11	0.13	0.13	0.12	0.10	0.08
Unemployment rate[1]									
Unskilled	−2.38	−2.39	−2.39	−2.41	−2.43	−2.46	−2.50	−2.53	−2.57	−2.61
Skilled	−0.01	−0.02	−0.03	−0.03	−0.04	−0.04	−0.05	−0.05	−0.05	−0.05
Real wage ratios[1]									
Expected urban-rural	0.00	−0.68	−0.57	−0.40	−0.21	−0.02	0.15	0.27	0.35	0.36
Expected formal-informal	0.00	−1.98	−2.32	−2.83	−3.38	−3.84	−4.16	−4.30	−4.26	−4.07
International-expected formal	0.00	2.04	1.80	1.39	0.90	0.42	0.02	−0.26	−0.41	−0.44
Migration[1]									
Rural-urban (% of urban unskilled labor supply)	0.00	−0.05	−0.08	−0.09	−0.09	−0.07	−0.04	−0.01	0.03	0.05
Formal-informal (% of urban formal unskilled labor supply)	0.00	−0.01	−0.01	−0.01	−0.02	−0.02	−0.02	−0.03	−0.03	−0.03
International migration (% of urban unskilled labor supply)	0.00	0.02	0.04	0.04	0.04	0.04	0.03	0.01	0.00	0.00
Memorandum items[2]									
GDP at market prices	0.05	0.06	0.07	0.08	0.09	0.10	0.11	0.12	0.13	0.14
Value added at factor cost	0.04	0.05	0.06	0.07	0.08	0.10	0.11	0.12	0.13	0.14
Value added in traded agricultural sector	−0.01	0.00	0.02	0.04	0.07	0.09	0.11	0.12	0.12	0.11
Value added in non-traded agricultural sector	0.02	0.02	0.03	0.05	0.06	0.07	0.08	0.09	0.10	0.10
Value added in urban informal sector	0.00	−0.01	−0.04	−0.07	−0.09	−0.12	−0.14	−0.15	−0.15	−0.14
Value added in urban formal sector	0.07	0.08	0.10	0.11	0.13	0.14	0.16	0.17	0.18	0.19
Private Consumption	0.04	0.04	0.06	0.07	0.08	0.10	0.11	0.12	0.13	0.13
Private Investment	0.19	0.22	0.25	0.29	0.32	0.35	0.38	0.40	0.41	0.42
Disposable income	0.04	0.04	0.05	0.06	0.08	0.09	0.10	0.11	0.11	0.11

[1] Absolute deviations from baseline. [2] In real terms.

Table 4.2 Morocco: price, poverty, and distributional indicators 5-percent reduction in unskilled labor minimum wage (Percentage deviations from baseline, unless otherwise indicated)

	Periods									
	1	2	3	4	5	6	7	8	9	10
Consumer Prices and the Real Exchange Rate[1]										
Rural CPI	0.00	0.00	0.00	0.01	0.02	0.02	0.03	0.03	0.03	0.03
Urban CPI	-0.01	-0.01	0.00	0.01	0.01	0.02	0.03	0.03	0.03	0.02
Unskilled	-0.01	-0.01	0.00	0.01	0.02	0.02	0.03	0.03	0.03	0.02
Skilled	-0.01	-0.01	0.00	0.01	0.01	0.02	0.02	0.03	0.03	0.02
Real exchange rate	0.02	0.02	0.02	0.02	0.01	0.01	0.01	0.02	0.02	0.03
Value Added Prices[1]										
Rural traded agriculture	0.05	0.05	0.03	0.00	-0.02	-0.04	-0.05	-0.05	-0.04	-0.03
Rural non-traded agriculture	0.13	0.14	0.14	0.14	0.13	0.14	0.15	0.17	0.20	0.24
Urban private informal	0.04	0.08	0.15	0.22	0.30	0.37	0.42	0.45	0.46	0.44
Urban private formal	-0.04	-0.04	-0.04	-0.03	-0.02	-0.01	-0.01	-0.02	-0.03	-0.04
Urban public	0.01	0.01	0.01	0.01	0.01	0.01	0.01	0.01	0.01	0.02
Real Disposable Income[1]										
Rural households	0.04	0.05	0.06	0.07	0.08	0.09	0.10	0.12	0.14	0.16
Traded agriculture	0.04	0.05	0.04	0.04	0.04	0.04	0.05	0.05	0.07	0.08
Non-traded agriculture	0.04	0.05	0.07	0.08	0.10	0.12	0.14	0.16	0.18	0.20
Urban households	0.03	0.04	0.05	0.07	0.08	0.09	0.10	0.10	0.10	0.09
Informal	0.05	0.07	0.10	0.14	0.18	0.21	0.24	0.26	0.26	0.26
Formal unskilled	-0.24	-0.24	-0.22	-0.20	-0.18	-0.17	-0.16	-0.16	-0.16	-0.17
Formal skilled	0.03	0.04	0.05	0.07	0.09	0.10	0.12	0.14	0.16	0.18
Capitalists and rentiers	0.07	0.07	0.08	0.09	0.10	0.10	0.10	0.10	0.09	0.08
Real Private Consumption[1]										
Rural households	0.04	0.05	0.06	0.07	0.08	0.09	0.10	0.12	0.14	0.16
Traded agriculture	0.04	0.05	0.04	0.04	0.04	0.04	0.05	0.05	0.07	0.08
Non-traded agriculture	0.04	0.05	0.07	0.08	0.10	0.12	0.14	0.16	0.18	0.20

Urban households	0.03	0.04	0.05	0.06	0.08	0.09	0.10	0.10	0.10	0.10	0.09
Informal	0.05	0.07	0.10	0.14	0.18	0.21	0.24	0.26	0.26	0.26	0.26
Formal unskilled	−0.24	−0.24	−0.22	−0.20	−0.18	−0.17	−0.16	−0.16	−0.16	−0.16	−0.17
Formal skilled	0.03	0.04	0.05	0.07	0.09	0.10	0.12	0.14	0.14	0.16	0.18
Capitalists and rentiers	0.07	0.07	0.08	0.09	0.10	0.10	0.10	0.10	0.10	0.09	0.08
Production Structure											
Size of informal sector (% of total output)	0.00	0.00	0.00	−0.01	−0.01	−0.01	−0.01	−0.01	−0.01	−0.01	−0.01
Size of agricultural sector (% of total output)	−0.01	−0.01	−0.01	−0.01	0.00	0.00	0.00	0.00	0.00	0.00	−0.01
Composition of Employment											
Employment in rural sector (% of total employment)	−0.04	−0.03	−0.02	−0.01	0.00	0.01	0.02	0.02	0.02	0.02	0.02
Employment in informal sector (% of total employment)	−0.01	−0.01	−0.03	−0.04	−0.06	−0.07	−0.08	−0.08	−0.08	−0.08	−0.07
Employment in informal sector (% of urban employment)	−0.01	−0.02	−0.04	−0.06	−0.07	−0.09	−0.10	−0.10	−0.10	−0.10	−0.09
Employment in public sector (% of total employment)	0.00	0.00	0.00	0.00	0.00	0.00	0.00	0.00	0.00	0.00	0.00
Employment in public sector (% of urban employment)	0.00	0.00	0.00	0.00	0.00	0.00	0.00	0.00	0.00	0.00	0.00
Private Expenditures											
Consumption (% of GDP)	0.00	−0.01	−0.01	0.00	0.00	0.00	0.00	0.00	−0.01	−0.01	−0.01
Consumption (% of total consumption)	0.00	0.01	0.01	0.01	0.01	0.02	0.02	0.02	0.02	0.02	0.02
Investment (% of GDP)	0.02	0.02	0.02	0.03	0.03	0.03	0.04	0.04	0.04	0.04	0.04
Investment (% of total investment)	0.05	0.05	0.06	0.07	0.08	0.08	0.09	0.10	0.10	0.10	0.10
Public Expenditures											
Consumption (% of GDP)	−0.01	−0.01	−0.01	−0.01	−0.02	−0.02	−0.02	−0.02	−0.02	−0.02	−0.02
Investment (% of GDP)	−0.01	−0.01	−0.01	−0.01	−0.02	−0.02	−0.02	−0.02	−0.02	−0.02	−0.02
Infrastructure (% of public investment)	0.00	0.00	0.00	0.00	0.00	0.00	0.00	0.00	0.00	0.00	0.00
Health (% of public investment)	0.00	0.00	0.00	0.00	0.00	0.00	0.00	0.00	0.00	0.00	0.00
Education (% of public investment)	0.00	0.00	0.00	0.00	0.00	0.00	0.00	0.00	0.00	0.00	0.00
Public sector wage bill (% of public expenditure)	0.00	0.00	0.00	0.00	0.00	0.00	0.00	0.01	0.01	0.01	0.01
External Sector											
Agricultural exports (% of total exports)	−0.03	−0.03	−0.02	−0.01	0.00	0.01	0.02	0.02	0.02	0.01	0.00
Imports of non-agricultural goods (% of total imports)	0.00	0.00	0.00	0.00	0.00	0.00	0.00	0.00	0.00	0.00	0.00
External debt (% of GDP)	−0.05	−0.07	−0.10	−0.13	−0.17	−0.21	−0.25	−0.27	−0.30	−0.30	−0.31
Degree of openness (total trade in % of GDP)	0.00	0.01	0.01	0.01	0.01	0.01	0.01	0.01	0.02	0.02	0.02

[1] Percentage deviations from baseline.

We limit our analysis to the first 10 periods (or years) after the shock, a time span that we refer to below as the "adjustment period." The experiment assumes, as noted earlier, that any fiscal imbalance is offset by an adjustment in private investment.

The impact effect of the reduction in the minimum wage is an increase in the demand for unskilled labor in the private sector by about 3.7 percent in the first year. This increase in demand is met by the existing pool of unskilled workers seeking employment in the urban sector.

As a result, the unskilled unemployment rate drops significantly, by about 2.4 percentage points. Both the increase in employment and the reduction in the unemployment rate of the unskilled display strong persistence over time.

In the medium and longer term, as the expected unskilled wage in the formal economy falls, formal–informal, rural–urban, and domestic–international migration dynamics set in. First, the increase in private formal sector employment (at the initial supply of unskilled workers in the formal sector) raises the probability of finding a job in that sector; however, this is not sufficient to offset the reduction in the minimum wage itself, and the expected formal sector wage for unskilled workers falls (by about 2 percentage points in the second year, for instance), relative to the informal sector wage. This leads to a reduction in the number of workers willing to queue for employment in the formal economy. After 10 years, the reduction in unskilled unemployment is about 2.6 percentage points, slightly higher than the impact effect. The reduction in the number of unskilled workers seeking employment in the formal private sector is accompanied by an increase in labor supply in the informal economy, which tends to push wages down in that sector. However, at the same time, the expected urban–rural wage falls, thereby reducing migration flows to urban areas and the supply of labor in the informal sector. The net effect is a reduction in the supply of workers in the informal economy (with employment falling by about 0.5 percent in period 3, 1.1 percent in period 5, and 1.7 percent in periods 8 to 10), which tends to put upward pressure on informal sector wages. This tends to further dampen the incentive to queue for employment in the formal private sector. Overall, both employment and activity fall in the informal sector, with real value added dropping by 0.14 percent by the end of the adjustment period. At the same time, the reduction in rural-to-urban migration flows is accompanied by higher employment, lower wages, and higher output in agriculture in the longer run, with real value added in both the traded and nontraded sectors increasing by about 0.1 percent after 10 years.

The initial reduction in the expected unskilled urban wage relative to the foreign wage increases incentives to migrate abroad; but due to the parameters of the model (the wage elasticity of these flows is assumed to be relatively small, and there is a high degree of persistence) international migration flows rise by only a small amount (when measured in proportion of the total urban unskilled labor force). The increase in the number of international migrants means also a reduction in the domestic supply of unskilled labor, which exerts upward pressure on informal sector wages (and thus the expected unskilled urban wage), thereby mitigating the initial incentive to migrate.

The reduction in the minimum wage, by reducing the relative cost of unskilled labor, also leads to some substitution among production factors over time. Because unskilled labor has a relatively high degree of substitution relative to the composite factor consisting of skilled labor and physical capital, the lower cost of that category of labor gives firms an incentive to substitute away from the skilled labor–physical capital bundle. However, this effect is not large, despite the fact that the skilled wage rises slightly after period 3, as a result of an increase in the price of the consumption basket of the skilled household (see equation (32) and Table 4.2).

In fact, the supply of skilled labor barely changes during the simulation period, given that the public stock of capital in education is exogenous and the elasticity of the education technology with respect to the skilled–unskilled expected wage differential is relatively low. However, because of the overall effect of output growth on labor demand (real value added in the urban formal sector rises over time, to about 0.2 by the end of the adjustment period), skilled employment tends to increase. As a result, the skilled unemployment rate also falls slightly over time.

The effect on real GDP is negligible during the first few years but tends to increase somewhat over time, as a result of the growth in real value added in agriculture and the urban formal sector. Aggregate disposable income, and private consumption and investment also tend to increase. Real disposable income and private consumption follow a similar pattern for each group, except for unskilled workers in the formal urban sector.

Regarding the government budget, there are two effects to consider. First, the price of the consumption basket for the urban skilled and unskilled households rises slightly over time (as a result of an increase in the demand for private formal goods), the nominal wage at which the government pays its workers increases also slightly over time (see equations (21) and (28)). Given that employment of both categories of workers is exogenous, the wage bill increases slightly (see Table 4.2), but this has no effect on the government current fiscal balance, as indicated in equation (81). Second, both public consumption and investment spending fall as a proportion of GDP, thereby reducing government borrowing from domestic agents.

Thus, given the macroeconomic "closure" rule adopted here, there is a "crowding in" effect on private investment, which increases in real terms by 0.4 percent after 10 years. The gradual increase in private physical capital accumulation has both short-term effects (which take the form of upward pressures on aggregate demand and prices) but also longer-term, supply-side effects, because it affects the marginal productivity of (and thus the demand for) all categories of labor.

4.3.2 Reduction in Payroll Taxes on Unskilled Labor

The simulation results associated with a permanent, 5 percentage point reduction in the payroll tax rate on unskilled labor are illustrated in Tables 4.3 and 4.4. As indicated earlier, we assume that the shock is nonneutral, implying that domestic borrowing by the government exerts (everything else equal) a full crowding out effect on private investment.

The impact effect of this shock is qualitatively similar to a cut in the minimum wage: by reducing the effective cost of unskilled labor, it tends to increase immediately the demand for that category of labor, by an average of 3.3 percent in the first and subsequent three years. The unskilled unemployment rate drops by 2 percentage points on impact.

Over time, the adjustment process of the labor market follows the same type of dynamics described earlier, except that now these dynamics operate in reverse: because the minimum wage does not change, and the probability of employment rises (as a result of the increase in unskilled labor demand induced by the tax cut), the expected formal–informal sector unskilled wage differential *increases*, by about 4.1 percent in period 2, and by larger amounts over time. This tends to draw labor out of the informal sector and to raise the number of unskilled job seekers in the formal sector.

At the same time, the increase in the expected urban wage (relative to the rural wage) draws labor out of the rural sector and into the informal economy. The net result is an increase in informal sector employment and a fall in informal sector wages. The reduction in employment in agriculture also leads to higher wages there, dampening over time (and eventually reversing) migration flows. The increase in the expected urban unskilled wage (due almost entirely to the increase in the employment probability in the formal sector) relative to the foreign wage leads to a fall in international migration flows.

In the longer run, real value added falls in all sectors – except the informal economy, which ends up absorbing part of the labor force that previously was seeking employment abroad. The reason is that the increase in government borrowing needs entailed by the reduction in the payroll tax tends to crowd out private investment, thereby reducing demand for formal sector goods and activity there. This tends to have also an adverse effect on tax revenue over time, thereby compounding the problem. Indeed, as the public deficit increases, the rate at which real private investment falls also increases over time (from −0.3 percent in period 2 to −0.9 percent in period 5, −1.9 percent in period 8, and −3.0 percent in period 10), generating therefore an unsustainable "downward" spiral of low activity, low employment and rising deficits.

In fact, after falling initially by 2 percentage points relative to its baseline value, the unskilled unemployment rate starts increasing again as a result of the reduction in the overall demand for labor in the formal economy, in addition to the increase in the number of job seekers in the formal economy. By the end of the adjustment period, the drop in the unskilled unemployment rate amounts to only 1.2 percentage points. The reduction in private investment lowers aggregate demand, puts downward pressure on prices, and slows physical capital accumulation – thereby reducing growth in the demand for all categories of labor over time. Indeed, skilled employment in the private sector falls at an increasing rate over time, due to its high degree of complementarity with physical capital, pushing unemployment up.

Thus, an important policy lesson can be drawn from this simulation: given the link between government borrowing needs and the private savings–investment balance, labor market reforms that entail an initial adverse effect on the government budget may do more harm than good if they are not accompanied by adequate fiscal reforms.

Table 4.3 Morocco: simulation results 5-percentage point reduction in unskilled payroll tax rate (Percentage deviations from baseline, unless otherwise indicated)

	Periods									
	1	2	3	4	5	6	7	8	9	10
Real Sector										
Total resources	0.03	0.01	−0.02	−0.06	−0.11	−0.15	−0.19	−0.23	−0.26	−0.28
Gross domestic product	0.03	0.01	−0.02	−0.06	−0.10	−0.15	−0.19	−0.22	−0.25	−0.28
Imports of goods and NFS	0.03	0.02	−0.02	−0.07	−0.12	−0.17	−0.21	−0.25	−0.27	−0.30
Total expenditure	0.03	0.01	−0.02	−0.06	−0.11	−0.15	−0.19	−0.23	−0.25	−0.27
Total consumption	0.06	0.04	0.02	−0.02	−0.06	−0.10	−0.13	−0.15	−0.16	−0.17
Private consumption	0.07	0.05	0.02	−0.02	−0.07	−0.12	−0.15	−0.18	−0.20	−0.21
Public consumption	0.00	0.00	0.00	0.00	0.00	0.00	0.00	0.00	0.00	0.00
Total investment	−0.07	−0.10	−0.14	−0.21	−0.28	−0.35	−0.43	−0.50	−0.57	−0.64
Private investment	−0.22	−0.31	−0.47	−0.69	−0.97	−1.27	−1.59	−1.95	−2.36	−2.88
Public investment	0.00	0.00	0.00	0.00	0.00	0.00	0.00	0.00	0.00	0.00
Exports of goods and NFS	0.03	0.02	−0.02	−0.07	−0.12	−0.17	−0.21	−0.25	−0.27	−0.30
External Sector (% of GDP)[1]										
Current account	0.00	0.00	0.01	0.01	0.02	0.02	0.03	0.02	0.02	0.01
Exports of goods and NFS	0.00	0.00	0.00	0.00	0.00	0.00	−0.01	−0.01	−0.02	−0.02
Imports of goods and NFS	0.00	0.00	0.00	0.00	0.00	−0.01	−0.01	−0.01	−0.01	−0.01
Factor services	0.00	0.00	0.00	−0.01	−0.02	−0.02	−0.02	−0.03	−0.02	−0.02
Capital account	0.00	0.00	0.00	0.01	0.01	0.02	0.02	0.03	0.03	0.04
Private borrowing	0.00	0.00	0.00	0.00	0.00	0.00	0.01	0.01	0.01	0.01
Public borrowing	0.00	0.00	0.00	0.00	0.01	0.01	0.02	0.02	0.03	0.03
Government Sector (% of GDP)[1]										
Total revenue	−0.04	−0.04	−0.03	−0.03	−0.03	−0.03	−0.03	−0.04	−0.04	−0.05
Direct taxes	0.00	0.01	0.01	0.01	0.01	0.01	0.01	0.01	0.01	0.00
Indirect taxes	−0.04	−0.04	−0.04	−0.04	−0.04	−0.04	−0.05	−0.05	−0.05	−0.05

Total expenditure	-0.01	-0.01	0.01	0.02	0.04	0.06	0.07	0.09	0.10	0.11
Consumption	0.00	0.00	0.00	0.01	0.02	0.03	0.03	0.04	0.05	0.05
Investment	-0.01	0.00	0.00	0.01	0.02	0.03	0.03	0.04	0.05	0.05
Transfers to households	0.00	0.00	0.00	0.00	0.00	0.00	0.00	0.00	0.01	0.01
Foreign interest payments	0.00	0.00	0.00	0.00	0.00	0.00	0.00	0.00	0.00	0.00
Total financing	0.02	0.03	0.04	0.06	0.08	0.10	0.12	0.14	0.16	0.18
Foreign financing	0.00	0.00	0.00	0.00	0.01	0.01	0.02	0.02	0.03	0.03
Domestic borrowing	0.02	0.03	0.04	0.05	0.07	0.09	0.10	0.12	0.13	0.15
Labor Market										
Nominal wages										
Agricultural sector	0.05	0.11	0.22	0.35	0.48	0.58	0.64	0.65	0.60	0.51
Informal sector	0.00	-0.47	-1.22	-2.06	-2.88	-3.57	-4.05	-4.29	-4.28	-4.05
Private formal sector										
Unskilled	-0.01	-0.02	-0.03	-0.05	-0.07	-0.09	-0.10	-0.09	-0.07	-0.04
Skilled	0.00	-0.01	-0.04	-0.07	-0.10	-0.12	-0.14	-0.14	-0.14	-0.12
Public sector										
Unskilled	-0.01	-0.02	-0.03	-0.05	-0.07	-0.09	-0.10	-0.09	-0.07	-0.04
Skilled	-0.01	-0.02	-0.03	-0.05	-0.07	-0.09	-0.09	-0.09	-0.07	-0.04
Employment										
Agricultural sector										
Traded	-0.02	-0.07	-0.17	-0.28	-0.39	-0.49	-0.56	-0.60	-0.60	-0.56
Non-traded	0.08	0.04	-0.04	-0.13	-0.24	-0.35	-0.46	-0.56	-0.66	-0.76
Informal sector	0.00	0.42	1.09	1.86	2.61	3.23	3.67	3.87	3.82	3.55
Private formal sector										
Unskilled	3.36	3.35	3.32	3.30	3.26	3.22	3.18	3.13	3.08	3.02
Skilled	0.02	0.01	0.00	-0.03	-0.06	-0.09	-0.14	-0.19	-0.25	-0.33
Public sector										
Unskilled	0.00	0.00	0.00	0.00	0.00	0.00	0.00	0.00	0.00	0.00
Skilled	0.00	0.00	0.00	0.00	0.00	0.00	0.00	0.00	0.00	0.00
Labor supply (urban formal)										
Unskilled	0.00	0.01	0.03	0.06	0.10	0.14	0.20	0.25	0.31	0.37
Skilled	0.00	0.00	0.00	0.00	-0.01	-0.01	-0.01	-0.01	-0.01	-0.01
Workers abroad	0.00	-0.05	-0.12	-0.18	-0.23	-0.26	-0.25	-0.23	-0.18	-0.13

Continued

Table 4.3 Continued

	Periods									
	1	2	3	4	5	6	7	8	9	10
Unemployment rate[1]										
Unskilled	−2.00	−1.95	−1.89	−1.81	−1.73	−1.63	−1.53	−1.43	−1.33	−1.22
Skilled	−0.01	−0.01	0.00	0.01	0.02	0.04	0.06	0.09	0.11	0.14
Real wage ratios[1]										
Expected urban-rural	0.00	1.45	1.20	0.82	0.39	−0.03	−0.38	−0.63	−0.75	−0.75
Expected formal-informal	0.00	4.06	4.91	6.18	7.53	8.70	9.51	9.88	9.80	9.35
International-expected formal	0.00	−4.85	−4.37	−3.46	−2.35	−1.25	−0.30	0.37	0.73	0.79
Migration[1]										
Rural-urban (% of urban unskilled labor supply)	0.00	0.11	0.18	0.19	0.17	0.12	0.06	−0.02	−0.09	−0.15
Formal-informal (% of urban formal unskilled labor supply)	0.00	0.01	0.02	0.03	0.04	0.05	0.05	0.06	0.06	0.05
International migration (% of urban unskilled labor supply)	0.00	−0.06	−0.09	−0.10	−0.10	−0.08	−0.06	−0.04	−0.02	0.00
Memorandum items[2]										
GDP at market prices	0.04	0.03	0.02	0.01	−0.01	−0.04	−0.07	−0.11	−0.16	−0.21
Value added at factor cost	0.04	0.03	0.02	0.00	−0.02	−0.05	−0.08	−0.12	−0.16	−0.21
Value added in traded agricultural sector	−0.01	−0.03	−0.07	−0.12	−0.17	−0.21	−0.23	−0.25	−0.25	−0.23
Value added in non-traded agricultural sector	0.02	0.01	−0.01	−0.03	−0.05	−0.08	−0.10	−0.12	−0.14	−0.17
Value added in urban informal sector	0.00	0.03	0.09	0.15	0.21	0.27	0.30	0.32	0.31	0.29
Value added in urban formal sector	0.07	0.05	0.04	0.02	−0.02	−0.06	−0.11	−0.17	−0.24	−0.33
Private Consumption	0.08	0.07	0.05	0.03	0.00	−0.03	−0.06	−0.09	−0.12	−0.16
Private Investment	−0.20	−0.27	−0.41	−0.62	−0.87	−1.17	−1.51	−1.91	−2.39	−3.01
Disposable income	0.08	0.07	0.05	0.03	0.00	−0.03	−0.06	−0.09	−0.13	−0.16

[1] Absolute deviations from baseline. [2] In real terms.

Table 4.4 Morocco: price, poverty, and distributional indicators 5-percentage point reduction in unskilled labor payroll tax rate (Percentage deviations from baseline, unless otherwise indicated)

					Periods					
	1	2	3	4	5	6	7	8	9	10
Consumer Prices and the Real Exchange Rate[1]										
Rural CPI	-0.01	-0.01	-0.03	-0.05	-0.06	-0.08	-0.09	-0.08	-0.07	-0.04
Urban CPI	-0.01	-0.02	-0.03	-0.05	-0.07	-0.09	-0.09	-0.09	-0.07	-0.04
Unskilled	-0.01	-0.02	-0.03	-0.05	-0.07	-0.09	-0.09	-0.09	-0.07	-0.04
Skilled	-0.01	-0.02	-0.03	-0.05	-0.07	-0.09	-0.09	-0.09	-0.07	-0.04
Real exchange rate	0.02	0.03	0.04	0.06	0.07	0.08	0.08	0.06	0.02	-0.03
Value Added Prices[1]										
Rural traded agriculture	0.05	0.07	0.11	0.16	0.21	0.23	0.24	0.21	0.16	0.08
Rural non-traded agriculture	0.15	0.16	0.19	0.22	0.24	0.22	0.17	0.07	-0.07	-0.27
Urban private informal	0.00	-0.09	-0.24	-0.41	-0.59	-0.74	-0.86	-0.94	-0.97	-0.97
Urban private formal	-0.04	-0.05	-0.07	-0.10	-0.12	-0.13	-0.12	-0.10	-0.05	0.03
Urban public	0.01	0.01	0.02	0.03	0.03	0.03	0.03	0.02	0.01	-0.02
Real Disposable Income[1]										
Rural households	0.04	0.04	0.03	0.03	0.02	0.00	-0.04	-0.08	-0.13	-0.20
Traded agriculture	0.04	0.04	0.06	0.07	0.07	0.07	0.05	0.01	-0.05	-0.13
Non-traded agriculture	0.04	0.03	0.02	0.00	-0.02	-0.05	-0.09	-0.13	-0.18	-0.24
Urban households	0.10	0.09	0.06	0.03	0.00	-0.04	-0.07	-0.10	-0.12	-0.15
Informal	0.01	-0.03	-0.10	-0.18	-0.27	-0.35	-0.43	-0.49	-0.54	-0.58
Formal unskilled	0.54	0.53	0.50	0.45	0.40	0.35	0.32	0.30	0.29	0.28
Formal skilled	0.02	0.01	0.00	-0.02	-0.05	-0.08	-0.11	-0.14	-0.18	-0.22
Capitalists and rentiers	0.07	0.06	0.04	0.02	-0.01	-0.04	-0.07	-0.10	-0.12	-0.15

Continued

Table 4.4 Continued

	Periods									
	1	2	3	4	5	6	7	8	9	10
Real Private Consumption[1]										
Rural households	0.04	0.04	0.03	0.03	0.02	0.00	−0.03	−0.08	−0.13	−0.20
Traded agriculture	0.04	0.04	0.06	0.07	0.07	0.07	0.05	0.01	−0.05	−0.13
Non-traded agriculture	0.04	0.03	0.02	0.00	−0.02	−0.05	−0.09	−0.13	−0.18	−0.24
Urban households	0.10	0.09	0.07	0.04	0.00	−0.03	−0.06	−0.09	−0.12	−0.15
Informal	0.01	−0.03	−0.10	−0.18	−0.27	−0.35	−0.43	−0.49	−0.54	−0.58
Formal unskilled	0.54	0.53	0.50	0.45	0.40	0.35	0.32	0.30	0.29	0.28
Formal skilled	0.02	0.01	0.00	−0.02	−0.05	−0.08	−0.11	−0.14	−0.18	−0.22
Capitalists and rentiers	0.07	0.06	0.04	0.02	−0.01	−0.04	−0.07	−0.10	−0.12	−0.15
Production Structure										
Size of informal sector (% of total output)	0.00	0.00	0.00	0.01	0.01	0.01	0.02	0.02	0.02	0.02
Size of agricultural sector (% of total output)	−0.01	−0.01	−0.01	−0.02	−0.02	−0.02	−0.02	−0.01	−0.01	0.00
Composition of Employment										
Employment in rural sector (% of total employment)	−0.03	−0.05	−0.07	−0.09	−0.12	−0.14	−0.15	−0.15	−0.14	−0.13
Employment in informal sector (% of total employment)	−0.01	0.01	0.04	0.08	0.11	0.14	0.16	0.16	0.16	0.15
Employment in informal sector (% of urban employment)	−0.01	0.01	0.05	0.09	0.14	0.17	0.19	0.20	0.20	0.19
Employment in public sector (% of total employment)	0.00	0.00	0.00	0.00	0.00	0.00	0.00	0.00	0.00	0.00
Employment in public sector (% of urban employment)	0.00	0.00	0.00	0.00	0.00	0.00	0.00	0.00	0.00	0.00

Private Expenditures										
Consumption (% of GDP)	0.03	0.03	0.03	0.02	0.02	0.02	0.02	0.03	0.04	0.05
Consumption (% of total consumption)	0.01	0.01	0.00	0.00	-0.01	-0.02	-0.02	-0.03	-0.03	-0.03
Investment (% of GDP)	-0.02	-0.03	-0.04	-0.05	-0.06	-0.08	-0.10	-0.11	-0.13	-0.14
Investment (% of total investment)	-0.05	-0.07	-0.10	-0.15	-0.20	-0.26	-0.31	-0.37	-0.43	-0.50
Public Expenditures										
Consumption (% of GDP)	0.00	0.00	0.00	0.01	0.02	0.03	0.03	0.04	0.05	0.05
Investment (% of GDP)	-0.01	0.00	0.00	0.01	0.02	0.03	0.03	0.04	0.05	0.05
Infrastructure (% of public investment)	0.00	0.00	0.00	0.00	0.00	0.00	0.00	0.00	0.00	0.00
Health (% of public investment)	0.00	0.00	0.00	0.00	0.00	0.00	0.00	0.00	0.00	0.00
Education (% of public investment)	0.00	0.00	0.00	0.00	0.00	0.00	0.00	0.00	0.00	0.00
Public sector wage bill (% of public expenditure)	0.00	-0.01	-0.01	-0.02	-0.02	-0.03	-0.03	-0.03	-0.02	-0.01
External Sector										
Agricultural exports (% of total exports)	-0.03	-0.05	-0.07	-0.10	-0.12	-0.14	-0.14	-0.12	-0.08	-0.03
Imports of non-agricultural goods (% of total imports)	0.00	0.00	0.00	0.00	0.00	0.00	-0.01	-0.01	-0.01	0.00
External debt (% of GDP)	-0.04	-0.02	0.03	0.09	0.17	0.25	0.34	0.42	0.49	0.57
Degree of openness (total trade in % of GDP)	0.00	0.00	0.00	0.00	0.00	-0.01	-0.01	-0.02	-0.02	-0.03

[1] Percentage deviations from baseline.

4.4   Concluding Remarks

Reducing unemployment and raising the rate of economic growth are key policy challenges in Morocco today. The purpose of this chapter has been to adapt the Mini-IMMPA framework presented in Chapter 3 to propose a tool that could be used to analyze the impact of a variety of macroeconomic and structural policies on growth and the labor market in Morocco. The first part of the chapter provided an overview of the Moroccan labor market, and identified some of the constraints and challenges that the country will continue to face in the coming years. The second part presented the model, which captures many of the characteristics of Morocco's labor market (already present in Mini-IMMPA), such as skilled and unskilled urban unemployment, the existence of firing costs, a signaling role of public sector wages on the union's target wage, payroll taxation in the private urban formal sector, as well as international labor migration. The extent to which high payroll taxes have tended to discourage the demand for unskilled labor has been an important policy issue in Morocco. Our framework allows us to consider how changes in these taxes affect employment and wages, taking into account their fiscal effects.

The third part of the chapter presented simulation results associated with a cut in the minimum wage and a reduction in payroll taxation on unskilled labor, under the assumption that government domestic borrowing exerts a crowding out effect on private investment. We showed that both policies may lead to a reduction in unskilled unemployment in the short term, and that the process of adjustment of the labor market involves similar sources of dynamics: rural-to-urban migration, formal–informal sector labor movements, and domestic–international migration flows. However, our second experiment also illustrates the potential problem associated with labor market reforms – the increase in government borrowing needs due initially to the reduction in the payroll tax was shown to crowd out private investment, thereby reducing demand for formal sector goods, activity, and demand for both categories of labor. The fall in output tends also to reduce tax revenue, thereby leading to an unsustainable increase in fiscal deficits over time. Moreover, the fall in investment translates over time into lower private capital, which hampers growth and the expansion of employment. Thus, tax-based labor market reforms in Morocco may bring few benefits in the long run if they are not accompanied by adequate fiscal adjustment.

The policy experiments considered here could be extended in a variety of directions. For instance, as in the previous chapter, one could consider budget-neutral changes in payroll taxation on unskilled labor involving adjustment in income taxes, reductions in transfers, or taxes on domestic sales. Although the qualitative implications of these alternative budget closure rules may be similar to those described earlier, the quantitative effects may differ significantly, particularly on the composition of employment in the formal sector. In addition, there are a variety of other labor market policies that can be analyzed in the present setting, such as the impact of reductions in firing costs, public sector layoffs (possibly coupled with an increase in employment subsidies to private, formal sector firms), changes in trade unions' preferences between wages and employment (see Agénor, Nabli, Yousef, and Jensen

(2004)). As noted earlier, in Morocco as well as in many other countries, firing costs have often been considered to be a major obstacle to labor market flexibility, because by constraining the ability of firms to react to adverse shocks they lead them to restrain (permanent) hiring in "good" times and to rely more on casual or temporary labor. Another important policy exercise would be to examine the effects of changes in the composition of public expenditure (that is, the allocation between investment in infrastructure, education, and health) on growth and employment.

Although some of these policy experiments would be useful in designing an appropriate sequence of labor market reforms for Morocco, the key policy message of the simulations reported in this chapter is likely to remain valid: labor market reforms that are associated with large (general equilibrium) fiscal effects may not be sufficient, by themselves, to increase employment durably. They must be devised in the context of a broader policy package (most likely involving significant changes in the allocation of public investment) designed to spur growth and employment.

Appendix
Calibration and Parameter Values

This Appendix presents a brief overview of the characteristics of the data underlying the model's social accounting matrix (SAM) and discusses the parameter values.[13]

The basic data set consists of a SAM and a set of initial levels and lagged variables. The SAM encompasses 27 accounts including production and retail sectors (4 accounts), labor production factors and profits (3 accounts), enterprises (1 account), households (5 accounts), government current expenditures and taxes (9 accounts), government investment expenditures (3 accounts), private investment expenditures (1 account), and the rest of the world (1 account). The actual SAM data are presented in Table A4.1.

The characteristics of the SAM data are summarized in the following. On the output side, agricultural and informal sectors are very small accounting for respectively 3 and 11 percent of total output. In contrast, private urban formal production account for almost 75 percent of total output. On the demand side, private current expenditures account for 68 percent of GDP, while government current expenditures account for 15 percent of GDP. At the same time, total investment expenditures represent 25 percent of GDP, implying that Morocco is running a trade deficit equivalent to 8 percent of GDP.

Looking at the balance of payments, total net remittances to households and net factor income to enterprises amounts to 2 percent of GDP. The ensuing current account deficit, amounting to 6 percent of GDP, is financed equally by private and public foreign borrowing. The trade balance are dominated by nonagricultural imports and exports; agricultural exports account for only 14 percent of total export earnings,

---

[13]The first part of this Appendix draws heavily on an unpublished note by Dr. Touhami, who built the SAM that we use for calibrating our model. A comprehensive description of the SAM is available in Touhami (2003).

Table A4.1 Morocco: social accounting matrix (Data in millions of 1990 dirhams)

Ressources	Dépenses N°	Facteurs de production 1	2	3	4	Agents économiques 5	6	7	8	9	10	11	12	13
Facteurs de production														
Travail rural non qualifié	1													
Travail urbain non qualifié	2													
Travail qualifié (urbain)	3													
Capital	4													
Agents économiques														
Ménages ruraux occupés dans des productions N.E.	5	1605.35		32569.17	6166.59	136.74	106.35	13.91	6.96	54.78	242.19		0.00	0.04
Ménages ruraux occupés dans des productions E.	6	10617.40		4071.15	13104.81	17.09	35.45	3.48	3.48	13.69	161.46		0.00	616.75
Ménages urbains non qualifiés employés dans l'informel	7		1040.26		7576.43	68.37	70.90	20.87	13.91	27.39	322.92		0.00	308.38
Ménages urbains non qualifiés employés dans le formel	8		2379.00			119.65	319.04	27.82	41.73	116.40	645.84		0.00	6834.34
Ménages urbains qualifiés	9			24426.87	38327.63	0.00	35.45	3.48	3.48	13.69	80.73	63.95	538.40	1294.72
Ménages capitalistes	10			20355.74	11058.59	0.00	141.80	0.00	0.00	47.93	161.46	703.49	2153.60	4140.48
Entreprises	11				2258.54	0.00	0.50	109.20	536.00	4038.80	2949.50	14552.00	3713.00	914.65
Etat	12				1605.00	0.00	0.00	0.00	0.00	69.60	116.00	−144.83	2330.00	6265.00
Reste du monde	13			67.60		0.00	0.00	0.00	0.00	0.00			7816.00	
Secteurs														
Production rurale N.E.	14													
Production rurale E.	15													
Production urbaine informelle	16													
Production urbaine formelle (privée)	17													
Production non marchande	18													
Demande de biens composites														
Produits ruraux N.E.	19					4547.05	2864.21	514.23	514.23	1121.79	1904.10			
Produits ruraux E.	20					8521.38	5192.72	1844.93	1844.93	4577.68	10075.50			
Produits urbains informels	21					2147.33	1473.85	560.48	560.48	1320.21	4078.65			
Produits urbains formels (privés)	22					19839.11	14516.74	5724.55	5724.55	13900.41	41902.89		33280.80	
Services non marchands	23					187.83	154.14	62.25	62.25	248.67	517.87			
Exportations														
Produits ruraux N.E.	24													0.85
Produits ruraux E.	25													5628.17
Produits urbains formels (privés)	26													35191.75
Accumulation	27					5317.49	3733.62	564.22	1171.82	909.74	2873.01	511.63	34560.77	7782.21
Total		12222.75	3419.26	81490.53	80097.59	40902.03	28644.76	9449.42	10483.82	26460.77	66032.12	15686.24	84392.57	68977.29

Continued

Table **A4.1** Continued

Ressources	N°	14	15	16	17	18	19	20	21	22	23	24	25	26	27	Total
		Secteurs de production					Produits destinés au marché domestique					Exportations			Accumulation	Total
Facteurs de production																
Travail rural non qualifié	1	1605.35	10617.40													12222.75
Travail urbain non qualifié	2			1040.26	1836.56	542.44										3419.26
Travail qualifié (urbain)	3				57376.76	24113.77										81490.53
Capital	4	6166.59	15417.42	12627.39	45839.37	46.82										80097.59
Agents économiques																
Ménages ruraux occupés dans des productions N.E.	5															40902.03
Ménages ruraux occupés dans des productions E.	6															28644.76
Ménages urbains non qualifiés employés dans l'informel	7															9449.42
Ménages urbains non qualifiés employés dans le formel	8															10483.82
Ménages urbains qualifiés	9															26460.77
Ménages capitalistes	10															66032.12
Entreprises	11															15686.24
Etat	12	464.23	1599.11	332.35			56.07	630.03		18905.00						84392.57
Reste du monde	13				29352.59	13.66	1780.54	1363.31		56304.07						68977.29
Secteurs																
Production rurale N.E.	14						14548.38					0.85				14549.23
Production rurale E.	15							43187.25					5628.17			48815.42
Production urbaine informelle	16								20000.00							20000.00
Production urbaine formelle (privée)	17									292751.12				35191.75		327942.86
Production non marchande	18										34513.80					34513.80
Demande de biens composites																
Produits ruraux N.E.	19	253.43	358.50	0.00	6001.83	13.78									-1708.14	16384.99
Produits ruraux E.	20	436.57	4130.69	0.00	8911.60	20.45									-375.86	45180.59
Produits urbains informels	21	0.00	0.00	6000.00	0.00	0.00									3859.00	20000.00
Produits urbains formels (privés)	22	5623.06	16692.31	0.00	178624.16	9762.89									55649.51	367960.18
Services non marchands	23	0.00	0.00	0.00	0.00	0.00									0.00	34513.80
Exportations																
Produits ruraux N.E.	24															0.85
Produits ruraux E.	25															5628.17
Produits urbains formels (privés)	26															35191.75
Accumulation	27															57424.51
Total		14549.23	48815.42	20000.00	327942.86	34513.80	16384.99	45180.59	20000.00	367960.18	34513.80	0.85	5628.17	35191.75	57424.51	

whereas non-agricultural imports account for 95 percent of total import expenditures. The level of trade openness, measured by the ratio of the sum of imports and exports to GDP, amounts to a moderate 44 percent.

Looking at the government budget, indirect taxes in the form of production and retail level taxes account for 62 percent of total government revenues excluding intergovernment transfers. Enterprise tax revenues, amounting to 18 percent of total government income, represent the largest revenue item among direct tax items, while combined factor and household taxes account for only 12 percent of revenues. Foreign borrowing accounts for the remaining 8 percent of government revenues. On the expenditure side, domestic and foreign transfers account for respectively 8 and 9 percent of the budget, while consumption and savings for investment purposes amount to respectively 40 and 42 percent of the budget. Overall, the Moroccan government relies heavily on indirect taxes for revenue collection, while maintaining almost equal proportions between consumption and saving for investment purposes.

Consider now the behavioral parameters. The elasticity of substitution of the public capital stock with the private capital–skilled labor bundle in the production of the private good, σ_{XP}, is set to zero, implying perfect complementarity. The elasticities of substitution of public capital with unskilled labor in production of agricultural goods, σ_{XAN} and σ_{XAT}, are both equal to 0.75. The elasticity of substitution between unskilled labor and the capital–skilled labor bundle in the private formal sector, σ_{XP1}, is 0.7. The elasticity of substitution between skilled labor and private capital, σ_{XP2}, is 0.3. The Armington elasticities, ρ_{QA} and ρ_{QP}, are taken to be 0.25 and zero respectively. σ_{QA} and σ_{QP} are 0.8 and 1 respectively. The CET transformation elasticity, σ_{TP}, is 1, and the export demand elasticity, σ_{TP}, is also 1.

The depreciation rate of private capital, δ_P, is 0.08. The congestion effect on the use of public goods in production, $dcop$, is zero. Nominal wages are fully indexed on the relevant price index. The elasticity of the skilled wage with respect to unemployment, ϕ_1, and with respect to firing costs, ϕ_2, are both equal to 0.1, whereas the elasticity with respect to the public sector wage, ϕ_3, is 0.5. The relative weight of wages in the trade union's utility function, υ, is 0.1, which indicates that the union cares more about employment than wages. The weight of relative wages in the migration equation, λ_m, is 0.3. The elasticity of migration with respect to the expected wage differential, σ_m, is 0.1. The degree of persistence in international migration flows, λ_{im}, is 0.1. The elasticity of international migration with respect to the expected wage differential, σ_{im}, is 0.1. The adjustment coefficient on skills acquisition, λ_s, is 0.1. The impact of relative wages on skills acquisition, σ_w, is 0.5. The elasticity of skills acquisition with respect to the public capital stock in education, σ_E, is 0.8273. The degree of persistence of migration flows to the formal sector, β_F, is 0.1. The elasticity of substitution between infrastructure capital and health, σ_G, is equal to 0.75. Finally, the initial share parameter for the infrastructure component, β_G, is 0.75.

Chapter 5

The Complete IMMPA Framework for Low-Income Countries

Pierre-Richard Agénor, Alejandro Izquierdo, and Hippolyte Fofack

This chapter presents the complete IMMPA prototype for low-income countries.[1] Just like Mini-IMMPA, it dwells on the extensive analytical and applied research conducted in academic and policy circles over the past two decades on macroeconomic and structural adjustment issues in developing economies. It emphasizes, most notably, the role of labor market segmentation (induced either by government legislation or firms' wage-setting decisions) and the role of informal employment in the transmission of policy and exogenous shocks to the poor. The detailed treatment of the labor market is particularly important, as noted in previous chapters, to assess the poverty effects of adjustment programs, because the poor often generate their main source of income from wages, and the latter depend on available employment opportunities. It also accounts for the role of public capital on private production and the accumulation of physical and human capital, with public investment decomposed into infrastructure, education, and health.

At the same time, it goes beyond Mini-IMMPA by adding a fairly detailed financial side. In particular, it accounts for credit market imperfections and linkages between the financial system and the real side of the economy, by relating firms' borrowing needs (for both working capital and physical capital formation) to bank lending.

---

[1]As discussed in the concluding section and the next two chapters, most of the building blocks of the low-income IMMPA prototype are also relevant for policy analysis in middle-income economies.

Because of its integrated treatment of the real and financial sides, the model allows policy analysts to study not only the impact of structural reforms (such as changes in tariffs or increases in tax rates) on growth, income inequality, and poverty, but also the effect of short-term stabilization policies (such as a cut in domestic credit or a rise in policy interest rates) as well as other financial shocks (such as an outflow of private capital or a rise in world interest rates).

The prototype also accounts for a possible negative effect of external debt on private investment. Such a relationship can result from various channels, including disincentive effects associated with a large external debt. Indeed, several studies, evolving from Krugman (1988) and Sachs (1989), have argued that an excessive amount of debt raises expectations of higher future (implicit or explicit) taxation and confiscation risk to satisfy debt service payments. This, in turn, creates disincentives to invest – most notably by lowering the expected after-tax rate of return on capital – and may generate capital flight and lower net private capital inflows, as well as, in the longer term, lower growth.[2] Studies by Elbadawi, Ndulu, and Ndungu (1997), Iyoha (2000), Pattillo, Poirson, and Ricci (2002), and Clements, Bhattacharya, and Nguyen (2003), provide some recent empirical evidence of a negative relationship between external debt and private capital formation, or between external debt and growth, for Sub-Saharan Africa. Iyoha (2000) for instance, in a study covering the period 1970–94, found that the ratio of external debt to GDP had a significant and negative effect on gross domestic investment. Pattillo, Poirson, and Ricci (2002), in a study covering 93 developing countries over 1969-98, found that on average external debt begins to have a negative marginal impact on growth – possibly as a result of lower public, as well as private, investment – when it reaches about 160–70 percent of exports or 35–40 percent of GDP. Clements, Bhattacharya, and Nguyen (2003), focusing on low-income countries only, found a critical threshold of 50 percent when the face value of debt is used. In the IMMPA prototype presented in this chapter, we capture adverse incentive effects of a debt overhang by introducing a nonlinear effect of the ratio of debt service to taxes on private investment. As a result, the higher the initial level of public external debt, the stronger the negative marginal effect of a further increase in foreign borrowing on private capital formation.

The remainder of the chapter is organized as follows. Section 5.1 describes in detail the structural component of the low-income IMMPA prototype. Section 5.2 explains the link between the structural component of IMMPA and a household expenditure survey. Section 5.3 discusses issues associated with the calibration and solution of the model and the extent to which our parameters and initial values can be deemed "representative" of a poor, highly-indebted economy. Section 5.4 presents the simulation results of various shocks (both exogenous and policy-induced) and discusses their real, financial, distributional, and poverty effects. We analyze, in turn, the short- and long-run impact of a temporary terms-of-trade shock, a permanent cut in domestic credit to the government, and a poverty-reduction program consisting of partial external debt forgiveness coupled with a reallocation of savings made on debt

---

[2] As pointed out by Husain (1997), the taxation ability of the debtor government may be important in determining the magnitude of the debt overhang effect on private investment.

service payments to three alternative forms of government expenditure: lump-sum transfers to households, spending on infrastructure and outlays on education. This last experiment is of particular interest in light of the current international debate (alluded to in the introduction to this volume) on the need for debt relief for low-income countries – conditional on a productive use of associated savings. The last section summarizes the main results and suggests various extensions.

5.1   Model Structure

This section reviews the various building blocks of the structural component of the low-income IMMPA prototype. We consider in turn the production side, employment, the demand side, external trade, sectoral and aggregate prices, income formation, the financial sector and asset allocation decisions, and the public sector. We specify behavioral functions for each of the six broad categories of agents included in IMMPA: households (disaggregated by levels of skills and location into various types of rural and urban households), firms, the government, the central bank, commercial banks, and the rest of the world. Throughout the discussion, as in Chapter 4, we often use "generic" forms to specify functional relationships.[3]

5.1.1   Production

In many low-income countries, the majority of the poor lives in rural areas; it is therefore essential for a framework whose aim is to help policymakers design poverty-reduction programs to be able to trace differences in economic performance between the rural and urban sectors. We therefore begin with a distinction on the production side between these sectors. The rural economy (or agriculture, for short) is itself divided between a tradable sector, which produces a homogeneous good sold only abroad, and a nontraded goods sector, which produces a good sold only domestically. The rationale that underlies this distinction can be found in the available evidence on the structure of the rural labor market, which suggests the existence of an often large wage differential between workers employed in the production of predominantly exported agricultural goods and workers producing mainly for the domestic market – many of whom are involved in subsistence agriculture (see for instance Bigsten and Horton (1998)). Because the poverty implications of such differentials can be large, our strategy is to model them separately – unlike the specification adopted in the Mini-IMMPA framework presented in Chapter 3, which assumes that only one good is produced in the rural sector. There is therefore no smooth transformation curve (with a conventional concave shape) between domestic sales and exports of agricultural goods.

---

[3]Explicit functional forms (as well as variable names and definitions) are provided in Appendices A and B of the original paper, which can be downloaded from the World Bank website (Working Paper No. 3092).

Although income in the urban economy tends on average to be higher than in the rural sector, the incidence of poverty has increased significantly (and sometimes dramatically) in urban areas in many low-income countries. Concomitantly, the informal economy has grown in size in these countries, in part as a result of the lack of employment opportunities in the formal sector and the pervasiveness of labor market segmentation. We account for these characteristics by including both formal and informal components when specifying urban production. Furthermore, we separate the formal urban economy into production of private goods (which are sold abroad and domestically) and a public good.

Rural Production

Gross output of nontraded goods, X_{AN}, and exported agricultural goods, X_{AT}, are given by the sum of value added (V_{AN} and V_{AT}, respectively) and intermediate consumption:

$$X_j = V_j + X_j \sum_i a_{ij}, \quad j = AN, AT \tag{1}$$

where the a_{ij} are conventionally-defined input-output coefficients (sales from sector i to sector j) and AN, AT, I, P, G are used in what follows to refer, respectively, to the nontraded agricultural sector, the traded agricultural sector, the informal sector, the private urban sector, and the public sector. As in previous chapters, use of the index i or j without precision will refer to all five sectors.

Value added in each sector is assumed to be produced with a Cobb-Douglas (CD) function of land, *LAND*, and a composite factor, defined as a constant elasticity of substitution (CES) function that depends on the number of unskilled rural workers employed (U_{AN} in the nontraded-good sector and U_{AT} in the traded-good sector) and the economy-wide stock of public physical capital, K_G:

$$V_j = CD[LAND_j, CES(U_j, K_G)], \quad j = AN, AT \tag{2}$$

Land available for each production activity in the rural sector is assumed to be in fixed supply and there is no market to trade property claims on it. As noted above, we assume that land is a fixed input in each sector; and for simplicity, we normalize the area of land allocated to production to unity in what follows. Given the CD specification, agricultural production exhibits decreasing returns to scale in the remaining (composite) input.

The introduction of K_G in the production functions (2) is based on the view that public capitgal in the economy improves the productivity of private firms and other production units in agriculture, because it facilitates not only trade and domestic commerce but also the production process itself. Thus, our concept of public capital includes not only roads and public transportation that may increase access to markets, but also power plants and similar public goods that may contribute to an increase in productivity.

As discussed later, the private, formal urban sector produces a single tradable good that may be either sold domestically or abroad. By contrast, the structure of the rural economy is rather different: we assume that production of the rural traded good, X_{AT}, is exclusively allocated to exports, whereas the nontraded agricultural good is exclusively produced for the domestic market ($X_{AN} = D_{AN}$). The reason for choosing this approach is that in some countries, there is often a sharp contrast between the "external" component of the agricultural sector, where production is mostly targeted to foreign markets, and the "domestic" component, where production is targeted mainly toward domestic consumers. The production process, access to bank credit, and wage formation mechanisms often differ significantly across these components, making the assumption of a smooth production possibility frontier inappropriate. This formulation therefore extends the specification adopted in Mini-IMMPA.

Urban Informal Production

Gross production in the urban informal sector, X_I, is given as the sum of value added, V_I, and intermediate consumption,

$$X_I = V_I + X_I \sum_i a_{iI}, \qquad (3)$$

with value added given as a function of the number of unskilled workers employed in the informal economy, U_I, with decreasing returns to scale:

$$V_I = \alpha_{XI} U_I^{\beta_{XI}}, \quad \alpha_{XI} > 0, \ 0 < \beta_{XI} < 1. \qquad (4)$$

Given that the available evidence suggests that production in the informal sector is relatively intensive in labor, we take β_{XI} to be relatively high in our policy experiments.

Production of the Public Good

Gross production of the composite public good, X_G, is given by the sum of value added, V_G, and intermediate consumption:

$$X_G = V_G + X_G \sum_i a_{iG}, \qquad (5)$$

Production of value added requires both types of labor (skilled and unskilled) and is given by a two-level CES function. At the lower level, unskilled workers, U_G, and skilled workers, S_G, combine to produce "effective" employment in the public sector. At the second level, effective labor and public capital, K_G combine to produce net output:

$$V_G = CES[CES(S_G, U_G), K_G]. \qquad (6)$$

Employment levels of both categories of workers are treated as predetermined. This specification of the production process of the public sector good makes it possible to analyze the effects of changes in government employment. Public sector layoffs, for instance, will influence the rest of the economy through changes in both labor supply to other segments of the labor market, and a reduction in public sector output.

As indicated later, wages for skilled workers in the public sector are set equal to the efficiency wage paid to that category of workers in the private formal sector. Wages for unskilled workers in the public sector are, by contrast, set equal to the minimum wage; unskilled workers are therefore "off" their labor supply curve. We will assume that "excess" employment (or disguised unemployment) of unskilled labor prevails in the public sector, as documented in some studies of the labor market in developing countries.[4] As a result, output is never constrained.

Urban Formal Private Production

Gross production of the private formal urban sector, X_P, is the sum of value added, V_P, and intermediate consumption:

$$X_P = V_P + X_P \sum_i a_{iP}. \tag{7}$$

As with the production of the public good, private formal production also uses skilled and unskilled labor. In addition, physical capital is also included as an input in the production process. An important step in specifying the production technology consists of defining the degree of substitutability among inputs. We assume – as suggested by some of the empirical evidence reviewed in Chapter 1 – that skilled labor and private physical capital have a higher degree of complementarity (lower degree of substitution) than physical capital and unskilled workers. In order to account explicitly for these differences in the degree of substitutability among inputs, we adopt a nested CES production structure. Specifically,

$$V_P = CES\{CES[CES(ef \cdot S_P, K_P), U_P], K_G\}, \tag{8}$$

where ef, as discussed below, denotes the level of on-the-job effort provided by skilled workers.

At the lowest level of equation (8), the effective supply of skilled labor, $ef \cdot S_P$, and private capital, K_P, are used in the production of the composite input T_2 (assuming a low elasticity of substitution between them). At the second level, this composite input is used, together with unskilled labor, U_P, to produce the composite input T_1. With this specification it is possible to choose a higher elasticity of substitution between T_2, and unskilled workers, U_P. In other words, whereas skilled labor and private physical capital are essentially complements, either one of these inputs is a substitute to unskilled labor in the production process. The final layer of this nested CES has T_1 and K_G (the stock of government capital) as inputs in the production of private formal urban output.

Given our assumption that both the public and informal goods are not traded (that is, they are sold only on the domestic market), the private formal urban good is the only component of urban production that can be exported abroad. In line with conventional CGE models (see, for instance, Dervis, De Melo, and Robinson (1982), Devarajan et al. (1997), and Robinson et al. (1999)), we assume that firms choose to allocate their output either to exports, E_P, or to the domestic market, D_P, according to a production possibility frontier, defined by a Constant Elasticity of Transformation (CET) function:

$$X_P = CET(E_P, D_P). \tag{9}$$

---

[4]See Agénor (1996), who discusses the role of political factors in the determination of public sector employment, and Rodrik (2000) for an alternative view.

As discussed later, the actual ratio of E_P over D_P depends on the relative prices of exported and domestic goods.

5.1.2   Wage Formation, Employment, Migration, and Skills Acquisition

As mentioned earlier, there are two types of workers in this model: skilled and unskilled. In practice, of course, there is a continuum of skills, but one may want to think of our distinction as a broad one that suffices for analytical purposes.

Unskilled workers may be employed either in the rural economy, U_R, or in the urban sector, U_U, whereas skilled workers are employed only in the urban economy.[5] We also assume that skilled workers are not employed in the informal economy either – perhaps as a result of signaling considerations, as discussed in previous chapters. In practice, there may obviously be many cases in which (semi-)skilled workers take part in the informal labor force. However, their productivity should not differ much from that of unskilled workers, at least in part because monitoring is relatively easier than in the formal economy (this being in turn related to the smaller size of production units in the informal sector). As a result, modeling them differently would not substantially alter the results of a a broad range of experiments.

Rural Wages and Employment

The available empirical evidence on wages in the rural economy of many low-income developing countries suggests that there is a significant discrepancy between wages paid in the export sector (cash crops and other agricultural products), and wages paid in the nontraded sector (namely, food crops). Because of higher wages in the export sector, all workers in rural areas will opt to seek employment there first. In general, nominal wages in the export sector, W_{AT}, can be indexed on either the value added price or gross output price in that sector, or the economy-wide consumer price, so that

$$W_{AT} = w_{AT}(PIND_{AT})^{ind_{AT}}, \tag{10}$$

where $PIND_{AT} = PV_{AT}, PX_{AT},$ or $PLEV$, and $0 \le ind_{AT} \le 1$, with PV_{AT} (PX_{AT}) being the price of value added (gross output) in the export sector, and $PLEV$ the consumer price index.

In the simulations reported later, we take the degree of indexation to be perfect with respect to the price of value added (as a result, say, of strong bargaining power of workers), so that $PIND_{AT} = PV_{AT}$, and $ind_{AT} = 1$. Thus, the product wage, w_{AT}, is fixed and firms are assumed to hire workers up to the optimal level given by their labor demand curve. From (2), the profit-maximizing demand function for labor in

---

[5] This is of course a simplification, as there are some firms, located in the rural area, which may require skilled labor.

the export sector, U^d_{AT}, is thus

$$U^d_{AT} = \left\{ V^{1+\rho_{XAT}/(1-\eta_{XAT})}_{AT} \frac{1-\eta_{XAT}}{(1+IL_{-1})w_{AT}} \cdot \frac{\beta_{XAT}}{\alpha^{\rho_{XAT}}_{XAT}} \right\}^{1/(1+\rho_{XAT})}, \qquad (11)$$

where $w_{AT} = W_{AT}/PV_{AT}$. Equation (11) indicates that labor demand in the rural export sector is positively related to the level of net output, V_{AT}, and negatively related to the effective product wage, $(1+IL_{-1})w_{AT}$. Labor demand does not depend directly on the price of the exported agricultural good, PX_{AT} (which is proportional to the value added price, as shown below in equation (46)), because the nominal wage paid to workers, W_{AT}, varies proportionally to PV_{AT} in order to keep the real wage rate fixed at w_{AT}. Of course, the assumption of perfect real (product) wage rigidity is not necessarily appropriate for all countries; there are cases where partial indexation of nominal wages might be more appropriate.

Note also that the product wage rate is multiplied by $(1+IL_{-1})$, where IL_{-1} is the one-period lagged bank lending rate, to account for the fact that firms in this sector rely on working capital to pay wages in advance of the sale of output. As a result, firms consider the *effective* price of labor, which includes the cost of borrowing, when making labor hiring decisions.[6] We assume that the cost of credit specified in loan contracts negotiated for the current period is based on the interest rate prevailing in the previous period.[7]

The supply of labor to the nontraded agricultural sector is determined residually, as the number of workers who are unable to find a job in the better-paying sector seek employment in the nontraded sector:

$$U^s_{AN} = U_R - U^d_{AT}. \qquad (12)$$

The wage rate in the nontraded agricultural sector is flexible and determined so as to equate labor demand (derived from standard profit maximization conditions), U^d_{AN}, and labor supply, given by (12). The market-clearing equilibrium product wage, w_{AN}, is thus given by

$$w_{AN} = \frac{\beta_{XAN}(1-\eta_{XAN})}{\alpha^{\rho_{XAN}}_{XAN}} \left\{ \frac{V^{1+\rho_{XAN}/(1-\eta_{XAN})}_{AN}}{(U_R - U^d_{AT})^{1+\rho_{XAN}}} \right\}, \qquad (13)$$

where $w_{AN} = W_{AN}/PV_{AN}$.

The size of the labor force in the rural sector, U_R, is predetermined at any given point in time. Over time, U_R grows at the exogenous population growth rate, net of worker migration to urban areas, $MIGR$:

$$U_R = (1+g_R)U_{R,-1} - MIGR. \qquad (14)$$

---

[6]There is a large literature emphasizing the role of interest rates in a credit-in-advance economy on the supply side; New Structuralist economists (see, for instance, van Wijnbergen (1982) and Taylor (1983)) were very early on strong advocates of the necessity to take this effect into account when specifying macroeconomic models. See also Izquierdo (2000) for a more recent discussion.

[7]In this chapter, as in the rest of the book, one period corresponds to one year.

In line with the traditional analysis of Harris and Todaro (1970), the incentives to migrate are taken to depend negatively on the ratio of the average expected *consumption* wage in rural areas to that prevailing in urban areas. As in Chapters 3 and 4, we assume that costs associated with migration or other frictions may delay the migration process, introducing significant persistence in migration flows.

Unskilled workers in the urban economy may be employed either in the formal sector, in which case they are paid a minimum wage, W_M, or they can enter the informal economy and receive the market-determined wage in that sector, W_I. When rural workers make the decision to migrate to urban areas, they are uncertain as to which type of job they will be able to get, and therefore weigh wages in each sector by the probability of finding a job in that sector.

Suppose, for simplicity, that the rural labor market operates as a sequential "auction" market – all rural workers are laid-off at the end of each production period and rehired randomly at the beginning of the next. In such conditions, the probability of employment in each sector subject to entry restrictions (that is, sectors where employment is demand determined) can be approximated by prevailing employment ratios. Moreover, potential migrants also consider what their expected purchasing power in rural and urban areas will be, depending on whether they stay in the rural sector and consume the "typical" basket of goods of rural households, or migrate and consume the "typical" urban basket of goods.

Combining these hypotheses implies that the average expected urban consumption wage is a weighted average of the minimum wage in the formal sector and the going wage in the informal sector, deflated by an urban consumption price index, P_{UU}. Weights are given by θ_U and $1 - \theta_U$, where $0 < \theta_U < 1$ is the probability of finding a job in the urban formal sector. Assuming a one-period lag, the expected, unskilled urban real wage, $\mathrm{E}w_U$, is thus

$$\mathrm{E}w_U = \frac{\theta_U W_{M,-1} + (1 - \theta_U) W_{I,-1}}{P_{UU,-1}}, \tag{15}$$

where θ_U is measured by the proportion of unskilled workers in the private formal sector relative to the total number of unskilled urban workers net of government employment prevailing in the previous period,[8]

$$\theta_U = \frac{U_{P,-1}}{U_{U,-1} - U_{G,-1}}, \tag{16}$$

where U_U measures the size of the urban unskilled labor force.

A similar reasoning is used to calculate the expected rural consumption real wage, $\mathrm{E}w_A$:

$$\mathrm{E}w_A = \frac{\theta_R W_{AT,-1} + (1 - \theta_R) W_{AN,-1}}{P_{R,-1}},$$

---

[8]Note that this expression for θ_U assumes that there is no "auctioning" of public sector jobs, that is, the government does not turn over its employees over every period as occurs in the private sector. This assumption captures the view that public jobs are not "randomly" distributed but result rather from various non-economic considerations, such as political patronage. If there is turnover in the public sector, however, the probability of finding a job would be $(U_{P,-1} + U_{G,-1})/U_{U,-1}$, instead of (16).

where P_R is the consumption index for the rural sector and $0 < \theta_R < 1$ is approximated by the proportion of the rural unskilled labor force employed in the export sector:

$$\theta_R = \frac{U_{AT,-1}}{U_{R,-1}}. \tag{17}$$

The migration function can therefore be specified as

$$MIGR = U_{R,-1}\lambda_m \left[\sigma_M \ln \left(\frac{Ew_U}{Ew_A} \right) \right] + (1 - \lambda_m)\frac{U_{R,-1}}{U_{R,-2}}MIGR_{-1}, \tag{18}$$

where $0 < \lambda_m < 1$ measures the speed of adjustment and $\sigma_M > 0$ measures the elasticity of migration flows with respect to expected wages.

It should be noted that we have abstracted in the above discussion from the role of risk aversion in individual migration decisions, by focusing on "expected income" differentials rather than "expected utility" differentials. For a risk-averse worker, for instance, the probability of employment is a more important determinant of migration than the wage rate. More generally, we have not captured in our specification some of the other factors that may affect the decision to migrate, as emphasized in the recent analytical and empirical literature (see for instance Stark (1991) and Ghatak, Levine, and Price (1996)). Wage uncertainty in agriculture or the urban sector (resulting, in the former case, from output variability, and in the latter, from imperfect information about labor market conditions), income inequality and relative deprivation in the rural sector, the joint nature of the decision process in households, and the lack of access to credit markets, may all affect migration decisions and lead potential migrants to alter their decision to move.[9] For instance, imperfect (and costly) information about urban labor market conditions may lead potential migrants to attach a greater weight to the available information regarding the rural sector and may lead them to postpone their decision to move – despite the existence of a large (expected) wage differential.[10] However, some of these factors may be country-specific and we have opted in building the IMMPA prototype framework to focus on a more parsimonious specification that highlights the role of relative income opportunities.

Urban Unskilled Wages and Employment

Unskilled employment in the public sector, U_G, is assumed to be exogenous. For simplicity, the wage rate paid by the government to these workers is set at the same level as the wage rate paid to that category of labor in the private formal sector. Furthermore, we assume that there is a legally-binding minimum wage in place, which is indexed to either the consumer price index or an alternative price:

$$W_M = w_M(PIND_M)^{ind_M},$$

---

[9] Stark (1991) also emphasized that individual migration can be the outcome of a family decision, often as a response to uninsurable risks.

[10] We also abstract from the negative externalities associated with rural to urban migration, such as congestion costs or pollution in shanty towns.

where $PIND_M = PLEV$ for instance, and $0 \leq ind_M \leq 1$. In the simulation exercises reported later, we assume that the minimum wage is fully indexed (so that $ind_M = 1$) on the price of the composite factor T_1.[11]

Unskilled labor demand in the formal private sector, U_P^d, is determined by firms' profit maximization. Given that formal private sector firms also borrow to finance their wage bill prior to the sale of output, the effective price of labor accounts again for the bank lending rate; thus

$$U_P^d = T_1 \left\{ \frac{1}{(1 + IL_{-1})w_M} \frac{\beta_{XP1}}{\alpha_{XP1}^{\rho_{XP1}}} \right\}^{\sigma_{XP1}}, \quad w_M = \frac{W_M}{PT_1}. \tag{19}$$

As was the case with the rural sector (and in order to avoid corner solutions), we assume that the wage rate paid to unskilled labor in the formal urban sector is systematically greater than the real wage rate paid in the informal sector. Consequently, unskilled urban workers will first seek employment in the private formal sector. The actual level of employment in that sector is determined according to equation (19).

The remainder of the urban unskilled labor force will thus seek employment in the informal economy, where there are no barriers to entry:

$$U_I^s = U_U - U_P^d - U_G. \tag{20}$$

From (4), the demand for labor in the informal sector is given by $U_I^d = \beta_{XI}(V_I/w_I)$, where w_I is the product wage defined as W_I/PV_I. Because the informal labor market clears continuously ($U_I^d = U_I^s$), the equilibrium product wage is given by

$$w_I = \beta_{XI} \frac{V_I}{U_I^s}, \quad w_I = \frac{W_I}{PV_I}. \tag{21}$$

There is therefore no open unskilled unemployment, as in the analytical model developed in Chapter 2.

The urban unskilled labor supply, U_U, grows as a result of "natural" urban population growth and migration of unskilled labor from the rural economy, as discussed earlier. Moreover, a fraction of the urban unskilled population acquires skills (SKL) and leaves the unskilled labor force to augment the supply of skilled labor in the economy. We make the additional assumption that individuals are born unskilled, and therefore natural growth in the urban population (not resulting from migration or skills acquisition factors) results only from an expansion in the urban unskilled labor force, at the rate g_U. Thus, total supply of unskilled labor in the urban sector evolves according to

$$U_U = (1 + g_U)U_{U,-1} + MIGR - SKL. \tag{22}$$

We treat the growth rate of the urban unskilled population endogenously. We do so by dwelling on the various studies have documented the existence of a negative association between population growth rates and income levels; fertility rates tend to

---

[11] An alternative would be to assume that the minimum wage is fixed in nominal terms ($ind_M = 0$). As one would expect, simulation results of particular shocks may differ significantly under the two assumptions (see for instance Devarajan, Ghanem, and Thierfelder (1999)).

fall as the level of income increases (see for instance Barro and Becker (1989), and Becker, Murphy, and Tamura (1990) for the growth implications of this relationship). Specifically, we assume that the growth rate of the urban unskilled population is related to a distributed lag of current and past values of the ratio of average income in the urban economy for skilled and unskilled workers. Assuming that these lags follow a declining geometric pattern and using the Koyck transformation, we get

$$g_U = \lambda_g \alpha_{gu} \left[\frac{(S_P + S_G) W_S / S}{[U_I W_I + (U_P + U_G) W_M]/U_U} \right]^{-\gamma_{gu}} + (1 - \lambda_g) g_{U,-1}, \qquad (23)$$

where $\alpha_{gu} > 0$, $0 \leq \lambda_g \leq 1$, and $\gamma_{gu} > 0$ is the absolute value of the elasticity of the growth rate of the urban unskilled population with respect to the wage ratio.

The acquisition of skills by unskilled workers is assumed to depend on three factors: *a*) relative expected consumption wages of skilled and unskilled urban workers (as a proxy for the future stream of earnings associated with higher levels of education); *b*) the government stock of education capital, K_E, which affects the ability to invest in skills; and *c*) the average level of wealth held by each unskilled worker, which may play an important role in the presence of liquidity constraints – that is, the inability to borrow to finance human capital accumulation (a well-documented feature of the financial system in many developing countries).

Consider first the effect of wages. In case they acquire skills, an unskilled worker expects to earn a wage of W_S if he/she is employed (with probability θ_S) and nothing if he/she remains unemployed. The purchasing power of this wage is obtained by deflating it by the skilled household's consumption price index, $P_{US,-1}$:

$$\mathrm{E} w_S = \theta_S \frac{W_{S,-1}}{P_{US,-1}} + (1 - \theta_S) \cdot 0, \qquad (24)$$

where $0 < \theta_S < 1$ is, as before, approximated by the one-period lagged ratio of the number of skilled workers employed in the private sector, over the total number of skilled workers that are not employed in the public sector seeking a job in the private sector:

$$\theta_S = \frac{S_{P,-1}}{S_{-1} - S_{G,-1}}. \qquad (25)$$

In contrast, if they remain unskilled, they expect to get the average unskilled wage, which is a weighted average of the minimum wage W_M and the informal wage rate. Assuming, again, that there is no job turnover in the public sector, the average expected real wage is given by (15), with θ_U defined in (16).

Consider now the effect of initial wealth. As can be inferred, for instance, from various studies in the endogenous growth literature (see for instance De Gregorio (1996)), the existence of constraints in obtaining credit to fund the cost of acquiring skills may completely outweigh the impact of relative wages and the availability of government capital in education on workers' decisions. Indeed, in the framework that we consider here, only firms have access to bank credit; no matter how high the wage differential is or is expected to be, workers simply cannot borrow to finance human capital accumulation.[12] To capture the existence of these credit constraints we assume that the decision to acquire skills is a function of the (lagged) ratio of the level of wealth of urban formal and informal unskilled households divided by the number of unskilled workers in the urban sector, $(WT_{UI} + WT_{UF})/U_U$. Admittedly, this is a rather simplistic way of modeling these frictions; an alternative, but less tractable approach in numerical models would be to assume that access to the credit market is subject to a threshold effect, with financial wealth playing a "signaling" role because of workers' ability to pledge a fraction of it as collateral.

Given these three effects, the flow increase in the supply of skilled labor can be written as:

$$SKL = \lambda_S \left[\kappa_e WU_{-1}^{\alpha_{edu}} \left\{ \frac{Ew_S}{Ew_U} \right\}^{\sigma_W} (K_{E,-1})^{\sigma_E} \right] + (1 - \lambda_S)SKL_{-1}, \qquad (26)$$

where $WU_{-1} = (WT_{UI,-1} + WT_{UF,-1})/U_{U,-1}, 0 < \lambda_S < 1, \kappa_e$ is a shift parameter, and $\alpha_{edu}, \sigma_W, \sigma_E > 0$. For simplicity, we treat as constant the cost of acquiring skills (as measured by the number of years of schooling multiplied by the average cost of education per year).

Urban Skilled Wages and Employment

As indicated earlier, we assume that wage-setting behavior for skilled labor is based on efficiency considerations. Specifically, we assume that in order to provide incentives for employees to provide maximum effort, firms must set a sufficiently high (product) wage. Along the lines of the Agénor-Aizenman functional form discussed in Chapter 1, we assume that the level of effort skilled workers provide depends negatively on the ratio of their real opportunity cost, Ω_W, to their *consumption* wage, that is, the nominal wage W_S deflated by the skilled consumption price index, P_{US}:

$$ef = 1 - ef_m \left[\frac{\Omega_W}{W_S/P_{US}} \right]^{\gamma_{ef}}, \quad \gamma_{ef} > 0, \qquad (27)$$

and where $0 < ef_m < 1$ denotes the "minimum" level of effort. The opportunity cost of effort is taken to be constant in what follows.

Firms determine the levels of skilled and unskilled employment, as well as the *product* wage for skilled labor, w_S, so as to maximize profits, taking as given the real minimum wage paid and the production technology (8). It can be established that the demand for skilled labor is given by

$$S_P^d = T_2 \kappa_S \left\{ \frac{1}{(1 + IL_{-1})w_S} \cdot \frac{\beta_{XP2}}{\alpha_{XP2}^{\rho_{XP2}}} \right\}^{\sigma_{XP2}}, \quad w_S = \frac{W_S}{PT_2}, \qquad (28)$$

whereas the optimal wage-setting equation is given by

$$w_S = \frac{\beta_{XP2}\gamma_{ef}(1 - ef)}{\alpha_{XP2}^{\rho_{XP2}}} \left\{ \frac{T_2}{ef \cdot S_P} \right\}^{1+\rho_{XP2}} \frac{P_{US}}{PT_2}. \qquad (29)$$

---

[12]This assumption is well supported by the evidence on the composition of bank credit in low-income countries, which suggests that only a small fraction of bank loans is allocated to households.

Note that in this equation the ratio of the consumption price index for skilled workers, P_{US}, over the price of the composite input, PT_2, appears because firms set the *product* wage whereas effort depends on the *consumption* wage. This creates an important channel (seldom accounted for in empirical models) through which changes in relative prices affect wage formation.

Given that firms set wages and are on their labor demand curve, open skilled unemployment may emerge. The rate of skilled unemployment, $UNEMP_S$, is given by the ratio of skilled workers who are not employed either by the private or the public sector, divided by the total population of skilled workers:

$$UNEMP_S = \frac{S - S_G - S_P^d}{S}. \tag{30}$$

Note that here we assume that skilled workers who are unable to find a job in the formal economy do not enter the informal sector, in contrast to unskilled workers. In principle, any worker who is not hired in the formal economy could get a job in the informal sector at the going wage. However, there are several reasons why they may choose not to do so. An important consideration may be that skilled workers are concerned about possible adverse signaling effects associated with employment in the informal economy and may prefer instead to remain openly unemployed, as noted by Gottfries and McCormick (1995). Indeed, the existence of "luxury" unemployment, as discussed in Chapter 1, is a well-documented feature of the labor market in developing countries.

The skilled labor force evolves over time according to:

$$S = S_{-1} + SKL. \tag{31}$$

Because we assumed that workers are born unskilled, the skilled workforce does not grow at the natural growth rate of the urban population, but rather at the rate at which unskilled workers choose to acquire skills. Note also that, for simplicity, we assume no "deskilling" (or obsolescence) effect, although this could be easily introduced.

It is important, to conclude this discussion of wage formation mechanisms, to return to our assumption that skilled workers' wage is determined on the basis of an efficiency effect of compensation on productivity. In practice, it is notoriously difficult to discriminate among various forms of efficiency wage theories; these theories tend to be "observationally equivalent." At the same time, however, this makes our choice here of an explicit formulation based on the wage–productivity link less restrictive than it appears at first glance; in fact, a wage-setting equation fundamentally similar to (29) can also be derived by considering, say, turnover costs (see Agénor (2001) and Chapter 1). A bargaining framework between firms and a centralized trade union could also lead to a similar wage-setting specification. The important point is to assume in each case that, whereas firms are concerned with the *product* wage, workers (or the union that represents them) are concerned with the *consumption* wage. This creates a wedge, as derived above, through which relative prices affect wage-setting decisions.

Although our treatment above provides a tractable specification of the wage–productivity link, a more general specification of wage formation for skilled labor may also be warranted in some applications. Such a specification consists of replacing (29) by the "generic" formulation

$$W_S = w_S (PIND_S)^{ind_S} (UNEMP_S)^{-\phi_U} \Omega_W^{\phi_1} \left(\frac{P_{US}}{PT_2} \right)^{\phi_2} (1 + IL_{-1})^{-\phi_3}, \qquad (32)$$

where $PIND_S = PLEV$ or PT_2 (depending on whether the nominal wage is indexed to the overall level of prices or the composite "product" price), $0 \leq ind_S \leq 1$, and $\Omega_W, \phi_U, \phi_1, \phi_2, \phi_3 > 0$.

If this specification is used, w_S in equation (28) must be defined as $w_S = W_S/PT_2$, with W_S given in (32), and the production technology, equation (8), must be replaced by

$$V_P = CES\{CES[CES(S_P, K_P), U_P], K_G\}. \qquad (33)$$

Specification (32) is quite flexible; for instance, full indexation on the consumer price index only requires setting $PIND_S = PLEV$, $ind_S = 1$, and $\phi_U = \phi_1 = \phi_2 = \phi_3 = 0$. To assume that the product wage depends only on the ratio P_{US}/PT_2 (as above) requires setting $PIND_S = PT_2$, $ind_S = 1$, $\phi_2 > 0$, and $\phi_U = \phi_1 = \phi_3 = 0$. Note also that in (32), as long as $\phi_U > 0$, the level of skilled unemployment will affect (negatively) the *level* of nominal wages, instead of the *rate of growth* of wages (as would be the case with a Phillips curve formulation). This level effect is consistent with various forms of efficiency wage theories in which unemployment acts as a "worker discipline device," such as the effort elicitation model of Shapiro and Stiglitz (1984) discussed in Chapter 1; evidence supporting it has been provided for instance by Hoddinot (1996) for Côte d'Ivoire.

Note that the gross lending rate, $1 + IL_{-1}$, enters in this specification because an increase, say, in the cost of borrowing raises the effective price of labor, which firms try to offset, at least in part, by reducing the nominal wage. If $\phi_3 < 1$ ($\phi_3 > 1$) the net effect is an increase (reduction) in the effective cost of skilled labor, and the demand for skilled labor will fall (increase), everything else equal.

Finally, note also that the inverse relationship between the level of skilled unemployment and the skilled workers' wage can be introduced in either (27) or (29), by assuming that the reservation wage, Ω_W, is inversely related to the unemployment rate:

$$\Omega_W = \overline{\Omega}_W (UNEMP_S)^{-\phi_U},$$

where $\phi_U \geq 0$. Put differently, unemployment acts as a "disciplining device" by reducing the perceived opportunity cost of working and/or in reducing wage demands. In the simulation experiments reported below, however, we focus on the case where $\phi_U = 0$.

5.1.3   Supply and Demand

As noted earlier, we assume that both the informal and public sector goods are nontraded. As a result, total supply in each sector, Q_i^s, is equal to gross production:

$$X_i = Q_i^s, \quad i = I, G \qquad (34)$$

Nontraded agricultural and private formal urban goods, by contrast, compete with imported goods. The supply of the composite good for each of these sectors consists of a CES combination of imports and domestically-produced goods:

$$Q_i^s = CES(M_i, D_i), \quad i = AN, P \tag{35}$$

where $D_{AN} = X_{AN}$.

Aggregate demand for each of these sectors, Q_i^d, consists of intermediate and final consumption, government spending, and investment demand:

$$Q_{AN}^d = C_{AN} + INT_{AN}, \tag{36}$$

$$Q_I^d = C_I + INT_I, \tag{37}$$

$$Q_G^d = C_G + G_G + Z_G + INT_G, \tag{38}$$

$$Q_P^d 7 = C_P + G_P + Z_P + INT_P, \tag{39}$$

where INT_j is defined as total demand (by all productions sectors) for intermediate consumption of good j:

$$INT_j = \sum_i a_{ji} X_i, \quad j = AN, I, G, P \tag{40}$$

Government expenditure on good j, G_j, is expressed in real terms as:

$$G_j = gg_j \frac{NG}{PQ_j}, \quad j = G, P \tag{41}$$

where NG represents total nominal government expenditure, PQ_h is the market price of goods purchased by the government, and $gg_G + gg_P = 1$. Note that the government is assumed not to spend on nontraded agricultural and informal sector goods.

Equations (36) to (39) indicate that for the nontraded agricultural and informal sectors, aggregate demand consists of intermediate consumption and demand for final consumption, C_{AN} and C_I, whereas aggregate demand for the public good consists not only of intermediate consumption and demand (both private and public) for final consumption, $C_G + G_G$, but also investment demand, Z_G. Similarly, demand for the private formal good consists of intermediate consumption, as well as demand for final consumption, $C_P + G_P$, and private investment, Z_P.

Final consumption for each production sector i, C_i, is the summation across all categories of households of nominal consumption of good i, deflated by the composite price of good i:

$$C_i = \sum_h C_{ih} = \frac{\sum_h cc_{ih} \cdot CON_h}{PQ_i}, \quad 0 < cc_{ih} < 1, \quad \sum_i cc_{ih} = 1, \ \forall i, h. \tag{42}$$

where C_{ih} is consumption of good i by household h, and PQ_i is the composite sales price of good i. Coefficients cc_{ih} indicate how total nominal consumption spending by household h, CON_h, is allocated to each type of good. Equations (42) can be derived by maximization of a Stone-Geary utility function (see for instance Deaton and Muellbauer (1980)). They represent a linear expenditure system in which, for simplicity, the subsistence level of consumption is set to zero (see Chapter 4).

Finally, total private investment, Z, consists of purchases of both public and private goods (Z_G and Z_P respectively):

$$Z_i = zz_i \frac{Z \cdot PK}{PQ_i}, \quad zz_G + zz_P = 1.$$

Coefficients zz_i measure the allocation of total investment demand to public and private goods.

5.1.4   External Trade

As indicated earlier, firms in the private formal sector allocate their output to exports or the domestic market according to the production possibility frontier (PPF) specified in equation (9) and the relative price of exports, PE_P, vis-à-vis domestic goods, PD_P. Efficiency conditions require that firms equate this relative price to the opportunity cost in production. This yields:

$$E_P = D_P \left\{ \frac{PE_P}{PD_P} \cdot \frac{1 - \beta_{TP}}{\beta_{TP}} \right\}^{\sigma_{TP}}. \tag{43}$$

The agricultural traded good is fully exported, as also indicated earlier; given that this sector is the only one using only its own good as intermediate consumption, we have

$$E_{AT} = V_{AT} = (1 - a_{AT,AT})X_{AT}. \tag{44}$$

A similar reasoning applies to the determination of the demand for imports. We assume that imports compete with domestic goods in the agricultural nontraded sector as well as in the private formal sector. Making use of Armington functions for the demand for imported vs. domestic goods and relative prices, import demand for both sectors (M_{AN} and M_P) can be written as:

$$M_i = D_i \left\{ \frac{PD_i}{PM_i} \cdot \frac{\beta_{Qi}}{1 - \beta_{Qi}} \right\}^{\sigma_{Qi}}, \quad i = AN, P \tag{45}$$

These equations indicate that the ratio of imports to domestic supply of both categories of domestic goods depends on the relative prices of these goods and the elasticity of substitution, σ_{QAN} and σ_{QP}, between these goods.

5.1.5   Prices

As indicated previously, production requires both factor inputs and intermediate inputs; we therefore define the net or value added price of output as:

$$PV_i = V_i^{-1} \left\{ PX_i(1 - indtax_i) - \sum_j a_{ji} PQ_j \right\} X_i, \tag{46}$$

where *indtax$_i$* is the rate of indirect taxation of output in sector i (with *indtax$_I$* $= 0$ because there is no indirect taxation of informal sector output). This equation relates the value added price of output of sector i to the price of gross output, PX_i, net of indirect taxes, less the cost of intermediate inputs, purchased at composite prices.

We are considering a small economy and therefore assume that the world prices of imported and exported goods are exogenously given. The domestic currency price of these goods is obtained by adjusting the world price by the exchange rate, the import tariff rate, *tm*, or the export subsidy rate, *te*:

$$PE_i = wpe_i(1 + te_i)ER, \quad i = AT, P, \tag{47}$$

$$PM_i = wpm_i(1 + tm_i)ER, \quad i = AN, P, \tag{48}$$

where ER is the nominal exchange rate.

Because the transformation function between exports and domestic sales of the urban private good is linear homogeneous, the sales price, PX_P, is derived from the expenditure identity:[13]

$$PX_P X_P = PD_P D_P + PE_P E_P,$$

that is,[14]

$$PX_P = \frac{PD_P D_P + PE_P E_P}{X_P}. \tag{49}$$

In the agricultural sector, prices of domestic sales and gross output of the traded agricultural good is simply the domestic-currency price of agricultural exports, PE_{AT}, whereas the price of domestic sales of the nontraded good, PD_{AN}, is equal to the gross output price of these goods, PX_{AN}:

$$PD_{AT} = PX_{AT} = PE_{AT}, \tag{50}$$

$$PD_{AN} = PX_{AN}. \tag{51}$$

For the nontraded agricultural sector and private urban production, the substitution function between imports and domestic goods is also linearly homogeneous, and the composite market price is determined accordingly by the expenditure identity:

$$PQ_i Q_i = PD_i D_i + PM_i M_i, \quad i = AN, P,$$

that is

$$PQ_i = \frac{PD_i D_i + PM_i M_i}{Q_i}, \quad i = AN, P. \tag{52}$$

---

[13] An alternative approach to price formation in the private formal sector is to assume, as noted in Chapter 3, that prices are set monopolistically, as markups over input costs. With a fixed markup, and a demand determined level of output, the production function would need to be dropped from the system.

[14] In solving the model, we use equation (45) to solve for PD_P, and, because $Q_P^s = Q_P^d$, we use (39) to solve for the equilibrium value of Q_P. We then invert the composite good CES equation (35) to solve for M_P and invert the CET function to solve for D_P. This procedure ensures that the composite price (and thus indirectly the price of domestic sales) adjusts to equilibrate supply and demand.

For the informal and public sectors (both of which produce goods that are not exported and do not compete with imports), the composite sales price is identical to the price of domestic sales, which in turn is equal to the price of gross output:

$$PQ_i = PD_i = PX_i, \quad i = I, G. \tag{53}$$

The nested CES production function of private formal urban goods is also linearly homogeneous; prices of the composite inputs are therefore derived in similar fashion:

$$T_1 PT_1 = T_2 PT_2 + (1 + IL_{-1}) WM U_P, \tag{54}$$

$$T_2 PT_2 = PROF_P + (1 + IL_{-1}) W_S S_P, \tag{55}$$

where $PROF_P$ denotes profits of private firms in the urban formal sector.

The price of capital is constructed by using the investment expenditure identity, which involves those goods for which there is investment demand, namely, the public and private-formal urban goods (see equations (38) and (39)):

$$PK = \frac{\sum_i PQ_i Z_i}{Z} = \frac{PQ_G Z_G + PQ_P Z_P}{Z}. \tag{56}$$

Markets for informal goods and government services clear continuously; equilibrium conditions are thus given by

$$Q_I^s = Q_I^d, \quad Q_G^s = Q_G^d.$$

In solving the model, we use equations (34) to determine the equilibrium quantities $Q_I = X_I$ and $Q_G = X_G$, that is, equations (3) and (5). We also use the demand equations (37) and (38) to solve residually for C_I and C_G, that is:

$$X_I - INT_I = C_I, \tag{57}$$

$$X_G - G_G - Z_G - INT_G = C_G. \tag{58}$$

Equation (42) for $i = I, G$, is then solved for $PQ_I = PX_I$ and $PQ_G = PX_G$, respectively. This yields:

$$PX_i = \frac{\sum_h cc_{ih} CON_h}{C_i}, \quad i = I, G. \tag{59}$$

The aggregate price level, $PLEV$, or consumer price index, is a weighted average of individual goods market prices, PQ_i:

$$PLEV = \sum_i wt_i PQ_i, \tag{60}$$

where $0 < wt_i < 1$ denotes the relative weight of good i in the index, and $PQ_I = PX_I$ and $PQ_G = PX_G$. These weights are fixed according to the share of each of these goods in aggregate consumption in the base period. Inflation is defined as the percentage change in the price level:

$$PINF = \frac{PLEV - PLEV_{-1}}{PLEV_{-1}}. \tag{61}$$

The consumption price index for the rural sector is given by

$$P_R = \sum_i wr_i PQ_i, \tag{62}$$

whereas the consumption price indexes for urban unskilled and skilled workers are given by

$$P_{UU} = \sum_i wu_i PQ_i, \tag{63}$$

$$P_{US} = \sum_i ws_i PQ_i, \tag{64}$$

where the wr_i, wu_i and ws_i are relative weights with $\sum_i wr_i$, $\sum_i wu_i$ and $\sum_i ws_i$ summing to unity. The deflator of GDP at factor cost, $PGDP_{FC}$, is given by

$$PGDP_{FC} = \Sigma_i v_i PV_i, \tag{65}$$

where, again, the v_i are relative weights corresponding to some base period $t = 0$ (that is, $v_i = PV_{i,0}X_{i,0}/\Sigma_j PV_{j,0}X_{j,0}$), with $\Sigma_i v_i = 1$.

5.1.6 Profits and Income

Firms' profits are defined as revenue minus total labor costs (inclusive of interest payments). In the case of agricultural nontraded sector firms and urban informal sector firms, profits are simply given by

$$PROF_i = PV_i V_i - W_i U_i, \quad i = AN, I. \tag{66}$$

Firms producing in the traded agricultural sector must include working capital costs as well, in measuring their production costs, that is, interest payments on their wage bill. Their profits (at current prices) are therefore given by

$$PROF_{AT} = PV_{AT} V_{AT} - (1 + IL_{-1})W_{AT} U_{AT}. \tag{67}$$

Similarly, profits of private-urban sector firms account for both working capital costs and salaries paid to both categories of workers:

$$PROF_P = PV_P V_P - (1 + IL_{-1})(W_M U_P + W_S S_P), \tag{68}$$

where, as noted earlier, the nominal wage paid to unskilled workers is the legally-imposed minimum wage, W_M.

Firms' income is, in principle, equal to profits minus interest payments on loans for investment purposes. Firms' income and profits are defined separately, because not all sectors are assumed to borrow on the credit market to finance investment. Specifically, we assume that only firms in the formal urban economy accumulate capital.[15] Firms' income, YF_i, can thus be defined as

$$YF_i = PROF_i, \quad i = AN, AT, I, \tag{69}$$

$$YF_P = PROF_P - IL_{-1}DL_{P,-1} - IF \cdot FL_{P,-1}ER, \tag{70}$$

---

[15] Of course, this assumption can be relaxed in specific country applications.

where IF is the interest rate paid on foreign loans, and DL_P and FL_P are the amounts borrowed domestically and abroad by private urban firms to finance investment needs.

Commercial banks' profits must also be taken into account. They are defined as the difference between revenues from loans to firms (be it for working capital or investment needs) and the government, DL_G, and interest payments on both households' deposits, $\sum_h DD_h$, and foreign loans received from international creditors, FL_B, measured in domestic-currency terms:

$$YF_{PB} = IL_{-1}(DL_{P,-1} + DL_{G,-1} + U_{AT}W_{AT} + W_M U_P + W_S S_P)$$

$$- ID \sum_h DD_{h,-1} - IF \cdot ER \cdot FL_{B,-1}, \qquad (71)$$

where ID is the interest rate on bank deposits, set by the central bank.

Household income is based on salaried labor, distributed profits, transfers, and net interest receipts on holdings of financial assets. Households are defined according to both labor categories and their sector of location. There are two types of rural households: one comprising workers employed in the traded sector, and the other workers in the nontraded sector. In the urban sector there are two types of unskilled households, those working in the informal sector and those employed in the formal sector (public or private). The fifth type of households consists of skilled workers employed in the formal urban economy, in both the private and public sectors). Finally, there are "capitalist" households (including rentiers) whose income comes from firms' earnings in the formal private sector, the agricultural traded sector and commercial banks. We further assume that households in both the nontraded agricultural sector and in the informal urban economy own the firms in which they are employed – an assumption that captures the fact that firms in these sectors tend indeed to be small, family-owned enterprises.

Income of agricultural nontraded and urban informal groups is given by

$$YH_i = \gamma_i TRH + W_i U_i + ID \cdot DD_{i,-1} + IF \cdot FD_{i,-1}ER + YF_i, \quad i = AN, I, \quad (72)$$

where γ_i is the portion of total government transfers (TRH) each group receives, $W_i U_i$ denote wage earnings, DD_i domestic bank deposits, FD_i foreign bank deposits (taken to be a fairly small share of assets in the simulations reported below), and YF_i firms' income in these sectors. Given (69) and (66), these equations are equivalent to

$$YH_i = \gamma_i TRH + PV_i V_i + ID \cdot DD_{i,-1} + IF \cdot FD_{i,-1}ER, \quad i = AN, I.$$

Income of the agricultural traded sector household, as well as that of the urban formal unskilled and skilled households, depends on government transfers, salaries and interests on deposits; firms provide no source of income, because these groups do not own the production units in which they are employed:

$$YH_{AT} = \gamma_{AT} TRH + W_{AT} U_{AT} + ID \cdot DD_{AT,-1} + IF \cdot FD_{AT,-1}ER, \qquad (73)$$

$$YH_{UF} = \gamma_{UF} TRH + W_M(U_P + U_G) + ID \cdot DD_{UF,-1} + IF \cdot FD_{UF,-1}ER, \qquad (74)$$

$$YH_S = \gamma_S TRH + W_S(S_P + S_G) + ID \cdot DD_{S,-1} + IF \cdot FD_{S,-1}ER. \qquad (75)$$

Firms' income in the traded agricultural and private urban sectors are assumed to go to capitalist households, along with commercial banks' income, and interest on deposits. Because there is no capital accumulation in the traded agricultural sector to be financed, the entire amount of firms' profits from that sector is transferred to capitalist households. By contrast, firms in the private urban sector retain a portion of their earnings, *re*, for investment financing purposes, and transfer the remainder to their owners. Capitalist households' income is thus:

$$YH_{KAP} = \gamma_{KAP}TRH + ID \cdot DD_{KAP,-1} + IF \cdot FD_{KAP,-1}ER$$

$$+ YF_{AT} + (1 - re)YF_P + YF_{PB}. \tag{76}$$

5.1.7 Savings, Consumption, and Investment

Each category of household h saves a fraction, $0 < savrate_h < 1$, of its disposable income:

$$SAV_h = savrate_h YH_h(1 - inctax_h), \tag{77}$$

where $0 < inctax_h < 1$ is the income tax rate applicable to household h, with $inctax_I = 0$, because the government is unable to collect direct taxes in the informal sector.

The savings rate is a positive function of the real interest rate on deposits:

$$savrate_h = s_{0,h} \left(\frac{1 + ID}{1 + PINF} \right)^{\sigma_{S,h}}, \quad s_{0,h}, \ \sigma_{S,h} > 0. \tag{78}$$

In practical applications, the propensity to save could be made a function of not only the real deposit rate, which implies that inflation and the savings rate are inversely related, but also of the inflation rate itself, as a result of a precautionary motive (with higher inflation acting as a signal of greater uncertainty about future real income). The evidence on the latter effect is quite significant for some countries (see Agénor (2004b) and Loayza, Schmidt-Hebbel, and Servén (1999)).

The portion of disposable income that is not saved is allocated to consumption:[16]

$$CON_h = (1 - inctax_h)YH_h - SAV_h.$$

For each household group, the flow of savings is channeled into the accumulation of financial wealth, WT_h, which also accounts for valuation effects on the stock of foreign-currency deposits, FD_h, associated with changes in the nominal exchange rate:

$$WT_h = WT_{h,-1} + SAV_h + \Delta ER \cdot FD_{h,-1}. \tag{79}$$

---

[16]Note that we do not account for any real balances effect (or wealth effect) on consumption, as in Easterly (1990) and others. However, this effect can be easily added if warranted by the empirical evidence – for instance by making the savings rate a function of wealth as well. It could prove important in assessing the effects of exchange-rate induced valuation changes on domestic expenditure.

Capital accumulation occurs only in the private urban sector. The investment function of firms operating in that sector takes the general form

$$
\frac{Z}{K_{P,-1}} = \left\{ \frac{K_{INF}}{K_{INF,-1}} \right\}^{\sigma_K} \left\{ \left(1 + \frac{\Delta RGDP_{FC}}{RGDP_{FC,-1}} \right)^{\sigma_{ACC}} \right.
$$

$$
+ \frac{\phi_Z}{(1 + PINF_{-1})^{\sigma_P}} \left[\frac{(1 + IK)(1 - inctax_{KAP})}{1 + IL} \right]^{\sigma_{IK}}
$$

$$
\left. -\phi_D \left[\frac{IF_G \cdot ER \cdot FL_{G,-1}}{TXREV} \right] - \phi_{DD} \left[\frac{IF_G \cdot ER \cdot FL_{G,-1}}{TXREV} \right]^2 \right\}. \tag{80}
$$

Equation (80) indicates that the ratio of private investment, Z, to the (lagged) stock of private capital, K_P, is related to a number of factors. First, it depends on the growth rate of the public capital stock in infrastructure, K_{INF}. There is substantial empirical evidence supporting the view that public and private sector capital in infrastructure (railroads, paved roads, water systems, telecommunications, and power) tend to be complements (see Agénor (2004b) and Agénor and Montiel (1999)).

Second, equation (80) integrates the "flexible" accelerator effect on private investment, which aims to capture the impact of the desired capital stock on current investment. The ability of the firm to respond to changes in its desired capital stock is reflected in the positive effect on investment of the growth in value added, which is measured by changes in real GDP evaluated at factor cost, $RGDP_{FC}$, defined as

$$
RGDP_{FC} = \Sigma_i PV_i X_i / PGDP_{FC}, \tag{81}
$$

where $PGDP_{FC}$, the deflator of GDP at factor cost, is defined in (65).

There is considerable evidence supporting this effect, particularly for Sub-Saharan Africa, as discussed for instance by Agénor (2004b, Chapter 2).

Third, high inflation has a negative effect on investment decisions. This variable captures the impact of increased uncertainty about relative prices under higher inflation, which makes investment decisions riskier. It also acts as a proxy for macroeconomic instability. Several recent studies – see, for instance, Servén (1997, 1998) and Zeufack (1997) – have indeed shown that macroeconomic instability may have a significant detrimental effect on the decision to invest, particularly when capital outlays are irreversible.

Fourth, the growth rate of private capital is positively related to the (gross) rate of return to capital, IK, net of the income tax rate that capitalists are subject to, relative to the (gross) lending rate. High taxes on capitalists therefore has a negative impact on investment. The introduction of the lending rate captures the adverse effect of the marginal cost of borrowing on capital accumulation.

Fifth, there is a negative effect of the economy's level of debt. In general, as noted earlier, this effect may operate through several channels: *a*) the risk of confiscation associated with a debt overhang (as discussed earlier); *b*) the diversion of foreign exchange to service foreign debt and consequently insufficient amounts of foreign currency to import capital goods; and *c*) the possibility that a high external debt may force a reallocation of public expenditure away from productive uses (maintenance and infrastructure investment, most notably) and toward debt service. In the second case the inclusion of foreign debt acts as a "proxy" for foreign exchange availability, whereas in the third it is a proxy for the composition of (future) public spending.[17] The last two terms in equation (80) indicate that investment is inversely related to the ratio of interest payments on public sector debt to tax revenues; thus, in line with the evidence, we emphasize channels *a*) and *c*). Regarding *a*), for instance, when government revenues fall, investors may infer that there is a higher probability that private sector capital may be either taxed or confiscated to finance existing debt service.

This particular form of the investment function introduces an important role for fiscal policy. For instance, increasing the tax rate on income of capitalists will increase revenues and therefore stimulate private investment by reducing confiscation risk; because at the same time it also reduces the after-tax return to physical capital, the net effect will be ambiguous in general. A debt reduction program combined with suitable fiscal policies may both reduce interest payments and improve tax collection, thereby reducing confiscation risk and boosting private investment. The specific formulation that we have adopted here (which includes both linear and quadratic terms in the debt service-to-taxes ratio) implies that the marginal effect on private investment of a reduction in the debt–revenue ratio is magnified if the initial level of that ratio is high. We could also have assumed that the relationship between investment and external debt has a concave form, as suggested by the econometric results of Elbadawi, Ndulu, and Ndungu (1997) and Clements, Bhattacharya, et Nguyen (2003); in that case, the coefficient ϕ_D should be negative, implying that external debt has at first a positive impact and a negative one only when the it becomes relatively large.

The rate of return on capital is defined as the ratio of profits to the stock of capital:

$$IK = \frac{PROF_P}{PK \cdot K_P}. \tag{82}$$

Capital accumulation depends on the flow level of investment, Z, and the depreciation rate of capital from the previous period, δ_P:

$$K_P = K_{P,-1}(1 - \delta_P) + Z_{-1}, \tag{83}$$

where $0 < \delta_P < 1$.

5.1.8 Financial Sector

The financial balance sheets of each group of agents are presented in summary form in Table 5.1. In what follows we consider in turn the determination of the portfolio structure of households, the demand for credit by firms, and the behavior of commercial banks.

---

[17]It should be noted that external debt may exert disincentive effects not only on domestic private investment but also on international capital flows. As discussed by Khan and Haque (1985), high public external debt can lead to capital flight if domestic investment is subject to "expropriation risk." Conversely, debt reduction may not only stimulate private domestic capital formation but also net capital inflows; see for instance, Bhattacharya, Montiel and Sharma (1997) for Sub-Saharan Africa. This may be an important source of positive externality associated with debt relief, which suggests that the benefits of this shock, as discussed later, may be underestimated.

Table 5.1   IMMPA prototype for low-income countries: financial
balance sheets (in domestic-currency terms, at current prices)

Households

Assets	Liabilities
Cash holdings (H)	Financial wealth (WT)
Domestic deposits (DD)	
Foreign deposits ($ER \cdot FD$)	

Firms

Assets	Liabilities
Stock of capital ($PK \cdot K_P$)	Borrowing from banks (DL_P)
	Foreign borrowing ($ER \cdot FL_P$)
	Net worth (NW_P)

Commercial Banks

Assets	Liabilities
Loans to government (DL_G)	Household deposits (DD)
Loans to firms (DL_P)	Foreign liabilities ($ER \cdot FL_B$)
Reserve requirements (RR)	Net worth (NW_B)

Central Bank

Assets	Liabilities
Loans to government (DC_G)	Cash in circulation (H)
Foreign reserves ($ER \cdot FF$)	Reserve requirements (RR)
	Net worth (NW_{CB})

Government

Assets	Liabilities
Capital in education ($PK \cdot K_E$)	Loans from central bank (DC_G)
Capital in health ($PK \cdot K_H$)	Loans from banks (DL_G)
Capital in infra. ($PK \cdot K_{INF}$)	Foreign borrowing ($ER \cdot FL_G$)
	Net worth (NW_G)

Consolidated Public Sector

Assets	Liabilities
Capital in education ($PK \cdot K_E$)	Cash in circulation (H)
Capital in health ($PK \cdot K_H$)	Reserve requirements (RR)
Capital in infra. ($PK \cdot K_{INF}$)	Loans from banks (DL_G)
Foreign reserves ($ER \cdot FF$)	Foreign borrowing ($ER \cdot FL_G$)
	Net worth (NW_{PS})

Households

Households can freely alter the desired composition of their financial wealth, subject
to the overall constraint that initial or beginning-of-period wealth is predetermined
at any given moment in time. Each category of household allocates instantaneously
its stock of wealth to either money (in the form of cash holdings that bear no interest),

H_h, domestic bank deposits, DD_h, or foreign bank deposits, FD_h:

$$WT_h = H_h + ER \cdot FD_h + DD_h. \tag{84}$$

Note that in our definition of private wealth we have excluded land and other types of real assets (such as livestock), which can be important for households located in the rural sector. Some of these assets are often held in "unproductive" form and no market *per se* exists to measure their relative price. Thus, in practice, accounting for real assets is likely to raise some insurmountable measurement problems, involving both values and quantities. Nevertheless, it should be kept in mind that in a setting in which such assets are accounted for, a reallocation of wealth away from (say) real to financial assets would have significant real effects, by affecting interest income on interest-bearing assets (such as bank deposits), disposable income, and thus expenditure.

Real money demand functions for each household category are taken to depend positively on real income (measured in terms of the overall price level, which is nothing but the inverse of the purchasing power of one unit of currency), and negatively on inflation (as a proxy for the opportunity cost of holding money instead of real assets) and the rates of return on domestic and foreign deposits (which measure the opportunity cost of holding money instead of interest-bearing financial assets):

$$H_h^d = PLEV \left(\frac{YH_h}{PLEV} \right)^{\sigma_H} (1 + ID)^{-\beta_{hD}} [(1 + IF)(1 + dev)]^{-\beta_{hF}}$$

$$\times (1 + PINF)^{-\beta_{hPINF}}, \tag{85}$$

where *dev* denotes the expected devaluation rate, that is, the expected rate of change in *ER*, which is taken as exogenous (see Chapters 6 and 7 for an alternative treatment under flexible exchange rates). This specification of money demand allows us not only to account for different elasticities between domestic and foreign deposits, but also for different elasticities across households.

An alternative, simpler specification is to assume that the demand for money balances is proportional to total consumption, as a result of a "cash-in-advance" constraint:

$$H_h^d = CONS_h.$$

Because of our assumptions of a fixed exchange rate and incomplete sterilization, the nominal money supply (which is derived later from the base money stock), H^s, is determined endogenously. In equilibrium, this stock is equal to the total sum of money demanded by households:[18]

$$H^s = \sum_h H_h^d. \tag{86}$$

The portion of wealth that is not held in the form of noninterest-bearing currency is allocated between domestic and foreign deposits. The relative proportions of holdings

---

[18]When computing the solution of our model, this equation is dropped. Given Walras' law, if all other markets but the money market are in equilibrium, then the money market must be in equilibrium as well. Our computer program checks that this equation indeed holds continuously.

of each of these two categories of assets are taken to depend on their relative rates of return:

$$\frac{\gamma_{Bh}}{1 - \gamma_{Bh}} = \phi_{Bh} \left\{ \frac{1 + ID}{(1 + IF)(1 + dev)} \right\}^{\sigma_{Bh}}, \tag{87}$$

where γ_{Bh} represents the proportion of domestic deposits held in total deposits:

$$\gamma_{Bh} = \frac{DD_h}{DD_h + ER \cdot FD_h}. \tag{88}$$

In solving the model, we use equation (87) to determine the optimal level of domestic bank deposits, whereas we use equation (84) to determine residually the level of foreign deposits.

Firms

Firms finance their investment plans through retained earnings, as well as domestic and foreign loans (DL_P and FL_P, respectively):

$$PK \cdot Z = \Delta DL_P + ER \cdot \Delta FL_P + re \cdot YF_P.$$

Solving this equation for DL_P gives us the demand for bank loans:

$$DL_P = DL_{P,-1} - ER \cdot \Delta FL_P + PK \cdot Z - re \cdot YF_P. \tag{89}$$

The path of foreign loans is set exogenously. This implicitly accounts for ceilings that firms may face in their access to foreign markets.

Commercial Banks

Banks are at the heart of the financial system in our archetype economy, as is indeed the case in many low- and middle-income developing countries. Commercial banks are required to keep a portion $0 < rreq < 1$ of the deposits that they collect as reserve requirements:

$$RR = rreq \sum_h DD_h. \tag{90}$$

The balance sheet of commercial banks is

$$NW_{PB} = DL_P + DL_G + RR - \sum_h DD_h - ER \cdot FL_B, \tag{91}$$

where NW_{PB} denotes banks' net worth, which is essentially the difference between assets (loans and required reserves held at the central bank) and liabilities (household deposits and foreign borrowing).

Equation (89) represents the demand for loans. We assume that the actual stock of loans is demand determined, and that banks borrow on world capital markets the required "shortfall" given their domestic sources of funds. In flow terms, therefore, foreign borrowing is is given by

$$ER \cdot \Delta FL_B = \Delta DL_P + \Delta DL_G - (1 - rreq) \sum_h \Delta DD_h. \tag{92}$$

Given (92), and because all bank profits are distributed to households, the net worth of commercial banks evolves over time according to

$$NW_{PB} = NW_{PB,-1} - \Delta ER \cdot FL_{B,-1},\qquad(93)$$

where the second term on the right-hand side represents again valuation effects associated with nominal exchange rate changes.

Banks set the loan interest rate as a premium over the average cost of funds (including the devaluation rate, which affects the cost of foreign borrowing), taking into account the implicit cost of holding reserve requirements:

$$IL = \frac{ID^{\alpha_b}[(1 + IF)(1 + dev) - 1]^{1-\alpha_b}}{1 - rreq}PR,\qquad(94)$$

where $0 < \alpha_b < 1$ is measured by the initial share of domestic deposits in banks' total funds (that is, $\alpha_b = \sum_h DD_{h,0}/(\sum_h DD_{h,0} + FL_{B,0}ER_0)$), and PR denotes the finance premium, which is assumed to be set according to:[19]

$$PR = \xi_{pr}\left[\lambda_{pr}\left(\frac{\delta_c(NW_P + DL_P)}{DL_P}\right)^{-\gamma_{pr}}\right] + (1 - \xi_{pr})PR_{-1},\qquad(95)$$

where $0 < \xi_{pr} < 1$ is the speed of adjustment, $0 < \delta_c \leq 1$, and NW_P is the net worth of private urban firms in nominal terms, defined as

$$NW_P = PK \cdot K_P - DL_P - ER \cdot FL_P.$$

NW_P changes over time according to

$$\Delta NW_P = PK \cdot \Delta K_P - \Delta DL_P - ER \cdot \Delta FL_P$$
$$- \Delta ER \cdot FL_{P,-1} + \Delta PK \cdot K_{P,-1}\qquad(96)$$

The last two terms on the right-hand side of this expression represent, respectively, capital losses associated with depreciations of the nominal exchange rate, and capital gains associated with changes in the price of capital.

Our specification of pricing decisions by commercial banks allows us to capture balance sheet effects in the determination of loan rates. It is consistent with the current line of research emphasizing the role of collateral and the impact of borrowers' net worth on the "finance premium," as illustrated in the work of Bernanke, Gertler, and Gilchrist (2000), Kiyotaki and Moore (1997), and Izquierdo (2000). The higher the value of the private capital stock net of foreign borrowing (that is, "pledgeable" collateral, $PK \cdot K_P - ER \cdot FL_P$, or an "effective" fraction δ_c of that amount) relative to the amount of domestic loans, DL_P, the higher the proportion of total lending that banks can recoup in the event of default by seizing borrowers' assets. This reduces the finance premium and the cost of borrowing, stimulating the demand for credit.

---

[19]The coefficient α_b could be made time varying, by relating it for instance to the lagged ratio of domestic deposits in banks' total funds. Alternatively, given that the marginal cost of funds is given by the interest rate (inclusive of devaluation) on foreign borrowing, we could set $\alpha_b = 0$.

The dependence of the cost of funds on net worth is a critical aspect of the model; for instance, a nominal exchange rate devaluation (a rise in ER), would reduce firms' net worth and dampen private investment, by increasing the cost of capital (see (80)).

An alternative justification for the finance premium equation (95) can be found in the models of credit market imperfections recently developed by Agénor and Aizenman (1998, 1999b). These models, following Townsend (1979) and Helpman (1989), emphasize the importance of monitoring and enforcement costs of loan contracts that lenders face in a weak legal environment – as is so often the case in developing countries. In such an environment, these costs may be an *increasing* function of the amount lent (even against "good" collateral) because of congestion in courts and the difficulty of settling legal claims, which make it hard for lenders to actually seize borrowers' assets in case of default. This approach amounts to specifying the premium as a positive function of the ratio of the amount lent DL_P over "effective" collateral (as is done here), or separately as a negative function of $P_K \cdot K_P - ER \cdot FL_P$, with possibly a lower elasticity than that associated with DL_P.

Finally, it should be noted that the assumption that banks, given their deposit base, can borrow at will on world capital markets to satisfy the demand for domestic loans, may not be appropriate for all low-income countries. The reason is that in some countries domestic financial intermediaries (even local subsidiaries of foreign banks) may have either limited access to these markets – and thus be subject to quantity rationing – or may face themselves a rising risk premium on external funds (as, for instance, in Agénor and Aizenman (1998)). An alternative approach, which avoids introducing explicitly credit rationing of some categories of domestic borrowers, is to assume that commercial banks hold excess liquid reserves (above and over required reserves), and that movements in such reserves adjust endogenously to equilibrate the credit market – with foreign borrowing taken as exogenous. Yet another approach, as in the models of Chapters 6 and 7, would be to assume that banks borrow freely from the central bank at the prevailing policy rate, with foreign borrowing again taken as exogenous.

5.1.9   Public Sector

The public sector in our framework consists of the government and the central bank. We consider them in turn and relate changes in official reserves to the balance of payments.

Central Bank and the Balance of Payments

From the central bank's balance sheet, its net worth, NW_{CB}, is given by

$$NW_{CB} = DC_G + ER \cdot FF - MB, \tag{97}$$

where DC_G denotes domestic credit to the government, FF the stock of foreign reserves, and MB the monetary base. Assuming that capital gains and losses are not monetized, changes in the monetary base reflect changes in credit to the government, as well as changes in official reserves:

$$MB = MB_{-1} + \Delta DC_G + ER \cdot \Delta FF. \tag{98}$$

Assuming no operating costs, net profits of the central bank, $PROF^{CB}$, are given by the sum of interest payments on loans to the government, and interest receipts on holdings of foreign assets:

$$PROF^{CB} = IL_{-1} \cdot DC_{G,-1} + IF_G \cdot FF_{-1}. \tag{99}$$

where IF_G is the interest rate on foreign loans to the government. We assume that net profits of the central bank are transferred to the government.

Domestic credit to the government, DC_G, is treated as an exogenous policy variable. The accumulation of foreign reserves depends on the balance of payments, as any current account surplus (or deficit) must be compensated by a net flow of foreign capital:

$$\Delta FF = \sum_i (wpe_i E_i - wpm_i M_i) + IF \cdot \sum_h FD_{h,-1}$$
$$- IF \cdot FL_{P,-1} - IF_G(FL_{G,-1} - FF_{-1}) - IF \cdot FL_{B,-1}$$
$$- \sum_h \Delta FD_h + \Delta FL_G + \Delta FL_P + \Delta FL_B. \tag{100}$$

Equation (100) determines the change in the foreign-currency value of official reserves, ΔFF, required to clear the balance of payments, given changes in households' holdings of foreign assets, $\sum_h \Delta FD_h$, changes in foreign loans made to the government, ΔFL_G, and to private firms, ΔFL_P (both taken to be exogenous), changes in loans to domestic banks, ΔFL_B, and the current account.

The monetary base consists of currency in circulation, H^s, and reserve requirements, RR. The supply of currency to households is thus given by

$$H^s = MB - RR. \tag{101}$$

Note that the model could also be solved with a flexible exchange rate (as opposed to a fixed exchange rate), in which case FF would be kept constant (that is, $\Delta FF = 0$) and equation (100) would be solved for the nominal exchange rate (which affects trade volumes). Under this regime, currency fluctuations would have sizable effects not only on the banking system but also on the private sector's balance sheet and the economy in general; as discussed earlier, the "finance premium" depends on the net worth of private borrowers, which accounts for foreign indebtedness.

Finally, given (97) and (98), the central bank's net worth evolves over time according to:

$$NW_{CB} = NW_{CB,-1} + \Delta ER \cdot FF_{-1}, \tag{102}$$

where the last term represents valuation effects.

Government

We assume that government expenditures consist of government consumption, which only has demand-side effects, and public investment, which has both demand- and supply-side effects.

Government saving is defined as minus the government budget deficit:

$$-DEFa7 = PV_G X_G - W_M U_G - W_S S_G + PROF^{CB} + TXREV - TRH$$
$$- NG - IF_G \cdot ER \cdot FL_{G,-1} - IL_{-1}(DC_{G,-1} + DL_{G,-1}). \quad (103)$$

The term in square brackets on the right-hand side of this equation represents profits by the government from sales of the public good. $TXREV$ denotes total tax revenues, TRH government transfers to households, NG total government (current and capital) expenditures, and $PROF^{CB}$ profits from the central bank. The final two terms in the government budget include interest payments on loans from abroad, and interest payments on domestic loans by the central bank and commercial banks.

Using the definition of net profits of the central bank given in equation (99), government saving can be rewritten as

$$-DEF = PV_G X_G - W_M U_G - W_S S_G + TXREV - TRH - NG$$
$$- IF_G \cdot ER \cdot (FL_{G,-1} - FF_{-1}) - IL_{-1}DL_{G,-1}. \quad (104)$$

Total tax revenues, $TXREV$, consist of revenue generated by import tariffs (net of export subsidies), sales taxes, and income taxes:

$$TXREV = wpm_{AN} tm_{AN} M_{AN} ER + wpm_P tm_P M_P ER$$
$$- wpe_{AT} te_{AT} E_{AT} ER - wpe_P te_P E_P ER$$
$$+ \sum_i indtax_i PX_i X_i + \sum_h inctax_h YH_h, \quad (105)$$

where again $inctax_I = 0$.

Note that in this prototype framework we do not account explicitly for payroll taxes, although this could be important to study complementarities between tax and labor market reforms, as discussed in Chapters 3 and 4.

Public investment consists of investment in infrastructure, education, and health.[20] As in previous chapters, we define investment in infrastructure as the expenditure affecting the accumulation of public infrastructure capital, which includes public assets such as roads, power plants and railroads. Investment in education affects the stock of public education capital, which consists of assets such as school buildings and other infrastructure affecting skills acquisition, but does not represent human capital. In a similar fashion, investment in health adds to the stock of public assets such as hospitals, clinics, and other government infrastructure affecting health.

Formally, total government expenditure can thus be defined as

$$NG = I_{INF} + I_E + I_H + G_C, \quad (106)$$

where I_{INF}, I_E, I_H, denote investment in, respectively, infrastructure, education, and health, and G_C current expenditures besides labor costs.

---

[20]It should be noted that this treatment of public investment differs from standard data classification reported in national accounts; in many instances these investments are classified as current expenditures.

Accumulation of each type of public capital is defined as:

$$K_j = (1 - \delta_j)K_{j,-1} + \frac{I_{j,-1}}{PQ_{P,-1}}, \quad j = INF, E, H, \tag{107}$$

where $0 < \delta_j < 1$ is a depreciation rate. We assume that only the private good is used to invest and therefore deflate nominal investment by the demand price PQ_P.

The main reason for treating government capital at a disaggregated level is that, as noted earlier, we want to capture the different long-run effects that the allocation of public resources may have on the economy and ultimately on the poor. For instance, the stock of capital in education affects skills acquisition according to equation (26). Infrastructure and health capital affect the production process in the private sector as they both combine to produce the (composite) stock of government capital, K_G:

$$K_G = CES(K_{INF}, K_H). \tag{108}$$

As discussed below, the various channels through which different forms of government investment flows affect the economy figure prominently in our analysis of the impact of debt reduction, budget savings, and expenditure reallocation.

The government budget deficit is financed by either foreign or domestic borrowing:

$$DEF = ER \cdot \Delta FL_G + \Delta DL_G + \Delta DC_G. \tag{109}$$

In general, a variety of financing rules can be specified. For instance, it could be assumed that the deficit is financed by domestic loans (through either commercial banks or the central bank) or foreign borrowing, or that it be closed by cuts in government spending. Considering domestic financing alternatives could be useful for analyzing the crowding-out effects of public spending on private investment, as is done for instance in Chapter 4. In the policy experiments reported in this chapter, we assume that the sources of deficit financing are set exogenously. Thus, the public sector deficit is determined from "below the line." The variable that adjusts expenditures to make them consistent with the available financing and the revenues collected is the level of lump-sum transfers to households. The choice of a specific financing rule (which is critical for simulations of many shocks) is an important aspect of adapting the IMMPA prototype to specific countries.

The net worth of the government, NW_G, is defined as:

$$NW_G = PK(K_G + K_E) - (DL_G + DC_G) - ER \cdot FL_G, \tag{110}$$

and evolves over time according to

$$\Delta NW_G = PK(\Delta K_G + \Delta K_E) - (\Delta DL_G + \Delta DC_G) - ER \cdot \Delta FL_G$$
$$+ \Delta PK(K_{G,-1} + K_{E,-1}) - \Delta ER \cdot FL_{G,-1}, \tag{111}$$

with the last two terms on the right-hand side representing again valuation effects associated with changes in the price of capital and the nominal exchange rate.

Finally, from (97) and (110), the net worth of the consolidated public sector, NW_{PS}, is given by

$$NW_{PS} = PK(K_G + K_E) - DL_G + ER \cdot (FF - FL_G) - MB. \tag{112}$$

The logical structure of the IMMPA prototype is summarized in Figure 5.1.

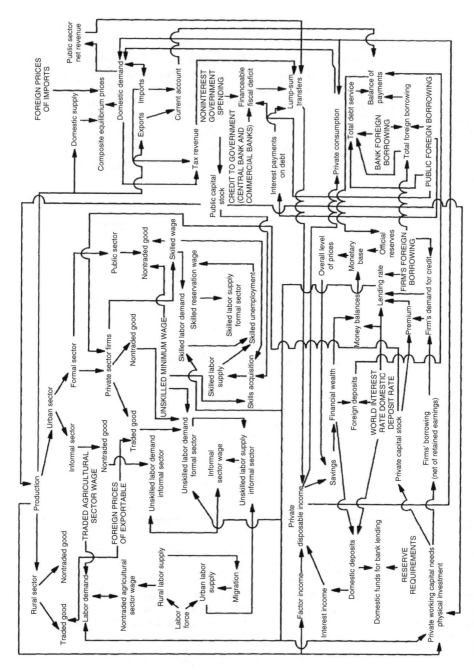

Figure 5.1 IMMPA prototype for low-income countries: analytical structure.

5.2   Poverty and Income Distribution Indicators

There are several alternative approaches to the analysis of the poverty and distributional effects of policy and exogenous shocks in applied general equilibrium models. A popular approach in the CGE literature consists in specifying a relatively large number of homogeneous household groups and calculating average income for each group following a shock, and treating the group as a whole as being poor if average income is lower than a given poverty line. This is the procedure followed, for instance, by Löfgren (2001), in a study based on a classification of households in fourteen groups. In IMMPA, the distributional and poverty effects of shocks are assessed in two ways: first by calculating a set of indicators (for income distribution) based directly on the model's simulation results; second, by linking IMMPA simulation results to a household expenditure survey.

Specifically, two measures of income distribution are generated directly from IMMPA: the Gini coefficient and the Theil inequality index.[21] Both are based on the six categories of households that were identified earlier, that is, workers located in the rural traded sector, rural nontraded sector, urban (unskilled) informal economy, urban unskilled formal sector, urban skilled formal sector, and capitalists-rentiers. Thus, these indicators allow the analyst to study changes in income distribution and poverty between groups, under the assumption of complete homogeneity *within* groups (or representative households). Formally, they are defined as

$$\text{Gini} = \frac{1}{2n^2 \cdot YH_M} \sum_h \sum_j |YH_h - YH_j|,$$

where $n = 6$ is the number of household categories, $h, j = AN, AT, UI, UF, S,$ KAP, and $YH_M = \sum_h YH_h/n$ is the arithmetic mean level of disposable income for household categories.

Using the same definitions, the Theil inequality index is measured as

$$\text{Theil} = \frac{1}{n} \sum_i \frac{YH_i}{\overline{YH}} \log \left(\frac{YH_i}{YH_M} \right).$$

We also calculate these two indicators using consumption, instead of disposable income. In the base period that we consider here, the initial values of the consumption- and income-based Gini coefficients are 0.512 and 0.515, respectively, whereas the consumption- and income-based Theil indexes are 0.199 and 0.203.

Following a shock, IMMPA generates three measures for these indicators (as well as those derived from household surveys, as discussed below): a *short-term* measure (first two periods following a shock), a *medium-term* measure (between 3 and

---

[21] Other commonly-used indicators include the Atkinson index which, like the Gini index, ranges from 0 to 1. For a detailed analytical discussion of the pros and cons of various measures of income inequality, see Cowell (1999). For instance, the Atkinson index is sensitive to inequality changes in the lowest part of the income distribution; the Gini coefficient is sensitive to inequality changes around the median; and the Theil index and coefficient of variation are both sensitive to inequality changes in the top part of the income distribution.

5 periods), and a *long-term* measure (between 6 and 10 periods).[22] While somewhat arbitrary in the choice of intervals, the importance of these measures (which can obviously be calculated only with a dynamic model) is clear: they allow the analyst to identify and discuss possible *dynamic trade-offs* associated with specific policy choices, by contrasting their short- and longer-run effects on inequality and the poor.

To assess the poverty effects of alternative shocks, IMMPA must be linked to a household income and expenditure survey, such as an Integrated Survey (IS) or Living Standards Measurement Survey (LSMS), which typically collect extensive information on migration, household income and expenditure (including own consumption), household assets, credits and savings, levels of education, apprenticeship and training, employment, occupational characteristics and status, as well as geographical location.[23] To begin with, we assume that the available survey consists of a relative large sample. This is needed to reduce nonsampling errors that may cause household income and expenditure to be underestimated – particularly in the least monetized regions of predominantly nontraded agricultural production (see Fofack (2000)) – and ensure sound inference on poverty effects following changes in factor allocation and resource flows across sectors. The approach that we propose proceeds as follows:

Step 1. Using the information provided in the household survey (presumably the most recent information available), classify the available sample into the six categories of households contained in the IMMPA framework (using, say, information on the main source of income of household heads) so as to establish an interface between the model's predictions and actual household income and expenses.

Step 2. For a given shock, generate with IMMPA real growth rates in per capita consumption and disposable income for all six categories of households in the economy, up to the end of the simulation horizon (say, T periods).

Step 3. Apply these growth rates separately to the per capita (disposable) income and consumption expenditure of each household (in each of the six groups) in the survey. This gives absolute income and consumption levels for each individual (and averages for each group) following the shock, for T periods.

---

[22] Specifically, let x_0^h denote the initial (base period) value of consumption (or income) for household group h and $\{g_t\}_{t=1}^{10}$ the (discounted) growth rate in consumption (or income) generated by the model for the first 10 years following a shock. The short-run measure of consumption, x_{SR}^h, is calculated as a geometric average of period-1 and period-2 values of x^h, $x^h(1)$ and $x^h(2)$, themselves obtained by applying the average growth rate for the period $x_{SR}^h = \sqrt{x^h(1)x^h(2)} = \sqrt{x_0^h(1+g_{SR})x_0^h(1+g_{SR})^2}$, where $g_{SR} = \sqrt{(1+g_1)(1+g_2)}-1$. Thus, $x_{SR}^h = x_0^h(1+g_{SR})^{1.5}$. Similarly, it can be shown that the medium-run value of consumption, x_{MR}^h, is given by $x_{MR}^h = x_2^h(1+g_{MR})^2$, where $g_{MR} = \sqrt[3]{\Pi_{t=3}^5(1+g_t)}-1$, whereas the long-run level of consumption, x_{LR}^h, is given by $x_{LR}^h = x_5^h(1+g_{LR})^3$, with $g_{LR} = \sqrt[5]{\Pi_{t=6}^{10}(1+g_t)}-1$. See Chen et al. (2001) for more details on this procedure.

[23] For more details on the scope and content of these surveys, see Delaine et al. (1992) for Integrated Surveys and Grosh and Glewwe (2000) for LSMS surveys. See also Deaton (1997) for a general discussion.

Step 4. Assuming different initial poverty lines for the rural and urban sectors (expressed in monetary units and adjusted over time to reflect increases in rural and urban price indexes), and using the new absolute nominal levels of income and consumption for each individual and each group, calculate a poverty headcount index, a poverty gap index, as well as the two indicators of income distribution described above (the Gini coefficient and the Theil inequality index), for the three different horizons identified earlier.

Step 5. Compare the postshock poverty and income distribution indicators with the baseline values to assess the impact of the shock on the poor.[24]

The two poverty indexes that are described in Step 4 are defined as follows. The poverty headcount index is the ratio of the number of individuals in the group whose income is below the poverty line to the total number of individuals in that group.[25] The poverty gap index is defined as:

$$P_G = \frac{1}{m \cdot YH^*} \sum_{k=1}^{m} (YH^* - YH_k),$$

where k is an individual whose income is below the poverty line, m the total number of people in the group below the poverty line, YH_k the income of individual k, and YH^* the poverty line.

We also use expenditure data to calculate our poverty measures. In practice, of course, whether income or expenditure data should be preferred depends on the scope and quality of the data in the available household survey.

In the illustrative simulations reported later in this chapter, we use instead of an actual household income and expenditure survey a "fictitious" one, that we built as follows.

First, we calculated real per capita disposable income and consumption expenditure for each of our six household categories, based on the initial values used to calibrate the model in the base period.

Second, using a random number generator and a log-normal distribution, we produced a sample of 1,397 observations, corresponding to the total number of workers and capitalists in the initial data set. We thus considered each individual as one household.

---

[24]To the extent that the initial poverty lines for the rural and urban sectors are adjusted over time to fully reflect increases in rural and urban price indexes (as we do in all experiments reported in this book) the comparisons involved in Step 5 would implicitly assume that the poverty line is constant in real terms in both sectors.

[25]As is well known, the headcount index suffers from several limitations (see for instance Blackwood and Lynch (1994) and Ravallion (1994)). In particular, it does not indicate how poor the poor really are – it remains unchanged even if all people with incomes below the poverty line were to experience, say, a 50 percent drop in income. Put differently, when a poor person becomes poorer, the index does not increase. Moreover, it implies that the distribution of income among the poor is homogeneous (it does not distinguish between a poor person who earns one monetary unit less than the poverty line and a poor person who earns 100 monetary units less than the poverty line). But to the extent that the analyst is interested only in the number of poor, the headcount index is a useful measure.

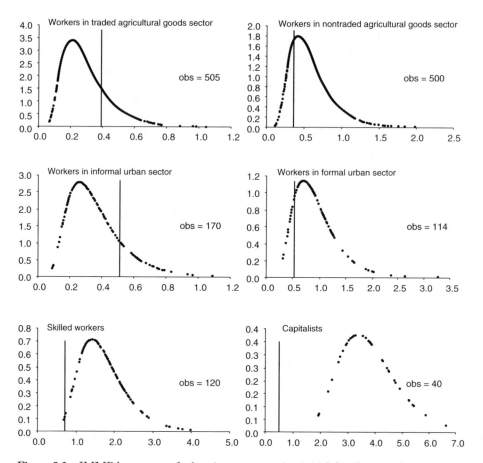

Figure 5.2   IMMPA prototype for low-income countries: initial distribution of income.

Third, we used the initial per capita income and consumption data as mean values and imposed a standard error of 0.5 for all household categories, except for skilled workers and capitalists, for which we chose a standard error of 0.35. We set (somewhat arbitrarily) the income poverty line at 0.45 for the rural sector and 0.5175 for the urban sector (or 15 percent higher than the rural poverty line). For the consumption data, we used initial poverty lines of 0.4 and 0.46 for the rural and urban sectors (again, with the latter being 15 percent higher than the former). We assume that these poverty lines remain constant in real terms for the whole horizon of the simulation period (10 periods); their behavior over time reflects therefore only changes in rural and urban prices levels.

Figures 5.2 and 5.3 show the initial data on income and consumption that we generated for each of our six categories of households, as well as a log-normal approximation. This parametric approximation is of course very good, given that the artificial samples that we generated were based on the log-normal distribution

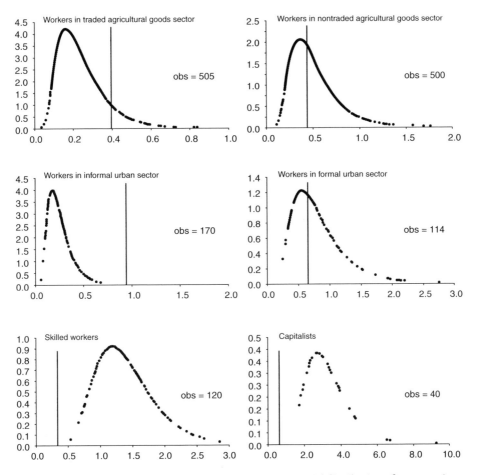

Figure 5.3   IMMPA prototype for low-income countries: initial distribution of consumption.

itself. But as discussed in Chapter 8, a number of alternative statistical distributions – such as the beta distribution – could be specified to approximate the actual distribution of any given income group.

The data that we generated produced an income-based headcount index of 61.8 percent in the agricultural sector (86.1 percent in the nontraded sector and 37.2 percent in the traded sector), 52.8 percent for urban unskilled households (78.8 percent in the informal sector and 14.0 percent for unskilled workers in the formal sector), and 0 percent for skilled workers and capitalists. For the economy as a whole, the income-based poverty rate amounts to 53.2 percent. With the income-based poverty gap, the results obtained are 38.9 percent for the agricultural sector (44.0 percent in the nontraded sector and 26.8 percent in the traded sector), 40.8 percent for urban unskilled households (43.8 percent in the informal sector and

15.7 percent for unskilled workers in the formal sector), and again 0 percent for skilled workers and capitalists. The aggregate poverty gap index is 38.7 percent.

For the consumption-based headcount index, the results are 64.4 percent in the agricultural sector (88.7 percent in the nontraded sector and 39.8 percent in the traded sector), 62.3 percent for urban unskilled households (91.8 percent in the informal sector and 18.4 percent for unskilled workers in the formal sector), and 0 percent for skilled workers and capitalists. For the economy as a whole, the consumption-based poverty rate amounts to 56.9 percent. With the consumption-based poverty gap, we obtain 40.6 percent for the agricultural sector (47.0 percent in the nontraded sector and 26.1 percent in the traded sector), 46.3 percent for urban unskilled households (50.0 percent in the informal sector and 18.9 percent for unskilled workers in the formal sector), and again 0 percent for skilled workers and capitalists. The aggregate poverty gap index is 41.4 percent. These numbers are broadly in line with the evidence for Sub-Saharan Africa and low-income countries in general.

For each policy or exogenous shock, therefore, the user can assess the short-, medium-, and long-term effects on poverty and income distribution and thus examine possible trade-offs with other policy objectives.

The main benefit of this approach is that it allows us to link IMMPA simulation results with actual, survey-based patterns of income and expenditure and to provide a more accurate derivation of poverty indicators.

The procedure described above assumes that the modeler matches households as defined in the macro component of IMMPA and a household survey using information on the main source of income of household heads.

An alternative treatment is also possible and depends on whether or not the household survey provides sufficient detail regarding the composition of income among individual members of each household; "light" surveys tend to concentrate on the household head, whereas more in-depth surveys (which tend to be conducted less frequently) provide richer information.

To the extent that the information is detailed enough, and as long as each member of a household can be "allocated" to one of the six income groups identified earlier, growth rates of income and consumption can be applied separately to each individual income earner (as in Step 3 above). A more accurate measure of the change in each household's income can therefore be calculated and poverty and income indicators can be generated using either "individual" income earners or "composite" households. However, whether accounting for heterogeneity in the sources of income among individual household members makes a difference or not is generally case specific; it depends on both the characteristics of the intra-household distribution of income (which depends on each household's risk diversification strategies) and the extent to which the growth rates of income and consumption generated by the macro component of IMMPA, following a given shock, differ among the various income groups on which it is based. If, for instance, the intra-household distribution as given in the survey is such that most of the income of each composite unit is generated by the household head, treating the household as a homogeneous unit and applying the same growth rate of income to each member should not result in significant errors.

Perhaps more problematic for our approach is the assumption, as noted earlier, that intra-group distribution (among homogeneous households) is constant. In turn, the assumption of within-group homogeneity implies that the within-group rank ordering of households remains unchanged following any shock. As noted by Kanbur (1987) and Demery and Addison (1993) in a related context, the assumption that within-group distributions are unchanged and unaffected by policy shocks implies that workers are withdrawn from the sector of origin in a representative manner (leaving the distribution of income there unchanged) and that, as they move from one sector to another, they assume immediately the income distribution characteristics of the sector of destination (in particular, the variance of income in that sector is assumed to apply to all new entrants).[26] Thus, some workers may be poor not because of their personal characteristics but because of the economic circumstances that characterize their sector of employment. Whether the assumption of constant within-group distributions is always warranted is not entirely clear; it represents therefore a potential weakness in this approach.

Several recent studies have attempted to drop the assumption of a stable within-group distribution to analyze the poverty and distributional effects of policy and exogenous shocks in applied general equilibrium models; they include Cockburn (2002), Decaluwé, Dumont, and Savard (1999), and Decaluwé, Patry, Savard, and Thorbecke (1999). Individual data in these studies are included directly in the general equilibrium model and (assuming that the within-group distribution follows a well-defined statistical distribution, such as the log-normal or a beta distribution) micro-simulation techniques are used to exploit intra-group information. This approach has the benefit of allowing the analyst to distinguish, in the evolution of poverty indicators, the specific contribution of three factors: changes in the poverty line (when it is treated as endogenous), average income variations, and income distribution. It provides therefore a potentially important direction for future research. At the same time, however, it must be recognized that it is relatively complex to implement (particularly in conjunction with a fully specified macroeconomic model, like a complete IMMPA framework), because it requires manipulating a sizable amount of data. Moreover, whether changes in the intra-group distribution matter appears to be shock dependent; indeed, in some of the simulation results reported by Decaluwé, Dumont and Savard (1999), such changes account for only a small proportion in changes in poverty measures.[27]

It is also worth noting that in the artificial survey that we constructed, we did not account for openly unemployed workers, of either variety. In practice, however, surveys may report a head of household as being unemployed (and therefore with no

---

[26] It also implies that income transfers between households in any given group are ignored. In practice, intra-group income reallocation may be large in periods of hardship and may represent an important factor in understanding the poverty effects of adverse economic shocks.

[27] A possible way of testing for whether this type of techniques should be used is to compare the aggregated results of two (or more, where feasible) household surveys and test statistically (using parametric or non-parametric tests) for any evidence of a shift in intra-group distributions. This test is not, however, fully satisfactory, because evidence of stability across surveys cannot necessarily be construed as providing definite support to any model-based experiment – particularly those involving "atypical" shocks.

declared wage income), while at the same time receiving nonwage income from, say, holdings of financial assets, government transfers, or a share of distributed profits by firms in the private sector. Instead of simply assuming that the rate of growth of income or consumption is zero for the unemployed (an assumption that may lead to unrealistic results for medium-term exercises), our inclination would be to treat these observations as follows. For unskilled workers, it would seem reasonable to assume that the openly unemployed are actually employed in the informal sector or the nontradable agricultural sector (even if they don't declare it), depending on the sector of occupation, at the going wage. One can thus apply the growth rates of consumption and "full" disposable income taken from the macro component of IMMPA to that category of workers, as in the sequence described previously. By contrast, for skilled workers, the assumption that the unemployed are actually working in the informal sector may not be very satisfactory, for the reasons discussed earlier and in Chapter 1. We would suggest using the growth rate of pre-tax, nonwage income only, for that category of workers, and adjust the rate of growth of consumption taken from the macro component of IMMPA in proportion to the differential between disposable income of employed workers and pre-tax non-wage income.

Finally, it should be noted that we have abstracted in the above discussion from issues associated with differences between national accounts data (on which IMMPA is based) and survey data (from which poverty measures are calculated). However, in practice, large discrepancies can arise between these two sets of data. In particular, it is possible that the composition of employment, output, and the inter-group income distribution generated by IMMPA and the household survey (following Step 1 above) are different.[28] Indeed, it is well recognized that national accounts and survey estimates of income and consumption patterns can differ significantly. Moreover, these differences may even be increasing in some cases, as appears to be the case in India (see Deaton (2001)). In general, the evidence suggests that nominal consumption growth rates estimated from survey data tends to be substantially lower than those estimated from national accounts data. Various factors may account for these discrepancies, as discussed by Deaton (2001, 2005) and Ravallion (2000). For instance, consumption in national accounts is typically determined as a residual and is thus contaminated by errors and omissions elsewhere in the accounts. In practice, researchers often end up treating one source or the other as the "correct" or "most reliable" one – despite the fact that it is likely that both sources of information are subject to error. In the present context, because both sources are used jointly, the issue of reconciling them arises. For instance, if it is believed that the national accounts data provide a more accurate measure of the level of consumption, one approach could be to scale up survey data so as to match the former, and use the rescaled data for poverty assessment. There are several potential problems, of course, with this approach – the assumption that

---

[28] As indicated earlier, for the simulation exercises reported in this paper, we generated an artificial sample (based on a log-normal distribution) using the mean per capita real income data obtained from the calibration of the model in the base period. The inter-group Gini coefficients that are calculated from the model and from the household survey are thus very close, given the relatively large number of replications. In practice, however, this may not be the case.

household consumption levels as measured in the survey are correct up to a multiplicative constant is by no means a reliable one, given the likely discrepancies between urban and rural data. More generally, the decision as to which data are correct is a difficult one, and the reconciliation process is likely to be country specific.

5.3 Calibration

Assessing the properties of the model presented in the previous section requires calibration and numerical simulations. Given that the objective of the model is to analyze the poverty and distributional impact of adjustment policies in highly-indebted, low-income countries, we have calibrated it to reflect what we believe to be a "representative" country with those characteristics. A complete list of parameters and initial values for each of the variables in the model is provided in Chen et al. (2001); here a brief summary is provided. Many of these parameters (such as demand and supply elasticities) reflect conventional values used in the literature. A financial social accounting matrix (FSAM) presents all initial values in a pedagogical format. Emini and Fofack (2004) provide a detailed FSAM of Cameroon that follows closely the IMMPA structure described in the previous sections.

5.3.1 Initial Values

Endogenous Variables

For the first period, we assume that our "representative" economy has a nominal GDP of approximately 850 units and we set agricultural production to about 30 percent of GDP, with slightly more than four-fifths of it being traded and the remainder being nontraded. We further assume that the private, formal urban sector produces 15 percent, the informal sector about 43 percent, and the public sector 12 percent of the country's total output.

The size of the total workforce in the first period is set to 1,416, with 829 persons residing in rural areas, about 40 percent of which are employed in the traded agricultural sector. There are about 467 urban unskilled workers, eighty percent of which are employed in the informal economy. There are 121 skilled workers, with 46 of them employed in the private urban formal sector, and another 50 working in the public sector. This implies that the initial open unemployment rate for skilled workers is about 20.6 percent. The growth rate of the urban unskilled population is set to 2.2 percent.

The skilled nominal wage is set to approximately 30 percent above the minimum wage paid to unskilled workers employed in the formal urban economy. Rural workers employed in the traded agricultural sector receive about 35 percent of the urban minimum wage.

Aggregate demand consists of households' consumption, private investment and government expenditures. Demand for the formal, private urban good is approximately 600 units, whereas demand for the nontraded agricultural good is

190 units. Demand for the public good is 286 units, and demand for informal goods is 152 units.

The level of agricultural goods exported is 371 units and imports of nontraded agricultural goods is assumed to be 75 units in the first period. Domestic demand for nontraded agricultural goods is set at 123 units. Imports of the formal private good are assumed to be 486 units. Also, we have assumed exports and domestic demand of the private formal good to be 215 units and 114 units, respectively.

First-period values for household incomes range from a value of 61 for the nontraded agricultural sector household to 217 for the capitalist household. Private urban formal firms make the highest profits with a profit level of 179. The nontraded agricultural firms are assumed to have the lowest profit levels, at about 30. Firms' incomes mirror that of profits with private urban firms earning the highest income (168 units), and nontraded agricultural firms the lowest income (30 units).

The return to capital is initially set to 12 percent, whereas the lending rate is set to 7 percent, with a financial premium of 1.07. Domestic loans to private urban firms amount to 154, whereas banks have foreign liabilities of 62. The initial stock of private capital is set to 1,500, whereas the initial stocks of public capital in infrastructure, education, and health, are set to 500, 50, and 50, respectively. The initial stock of "composite" public capital is also set at 50 units. With a reserve requirement ratio of 10 percent, and total bank deposits of 213, the level of required reserves is 21. The money supply is initially set at 152. The initial values of tax revenue, transfers to households, the budget balance, and total government expenditure, as shares of GDP, are 23 percent, 15 percent, −1.3 percent, and 37 percent, respectively.

Exogenous Variables

Both the initial numbers of skilled and unskilled workers in the public sector are set to 50 and grow at a constant rate of 2 percent annually. The real minimum wage rate of urban workers and the real wage rate paid to workers in the rural traded sector are kept constant throughout. The growth rate of the rural population is set at 2 percent per annum.

Skilled workers, unskilled workers (in both rural and urban areas), and capitalists, are subject to Constant income tax rates of 15 percent, 23 percent, and 33 percent, respectively. There are no tariffs on, or export subsidies to, agricultural goods. A 4 percent tariff is imposed on imports of private formal urban goods, but at the same time they also benefit from a 5 percent export subsidy.

Foreign loans to private firms amount initially to 136.6 and grow at 9 percent in every period. The initial values of public investment in infrastructure, health and education are set to 10 and each grows at a fixed rate of 2 percent per period. Depreciation for infrastructure capital occurs at 1 percent per annum.

Government consumption has an initial value of 40 and grows at 2 percent thereafter. Domestic credit to government has an initial value of 50 and grows also at an annual rate of 2 percent in subsequent periods. Domestic loans to the government have an initial value of 100 and are kept constant over time, whereas foreign loans to the government have a starting value of 1,567 and grow at 1 percent annually. Indirect tax rates on output have been all set to zero in the base period.

5.3.2   Parameter Values

Recall that all sectors, with the exception of the informal sector, have CES production functions. Elasticities of substitution between the various inputs in these production functions are calibrated to values between 0.4 and 1.2, reflecting low to medium values.

Input share parameters are chosen to reflect labor-intensive production technologies, typical of a low-income developing country. In the rural sector, the labor share parameter is 0.92 for the traded good and 0.63 for the nontraded good. Similarly, the labor share parameter in the public good production function is also high, at 0.90. Production of the private formal sector good not only leans heavily toward usage of labor, with the skilled labor-private capital composite input share parameter being 0.90, but also uses more unskilled labor rather than skilled labor or capital, with the unskilled labor share parameter having a value of 0.97. The growth rate of the population of urban unskilled workers has an elasticity with respect to expected wages of 0.3.

Recall that only the agricultural goods and private formal goods can be traded. The demand functions for these goods are therefore expressed as Armington functions over import and domestic demand. The values for the share parameter (for import demand) and elasticity of substitution for the demand for agricultural goods are 0.5 and 0.8, respectively, whereas those for the demand for private formal goods are 0.8 and 1.01, respectively. For all households, the largest consumption share is on goods produced by the sectors in which they are employed. With the exception of the urban informal household, for all households the smallest share of consumption goes to informal goods.

For the construction of consumer price indexes, and in order to capture different consumption patterns, private formal urban sector goods are assigned the largest share in the urban price index, whereas agricultural goods have the largest weight in the construction of the rural price index. For the urban unskilled price index, informal sector goods have the largest share. for the construction of the urban skilled price index, private urban goods are weighted most heavily. Lastly, elasticities of money demand with respect to domestic and foreign interest rates are all set at 0.5, whereas the elasticity to real income is assigned a uniform value of 1.0.

5.4   Some Illustrative Experiments

This section presents and discusses the numerical results associated with three types of shocks: a temporary terms-of-trade shock, a permanent cut in domestic credit to the government, and a debt relief-expenditure reallocation program, consisting of partial external debt forgiveness coupled with a reallocation of savings on debt service payments to three alternative forms of government expenditure: lump-sum transfers to households, spending on infrastructure, and outlays on education.[29],[30] Both the short- and longer-run effects of these shocks are analyzed, with a particular focus on poverty as measured by the indicators described earlier.[31]

5.4.1 Terms-of-Trade Shock

We first simulate the impact of a temporary terms-of-trade shock that takes the form of a transitory (one period only) 10 percent increase in the world market price of the agricultural traded good. The results are summarized in Tables 5.2 and 5.3. This type of shocks has indeed played a pervasive role in explaining changes in real incomes in sub-Saharan Africa and has been analyzed in a number of empirical studies (see, for instance, Dorosh and Sahn (2000)). Because we have assumed that the product wage in the traded rural sector is fixed (that is, the ratio of the nominal wage to the value added price of the good is constant), nominal wages will tend to match the increase in the producer price.[32] Had we excluded financial sector effects from the model, the demand for labor would remain constant and so would production of the traded good.

But because firms in this sector borrow to finance wage payments, the effective price of labor includes the lending rate, as noted earlier. As we shall explain later, lending rates experience an initial decline after the positive terms-of-trade shock, implying that the effective price of labor falls. By itself, this tends to increase the demand for labor in that sector. However, a decline in the real value of public investment, due to increasing formal sector goods prices, leads to an overall reduction in value added and output in that sector, lowering labor demand. Given that at any point in time the supply of labor in the rural sector is predetermined, and that this segment of the labor market must clear at the aggregate level, workers laid off from the traded sector are absorbed by the nontraded sector. But because of the decline in public investment, output also declines over time in the nontraded agricultural sector.

All these dynamics occur in the period following that of the shock, given our assumption that the cost of credit in loan contracts is agreed upon one period in advance and therefore interest rate effects take one period to materialize. However, at the very moment the shock occurs, interest rate effects are absent; as a result, value added in both components of the rural sector remains constant on impact, implying no changes in the rural traded and rural nontraded workforce. This occurs because the product wage in both segments remains constant, implying that nominal wages match exactly the increase in the value added price of their respective good.

---

[29] For a description of the IMMPA simulation program, which consists of both Eviews and GAMS versions combined with Excel input and output sheets, see Chen et al. (2001).

[30] In principle, as implied by (16) and (17), both θ_U and θ_R vary over time. In the simulations, however, we treat them as constant.

[31] It should be kept in mind that the choice of a particular set of poverty measures always involves a value judgement and can have considerable bearing on simulation results and policy choices. The open architecture of IMMPA, however, allows users to program alternative measures if deemed necessary.

[32] They do not match the increase in the price of the agricultural good one to one, because producer prices also reflect changes in intermediate input prices.

Table 5.2 IMMPA: Macroeconomic indicators 10-percent increase in the world price of the agricultural traded good (Absolute deviations from baseline, unless otherwise indicated)

					Periods					
	1	2	3	4	5	6	7	8	9	10
Real Sector										
Total resources	5.171	−0.184	0.025	0.020	0.019	0.020	0.021	0.021	0.021	0.022
Gross domestic product	5.889	−0.205	0.036	0.025	0.026	0.027	0.028	0.028	0.029	0.030
Imports of goods & NFS	4.007	−0.149	0.006	0.010	0.008	0.009	0.009	0.009	0.009	0.009
Total expenditures										
Private consumption	7.290	−0.492	0.089	0.054	0.055	0.056	0.057	0.057	0.058	0.058
Public consumption	0.000	0.000	0.000	0.000	0.000	0.000	0.000	0.000	0.000	0.000
Private investment	1.449	0.362	−0.087	0.010	−0.005	−0.004	−0.005	−0.005	−0.005	−0.006
Public investment	0.000	0.000	0.000	0.000	0.000	0.000	0.000	0.000	0.000	0.000
Exports of goods & NFS	4.411	−0.019	−0.012	−0.017	−0.014	−0.014	−0.013	−0.012	−0.012	−0.011
Memorandum item										
Private disposable income	7.017	−0.206	0.065	0.054	0.054	0.055	0.056	0.056	0.056	0.057
External Sector										
Current account	−4.557	−1.650	−0.050	0.039	−0.001	0.003	0.001	0.000	−0.001	−0.002
Exports of goods & NFS (excl. subsidies)	4.545	−0.019	−0.012	−0.017	−0.014	−0.014	−0.013	−0.012	−0.012	−0.011
Imports of goods & NFS (excl. tariffs)	4.027	−0.151	0.007	0.011	0.009	0.009	0.010	0.010	0.010	0.010
Factor services	0.000	−0.204	−0.261	−0.253	−0.241	−0.231	−0.222	−0.213	−0.204	−0.188
Capital account	7.581	−8.572	−4.522	0.411	−0.004	0.017	0.015	0.013	0.012	0.010
NFPS financing	0.000	0.000	0.000	0.000	0.000	0.000	0.000	0.000	0.000	0.000
Central bank financing	0.000	0.000	0.000	0.000	0.000	0.000	0.000	0.000	0.000	0.000
Private financing	9.092	−10.519	−5.600	0.504	−0.005	0.020	0.018	0.016	0.014	0.012
Change in net international reserves	48.995	−34.008	−30.693	2.450	−0.025	0.095	0.100	0.095	0.094	0.093

Continued

Table 5.2 Continued

					Periods					
	1	2	3	4	5	6	7	8	9	10
Nonfinancial Public Sector										
Total revenue	6.328	0.057	0.008	−0.001	−0.003	−0.002	−0.002	−0.002	−0.002	−0.003
Total expenditures	6.095	0.055	0.008	−0.001	−0.003	−0.002	−0.002	−0.002	−0.002	−0.003
Consumption	0.000	0.000	0.000	0.000	0.000	0.000	0.000	0.000	0.000	0.000
Investment	0.000	0.000	0.000	0.000	0.000	0.000	0.000	0.000	0.000	0.000
Transfers to households	8.852	0.082	0.010	−0.003	−0.005	−0.004	−0.003	−0.003	−0.004	−0.004
Domestic interest payments	0.000	−0.035	0.057	0.039	0.032	0.027	0.023	0.021	0.019	0.016
Foreign interest payments	0.000	0.000	0.000	0.000	0.000	0.000	0.000	0.000	0.000	0.000
Total financing	0.000	0.000	0.000	0.000	0.000	0.000	0.000	0.000	0.000	0.000
Net foreign financing	0.000	0.000	0.000	0.000	0.000	0.000	0.000	0.000	0.000	0.000
Net domestic credit, central bank	0.000	0.000	0.000	0.000	0.000	0.000	0.000	0.000	0.000	0.000
Net domestic credit, commercial banks	0.000	0.000	0.000	0.000	0.000	0.000	0.000	0.000	0.000	0.000
Central Bank										
Total assets	4.305	1.620	0.195	0.299	0.283	0.274	0.266	0.258	0.251	0.237
Net foreign assets	5.445	2.021	0.241	0.367	0.346	0.333	0.321	0.310	0.300	0.281
Net domestic assets	0.000	0.000	0.000	0.000	0.000	0.000	0.000	0.000	0.000	0.000
Loans to government	0.000	0.000	0.000	0.000	0.000	0.000	0.000	0.000	0.000	0.000
Loans to commercial banks	0.000	0.000	0.000	0.000	0.000	0.000	0.000	0.000	0.000	0.000
Other domestic assets	0.000	0.000	0.000	0.000	0.000	0.000	0.000	0.000	0.000	0.000
Total liabilities/reserve money	4.305	1.620	0.195	0.299	0.283	0.274	0.266	0.258	0.251	0.237
Currency in circulation	4.976	1.690	−0.098	0.053	0.046	0.047	0.048	0.048	0.048	0.049
Reserve requirements	−0.762	1.213	1.567	1.263	1.084	0.950	0.845	0.762	0.694	0.590

Memorandum items									
Money demand (M1)	4.976	1.690	−0.098	0.053	0.046	0.047	0.048	0.048	0.048	0.049
Gross reserves in months of imports	1.363	2.175	0.235	0.357	0.337	0.323	0.311	0.300	0.290	0.271
Commercial Banks									
Total assets	0.903	0.912	0.731	0.609	0.523	0.459	0.410	0.371	0.339	0.291
Net foreign assets	0.000	0.000	0.000	0.000	0.000	0.000	0.000	0.000	0.000	0.000
Net domestic assets	0.903	0.912	0.731	0.609	0.523	0.459	0.410	0.371	0.339	0.291
Loans to government	0.000	0.000	0.000	0.000	0.000	0.000	0.000	0.000	0.000	0.000
Loans to firms	1.303	1.066	0.778	0.635	0.535	0.464	0.411	0.369	0.336	0.286
Other domestic assets	−0.762	1.213	1.567	1.263	1.084	0.950	0.845	0.762	0.694	0.590
Total liabilities	0.903	0.912	0.731	0.609	0.523	0.459	0.410	0.371	0.339	0.291
Banks' foreign liabilities	3.437	0.495	−0.386	−0.241	−0.194	−0.157	−0.130	−0.108	−0.091	−0.065
Deposits	−0.762	1.213	1.567	1.263	1.084	0.950	0.845	0.762	0.694	0.590
Memorandum items [1]									
Real GDP growth rate	−0.124	0.104	0.011	−0.002	0.002	0.001	0.001	0.001	0.001	0.001
Inflation rate (economy-wide)	3.778	−3.636	0.307	−0.016	−0.001	0.000	−0.001	−0.001	−0.001	0.000
Deposit rate	0.000	0.000	0.000	0.000	0.000	0.000	0.000	0.000	0.000	0.000
Lending rate	−0.237	−0.149	−0.102	−0.082	−0.068	−0.059	−0.052	−0.047	−0.043	−0.040
Risk premium	−0.001	0.001	0.000	0.000	0.000	0.000	0.000	0.000	0.000	0.000

[1] Absolute deviations from baseline.

Table 5.3 IMMPA: structural, poverty, and income distribution indicators 10-percent increase in the world price of the agricultural traded good (Absolute deviations from baseline, unless otherwise indicated)

					Periods					
	1	2	3	4	5	6	7	8	9	10
Production Structure										
Size of informal sector (% of total output)	0.809	−0.161	0.050	0.034	0.036	0.036	0.037	0.037	0.037	0.038
Size of rural sector (% of formal sector output)	5.069	−0.063	0.015	0.003	0.005	0.005	0.005	0.005	0.005	0.005
Composition of Employment and Wages										
Employment in rural sector (% of total employment)	0.000	0.007	0.011	0.015	0.018	0.021	0.023	0.024	0.025	0.027
Employment in rural nontraded sector (% of rural employment)	0.000	0.014	0.024	0.028	0.033	0.038	0.042	0.047	0.051	0.055
Employment in informal sector (% of total employment)	0.023	−0.005	−0.012	−0.015	−0.019	−0.021	−0.023	−0.025	−0.027	−0.028
Employment in informal sector (% of urban employment)	0.050	−0.002	−0.008	−0.009	−0.010	−0.011	−0.012	−0.013	−0.013	−0.014
Employment in public sector (% of total employment)	0.000	0.000	0.000	0.000	0.000	0.000	0.000	0.000	0.000	0.000
Employment in public sector (% of urban employment)	0.000	0.002	0.003	0.003	0.004	0.004	0.004	0.004	0.004	0.004
Rural traded and rural nontraded sector wage differential[1]	12.588	0.153	−0.011	0.005	0.020	0.038	0.062	0.093	0.131	0.176
Urban unskilled formal and informal sector wage differential[1]	−0.489	0.068	−0.023	−0.013	−0.013	−0.012	−0.011	−0.010	−0.010	−0.009
Public sector wages (% of total public expenditure)	−0.437	−0.026	0.014	0.008	0.008	0.008	0.008	0.008	0.008	0.008

Aggregate Demand

Private consumption (% of GDP)	0.978	−0.212	0.039	0.021	0.022	0.022	0.022	0.021	0.021	0.021
Private consumption (% of total consumption)	0.274	−0.020	0.004	0.002	0.002	0.002	0.002	0.002	0.002	0.002
Private investment (% of GDP)	−0.910	0.121	−0.026	−0.003	−0.006	−0.006	−0.007	−0.007	−0.007	−0.007
Private investment (% of total investment)	0.135	0.035	−0.008	0.001	−0.001	0.000	0.000	−0.001	−0.001	−0.001

Fiscal Indicators

Public investment in infrastructure (% of total public investment)	0.000	0.000	0.000	0.000	0.000	0.000	0.000	0.000	0.000	0.000
Public investment in health (% of total public investment)	0.000	0.000	0.000	0.000	0.000	0.000	0.000	0.000	0.000	0.000
Public investment in education (% of total public investment)	0.000	0.000	0.000	0.000	0.000	0.000	0.000	0.000	0.000	0.000

Financial Indicators

Currency (% of M2)	1.383	0.110	−0.358	−0.243	−0.194	−0.158	−0.131	−0.111	−0.095	−0.082
M2 (% of GDP)	−1.602	0.778	0.561	0.571	0.566	0.562	0.557	0.554	0.550	0.546
Bank credit to private sector (% of GDP)	0.004	0.005	0.005	0.005	0.005	0.005	0.005	0.005	0.005	0.005
Lending – deposit rate differential	0.000	0.000	0.000	0.000	0.000	0.000	0.000	0.000	0.000	0.000

External Sector

Agricultural exports (% of total exports)	2.627	0.001	−0.003	0.001	0.001	0.001	0.002	0.002	0.002	0.002
Imports of non-agricultural goods (% of total imports)	−0.488	0.041	−0.012	−0.007	−0.007	−0.007	−0.007	−0.007	−0.007	−0.007
External debt (% of GDP)	−7.143	0.263	−0.046	−0.032	−0.033	−0.034	−0.034	−0.035	−0.035	−0.036
Degree of openness (exports plus imports divided by GDP)	−1.939	0.147	−0.047	−0.035	−0.035	−0.035	−0.036	−0.036	−0.036	−0.036

Continued

Table 5.3 Continued

Poverty Indicators		Periods									
	1	2	3	4	5	6	7	8	9	10
	SR	MR	LR							
Rural poverty line (consumption-based) in real terms[1]	0.0000	0.0000	0.0000							
Rural poverty line (consumption-based) in nominal terms[1]	2.6808	1.2985	0.1656							
Rural poverty line (income-based) in real terms[1]	0.0000	0.0000	0.0000							
Rural poverty line (income-based) in nominal terms[1]	2.6808	1.2985	0.1656							
Urban poverty line (consumption-based) in real terms[1]	0.0000	0.0000	0.0000							
Urban poverty line (consumption-based) in nominal terms[1]	4.5274	2.2342	0.3645							
Urban poverty line (income-based) in real terms[1]	0.0000	0.0000	0.0000							
Urban poverty line (income-based) in nominal terms[1]	4.5274	2.2342	0.3645							
Rural nontraded household (consumption-based) poverty headcount index	−0.0220	−0.0180	−0.0020							
Rural traded household (consumption-based) poverty headcount index	−0.0486	−0.0243	−0.0030							

Urban informal household (consumption-based) poverty headcount index	−0.0125	−0.0093	0.0000
Urban formal unskilled household (consumption-based) poverty headcount index	0.0067	0.0000	0.0067
Urban formal skilled household (consumption-based) poverty headcount index	0.0000	0.0000	0.0000
Capitalists household poverty (consumption-based) headcount index	0.0000	0.0000	0.0000
Rural nontraded household (consumption-based) poverty gap index	−0.0139	−0.0047	−0.0003
Rural traded household (consumption-based) poverty gap index	−0.0033	−0.0016	−0.0005
Urban informal household (consumption-based) poverty gap index	−0.0123	−0.0038	−0.0022
Urban formal unskilled household (consumption-based) poverty gap index	0.0072	0.0075	−0.0062
Urban formal skilled household (consumption-based) poverty gap index	0.0000	0.0000	0.0000
Capitalists household (consumption-based) poverty gap index	0.0000	0.0000	0.0000
Rural nontraded household (income-based) poverty headcount index	−0.0220	−0.0120	−0.0020
Rural traded household (income-based) poverty headcount index	−0.0426	−0.0304	−0.0061

Continued

Table 5.3 Continued

		Periods								
	1	2	3	4	5	6	7	8	9	10
Urban informal household (income-based) poverty headcount index	−0.0156	−0.0031	0.0000							
Urban formal unskilled household (income-based) poverty headcount index	0.0201	0.0000	0.0000							
Urban formal skilled household (income-based) poverty headcount index	0.0000	0.0000	0.0000							
Capitalists household poverty (income-based) headcount index	0.0000	0.0000	0.0000							
Rural nontraded household (income-based) poverty gap index	−0.0127	−0.0071	−0.0002							
Rural traded household (income-based) poverty gap index	−0.0082	0.0013	0.0011							
Urban informal household (income-based) poverty gap index	−0.0092	−0.0068	−0.0021							
Urban formal unskilled household (income-based) poverty gap index	−0.0024	0.0081	0.0016							
Urban formal skilled household (income-based) poverty gap index	0.0000	0.0000	0.0000							
Capitalists household (income-based) poverty gap index	0.0000	0.0000	0.0000							
Income Distribution Indicators[2]										
Gini coefficient (consumption-based)	−0.0029	−0.0016	−0.0006							
Gini coefficient (income-based)	−0.0025	−0.0014	−0.0004							
Theil index (consumption-based)	0.0300	0.0141	0.0024							
Theil index (income-based)	0.0303	0.0143	0.0012							

[1] Percentage deviations from baseline. [2] Gini Coefficients and Theil Indices measure between-group inequality.
Note: SR, MR and LR stand for short run, medium run, and long run, respectively.

The increase in nominal wages in the agricultural sector yields higher income and higher consumption for households in that sector; this raises aggregate demand and put upward pressure on domestic prices.

A strong price increase actually leads to a switch in the demand for formal sector goods, away from domestic production and toward imported goods. Production in the private formal sector therefore decreases in response to the expansion in spending. The supply response is partly brought about by a decline in the public capital stock and partly by price-driven increases in the skilled (product) wage, which lowers the demand for skilled labor. As a result, unemployment of skilled workers increases. The decline in skilled employment, in turn, lowers the marginal product of unskilled labor in the private formal sector, lowering demand for that category of labor as well. Because a constant minimum real wage prevails for unskilled formal sector workers, the probability of employment in that sector falls. The formal–informal unskilled wage differential therefore falls, and this translates into a shift in the supply of unskilled labor from the formal to the informal sector. As a consequence, the product wage falls in that sector and the size of the informal economy expands.

We next focus on the effects of this shock on migration between rural and urban areas. The main determinant of this decision is the ratio of average expected rural consumption wages to average expected urban consumption wages.[33] In the case at hand, the increase in the price of the agricultural traded good raises the average rural wage by more than the average urban wage, providing incentives to remain in the agricultural sector. This brings migration down after the shock, but the situation is gradually reversed as the effect of the shock dies out. In a similar fashion, skills acquisition depends on relative expected consumption wages of urban skilled versus unskilled workers. The fact that the expected consumption wage of skilled workers goes up whereas that of unskilled workers goes down leads to an increase in the rate of skills acquisition and an increase in unemployment. This increase is gradually reversed as the effect of the shock fades away.

Higher incomes and aggregate demand lead to a rise in tax collection. Because the public sector deficit is determined by its sources of financing (which are taken as exogenous), and the selected closure rule implies that additional revenue is devoted to an increase in government transfers to households (which increase by almost 9 percent on impact), the initial positive effect of the terms-of-trade shock is reinforced by an expansionary fiscal policy. But there is also an additional effect of public sector finances: higher taxes relative to the existing debt service are interpreted by investors as a reduction in confiscation risk, resulting thereby in a rise in private investment. This in turn generates an increase in the demand for loans by firms which, in itself, puts upward pressure on the domestic bank lending rate (as noted earlier, banks charge a premium over the cost of funds, which depends inversely on the effective value of collateral relative to the size of loans). Nevertheless, because the price of capital jumps up by more than the increase in loans, the premium goes down and so does the lending rate on impact.

---

[33] As noted earlier, consumption wages are defined as nominal wages deflated by the price index corresponding to the consumption basket of workers in a particular sector.

On the financial side, money holdings for all households are higher on impact, and eventually go back to their original levels as the effects of the shock vanish. Although savings across households increase as a consequence of higher incomes, they do not rise proportionally to income because savings rates are smaller on impact due to the temporary increase (by almost 3.4 percent) in inflation. Given that the allocation of savings between domestic and foreign deposits is made after choosing the desired level of money holdings, and that the latter increases at a higher rate than total financial savings, then holdings of domestic and foreign deposits fall on impact, but quickly increase relative to the base scenario once inflation drops and savings rates go up again.

Higher export prices for the agricultural good, coupled with the increase in loans from abroad to domestic banks to finance the higher level of private investment, more than offset the increase in imports. As a result, the central bank accumulates foreign reserves and this in turn leads to an expansion of money supply (given our assumption that changes in the "external" component of the monetary base are not sterilized). These variables also return close to their baseline values as the effects of the shock fade away.

We now turn to poverty and income distribution effects, indices based on our household survey data. The impact and short-run effects of the terms-of-trade shock are generally reductions in consumption-based poverty headcount indices. There is a decrease in the poverty headcount index of the rural nontraded sector, but the largest decrease occurs in the rural traded sector. The decrease in the latter index is expected, given the 10 percent increase in the world price of the exported agricultural good and the existence of fixed real wages in that sector. The decrease in poverty in the rural nontraded sector is mainly due to higher labor earnings, because increasing demand for nontraded agricultural goods leads to higher demand for production inputs in that sector. Because there are only smaller changes in consumption poverty headcount indices for the remaining sectors, there is a negative net effect on the economy-wide consumption poverty index in the short run. In the long run, however, there is only a slight decrease in the poverty index for the agricultural traded and nontraded sectors (given the size and temporary nature of the shock), which leads to a slight decrease in the consumption-based poverty headcount indices for the rural sector and the economy as a whole. Poverty headcount indices based on disposable income depict similar results: there is a relatively strong decline in the economy-wide poverty index in the short run, and a small decrease in the long run.

Consumption-based poverty gap indices indicate that poverty decreases in the rural traded and nontraded sectors and in the urban informal sectors in the short run. Given these decreases, the economy-wide poverty gap index also decreases, despite a slight increase in poverty in the formal unskilled labor group. In the long run, there is also a decrease in the poverty gap index, although its magnitude is much smaller. A similar picture emerges when income-based poverty gap indices are used instead: the economy experiences a decrease in poverty in the short run, which reverses itself in the long run.

In summary, a favorable temporary terms-of-trade shock has relatively unambiguous effects on poverty. Both headcount and poverty gap indices indicate that declines in poverty rates in the short run are reversed in the longer run.

With regard to income distribution indicators, the Gini coefficients generally indicate short and long run declines in income inequality, whereas the Theil indices show short- and long-run increases in income inequality. Long-run effects are generally much smaller than short-run effects. Again, this is not surprising, given the temporary nature of the shock.

5.4.2 Cut in Domestic Credit to Government

We next exploit the financial nature of the model to track the impact of a permanent, 30 percent cut in the stock of domestic credit by the central bank to the nonfinancial public sector, keeping its growth rate constant after the first period (see Tables 5.4 and 5.5).

This has two effects on impact. First, the fall in credit reduces the financing available for the public sector, therefore requiring a reduction in the deficit "above the line"; and second, there is a fall in the monetary base (and consequently the money supply), which creates deflationary pressures.

The reduction in the deficit is accomplished by a proportional cut in total lump-sum transfers to households.[34] This lowers households' income and consumption of all goods (with the exception of the informal good). Lower government revenue relative to the existing level of debt service payments increases the perceived risk of confiscation on impact and leads to a fall in both investment and the demand for domestic loans.

The drop in firms' domestic borrowing is larger than the initial fall in the price of collateral, providing incentives for banks to reduce the premium on the cost of funds, thereby lowering the lending rate. This has a positive effect on output in production sectors that rely on bank credit to finance working capital needs (wage payments here), namely the agricultural traded and urban private formal sectors. In addition, the skilled product wage declines, given that the fall in the price of the composite factor is much smaller than that of nominal skilled wages.

This decline compounds the downward effect of the drop in the lending rate on the effective cost of labor and leads to an increase in demand for skilled labor, as well as an increase in output, in the private formal sector. The urban unskilled workforce also expands, because the rise in the (expected) urban consumption wage is larger than the rise in the (expected) rural wage.

As a result of lower lending rates, labor demand is also higher in the rural traded sector. This increase is matched in part by an initial transfer of workers from the rural nontraded sector to the rural traded sector. As a result of the increase in rural sector wages, migration flows from urban areas increase and translate into a rise in labor supply (and this output) in both sectors in agriculture. In subsequent periods, wage increases lead to increases in the product wage. But because households in the rural nontraded sector consume a bundle of goods whose price index increases more than nominal wages, consumption wages fall for workers employed there. This dampens urban to rural migration over time.

---

[34]Of course, transfers could be negative, in which case they can be interpreted as non-distortionary taxes.

Table 5.4 IMMPA: macroeconomic indicators 30-percent cut in domestic credit to government (Absolute deviations from baseline, unless otherwise indicated)

	Periods									
	1	2	3	4	5	6	7	8	9	10
Real Sector										
Total resources	-1.516	0.129	0.011	0.015	0.016	0.016	0.016	0.016	0.016	0.017
Gross domestic product	-1.509	0.141	0.002	0.009	0.009	0.009	0.009	0.010	0.010	0.010
Imports of goods & NFS	-1.528	0.110	0.027	0.025	0.026	0.026	0.026	0.027	0.027	0.027
Total expenditures										
Private consumption	-3.345	0.335	0.005	0.027	0.027	0.027	0.027	0.028	0.029	0.030
Public consumption	0.000	0.000	0.000	0.000	0.000	0.000	0.000	0.000	0.000	0.000
Private investment	-0.487	-0.191	0.066	0.010	0.019	0.018	0.019	0.019	0.019	0.019
Public investment	0.000	0.000	0.000	0.000	0.000	0.000	0.000	0.000	0.000	0.000
Exports of goods & NFS	0.209	0.006	0.001	0.004	0.003	0.002	0.002	0.002	0.001	0.001
Memorandum item										
Private disposable income	-3.193	0.174	0.019	0.027	0.027	0.028	0.028	0.029	0.029	0.031
External Sector										
Current account	-17.524	0.397	-0.442	-0.481	-0.449	-0.441	-0.429	-0.418	-0.407	-0.386
Exports of goods & NFS (excl. subsidies)	0.204	0.006	0.002	0.004	0.003	0.003	0.002	0.002	0.002	0.001
Imports of goods & NFS (excl. tariffs)	-1.537	0.111	0.026	0.025	0.026	0.026	0.026	0.027	0.027	0.027
Factor services	0.000	-0.784	-0.737	-0.725	-0.715	-0.705	-0.694	-0.683	-0.672	-0.651
Capital account	-1.970	3.158	2.517	-0.250	-0.010	-0.023	-0.022	-0.021	-0.021	-0.020
NFPS financing	0.000	0.000	0.000	0.000	0.000	0.000	0.000	0.000	0.000	0.000
Central bank financing	0.000	0.000	0.000	0.000	0.000	0.000	0.000	0.000	0.000	0.000
Private financing	-2.363	3.876	3.118	-0.307	-0.012	-0.027	-0.026	-0.025	-0.024	-0.023
Change in net international reserves	51.105	13.304	19.833	1.015	2.487	2.418	2.423	2.433	2.440	2.456

Nonfinancial Public Sector

Total revenue	−2.020	0.159	0.188	0.196	0.200	0.203	0.206	0.209	0.213	0.221
Total expenditures	−5.327	0.085	0.111	0.118	0.121	0.122	0.124	0.126	0.128	0.132
Consumption	0.000	0.000	0.000	0.000	0.000	0.000	0.000	0.000	0.000	0.000
Investment	0.000	0.000	0.000	0.000	0.000	0.000	0.000	0.000	0.000	0.000
Transfers to households	−7.737	0.125	0.165	0.175	0.180	0.183	0.188	0.192	0.196	0.206
Domestic interest payments	0.000	0.016	−0.024	−0.015	−0.013	−0.011	−0.009	−0.008	−0.007	−0.006
Foreign interest payments	0.000	0.000	0.000	0.000	0.000	0.000	0.000	0.000	0.000	0.000
Total financing	−1.800	−1.816	−1.833	−1.850	−1.867	−1.884	−1.902	−1.919	−1.937	−1.973
Net foreign financing	0.000	0.000	0.000	0.000	0.000	0.000	0.000	0.000	0.000	0.000
Net domestic credit, central bank	−30.000	−30.000	−30.000	−30.000	−30.000	−30.000	−30.000	−30.000	−30.000	−30.000
Net domestic credit, commercial banks	0.000	0.000	0.000	0.000	0.000	0.000	0.000	0.000	0.000	0.000

Central Bank

Total assets	−1.795	−0.854	−0.055	−0.115	−0.105	−0.098	−0.093	−0.088	−0.083	−0.073
Net foreign assets	5.680	6.342	7.075	6.729	6.499	6.284	6.088	5.909	5.744	5.451
Net domestic assets	−30.000	−30.000	−30.000	−30.000	−30.000	−30.000	−30.000	−30.000	−30.000	−30.000
Loans to government	−30.000	−30.000	−30.000	−30.000	−30.000	−30.000	−30.000	−30.000	−30.000	−30.000
Loans to commercial banks	0.000	0.000	0.000	0.000	0.000	0.000	0.000	0.000	0.000	0.000
Other domestic assets	0.000	0.000	0.000	0.000	0.000	0.000	0.000	0.000	0.000	0.000
Total liabilities/reserve money	−1.795	−0.854	−0.055	−0.115	−0.105	−0.098	−0.093	−0.088	−0.083	−0.073
Currency in circulation	−2.042	−0.890	0.111	0.024	0.029	0.029	0.029	0.030	0.031	0.032
Reserve requirements	0.065	−0.639	−0.832	−0.657	−0.555	−0.478	−0.417	−0.369	−0.330	−0.270

Continued

Table 5.4 Continued

					Periods					
	1	2	3	4	5	6	7	8	9	10
Memorandum items										
Money demand (M1)	-2.042	-0.890	0.111	0.024	0.029	0.029	0.029	0.030	0.031	0.032
Gross reserves in months of imports	7.330	6.224	7.047	6.703	6.471	6.257	6.060	5.881	5.716	5.422
Commercial Banks										
Total assets	-0.341	-0.366	-0.288	-0.235	-0.197	-0.169	-0.148	-0.130	-0.116	-0.095
Net foreign assets	0.000	0.000	0.000	0.000	0.000	0.000	0.000	0.000	0.000	0.000
Net domestic assets	-0.341	-0.366	-0.288	-0.235	-0.197	-0.169	-0.148	-0.130	-0.116	-0.095
Loans to government	0.000	0.000	0.000	0.000	0.000	0.000	0.000	0.000	0.000	0.000
Loans to firms	-0.474	-0.417	-0.292	-0.234	-0.192	-0.163	-0.141	-0.124	-0.110	-0.089
Other domestic assets	0.065	-0.639	-0.832	-0.657	-0.555	-0.478	-0.417	-0.369	-0.330	-0.270
Total liabilities	-0.341	-0.366	-0.288	-0.235	-0.197	-0.169	-0.148	-0.130	-0.116	-0.095
Banks' foreign liabilities	-0.961	0.011	0.438	0.314	0.260	0.218	0.187	0.162	0.143	0.113
Deposits	0.065	-0.639	-0.832	-0.657	-0.555	-0.478	-0.417	-0.369	-0.330	-0.270
Memorandum items[1]										
Real GDP growth rate	0.062	-0.053	-0.006	0.001	-0.001	0.000	0.000	0.000	0.000	0.000
Inflation rate (economy-wide)	-2.044	2.117	-0.178	0.010	0.001	0.000	0.001	0.001	0.001	0.001
Deposit rate	0.000	0.000	0.000	0.000	0.000	0.000	0.000	0.000	0.000	0.000
Lending rate	-0.237	-0.146	-0.108	-0.086	-0.072	-0.062	-0.055	-0.049	-0.045	-0.042
Risk premium	0.000	0.000	0.000	0.000	0.000	0.000	0.000	0.000	0.000	0.000

[1] Absolute deviations from baseline.

Table 5.5 IMMPA: structural, poverty, and income distribution indicators 30-percent cut in domestic credit to government (Absolute deviations from baseline, unless otherwise indicated)

					Periods					
	1	2	3	4	5	6	7	8	9	10
Production Structure										
Size of informal sector (% of total output)	−1.000	0.108	−0.018	−0.008	−0.008	−0.008	−0.008	−0.008	−0.007	−0.007
Size of rural sector (% of formal sector output)	−0.058	0.034	−0.011	−0.004	−0.005	−0.005	−0.005	−0.005	−0.005	−0.005
Composition of Employment and Wages										
Employment in rural sector (% of total employment)	0.000	−0.001	−0.001	−0.002	−0.002	−0.002	−0.003	−0.003	−0.003	−0.003
Employment in rural nontraded sector (% of rural employment)	0.000	−0.004	−0.006	−0.006	−0.006	−0.006	−0.007	−0.007	−0.007	−0.007
Employment in informal sector (% of total employment)	−0.012	0.000	0.002	0.002	0.003	0.003	0.004	0.004	0.004	0.004
Employment in informal sector (% of urban employment)	−0.025	−0.001	0.002	0.001	0.002	0.002	0.003	0.003	0.003	0.003
Employment in public sector (% of total employment)	0.000	0.000	0.000	0.000	0.000	0.000	0.000	0.000	0.000	0.000
Employment in public sector (% of urban employment)	0.000	0.000	0.000	0.000	0.000	0.000	−0.001	−0.001	−0.001	−0.001
Rural traded and rural nontraded sector wage differential[1]	1.183	−0.107	−0.016	−0.024	−0.030	−0.037	−0.045	−0.054	−0.066	−0.078
Urban unskilled formal and informal sector wage differential[1]	0.420	−0.046	0.009	0.003	0.003	0.002	0.002	0.002	0.002	0.001
Public sector wages (% of total public expenditure)	0.587	0.024	0.000	0.003	0.003	0.004	0.004	0.004	0.004	0.005

Continued

Table 5.5 Continued

					Periods					
	1	2	3	4	5	6	7	8	9	10
Aggregate Demand										
Private consumption (% of GDP)	-1.377	0.142	0.002	0.013	0.013	0.013	0.013	0.014	0.014	0.014
Private consumption (% of total consumption)	-0.139	0.014	0.000	0.001	0.001	0.001	0.001	0.001	0.001	0.001
Private investment (% of GDP)	0.225	-0.071	0.013	0.000	0.002	0.002	0.002	0.002	0.002	0.002
Private investment (% of total investment)	-0.046	-0.018	0.006	0.001	0.002	0.002	0.002	0.002	0.002	0.002
Fiscal Indicators										
Public investment in infrastructure (% of total public investment)	0.000	0.000	0.000	0.000	0.000	0.000	0.000	0.000	0.000	0.000
Public investment in health (% of total public investment)	0.000	0.000	0.000	0.000	0.000	0.000	0.000	0.000	0.000	0.000
Public investment in education (% of total public investment)	0.000	0.000	0.000	0.000	0.000	0.000	0.000	0.000	0.000	0.000
Financial Indicators										
Currency (% of M2)	-0.521	-0.059	0.206	0.138	0.111	0.090	0.074	0.062	0.053	0.046
M2 (% of GDP)	0.275	-0.425	-0.299	-0.302	-0.296	-0.291	-0.286	-0.281	-0.276	-0.271
Bank credit to private sector (% of GDP)	-0.002	-0.002	-0.002	-0.002	-0.002	-0.002	-0.002	-0.002	-0.002	-0.002
Lending – deposit rate differential	0.000	0.000	0.000	0.000	0.000	0.000	0.000	0.000	0.000	0.000
External Sector										
Agricultural exports (% of total exports)	-0.102	0.000	0.003	0.001	0.001	0.001	0.001	0.000	0.000	0.000
Imports of non-agricultural goods (% of total imports)	0.242	-0.027	0.003	0.000	0.000	0.000	0.000	0.000	0.000	0.000
External debt (% of GDP)	1.968	-0.181	-0.003	-0.012	-0.012	-0.012	-0.012	-0.012	-0.012	-0.012
Degree of openness (exports plus imports divided by GDP)	1.040	-0.101	0.015	0.006	0.006	0.006	0.006	0.005	0.005	0.005

Poverty Indicators	SR	MR	LR
Rural poverty line (consumption–based) in real terms[1]	0.0000	0.0000	0.0000
Rural poverty line (consumption–based) in nominal terms[1]	−1.2386	−0.5860	−0.0487
Rural poverty line (income–based) in real terms[1]	0.0000	0.0000	0.0000
Rural poverty line (income–based) in nominal terms[1]	−1.2386	−0.5860	−0.0487
Urban poverty line (consumption–based) in real terms[1]	0.0000	0.0000	0.0000
Urban poverty line (consumption–based) in nominal terms[1]	−2.9243	−1.4146	−0.1562
Urban poverty line (income–based) in real terms[1]	0.0000	0.0000	0.0000
Urban poverty line (income–based) in nominal terms[1]	−2.9243	−1.4146	−0.1562
Rural nontraded household (consumption–based) poverty headcount index	0.0140	0.0040	0.0000
Rural traded household (consumption–based) poverty headcount index	0.0030	0.0030	0.0000
Urban informal household (consumption–based) poverty headcount index	0.0280	0.0031	0.0000
Urban formal unskilled household (consumption–based) poverty headcount index	−0.0067	0.0000	0.0000

Continued

Table 5.5 Continued

	Periods									
	1	2	3	4	5	6	7	8	9	10
Urban formal skilled household (consumption-based) poverty headcount index	0.0000	0.0000	0.0000							
Capitalists household poverty (consumption-based) headcount index	0.0000	0.0000	0.0000							
Rural nontraded household (consumption-based) poverty gap index	0.0097	0.0073	0.0007							
Rural traded household (consumption-based) poverty gap index	0.0007	−0.0008	0.0000							
Urban informal household (consumption-based) poverty gap index	0.0045	0.0068	0.0012							
Urban formal unskilled household (consumption-based) poverty gap index	0.0017	−0.0033	−0.0006							
Urban formal skilled household (consumption-based) poverty gap index	0.0000	0.0000	0.0000							
Capitalists household (consumption-based) poverty gap index	0.0000	0.0000	0.0000							
Rural nontraded household (income-based) poverty headcount index	0.0040	0.0100	0.0020							
Rural traded household (income-based) poverty headcount index	0.0000	0.0000	0.0000							
Urban informal household (income-based) poverty headcount index	0.0249	0.0031	0.0000							
Urban formal unskilled household (income-based) poverty headcount index	−0.0134	−0.0134	−0.0067							

	SR	MR	LR
Urban formal skilled household (income-based) poverty headcount index	0.0000	0.0000	0.0000
Capitalists household poverty (income-based) headcount index	0.0000	0.0000	0.0000
Rural nontraded household (income-based) poverty gap index	0.0144	0.0035	−0.0006
Rural traded household (income-based) poverty gap index	0.0021	0.0009	0.0000
Urban informal household (income-based) poverty gap index	0.0056	0.0066	0.0012
Urban formal unskilled household (income-based) poverty gap index	0.0060	0.0084	0.0049
Urban formal skilled household (income-based) poverty gap index	0.0000	0.0000	0.0000
Capitalists household (income-based) poverty gap index	0.0000	0.0000	0.0000
Income Distribution Indicators[2]			
Gini coefficient (consumption-based)	0.0044	0.0022	0.0004
Gini coefficient (income-based)	0.0040	0.0021	0.0002
Theil index (consumption-based)	−0.0045	−0.0020	−0.0006
Theil index (income-based)	−0.0037	−0.0016	0.0002

[1] Percentage deviations from baseline. [2] Gini Coefficients and Theil Indices measure between-group inequality.
Note: SR, MR and LR stand for short run, medium run, and long run, respectively.

The contraction in aggregate demand, together with the increase in output in the urban private formal sector, leads intially to a strong decline in imports and a smaller expansion in exports. The resulting improvement in the trade balance leads to higher official reserves, which tend to mitigate the impact of the original reduction in domestic credit to the government on domestic liquidity. In subsequent periods, the fall in both private investment and the associated demand for domestic loans reduce the need for external financing of banks, thereby reducing the rate of accumulation of foreign reserves. The initial fall in money demand leads to a reallocation of financial assets, namely, an increase in holdings of both domestic and foreign deposits.[35] The increase in domestic deposits lessens further the need for external financing of domestic banks, whereas the increase in foreign deposits abroad by domestic households generates a capital outflow. Both factors put further downward pressure on foreign reserves. The final outcome of all these forces is a fall in money supply, which has deflationary effects that are consistent with the observed initial fall in the price level.

Because we assume that domestic credit grows at the same rate as in the base scenario beyond the initial period, most variables converge to their pre-shock levels in the long run. The reason for a relatively rapid convergence is that the initial value of domestic credit to the government as a share of GDP is relatively small, implying that (given our assumption of a constant deficit) the initial level cut does not alter significantly the path of domestic credit for government budget financing purposes in future periods.

Consumption per capita falls temporarily for all categories of workers. On the one hand, consumption wages of workers in the rural sector as well as unskilled workers in the urban formal sector increase, whereas those of workers in the urban informal sector and skilled workers in the formal sector decrease. On the other, all households face lower transfer receipts from the government, mainly as a direct consequence of the drop in government domestic credit, but also because of lower tax revenues resulting from the fall in aggregate demand. This impact of lower transfer receipts counteracts any wage gains, leading to falls in household income and lower consumption levels.

Consumption-based poverty headcount indices show that poverty decreases only in the formal unskilled labor group in the short run. Moreover, poverty is unchanged for all groups in the long run. Turning to income-based poverty headcount indices, we can observe that poverty decreases in the formal unskilled labor group in both the short and the long run. The economy-wide income-based poverty headcount index increases less than its consumption-based counterpart in the short run, whereas both indices are unchanged in the long run. Poverty gap indices, both consumption and income-based, show that poverty at the aggregate level increases both in the short and the long run. However, they also indicate that the increase in poverty is greater in the short run than in the long run. Hence, all four poverty indices show that poverty changes, resulting from the domestic credit shock, are relatively small in the long run.

---

[35] Even though savings fall as a consequence of lower income, the reduction in the inflation rate increases savings rates on impact. This, coupled with the fall in money demand, leads to higher resources available for investment into other financial assets, such as domestic and foreign deposits.

Both consumption- and income-based Gini coefficients indicate that the domestic credit shock has a negative effect on income distribution, in the short as well as the long run. However, Theil indices generally imply that income distribution becomes more equal with the domestic credit shock. Thus, the effect of the shock on income distribution is ambiguous.

5.4.3   Debt Reduction and Expenditure Reallocation

An important policy experiment for highly-indebted low-income countries involves debt relief and fiscal adjustment. We analyze three different deficit-neutral scenarios that differ in the allocation of the savings resulting from a permanent, 5 percent reduction in the stock of public external debt.[36] The first scenario (which we take as our benchmark) corresponds to the case where savings are allocated to an increase in lump-sum transfers to households, in proportion to their initial shares. The next two scenarios focus on the allocation of savings to investment in education and investment in infrastructure, respectively.[37] The model also permits the analysis of the effects of mixed policies – a combination, for instance, of investment in education with investment in infrastructure – a particularly relevant consideration for policymakers who must determine the allocation of public expenditure. We contrast the effects of a mixed policy package with those of "pure" policies that imply full allocation to just one type of investment, but for brevity we do not go over a detailed account of this additional simulation.

Throughout the discussion we assume that the non-financial public sector deficit remains constant at base scenario levels. For many developing countries, the initial position may be one in which the fiscal deficit is unsustainable and creating undue pressure on inflation and interest rates. In such conditions, there is a good case for using savings from debt reduction to bring the deficit down to sustainable levels, if increases in taxation are not feasible. We abstract, however, from these considerations and examine the effects of alternative ways of spending the income saved from debt reduction, because our interest lies in understanding the effects of alternative strategies for expenditure allocation. Thus, we implicitly assume that the starting fiscal position is sustainable, be it because of continuing foreign aid or proper fiscal management, although this can be easily modified (by considering alternative sources of financing) to consider jointly the case of debt reduction coupled with a cut in the fiscal deficit.

Transfers to Households

We first consider the case where the savings (current and future) associated with the reduction in interest payments on external debt are rebated to all households in the

---

[36] Because we assume that contracted foreign public sector debt has infinite maturity, debt service consists of interest payments only. We therefore focus on the "cash flow" effect of debt relief.

[37] As noted earlier, the model also incorporates investment in health; but because its effects are similar to investment in infrastructure (that is, both types of investment increase labor productivity) they are not reported separately. Had we adopted the specification proposed in Agénor, Bayraktar, and El Aynaoui (2005), where health capital increases the "effective" supply of labor, the results would be different.

300 *Chapter 5*

form of lump-sum transfers (see Tables 5.6 and 5.7). Specifically, we assume that the government allocates these transfers according to initial household shares.[38]

This policy has immediate demand-side effects: the positive impact on households' incomes leads to an increase in consumption (mostly of agricultural traded and private formal sector goods) and money holdings. The increase in activity yields higher government revenues. This effect combines with the reduction in interest payments to exert a positive impact on private capital formation, because both contribute to a reduction in confiscation risk. Although private investment (as a share of GDP) falls on impact, it rises gradually in subsequent periods. Higher private investment implies a higher demand for domestic loans by firms, which tends to reduce their net worth.

At the same time, however, the composite price of formal sector goods (and thus the price of capital goods) increases, which raises the value of firms' collateral; the net effect is an increase in firms' net worth, a fall in the risk premium, and a drop in the bank lending rate. This effect tends to decline over time, as firms' borrowing from commercial banks tend to increase.

The fall in the lending rate tends to reduce the effective price of labor in the rural traded sector, thereby increasing labor demand and output. Workers are drawn from the rural nontraded sector, leading to a fall in output and a rise in the product wage there. As a result, the traded–nontraded sector wage differential falls.

In the formal urban sector, the initial reduction in the effective cost of labor tends at first to increase the demand for both categories of workers. In addition, the rise in investment increases the private capital stock over time; because skilled labor is complementary to physical capital, this stimulates further the demand for skilled labor. As a result of both factors, skilled wages tend to increase over time, thereby dampening the rise in skilled employment.

Despite the initial increase in the demand for unskilled labor in the formal sector (induced by the drop in the lending rate), over time firms tend to substitute away from that category of labor. This tends to reduce the probability of employment for unskilled workers in the urban sector. The resulting smaller differential between average expected urban consumption wages and rural wages eventually leads to a dampening of migration flows into urban areas, which tend to support the initial increase in informal sector wages. Over time, employment in the informal economy tends therefore to fall (following a slight intital increase), and so does output in that sector. There is also an increase in the expected skilled consumption wage and a fall in the expected unskilled consumption wage. In the case of the latter, this is due to the increase in the price index of the unskilled consumption basket. The combined effect of these movements in wages is to lead to a higher rate of skills acquisition and increased unemployment relative to the baseline scenario. In terms of real per capita consumption, all working households benefit from the increase in transfers, except the urban formal unskilled labor group.

Poverty, as measured by the economy-wide consumption-based poverty headcount index, decreases in the short run when savings from lower debt service are applied

---

[38]This implies that as long as groups differ in size, transfers per capita are not the same across groups. An alternative scenario would be to assume that only poor households receive transfers.

Table 5.6 [...] macroeconomic indicators 3-percent foreign debt reduction with increased transfers to households (Absolute deviations from baseline, unless otherwise indicated)

	Periods									
	1	2	3	4	5	6	7	8	9	10
Real Sector										
Total resources	0.357	0.333	0.345	0.354	0.362	0.371	0.380	0.389	0.398	0.415
Gross domestic product	0.348	0.323	0.337	0.347	0.358	0.369	0.379	0.390	0.400	0.421
Imports of goods & NFS	0.370	0.351	0.358	0.364	0.370	0.376	0.382	0.388	0.393	0.405
Total expenditures										
Private consumption	0.736	0.670	0.685	0.693	0.701	0.709	0.717	0.726	0.734	0.750
Public consumption	0.000	0.000	0.000	0.000	0.000	0.000	0.000	0.000	0.000	0.000
Private investment	0.290	0.333	0.342	0.360	0.376	0.392	0.408	0.423	0.438	0.468
Public investment	0.000	0.000	0.000	0.000	0.000	0.000	0.000	0.000	0.000	0.000
Exports of goods & NFS	−0.051	−0.042	−0.035	−0.029	−0.022	−0.016	−0.009	−0.003	0.004	0.016
Memorandum item										
Private disposable income	0.701	0.671	0.682	0.689	0.697	0.706	0.714	0.722	0.730	0.746
External Sector										
Current account	−0.051	−0.337	−0.259	−0.203	−0.150	−0.098	−0.050	−0.003	0.041	0.124
Exports of goods & NFS (excl. subsidies)	−0.050	−0.041	−0.034	−0.028	−0.022	−0.015	−0.009	−0.003	0.003	0.016
Imports of goods & NFS (excl. tariffs)	0.372	0.352	0.359	0.365	0.371	0.377	0.383	0.389	0.395	0.406
Factor services	−5.024	−4.802	−4.625	−4.450	−4.280	−4.114	−3.952	−3.793	−3.639	−3.341
Capital account	0.952	0.397	−0.130	−0.014	0.022	0.064	0.104	0.142	0.178	0.246
NFPS financing	0.000	0.000	0.000	0.000	0.000	0.000	0.000	0.000	0.000	0.000

Continued

Table 5.6 Continued

				Periods						
	1	2	3	4	5	6	7	8	9	10
Central bank financing	0.000	0.000	0.000	0.000	0.000	0.000	0.000	0.000	0.000	0.000
Private financing	1.142	0.487	−0.161	−0.018	0.027	0.078	0.125	0.169	0.211	0.288
Change in net international reserves	4.377	3.092	0.629	1.017	1.001	1.014	1.026	1.037	1.048	1.068
Nonfinancial Public Sector										
Total revenue	0.500	0.510	0.523	0.534	0.544	0.554	0.563	0.573	0.582	0.599
Total expenditures	0.481	0.491	0.504	0.513	0.523	0.532	0.541	0.550	0.559	0.575
Consumption	0.000	0.000	0.000	0.000	0.000	0.000	0.000	0.000	0.000	0.000
Investment	0.000	0.000	0.000	0.000	0.000	0.000	0.000	0.000	0.000	0.000
Transfers to households	1.705	1.742	1.763	1.785	1.806	1.828	1.851	1.874	1.898	1.947
Domestic interest	0.000	0.002	0.007	0.008	0.009	0.009	0.010	0.009	0.009	0.009
Foreign interest payments	−4.996	−4.947	−4.898	−4.849	−4.801	−4.754	−4.707	−4.660	−4.614	−4.523
Total financing	0.000	0.000	0.000	0.000	0.000	0.000	0.000	0.000	0.000	0.000
Net foreign financing	0.000	0.000	0.000	0.000	0.000	0.000	0.000	0.000	0.000	0.000
Net domestic credit, central bank	0.000	0.000	0.000	0.000	0.000	0.000	0.000	0.000	0.000	0.000
Net domestic credit, commercial banks	0.000	0.000	0.000	0.000	0.000	0.000	0.000	0.000	0.000	0.000
Central Bank										
Total assets	0.385	0.572	0.572	0.591	0.607	0.622	0.637	0.651	0.665	0.691
Net foreign assets	0.486	0.713	0.708	0.726	0.741	0.755	0.769	0.782	0.795	0.819
Net domestic assets	0.000	0.000	0.000	0.000	0.000	0.000	0.000	0.000	0.000	0.000
Loans to government	0.000	0.000	0.000	0.000	0.000	0.000	0.000	0.000	0.000	0.000
Loans to commercial banks	0.000	0.000	0.000	0.000	0.000	0.000	0.000	0.000	0.000	0.000
Other domestic assets	0.000	0.000	0.000	0.000	0.000	0.000	0.000	0.000	0.000	0.000

Total liabilities/reserve money	0.385	0.572	0.572	0.591	0.607	0.622	0.637	0.651	0.665	0.691
Currency in circulation	0.437	0.648	0.633	0.643	0.650	0.658	0.666	0.673	0.681	0.697
Reserve requirements	−0.014	0.123	0.284	0.386	0.460	0.516	0.561	0.598	0.630	0.680
Memorandum items										
Money demand (M1)	0.437	0.648	0.633	0.643	0.650	0.658	0.666	0.673	0.681	0.697
Gross reserves in months of imports	0.114	0.359	0.347	0.359	0.368	0.376	0.384	0.391	0.398	0.410
Commercial Banks										
Total assets	0.179	0.284	0.350	0.398	0.435	0.466	0.493	0.517	0.538	0.578
Net foreign assets	0.000	0.000	0.000	0.000	0.000	0.000	0.000	0.000	0.000	0.000
Net domestic assets	0.179	0.284	0.350	0.398	0.435	0.466	0.493	0.517	0.538	0.578
Loans to government	0.000	0.000	0.000	0.000	0.000	0.000	0.000	0.000	0.000	0.000
Loans to firms	0.248	0.350	0.405	0.444	0.474	0.500	0.522	0.542	0.561	0.597
Other domestic assets	−0.014	0.123	0.284	0.386	0.460	0.516	0.561	0.598	0.630	0.680
Total liabilities	0.179	0.284	0.350	0.398	0.435	0.466	0.493	0.517	0.538	0.578
Banks' foreign liabilities	0.473	0.506	0.439	0.414	0.404	0.403	0.408	0.416	0.428	0.456
Deposits	−0.014	0.123	0.284	0.386	0.460	0.516	0.561	0.598	0.630	0.680
Memorandum items[1]										
Real GDP growth rate	−0.014	0.004	0.005	0.004	0.004	0.004	0.004	0.004	0.004	0.004
Inflation rate (economy-wide)	0.464	−0.038	0.012	0.008	0.008	0.008	0.009	0.009	0.009	0.009
Deposit rate	0.000	0.000	0.000	0.000	0.000	0.000	0.000	0.000	0.000	0.000
Lending rate	−0.237	−0.147	−0.106	−0.084	−0.070	−0.060	−0.053	−0.048	−0.044	−0.041

[1] Absolute deviations from baseline.

Table 5.7 IMMPA: structural, poverty, and income distribution indicators 5–percent foreign debt reduction with increased transfers to households (Absolute deviations from baseline, unless otherwise indicated)

	Periods									
	1	2	3	4	5	6	7	8	9	10
Production Structure										
Size of informal sector (% of total output)	0.211	0.185	0.191	0.194	0.197	0.200	0.203	0.206	0.209	0.212
Size of rural sector (% of formal sector output)	−0.015	−0.027	−0.030	−0.034	−0.038	−0.042	−0.045	−0.048	−0.052	−0.055
Composition of Employment and Wages										
Employment in rural sector (% of total employment)	0.000	0.000	0.000	0.001	0.001	0.002	0.003	0.004	0.004	0.005
Employment in rural nontraded sector (% of rural employment)	0.000	0.001	0.003	0.004	0.005	0.007	0.009	0.011	0.013	0.016
Employment in informal sector (% of total employment)	0.003	0.001	0.000	−0.001	−0.003	−0.005	−0.007	−0.009	−0.011	−0.013
Employment in informal sector (% of urban employment)	0.006	0.003	0.001	−0.001	−0.003	−0.005	−0.007	−0.010	−0.012	−0.014
Employment in public sector (% of total employment)	0.000	0.000	0.000	0.000	0.000	0.000	0.000	0.000	0.000	0.000
Employment in public sector (% of urban employment)	0.000	0.000	0.000	0.000	0.000	0.000	0.001	0.001	0.001	0.001
Rural traded and rural nontraded sector wage differential[1]	−0.275	−0.288	−0.337	−0.391	−0.454	−0.527	−0.609	−0.700	−0.800	−0.905
Urban unskilled formal and informal sector wage differential[1]	−0.088	−0.070	−0.070	−0.071	−0.073	−0.076	−0.079	−0.083	−0.087	−0.091
Public sector wages (% of total public expenditure)	−0.017	−0.023	−0.023	−0.023	−0.023	−0.023	−0.023	−0.023	−0.023	−0.023

Aggregate Demand

Private consumption (% of GDP)	0.286	0.255	0.256	0.254	0.253	0.251	0.250	0.248	0.247	0.246
Private consumption (% of total consumption)	0.029	0.027	0.028	0.028	0.028	0.029	0.029	0.030	0.030	0.030
Private investment (% of GDP)	−0.013	0.002	0.001	0.003	0.004	0.005	0.006	0.007	0.008	0.009
Private investment (% of total investment)	0.027	0.032	0.033	0.035	0.037	0.039	0.040	0.042	0.044	0.046
Fiscal Indicators										
Public investment in infrastructure (% of total public investment)	0.000	0.000	0.000	0.000	0.000	0.000	0.000	0.000	0.000	0.000
Public investment in health (% of total public investment)	0.000	0.000	0.000	0.000	0.000	0.000	0.000	0.000	0.000	0.000
Public investment in education (% of total public investment)	0.000	0.000	0.000	0.000	0.000	0.000	0.000	0.000	0.000	0.000
Financial Indicators										
Currency (% of M2)	0.110	0.122	0.076	0.052	0.036	0.025	0.017	0.012	0.008	0.005
M2 (% of GDP)	−0.068	−0.002	0.033	0.070	0.106	0.141	0.174	0.207	0.238	0.269
Bank credit to private sector (% of GDP)	0.001	0.002	0.002	0.003	0.004	0.005	0.006	0.007	0.008	0.009
Lending–deposit rate differential	0.000	0.000	0.000	0.000	0.000	0.000	0.000	0.000	0.000	0.000
External Sector										
Agricultural exports (% of total exports)	0.025	0.020	0.015	0.012	0.008	0.005	0.001	−0.002	−0.005	−0.008
Imports of non-agricultural goods (% of total imports)	−0.046	−0.041	−0.042	−0.042	−0.042	−0.042	−0.042	−0.042	−0.042	−0.043
External debt (% of GDP)	−6.777	−6.687	−6.587	−6.493	−6.402	−6.314	−6.228	−6.144	−6.063	−5.983
Degree of openness (exports plus imports divided by GDP)	−0.227	−0.204	−0.211	−0.216	−0.221	−0.226	−0.230	−0.235	−0.239	−0.244

Continued

Table 5.7 Continued

					Periods					
	1	2	3	4	5	6	7	8	9	10
Poverty Indicators	**SR**	**MR**	**LR**							
Rural poverty line (consumption–based) in real terms[1]	0.0000	0.0000	0.0000							
Rural poverty line (consumption–based) in nominal terms[1]	0.2799	0.3649	0.3746							
Rural poverty line (income–based) in real terms[1]	0.0000	0.0000	0.0000							
Rural poverty line (income–based) in nominal terms[1]	0.2799	0.3649	0.3746							
Urban poverty line (consumption–based) in real terms[1]	0.0000	0.0000	0.0000							
Urban poverty line (consumption–based) in nominal terms[1]	0.6455	0.8271	0.8408							
Urban poverty line (income–based) in real terms[1]	0.0000	0.0000	0.0000							
Urban poverty line (income–based) in nominal terms[1]	0.6455	0.8271	0.8408							
Rural nontraded household (consumption–based) poverty headcount index	−0.0020	−0.0060	−0.0020							
Rural traded household (consumption–based) poverty headcount index	0.0000	0.0000	0.0000							
Urban informal household (consumption–based) poverty	−0.0031	−0.0062	−0.0031							

Urban formal unskilled household (consumption-based) poverty headcount index	0.0000	0.0000	0.0067
Urban formal skilled household (consumption-based) poverty headcount index	0.0000	0.0000	0.0000
Capitalists household poverty (consumption-based) headcount index	0.0000	0.0000	0.0000
Rural nontraded household (consumption-based) poverty gap index	−0.0025	−0.0020	−0.0042
Rural traded household (consumption-based) poverty gap index	−0.0005	−0.0006	−0.0005
Urban informal household (consumption-based) poverty gap index	−0.0023	−0.0009	−0.0018
Urban formal unskilled household (consumption-based) poverty gap index	0.0014	0.0018	−0.0057
Urban formal skilled household (consumption-based) poverty gap index	0.0000	0.0000	0.0000
Capitalists household (consumption-based) poverty gap index	0.0000	0.0000	0.0000
Rural nontraded household (income-based) poverty headcount index	−0.0040	0.0000	−0.0060
Rural traded household (income-based) poverty headcount index	−0.0030	−0.0030	0.0000

Continued

Table 5.7 Continued

	Periods									
	1	2	3	4	5	6	7	8	9	10
Urban informal household (income–based) poverty headcount index	0.0000	−0.0031	0.0000							
Urban formal unskilled household (income–based) poverty headcount index	0.0000	0.0000	0.0000							
Urban formal skilled household (income–based) poverty headcount index	0.0000	0.0000	0.0000							
Capitalists household poverty (income–based) headcount index	0.0000	0.0000	0.0000							
Rural nontraded household (income–based) poverty gap index	−0.0013	−0.0051	−0.0016							
Rural traded household (income–based) poverty gap index	0.0015	0.0013	−0.0004							
Urban informal household (income–based) poverty gap index	−0.0038	−0.0026	−0.0037							
Urban formal unskilled household (income–based) poverty gap index	0.0015	0.0019	0.0021							
Urban formal skilled household (income–based) poverty gap index	0.0000	0.0000	0.0000							
Capitalists household (income–based) poverty gap index	0.0000	0.0000	0.0000							
Income Distribution Indicators[2]										
Gini coefficient (consumption–based)	−0.0009	−0.0013	−0.0013							
Gini coefficient (income–based)	−0.0009	−0.0012	−0.0011							
Theil index (consumption–based)	0.0010	0.0012	0.0012							
Theil index (income–based)	0.0008	0.0011	0.0011							

1 Percentage deviations from baseline. 2 Gini Coefficients and Theil Indices measure between-group inequality.

to transfers to households. The reduction in poverty becomes somewhat larger in the medium run, but is reduced in the long run. In both the short and the long run, poverty reduction only occurs in the rural and urban informal sectors.[39] Short- and long-run poverty reduction is somewhat larger when using income-based poverty measures, but remains confined mainly to the rural sector. When using consumption-based poverty gap indices as indicators, poverty again falls in the short and the long run, with a larger decrease at a longer horizon. However, in contrast to headcount indices, poverty reduction here occurs across all unskilled labor groups in the long run. In the case of income-based poverty gap measures, economy-wide poverty decreases in the short and long run, confirming results obtained from the consumption-based poverty gap measure. The Gini coefficients show that debt reduction reduces income inequality, whereas the Theil indices show again the opposite result.

Investment in Infrastructure

The use of savings from debt reduction to increase the stock of capital in infrastructure has not only demand-side effects but also supply-side effects (see Tables 5.8 and 5.9). We focus on the latter, because demand-side effects are similar to those already described above. In particular, higher infrastructure provides a boost to production in the rural traded, rural nontraded, and private formal sectors. It increases the marginal product of all factors of production in these sectors, given our assumption that infrastructure facilitates a more efficient use of available resources. Thus, demand for labor goes up, as well as private investment. But there is also an additional channel that contributes to the rise in capital formation, as noted earlier: the reduction in confiscation risk resulting from the long-run increase in tax revenue, paired with a cut in interest payments following the reduction in external debt. These two channels of transmission have a compounded effect on output in the private formal sector, which increases strongly when compared to the case in which savings from debt relief are used to finance lump-sum transfers. Skilled unemployment is now lower, in contrast to the transfers scenario. The behavior of the rural sector is quite different as well: increased productivity both in the agricultural traded and nontraded sectors leads to an expansion in total agricultural output. Similar results to those of the transfers policy apply to consumption per capita levels among households – except for agricultural traded households, whose consumption levels tend to decline.

Consumption-based poverty headcount indices show that debt reduction has no effect on poverty in the short run, but it does have some positive effects in the long run. The latter is mainly due to poverty reduction in the rural nontraded sector. Similarly, income-based poverty headcount indices show that poverty is reduced only in the long run, and that the main gains accrue to households in the rural nontraded sector. The consumption-based poverty gap index indicates that poverty decreases in both the short and long run, with long-run gains being significantly larger. This reduction in poverty occurs for most unskilled labor groups in the long run. By contrast, income-based poverty gap measures show that poverty increases in the rural traded and urban

---

[39]This is mainly due to the fact that, in our base-period calibration, the share of total transfers allocated to rural households is assumed to be higher.

Table 5.8 IMMPA: macroeconomic indicators 5-percent foreign debt reduction with increased infrastructure investment (Absolute deviations from baseline, unless otherwise indicated)

	Periods									
	1	2	3	4	5	6	7	8	9	10
Real Sector										
Total resources	0.236	0.329	0.416	0.504	0.589	0.673	0.755	0.835	0.913	1.062
Gross domestic product	0.105	0.206	0.306	0.406	0.503	0.598	0.691	0.781	0.869	1.036
Imports of goods & NFS	0.448	0.528	0.595	0.663	0.730	0.796	0.860	0.924	0.985	1.105
Total expenditures										
Private consumption	0.136	0.242	0.353	0.465	0.575	0.682	0.788	0.891	0.991	1.185
Public consumption	0.000	0.000	0.000	0.000	0.000	0.000	0.000	0.000	0.000	0.000
Private investment	0.250	0.301	0.285	0.278	0.274	0.271	0.270	0.272	0.275	0.287
Public investment	9.966	9.770	9.579	9.391	9.207	9.026	8.849	8.676	8.506	8.175
Exports of goods & NFS	−0.046	0.061	0.170	0.276	0.378	0.476	0.571	0.663	0.751	0.917
Memorandum item										
Private disposable income	0.128	0.241	0.351	0.462	0.571	0.679	0.784	0.886	0.987	1.180
External Sector										
Current account	0.651	0.462	0.074	−0.253	−0.553	−0.822	−1.064	−1.278	−1.467	−1.778
Exports of goods & NFS (excl. subsidies)	−0.045	0.064	0.175	0.281	0.385	0.485	0.581	0.674	0.763	0.931
Imports of goods & NFS (excl. tariffs)	0.446	0.526	0.593	0.662	0.729	0.795	0.860	0.924	0.986	1.106
Factor services	−5.024	−4.771	−4.564	−4.378	−4.212	−4.065	−3.934	−3.817	−3.714	−3.540
Capital account	0.656	0.795	0.389	0.122	−0.125	−0.352	−0.557	−0.742	−0.908	−1.186
NFPS financing	0.000	0.000	0.000	0.000	0.000	0.000	0.000	0.000	0.000	0.000
Central bank financing	0.000	0.000	0.000	0.000	0.000	0.000	0.000	0.000	0.000	0.000
Private financing	0.786	0.976	0.482	0.149	−0.153	−0.426	−0.670	−0.887	−1.078	−1.392

Change in net international reserves	0.672	2.019	2.237	2.174	2.302	2.393	2.484	2.570	2.653	2.808

Nonfinancial Public Sector

Total revenue	0.192	0.295	0.380	0.466	0.552	0.637	0.720	0.803	0.884	1.045
Total expenditures	0.184	0.284	0.365	0.449	0.531	0.612	0.692	0.771	0.849	1.003
Consumption	0.000	0.000	0.000	0.000	0.000	0.000	0.000	0.000	0.000	0.000
Investment	9.966	9.770	9.579	9.391	9.207	9.026	8.849	8.676	8.506	8.175
Transfers to households	0.268	0.417	0.539	0.665	0.791	0.918	1.045	1.172	1.299	1.556
Domestic interest payments	0.000	0.003	0.008	0.010	0.011	0.011	0.011	0.011	0.011	0.010
Foreign interest payments	−4.996	−4.947	−4.898	−4.849	−4.801	−4.754	−4.707	−4.660	−4.614	−4.523
Total financing	0.000	0.000	0.000	0.000	0.000	0.000	0.000	0.000	0.000	0.000
Net foreign financing	0.000	0.000	0.000	0.000	0.000	0.000	0.000	0.000	0.000	0.000
Net domestic credit, central bank	0.000	0.000	0.000	0.000	0.000	0.000	0.000	0.000	0.000	0.000
Net domestic credit, commercial banks	0.000	0.000	0.000	0.000	0.000	0.000	0.000	0.000	0.000	0.000

Central Bank

Total assets	0.059	0.195	0.284	0.371	0.456	0.538	0.618	0.696	0.772	0.917
Net foreign assets	0.075	0.243	0.352	0.456	0.556	0.653	0.746	0.835	0.922	1.086
Net domestic assets	0.000	0.000	0.000	0.000	0.000	0.000	0.000	0.000	0.000	0.000
Loans to government	0.000	0.000	0.000	0.000	0.000	0.000	0.000	0.000	0.000	0.000
Loans to commercial banks	0.000	0.000	0.000	0.000	0.000	0.000	0.000	0.000	0.000	0.000
Other domestic assets	0.000	0.000	0.000	0.000	0.000	0.000	0.000	0.000	0.000	0.000

Continued

Table 5.8 Continued

	Periods									
	1	2	3	4	5	6	7	8	9	10
Total liabilities/reserve money	0.059	0.195	0.284	0.371	0.456	0.538	0.618	0.696	0.772	0.917
Currency in circulation	0.068	0.229	0.335	0.440	0.544	0.647	0.747	0.846	0.942	1.129
Reserve requirements	-0.005	-0.002	0.046	0.099	0.156	0.215	0.276	0.336	0.398	0.520
Memorandum items										
Money demand (M1)	0.068	0.229	0.335	0.440	0.544	0.647	0.747	0.846	0.942	1.129
Gross reserves in months of imports	-0.370	-0.282	-0.240	-0.205	-0.172	-0.141	-0.113	-0.088	-0.063	-0.019
Commercial Banks										
Total assets	0.127	0.196	0.226	0.241	0.247	0.248	0.247	0.245	0.243	0.237
Net foreign assets	0.000	0.000	0.000	0.000	0.000	0.000	0.000	0.000	0.000	0.000
Net domestic assets	0.127	0.196	0.226	0.241	0.247	0.248	0.247	0.245	0.243	0.237
Loans to government	0.000	0.000	0.000	0.000	0.000	0.000	0.000	0.000	0.000	0.000
Loans to firms	0.175	0.249	0.271	0.278	0.276	0.270	0.263	0.254	0.246	0.230
Other domestic assets	-0.005	-0.002	0.046	0.099	0.156	0.215	0.276	0.336	0.398	0.520
Total liabilities	0.127	0.196	0.226	0.241	0.247	0.248	0.247	0.245	0.243	0.237
Banks' foreign liabilities	0.328	0.471	0.468	0.425	0.362	0.290	0.213	0.133	0.054	-0.100
Deposits	-0.005	-0.002	0.046	0.099	0.156	0.215	0.276	0.336	0.398	0.520
Memorandum items[1]										
Real GDP growth rate	-0.001	0.104	0.103	0.099	0.095	0.092	0.088	0.085	0.081	0.076
Inflation rate (economy-wide)	0.117	0.008	0.012	0.018	0.022	0.026	0.030	0.034	0.036	0.039
Deposit rate	0.000	0.000	0.000	0.000	0.000	0.000	0.000	0.000	0.000	0.000
Lending rate	-0.237	-0.147	-0.106	-0.084	-0.070	-0.060	-0.053	-0.048	-0.044	-0.041

[1] Absolute deviations from baseline.

Table 5.9 IMMPA: structural, poverty and income distribution indicators 5-percent foreign debt reduction with increased infrastructure investment (Absolute deviations from baseline, unless otherwise indicated)

	Periods									
	1	2	3	4	5	6	7	8	9	10
Production Structure										
Size of informal sector (% of total output)	0.023	0.038	0.057	0.076	0.093	0.109	0.125	0.139	0.153	0.166
Size of rural sector (% of formal sector output)	−0.064	0.005	0.082	0.158	0.234	0.309	0.382	0.453	0.522	0.589
Composition of Employment and Wages										
Employment in rural sector (% of total employment)	0.000	0.000	0.000	0.000	0.000	0.001	0.001	0.003	0.004	0.006
Employment in rural nontraded sector (% of rural employment)	0.000	−0.090	−0.190	−0.297	−0.409	−0.524	−0.639	−0.754	−0.866	−0.975
Employment in informal sector (% of total employment)	0.000	−0.002	−0.004	−0.006	−0.008	−0.011	−0.014	−0.017	−0.020	−0.024
Employment in informal sector (% of urban employment)	0.000	−0.003	−0.007	−0.011	−0.014	−0.017	−0.020	−0.024	−0.027	−0.031
Employment in public sector (% of total employment)	0.000	0.000	0.000	0.000	0.000	0.000	0.000	0.000	0.000	0.000
Employment in public sector (% of urban employment)	0.000	0.000	0.000	0.000	0.000	0.000	0.000	0.000	0.001	0.001
Rural traded and rural nontraded sector wage differential[1]	−0.073	−0.132	−0.241	−0.420	−0.692	−1.081	−1.614	−2.315	−3.203	−4.284
Urban unskilled formal and informal sector wage differential[1]	0.075	0.108	0.135	0.161	0.186	0.208	0.228	0.246	0.263	0.277
Public sector wages (% of total public expenditure)	−0.016	−0.039	−0.057	−0.075	−0.092	−0.108	−0.123	−0.138	−0.151	−0.164

Continued

Table 5.9 Continued

					Periods					
	1	2	3	4	5	6	7	8	9	10
Aggregate Demand										
Private consumption (% of GDP)	0.023	0.026	0.035	0.043	0.053	0.062	0.071	0.081	0.090	0.100
Private consumption (% of total consumption)	0.005	0.010	0.014	0.019	0.023	0.028	0.032	0.036	0.040	0.045
Private investment (% of GDP)	0.032	0.020	−0.005	−0.027	−0.048	−0.068	−0.087	−0.105	−0.121	−0.137
Private investment (% of total investment)	−0.902	−0.899	−0.888	−0.877	−0.865	−0.853	−0.841	−0.829	−0.817	−0.804
Fiscal Indicators										
Public investment in infrastructure (% of total public investment)	−2.962	−2.852	−2.746	−2.644	−2.545	−2.451	−2.359	−2.271	−2.186	−2.105
Public investment in health (% of total public investment)	−3.021	−2.967	−2.914	−2.862	−2.810	−2.760	−2.710	−2.661	−2.613	−2.566
Public investment in education (% of total public investment)	−3.021	−2.967	−2.914	−2.862	−2.810	−2.760	−2.710	−2.661	−2.613	−2.566
Financial Indicators										
Currency (% of M2)	0.018	0.054	0.063	0.069	0.073	0.076	0.078	0.079	0.080	0.080
M2 (% of GDP)	−0.032	−0.060	−0.094	−0.133	−0.176	−0.222	−0.270	−0.319	−0.370	−0.422
Bank credit to private sector (% of GDP)	0.001	0.001	0.000	0.000	−0.001	−0.002	−0.004	−0.005	−0.007	−0.009
Lending–deposit rate differential	0.000	0.000	0.000	0.000	0.000	0.000	0.000	0.000	0.000	0.000
External Sector										
Agricultural exports (% of total exports)	0.023	0.056	0.086	0.115	0.142	0.169	0.194	0.219	0.242	0.264
Imports of non-agricultural goods (% of total imports)	0.051	0.045	0.037	0.029	0.021	0.014	0.006	−0.001	−0.007	−0.014
External debt (% of GDP)	−6.481	−6.545	−6.551	−6.564	−6.574	−6.584	−6.592	−6.599	−6.603	−6.606
Degree of openness (exports plus imports divided by GDP)	0.120	0.109	0.094	0.078	0.063	0.047	0.031	0.016	0.000	−0.014

Poverty Indicators	SR	MR	LR
Rural poverty line (consumption-based) in real terms[1]	0.0000	0.0000	0.0000
Rural poverty line (consumption-based) in nominal terms[1]	0.0680	0.0910	0.1595
Rural poverty line (income-based) in real terms[1]	0.0000	0.0000	0.0000
Rural poverty line (income-based) in nominal terms[1]	0.0680	0.0910	0.1595
Urban poverty line (consumption-based) in real terms[1]	0.0000	0.0000	0.0000
Urban poverty line (consumption-based) in nominal terms[1]	0.1191	0.2798	0.5208
Urban poverty line (income-based) in real terms[1]	0.0000	0.0000	0.0000
Urban poverty line (income-based) in nominal terms[1]	0.1191	0.2798	0.5208
Rural nontraded household (consumption-based) poverty headcount index	0.0000	−0.0040	−0.0080
Rural traded household (consumption-based) poverty headcount index	0.0000	0.0000	0.0000
Urban informal household (consumption-based) poverty headcount index	0.0000	0.0000	0.0000

Continued

Table 5.9 Continued

		Periods								
	1	2	3	4	5	6	7	8	9	10
Urban formal unskilled household (consumption-based) poverty headcount index	0.0000	0.0000	0.0067							
Urban formal skilled household (consumption-based) poverty headcount index	0.0000	0.0000	0.0000							
Capitalists household poverty (consumption-based) headcount index	0.0000	0.0000	0.0000							
Rural nontraded household (consumption-based) poverty gap index	−0.0004	−0.0022	−0.0094							
Rural traded household (consumption-based) poverty gap index	0.0002	0.0004	0.0011							
Urban informal household (consumption-based) poverty gap index	−0.0005	−0.0016	−0.0027							
Urban formal unskilled household (consumption-based) poverty gap index	0.0001	0.0002	−0.0069							
Urban formal skilled household (consumption-based) poverty gap index	0.0000	0.0000	0.0000							
Capitalists household (consumption-based) poverty gap index	0.0000	0.0000	0.0000							
Rural nontraded household (income-based) poverty headcount index	0.0000	0.0000	−0.0160							
Rural traded household (income-based) poverty headcount index	0.0000	0.0000	0.0000							

	SR	MR	LR
Urban informal household (income-based) poverty headcount index	0.0000	0.0000	0.0000
Urban formal unskilled household (income-based) poverty headcount index	0.0000	0.0000	0.0000
Urban formal skilled household (income-based) poverty headcount index	0.0000	0.0000	0.0000
Capitalists household poverty (income-based) headcount index	0.0000	0.0000	0.0000
Rural nontraded household (income-based) poverty gap index	−0.0004	−0.0043	−0.0041
Rural traded household (income-based) poverty gap index	0.0002	0.0004	0.0011
Urban informal household (income-based) poverty gap index	−0.0004	−0.0016	−0.0027
Urban formal unskilled household (income-based) poverty gap index	0.0001	0.0002	0.0009
Urban formal skilled household (income-based) poverty gap index	0.0000	0.0000	0.0000
Capitalists household (income-based) poverty gap index	0.0000	0.0000	0.0000
Income Distribution Indicators[2]			
Gini coefficient (consumption-based)	−0.0001	−0.0002	−0.0004
Gini coefficient (income-based)	−0.0001	−0.0002	−0.0003
Theil index (consumption-based)	0.0004	0.0019	0.0044
Theil index (income-based)	0.0003	0.0020	0.0046

[1] Percentage deviations from baseline. [2] Gini Coefficients and Theil Indices measure between-group inequality.
Note: SR, MR and LR stand for short run, medium run, and long run, respectively.

unskilled households almost outweigh poverty decreases among rural nontraded and urban informal labor households in the long run, resulting in a small decrease in the aggregate poverty gap index. Finally, the results indicate that income distribution, both in the short and the long run, becomes more (less) egalitarian when we use the Gini coefficient (Theil index), and that improvements are more significant at a longer horizon. These conflicting results across inequality indicators are similar to those obtained with previous shocks. If anything, they help to illustrate the importance of using a range of measures to assess changes in income distribution.

In sum, on comparing the effects of poverty reduction when savings are allocated to infrastructure relative to the effects obtained under a transfers policy, we find that every poverty indicator under the first scenario (except for the income-based poverty gap) outperforms indicators under the transfers scenario in the long run.

The fact that investment in infrastructure shifts the private sector production possibility frontier (whereas the transfers policy does not) explains why poverty reduction may be more significant when resources are devoted to infrastructure instead of transfers. By increasing its stock of assets the government creates positive supply-side externalities. These externalities translate over time into higher employment and higher income for workers.

Investment in Education

Investment in education provides incentives for higher skills acquisition by unskilled urban workers and this has a direct impact on the supply of skilled labor (see Tables 5.10 and 5.11). However, skills acquisition grows at a faster pace than labor demand over time, implying that skilled open unemployment accelerates over time. Debt reduction leads therefore to smaller employment gains for skilled workers, in spite of the high degree of complementarity between private capital (which increases over time due lower confiscation risk and higher investment) and skilled labor in production.

This result is important because it highlights the need to consider both demand- and supply-side effects in designing policy reforms. For instance, we have performed a simulation in which half the savings from debt reduction are applied to investment in education whereas the other half is allocated to investment in infrastructure. This mixed policy yields better results (in the sense of skilled unemployment being much lower) than the case in which public savings associated with debt relief are fully allocated to investment in education.

As urban unskilled workers enter the skilled labor force, and informal workers are absorbed into the formal sector, the expected average wage for unskilled workers in the urban labor market decreases (despite the fact that higher demand for labor in the informal sector drives wages up in that sector), but a larger initial decline in rural sector wages creates incentives to migrate from rural areas. This pushes workers out of the rural sector and into the urban unskilled labor market. However, migration flows are reversed in the long run, as (expected) urban unskilled wages start to decline.

Consumption-based poverty headcount indices show increases in poverty in the short run, but no change in poverty in the long run. The aggregate income-based poverty headcount index show increases in poverty in the short run, but a small

Table 5.10 IMMPA: macroeconomic indicators 5-percent foreign debt reduction with increased investment in education (Absolute deviations from baseline, unless otherwise indicated)

	Periods									
	1	2	3	4	5	6	7	8	9	10
Real Sector										
Total resources	0.236	0.234	0.242	0.250	0.258	0.266	0.274	0.282	0.290	0.306
Gross domestic product	0.105	0.104	0.116	0.127	0.137	0.148	0.158	0.169	0.179	0.200
Imports of goods & NFS	0.448	0.444	0.448	0.452	0.457	0.461	0.465	0.469	0.474	0.482
Total expenditures										
Private consumption	0.136	0.125	0.139	0.149	0.160	0.171	0.182	0.192	0.203	0.223
Public consumption	0.000	0.000	0.000	0.000	0.000	0.000	0.000	0.000	0.000	0.000
Private investment	0.250	0.259	0.280	0.299	0.319	0.338	0.356	0.374	0.392	0.427
Public investment	9.966	9.770	9.579	9.391	9.207	9.026	8.849	8.676	8.506	8.175
Exports of goods & NFS	−0.046	−0.037	−0.029	−0.022	−0.014	−0.006	0.001	0.009	0.017	0.032
Memorandum item										
Private disposable income	0.128	0.126	0.138	0.148	0.159	0.170	0.181	0.191	0.202	0.222
External Sector										
Current account	0.651	0.620	0.665	0.700	0.732	0.760	0.786	0.810	0.832	0.871
Exports of goods & NFS (excl. subsidies)	−0.045	−0.036	−0.029	−0.021	−0.014	−0.006	0.001	0.009	0.016	0.031
Imports of goods & NFS (excl. tariffs)	0.446	0.442	0.446	0.450	0.455	0.459	0.463	0.467	0.472	0.480
Factor services	−5.024	−4.771	−4.557	−4.348	−4.146	−3.949	−3.759	−3.574	−3.396	−3.055
Capital account	0.656	0.651	0.602	0.646	0.675	0.702	0.727	0.751	0.773	0.812
NFPS financing	0.000	0.000	0.000	0.000	0.000	0.000	0.000	0.000	0.000	0.000
Central bank financing	0.000	0.000	0.000	0.000	0.000	0.000	0.000	0.000	0.000	0.000
Private financing	0.786	0.799	0.745	0.792	0.822	0.850	0.875	0.897	0.917	0.953

Continued

Table 5.10 Continued

					Periods					
	1	2	3	4	5	6	7	8	9	10
Change in net international reserves	0.672	0.765	0.231	0.348	0.350	0.363	0.374	0.385	0.396	0.417
Nonfinancial Public Sector										
Total revenue	0.192	0.197	0.214	0.230	0.245	0.260	0.275	0.290	0.305	0.333
Total expenditures	0.184	0.190	0.206	0.221	0.236	0.250	0.265	0.279	0.293	0.320
Consumption	0.000	0.000	0.000	0.000	0.000	0.000	0.000	0.000	0.000	0.000
Investment	9.966	9.770	9.579	9.391	9.207	9.026	8.849	8.676	8.506	8.175
Transfers to households	0.268	0.279	0.304	0.328	0.352	0.376	0.400	0.424	0.448	0.496
Domestic interest payments	0.000	0.003	0.005	0.006	0.006	0.006	0.006	0.005	0.005	0.004
Foreign interest payments	−4.996	−4.947	−4.898	−4.849	−4.801	−4.754	−4.707	−4.660	−4.614	−4.523
Total financing	0.000	0.000	0.000	0.000	0.000	0.000	0.000	0.000	0.000	0.000
Net foreign financing	0.000	0.000	0.000	0.000	0.000	0.000	0.000	0.000	0.000	0.000
Net domestic credit, central bank	0.000	0.000	0.000	0.000	0.000	0.000	0.000	0.000	0.000	0.000
Net domestic credit, commercial banks	0.000	0.000	0.000	0.000	0.000	0.000	0.000	0.000	0.000	0.000
Central Bank										
Total assets	0.059	0.108	0.113	0.123	0.133	0.143	0.152	0.161	0.170	0.187
Net foreign assets	0.075	0.135	0.140	0.152	0.163	0.173	0.183	0.193	0.203	0.221
Net domestic assets	0.000	0.000	0.000	0.000	0.000	0.000	0.000	0.000	0.000	0.000
Loans to government	0.000	0.000	0.000	0.000	0.000	0.000	0.000	0.000	0.000	0.000
Loans to commercial banks	0.000	0.000	0.000	0.000	0.000	0.000	0.000	0.000	0.000	0.000
Other domestic assets	0.000	0.000	0.000	0.000	0.000	0.000	0.000	0.000	0.000	0.000

Total liabilities/reserve money	0.059	0.108	0.113	0.123	0.133	0.143	0.152	0.161	0.170	0.187
Currency in circulation	0.068	0.125	0.129	0.140	0.150	0.160	0.171	0.181	0.191	0.210
Reserve requirements	−0.005	0.010	0.040	0.060	0.076	0.090	0.102	0.113	0.124	0.143
Memorandum items										
Money demand (M1)	0.068	0.125	0.129	0.140	0.150	0.160	0.171	0.181	0.191	0.210
Gross reserves in months of imports	−0.370	−0.306	−0.305	−0.297	−0.291	−0.285	−0.279	−0.273	−0.268	−0.257
Commercial Banks										
Total assets	0.127	0.187	0.228	0.260	0.287	0.310	0.331	0.350	0.369	0.404
Net foreign assets	0.000	0.000	0.000	0.000	0.000	0.000	0.000	0.000	0.000	0.000
Net domestic assets	0.127	0.187	0.228	0.260	0.287	0.310	0.331	0.350	0.369	0.404
Loans to government	0.000	0.000	0.000	0.000	0.000	0.000	0.000	0.000	0.000	0.000
Loans to firms	0.175	0.236	0.274	0.303	0.327	0.348	0.368	0.386	0.404	0.437
Other domestic assets	−0.005	0.010	0.040	0.060	0.076	0.090	0.102	0.113	0.124	0.143
Total liabilities	0.127	0.187	0.228	0.260	0.287	0.310	0.331	0.350	0.369	0.404
Banks' foreign liabilities	0.328	0.431	0.480	0.521	0.555	0.586	0.614	0.641	0.667	0.715
Deposits	−0.005	0.010	0.040	0.060	0.076	0.090	0.102	0.113	0.124	0.143
Memorandum items[1]										
Real GDP growth rate	−0.001	0.005	0.005	0.005	0.005	0.005	0.005	0.005	0.005	0.005
Inflation rate (economy-wide)	0.117	−0.007	0.008	0.007	0.007	0.007	0.007	0.007	0.007	0.007
Deposit rate	0.000	0.000	0.000	0.000	0.000	0.000	0.000	0.000	0.000	0.000
Lending rate	−0.237	−0.147	−0.106	−0.084	−0.070	−0.061	−0.054	−0.048	−0.044	−0.041

[1] Absolute deviations from baseline.

Table 5.11 IMMPA: structural, poverty and income distribution indicators 5-percent foreign debt reduction with increased investment on education (Absolute deviations from baseline, unless otherwise indicated)

	Periods									
	1	2	3	4	5	6	7	8	9	10
Production Structure										
Size of informal sector (% of total output)	−1.000	0.108	−0.018	−0.008	−0.008	−0.008	−0.008	−0.008	−0.007	−0.007
Size of rural sector (% of formal sector output)	−0.058	0.034	−0.011	−0.004	−0.005	−0.005	−0.005	−0.005	−0.005	−0.005
Composition of Employment and Wages										
Employment in rural sector (% of total employment)	0.000	−0.001	−0.001	−0.002	−0.002	−0.002	−0.003	−0.003	−0.003	−0.003
Employment in rural nontraded sector (% of rural employment)	0.000	−0.004	−0.006	−0.006	−0.006	−0.006	−0.007	−0.007	−0.007	−0.007
Employment in informal sector (% of total employment)	−0.012	0.000	0.002	0.002	0.003	0.003	0.004	0.004	0.004	0.004
Employment in informal sector (% of urban employment)	−0.025	−0.001	0.002	0.001	0.002	0.002	0.003	0.003	0.003	0.003
Employment in public sector (% of total employment)	0.000	0.000	0.000	0.000	0.000	0.000	0.000	0.000	0.000	0.000
Employment in public sector (% of urban employment)	0.000	0.000	0.000	0.000	0.000	0.000	−0.001	−0.001	−0.001	−0.001
Rural traded and rural nontraded sector wage differential[1]	1.183	−0.107	−0.016	−0.024	−0.030	−0.037	−0.045	−0.054	−0.066	−0.078
Urban unskilled formal and informal sector wage differential[1]	0.420	−0.046	0.009	0.003	0.003	0.002	0.002	0.002	0.002	0.001
Public sector wages (% of total public expenditure)	0.587	0.024	0.000	0.003	0.003	0.004	0.004	0.004	0.004	0.005

Aggregate Demand										
Private consumption (% of GDP)	-1.377	0.142	0.002	0.013	0.013	0.013	0.013	0.014	0.014	0.014
Private consumption (% of total consumption)	-0.139	0.014	0.000	0.001	0.001	0.001	0.001	0.001	0.001	0.001
Private investment (% of GDP)	0.225	-0.071	0.013	0.000	0.002	0.002	0.002	0.002	0.002	0.002
Private investment (% of total investment)	-0.046	-0.018	0.006	0.001	0.002	0.002	0.002	0.002	0.002	0.002
Fiscal Indicators										
Public investment in infrastructure (% of total public investment)	0.000	0.000	0.000	0.000	0.000	0.000	0.000	0.000	0.000	0.000
Public investment in health (% of total public investment)	0.000	0.000	0.000	0.000	0.000	0.000	0.000	0.000	0.000	0.000
Public investment in education (% of total public investment)	0.000	0.000	0.000	0.000	0.000	0.000	0.000	0.000	0.000	0.000
Financial Indicators										
Currency (% of M2)	-0.521	-0.059	0.206	0.138	0.111	0.090	0.074	0.062	0.053	0.046
M2 (% of GDP)	0.275	-0.425	-0.299	-0.302	-0.296	-0.291	-0.286	-0.281	-0.276	-0.271
Bank credit to private sector (% of GDP)	-0.002	-0.002	-0.002	-0.002	-0.002	-0.002	-0.002	-0.002	-0.002	-0.002
Lending – deposit rate differential	0.000	0.000	0.000	0.000	0.000	0.000	0.000	0.000	0.000	0.000
External Sector										
Agricultural exports (% of total exports)	-0.102	0.000	0.003	0.001	0.001	0.001	0.001	0.000	0.000	0.000
Imports of non-agricultural goods (% of total imports)	0.242	-0.027	0.003	0.000	0.000	0.000	0.000	0.000	0.000	0.000
External debt (% of GDP)	-0.181	-0.101	-0.003	-0.012	-0.012	-0.012	-0.012	-0.012	-0.012	-0.012
Degree of openness (exports plus imports divided by GDP)	1.968	1.040	0.015	0.006	0.006	0.006	0.006	0.005	0.005	0.005

Continued

Table 5.11 Continued

Poverty Indicators	Periods									
	1	2	3	4	5	6	7	8	9	10
	SR	MR	LR							
Rural poverty line (consumption-based) in real terms[1]	0.0000	0.0000	0.0000							
Rural poverty line (consumption-based) in nominal terms[1]	−1.2386	−0.5860	−0.0487							
Rural poverty line (income-based) in real terms[1]	0.0000	0.0000	0.0000							
Rural poverty line (income-based) in nominal terms[1]	−1.2386	−0.5860	−0.0487							
Urban poverty line (consumption-based) in real terms[1]	0.0000	0.0000	0.0000							
Urban poverty line (consumption-based) in nominal terms[1]	−2.9243	−1.4146	−0.1562							
Urban poverty line (income-based) in real terms[1]	0.0000	0.0000	0.0000							
Urban poverty line (income-based) in nominal terms[1]	−2.9243	−1.4146	−0.1562							
Rural nontraded household (consumption-based) poverty headcount index	0.0140	0.0040	0.0000							
Rural traded household (consumption-based) poverty headcount index	0.0030	0.0030	0.0000							
Urban informal household (consumption-based) poverty headcount index	0.0280	0.0031	0.0000							

Urban formal unskilled household (consumption-based) poverty headcount index	−0.0067	0.0000	0.0000
Urban formal skilled household (consumption-based) poverty headcount index	0.0000	0.0000	0.0000
Capitalists household poverty (consumption-based) headcount index	0.0000	0.0000	0.0000
Rural nontraded household (consumption-based) poverty gap index	0.0097	0.0073	0.0007
Rural traded household (consumption-based) poverty gap index	0.0007	−0.0008	0.0000
Urban informal household (consumption-based) poverty gap index	0.0045	0.0068	0.0012
Urban formal unskilled household (consumption-based) poverty gap index	0.0017	−0.0033	−0.0006
Urban formal skilled household (consumption-based) poverty gap index	0.0000	0.0000	0.0000
Capitalists household (consumption-based) poverty gap index	0.0000	0.0000	0.0000
Rural nontraded household (income-based) poverty headcount index	0.0040	0.0100	0.0020
Rural traded household (income-based) poverty headcount index	0.0000	0.0000	0.0000
Urban informal household (income-based) poverty headcount index	0.0249	0.0031	0.0000
Urban formal unskilled household (income-based) poverty headcount index	−0.0134	−0.0134	−0.0067

Continued

Table 5.11 Continued

	Periods									
	1	2	3	4	5	6	7	8	9	10
Urban formal skilled household (income-based) poverty headcount index	0.0000	0.0000	0.0000							
Capitalists household poverty (income-based) headcount index	0.0000	0.0000	0.0000							
Rural nontraded household (income-based) poverty gap index	0.0144	0.0035	−0.0006							
Rural traded household (income-based) poverty gap index	0.0021	0.0009	0.0000							
Urban informal household (income-based) poverty gap index	0.0056	0.0066	0.0012							
Urban formal unskilled household (income-based) poverty gap index	0.0060	0.0084	0.0049							
Urban formal skilled household (income-based) poverty gap index	0.0000	0.0000	0.0000							
Capitalists household (income-based) poverty gap index	0.0000	0.0000	0.0000							
Income Distribution Indicators[2]										
Gini coefficient (consumption-based)	0.0044	0.0022	0.0004							
Gini coefficient (income-based)	0.0040	0.0021	0.0002							
Theil index (consumption-based)	−0.0045	−0.0020	−0.0006							
Theil index (income-based)	−0.0037	−0.0016	0.0002							

[1] Percentage deviations from baseline. [2] Gini Coefficients and Theil Indices measure between-group inequality.
Note: SR, MR and LR stand for short run, medium run, and long run, respectively.

decrease in the long run. The aggregate consumption-based poverty gap index show a rise in poverty in the short run, and a small increase in poverty in the long run. The aggregate income-based poverty gap index shows an increase in poverty in the short run and, to lesser extent, in the long run.

Finally, the indices of income distribution again convey again a mixed picture; the Gini coefficient shows a less egalitarian distribution, whereas the Theil index indicates the opposite.

Poverty reduction under this scenario is clearly not as substantial as in the case where savings are allocated to infrastructure. This is due in part to the fact that investment in education does not necessarily translate into a shift in the private sector production possibilities frontier (PPF) as long as newly-skilled workers remain unemployed, whereas investment in infrastructure (as indicated earlier) does so unambiguously. Comparison between investment in education versus a transfers policy is more ambiguous, as results vary depending on the chosen indicators.

5.5 Conclusions

The purpose of this chapter has been to present the complete IMMPA framework and to illustrate its use for analyzing the impact of policy and external shocks on income distribution and poverty. The prototype described in this chapter captures important structural features of low-income, highly-indebted countries: the existence of a negative relation between external debt and private investment, a large urban informal economy, a limited menu of financial assets, the impact of credit constraints on the decision to acquire skills, and a predominant role of banks in the economy. Taken together, these features create a variety of channels through which adjustment policies may affect growth, employment, and poverty in the short and the long run.

Section 5.1 provided a detailed analytical presentation of the model's structure and Section 5.2 explained how poverty and distributional analysis is performed. Section 5.3 discussed calibration. Section 5.4 presented the results of several simulation experiments. In particular, we used the model to analyze a temporary terms-of-trade shock, a permanent cut in domestic credit to the government, and a poverty-reduction program consisting of partial external debt forgiveness coupled with a reallocation of savings on debt service payments. The latter experiment is particularly important for many low-income countries. Recent evidence suggests that external debt remains at unsustainable levels in many of these countries. The direct short-term impact of debt reduction is to reduce pressure on the government budget constraint; and if one considers a country starting from an initially high fiscal deficit (with a high degree of monetization and inflation, or a significant crowding-out effect on the private sector) then it might indeed be best to allocate savings from debt reduction to reducing the deficit. But in more general circumstances, the question remains as to what the allocation of expenditure should be in order to maximize the impact of debt relief on poverty reduction.

Our model allows us to address this question. Specifically, we considered an experiment that consists of a permanent cut in the level of external debt, with the savings resulting from lower debt service being allocated to either lump-sum transfers to households, expenditure on infrastructure (which has complementary effects on private investment and a direct effect on the productivity of private inputs), education (which affects incentives to acquire skills), or education and health (which combine to raise productivity of the labor force). The results illustrated the importance of accounting for the various channels through which poverty alleviation programs based on external debt reduction and public expenditure reallocation may ultimately affect the poor.

The IMMPA framework presented in this chapter can be used to analyze a variety of other policy shocks – such as a reduction in external tariffs, fiscal adjustment (such as public sector layoffs or changes in the structure of income taxes), labor market reforms (such as changes in the minimum wage), a devaluation of the nominal exchange rate, or a financial liberalization program based on an increase in bank deposit rates. An important point that we want to emphasize is that IMMPA is not meant to be applied "blindly" to any particular country. Although the prototype version described in this chapter is general enough to be applied to a variety of cases (at least as a "first pass") we view our framework as a flexible tool that can (and should) be amended or extended to fit particular circumstances and needs. For instance, regarding the credit market, whether the "collateral" view or the "monitoring and enforcement costs" view are appropriate should be gauged on the basis of the evidence on the determinants of interest rate spreads.

More generally, we have assumed that the credit market clears because commercial banks can borrow (and lend) as much as they desire on world capital markets; if banks are unable to do so, it could be assumed that they carry significant excess liquid reserves that would play the equilibrating role. Alternatively, credit rationing can be introduced (see, for instance, Decaluwé and Nsengiyumva (1994)), with possibly significant implications for the behavior of private investment and the behavior of output in the short term. Finally, we have completely ignored informal financial markets. A good argument for doing so is that financial liberalization in many developing countries has proceeded to such an extent that these markets play a much less prominent role than they used to. However, it is also true that in some countries (mostly in Sub-Saharan Africa) informal *credit* markets continue to play a significant role in the financial system. Modeling the channels through which such markets operate could proceed along the lines of Agénor, Haque, and Montiel (1993), but doing so would add another layer of complexity. The next two chapters will, instead, focus on adjusting the low-income IMMPA prototype to better reflect the financial features that characterize middle-income countries, such as bond financing, flexible exchange rates, a monetary policy based on setting short-term interest rates, and dollarization of the banking system.

Chapter 6

Stabilization Policy, Poverty, and Unemployment in Brazil

Pierre-Richard Agénor, Reynaldo Fernandes, Eduardo Haddad, and Henning Tarp Jensen

Since the Real Plan was implemented in July 1994, Brazil has achieved much progress in taming inflation. Despite the currency crisis of January 1999 (which led to the abandonment of the band regime and the adoption of a flexible exchange rate, followed by the introduction of an inflation targeting framework), and the turmoil on world capital markets that followed the Russian default of August 1998 and the Argentina crisis of 2001–2, inflation has remained at or below double digit levels for the past few years (with the exception of 2002), in large part due to prudent fiscal policies and active management of short-term interest rates by the Brazilian central bank. The era of low inflation has been accompanied by improved financial intermediation (as measured by an increase in the share of credit to GDP), significant progress in reducing fiscal deficits and the burden of domestic public debt. Brazil's net public sector debt, after increasing continuously from 30.6 percent of GDP in 1995 to 57.2 percent in 2002, dropped to 51.3 percent in February 2005.[1] On average, the annual growth rate of the economy remained at about 2 percent per annum between 1994 and 2001, despite the recession of 1998–9 (Da Fonseca (2001)). Following a lackluster performance in 2002 and 2003, real GDP growth improved to 5 percent in 2004.

However, progress in reducing unemployment, poverty, and income inequality has been mixed. After peaking at 12.3 percent of the labor force in 2003, unemployment

---

[1] See Bevilaqua and Garcia (2002) for an analysis of the evolution of Brazil's net public debt (domestic and external) in the second half of the 1990s.

has declined only slightly in 2004 to 11.5 percent. The degree of income inequality in Brazil is one of the worst in the world; despite a slight reduction in the immediate aftermath of the Real Plan, the Gini coefficient has remained at around 0.6 during the 1990s. Significant gains were achieved in reducing poverty after the Real Plan, with the share of the poor in the population falling by almost 10 percentage points between 1992 and 1995, as a result of the pickup in growth and the rise in per capita income that followed. Nevertheless, little progress has been achieved since then; a significant percentage of the population remains in deep poverty, with the headcount poverty index exceeding 35 during much of the second half of the 1990s and early 2000s. One reason has been the slowdown in growth rates in income; after increasing at a rate of almost 6 percent during the 1970s, real per capita income increased by only 0.7 percent during the period 1980–2004. Thus, reducing unemployment and poverty remain key policy issues in Brazil today.

The purpose of this chapter is to develop a quantitative framework for analyzing the impact of adjustment policies on unemployment, poverty and income distribution in Brazil. Our point of departure is the IMMPA prototype described in the previous chapter. The IMMPA prototype captures several structural features that are common to many developing countries: the pervasive role of the informal economy and the relative scarcity of "good jobs" for unskilled workers in the urban sector, labor market segmentation, and the links between the financial sector and the supply side through the credit market. In addition, however, there are several important characteristics of the Brazilian economy that are not well captured in the low-income IMMPA prototype. Accounting for these characteristics is essential to make the model useful for policy analysis.

We therefore extend the low-income IMMPA framework in several directions. First, we allow for open unskilled urban unemployment, by introducing, as discussed in Chapters 1, 3, and 4, a Harris-Todaro type mechanism to determine the supply of unskilled labor in the formal sector. This extension is very important for a country like Brazil, where unskilled workers account for a large fraction of employment (61.8 percent of total employment in 1996 an 55.2 percent in 2003) and unemployment: in 2003, the overall open unemployment rate stood at 8.1 percent up from 7.4 percent in 1996. The skilled unemployment rate amounted to 3.8 percent, whereas the unemployment rate for unskilled labor represented 4.3 percent. Second, we specify a more general and flexible form for the determination of skilled workers' wage in the private formal sector. Our specification dwells on the distinction between the product wage (which firms are concerned with) and the consumption wage (which matters for workers or those who represent them), as well as a *level* effect of unemployment on wages, which is consistent with various forms of efficiency wage theories, such as those emphasizing the wage–productivity link or turnover costs (see Chapter 1). In particular, it is consistent with a negative effect of unemployment on workers' reservation wage, and wage-setting models based on a bargaining framework between firms and trade unions. In addition, the wage specification accounts for the effect of payroll taxation on firms' wage bill and the cost of borrowing for financing workers' compensation. Third, as in Chapter 3, we account for the possibility of congestion effects associated with the use of public sector services in the urban sector. Fourth, we introduce the possibility of bond financing of public sector deficits and preclude at the same time public sector borrowing from the central bank. This modification is important for many middle-income countries, where (in addition to foreign borrowing) governments have increasingly issued domestic bonds to finance their fiscal deficits. Of course, we model not only the supply side of the bonds market but also the demand side, that is, holdings of bonds by households and the financial system. Fifth, we assume that the exchange rate is fully flexible and equilibrates the balance of payments. Official reserves are therefore exogenous, in the absence of central bank intervention in the foreign exchange market. Finally, we model monetary policy by assuming that the central bank sets a policy interest rate (or, more directly in the case of Brazil, a short-term market interest rate) and has a perfectly elastic supply curve of liquidity to commercial banks at that rate. Domestic borrowing by commercial banks is thus the equilibrating variable on the credit market.

We also make other (less significant) modifications to reflect Brazil's institutional characteristics and the type of policy issues that we want to address. First, we assume that nominal wages are fully flexible in the rural sector and adjust continuously to equilibrate overall supply and demand for labor. Second, we exclude borrowing from the financial system in the rural sector, given its relatively limited empirical importance. This has an important effect, of course, on the transmission process of financial shocks to rural areas and rural production. Third, we keep public sector wages for skilled workers constant in real terms and assume that there is a nonpecuniary benefit (in terms of, say, increased job security) that leads to zero turnover for that category of workers. Finally, we also introduce payroll taxation on both categories of labor in the private urban formal sector. The extent to which high payroll taxes have tended to discourage the demand for labor (particularly unskilled labor) has remained an important policy issue in Brazil; in the present framework, these taxes influence simulation results partly through their "pure" fiscal effects, and partly through their effect on hiring decisions in the formal sector.

Section 6.1 describes the macroeconomic component of the model, whereas Section 6.2 explains the data and indicators used for poverty and income distribution analysis. Section 6.3 and the Appendix discuss briefly the calibration procedure, including the structure of the financial SAM that underlies the model. Section 6.4 considers a policy experiment consisting of a permanent increase in official interest rates and discusses the response of production, wages, employment, and poverty. The last section summarizes the main results and considers some possible extensions of our analysis.

6.1   An IMMPA Framework for Brazil

In this section we review the various building blocks of the model. We consider in turn the production side, employment, the demand side, external trade, sectoral and aggregate prices, income formation, the financial sector and asset allocation decisions, and the public sector. Given that the structure of the model differs significantly from existing applied general equilibrium models for Brazil, a detailed justification is provided.[2] Throughout the discussion, as in Chapters 4 and 5, we often use generic forms to specify functional relationships.[3]

6.1.1   Production

The basic distinction on the production side is that between rural and urban sectors. As in the Mini-IMMPA framework described in Chapter 3, the rural sector produces only one good, which is sold both on domestic markets and abroad. Urban production includes both formal and informal components; in addition, the formal urban economy consists of a private sector (which produces a good sold on both domestic markets and abroad) and a consolidated public sector (which produces a good sold only on domestic markets).

Rural Sector

Land available for production in the rural sector is in fixed supply and non marketable. Gross output of the rural good, X_A, is given by the sum of value added, V_A, and intermediate consumption:

$$X_A = V_A + \sum_i a_{iA} X_A, \tag{1}$$

where the a_{ij} are conventionally-defined input–output coefficients (sales from sector i to sector j) and $i = A, I, P, G$, with A referring to the rural sector, I the informal sector, P the private urban sector, and G the public sector.[4]

Value added is produced with a Cobb-Douglas (CD) function of land, $LAND$, and a composite factor, defined as a constant elasticity of substitution (CES) function that depends on the number of unskilled rural workers employed in the rural sector, U_A, and the economy-wide stock of public physical capital, K_G:

$$V_A = CD[LAND, CES(U_A, K_G)], \tag{2}$$

Given the CD specification, and that the area of land allocated to production is constant, rural production exhibits decreasing returns to scale in the composite input.

As discussed in previous chapters, the presence of K_G in the production functions (2) and (8) is based on the view that a greater availability of public physical capital in the economy (such as highways and airports, or water treatment plants) raises the productivity of private firms and other production units in the rural sector.

Allocation of rural sector output to domestic consumption, D_A, and exports, E_A, occurs according to a production possibility frontier, defined by a constant elasticity

---

[2] For a review of computable general equilibrium models for the Brazilian economy since the mid-1990s, see Domingues (2002). For earlier models, see Guilhoto (1995).

[3] Explicit functional forms, as well as variable names and definitions, are provided in Appendices A and B, available in the more detailed version of this chapter that can be downloaded from RePEC.

[4] In what follows, whenever the indexes i and j are not explicitly defined, they will be taken to refer to all of these sectors.

of transformation (CET) function:

$$X_A = CET(D_A, E_A). \tag{3}$$

where the ratio E_A/D_A depends, as discussed later, on relative prices.

Urban Informal Sector

Gross production in the urban informal sector, X_I, is given as the sum of value added, V_I, and intermediate consumption:

$$X_I = V_I + \sum_i a_{iI} X_I. \tag{4}$$

There is no physical capital in the informal sector, and production requires only unskilled labor. Assuming decreasing returns to scale, value added depends only on the number of unskilled workers employed in the informal economy, U_I:

$$V_I = \alpha_{XI} U_I^{\beta_{XI}}, \qquad \alpha_{XI} > 0, \ 0 < \beta_{XI} < 1. \tag{5}$$

From (5), the demand for labor in the informal sector is given by

$$U_I^d = \beta_{XI}(V_I/w_I), \tag{6}$$

where w_I is the product wage given by $w_I = W_I/PV_I$, with PV_I denoting the price of value added in the informal sector.

Public Sector

Gross production of the public good, X_G, is given by the sum of value added, V_G, and intermediate consumption:

$$X_G = V_G + \sum_i a_{iG} X_G. \tag{7}$$

Production of value added requires both types of labor (skilled and unskilled) and is given by a two-level CES function. At the lower level, unskilled workers, U_G, and skilled workers, S_G, combine to produce a composite labor input. At the second level, the labor input and public capital, K_G, combine to produce net output:

$$V_G = CES[CES(S_G, U_G), K_G]. \tag{8}$$

Employment levels of both categories of workers are treated as exogenous.

Urban Formal Private Sector

Gross production of the private formal urban sector, X_P, is the sum of value added, V_P, and intermediate consumption:

$$X_P = V_P + \sum_i a_{iP} X_P. \tag{9}$$

Value added is created by combining skilled labor, S_P, unskilled labor, U_P, and physical capital, K_P. Skilled labor and physical capital have a higher degree of complementarity (lower degree of substitution) than physical capital and unskilled labor. In order to account explicitly for these differences in the degree of substitutability among inputs, as in previous chapters, we adopt a nested CES production structure:

$$V_P = CES\left\{CES[CES(S_P, K_P), U_P], \frac{K_{G,-1}}{L_{U,-1}^{pc}}\right\}, \tag{10}$$

where $pc \geq 0$.

At the lowest level of equation (10), skilled labor and physical capital are combined to form the composite input T_2, with a low elasticity of substitution between them. At the second level, this composite input is used together with unskilled labor to form the composite input T_1. The elasticity of substitution between T_2 and unskilled labor, U_P, is higher than the elasticity between S_P and K_P. The final layer involves combining T_1 and the (lagged) value of the ratio of the stock of government capital to the total size of the labor force in the urban sector, L_U. The presence of this ratio can be rationalized as follows. As noted earlier, a greater stock of public capital raises the productivity of private production. However, due to congestion effects, this positive externality of public capital decreases as its usage increases. As in Chapter 3, the size of the urban labor force is used as a proxy for usage. When $pc = 0$, public capital is a pure public good. Otherwise, the higher the size of the labor force in urban areas, the lower is the contribution of the public capital stock to private production.

Private firms in the urban formal sector allocate their output to exports, E_P, or the domestic market, D_P, according to a production possibility frontier, which is also defined by a CET function:

$$X_P = CET(E_P, D_P). \tag{11}$$

As shown later, the ratio E_P/D_P depends also on relative prices.

6.1.2 Wages, Employment, Migration, and Skills Acquisition

Unskilled workers in the economy may be employed either in the rural sector, U_R, or in the urban sector, U_U, whereas skilled workers are employed only in the urban sector.

Rural Wages and Employment

From (2), the demand curve for unskilled labor consistent with profit maximization in the rural sector, U_A^d, can be derived as

$$U_A^d = \left\{V_A^{1+\rho_{XA}/(1-\eta_{XA})}\frac{1-\eta_{XA}}{w_A}\cdot\frac{\beta_{XA}}{\alpha_{XA}^{\rho_{XA}}}\right\}^{1/1+\rho_{XA}}, \qquad w_A = \frac{W_A}{PV_A}, \tag{12}$$

where W_A denotes the nominal wage and PV_A the net output price in the rural sector.

Nominal wages in the rural sector adjust to clear the labor market. Let U_R^s denote labor supply in the rural sector; the equilibrium condition is thus given by

$$U_R^s = U_A^d \left(V_A, \frac{W_A}{PV_A} \right), \tag{13}$$

which can be solved for W_A.

The size of the labor force in the rural sector expands as a result of exogenous population growth, at the rate g_R, net of worker migration to urban areas, $MIGR$:

$$U_R^s = (1 + g_R) U_{R,-1}^s - MIGR. \tag{14}$$

Following Harris and Todaro (1970), and as discussed in previous chapters, rural workers choose to migrate depending on the perceived wage differential between rural areas and urban areas. Unskilled workers in the urban economy may be employed either in the private formal sector, in which case they are paid a minimum wage, W_M, or they can enter the informal economy and receive the market-determined wage in that sector, W_I.[5] When rural workers make the decision to migrate to urban areas, they are uncertain as to which type of job they will be able to get, and therefore weigh wages in each sector by the probability of finding a job there. Assuming, for simplicity, complete job turnover in the urban formal private sector, these probabilities can be approximated by prevailing employment ratios.

The expected, unskilled urban wage, EW_U, is thus a weighted average of the minimum wage in the formal sector and the going wage in the informal sector:

$$EW_U = \theta_U W_{M,-1} + (1 - \theta_U) W_{I,-1}, \tag{15}$$

where θ_U is the probability of employment in the formal private sector, measured by the (lagged) ratio of employment in that sector to the number of unskilled workers (net of public employment) looking for a job there:

$$\theta_U = \frac{U_{P,-1}^d}{U_{F,-1}^s - U_{G,-1}}. \tag{16}$$

In the rural sector, the employment probability is equal to unity, because workers can always find a job at the going wage. Assuming a one-period lag, the expected rural wage, EW_A, is thus given by

$$EW_A = W_{A,-1}.$$

The migration function can therefore be specified as

$$\frac{MIGR}{U_{R,-1}} = \lambda_m \left\{ \sigma_M \ln \left(\frac{EW_U}{EW_A} \right) \right\} + (1 - \lambda_m) \frac{MIGR_{-1}}{U_{R,-2}}, \tag{17}$$

where $0 < \lambda_m < 1$ measures the speed of adjustment and $\sigma_M > 0$ the elasticity of migration flows with respect to the expected wage ratio. This specification assumes

---

[5] As indicated earlier, there is no job turnover for either category of workers in the public sector. Note also that in the present chapter, we assume that migrants compare relative wages in nominal terms.

again that costs associated with migration or other frictions may delay the migration process, introducing persistence in migration flows.

Urban Unskilled Wages, Employment, and Unemployment

Unskilled labor is used in all urban production activities. The public sector hires a fixed number of unskilled workers, U_G, at the given nominal wage rate $W_{UG} \geq W_M$. By contrast, the demand for unskilled labor by the formal private sector is determined by firms' profit maximization subject to the given minimum wage, W_M. As discussed later, many unskilled workers in Brazil actually earn a wage that exceeds the official minimum wage. At the same time, however, the wedge has remained relatively stable over time. Consequently, we simply assume that workers earn the legally-set minimum wage. We further assume that the real minimum wage is fixed, that is, that the nominal minimum wage is fully indexed to the urban unskilled price index.

Formal private sector firms cannot issue securities or equity claims on their stock of physical capital. To finance their wage bill (inclusive of payroll taxes), prior to the sale of output, they must borrow from domestic banks. As a result, the effective price of labor includes the bank lending rate. As in Chapters 3 and 4, we also assume that firms pay a payroll tax, at the rate $0 < ptax_U < 1$, which is proportional to the unskilled wage bill, $W_M U_P$. Unskilled labor demand by the private sector is thus given by

$$
U_P^d = T_1 \left\{ \frac{1}{(1 + IL_{-1})(1 + ptax_U)w_M} \frac{\beta_{XP1}}{\alpha_{XP1}^{\rho_{XP1}}} \right\}^{\sigma_{XP1}}, \quad w_M = \frac{W_M}{PT_1}, \quad (18)
$$

where IL is the lending rate. We assume that the cost of credit specified in loan contracts negotiated for the current period is based on the interest rate prevailing in the previous period.

In order to avoid corner solutions, we assume that the minimum wage is greater than the wage earned in the informal sector, $W_I < W_M$. Consequently, unskilled urban workers will first seek employment in the private formal sector. The actual level of employment in that sector is determined according to equation (18).

As in Chapters 3 and 4, we also assume that, as a result of relocation and congestion costs, mobility of the unskilled labor force between the formal and the informal sectors is imperfect. Migration flows are determined by expected income opportunities, along the lines of Harris and Todaro (1970). Specifically, total supply of unskilled labor in the formal sector, U_F^s, is assumed to change gradually over time as a function of the expected wage differential across sectors. Wage and employment prospects are formed on the basis of prevailing conditions in the labor market. Because there is no job turnover in the public sector, the expected nominal wage in the formal economy is equal to the minimum wage weighted by the probability of being hired in the private urban sector. Assuming that hiring in that sector is random, this probability can be approximated by the ratio of currently employed workers to those seeking employment in private firms, $U_P^d/(U_F^s - U_G)$. The expected nominal wage in the informal economy is simply the going wage, because there are no barriers to entry in that sector. Assuming a one-period lag, the supply of unskilled workers in the formal sector thus evolves over time according to

$$\Delta U_F^s = \beta_F \left\{ \frac{U_{P,-1}^d}{U_{F,-1}^s - U_{G,-1}} W_{M,-1} - W_{I,-1} \right\}, \tag{19}$$

where $\beta_F > 0$. The unskilled unemployment rate in the formal urban sector, $UNEMP_U$, is thus given by

$$UNEMP_U = 1 - \frac{(U_G + U_P^d)}{U_F^s}. \tag{20}$$

With U_U denoting the urban unskilled labor force, the supply of labor in the informal economy, U_I^s, is given by

$$U_I^s = U_U - U_F^s. \tag{21}$$

The informal labor market clears continuously, so that $U_I^d = U_I^s$. Equation (6) can therefore be solved for the equilibrium wage:

$$W_I = \beta_{XI} \left(\frac{PV_I \cdot V_I}{U_I^s} \right). \tag{22}$$

The urban unskilled labor supply, U_U, grows as a result of *a*) "natural" urban population growth, which occurs at the exogenous rate g_U; *b*) migration of unskilled labor from the rural economy; and *c*) the flow of unskilled workers, *SKL*, who acquire skills and leave the unskilled labor force:

$$U_U = U_{U,-1}(1 + g_U) + MIGR - SKL. \tag{23}$$

Urban Skilled Wages and Employment

As noted earlier, employment levels of both skilled and unskilled workers in the public sector are taken as exogenous. We also take as given the real wage rate that skilled workers are paid in the public sector, ω_{SG}. With W_{SG} denoting the nominal wage, and P_{US} the consumption price index for (urban) skilled workers, full indexation therefore implies that

$$W_{SG} = \omega_{SG} P_{US}. \tag{24}$$

To avoid a corner solution in which no worker would want to seek employment in the public sector, we assume that working for the government provides a nonpecuniary benefit, such as a lower risk of unemployment (see Chapter 1). As in Chapter 3, this benefit is measured as a proportion $b_G > 0$ of the wage, which must therefore be large enough to ensure that $(1 + b_G)W_{SG} > W_S$.

We assume again that private urban firms pay a payroll tax, at the rate $0 < ptax_S < 1$, which is proportional to the skilled wage bill, $W_S S_P$. The wage-setting equation for skilled labor in the private sector is given by

$$W_S = \overline{w}_S (P_{US})^{inds} (UNEMP_S)^{-\phi_U} \Omega_S^{\phi_1} \left(\frac{P_{US}}{PT_2} \right)^{\phi_2}, \tag{25}$$

where $\Omega_S > 0$ is the reservation wage, $UNEMP_S$ the skilled unemployment rate, and $\phi_U, \phi_1, \phi_2 > 0$.

This specification is quite flexible. For instance, full indexation on the consumer price index for (urban) skilled workers only requires setting $ind_S = 1$, and $\phi_U = \phi_1 = \phi_2 = 0$. This case is important because it implies that whereas firms are concerned with the *product* wage, workers are concerned with the *consumption* wage. This creates a wedge through which relative prices affect wage-setting decisions. To assume that the wage-setting depends only on the ratio P_{US}/PT_2 requires setting $\phi_2 > 0$, and $ind_S = \phi_U = \phi_1 = 0$. Note also that in (25), as long as $\phi_U > 0$, the level of skilled unemployment will affect (negatively) the *level* of nominal wages, instead of the *rate of growth* of wages (as would be the case with a Phillips curve-type formulation). as discussed at length in Chapter 1, this level effect is consistent with various forms of efficiency wage theories (such as those emphasizing the wage–productivity link or turnover costs), in which unemployment acts as a "worker discipline device", by moderating wage demands, eliciting a higher level of effort, and by reducing the incentive to quit and thus lowering turnover costs.[6]

From (10), the demand for skilled labor is given by

$$S_P^d = T_2 \kappa_S \left\{ \frac{1}{(1 + IL_{-1})(1 + ptax_S)w_S} \cdot \frac{\beta_{XP2}}{\alpha_{XP2}^{\rho_{XP2}}} \right\}^{\sigma_{XP2}}, \tag{26}$$

where $w_S = W_S/PT_2$.

As in previous chapters, signaling considerations provide incentives for skilled workers to remain openly unemployed (if they cannot be hired in the formal sector), instead of seeking employment in the informal economy. Given that wages are determined by the wage-setting equation (25) and that firms are on their labor demand curve, open skilled unemployment may emerge. The skilled unemployment rate, $UNEMP_S$, is given by the ratio of skilled workers who are not employed either by the private or the public sector, divided by the total population of skilled workers:

$$UNEMP_S = 1 - \frac{(S_G + S_P^d)}{S}. \tag{27}$$

The skilled labor force "depreciates" at the rate $0 < \delta_S < 1$ and expands as a result of unskilled workers acquiring skills:

$$S = (1 - \delta_S)S_{-1} + SKL. \tag{28}$$

The total size of the labor force in the urban sector, L_U, is given by

$$L_U = U_U + S. \tag{29}$$

Acquisition of Skills

All individuals are born unskilled. The acquisition of skills by unskilled workers is assumed to depend on two factors: *a*) relative expected consumption wages of skilled

---

[6]As also discussed in Chapter 1, a bargaining framework between firms and a centralized trade union could also lead to a similar wage-setting specification.

and unskilled urban workers (as a proxy for the future stream of earnings associated with higher levels of education); and *b*) the government stock of education capital, K_E, which limits the ability to invest in skills.

Consider first the effect of wages. In case they acquire skills, current unskilled workers expect to earn wage W_S if they are employed (with probability θ_S) and nothing if they are unemployed. Assuming that the lagged wage is a good proxy for future wages, the expected wage is thus

$$\mathbb{E} w_S = \theta_S W_{S,-1},$$

where θ_S is measured by the (lagged) ratio of the number of skilled workers employed in the private sector, over the total number of those workers who are not employed in the public sector:

$$\theta_S = \frac{S_{P,-1}}{S_{-1} - S_{G,-1}}. \tag{30}$$

If they remain unskilled, workers expect to get the average unskilled wage, which is a weighted average of the minimum wage W_M and the informal wage rate. Assuming, again, that there is no job turnover in the public sector, the expected wage is given by (15).

Thus, the flow increase in the supply of skilled labor can be written as:

$$SKL = \lambda_S \left\{ \kappa_e \left(\frac{\mathbb{E} w_S}{\mathbb{E} w_U} \right)^{\sigma_W} (K_{E,-1})^{\sigma_E} \right\} + (1 - \lambda_S) SKL_{-1}, \tag{31}$$

where $0 < \lambda_S < 1$, σ_W and $\sigma_E > 0$, and κ_e is a shift parameter.[7]

6.1.3 Supply and Demand

Both the informal and public sector goods are nontraded. Total supply in each sector is thus equal to gross production, that is

$$X_i = Q_i^s, \quad i = I, G. \tag{32}$$

Rural and private formal urban goods, by contrast, compete with imported goods. The supply of the composite good for each of these sectors consists of a CES combination of imports and domestically produced goods:

$$Q_i^s = CES(M_i, D_i), \quad i = A, P. \tag{33}$$

For the informal sector, aggregate demand (Q_I^d) consists of intermediate consumption and demand for final consumption (by the private sector), whereas aggregate demand for rural, public, and private goods (Q_A^d, Q_G^d and Q_P^d) consists not only of

---

[7]Note that we abstract from the cost of acquiring skills (as measured by the number of years of schooling multiplied by the average cost of education per year), which may also affect the propensity to invest in skills acquisition. Education is thus implicitly a free public good. We also do not explicitly account for the role of teachers, as in Chapter 3.

intermediate consumption and final consumption but also of investment demand (including changes in inventories):

$$Q_A^d = C_A + Z_P^A + INT_A, \tag{34}$$

$$Q_I^d = C_I + INT_I, \tag{35}$$

$$Q_G^d = C_G + G_G + (Z_P^G + Z_G) + INT_G, \tag{36}$$

$$Q_P^d = C_P + Z_P^P + INT_P, \tag{37}$$

where INT_j is defined as total demand (by all productions sectors) for intermediate consumption of good j:

$$INT_j = \sum_i a_{ji} X_i. \tag{38}$$

Government spending on goods and services consists only of expenditure on the public formal sector good, in quantity G_G.

Private final consumption for each production sector i, C_i, is the summation across all categories of households of nominal consumption of good i, deflated by the demand price of good i:

$$C_i = \sum_h C_{ih} = \sum_h x_{ih} + \frac{\sum_h cc_{ih}(CON_h - \sum_j PQ_j x_{jh})}{PQ_i}, \tag{39}$$

where C_{ih} is consumption of good i by household h, x_{ih} is the subsistence (or autonomous) level of consumption of good i by household h, CON_h total nominal consumption expenditure by household h, and PQ_i the (composite) sales price of good i. Equations (39) are based on the linear expenditure system. Coefficients cc_{ih} indicate how total nominal consumption expenditure by household h, CON_h, is allocated to each type of good and satisfy the restrictions $0 < cc_{ih} < 1$, $\forall i, h$, as well as $\sum_i cc_{ih} = 1$, $\forall h$.

Private investment, Z_P, consists of purchases of both rural, public, and private goods and services (Z_P^A, Z_P^G and Z_P^P respectively):

$$Z_P^i = zz_i \frac{PK \cdot Z_P}{PQ_i}, \quad i = A, G, P, \tag{40}$$

where $zz_A + zz_G + zz_P = 1$. Coefficients zz_i measure the allocation of total investment demand to rural, public and private goods.

6.1.4 External Trade

As indicated earlier, firms in the rural and private formal sectors allocate their output to the domestic market or exports according to the production possibility frontier specified in equations (3) and (11). Efficiency requires that the ratio of exports to domestic sales be positively related to the ratio of export prices (PE_A and PE_P, respectively) to domestic prices (PD_A and PD_P, respectively):

$$\frac{E_i}{D_i} = \left\{ \frac{PE_i}{PD_i} \cdot \frac{1 - \beta_{Ti}}{\beta_{Ti}} \right\}^{\sigma_{Ti}}, \quad i = A, P, \tag{41}$$

where $0 < \beta_{Ti} < 1$ and $\sigma_{Ti} > 0$ is the elasticity of transformation.

As noted earlier, imports compete with domestic goods in both the rural and private formal sectors. Using standard Armington aggregation functions, optimality requires that the ratio of imports to domestic production depends on the relative price of these goods and the ease with which these goods can be substituted for each other:

$$\frac{M_i}{D_i} = \left\{ \frac{PD_i}{PM_i} \cdot \frac{\beta_{Qi}}{1 - \beta_{Qi}} \right\}^{\sigma_{Qi}}, \quad i = A, P, \tag{42}$$

where $0 < \beta_{Qi} < 1$ and $\sigma_{Qi} > 0$ is the elasticity of substitution.

6.1.5 Prices

The price of value added is given by the gross price, PX_i, net of indirect taxes, less the cost of intermediate inputs (purchased at composite prices):

$$PV_i = V_i^{-1}[(1 - dtax_i)PX_i - \sum_j a_{ji}PQ_j]X_i, \tag{43}$$

where $dtax_i$ is the rate of indirect taxation of output in sector i. There is no indirect taxation of informal sector output, so that $dtax_I = 0$.

The world prices of imported and exported goods are taken as exogenously given. The domestic currency price of these goods is obtained by adjusting for the exchange rate and import tariff rates, tm_i:

$$PE_i = wpe_i ER, \quad i = A, P, \tag{44}$$

$$PM_i = wpm_i(1 + tm_i)ER, \quad i = A, P. \tag{45}$$

Because the transformation function between exports and domestic sales of the rural and urban private goods is linear homogeneous, the gross output prices, PX_A and PX_P, are derived from the expenditure identity:

$$PX_i X_i = PD_i D_i + PE_i E_i, \quad i = A, P,$$

that is,

$$PX_i = \frac{PD_i D_i + PE_i E_i}{X_i}, \quad i = A, P. \tag{46}$$

For the informal and public sectors (both of which do not export and produce a good that does not compete with imports), the composite price is simply the domestic price, PD_i, which is in turn equal to the gross output price, PX_i:

$$PD_i = PX_i, \quad i = I, G. \tag{47}$$

For the rural sector and private urban production, the substitution function between imports and domestic goods is also linearly homogeneous, and the composite market price is determined accordingly by the expenditure identity:

$$PQ_i Q_i = PD_i D_i + PM_i M_i, \quad i = A, P,$$

that is

$$PQ_i = \frac{PD_i D_i + PM_i M_i}{Q_i}, \quad i = A, P. \tag{48}$$

The nested CES production function of private formal urban goods is also linearly homogeneous; prices of the composite inputs are therefore derived in similar fashion:

$$T_1 PT_1 = T_2 PT_2 + (1 + IL_{-1})(1 + ptax_U) W_M U_P, \tag{49}$$

$$T_2 PT_2 = PROF_P + (1 + IL_{-1})(1 + ptax_S) W_S S_P, \tag{50}$$

where $PROF_P$ denotes profits of private firms in the urban formal sector. These equations can be solved for PT_1 and PT_2, as in (48).

The price of capital is constructed as a geometric weighted average of the composite prices of the goods for which there is investment demand, namely, the rural, public, and private formal urban goods (see equations (34), (36), and (37)):

$$PK = \Pi_i PQ_G^{zz_i}, \quad i = A, G, P. \tag{51}$$

Markets for informal goods and government services clear continuously; equilibrium conditions are thus given by

$$Q_i^s = Q_i^d, \quad i = I, G.$$

The aggregate price level, $PLEV$, or consumer price index, is a weighted average of individual goods market prices, PQ_i:

$$PLEV = \Pi_i PQ_i^{wt_i}, \tag{52}$$

where $0 < wt_i < 1$ denotes the relative weight of good i in the index, and $PQ_I = PD_I$ and $PQ_G = PD_G$. These weights are fixed according to the share of each of these goods in aggregate household consumption in the base period.

The consumption price index for workers from rural households, P_R, is given by

$$P_R = \Pi_i PQ_i^{wr_i},$$

whereas the consumption price indices for workers from urban unskilled and skilled households are given by

$$P_{UU} = \Pi_i PQ_i^{wu_i}, \quad P_{US} = \Pi_i PQ_i^{ws_i}, \tag{53}$$

where the wr_i, wu_i and ws_i are relative shares (and thus less than one) with $\sum_i wr_i$, $\sum_i wu_i$ and $\sum_i ws_i$ summing to unity.

The deflator of GDP at factor cost is given by

$$PGDP_{FC} = \Pi_i PV_i^{v_i}, \tag{54}$$

where v_i are base-period weights satisfying $\Sigma_i v_i = 1$.

6.1.6 Profits and Income

Firms' profits are defined as revenue minus total labor costs. In the case of rural sector firms and urban informal sector firms, profits are given by

$$PROF_i = PV_i V_i - W_i U_i, \quad i = A, I. \tag{55}$$

Profits of private urban sector firms account for both working capital costs and salaries paid to both categories of workers, as well as payroll taxes:

$$PROF_P = PV_P V_P - (1 + IL_{-1})[(1 + ptax_U)W_M U_P + (1 + ptax_S)W_S S_P]. \tag{56}$$

Firms' income is equal to profits minus interest payments on loans for investment purposes. Firms' income and profits are defined separately, because not all sectors are assumed to borrow to finance investment. Specifically, we assume that only firms in the formal urban economy accumulate capital. Firms' income can thus be defined as:

$$YF_i = PROF_i, \quad i = A, I, \tag{57}$$

$$YF_P = PROF_P - IL_{-1}DL_{P,-1} - IF \cdot ER \cdot FL_{P,-1}, \tag{58}$$

where IF is the (exogenous) interest rate on foreign loans, and DL_P and FL_P are the levels borrowed domestically and abroad by private urban firms for physical capital accumulation.[8]

Commercial banks' profits must also be taken into account. They are defined as the difference between revenues from loans to firms (be it for working capital or investment needs) and income from government bonds, BB^C, on the one hand, and interest payments on borrowing from the central bank plus interest payments on both households' deposits and foreign loans, on the other hand:

$$YF_{PB} = IL_{-1}[DL_{P,-1} + (1 + ptax_U)W_M U_P + (1 + ptax_S)W_S S_P$$
$$+ IB \cdot BB_{-1}^C - IR \cdot DL_{-1}^{BC} - ID \sum_h DD_{h,-1} - IF \cdot ER \cdot FL_{B,-1}, \tag{59}$$

where IB is the rate of interest on public bonds, IR The interest rate on borrowing from the central bank, and ID the interest rate on bank deposits. For simplicity, banks are assumed to face the same borrowing rate as private firms on world capital markets.

Household income is based on the return to labor (salaries), distributed profits, transfers, and net interest receipts on holdings of financial assets. Households are defined according to the skills composition of the workforce and the sector of employment. There is one rural household, comprising all workers employed in the rural sector. In the urban sector there are two types of unskilled households, those working in the informal sector and those employed in the formal sector. The fourth household consists of skilled workers employed in the formal urban economy (in both

---

[8]Note that in the model corporate income taxes on private sector firms (which represented about 2.4 percent of Brazilian GDP in 1996) are not explicitly accounted for in calculating net income. Given our assumption that rentiers and capitalists hold those firms, we have consolidated corporate income taxes and household income taxes for this category of household.

the private and public sectors). The fifth household consists of capitalists and rentiers, whose income comes from firms' earnings in the formal private and commercial banking sectors, and interest on bank deposits. They are also the only category of households to hold government bonds.

We further assume that households in both the rural sector and in the informal urban economy own the firms in which they are employed – an assumption (as noted in Chapter 5) that captures the fact that firms in these sectors tend indeed to be small, family-owned enterprises.

Using (55) and (57), income of the rural and informal sector households (identified with subscripts A and I, respectively) is given by

$$YH_i = \gamma_i TRH + PV_i X_i + ID \cdot DD_{i,-1} + IF \cdot ER \cdot FD_{i,-1}, \quad i = A, I. \quad (60)$$

where γ_i is the share of total government transfers, TRH, that each group receives, so that with $\sum_i \gamma_i = 1$, DD_i domestic bank deposits, and FD_i foreign bank deposits.

Income of the urban formal unskilled and skilled households (identified with subscripts UF and S, respectively) depends on government transfers, salaries and interests on deposits (domestic and foreign); firms provide no source of income, because these groups do not own the production units in which they are employed:

$$YH_{UF} = \gamma_{UF} TRH + (W_M U_P + W_{UG} U_G) + ID \cdot DD_{UF,-1} + IF \cdot ER \cdot FD_{UF,-1},$$
$$(61)$$

$$YH_S = \gamma_S TRH + (W_S S_P + W_{SG} S_G) + ID \cdot DD_{S,-1} + IF \cdot ER \cdot FD_{S,-1}. \quad (62)$$

Firms' income (or net earnings) in the private urban sector goes to capitalists and rentiers, (identified with the subscript KR, respectively) who also receive commercial bank's income, YF_{PB}, and interest on deposits. Firms retain a portion re of their earnings for investment financing purposes, and transfer the remainder to capitalists and rentiers. Thus, income of capitalists and rentiers is:

$$YH_{KR} = \gamma_{KR} TRH + ID \cdot DD_{KR,-1} + IF \cdot ER \cdot FD_{KR,-1}$$
$$+ IB \cdot BB_{KR,-1} + (1 - re)YF_P + YF_{PB}, \quad (63)$$

where BB_{KR} denote government bond holdings by capitalists and rentiers.

6.1.7   Savings, Financial Wealth, and Investment

Each category of household h saves a fraction, $0 < srate_h < 1$, of its disposable income:

$$SAV_h = (1 - itax_h)srate_h YH_h, \quad (64)$$

where $0 < itax_h < 1$ is the income tax rate applicable to household h. Income in the informal sector is not taxed, so that $itax_I = 0$.

The savings rate is a positive function of the real interest rate on deposits:

$$srate_h = s_{0,h} \left(\frac{1 + ID}{1 + INFL} \right)^{\sigma_{sav,h}}, \quad (65)$$

where $INFL = \Delta PLEV / PLEV_{-1}$ is the inflation rate in terms of the overall price index.

The portion of disposable income that is not saved is allocated to consumption:

$$CON_h = (1 - itax_h)YH_h - SAV_h.$$

For each household category, savings serve to accumulate financial wealth, WT_h:

$$WT_h = WT_{h,-1} + SAV_h + \Delta ER \cdot FD_{h,-1}, \tag{66}$$

where the last term accounts for valuation effects on the stock of foreign-currency deposits, FD_h, associated with changes in the nominal exchange rate.

As noted earlier, capital accumulation occurs only in the private urban sector. The decision to invest is taken to depend on several factors. First, there is a positive effect of the after-tax rate of return to capital relative to the cost of funds. Second, there is an accelerator effect, which aims to capture the impact of the desired capital stock on current investment. Third, there is a negative effect of the inflation rate, which may be viewed as a measure of macroeconomic instability, or of increased uncertainty about relative prices under high inflation, which makes investment decisions riskier. And fourth, there is a positive effect of the public capital stock in infrastructure, in line with the "complementarity effect" identified in a number of empirical studies. Formally, the investment function is given by

$$\frac{Z_P}{K_{P,-1}} = \left(\frac{K_{INF}}{K_{INF,-1}}\right)^{\sigma_K} \left\{\left(1 + \frac{\Delta RGDP_{FC}}{RGDP_{FC,-1}}\right)^{\sigma_{ACC}} \right.$$
$$\left. \times (1 + INFL)^{-\sigma_P} \left[\frac{(1 + IK)(1 - itax_{KR})}{1 + IL}\right]^{\sigma_{IK}}\right\}, \tag{67}$$

where IK is the return to capital, IL the bank lending rate, and $itax_{KR}$ is the income tax rate that capitalists and rentiers are subject to.

The second term in equation (67) captures the accelerator effect on private investment associated with changes in real GDP measured at factor cost, $RGDP_{FC}$, defined as

$$RGDP_{FC} = \Sigma_i PV_i X_i / PGDP_{FC}, \tag{68}$$

where $PGDP_{FC}$, the deflator of GDP at factor cost, is defined in (54).

The rate of return on capital is defined as the ratio of profits to the stock of capital:

$$IK = \frac{PROF_P}{PK \cdot K_P}. \tag{69}$$

Capital accumulation depends on the flow level of investment and the depreciation rate of capital from the previous period, δ_P:

$$K_P = (1 - \delta_P)K_{P,-1} + Z_{P,-1}, \tag{70}$$

where $0 < \delta_P < 1$.

6.1.8 Asset Allocation and the Financial Sector

We now consider the determination of the portfolio structure of households, the demand for credit by firms, and the behavior of commercial banks.

Households

Each household allocates instantaneously its stock of wealth to either money (in the form of cash holdings that bear no interest), H_h, domestic bank deposits, DD_h, foreign bank deposits, FD_h, or holdings of government bonds, BB_h:

$$WT_h = H_h + ER \cdot FD_h + DD_h + BB_h. \tag{71}$$

As noted earlier, only capitalists and rentiers hold government bonds. Thus, in the above equation, $BB_h = 0$ for $h \neq KR$.

The demand function for currency is taken to be proportional to total consumption, as a result of a "cash-in-advance" constraint:

$$H_h^d = \psi_h CON_h, \tag{72}$$

where $\psi_h > 0$.[9]

The total demand for cash is thus

$$H^d = \sum_h H_h^d = \sum_h \psi_h CON_h. \tag{73}$$

The demand for interest-bearing assets by capitalists and rentiers proceeds in two stages. First, they allocate a fraction of their noncash financial wealth, $WT_{KR} - H_{KR}$, to government bonds. Second, they allocate the remaining part of wealth, between domestic and foreign currency deposits. For all other households, because they do not hold government bonds, their portfolio choices are limited to the second stage only.

In standard fashion, the demand for government bonds by capitalists and rentiers is assumed to depend on prevailing interest rates:

$$\frac{BB_{KR}^d}{WT_{KR} - H_{KR}^d} = \Psi_K \frac{(1+IB)^{\beta_{KB}}}{(1+ID)^{\beta_{KD}}}[(1+IF)(1+depr)]^{-\beta_{KF}}, \tag{74}$$

where $\Psi_K > 0$ is a shift factor and *depr* the expected rate of depreciation of the nominal exchange rate.

The portion of wealth that is not held in the form of noninterest-bearing currency and government bonds (for capitalists and rentiers) is allocated between domestic and foreign deposits. Thus, from (71),

$$DD_h + ER \cdot FD_h = WT_h - H_h^d - BB_h^d, \tag{75}$$

with $BB_h = 0$ for $h \neq KR$.

The relative proportions of holdings of each of these two categories of assets are taken to depend on their relative rates of return:

$$\frac{DD_h}{ER \cdot FD_h} = \phi_{Bh} \left\{ \frac{1+ID}{(1+IF)(1+depr)} \right\}^{\sigma_{Bh}}. \tag{76}$$

Equation (76) can be used to solve for DD_h, whereas equation (75) can be used to calculate FD_h residually.

---

[9]The assumption that the demand for cash depends only on a transactions motive is a reasonable one in a low-inflation environment. In addition, it allos us to estimate individual holdings of cash from our household survey, as explained later.

Firms

Firms finance their investment needs through retained earnings and domestic and foreign loans:

$$PK \cdot Z_P = \Delta DL_P + ER \cdot \Delta FL_{P,-1} + re \cdot YF_P.$$

Solving this equation for DL_P gives us the demand for bank loans:

$$DL_P^d = DL_{P,-1} + PK \cdot Z_P - ER \cdot \Delta FL_{P,-1} - re \cdot YF_P. \tag{77}$$

The path of foreign loans is set exogenously. This implicitly accounts for ceilings that firms may face in their access to foreign markets.

Commercial Banks

Commercial banks are required to keep a fraction $0 < rreq < 1$ of the deposits that they collect as reserves with the central bank, denoted RR:

$$RR = rreq \sum_h DD_h. \tag{78}$$

Banks do not lend to households. Their balance sheet is thus

$$NW_B = DL_P + BB^C + RR - \sum_h DD_h - DL^{BC} - ER \cdot FL_B, \tag{79}$$

where NW_B is commercial banks' net worth, DL_P loans to private firms, BB^C holdings of government bonds, DL^{BC} borrowing from the central bank, and $ER \cdot FL_B$ foreign borrowing (measured in domestic-currency terms). Commercial banks do not retain profits. NW_B therefore changes over time according to

$$NW_B = NW_{B,-1} - \Delta ER \cdot FL_{B,-1}, \tag{80}$$

where the second term on the right-hand side represents capital losses (gains) associated with nominal exchange rate depreciations (appreciations).

The supply of credit is assumed to be perfectly elastic at the prevailing lending rate. With equation (77) representing the demand for loans, we therefore exclude any possibility of credit rationing. At the same time, to ensure that banks do not face a liquidity shortfall (as a result of an inadequate domestic deposit base and insufficient foreign borrowing), we assume that the supply of funds by the central bank is perfectly elastic at the prevailing official interest rate. Thus, borrowing from the central bank is determined residually. Combining (78), (79), and (80) yields

$$DL^{BC} = DL_{-1}^{BC} + \Delta DL_P^d + \Delta BB^C - (1 - rreq) \sum_h \Delta DD_h - ER \cdot \Delta FL_B. \tag{81}$$

The demand for government bonds by commercial banks consists of two components. The first component, BB_p^C, corresponds to the fraction of the total supply of government bonds, BB^s, placed directly with banks:

$$BB_p^C = \phi_{C,p} BB^s, \tag{82}$$

where $0 < \phi_{C,p} < 1$. The second component is the demand for bonds based on market conditions, BB_m^C, which is given by

$$\frac{BB_m^C}{DL_P} = \phi_{C,m}\left(\frac{1+IB}{1+IL}\right)^{\sigma_C}, \tag{83}$$

where $\phi_{C,m} > 0$. Thus, the market-related demand for bonds by commercial banks (as a ratio of credit to the private sector) is related positively to the interest rate on these bonds and negatively to their opportunity cost, that is, the lending rate.[10] Of course,

$$BB^C = BB_p^C + BB_m^C. \tag{84}$$

Banks set both deposit and lending interest rates. The deposit rate is set equal to the cost of funds provided by the central bank:

$$ID = IR. \tag{85}$$

This specification implies that banks are indifferent as to their source of domestic funds – or, equivalently, household deposits and loans from the central bank are viewed (at the margin) as perfect substitutes.

The loan rate is set as a premium over the marginal cost of funds. We assume that foreign borrowing is at the constrained level, so that marginal borrowing on world capital markets cannot occur. Thus, given (85), the marginal cost of funds is simply the cost of borrowing from the central bank, IR, taking into account as well the (implicit) cost of holding reserves according to reserve requirements:

$$IL = \frac{IR}{1 - rreq} + PR, \tag{86}$$

where PR denotes the finance premium, which is assumed to be set according to:

$$PR = \xi_{pr}\left[\lambda_{pr}\left\{\frac{\delta_c(NW_{P,-1} + DL_{P,-1})}{DL_{P,-1}}\right\}^{-\gamma_{pr}}\right] + (1 - \xi_{pr})PR_{-1}, \tag{87}$$

where $\gamma_{pr} > 0, 0 < \xi_{pr} < 1$ is the speed of adjustment, $0 < \delta_c \leq 1$, and NW_P is the net worth of private urban formal sector firms in nominal terms, defined as

$$NW_P = PK \cdot K_P - DL_P - ER \cdot FL_P. \tag{88}$$

---

[10]Note that in the foregoing discussion we abstracted from "excess" liquid reserves, and considered only required reserves. In practice, commercial banks may also seek to hold "discretionary" reserves, in order to meet unexpected deposit withdrawals. Denoting by $ELIQ$, the demand for such reserves, equation (81) would be replaced by

$$\Delta DL^{BC} = \Delta DL_p^d + \Delta BB^C + \Delta ELIQ - (1 - rreq)\sum_h \Delta DD_h - ER \cdot \Delta FL_B,$$

with $ELIQ$ being determined by an equation similar to (83), with a negative sign on IB (as a measure of the opportunity cost of holding liquid assets), or more generally, through a joint process involving the decision to supply credit and to hold government bonds.

Specification (87) captures the impact of collateralizable wealth on bank pricing decisions, in line with recent models of credit market imperfections (see Bernanke, Gertler, and Gilchrist (2000)). Here, "pledgeable" collateral is defined as the private capital stock net of foreign borrowing, that is, $PK \cdot K_P - ER \cdot FL_P$. The higher the value of collateral (or an "effective" fraction δ_c of that amount) relative to the amount of domestic loans, DL_P, the higher the proportion of total lending that banks can recoup in the event of default by seizing borrowers' assets. This reduces the finance premium and the cost of borrowing, stimulating the demand for credit. A large nominal exchange rate depreciation (that is, a rise in ER), would reduce firms' net worth, thereby raising the cost of capital and leading to a contraction of private investment.

An alternative justification for the finance premium equation (87) can be found in the models of credit market imperfections recently developed by Agénor and Aizenman (1998, 1999*b*). These models, following Townsend (1979), emphasize the importance of monitoring and enforcement costs of loan contracts that lenders face in a weak legal environment – as is so often the case in developing countries. In such an environment, these costs may be an *increasing* function of the amount lent (even against "good" collateral) because of congestion in courts and the difficulty of settling legal claims, which make it hard for lenders to actually seize borrowers' assets in case of default. This approach amounts to specifying the premium as a positive function of the ratio of the amount lent DL_P over "effective" collateral.

There has been limited research on the link between collateral and bank interest rate spreads in Brazil. Afanasieff, Lhacer, and Nakane (2002) found that macroeconomic factors, such as inflation and economic factors, play a more important role in the determination of bank interest spreads than microeconomic factors.[11] Overall, however, their regressions explain only a fraction of the observed movement in spreads. As shown in the bottom panel of Figure 6.1, bank lending spreads appear to follow a countercyclical pattern in Brazil. This behavior is consistent with the view that in downswings, the value of borrowers' collateral tends to fall and the risk of default increases; as a result, banks tend to charge a higher premium, as hypothesized in equation (87).[12]

6.1.9   Public Sector

The public sector in our framework consists of the government and the central bank. We consider them in turn.

---

[11] Note that, in practice, although interest rate spreads reflect the riskiness of loans, they are not strictly speaking measures of borrowers' risk, because the amount lent may be rationed or may reflect lenders' perceptions of risk.

[12] Note that the level of the spread depends also on the degree of competition among banks and the overall efficiency of the financial intermediation process. See Belaisch (2003*a*) for evidence on both factors.

Central Bank and Monetary Policy

To model monetary policy we assume that the central bank exerts a direct influence over the rate at which it supplies (marginal) funds to commercial banks. Thus, monetary policy is operated via the central bank's control over a short-term interest rate, denoted IR. This instrument is the rate at which the central bank elastically supplies loans (or liquidity) to the commercial banking system in order for them to balance their overall sources of funds (including deposits and foreign borrowing) with their desired level of holdings of government bonds and loans to firms (which are demand determined). As noted earlier, the bank deposit rate is modeled as having a fixed relationship (in fact, one to one) with the official rate. Evidence of this relationship for Brazil is shown in the upper panel of Figure 6.1, which displays the behavior of deposit rates and the money market rate (itself closely linked to the Bank of Brazil's repurchase rate) over the period 1995–2003. Thus, monetary policy in Brazil can therefore be modeled by assuming that the central bank controls directly short-term interest rates, and thus bank deposit rates.

In principle, we could also endogenize the official interest rate by specifying a monetary policy rule that relates IR to deviations of output from target, along the lines of the "flexible inflation targeting framework" that Brazil has adopted since June 1999 (see Bogdanski, Tombini, and Werlang (2000) and Minella et al. (2003)). Such a rule could be specified, for instance, as

$$\Delta IR = \kappa_1(INFL_{-1} - INFL^*) - \kappa_2 \ln\left(\frac{RGDP_{-1}}{RGDP_{-1}^T}\right) + \kappa_3 \Delta \ln ER_{-1}, \qquad (89)$$

where $\kappa_1, \kappa_2, \kappa_3 > 0$, $INFL^*$ is the government's inflation target, $\Delta \ln ER$ the rate of depreciation of the nominal exchange rate, and $RGDP$ and $RGDP^T$ denote the actual and trend values of real GDP, with $\ln(RGDP_{-1}/RGDP_{-1}^T)$ measuring therefore the lagged value of the output gap, in percentage terms. Such a rule would be defined as "backward-looking", given that lagged inflation appears in its specification. Alternatively, using the one-period ahead inflation rate, $INFL_{+1}$, would make the rule forward-looking and more consistent with a "true" inflation targeting rule (see Agénor (2002*b*)). Evidence by Minella et al. (2003) suggests indeed that the Central Bank of Brazil has followed a forward-looking approach in setting short-term interest rates. Nevertheless, given our interest in examining the poverty and labor market impact of an exogenous change in official interest rates, we will take IR as predetermined in the policy experiment that we conduct later.

From the balance sheet of the central bank, its net worth, NW_{CB}, is given by

$$NW_{CB} = DL^{BC} + ER \cdot FF - MB, \qquad (90)$$

where DL^{BC} denotes loans to commercial banks, FF the stock of foreign reserves (taken as predetermined), and MB the monetary base.

Assuming no operating costs, net profits of the central bank, $PROF_{CB}$, are given by the sum of interest receipts on loans to commercial banks and interest receipts on holdings of foreign assets:

$$PROF_{CB} = IR \cdot DL_{-1}^{BC} + IF_G ER \cdot FF_{-1}. \qquad (91)$$

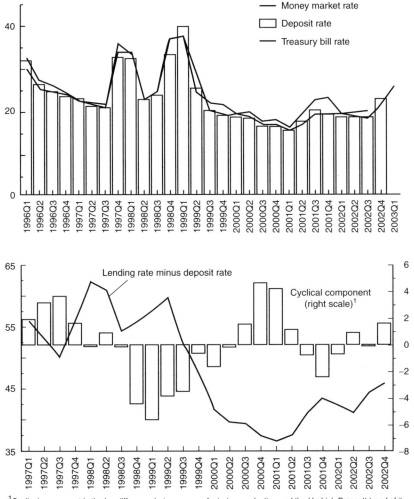

Figure 6.1   Brazil: interest rates and cyclical output, 1995–2003. *Source*: International Monetary Fund.

where IF_G is the interest rate on official reserves. We assume in what follows that net profits of the central bank are transferred entirely to the government. The central bank's net worth therefore evolves over time according to:

$$NW_{CB} = NW_{CB,-1} + \Delta ER \cdot FF, \qquad (92)$$

where the last term represents valuation effects. Put differently, capital gains and losses on the domestic-currency value of foreign reserves associated with exchange rate changes are absorbed via changes in the central bank's net worth, and do not affect the monetary base.

Taking first differences of equation (90), and combining the result with (92), implies that the base money stock evolves over time according to

$$MB = MB_{-1} + \Delta DL^{BC} + ER \cdot \Delta FF. \tag{93}$$

Government

We assume that government expenditures consist of government consumption, which only has demand-side effects, and public investment, which has both demand- and supply-side effects. Government saving is defined as minus the government budget deficit:

$$\begin{aligned} -DEF = & (PV_G V_G - W_{UG} U_G - W_{SG} S_G) + PROF_{CB} \\ & + TXREV - TRH - PQ_G(G_G + Z_G) \\ & - IF_G \cdot ER \cdot FL_{G,-1} - IB \cdot BB_{-1}, \end{aligned} \tag{94}$$

where BB denotes the total stock of bonds held by banks and households:[13]

$$BB = BB_{KR} + BB^C. \tag{95}$$

The first term in parentheses on the right-hand side of equation (94) represents profits by the government from sales of the public good. $PROF_{CB}$ represent profits transferred by the central bank. $TXREV$ denotes total tax revenues, whereas TRH is total government transfers to households. G_G represents government spending on goods and services, whereas Z_G represents investment. The final two terms in the government budget include interest payments on loans from abroad, and interest payments on government bonds held by commercial banks and the public.

Using the definition of net profits of the central bank given in equation (91), and the fact that government profits from production are zero in the current application, government saving can be rewritten as

$$\begin{aligned} -DEF = & TXREV - TRH - PQ_G(G_G + Z_G) \\ & + IR \cdot DL^{BC}_{-1} - IF_G \cdot ER(FL_{G,-1} - FF_{-1}) - IB \cdot BB_{-1}. \end{aligned} \tag{96}$$

Total tax revenues consist of revenue generated by import tariffs, sales taxes, income taxes, and payroll taxes:

$$\begin{aligned} TXREV = & ER \sum_{i=A,P} wpm_i tm_i M_i + \sum_i dtax_i PX_i X_i \\ & + itax_{KR} YH_{KR} + itax_r (YH_{AT} + YH_{AN}) + itax_{UU}(YH_{UF} + YH_S) \\ & + ptax_U W_M U_P + ptax_S W_S S_P. \end{aligned} \tag{97}$$

---

[13] Again, in the model only capitalists and commercial banks demand government bonds. Neither the central bank, nor non-residents, are assumed to hold these assets. These modifications can be easily added.

Public investment, Z_G, is the sum of public investment in infrastructure, I_{INF}, in health, I_H, and in education, I_E, all of them considered exogenous:

$$Z_G = I_{INF} + I_E + I_H. \tag{98}$$

As in previous chapters, we define investment in infrastructure as the expenditure affecting the accumulation of public infrastructure capital, which includes public assets such as roads, power plants and railroads. Investment in education affects the stock of public education capital, which consists of assets such as school buildings and other infrastructure affecting skills acquisition, but does not represent human capital. In a similar fashion, investment in health adds to the stock of public assets such as hospitals and clinics.

Investment increases the stock of public capital in each category:

$$K_i = (1 - \delta_i)K_{i,-1} + I_{i,-1}, \quad i = INF, H, E, \tag{99}$$

where $0 < \delta_i < 1$ is the depreciation rate of capital i.

Infrastructure and health capital combine to produce the stock of public capital, K_G:

$$K_G = CES(K_{INF}, K_H). \tag{100}$$

The government deficit is financed by either an increase in foreign loans, or by issuing bonds:

$$DEF = ER \cdot \Delta FL_G + \Delta BB. \tag{101}$$

For a given path of foreign borrowing, the supply of government bonds is thus

$$BB^s = BB^s_{-1} + DEF - ER \cdot \Delta FL_G. \tag{102}$$

The net worth of the government, NW_G, is defined as:

$$NW_G = PK(K_{INF} + K_H + K_E) - BB^s - ER \cdot FL_G. \tag{103}$$

From (90) and (103), the net worth of the consolidated public sector, NW_{PS}, is thus

$$NW_{PS} = PK(K_{INF} + K_H + K_E) + DL^{BC} - BB^s \tag{104}$$

$$+ER \cdot (FF - FL_G) - MB.$$

6.1.10 Balance of Payments and the Exchange Rate

Because foreign reserves are constant, the balance of payments constraint implies that any current account surplus (or deficit) must be compensated by a net flow of foreign capital, given by the sum of changes in foreign loans made to the government, ΔFL_G, private firms, ΔFL_P, and domestic banks, ΔFL_B, minus changes in households' holdings of foreign assets, $\sum_h \Delta FD_h$, all measured in foreign-currency terms:[14]

$$0 = \sum_{i=A,P} (wpe_i E_i - wpm_i M_i) + IF \sum_h FD_{h,-1}$$

$$- IF \cdot FL_{P,-1} - IF_G(FL_{G,-1} - FF) - IF \cdot FL_{B,-1}$$

$$+ \Delta FL_G + \Delta FL_P + \Delta FL_B - \sum_h \Delta FD_h. \tag{105}$$

Equation (105) determines implicitly the equilibrium nominal exchange rate.

As noted earlier, the expected rate of depreciation of the nominal exchange rate, *depr*, affects portfolio decisions and the pricing rule of commercial banks. We assume that the expected rate of depreciation is a weighted average of last period's expected depreciation rate and the lagged change in the "consumption" real exchange rate, defined as the difference between domestic inflation in terms of the overall price index, *INFL*, and foreign inflation, *FINFL*, measured in domestic-currency terms, and with $0 < \chi < 1$:[15]

$$depr = \chi\, depr_{-1} + (1 - \chi)[INFL_{-1} - (FINFL_{-1} + \Delta ER_{-1}/ER_{-2})], \tag{106}$$

6.1.11 Currency and Bond Market Equilibrium

The monetary base, *MB*, consists of the supply of currency in circulation, H^s, and reserve requirements, *RR*. With the monetary base determined from the balance sheet constraint (see equation (93), the supply of currency can be determined residually as

$$H^s = MB - rreq \sum_h DD_h.$$

Equality between the supply and demand for cash requires that, using (73):

$$H^s = H^d = \sum_h H_h^d. \tag{107}$$

Finally, from (95) and (102), the interest rate that equilibrates the market for government bonds, *IB*, is given as the solution of

$$BB^s = BB_{KR}^d + BB^C,$$

that is, using (82) and (84),

$$(1 - \phi_{C,p})BB^s = BB_{KR}^d + BB_m^C, \tag{108}$$

---

[14]It is not necessary, in fact, to set ΔFF equal to zero; it can simply be made exogenous. Doing so would allow the model to account for central bank intervention aimed at managing the exchange rate.

[15]Alternatively, it could be assumed that expectations are forward looking (or, more precisely, model consistent), so that the expected depreciation rate is equal to the one-period ahead "actual" rate, as derived from the model itself. This, however, is a lot more involved from a computational standpoint; see for instance Thissen (2000), Thissen and Lensink (2001), and Dixon et al. (2005).

or, using (74), (83),

$$(1 - \phi_{C,p})BB^s = \phi_{C,m}DL_P \left(\frac{1 + IB}{1 + IL}\right)^{\sigma_C}$$

$$+ \Psi_K(WT_{KR} - H_{KR}^d)\frac{(1 + IB)^{\beta_{KB}}}{(1 + ID)^{\beta_{KD}}}[(1 + IF)(1 + depr)]^{-\beta_{KF}}.$$

$$(109)$$

The financial balance sheets of each group of agents are presented in summary form in Table 6.1. The logical structure of IMMPA-Brazil is summarized in Figure 6.2. The Appendix discusses calibration and parameter values.

6.2 Poverty and Income Distribution Indicators

As discussed in Chapters 3 and 5, two measures of income distribution are generated directly from IMMPA: the Gini coefficient and the Theil inequality index.[16] Both are based on the five categories of households that were identified earlier, that is, workers located in the rural sector, urban (unskilled) informal economy, urban unskilled formal sector, urban skilled formal sector, and capitalists-rentiers.

The Gini index is defined as

$$\text{Gini} = \frac{1}{2n^2 \cdot YH_M} \sum_h \sum_j \left|YH_h - YH_j\right|,$$

where $n = 5$ is the number of household categories, $h, j = A, UI, UF, S, KR$, and $YH_M = \sum_h YH_h/n$ is the arithmetic mean level of disposable income for household categories.

Similarly, the Theil inequality index is measured as

$$\text{Theil} = \frac{1}{n} \sum_h \frac{YH_h}{YH_M} \log\left(\frac{YH_h}{YH_M}\right).$$

We also calculate these two indicators using consumption, instead of disposable income.

To assess the poverty effects of alternative shocks, we link IMMPA to a household income and expenditure survey. Our poverty indexes are the poverty headcount index (the ratio of the number of individuals in the group whose income is below the poverty line, relative to the total number of individuals in that group) and the poverty gap index, which is defined as:

$$P_G = \frac{1}{n \cdot YH^*} \sum_{k=1}^{n}(YH^* - YH_k),$$

---

[16]See Litchfield (1999) for a brief discussion of these measures. Cowell (1999) provides a detailed analytical discussion of the pros and cons of various measures of income inequality.

Table 6.1   IMMPA Brazil: Financial Balance Sheets (in domestic-currency terms, at current prices)

Households

Assets	Liabilities
Cash holdings (H)	Financial wealth (WT)
Domestic bank deposits (DD)	
Foreign bank deposits ($ER \cdot FD$)	
Government bonds (BB_{KR})	

Firms

Assets	Liabilities
Stock of private capital ($PK \cdot K_P$)	Domestic borrowing (DL_P)
	Foreign borrowing ($ER \cdot FL_P$)
	Net worth (NW_P)

Commercial Banks

Assets	Liabilities
Government bonds (BB^C)	Domestic bank deposits (DD)
Loans to domestic firms (DL_P)	Foreign liabilities ($ER \cdot FL_B$)
Reserve requirements (RR)	Borrowing, central bank (DL^{BC})
	Net worth (NW_B)

Central Bank

Assets	Liabilities
Loans to commercial banks (DL^{BC})	Cash in circulation (H)
Foreign reserves ($ER \cdot FF$)	Reserve requirements (RR)
	Net worth (NW_{CB})

Government

Assets	Liabilities
Capital in education ($PK \cdot K_E$)	Government bonds (BB)
Capital in health ($PK \cdot K_H$)	Foreign borrowing ($ER \cdot FL_G$)
Capital in infrastruc. ($PK \cdot K_{INF}$)	Net worth (NW_G)

Consolidated Public Sector

Assets	Liabilities
Loans to commercial banks (DL^{BC})	Cash in circulation (H)
Foreign reserves ($ER \cdot FF$)	Reserve requirements (RR)
Capital in education ($PK \cdot K_E$)	Government bonds (BB)
Capital in health ($PK \cdot K_H$)	Foreign borrowing ($ER \cdot FL_G$)
Capital in infrastruc. ($PK \cdot K_{INF}$)	Net worth (NW_{PS})

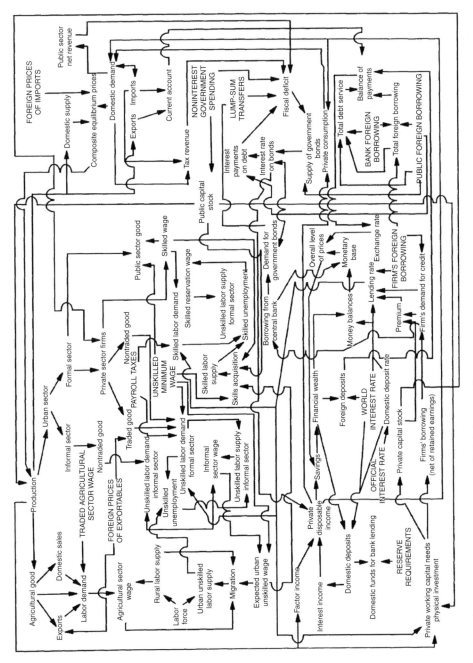

Figure 6.2 Brazil: analytical structure of IMMPA framework.

where k is an individual whose income is below the poverty line, n is the total number of people in the group below the poverty line, YH_k is the income of individual k, and YH^* is the poverty line.

The procedure for calculating these poverty and distributional indicators was described at length in the previous chapter and is discussed again in Chapter 8. It can be summarized as follows:

- **Step 1**. Classify the data in the household survey into the five categories of households contained in the structural component of the model.
- **Step 2**. Following a shock, generate real growth rates in per capita consumption and disposable income for all five categories of households, up to the end of the simulation horizon.
- **Step 3**. Apply these growth rates separately to per capita income and consumption expenditure for each household in the survey. This gives a new vector of absolute income and consumption levels for each household in each group.
- **Step 4**. Calculate poverty and income distribution indicators, using the new absolute nominal levels of income and consumption for each household, after updating the initial rural and urban poverty lines to reflect increases in rural and urban price indexes.
- **Step 5**. Compare the postshock poverty and income distribution indicators with the baseline values to assess the impact of the shock on the poor in each group.

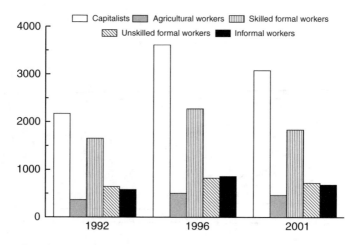

Figure 6.3   Brazil: average household income. *Source*: Author's calculations.

6.3 Calibration and Survey Characteristics

The Appendix to thic chapter provides a brief review of the structure of the financial SAM that underlies the model, our calibration procedure, and the parameter values (estimated and nonestimated) that we use in the behavioral equations. A more detailed description of the data and adjustment procedures used to construct the SAM is provided in Haddad, Fernandes, Domingues, Perobelli, and Afonso (2003).

Based on the household survey data discussed in the Appendix, Figure 6.3 shows the average household per capita income for each IMMPA income category for 1992, 1996, and 2001. Between 1992 and 1996, real income increased for all groups, whereas between 1996 and 2001 it went down. For the whole period, formal workers' income (skilled and unskilled) recorded the smallest growth rate (about 10 percent), whereas the capitalists-rentiers group experienced the largest increase: a growth rate of about 42 percent of income. An interesting aspect refers to the fact that income for informal workers household is very close to the income for unskilled formal workers, which seems to suggest that wages are paid more according to the qualification of workers, instead of the position in the urban labor market. It is worth pointing out, however, that household income, as defined here, includes the income of all the members of the household, as well as all the sources.

Figures 6.4 to 6.6 show the distribution of income within each group, as constructed from our sample of observations. A log-normal approximation is also shown. The figures indicate that the log-normal distribution provides an adequate characterization of income dispersion within each group.

6.4 Stabilization, Unemployment, and Poverty

This section examines the impact of a permanent, 10-percentage point increase in the official interest rate, *IR*, which the central bank charges for providing liquidity to commercial banks.[17] This policy experiment is important because it allows us to illustrate the output, poverty, and labor market effects of short-run stabilization policies.

Simulation results are summarized in Tables 6.2 and 6.3, where the horizon is set at 10 periods (or years), as in other chapters of this book. In Table 6.3, we defined the "trade-weighted" real exchange rate, as a weighted average of the domestic-currency price of exports and imports (with weights based on initial volumes of trade) divided by a weighted average of the price of domestic sales of agricultural and private sector goods (the only two sectors involved in external transactions).

A rise in the cost of refinancing from the central bank leads commercial banks to raise their deposit and lending rates – the deposit rate is increased in the exact same

---

[17] Since the implementation of the Real Plan in July 1994, the manipulation of short-term interest rates has been the major instrument through which Brazil's central bank conducts its monetary policy.

Chapter 6

proportion as the official rate, as implied by (85), whereas the lending rate is increased proportionately over and above the (initial) level of the risk premium.

The rise in the lending rate has important short-term implications for production and investment decisions. First, it raises the cost of working capital for producers, given its impact on the effective wage. This leads to an increase in private unskilled and skilled labor costs relative to the capital rental rate, and a short-term reduction in skilled and unskilled employment in the private urban sector. Second, it leads to a contraction in private investment, which translates over time into a lower rate of capital accumulation.

In turn, the reduction in the capital stock lowers private sector demand for labor. Unemployment tends to increase over time for both categories of labor, by about

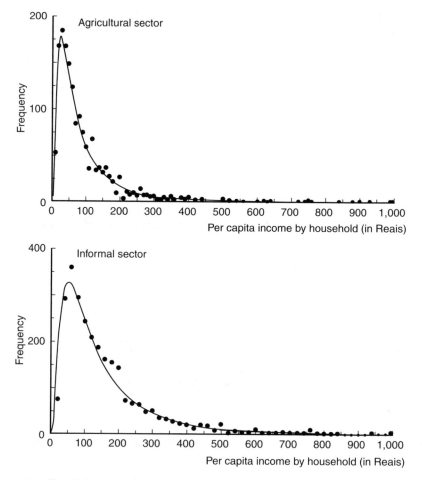

Figure 6.4 Brazil: frequency distributions of households by income per capita in agriculture and the informal sector.

Table 6.2 Brazil: Simulation results. 10-percentage point permanent increase in official interest rate. (Percentage deviations from baseline, unless otherwise indicated)

					Periods					
	1	2	3	4	5	6	7	8	9	10
Real Sector										
Total resources	-0.70	-0.98	-1.34	-1.71	-1.73	-1.46	-1.01	-0.21	1.17	3.33
Gross domestic product	-0.69	-0.96	-1.33	-1.70	-1.71	-1.44	-0.99	-0.18	1.21	3.38
Imports of goods and NFS	-0.76	-1.14	-1.50	-1.85	-1.93	-1.73	-1.32	-0.57	0.73	2.78
Total expenditure	-0.70	-0.98	-1.34	-1.71	-1.73	-1.46	-1.01	-0.21	1.17	3.33
Total consumption	-0.20	-0.26	-0.62	-0.56	-0.05	0.74	1.78	3.40	5.86	9.33
Private consumption	-0.14	-0.16	-0.52	-0.41	0.16	1.01	2.10	3.78	6.32	9.86
Public consumption	-0.57	-0.91	-1.26	-1.47	-1.31	-0.83	-0.07	1.17	3.16	6.15
Total investment	-2.25	-4.35	-4.58	-5.36	-6.72	-7.88	-8.73	-9.75	-10.98	-12.18
Private investment	-3.14	-6.08	-5.90	-6.83	-8.74	-10.44	-11.77	-13.53	-15.88	-18.57
Public investment	-0.58	-0.94	-1.31	-1.53	-1.40	-0.95	-0.23	0.95	2.86	5.74
Exports of goods and NFS	-0.32	1.30	1.78	0.74	1.07	2.17	3.05	4.25	6.37	9.48
External Sector (% of GDP)[1]										
Current account	0.04	0.27	0.36	0.32	0.40	0.52	0.59	0.64	0.71	0.77
Exports of goods and NFS	0.05	0.39	0.50	0.41	0.49	0.65	0.73	0.81	0.96	1.13
Imports of goods and NFS	-0.01	-0.02	-0.02	-0.01	-0.02	-0.03	-0.03	-0.03	-0.04	-0.05
Factor services	-0.02	-0.14	-0.16	-0.10	-0.11	-0.15	-0.17	-0.21	-0.28	-0.41
Capital account	-0.04	-0.27	-0.36	-0.32	-0.40	-0.52	-0.59	-0.64	-0.71	-0.77
Private borrowing (firms)	0.00	0.03	0.04	0.05	0.06	0.10	0.13	0.18	0.25	0.35
Commercial bank borrowing	0.00	0.00	0.00	0.00	0.00	0.00	0.00	0.00	0.00	0.00
Public borrowing	0.00	0.03	0.04	0.05	0.07	0.10	0.14	0.19	0.26	0.36
Household net foreign liabilities	-0.05	-0.33	-0.45	-0.41	-0.53	-0.72	-0.86	-1.01	-1.22	-1.48
Government Sector (% of GDP)[1]										
Total revenue	0.07	0.30	0.33	0.44	0.74	1.09	1.48	2.00	2.69	3.52
Direct taxes	0.08	0.35	0.39	0.50	0.81	1.16	1.56	2.09	2.80	3.64
Indirect taxes	-0.01	-0.06	-0.05	-0.06	-0.07	-0.07	-0.08	-0.09	-0.11	-0.12

Total expenditure	-0.09	1.08	1.74	2.49	3.34	4.42	5.66	6.98	8.24	9.17
Consumption	0.01	0.00	0.00	0.01	0.03	0.04	0.06	0.09	0.13	0.18
Investment	0.01	0.00	0.00	0.01	0.03	0.04	0.06	0.09	0.13	0.18
Transfers to households	0.08	0.10	0.13	0.16	0.15	0.12	0.08	0.01	-0.10	-0.26
Domestic interest payments	-0.19	0.97	1.58	2.28	3.10	4.15	5.36	6.64	7.88	8.78
Foreign interest payments	0.00	0.01	0.03	0.03	0.04	0.07	0.10	0.14	0.20	0.29
Total financing	-0.15	0.79	1.41	2.06	2.61	3.35	4.20	5.00	5.59	5.70
Foreign borrowing	0.00	0.03	0.04	0.05	0.07	0.10	0.14	0.19	0.26	0.36
Domestic borrowing	0.00	0.00	0.00	0.00	0.00	0.00	0.00	0.00	0.00	0.00
Bond financing	-0.16	0.76	1.36	2.01	2.54	3.25	4.07	4.81	5.33	5.33
Primary Budget Balance	-0.03	0.20	0.20	0.26	0.54	0.88	1.27	1.80	2.53	3.41
Labor Market										
Nominal wages										
Rural sector	-0.73	-1.69	-2.38	-3.13	-3.51	-3.75	-4.01	-4.05	-3.66	-2.77
Informal sector	-0.02	-1.78	-3.22	-4.08	-4.49	-5.18	-6.30	-7.29	-8.15	-9.37
Private formal sector										
Unskilled	-0.69	-0.79	-1.01	-1.16	-0.96	-0.40	0.49	1.85	3.98	7.15
Skilled	-0.73	-1.41	-1.96	-2.52	-2.80	-2.90	-2.89	-2.61	-1.89	-0.57
Public sector										
Unskilled	-0.69	-0.79	-1.01	-1.16	-0.96	-0.40	0.49	1.85	3.98	7.15
Skilled	-0.69	-0.79	-1.01	-1.16	-0.96	-0.40	0.49	1.85	3.98	7.15
Employment										
Rural sector	0.00	0.00	0.00	-0.01	-0.02	-0.04	-0.08	-0.14	-0.22	-0.33
Informal sector	0.00	0.04	0.06	0.05	0.03	0.01	-0.01	-0.04	-0.07	-0.09
Private formal sector										
Unskilled	-0.13	-0.78	-0.76	-0.90	-1.04	-1.21	-1.45	-1.81	-2.27	-2.89
Skilled	-0.03	-0.10	-0.12	-0.19	-0.27	-0.38	-0.52	-0.72	-0.99	-1.34
Public sector										
Unskilled	0.00	0.00	0.00	0.00	0.00	0.00	0.00	0.00	0.00	0.00
Skilled	0.00	0.00	0.00	0.00	0.00	0.00	0.00	0.00	0.00	0.00
Labor supply (urban formal)										
Unskilled	0.00	-0.03	-0.04	-0.03	-0.01	0.01	0.03	0.07	0.11	0.14
Skilled	0.00	0.00	0.00	0.00	0.00	0.00	0.00	0.00	0.00	0.00

Table 6.2 Continued

					Periods					
	1	2	3	4	5	6	7	8	9	10
Unemployment rate[1]										
Unskilled	0.11	0.65	0.62	0.75	0.87	0.99	1.19	1.46	1.80	2.24
Skilled	0.03	0.08	0.10	0.15	0.22	0.30	0.42	0.57	0.78	1.07
Real wage ratios[1]										
Expected urban–rural	0.00	0.25	0.22	0.66	1.43	2.22	3.20	4.47	5.93	7.53
Expected formal–informal	-0.18	-2.38	0.64	3.33	5.00	6.42	9.78	15.70	23.17	33.42
Migration[1]										
Rural–urban (% of urban unskilled labor supply)	0.00	0.00	0.00	0.00	0.00	0.00	0.01	0.01	0.01	0.02
Formal–informal (% of urban formal unskilled labor supply)	0.00	-0.03	-0.01	0.01	0.02	0.02	0.02	0.03	0.04	0.04
Financial Sector										
Risk premium	-0.01	0.07	0.26	0.55	0.94	1.45	2.09	2.91	3.94	5.27
Lending rate	11.10	11.19	11.37	11.66	12.05	12.56	13.20	14.02	15.05	16.39
Bond rate	5.48	5.45	5.46	5.35	5.36	5.61	5.79	5.85	5.84	5.66
Deposit rate	10.00	10.00	10.00	10.00	10.00	10.00	10.00	10.00	10.00	10.00
Inflation	-0.78	-0.11	-0.24	-0.16	0.21	0.59	0.91	1.39	2.12	3.09
Exchange rate depreciation	-0.80	0.92	0.14	-0.44	0.39	0.97	1.11	1.57	2.44	3.48
Memorandum items[2]										
GDP at market prices	-0.04	-0.32	-0.45	-0.60	-0.81	-1.11	-1.47	-1.92	-2.49	-3.22
Value added at factor cost	-0.03	-0.21	-0.32	-0.48	-0.66	-0.89	-1.21	-1.61	-2.11	-2.75
Value added in rural sector	0.00	0.00	0.00	0.00	-0.01	-0.01	-0.02	-0.03	-0.05	-0.08
Value added in urban informal sector	0.00	0.02	0.03	0.02	0.01	0.00	-0.01	-0.02	-0.03	-0.04
Value added in urban formal sector	-0.05	-0.32	-0.48	-0.71	-0.98	-1.34	-1.82	-2.41	-3.17	-4.13
Private Consumption	0.55	0.65	0.55	0.84	1.25	1.58	1.87	2.27	2.76	3.24
Private Investment	-2.45	-5.36	-4.98	-5.78	-7.89	-10.12	-12.23	-15.12	-19.09	-23.97
Disposable income	1.76	3.37	4.34	5.75	7.34	9.11	11.05	13.14	15.25	17.12

[1] Absolute deviations from baseline. [2] In real terms.

Table 6.3 Brazil: price, poverty, and distributional indicators. 10-percentage point permanent increase in official interest rate. (Percentage deviations from baseline, unless otherwise indicated)

	Periods									
	1	2	3	4	5	6	7	8	9	10
Consumer Prices and the Real Exchange Rate										
Rural and urban CPI	-0.7	-0.8	-1.0	-1.2	-1.0	-0.4	0.5	1.9	4.0	7.2
Real exchange rate	0.2	1.1	1.5	1.2	1.4	1.9	2.1	2.3	2.7	3.1
Value Added Prices										
Rural	-0.7	-1.7	-2.4	-3.1	-3.5	-3.8	-4.1	-4.2	-3.9	-3.1
Urban private informal	0.0	-1.8	-3.2	-4.1	-4.5	-5.2	-6.3	-7.3	-8.2	-9.4
Urban private formal	-0.8	-0.4	-0.5	-0.6	-0.2	0.5	1.6	3.3	5.7	9.3
Urban public	-0.7	-0.8	-1.0	-1.2	-1.0	-0.4	0.5	1.9	4.0	7.1
Real Disposable Income[1]										
Rural households	0.4	-0.5	-0.9	-1.3	-1.7	-2.5	-3.6	-4.9	-6.6	-8.7
Urban households	2.0	4.1	5.3	7.0	8.9	11.0	13.3	15.8	18.4	20.7
Informal	1.2	-0.2	-0.8	-1.0	-1.3	-2.3	-3.7	-5.3	-7.5	-10.6
Formal unskilled	1.8	0.7	0.5	0.3	0.1	-0.2	-0.5	-1.0	-1.6	-2.5
Formal skilled	3.4	3.0	2.9	2.9	2.7	2.3	1.6	0.7	-0.6	-2.5
Capitalists and rentiers	1.3	13.4	17.9	23.6	29.2	35.0	41.0	46.9	52.3	56.8
Real Consumption[1]										
Rural households	0.4	-0.5	-0.9	-1.3	-1.8	-2.5	-3.6	-4.9	-6.6	-8.7
Urban households	0.6	0.9	0.8	1.2	1.7	2.2	2.6	3.2	4.0	4.7
Informal	1.2	-0.2	-0.8	-1.0	-1.3	-2.3	-3.7	-5.3	-7.5	-10.6
Formal unskilled	1.7	0.7	0.5	0.2	0.0	-0.2	-0.6	-1.0	-1.6	-2.5
Formal skilled	3.3	2.9	2.8	2.8	2.6	2.2	1.5	0.6	-0.7	-2.6
Capitalists and rentiers	-13.1	-1.9	-0.7	3.3	8.6	13.9	19.3	25.4	32.1	39.1
Household Size[1]										
Rural households	0.0	0.0	0.0	0.0	0.0	0.0	0.0	-0.1	-0.2	-0.3
Urban households	0.0	0.0	0.0	0.0	0.0	0.0	0.0	0.0	0.0	0.0
Informal	0.0	0.0	0.1	0.0	0.0	0.0	0.0	0.0	-0.1	-0.1
Formal unskilled	0.0	0.0	0.0	0.0	0.0	0.0	0.0	0.1	0.1	0.1
Formal skilled	0.0	0.0	0.0	0.0	0.0	0.0	0.0	0.0	0.0	0.0
Capitalists and rentiers	0.0	0.0	0.0	0.0	0.0	0.0	0.0	0.0	0.0	0.0

Continued

		Periods									
		1	2	3	4	5	6	7	8	9	10
Poverty and Distributional Indicators											
Consumption-based											
Poverty Line[1]											
	Rural	−0.7	−0.8	−1.0	−1.2	−1.0	−0.4	0.5	1.9	4.0	7.2
	Urban	−0.7	−0.8	−1.0	−1.2	−1.0	−0.4	0.5	1.9	4.0	7.2
Poverty headcount											
	Rural households	−0.1	0.1	0.2	0.4	1.5	1.0	1.1	1.5	2.6	3.0
	Urban households	−0.6	0.0	−0.1	0.0	0.0	0.2	0.6	1.0	1.5	2.2
	Informal	−0.1	0.0	0.1	0.4	0.2	0.7	1.6	2.5	3.3	4.9
	Formal unskilled	−1.8	−0.1	0.0	−0.1	0.0	0.1	0.1	0.5	0.8	0.9
	Formal skilled	−0.1	−0.1	−0.4	−0.3	−0.2	−0.1	−0.1	0.0	0.2	0.3
	Capitalists and rentiers	0.5	0.5	0.0	−0.5	−0.3	−0.5	−1.2	−1.0	−1.0	−0.7
	Economy	−0.5	0.0	0.0	0.1	0.3	0.4	0.7	1.1	1.7	2.3
Poverty Gap											
	Rural households	−0.1	0.1	0.2	0.4	0.5	0.8	1.1	1.5	2.0	2.7
	Urban households	−0.1	0.0	0.0	0.1	0.1	0.2	0.4	0.6	1.0	1.5
	Informal	−0.2	0.0	0.2	0.2	0.3	0.6	1.0	1.6	2.3	3.5
	Formal unskilled	−0.1	−0.1	−0.1	0.0	0.0	0.0	0.1	0.1	0.2	0.4
	Formal skilled	−0.1	−0.1	−0.1	−0.1	−0.1	−0.1	−0.1	0.0	0.0	0.2
	Capitalists and rentiers	0.4	0.0	0.0	−0.1	−0.2	−0.2	−0.2	−0.2	−0.2	−0.2
	Economy	−0.1	0.0	0.1	0.1	0.2	0.3	0.5	0.8	1.2	1.7
Distributional Indicators[2]											
	Gini coefficient	−2.3	−0.3	0.0	0.6	1.4	2.3	3.1	3.8	4.6	5.3
	Theil index	−1.2	−0.3	−0.1	0.4	1.0	1.8	2.7	3.7	4.9	6.2
Distributional Indicators											
Income-based											
Distributional Indicators[2]											
	Gini coefficient	0.0	1.7	2.2	2.7	3.2	3.5	3.8	4.0	4.1	4.1
	Theil index	−0.1	1.9	2.7	3.5	4.3	5.0	5.8	6.4	7.0	7.4

[1] Percentage deviations from baseline. [2] Gini Coefficients and Theil Indices measure between-group inequality.

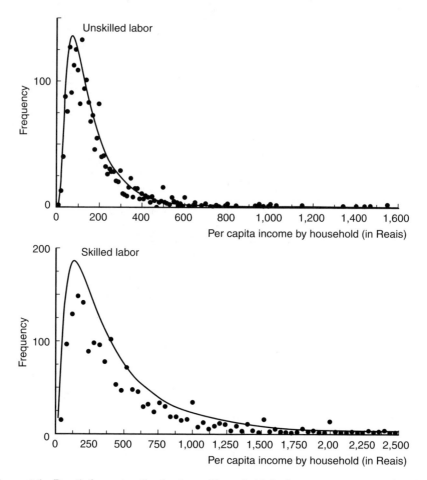

Figure 6.5   Brazil: frequency distributions of households by income per capita in the urban formal sector.

1.1 percentage points for skilled labor and 2.2 percentage points for unskilled labor in the long run.

Reduced inflation and increasing unemployment lead to relatively strong short-term reductions in nominal wage rates among private formal sector workers, and to a substantial reduction in the expected wage differential between formal and informal sectors (in the second period). This implies a reduction (albeit small) in the number of unskilled job seekers in the formal sector. The increase in informal sector labor supply combined with declining (intermediate) demand for informal sector products tends to reduce informal sector wages faster than other wages during the first three years of the simulation.

The reversal of the urban wage differential after the first couple of years leads to a subsequent reversal in migration flows between the informal and formal urban

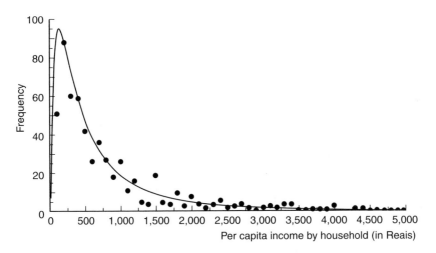

Figure 6.6 Brazil: frequency distributions of households by income per capita, capitalists and rentiers.

sectors. At the same time, the expected wage differential between rural and urban areas increases by a mere 0.2 percent over the initial three years. This implies virtually no change in migration flows between rural and urban areas given the low relative wage elasticity of rural–urban migration.

Rural wages are reduced in parallel with expected urban wages, leading to a 2.4 percent decline in nominal terms in the third period. Due to the small change in rural–urban migration flows, rural employment remains essentially unchanged over the short term. Production (or value added) in the rural sector is therefore unaffected initially by the interest rate hike. At the same time, the (slightly) increasing informal sector labor supply leads to a small short-term increase in value added in that sector.

The increase in formal sector labor costs, associated with the interest rate hike, lowers formal sector employment (at the same time that it lowers wages partially) and leads to a relatively strong decline in formal sector value added in the 2–3 years following the shock (by 0.5 percent in period 3). Real GDP at market prices declines by about the same amount over the same horizon.

On the demand side, real private investment drops sharply in the short term (by 2.5 percent in the first period) as a result of the increase in the real lending rate. This increase is exacerbated by the initial 0.8 percentage point drop in the overall inflation rate.

In the subsequent three periods, during which inflation impact drops to 0.2 percentage point, the permanent increase in (real) funding costs combines with the increasingly negative accelerator effect associated with negative real GDP growth rates; as a result, real private investment drops by a sharper 5.5 percent after three years. The drop is associated with a concomitant increase in real private consumption expenditures. Declining nominal wage rates and employment levels combined with declining profit levels in the formal sector lead to declining levels of factor income for all household categories. Nevertheless, the strong increase in deposit rates compensates formal sector households for the drop in factor income. In fact, nominal consumption increases on impact for formal sector skilled households (who hold large initial levels of deposits), and subsequently for capitalists and rentiers (who take advantage of increasing incentives to build up deposits). Aggregate nominal private consumption drops by 0.1–0.2 percent during the first two years, only to decline by 0.6 percent during the third year. The resilience of nominal consumption combined with declining prices leads to a 0.8 percent increase in real private consumption after three years.

Commercial banks initially need additional liquidity from the central bank, in order to finance the increase in interest payments to deposit holders. This borrowing need disappears, however, during the subsequent two periods. Accordingly, there is only a very limited need for additional central bank borrowing after three years. At the same time, the increasing inflow of deposits into the commercial banking sector leads to increasing reserve accumulation at the central bank. The combined effect is to keep the supply of high-powered money in the hands of the public unchanged during the two initial years, only to be followed by a 0.4 percent drop in the third period (in line with nominal consumption). Overall, the collapse of private investment demand means that money holdings are too low to allow for nominal consumer transactions to clear the goods market at unchanged prices. This explains the short-term drop in inflation rates. Inflation declines more moderately during the subsequent two years (0.1–0.2 percent), because prices are already low and in line with real output levels – there is less need for additional price corrections.

The bond rate increases by about 5.5 percentage points during the initial three-year period. This increase is driven by the rise in deposit and lending rates for households and commercial banks: households can make deposits with banks at a higher deposit rate, whereas banks can make loans at a higher lending rate. The bond rate increases by around half of the 10 percentage point increase in the official and deposit rates. The smaller increase in the bond rate is due to differences in demand elasticities. It implies that the government budget remains relatively unaffected in the short term. Domestic interest payments as a share of GDP increase by 1.6 percentage points during the third year, accounting for the major part of the 1.7 percentage point increase in the ratio of overall government expenditures to GDP in the same period.

With a constant stock of foreign exchange reserves (measured in foreign-currency units), the nominal exchange rate fluctuates to equilibrate the balance of payments. Although the nominal exchange rate appreciates in the first year, the drop in domestic prices is such that the trade-weighted real exchange rate depreciates immediately and continues to do so in subsequent years. The real depreciation underpins a relative expansion of exports at the expense of domestic sales, which decline with decreasing domestic demand. Imports, by contrast, tend to fall, albeit slightly in proportion of GDP. The trade balance and the current account tend therefore to improve over time, despite the fact that net factor payments from the rest of the world (relative to GDP) tend to decline. The counterpart to the improvement in the current account is a worsening of the capital account (a capital outflow), which takes the form of a reduction in households' net foreign liabilities, that is, an increase in their foreign currency deposits held abroad. This increase occurs despite the fact that, as implied by equation (76), the hike in domestic interest rates leads to a relative shift toward domestic bank deposits. It is essentially due to a a sharp increase in wealth of capitalists and rentiers. Capital outflows are accompanied by a continuous depreciation of the nominal exchange rate, which following a small appreciation on impact.

The medium- to long-term consequences of the increase in the official interest rate show signs of instability. Flexible nongovernment wage rates tend to decline at an accelerating pace at first and then a decelerating pace in the case of rural sector wages, and at an accelerating pace in the case of the informal sector. By the end of the simulation horizon, rural and urban informal wages fall by 2.8 and 9.4 percent, respectively. The decline in both wages is due to a strong reduction in (intermediate) demand from the private formal sector. Backward linkages from the private formal sector is the main mechanism for transmitting the effects of the official interest rate increase to the rural and urban informal sectors. Rural sector wages are, however, somewhat insulated because export earnings substitute to some extent for lower demand for rural sector goods.

In the long run, formal sector wages for skilled workers drop by 0.6 percent, whereas the urban price level increases (7.2 percent in year 10). Accordingly, the drop in formal sector wages for skilled workers derives principally from the increase in skilled unemployment; skilled workers lower their wage demands as unemployment increases. Formal sector wages for unskilled worker follow the urban price level (given the assumption of full indexation) and therefore increase also by about 7.2 percent in the long run.

The decline in skilled workers' (product) wages helps to maintain skilled employment in the formal private sector, in spite of the collapse of private investment and the accelerating drop in the private capital stock. Due to complementarity between capital and skilled labor inputs in formal sector production, the declining capital stock leads to a concomitant reduction in the demand for skilled labor. Nevertheless, the declining (product) wage level means that skilled employment only drops by 1.3 percent in the long run. By contrast, because the unskilled labor wage increased by as much as urban consumption prices, and the value added price in the urban private formal sector rises by about 9.3 percent in the long run, the unskilled product wage declines by only a small amount. As a result, the drop in the private capital stock over time has a larger effect on unskilled employment, which declines by a more significant 2.9 percent. Thus, unskilled employment is hurt more than skilled employment in the long run, due to real wage rigidity. Because migration flows are relatively modest, reduced employment leads to increasing open unemployment among skilled and unskilled workers. The strong decline in employment means that open unemployment among unskilled workers grows by 2.2 percent of the unskilled labor force in the formal sector in the long run.

Employment losses in the formal sector are also driven by a steady increase in the lending rate. The increasing lending rate makes borrowing for working capital purposes more expensive, and leads to increasing labor costs. The accelerating increase in the lending rate is driven by a rise in the risk premium, which is driven in turn by a reduction in the collateral value of the physical assets held by the private sector. The reduced collateral value of the private sector follows from *a*) a steady decline in retained profits; and *b*) a steadily increasing need for private sector borrowing to finance rising debt interest payments. Accordingly, the long-run collapse of investment demand is caused primarily by a vicious circle of cumulative causation whereby increasing interest rates lead to declining private sector profits and investment, and destabilization of the private sector balance sheet, which subsequently feeds back into accelerating interest rate increases and further destabilization of the private sector's net worth.

In addition to the accelerating increase in the lending rate due to powerful net worth effects, the 24 percent long-run drop in real private investment is also due to *a*) induced long-run relative price increases on formal sector (investment) goods, and *b*) the negative accelerator effect emanating from the steadily declining real GDP. The reductions in capital accumulation and induced reductions in formal sector employment lower formal sector value added by 4.1 percent and total value added by 2.7 percent in the long run.

The bond rate remains relatively constant in the long run, recording a 5.7 percentage point increase after 10 years. Nevertheless, a small upward pressure on the bond rate can be detected between the short and the long term. This upward pressure is due partly to the gradual increase in the lending rate (which tends to reduce the demand for bonds by commercial banks), and partly to a gradual rise in bond issuing resulting from an increase in the government borrowing requirements (following a decline in the first year). Overall, the increased bond rate and outstanding stock of debt lead to an 8.8 percentage point increase in the ratio of government domestic interest payments to GDP in the long run. Accordingly, the increase in domestic interest payments accounts for the majority of the 9.2 percent long-run increase in the ratio of government expenditures to GDP. Although the share of revenues in GDP increases by 3.5 percentage points in the long run, bond financing as a share of GDP increases by 5.3 percentage points.

The impact of the shock on poverty and income distribution is generally unfavorable. The rural and urban poverty lines drop by around 1.0 percent in the short term, but increases with the rural and urban price levels in the long-term – by about 7.2 percent after 10 years. In the short term, the poverty headcount index increases by 0.2 percent in rural areas and 0.6 percent in urban areas. In the long term, real consumption declines among all households, except for capitalists and rentiers. The poverty rate therefore increases by 3.0 percent in rural areas, and by 2.2 in urban areas. Urban informal sector households are the hardest hit, experiencing in the long term a 10.6 percent decline in real consumption and a 4.9 percent increase in the headcount ratio.

Changes in the poverty gap ratio mirror changes in the poverty headcount index; poverty gap indicators remain relatively unchanged in the short term and increase in the long term – by 1.5 percent in urban areas and 2.7 percent in rural areas. Again, the urban informal sector experiences a strong 3.5 percent increase in poverty. However, the rural sector also experiences a relatively strong 2.7 percent increase in the poverty gap ratio. The relatively larger changes in poverty gap indicators relative to poverty headcount ratios shows that increasing poverty comes both from increased depth of poverty (among people who were initially below the poverty line) as well as increasing numbers of newly-impoverished households.

Changes in between-household inequality measures indicate that inequality tends to increase in the long term. Both income- and consumption-based inequality measures support this conclusion. Changes in the income-based measures indicate a 4.1 percent increase in the Gini coefficient and a 7.4 percent increase in the Theil index in the long run, whereas changes in expenditure-based measures display changes of 5.3 and 6.2 percent for the two indicator types at the same horizon. The large long-term increases in inequality reflect the strongly increasing real income and consumption enjoyed by capitalists and rentiers, as compared to rural and urban informal sector households.

In the short-term (initial three years), changes in inequality show pronounced differences between income- and expenditure-based measures. While consumption-based inequality indicators decrease by 1.2–2.3 percent on impact and remain relatively unchanged during the third year, income-based inequality measures remain unchanged on impact and increase by 2.2–2.7 percent after three years. These differences reflect the fact that gradually increasing real income of capitalists and rentiers are not reflected in real consumption expenditures. This asymmetry between income and consumption is due to differences in interest rate elasticities of savings rates, among different household types. Capitalists and rentiers have the highest initial savings rate among households, as well as the highest savings rate elasticity. The increasing real return to deposits therefore raises savings among capitalists and rentiers relatively strongly. The less asymmetrical long-run impact follows from the fact that capitalists and rentiers face a relatively low direct tax rate as compared to other household types (excluding informal sector households, who do not pay taxes). Accordingly, the relative impact of higher savings rates by capitalists and rentiers diminishes as income increases over the long term.

6.5   Concluding Remarks

In this chapter we have developed a quantitative framework for analyzing the impact of adjustment policies on output, wages, unemployment, poverty, and income distribution in Brazil. To do so we modified and extended in several directions the low-income IMMPA prototype described in the previous chapter, and the Mini-IMMPA framework presented in Chapter 3. Specifically, we introduced several features that we believe are important to capture some of the most salient structural characteristics of the Brazilian economy, namely, open unskilled urban unemployment, bond financing of public sector deficits, a flexible exchange rate, and payroll taxation. After explaining the structural components of the model, we described its underlying accounting framework (namely, the financial SAM on which it is based), the household survey data used to assess poverty and distributional effects, and the choice of parameters. The properties of the model were illustrated by studying the effects of a permanent increase in the short-term official interest rate.

The analysis indicates that a shock of this type will only lower inflation in the short term. Inflation is driven by commercial banks' need for liquidity. The increase in the official rate spills over into increased deposit rates, higher savings accumulation rates, lower demand for liquidity by commercial banks, and, consequently, lower liquidity in the hands of the public. This lowers inflation in the short term. Lower inflation is, however, replaced by higher inflation in the medium to long term. Private sector borrowing for investment purposes declines strongly, as a result initially of an increase in borrowing costs. Subsequently, the significant increase in private sector interest payments leads to increasing private sector debt accumulation, lower private sector net worth/collateral value, an increased lending rate (premium), and, subsequently, further increases in private sector interest payments, which have to be financed by additional private sector borrowing. Increasing private sector borrowing requirements lead to higher demand for liquidity by commercial banks, increasing liquidity in the hands of the public and, consequently, increasing inflation. Accordingly, the vicious circle of cumulative causation whereby increasing lending rates leads to lower profits and investment demand, worsening private sector balance sheets, and further increasing lending rates, is simultaneously the cause of the short-term reduction of inflation (due to lower financing needs for private sector investment expenditures), and the long-term increase in inflation (due to higher financing needs for increasing private sector interest payments).

The analysis also indicates that open unemployment will increase strongly both in the short and the long term. The increase in the official refinancing rate leads immediately to higher lending rates. Moreover, subsequent increases in the risk premium, due to the worsening of private firms' net worth, leads to further increases in lending rates over the longer term. High lending rates leads to higher costs of working capital, which consist mainly of labor costs. In turn, higher labor costs, combined with lower private sector investment and capital accumulation, reduce formal sector employment and increase open unemployment in the long term. At the same time, reduced formal sector production lowers intermediate demand for rural and informal sector goods. Backward linkages from the private formal sector forms the main transmission channel through which a higher official interest rate influences employment and poverty in the rural and urban informal sectors. Lower intermediate demand for informal sector goods has a particularly strong negative impact, given the high degree of wage flexibility in that sector. Urban poverty therefore increases significantly. Increased export earnings dampens the negative impact of lower intermediate demand for rural sector goods; rural poverty therefore increases less strongly. Nevertheless, poverty headcount and poverty gap ratios increase significantly in both rural and urban informal sectors in the long term. Finally, inequality among household groups increases because capitalists and rentiers experience a relatively strong long-term increase in income and consumption. Capitalists and rentiers are the only household group able to raise savings rates and take advantage of the strongly increased real returns on bank deposits. Overall, a permanent 10 percent increase in the central bank official rate leads to lower inflation in the short term, at the expense of increased unemployment, higher poverty, and worsened inequality. In the long run, lower inflation is replaced by increasing inflation, whereas unemployment, income inequality, and poverty continue to increase.

The model can be used to address a variety of issues that are at the forefront of the policy agenda in Brazil. In particular, it can be used to examine the growth, employ-ment, and poverty effects of a reallocation of public expenditure, with a comparison between changes in transfers, spending on infrastructure, and spending on education or health (see Chapter 5), an increase in the minimum wage (as in Foguel, Ramos, and Carneiro (2001)), and a reduction in the payroll tax rate on unskilled labor.

Appendix
Calibration and Parameter Values

This Appendix briefly reviews the structure of the financial SAM that underlies the model, the household survey data that we used to link the macro component to our poverty and income distribution assessments, and the parameter values that we used to calibrate the behavioral equations.[18] As with the aplications discussed in Chapters 3, 4, and 5, the model itself is solved using a combination of GAMS and Excel.

To build the necessary data to calibrate the model involves two steps. First, a balanced aggregate SAM was constructed. Second, using the aggregate SAM and additional structural data, we constructed a balanced disaggregated SAM. This procedure guarantees that the disaggregated SAM matches the aggregate SAM, and provides controls over totals for each block. Tables A6.1 and A6.2 show the final form of the real and financial SAMs that together represent the balanced disaggregated SAM.

Brazilian national accounts data for 1996 were used to compile the macro data for the real part of the SAM. We collected aggregate data for intermediate consumption, exports, imports, investment (capital formation plus inventory changes), output taxes, import taxes, household consumption, government consumption, wage taxes, wages, and profits. Wage taxes are the required and imputed payments over labor and other payments to workers. Wages are the sum of labor payments and payments to autonomous workers. Profits correspond to the sum of gross surplus by activities. Working capital requirements were obtained as a residual. Information about direct taxes and property taxes, transfers to households (social security payments and other benefits) and interest payments (domestic and foreign) were taken from public administration accounts. Data on domestic and foreign interest payments by the Government were also collected.

Financial data used in the aggregate SAM were obtained from the database of the Central Bank of Brazil: currency in circulation, domestic deposits and bonds held by households; and domestic banks' holdings of domestic bonds. Information about the allocation of domestic banks' assets was completed with information about profits, credit to the private sector, changes in bank reserves, and holdings of foreign bonds. Foreign financing to domestic firms was calculated in "net" terms by adding loans by foreign banks to domestic firms (for investment purposes) plus foreign direct investment (plus stocks and derivatives) minus domestic bonds issued by domestic firms. Government foreign borrowing was obtained directly from the balance of payments.

---

[18] A detailed description of the data and adjustment procedures used to construct the financial SAM are provided in Haddad, Fernandes, Domingues, Perobelli, and Afonso (2003).

Table A6.1 Brazil: real SAM (in billions of Reais)

	Expenditures									
	Agriculture sector goods	Private informal sector goods	Private formal sector goods	Government sector goods	Unskilled labor	Skilled labor	Profit	Working capital costs	Product tax	Wage tax
Income										
Agriculture sector goods	21,093	700	81,139	6,599	0	0	0	0	0	0
Private informal sector goods	2,899	9,122	67,734	39,259	0	0	0	0	0	0
Private formal sector goods	17,005	28,582	269,181	73,623	0	0	0	0	0	0
Government sector goods	430	797	5,805	4,477	0	0	0	0	0	0
Unskilled labor	21,298	47,777	96,419	5,212	0	0	0	0	0	0
Skilled labor	0	0	81,785	16,634	0	0	0	0	0	0
Profit	69,487	50,694	224,889	0	0	0	0	0	0	0
Working capital costs	0	0	8,013	0	0	0	0	0	0	0
Product tax	4,822	0	71,666	3,394	0	0	0	0	0	0
Wage tax	1,002	0	66,823	8,192	0	0	0	0	0	0
Direct tax	0	0	0	0	0	0	0	0	0	0
Import tax	173	0	4,019	0	0	0	0	0	0	0
Rural agricultural households	0	0	0	0	21,298	0	69,487	0	0	0
Urban informal households	0	0	0	0	47,777	0	50,694	0	0	0
Urban formal unskilled households	0	0	0	0	101,630	0	0	0	0	0
Urban formal skilled households	0	0	0	0	0	98,419	0	0	0	0
Rentier households	0	0	0	0	0	0	54,981	0	0	0
Government	0	0	0	0	0	0	0	0	79,882	76,017
Savings (excl. Private enterprises)	0	0	0	0	0	0	0	0	0	0
Private savings-investment balance	0	0	0	0	0	0	99,625	0	0	0
Private investment allocation	0	0	0	0	0	0	0	0	0	0
Rest of the World	2,699	0	62,862	0	0	0	0	0	0	0
Money	0	0	0	0	0	0	0	0	0	0
Domestic Banks	0	0	0	0	0	0	82,881	8,013	0	0
Central Bank	0	0	0	0	0	0	0	0	0	0
Foreign Banks	0	0	0	0	0	0	12,111	0	0	0
Government Bonds	0	0	0	0	0	0	0	0	0	0
Total	140,909	137,672	1,040,334	157,389	170,705	98,419	369,780	8,013	79,882	76,017

Table A6.1 Continued

				Expenditures					
	Direct tax	Import tax	Rural agricultural households	Urban informal households	Urban formal unskilled households	Urban formal skilled households	Rentier households	Government	Savings (excl. Private enterprises)
Income									
Agriculture sector goods	0	0	4,515	5,860	5,228	6,576	1,787	0	0
Private informal sector goods	0	0	3,515	4,563	4,070	5,120	1,391	0	0
Private formal sector goods	0	0	83,352	108,201	96,517	121,409	32,987	0	0
Government sector goods	0	0	429	557	497	625	170	143,111	0
Unskilled labor	0	0	0	0	0	0	0	0	0
Skilled labor	0	0	0	0	0	0	0	0	0
Profit	0	0	0	0	0	0	0	0	0
Working capital costs	0	0	0	0	0	0	0	0	0
Product tax	0	0	0	0	0	0	0	0	0
Wage tax	0	0	0	0	0	0	0	0	0
Direct tax	0	0	11,927	0	13,352	12,930	7,223	0	0
Import tax	0	0	0	0	0	0	0	0	0
Rural agricultural households	0	0	0	0	0	0	0	12,498	0
Urban informal households	0	0	0	0	0	0	0	20,091	0
Urban formal unskilled households	0	0	0	0	0	0	0	15,444	0
Urban formal skilled households	0	0	0	0	0	0	0	41,824	0
Rentier households	0	0	0	0	0	0	0	8,239	0
Government	45,432	4,192	0	0	0	0	0	0	0
Savings (excl. Private enterprises)	0	0	216	295	1,233	3,055	50,486	−80,764	0
Private savings-investment balance	0	0	0	0	0	0	0	0	62,505
Private investment allocation	0	0	0	0	0	0	0	0	0
Rest of the World	0	0	0	0	0	0	0	0	0
Money	0	0	0	0	0	0	0	0	0
Domestic Banks	0	0	0	0	0	0	0	33,364	0
Central Bank	0	0	0	0	0	0	0	0	0
Foreign Banks	0	0	0	0	0	0	0	9,928	0
Government Bonds	0	0	0	0	0	0	0	25,719	0
Total	45,432	4,192	103,953	119,476	120,897	149,715	94,044	229,455	62,505

Continued

Table A6.1 Continued

				Expenditures					
	Private savings-investment balance	Private investment allocation	Rest of the World	Money	Domestic Banks	Central Bank	Foreign Banks	Government Bonds	Total
Income									
Agriculture sector goods	0	5,561	1,851	0	0	0	0	0	140,909
Private informal sector goods	0	0	0	0	0	0	0	0	137,672
Private formal sector goods	0	156,078	53,400	0	0	0	0	0	1,040,334
Government sector goods	0	491	0	0	0	0	0	0	157,389
Unskilled labor	0	0	0	0	0	0	0	0	170,705
Skilled labor	0	0	0	0	0	0	0	0	98,419
Profit	0	0	0	0	24,709	0	0	0	369,780
Working capital costs	0	0	0	0	0	0	0	0	8,013
Product tax	0	0	0	0	0	0	0	0	79,882
Wage tax	0	0	0	0	0	0	0	0	76,017
Direct tax	0	0	0	0	0	0	0	0	45,432
Import tax	0	0	0	0	0	0	0	0	4,192
Rural agricultural households	0	0	0	0	670	0	0	0	103,953
Urban informal households	0	0	0	0	914	0	0	0	119,476
Urban formal unskilled households	0	0	0	0	3,822	0	0	0	120,897
Urban formal skilled households	0	0	0	0	8,051	0	1,421	0	149,715
Rentier households	0	0	0	0	11,269	0	4,830	14,724	94,044
Government	0	0	5,270	0	18,663	0	0	0	229,455
Savings (excl. Private enterprises)	0	0	-10,740	0	24,709	0	74,015	0	62,505
Private savings-investment balance	0	0	0	0	0	0	0	0	162,130
Private investment allocation	162,130	0	0	0	0	0	0	0	162,130
Rest of the World	0	0	0	0	0	0	0	0	65,562
Money	0	0	0	0	0	0	0	0	0
Domestic Banks	0	0	0	0	0	0	0	10,995	135,254
Central Bank	0	0	0	0	0	0	0	0	0
Foreign Banks	0	0	15,780	0	42,446	0	0	0	80,266
Government Bonds	0	0	0	0	0	0	0	0	25,719
Total	162,130	162,130	65,562	0	135,254	0	80,266	25,719	

Table A6.2 Brazil: financial SAM (in billions of Reais)

Asset Accumulation

	Liability Accumulation							
	Private enterprises	Rural agricultural households	Urban informal households	Urban formal unskilled households	Urban formal skilled households	Rentier households	Government	Savings (excl. Private enterprises)
Private enterprises								
Rural agricultural households								
Urban informal households								
Urban formal unskilled households								
Urban formal skilled households								
Rentier households								
Government								
Savings (excl. Private enterprises)		216	295	1,233	3,055	50,486	−80,764	
Private savings-investment balance	99,625							62,505
Rest of the World								
Money								
Domestic Banks	37,200							
Central Bank								
Foreign Banks	25,305						19,030	
Government Bonds							61,735	
Total	162,130	216	295	1,233	3,055	50,486	0	62,505

Table A6.2 Continued

Asset Accumulation	Liability Accumulation							
	Private savings–investment balance	Rest of the World	Money	Domestic Banks	Central Bank	Foreign Banks	Government Bonds	Total
Private enterprises	162,130							162,130
Rural agricultural households			28	188				216
Urban informal households			39	256				295
Urban formal unskilled households			162	1,071				1,233
Urban formal skilled households			401	2,653				3,055
Rentier households			682	4,510			45,294	50,486
Government								0
Savings (excl. Private enterprises)		−10,740		24,709		74,015		62,505
Private savings–investment balance	162,130							162,130
Rest of the World								0
Money					1,313			1,313
Domestic Banks				−8,559	868		16,441	54,509
Central Bank		10,740		29,680				2,181
Foreign Banks								74,015
Government Bonds								61,735
Total	162,130	0	1,313	54,509	2,181	74,015	61,735	

The initial (unbalanced) aggregate SAM was compiled from the initial data. A posterior (balanced) aggregate SAM was then obtained by the application of a RAS procedure, to square out statistical errors. Changes in each cell, from the unbalanced to the balanced aggregate SAM, were checked to ensure consistency.

The second step was to obtain a more detailed financial SAM, disaggregating relevant cells into their components. As noted in the text, in the model, households are separated in five groups (rural, urban informal, urban formal unskilled, urban skilled, and capitalists and rentiers). Goods are disaggregated into four sectors: the rural sector, the urban informal sector, the urban private formal sector and the urban public sector. Labor payments are disaggregated in two components, skilled and unskilled labor.

The main data sources for compiling the disaggregated and sectoral information are the available input–output tables for Brazil. Sales and purchases for up to 42 sectors were available; this information was mapped into the four IMMPA sectors. The rural and public sectors were mapped directly to the IMMPA classification. A mapping structure was created from the PNAD household survey data in order to separate formal and informal activities. Shares in the industry and services sectors were used to measure the informal economy; the private formal sector was constructed as a residual. This mapping was also used to establish the distribution of household consumption and the composition of foreign trade.

Production taxes by sector were derived from the estimated production, taking into account that the informal component pays no taxes. Import taxes were calculated in proportion to import flows. Wage taxes were allocated to sectors using the effective tax rate for the rural sector, with the residual tax revenue allocated to the private and public sectors, in line with labor payments in these sectors (by definition, the informal economy pays no wage taxes). Borrowing for short-term working capital needs by the urban private sector was calculated by taking into account the sector's wage payments.

Following the cash-in-advance specification of money demand by households described above (see equation (72)), the allocation of currency in circulation and domestic bank deposits followed household consumption shares. Direct taxes were allocated in the same way, taking into account that urban informal sector households do not pay direct taxes. By assumption, all government bonds were assumed to be held by capitalists-rentiers. Finally, PNAD survey data were used to derive the composition of government transfers to households.

A preliminary, unbalanced disaggregated SAM showed differences in rows and column sums in the various sectors and households blocks. An important discrepancy was between households' income and expenditures. The estimated income for each household group was used as a benchmark to adjust the expenditure on goods. A RAS procedure was implemented to adjust the household consumption block, and subsequently the intermediate consumption block.

Other stock data, on household financial wealth and physical capital of the government and the private sector, were also necessary to calibrate the model. Some information on these stocks was obtained from the same sources from which the flow data were taken. Data for the stock of public capital in infrastructure, and the private capital stock, were taken from the IPEA (*Instituto de Pesquisa Economica Aplicada*) database. To calculate data for the stock of public capital in education and health, we used flow data from the government budget on these components and applied the perpetual inventory method (with an annual depreciation rate set at 4 percent).

To simulate the impact of policy and exogenous shocks on poverty and income distribution we used two Brazilian household surveys: the *Pesquisa Nacional por Amostra de Domicílios* – PNAD (National Household Survey) and the *Pesquisa de Padrões de Vida* – PPV (Living Standard Survey). The PNAD is the main Brazilian household survey, conducted by IBGE (*Instituto Brasileiro de Geografia e Estatística*) since 1976. The interviews are carried out in October and the information is relative to September. Each year the PNAD interviews around 100,000 households, randomly selected, in the whole country. The number of visits to households in PNAD is limited to one, making it difficult for someone to capture short-run fluctuations in the household income. Even though PNAD does not investigate consumption expenditure patterns of households, it contains a very rich information set on personal and household characteristics, such as those related to housing (such as quality, size, and ownership), durable goods, family composition, income, location, demography, education, and work status for each member of the household.

The PPV was carried out by IBGE in 1996. It contains information (also available in PNAD) on personal and household characteristics. Moreover, it has rich information on patterns of households consumption expenditures. PPV, however, has a limited coverage when compared to PNAD: it has been conducted only in the Southeast and Northeast regions (urban and rural areas), and the sample size is relatively small (about 5,000 households).

Estimates from PNAD for the year 1996 are used in simulations for income-based indicators, while PPV is used in simulations for consumption-based poverty and inequality measures. When using PPV, the entire sample was considered, but in the PNAD case, for operational reasons, a representative subsample of 10 percent of the original sample was drawn. The size of the subsample from PNAD includes about 10,000 households and the whole PPV sample about 5,000 households.

The information set on work status in PNAD allowed us to classify households into the five household income groups specified in the model. Specifically, we used information on years of schooling and occupational status for each household head. The division between skilled and unskilled workers was based on the number of years of schooling. Those workers with at least one year of high school (9 or more years of schooling) were considered skilled, and those with less than 9 years of schooling were considered unskilled.

To distinguish between rural and urban workers we used the activity sector (agriculture versus nonagriculture), instead of residence area (rural versus urban). Finally, the nature of urban employment was considered formal or informal according to both occupational status and years of schooling of the workers. When the head of the household was unemployed, we used information on the last job. Thus, the actual mapping between the survey data and the household classification used in the model is as follows:

- *Rural sector group.* It consists of all households whose head works in agricultural activities.

- *Unskilled informal sector group.* It consists of all households whose head is unskilled, works in nonagricultural activities, and does not have a formal labor contract.
- *Unskilled formal sector group.* It consists of *a*) all households whose head is unskilled and has a formal labor contract and his job is in the nonagricultural and nonpublic sector; and *b*) all households whose head is an unskilled public servant.
- *Skilled formal sector group.* It consists of *a*) all households whose head is skilled, works in the nonagricultural and nonpublic sector; *b*) all households whose head is a skilled public servant.
- *Capitalists-rentiers group.* It consists of all households whose head is an employer.

The urban poverty line was fixed at R$ 56.00, corresponding to half the minimum wage of September 1996. In the rural area, the poverty line was fixed at 60 percent of the urban poverty line (R$ 33.60).

Parameter values for rural and urban informal production were calibrated from SAM data. Parameter values for the private formal sector production structure include substitution elasticities between skilled labor and capital, between unskilled labor and the composite factor consisting of skilled labor and capital, T_1, and the substitution elasticity between the composite factor consisting of the three primary production factors, T_2, and government capital, K_G. The bottom level substitution elasticity between skilled labor and capital was set at 0.4, the middle-level substitution elasticity between the composite factor and unskilled labor was set at 1.2, while the top-level substitution elasticity between the composite factor and government capital was set at 0.75. The elasticity measuring congestion effects (in terms of the size of the urban population), pc, was set at 0.2.

Parameter values for the public production structure include substitution elasticities between skilled and unskilled labor, as well as between the composite factor consisting of skilled and unskilled labor and government capital. The bottom level substitution elasticity between skilled and unskilled labor was set at 1.2, whereas the top-level substitution elasticity between the composite labor input and government capital was set at 0.75.

Trade parameters used in the model include substitution elasticities for the Armington specifications on the import side and CET specifications on the export side. Specifications are given separately for rural and private formal imports and exports. Substitution elasticities on the import side was set at 1.2 for rural sector goods and 0.8 for private formal sector goods, whereas substitution elasticities on the export side was set at 1.2 for rural sector goods and 1.5 for private formal sector goods.

As discussed in the text, migration between labor market segments is governed by Harris-Todaro type specifications. The only parameter in the migration function between informal and formal (unskilled) urban labor is the coefficient β_F, which is calibrated at 307 (note that, unlike the specifications adopted in Chapters 3 and 4, for instance, this parameter is not constrained between 0 and 1). In the migration function between the rural and urban labor market segments, the elasticity with respect to relative expected wages was set at a modest 0.1, and the speed of adjustment to 0.1 as well.

In the skills acquisition function, the elasticity with respect to relative expected wages was set at 0.5 and the speed of adjustment to 0.1. In addition, the elasticity with respect to the government stock of education capital in the skills-upgrading technology was set at 0.8.

Fixed real wage rates for skilled and unskilled employees in the public sector, as well as the fixed real minimum wage rate for unskilled workers in the private formal sector, are calibrated from the SAM and auxiliary labor market data. Parameter values for the wage-setting equation relating to skilled workers in the formal urban sector includes elasticities with respect to *a*) the consumer price index for urban skilled workers; *b*) the price ratio between the consumer price index for urban skilled workers and the composite product price PT_2; and *c*) the unemployment rate among skilled workers in the urban formal sector. The two former elasticities with respect to the consumer price index and the price-ratio were set at 1.0, whereas the elasticity with respect to the unemployment rate was set at 0.5.

Minimum consumption levels were not included as part of the linear expenditure system. Accordingly, income elasticities of demand remain constant and equal to unity. The household savings rates were each specified as a function of the opportunity cost of holding money, taken to be the real rate of interest on domestic currency deposits. The elasticity of the savings rate with respect to the real deposit rate was set at 0.5 for each of the five household types, except for capitalists and rentiers, in which case the elasticity was set at 1.2. The elasticity of the relative household demand for domestic versus foreign deposits with respect to relative rates of return (that is, the ratio of the domestic deposit rate to the foreign deposit rate corrected for expected depreciation of the exchange rate, as shown in (76)), was set at 0.7 for each household type.

The specification of private sector demand for investment relies on *a*) the growth rate of the government stock of infrastructure capital; *b*) the growth rate of real GDP at factor cost (the accelerator effect); *c*) the level of overall inflation; and *d*) the after-tax rate of return to private capital relative to the cost of funds. The elasticities were set at 0.8 with respect to the growth rate of infrastructure capital, 0.1 with respect to the growth rate of real GDP, 5.0 with respect to the level of inflation, and 0.8 with respect to the net return to private capital.

Bonds are only demanded by capitalists and commercial banks. The specification of the demand for bonds by capitalists relies on *a*) the own rate of return on bonds, that is, the bond rate; *b*) the alternative cost relating to domestic currency deposits, that is, the domestic deposit rate; and *c*) the alternative cost relating to foreign deposits, that is, the foreign deposit rate corrected for expected depreciation of the exchange rate. The elasticities were set at 4.0 with respect to the bond interest rate, 2.5 with respect to the domestic currency deposit rate, and 0.7 with respect to the foreign interest rate. The specification of the commercial banks' market-related demand for bonds (relative to domestic loans) relies on the ratio between the bond interest rate and the private lending rate. The elasticity was set at 2.0. The placement ratio of bonds with the domestic financial system was set at 0.9. This captures the role of state-owned banks in absorbing government debt.

Chapter 7

Disinflation, Fiscal Sustainability, and Labor Market Adjustment in Turkey

Pierre-Richard Agénor, Henning Tarp Jensen, Mathew Verghis, and Erinç Yeldan

For much of the past two decades, Turkey's economy has suffered from persistent fiscal imbalances, high inflation, financial volatility, and sharp swings in economic activity (see Figure 7.1). Large budget deficits during the 1990s fueled a rapid expansion in domestic public debt and sharp increases in real interest rates, with deposit rates, for instance, averaging 12.8 percent in real terms during that decade. In turn, high interest rates had an adverse effect on private investment and contributed to unsustainable debt dynamics. The overall balance of the consolidated public sector rose from 5.2 percent of GNP to 13.1 percent in 1997 and 22.3 percent in 1999. The net debt of the public sector reached 61 percent in 1999.[1]

In late 1999, the government launched a 3-year disinflation program based on a pre-announced exchange rate path. Despite some progress in 2000, with inflation falling and the public sector recording a sizable primary surplus, unfavorable debt dynamics and financial sector weaknesses combined with the rigidities imposed by the exchange rate peg led to a currency collapse and a full-blown financial crisis.[2]

---

[1] In 1995, foreign debt represented two-thirds of total debt (or 30.7 percent of GNP), whereas in 2002 it amounted to 40 percent of the stock (or 32.1 percent of GNP). Moreover, a sizable fraction of the domestic debt became denominated in foreign currency or indexed on the exchange rate. In 2002 this debt amounted to 15.3 percent of GNP, with total domestic debt representing 47.7 percent. The sum of foreign debt and foreign-currency denominated domestic debt amounted therefore to 47.4 percent that same year.

[2] See Yilmaz and Boratav (2003) for an overview of developments leading up to the crisis.

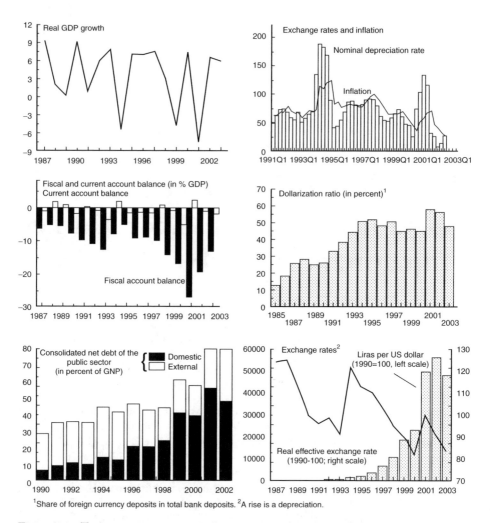

Figure 7.1   Turkey: macroeconomic indicators, 1987–2003. *Source*: International Monetary Fund and official estimates.

Between the end of 1995 and the end of 2001, Turkey's public debt almost doubled in proportion to GNP, from 41.3 percent to 80 percent (see Figure 7.1), with a significant portion of the increase coming in 2001, as the cost of bank restructuring was borne by the budget. Inflation hit 68.5 percent at the end of 2001 and interest rates on treasury bills reached 99.1 percent.

Although short-lived (the economy started to recover in 2002), the crisis had severe economic and social costs. Real GNP fell by 9.5 percent in 2001 alone, whereas per capita GDP contracted by 13 percent between 1998 and 2001. The officially recorded unemployment rate rose from 6.4 percent in 1998 to 8.5 percent in 2001 and 10.6 percent during 2002 (see Figure 7.2). Real wages in manufacturing remained

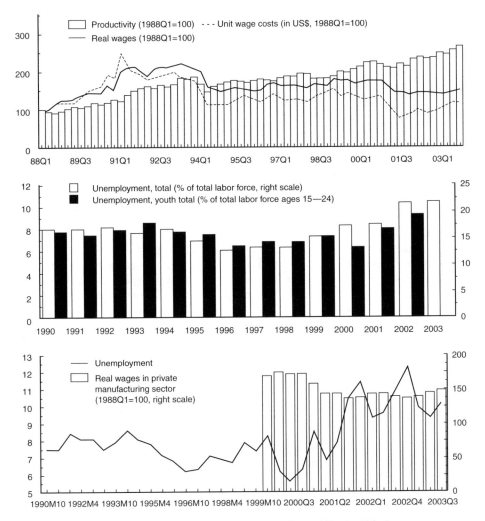

Figure 7.2 Turkey: wages and unemployment. *Source*: Central Bank of Turkey.

relatively constant throughout 2000 as nominal wage increases kept pace with inflation, but then declined sharply in 2001 – by 20 percent in the fourth quarter of that
year, compared to the same period of the previous year (World Bank (2003)).World
Bank estimates indicate that the urban headcount poverty index rose from 6.2 percent
in 1994 to 17.2 percent in 2001. Credit to the private sector (particularly firms in the
nontradables sector) fell sharply as a share of GDP and recovered only slowly – a typical pattern in the aftermath of financial crises in developing countries, as documented
for instance by Tornell and Westermann (2003) and Schneider and Tornell (2004).

   The development of the public debt overhang and the consequent need for continuous refinancing of the debt has led to a very close link between financial market

participants' perceptions of credibility of the Government's program, key macro-economic variables such as interest rates, exchange rates, and inflation, and real variables such as employment and growth. Our premise in this chapter is that a proper modeling of the structure of the labor market in Turkey, and a proper account of the linkages between the financial and real sides of the Turkish economy, are essential steps to understand the impact of the disinflation program on the evolution of output and employment. Accordingly, we develop an IMMPA framework for Turkey that shares many of the characteristics of the models presented in previous chapters, namely, a segmented labor market and a full-blown financial sector linked through various channels to the supply side. Our approach differs significantly from the existing literature on computable general equilibrium (CGE) models of the Turkish economy, which includes Lewis (1992), Yeldan (1997, 1998), Diao, Roe, and Yeldan (1998), Karadag and Westaway (1999), De Santis (2000), Voyvoda and Yeldan (2003), and Elekdag (2003). Those of Lewis (1992), Yeldan (1998), and Elekdag (2003) include a financial sector, whereas the others are "real" models focusing on tax and trade policy issues. In all of these models, however, the treatment of the labor market is fairly rudimentary and some important channels through which the real and financial sectors interact are absent. Indeed, as far as we are aware, some of these channels have been either ignored or improperly treated in the CGE literature in general; our framework should therefore be of independent interest to researchers focusing on other countries with large market-financed debt overhangs.

We pay particular attention to financial sector issues such as a high degree of exchange rate flexibility, risk premia in the banking sector, dollarization of loans and bank deposits, the link between market interest rates and official policy rates, and interactions between credibility, default risk on government debt, and inflation expectations. Understanding the link between credibility and inflation, in particular, is important to understand Turkey's experience in the immediate aftermath of the 2001 financial crisis. For instance, to the extent that inflation inertia is due to doubts about the commitment and ability of policymakers to keep prices in check, a disinflation program may entail a large output cost.

Accounting for default risk on public debt is another key feature of our analysis. It is well recognized that fiscal policy must be evaluated in a framework in which the government is subject to an intertemporal budget constraint (see, for instance, Uctum and Wickens (2000), Gunaydin (2003), and Salman (2003) for a discussion in Turkey's context).

If the real rate of interest is above the real growth rate of the economy, a fiscal deficit today (brought about by either an increase in expenditure or a reduction in taxes) must be accompanied at some point in the future by either a fiscal contraction or a rise in seigniorage revenue. Otherwise, the increase in public debt will feed upon itself as the government borrows to finance the interest payments on the liabilities that it previously issued. If the government cannot meet its debt service payments without further borrowing, investors may be unwilling after a certain point to continue to accumulate government bonds. As a result, the government will have to either reduce its primary deficit or engage in an outright default. Although we do not account explicitly for the government's intertemporal budget constraint in our framework, we capture this "unwillingness" of investors to provide indefinite financing by assuming that there is a nonzero probability of default that depends on the existing stock of debt (relative to tax revenues). In turn, the probability of default affects the expected rate of return on government bonds. The higher the perceived risk of default is, the higher will be the actual interest rate on these bonds, and the lower will be the degree of credibility of the fiscal stance. Lower credibility translates into higher inflation expectations and greater inflation persistence.[3]

Given our interest in understanding better the behavior of wages and unemployment in the context of adjustment, the labor market plays also an important role in our analysis. Indeed, as in the other IMMPA applications presented in Chapters 4 and 6, the framework developed in this chapter captures many important features of the Turkish labor market – such as a large informal urban economy, open unskilled urban unemployment, wage bargaining in the urban formal sector, and international migration, with remittance flows accounting for about 2 percent of GDP in 2002. As discussed in Chapters 1 and 2, in any model designed to study the response of the labor market to short-run macro shocks and structural policies, accounting for the informal sector is essential. In the case of Turkey, it is even more so. Some observers have argued that growth in that sector may explain the observed tendency for labor force participation to fall since the 1960s, that is, the growing gap between the labor force (the adult population either employed or looking for work, which was 22 million in 2001) and the adult population (of about 46 million adults in that same year).

The remainder of the chapter is organized as follows. Section 7.1 describes the model. Section 7.2 considers two policy experiments and discusses the response of production, wages and unemployment, as well as the behavior of the public debt-to-GDP ratio. The first consists of a temporary increase in official interest rates. The second focuses on fiscal adjustment and involves tax reform, namely an increase in the VAT rate and a rise in the tax rate on income of profit earners. These simulations are important because the sustainability of Turkey's public debt remains (at the time of this writing) a key policy issue. It has been argued by various observers that Turkey needs to run large primary surpluses over the medium and long term to lower its public debt burden, meet its disinflation targets, and convince markets that its debt is sustainable, for the risk premium embedded in interest rates on domestic debt to fall. In particular, the adjustment program introduced in May 2001 called for Turkey to maintain a primary surplus on the order of 6.5 percent of GNP over the medium term to lower its public debt to manageable proportions and achieve the goal of single digit inflation by 2005.[4] Although we do not assess explicitly the validity of this target, our simulations allow us to quantify the impact of fiscal adjustment not only on the

---

[3]Diao, Roe, and Yeldan (1998) analyzed fiscal management issues in Turkey using an explicit intertemporal CGE framework that accounts for the existence of a risk premium associated with large public sector borrowing requirements. Specifically, the domestic real interest rate, r, is taken to diverge from the world interest, r^*, by $r = (1 + \theta)r^*$, with θ being a function of the ratio of the fiscal deficit to GDP. However, the model is "real" only in nature; thus, the impact of interest rate changes on portfolio decisions and the supply side are not taken into account.

[4]These estimates are based on a variant of the consistency framework developed by Anand and van Wijnbergen (1989). However, this approach lacks a simultaneous determination of the rate of output growth, the real interest rate, fiscal variables, and the real exchange rate. Our analysis, by contrast, is cast in a general equilibrium setting.

budget and domestic inflation, but also on labor market outcomes and standards of living. The last section summarizes the main results of the chapter and offers some concluding remarks. The Appendix discusses the structure of the financial SAM that underlies the model, our calibration procedure, and the parameter values that are used in the behavioral equations.

7.1   Structure of the Model

Our IMMPA framework for the Turkish economy captures three features that we believe are essential to analyze the impact of disinflation and fiscal reforms on labor market adjustment and public debt sustainability. First, linkages between the financial and real sectors; second, the structure of the labor market; and third, the channels through which fiscal variables interact with financial variables to affect the economy. In addition, particular attention is paid to modeling monetary policy and the credit market. Specifically, we assume that the central bank sets a short-term policy interest rate (such as the repurchase rate) and has a perfectly elastic supply curve of liquidity to commercial banks at that rate. Credit to firms by commercial banks is also perfectly elastic (at the given lending rate), whereas lending to households is subject to rationing. As in the IMMPA application for Brazil developed in Chapter 6, foreign borrowing by commercial banks is exogenous and equilibrium of the credit market is obtained by domestic borrowing from the central bank, at the given policy rate.

In this section we review the various blocks of the model. We consider in turn the production side, the labor market, external trade, aggregate supply and demand, income formation, saving and investment, the financial sector and asset allocation, the balance sheets and flow budget constraints of the public sector (comprising the government and the central bank), the balance of payments, equilibrium conditions for the currency and bond markets, price formation, and the links between default risk, credibility, and inflation expectations.

7.1.1   Production

Given our focus on macroeconomic aspects, the production structure is kept fairly aggregate, as in Mini-IMMPA (see Chapter 3). The economy is divided between rural and urban sectors. The rural sector produces a homogeneous good, which is sold domestically and abroad. The urban sector consists of both formal and informal components; furthermore, the formal urban economy is separated between a private sector (which also produces a good sold on both domestic and foreign markets) and a public sector, which produces a single nontraded good.

Rural Sector

Gross output in the rural sector, X_A, is given by the sum of value added, V_A, and intermediate consumption:

$$X_A = V_A + \sum_i a_{iA} X_A, \tag{1}$$

where the a_{ij} are input–output coefficients measuring sales from sector i to sector j. We also have $i, j = A, I, P, G$ where A, I, P, G are used in what follows to refer, to the rural sector, the urban informal sector, the private urban formal sector, and the public sector, respectively. As in previous chapters, use of the index i or j without precision will refer to all five sectors.

Value added is produced with land, $LAND$ (available in fixed supply), unskilled labor, U_A (the only category of labor in the rural sector), and the economy-wide stock of public capital in infrastructure, K_{INF}, which is treated as a pure public good and consists not only of roads and public transportation that may increase access to markets, but also power plants, hospitals, and other public goods that may contribute to an increase in the productivity of factors in private production. A two-level production structure is assumed. Specifically, U_A and K_{INF} combine through a constant elasticity of substitution (CES) function to form a composite factor, which is then combined with land through a Cobb-Douglas technology:

$$V_A = LAND^{1-\eta_{X_A}}[\alpha_{X_A}\{\beta_{X_A}U_A^{-\rho_{X_A}} + (1-\beta_{X_A})K_{INF}^{-\rho_{X_A}}\}^{-1/\rho_{X_A}}]^{1-\eta_{X_A}}, \quad (2)$$

Thus, given the Cobb-Douglas specification, rural production exhibits decreasing returns to scale in the composite input. In what follows, the quantity of land is normalized to unity.

In standard fashion, output of the rural sector is allocated to domestic sales, D_A, and exports, E_A, through a constant elasticity of transformation (CET) function:

$$X_A = \alpha_{ED_A}[\beta_{ED_A}E_A^{\rho_{ED_A}} + (1-\beta_{ED_A})D_A^{\rho_{ED_A}}]^{1/\rho_{ED_A}}, \quad (3)$$

where, as discussed later, the ratio E_A/D_A depends on relative prices.

Urban Informal Sector

The second component of the production structure is the informal sector, whose share increased significantly in Turkey since the 1980s. The OECD (1996) estimated the size of the nonagricultural informal sector (defined as unpaid family workers, half of the self-employed, employers with fewer than four employees, and unregistered wage earners) to be 21 percent for 1993. Another study (cited by Onaran (2002)) using the same definition found 23 percent for 1997. The private formal sector was estimated at 19 percent of total employment, the public sector at 12 percent, with the rest (about 46 percent of total employment) being employed in the agricultural sector. Thus, the informal non-agricultural sector exceeded the size of the private formal sector. More recently, Taymaz and Ozler (2003) put the size of the informal sector at more than 30 percent of output and 40 percent of employment in the manufacturing sector. Similar estimates are cited in Tunali (2003).

Gross production in the informal sector, X_I, is given as the sum of value added, V_I, and intermediate consumption:

$$X_I = V_I + \sum_i a_{iI}X_I. \quad (4)$$

There is no physical capital in the informal sector, and value added is generated using only unskilled labor, U_I, with a decreasing returns to scale technology:

$$V_I = \alpha_{XI} U_I^{\beta_{XI}}, \qquad \alpha_{XI} > 0, \ 0 < \beta_{XI} < 1, \tag{5}$$

from which the demand for labor can be derived as

$$U_I^d = \beta_{XI} \left(\frac{PV_I V_I}{W_I} \right), \tag{6}$$

with W_I denoting the nominal wage and PV_I the price of value added.

Urban Formal Private Sector

Gross production in the private urban formal sector, X_P, is again given by the sum of value added, V_P, and intermediate consumption:

$$X_P = V_P + \sum_i a_{iP} X_P. \tag{7}$$

Value added is generated by combining both skilled and unskilled labor, as well as public and private physical capital, through a multi-level CES production structure. At the lowest level of factor combination, skilled labor, S_P, and private physical capital, K_P, are combined to form the composite input J_1, with a relatively low elasticity of substitution (as measured by $\sigma_{XP1} = 1/(1 + \rho_{X31})$) between them:

$$J_1(S_P, K_P) = \alpha_{XP1}[\beta_{XP1} S_P^{-\rho_{XP1}} + (1 - \beta_{XP1}) K_P^{-\rho_{XP1}}]^{-1/\rho_{XP1}}. \tag{8}$$

At the second level, this composite input is used together with unskilled labor, U_P, to form the composite input J_2:

$$J_2(J_1, U_P) = \alpha_{XP2}\{\beta_{XP2} J_1^{-\rho_{XP2}} + (1 - \beta_{XP2}) U_P^{-\rho_{XP2}}\}^{-1/\rho_{XP2}}. \tag{9}$$

In line with the evidence for middle-income developing countries (see Chapter 1), the elasticity of substitution between J_1 and unskilled labor, measured by $\sigma_{XP2} = 1/(1 + \rho_{XP2})$, is taken to be higher than the elasticity between S_P and K_P, that is

$$\sigma_{XP2} > \sigma_{XP1}.$$

The final layer combines J_2 and K_{INF} (the stock of government capital in infrastructure) as production inputs:[5]

$$V_P(J_2, K_{INF}) = \alpha_{XP}[\beta_{XP} J_2^{-\rho_{XP}} + (1 - \beta_{XP}) K_{INF}^{-\rho_{XP}}]^{-1/\rho_{XP}}. \tag{10}$$

As in the rural sector, firms in the private urban formal sector allocate their output to exports, E_P, or the domestic market, D_P, according to a CET function:

$$X_P = \alpha_{EDP}[\beta_{EDP} E_P^{\rho_{EDP}} + (1 - \beta_{EDP}) D_P^{\rho_{EDP}}]^{1/\rho_{EDP}}. \tag{11}$$

This specification also implies, as shown later, that the ratio E_P/D_P depends on relative prices.

---

[5] An alternative approach would be to follow Stokey (1996) and assume that physical capital (possibly defined as a composite of both public and private capital) and unskilled labor are substitutes, whereas both are complementary to skilled labor.

Public Production

Gross production of public services, X_G, is given by the sum of value added, V_G, and intermediate consumption:

$$X_G = V_G + \sum_i a_{iG} X_G. \tag{12}$$

Value added is generated by combining both categories of labor and public capital in infrastructure. Again, a two-level CES production structure is assumed. At the first level, skilled labor, S_G, and public capital in infrastructure, K_{INF}, combine to produce a composite input, J_G, with a relatively low elasticity of substitution between them:

$$J_G(S_G, K_{INF}) = \alpha_{X_{GJ}} [\beta_{X_{GJ}} S_G^{-\rho_{X_{PJ}}} + (1 - \beta_{X_{GJ}}) K_{INF}^{-\rho_{X_{GJ}}}]^{-1/\rho_{X_{GJ}}}. \tag{13}$$

At the second level, J_G is combined with unskilled labor, U_G, to produce net output:

$$V_G(J_G, U_G) = \alpha_{X_G} [\beta_{X_G} J_G^{-\rho_{X_G}} + (1 - \beta_{X_G}) U_G^{-\rho_{X_G}}]^{-1/\rho_{X_G}}. \tag{14}$$

We assume that the elasticity of substitution between S_G and K_{INF}, $\sigma_{X_{GJ}} = 1/(1 + \rho_{X_{GJ}})$, is lower than the elasticity of substitution between the composite input J_G and U_G, $\sigma_{X_G} = 1/(1 + \rho_{X_G})$, in order to capture the fact that there is a greater degree of complementarity between physical capital and skilled labor (as in the private sector), and a greater substitutability between these two factors and unskilled labor:

$$\sigma_{X_G} > \sigma_{X_{GJ}}.$$

7.1.2 The Labor Market

As noted earlier, modeling the main features of the labor market in Turkey is one of the key objectives of our IMMPA framework. Accounting for labor regulations and government-induced sources of labor market segmentation are thus important. Turkey's labor laws are widely considered to be the strictest in the OECD in terms of employment protection; the country's severance pay requirements are higher than in any other country (except Portugal) and restrictions on the use of temporary workers are severe.[6] In principle, employment protection rules are meant to enhance job security by making dismissals costly to the employer. They should therefore help to stabilize employment levels, by reducing layoffs in downturns. But they also reduce hiring as the economy recovers. The evidence for Turkey (see Tunali (2003)) suggests that employment protection laws may have increased the insecurity faced by workers, as employers avoid paying severance altogether and hire short-term workers illegally, and may have shifted activity to the informal sector – with adverse effects on tax revenue.

Turkey has implemented a minimum wage law nationwide since 1974. The minimum wage has been adjusted twice a year since 1999 to inflation. During the period

---

[6] As demonstrated formally by Saint-Paul (2002), employment protection is more likely to arise in economies with greater worker bargaining power.

2000–1, it represented only about 25 percent of the average daily wage in manufacturing (see Tunali (2003)). The extent to which it is enforced, even in the urban formal sector, remains a matter of debate. However, as noted in Chapter 1, even if it is not "binding" *per se*, changes in the minimum wage may well play an important signaling role for wage setters in general, including trade unions. Similarly, it is widely believed that public sector wages have a strong signaling effect on wage setting in the private sector (see Tunali (2003)). Collective agreements between the government and the major trade unions – almost all civil servants and employees of state-owned enterprises are unionized – tend to shape bargaining positions of unions and workers in the formal private sector.[7]

In modeling the labor market we attempt to capture in a stylized way several of these features. Given that the model integrates an informal urban sector, we account for the fact that labor market regulations and other "distortions" in the formal economy may not be binding for a large segment of the labor market. Wages may therefore exhibit a high degree of flexibility. In light of the evidence suggesting that the power of trade unions has eroded significantly during the past two decades (see Onaran (2002)), we focus on the case where workers in the private formal sector (as in Chapter 3) negotiate wages directly with firms. We also assume that workers' reservation wage depends on wages in the public sector. We thus capture the "signaling" effect alluded to above.[8]

Rural Wages, Employment, and Migration

Unskilled workers in the economy may be employed either in the rural or urban sector, whereas skilled workers are employed only in the urban sector. We also assume that skilled workers who are unable to find a job in the formal sector do not opt to work in the informal economy, either because of a high perceived disutility of work there, or because they fear an adverse signaling effect on future employers (see Chapter 1).

Assuming profit maximization, and using the production function (2), the demand for labor in the rural sector is

$$
U_A^d = U_A^d \left(V_A, \frac{W_A}{PV_A} \right) = \left\{ (1 - \eta_{XA}) V_A^{1+\rho_{XA}/(1-\eta_{XA})} \frac{PV_A}{W_A} \cdot \frac{\beta_{XA}}{\alpha_{XA}^{\rho_{XA}}} \right\}^{1/(1+\rho_{XA})},
$$

$$(15)$$

where W_A denotes the nominal wage and PV_A the net output price in the rural sector.

---

[7]Tunali (2003) reports that the pair-wise correlation between average wages in the public sector and the private manufacturing sector was 0.46 in the first period and 0.78 in the second period. Granger causality tests or impulse response functions from simple VAR models (involving, for instance, the rates of growth of public and private sector wages, inflation, and the cyclical component of output) could provide some useful additional information.

[8]As noted earlier, severance payments have long been a major source of frictions between unions and employers in Turkey. We do not explicitly introduce firing costs given the focus of our simulations in this paper; but this could be done along the lines suggested in Chapters 3 and 4.

Wages in the rural sector adjust to clear the labor market. Let U^s_{RUR} denote labor supply in rural areas; the equilibrium condition is thus given by

$$U^s_{RUR} = U^d_A \left(V_A, \frac{W_A}{PV_A} \right). \qquad (16)$$

Over time, labor supply in the rural sector grows at an exogenous rate, g_{RUR}, net of worker migration to urban areas, MIG:

$$U^s_{RUR} = U_{RUR,-1}(1 + g_{RUR}) - MIG. \qquad (17)$$

In the tradition of Harris and Todaro (1970), we assume that the incentives to migrate depend negatively on the ratio of the average expected wage in the rural sector to that prevailing in the urban sector. Unskilled workers in the urban economy may be employed either in the private formal sector, in which case they are paid a wage W_{UP}, or they can enter the informal economy and receive the going wage in that sector, W_I.[9] Assuming that unskilled workers in the private formal sector pay a social security tax at the rate $sstax_U$, the expected unskilled urban wage, EW_{URB}, is thus a weighted average of $(1 - sstax_U)W_{UP}$ and W_I:

$$EW_{URB} = \theta_U(1 - sstax_U)W_{UP,-1} + (1 - \theta_U)W_{I,-1}, \qquad (18)$$

where θ_U is the probability of finding a job in the private urban formal sector, which is approximated by the proportion of unskilled workers actually employed in the private formal sector, U_P, relative to the total number of unskilled urban workers looking for a job, U^s_F, minus those employed in government, U_G. Assuming a one-period lag yields

$$\theta_U = \frac{U_{P,-1}}{U^s_{F,-1} - U_{G,-1}}. \qquad (19)$$

In the rural sector, the employment probability is equal to unity, because workers can always find a job at the going wage. Assuming a one-period lag, the expected rural wage is thus $W_{A,-1}$.

The migration function can therefore be specified as

$$MIG = U_{RUR,-1}\lambda_M \left\{ \sigma_M \ln \left(\frac{EW_{URB}}{W_{A,-1}} \right) \right\} + (1 - \lambda_M)\frac{U_{RUR,-1}}{U_{RUR,-2}}MIG_{-1}, \qquad (20)$$

where $0 < \lambda_M < 1$ measures the speed of adjustment and $\sigma_M > 0$ the elasticity of migration flows with respect to expected wages. This specification assumes that costs associated with migration or other frictions may delay the migration process, introducing persistence in migration flows. Of course, other factors can be relevant in explaining these flows in Turkey. It has been argued, for instance, that the dramatic reductions in government subsidies to farming that started in the mid-1990s have

---

[9]As noted later, there is no job turnover for either category of workers in the public sector; the employment probability in that sector is therefore zero. Public sector wages therefore do not affect the expected urban wage.

made agriculture and the rural sector less and less attractive, encouraging rural-to-urban migration (see Tunali (2003)).[10] This could be captured by defining subsidies as negative production taxes – which would raise value added prices (as discussed later) and affect rural wages, through the labor demand function (15) and the market equilibrium condition (16)).

The Urban Labor Market

In the urban sector, as noted earlier, both public and private production require skilled and unskilled labor, whereas production in the informal urban sector requires only unskilled labor. We consider, in turn, the determination of wages and employment for both categories of labor, and then the determination of wages through bargaining.

Public Employment and Wage Formation   Both skilled and unskilled employment in the public sector, U_G and S_G^T, respectively, are considered exogenous.[11] Wages of both categories or workers, W_{UG} and W_{SG}, are assumed to be fully indexed on the urban consumption price index, P_{URB}:

$$W_{jG} = \omega_{jG} P_{URB}, \quad j = U, S, \tag{21}$$

where ω_{jG} is an exogenous real base wage. To avoid a corner solution in which no worker wants to seek employment in the public sector, we assume that working for the government provides a nonpecuniary benefit (perhaps in terms of higher job security or reduced volatility of earnings) that is sufficiently large to ensure that the differential between W_{jG} and W_{jP}, with $j = U, S$, is positive.

Private Sector Wage Formation   To determine the skilled and unskilled wage rates in the private formal sector, we assume direct bargaining between workers and employers over the nominal wage, as in Chapters 1 and 3.

Consider first the case of skilled workers. If a bargain is reached, each worker receives W_{SP}, whereas the producer receives $PJ_1 m_S - W_{SP}^E$, where W_{SP}^E is the effective cost of labor, defined as

$$W_{SP}^E = (1 + IL)(1 + paytax_S)W_{SP},$$

where IL is the bank lending rate on domestic-currency loans, $paytax_S$ the payroll tax rate on skilled labor, and $m_S = \partial J_1(S_P, K_P)/\partial S_P$ the physical marginal product of the worker, given by (from equation (8)):

$$m_S = \left(\frac{\beta_{Xp1}}{\alpha_{Xp1}^{\rho_{Xp1}}}\right)\left(\frac{J_1}{S_P}\right)^{1+\rho_{Xp1}}. \tag{22}$$

---

[10]Further reductions in subsidies to farming in agriculture may therefore continue to induce migration. Although this issue is beyond the scope of this chapter, it has important implications for the design of fiscal adjustment.

[11]A good theory of what determines the share of public employment in Turkey (as in many other developing countries) would involve considerations that are well beyond the scope of this study. See Chapter 1 for a brief discussion.

The Nash bargaining problem can be formulated as

$$\max_{W_{SP}}(W_{SP} - \Omega_S)^{\nu_S}(PJ_1 m_S - W^E_{SP})^{1-\nu_S}, \quad 0 < \nu_S < 1,$$

where Ω_S is the worker's reservation wage and $PJ_1 m_S - W^E_{SP}$ the firm's bargaining surplus. ν_S measures the bargaining strength of a skilled worker relative to the firm. The first-order condition is given by

$$\nu_S \left(\frac{PJ_1 m_S - W^E_{SP}}{W_{SP} - \Omega_S}\right)^{1-\nu_S} - \frac{(1 - \nu_S)(1 + IL)}{(1 + paytax_S)^{-1}} \left(\frac{PJ_1 m_S - W^E_{SP}}{W_{SP} - \Omega_S}\right)^{-\nu_S} = 0,$$

that is,

$$\nu_S \frac{PJ_1 m_S - W^E_{SP}}{W_{SP} - \Omega_S} - (1 - \nu_S)(1 + IL)(1 + paytax_S) = 0.$$

From this equation, and given the definition of W^E_{SP}, the (equilibrium) negotiated wage can be derived as

$$W_{SP} = (1 - \nu_S)\Omega_S + \frac{\nu_S PJ_1 m_S}{(1 + IL)(1 + paytax_S)}, \qquad (23)$$

which shows that the product wage is a weighted average of the reservation wage, Ω_S, and the marginal product of labor adjusted for the cost of borrowing and payroll taxes. An increase in the cost of borrowing, or in the payroll tax rate, lowers the equilibrium wage.

We also assume that the worker's reservation wage, Ω_S, is related positively to wages in the public sector, W_{SG}, and the expected level of prices in the urban sector, (measured by the quantity $P_{URB,-1}(1 + EINFL)$, where $EINFL$ is the expected inflation rate), and negatively to the skilled unemployment rate, $UNEMP_S$.[12] Wage-setting in the public sector is thus assumed to play a signaling role to wage setters in the rest of the economy, as discussed earlier. Given the exogeneity of public sector employment (which therefore cannot represent a job opportunity for those seeking employment), this signaling role may be the result of "fairness" considerations, rather than the perception of broader employment options.

The introduction of expected prices in the urban sector measures the extent to which the worker's reservation wage is driven by the desire to maintain its real purchasing power. To the extent that expectations of inflation display persistence (as a result of low credibility, itself resulting perhaps from a higher risk of default on public debt, as discussed later), real wage inertia may result. Finally, when unemployment is high, the probability of finding a job (at any given wage) is low. Consequently, the higher the unemployment rate, the greater the incentive for the worker to moderate his or

---

[12] Note that the reservation wage could be made a function of the unemployment benefit rate as well. However, an unemployment insurance scheme was introduced in Turkey only in August 1999; premium collections started in June 2000 and the first payments were made in March 2002. There is no evidence so far that these benefits have had a large impact on wage formation.

her wage demands. Thus

$$\Omega_S = \Omega_{S0} \frac{W_{SG}^{\phi_S^1}[P_{URB,-1}(1 + EINFL)]^{\phi_S^2}}{UNEMP_S^{\phi_S^3}}, \tag{24}$$

where $\Omega_{S0} > 0$ and the ϕ_S^k coefficients, with $k = 1, 2, 3$, are all positive. Equations (23) and (24) indicate that lower unemployment, higher public sector wages, and higher expected inflation raise the level of skilled wages in the private sector. The link between the levels of unemployment and private sector wages is consistent with the "wage curve" predicted by the various efficiency wage models discussed in Chapter 1, and has received some support in the empirical literature on labor markets in Turkey (see Ilkkaracan and Selim (2002)). This specification differs significantly from Phillips-curve type of wage equations, in which unemployment affects the *rate of growth* of nominal wages.

To the extent that the expected inflation rate depends on past inflation (as documented in various studies on Turkey, such as Agénor (2002b), Agénor and Bayraktar (2003), and Lim and Papi (1997)), our specification may generate some significant degree of real wage rigidity. And depending on the structure of the coefficients ϕ_S^k, a variety of alternative specifications of the behavior of skilled and unskilled wages can be obtained. For instance, to impose the assumption that the target wage for skilled workers is fully indexed on expected inflation and does not depend on any other variable would require setting $\phi_S^1 = \phi_S^3 = 0$ and $\phi_S^2 = 1$.

To determine unskilled wages in the private formal sector, we also assume that workers are engaged in individual bargaining with firms. Following the same reasoning as above, the wage-setting equation is thus

$$W_{UP} = (1 - v_U)\Omega_U + \frac{v_U P J_2 m_U}{(1 + IL)(1 + paytax_U)}, \tag{25}$$

where $paytax_U$ is the payroll tax rate on unskilled labor, $0 < v_U < 1$ measures the bargaining strength of unskilled workers and, from equation (9),

$$m_U = \left(\frac{\beta_{XP2}}{\alpha_{XP2}^{\rho_{XP2}}}\right)\left(\frac{J_2}{U_P}\right)^{1+\rho_{XP2}}. \tag{26}$$

The reservation wage is now given by

$$\Omega_U = \Omega_{U0} \frac{W_{UG}^{\phi_U^1}[P_{URB,-1}(1 + EINFL)]^{\phi_U^2} W_M^{\phi_U^4}}{UNEMP_U^{\phi_U^3}}. \tag{27}$$

Equation (27) has the same structure as (24), with $UNEMP_U$ denoting the unskilled open unemployment rate, except for an additional term in W_M, the legally-set unskilled minimum wage. This specification aims to capture the signaling role that changes in the minimum wage may have on wage-setting in the private sector. Thus, the minimum wage is implicitly assumed to be nonbinding; it could be made so by setting $\phi_U^k = 0$, for $k = 1, 2, 3$ $\phi_U^4 = \Omega_{U0} = 1$, and $v_U = 0$.

Private Sector Employment, Labor Supply, and Skills Formation   The demand for unskilled labor by firms in the formal private sector is determined by firms' profit maximization subject to the wage set through bargaining with workers, W_{UP}, as determined above. These firms have access only to bank credit to finance their working capital needs. Specifically, they borrow to finance their wage bill (inclusive of payroll taxes) prior to the sale of output. Moreover, we assume that banks can borrow only in domestic currency to finance working capital needs, unlike borrowing for capital accumulation, which (as discussed later) can be done in either domestic or foreign currency. As a result, the effective price of labor includes the bank lending rate on domestic-currency loans, IL.

We assume also that firms pay a payroll tax, at the rate $0 < paytax_U < 1$ for unskilled workers, which is proportional to the wage bill, $W_{UP}U_P$.[13] The demand for unskilled labor by (and actual unskilled employment in) the private formal sector is thus given by

$$U_P^d = J_2 \left\{ \frac{PJ_2}{(1 + IL)(1 + paytax_U)W_{UP}} \left(\frac{\beta_{X_P2}}{\alpha_{X_P2}^{\rho_{X_P2}}} \right) \right\}^{\sigma_{X_P2}}. \qquad (28)$$

As in previous chapters, mobility of the unskilled labor force between the formal and informal sectors is imperfect. Implicit in this assumption is the idea that the labor market in Turkey is characterized by the absence (or poor functioning) of institutions capable of processing and providing in a timely manner relevant information on job opportunities to potential applicants – particularly those with low levels of qualifications. As a result, low-skilled workers employed in the informal sector are unable to engage in on-the-job search. Looking for a job in the formal sector for that category of workers requires, literally, being physically present at the doors of potential employers.

Formally, migration flows between the formal and informal sectors are assumed to be determined (as for rural–urban migration) by expected income opportunities. Following a similar reasoning as before, the supply of unskilled workers in the formal sector thus evolves over time according to

$$\frac{\Delta U_F^s}{U_{I,-1}} = \beta_F \left[\sigma_F \ln \left\{ \frac{U_{P,-1}^d}{U_{F,-1}^s - U_{G,-1}} \frac{(1 - sstax_U)W_{UP,-1}}{W_{I,-1}} \right\} \right] + (1 - \beta_F) \frac{\Delta U_{F,-1}^s}{U_{I,-2}}, \qquad (29)$$

where $\beta_F > 0$ denotes the speed of adjustment and $U_{P,-1}^d / (U_{F,-1}^s - U_{G,-1})$ measures the probability of being hired in the private sector, approximated by the ratio of employed workers to those seeking employment (with a one-period lag). Note that expected income in the private formal sector is measured net of social security taxes, as in (18).

---

[13] In Turkey, payroll taxes are paid both by employees (in the form of social security contributions) and employers; see Tunali (2003). We capture employee contributions in our definition of "take home" pay.

The unskilled unemployment rate in the formal sector, $UNEMP_U$, is thus given by

$$UNEMP_U = 1 - \frac{(U_G + U_P^d)}{U_F^s}. \tag{30}$$

The supply of labor in the informal economy, U_I^s, is obtained by subtracting from the urban unskilled labor force, U_U, the quantity U_F^s:

$$U_I^s = U_{URB}^s - U_F^s. \tag{31}$$

The informal labor market clears continuously, so that $U_I^d = U_I^s$. From equations (6) and (31), the equilibrium wage is thus given by[14]

$$W_I = \beta_{XI} \left(\frac{PV_I \cdot V_I}{U_{URB}^s - U_F^s} \right). \tag{32}$$

The urban unskilled labor supply, U_{URB}^s, increases as a result of exogenous growth (at the rate g_{URB}), and rural-to-urban migration, net of "outflows" due to skills acquisition, SKL:

$$U_{URB}^s = (1 + g_{URB})U_{URB,-1}^s + MIG - SKL - IMIG. \tag{33}$$

As noted earlier, private urban firms pay a payroll tax, at the rate $0 < paytax_S < 1$, on their skilled wage bill, $W_S S_P$. From (8), the demand for skilled labor in the private formal sector is therefore given by

$$S_P^d = J_1 \left\{ \frac{PJ_1}{(1 + IL)(1 + paytax_S)W_{SP}} \left(\frac{\beta_{Xp1}}{\alpha_{Xp1}^{\rho_{Xp1}}} \right) \right\}^{\sigma_{Xp1}}. \tag{34}$$

As noted earlier, skilled workers who are unable to find a job in the formal economy opt to remain openly unemployed, instead of entering the informal economy. The skilled unemployment rate, $UNEMP_S$, is thus given by the ratio of skilled workers who are not employed either by the private or the public sector, divided by the total population of skilled workers:

$$UNEMP_S = 1 - \frac{(S_G^T + S_P^d)}{S}, \tag{35}$$

where S_G^T is total skilled employment in the public sector, defined as

$$S_G^T = S_G + S_G^E, \tag{36}$$

with S_G^E denoting the number of skilled workers involved in providing public education.

---

[14]To ensure that unskilled urban workers will always seek employment in the private formal sector first, we assume throughout that $W_I < W_{UP}$.

The acquisition of skills by unskilled workers takes place through an education system operated (free of charge) by the public sector.[15] Specifically, the flow of unskilled workers who become skilled, SKL, is taken to be a CES function of the number of skilled workers (teachers) in the public sector engaged in providing education, and the government stock of capital in education, K_{EDU}:

$$SKL = [\beta_E S_G^{E-\rho_E} + (1 - \beta_E)K_{EDU}^{-\rho_E}]^{-1/\rho_E}. \tag{37}$$

The evolution of the skilled labor force depends on the rate at which unskilled workers acquire skills:

$$S = (1 - \delta_S)S_{-1} + SKL, \tag{38}$$

where $0 < \delta_S < 1$ is the rate of "depreciation" of the skilled labor force.

International Labor Migration

In line with the evidence on international migration flows in Turkey, we assume that migrants are essentially unskilled workers, and that all potential migrants are in the urban sector (as captured in (33)). Moreover, international migration flows are taken to be determined (as in Chapter 4) by the expected urban wage for unskilled labor, EW_{URB}, given by (18), relative to the foreign wage measured in domestic-currency terms, EW_F. Assuming a one-period lag, we have

$$EW_F = ER_{-1} \cdot W_{F,-1},$$

with W_F denoting the foreign wage measured in foreign-currency terms, which is assumed exogenous. Adopting a specification similar to (20), the migration function is specified as

$$IMIG = U_{URB,-1}\lambda_{IM} \left\{ \sigma_{IM} \ln \left(\frac{ER_{-1}W_{F,-1}}{EW_{URB}} \right) \right\} + (1 - \lambda_{IM})\frac{U_{URB,-1}}{U_{URB,-2}}IMIG_{-1}, \tag{39}$$

where $0 < \lambda_{IM} < 1$ measures the speed of adjustment, and $\sigma_{IM} > 0$ the partial elasticity of migration flows with respect to expected wages. Because the employment probability affects the expected domestic wage, the prevailing unskilled unemployment rate in the formal urban sector affects indirectly the decision to migrate. Again, costs associated with migration (such as relocation costs, as discussed in pevious chapters) are assumed to introduce some degree of persistence. As discussed later, remittances associated with international migration flows of unskilled labor are assumed to benefit unskilled households in the urban formal and informal sectors.

---

[15] Note that we abstract from the cost of acquiring skills (as measured for instance by the number of years of schooling multiplied by the average cost of education per year), which should also affect the propensity to invest in human capital. We also do not account from privately-provided education. During the 1980s and 1990s, several new private universities were founded in Turkey. However, they still account for only a small fraction of the graduates produced by the higher education system as a whole.

7.1.3   Export Supply and Import Demand

Given the CET functions (3) and (11), the efficient allocation of production between domestic sales and exports in the rural and private urban formal sectors yields export supply equations that depend on the price of exports (PE_A and PE_P, respectively) vis-à-vis domestic prices (PD_A and PD_P, respectively):

$$E_i = D_i \left\{ \left(\frac{1 - \beta_{EDi}}{\beta_{EDi}} \right) \frac{PE_i}{PD_i} \right\}^{\sigma_{EDi}}, \quad i = A, P. \tag{40}$$

Imports in both of these sectors compete with domestic goods. In the Armington tradition, both categories of goods are combined through CES aggregation functions to give composite goods, Q_i^s:

$$Q_i^s = \alpha_{Qi} \{ \beta_{Qi} D_i^{-\rho_{Qi}} + (1 - \beta_{Qi}) M_i^{-\rho_{Qi}} \}^{-1/\rho_{Qi}}, \quad i = A, P. \tag{41}$$

Assuming cost minimization, import demand for both sectors, M_A and M_P, can be written solely as a function of relative prices:

$$M_i = D_i \left\{ \left(\frac{\beta_{Qi}}{1 - \beta_{Qi}} \right) \frac{PD_i}{PM_i} \right\}^{\sigma_{Qi}}, \quad i = A, P, \tag{42}$$

where PM_i is the domestic price of imports (inclusive of tariffs) and $\sigma_{Qi} = 1/(1+\rho_{Qi})$ the elasticity of substitution between domestic and imported goods.

7.1.4   Aggregate Supply and Demand

As noted earlier (see equation (41)), supply of rural and private urban formal sector goods consists of composite goods, which combine imports and domestically produced goods. Both the informal and public sector goods are nontraded; total supply in each sector is thus equal to gross production, that is

$$Q_i^s = X_i, \quad i = I, G. \tag{43}$$

Aggregate demand in the rural and informal sectors, Q_A^d and Q_I^d, consists of intermediate consumption and demand for final consumption – by both the government and households for the former, C_A and G_A, and by households only in the latter, C_I (the government does not spend on informal sector goods). Aggregate demand for the public and private goods, Q_G^d and Q_P^d, consists not only of intermediate consumption and final consumption, but also of investment demand by private firms in the urban formal sector, Z_P^G and Z_P^P, and the government, Z_G:

$$Q_A^d = C_A + G_A + INT_A, \tag{44}$$

$$Q_I^d = C_I + INT_I, \tag{45}$$

$$Q_G^d = C_G + G_G + Z_P^G + INT_G, \tag{46}$$

$$Q_P^d = C_P + G_P + Z_P^P + Z_G + INT_P, \tag{47}$$

where INT_j is defined as total demand (by all i productions sectors) for intermediate consumption of good j:

$$INT_j = \sum_i a_{ji} X_i. \tag{48}$$

Total real government consumption of goods and services, G, is allocated in fixed proportions to the rural, private formal, and public goods:

$$G_i = gg_i \frac{PG \cdot G}{PC_i}, \quad i = A, P, G, \tag{49}$$

where PG is the government consumption deflator, and PC_i the sales price of good i, and $\sum_i gg_i = 1$.

Private final consumption for each production sector i, C_i, is the summation across all categories of households of nominal consumption of good i, deflated by the sales price of good i:

$$C_i = \sum_h C_{ih} = \sum_h x_{ih} + \frac{\sum_h cc_{ih}(CON_h - \sum_i PC_i x_{ih})}{PC_i}, \tag{50}$$

where C_{ih} is consumption of good i by household h, x_{ih} is the autonomous level of consumption of good i by household h, and CON_h total nominal consumption expenditure by household h. Equations (50) are based on the linear expenditure system. Coefficients cc_{ih} indicate how total consumption expenditure by household h is allocated to each type of good. They satisfy the usual restrictions, $0 < cc_{ih} < 1$, $\forall i, h$, as well as $\sum_i cc_{ih} = 1$, $\forall h$.

Private investment by urban formal sector firms, Z_P, is allocated between purchases of both public services and private goods (Z_P^G and Z_P^P, respectively):

$$Z_P^i = zz_i \frac{PK \cdot Z_P}{PC_i}, \quad zz_G + zz_P = 1, \tag{51}$$

where PK is the price of capital goods.

7.1.5 Profits and Income

Firms' profits in the rural and urban informal sectors are given by

$$PROF_i = PV_i V_i - W_i U_i, \quad i = A, I. \tag{52}$$

In addition to wages paid to both categories of workers, firms in the private formal urban sector are subject to payroll taxes and pay interest on the loans that they receive for working capital needs. Their profits are thus

$$PROF_P = PV_P V_P - (1 + IL)[(1 + paytax_U) W_M U_P + (1 + paytax_S) W_S S_P]. \tag{53}$$

Firms in the formal urban economy also pay income taxes and interest on their domestic and foreign borrowing, which serves to finance investment. Their income therefore differs from profits, and is given by

$$YF_P = (1 - ftax_P)PROF_P - IL \cdot DL_{P,-1} - ILF \cdot DLF_{P,-1} - IF^W ER \cdot FL_{P,-1},$$
(54)

where $ftax_P$ is the corporate income tax rate, DL_P and DLF_P are investment-related domestic- and foreign-currency loans allocated by domestic banks, FL_P foreign borrowing for the purpose also of physical capital accumulation, ILF the interest rate charged on foreign-currency loans by domestic banks, and IF^W the interest rate on foreign loans.

Profits from public production are given by

$$PROF_G = PV_G V_G - (1 + paytax_U)W_{UG}U_G - (1 + paytax_S)W_{SG}S_G.$$
(55)

Commercial banks' profits, $PROF_B$, are defined as the difference between revenues from loans to firms (be it for working capital or investment needs, in domestic and foreign currencies) and formal sector households, DL_F, income from government bonds (perpetuities, whose nominal price is assumed fixed at unity), and interest payments on borrowing from the central bank plus interest payments on both households' deposits (denominated in domestic and foreign currencies) and foreign loans:

$$
\begin{aligned}
PROF_B = {} & IL \cdot (DL_{P,-1} + DL_{F,-1}) + ILF \cdot DLF_{P,-1} \\
& + IL \cdot [(1 + paytax_U)W_M U_P + (1 + paytax_S)W_S S_P] \\
& + IB \cdot GB_{B,-1}^T, -IR \cdot DL_{B,-1} - ID \sum_h DD_{h,-1} \\
& - IDF \cdot ER \sum_h FD_{h,-1} - IF^W ER \cdot FL_{B,-1},
\end{aligned}
$$
(56)

where IR (respectively ID) is the interest rate on central bank financing (respectively domestic-currency denominated bank deposits), IB the nominal rate of return on government bonds, IDF the domestic interest rate on foreign-currency deposits held in the domestic banking system by each category of household h, FD_h, GB_B^T total government bond holdings by commercial banks, DL_B (respectively FL_B) borrowing from the central bank (respectively abroad), and DD_h domestic-currency deposits by household h.

In contrast to the IMMPA applications developed in previous chapters, there are only four categories of households in the present framework. *Rural households*, identified with the sub-index A, consist of all workers employed in the rural sector. *Informal sector households*, identified with the sub-index I, consist of all the (unskilled) workers employed in the informal economy. *Formal sector households*, identified with the sub-index F, consist of all workers (skilled and unskilled) employed in the formal sector, both public and private. For all three groups, income is based on the return to labor (salaries), distributed profits, government transfers, remittances from abroad, and interest receipts on holdings of financial assets (net of borrowing from domestic banks). The fourth group consists of *profit earners*, identified with the sub-index E, whose income comes from firms' net earnings in the rural and formal private sectors, profits of commercial banks, interest on deposits, and government transfers.

Profits from rural production are assumed to be distributed in proportion $0 < shp_A < 1$ to rural households and $1 - shp_A$ to (urban) profit earners. Using (52), income of rural households is given by

$$YH_A = W_A U_A + shp_A PROF_A + \gamma_A TRH + ID \cdot DD_{A,-1}, \qquad (57)$$

where $0 < \gamma_h < 1$ is the portion of total government transfers (TRH) each household h receives, so that $\sum_h \gamma_h = 1$, and DD_h domestic-currency deposits in domestic banks by households h. Rural households, as well as informal sector households, are assumed not to hold foreign-currency deposits, either domestically or abroad.

To capture the fact that firms in the informal urban sector tend to be small, family-owned enterprises, we assume that households in that sector own the firms in which they are employed. Using again (52), income of the informal sector household is given by

$$YH_I = PV_I V_I + \gamma_I TRH + ID \cdot DD_{I,-1} + \tau_I ER \cdot REMIT, \qquad (58)$$

where $REMIT$ measures the foreign-currency value of the flow of remittances from (unskilled) workers employed abroad, and $0 < \tau_I < 1$ the fraction of these remittances that are allocated to households in the informal economy.

Income of the formal sector household consists of net salaries (that is, take-home pay) collected from private firms and the government, income from formal sector firms, transfers from the government, remittances from abroad, and interest receipts on deposits (in domestic and foreign currency, held both domestically and abroad), net of interest payments on borrowing from commercial banks:

$$YH_F = (1 - sstax_U) \sum_{j=P,G} W_{Uj} U_j + (1 - sstax_S) \sum_{j=P,G} W_{Sj} S_j + shp_P^F YF_P$$

$$+ W_{SG} S_G^E + \gamma_F TRH + ID \cdot DD_{F,-1} + ER(IDF \cdot FD_{F,-1} + IF_{RF}^W FD_{F,-1}^W)$$

$$- IL \cdot DL_{F,-1} + (1 - \tau_I) ER \cdot REMIT, \qquad (59)$$

where $0 < shp_P^F \leq 1$ is the share of private formal sector firms' net income distributed to households in that sector, FD_F foreign-currency deposits held domestically, IF_{RF}^W the risk-free foreign interest rate on foreign-currency deposits held abroad by household h, FD_h^W, and DL_F domestic borrowing from commercial banks. $sstax_U$ and $sstax_S$ are the social security taxes (assumed proportional to the wage) that workers employed in the private formal sector must pay.

Profit earners receive a fraction $0 < shp_P^E \leq 1 - shp_P^F$ of private formal sector firms' retained earnings, as well as a share $1 - shp_A$ of profits from the rural sector, a share $0 < shp_B^E < 1$ of commercial banks' income, $PROF_B$, and interest on bank deposits (held both domestically and abroad). Thus, profit earners' income is:

$$YH_E = (1 - shp_A) PROF_A + shp_P^E YF_P + shp_B^E PROF_B + \gamma_E TRH + ID \cdot DD_{E,-1}$$

$$+ ER(IDF \cdot FD_{E,-1} + IF_{RF}^W FD_{E,-1}^W) + IB \cdot GB_{E,-1}, \qquad (60)$$

where GB_{E} denotes government bond holdings by profit earners, who are the only category of households to hold such bonds. Note also that profit earners do not borrow directly from commercial banks or abroad.

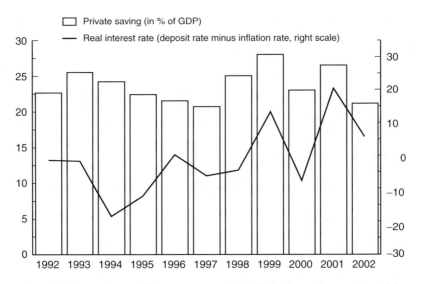

Figure 7.3 Turkey: saving and interest rates, 1992–2002. *Source*: International Monetary Fund.

7.1.6   Savings and Wealth Accumulation

Each category of household h saves a fraction, $0 < srate_h < 1$, of its disposable income:

$$SAV_h = srate_h(1 - inctax_h)YH_h, \tag{61}$$

where $0 < inctax_h < 1$ is the proportional income tax rate applicable to household category h.

The savings rate is a positive function of the expected real interest rate on domestic-currency deposits:

$$srate_h = s_0^h \left(\frac{1 + ID}{1 + EINFL} \right)^{\sigma_{SAV}^h}, \quad s_0^h > 0. \tag{62}$$

In principle, given the portfolio structure described later, the expected rate of return on other interest-bearing assets should also affect the propensity to save. However, as illustrated in Figure 7.3, the evidence for Turkey suggests that it is mostly the real interest rate on domestic-currency deposits that matters for private savings.[16] For simplicity, we therefore chose to exclude other rates of return from our specification.

The portion of disposable income that is not saved is allocated to consumption:

$$CON_h = (1 - inctax_h)YH_h - SAV_h. \tag{63}$$

The total flow of savings of each household category is channeled into the accumulation of financial wealth, WT_h, which also accounts for valuation effects on the stock

---

[16] See Ozcan, Gunay, and Ertac (2003).

of foreign-currency deposits held domestically and abroad, FD_h and FD_h^W, associated with changes in the nominal exchange rate:

$$WT_h = WT_{h,-1} + SAV_h + \Delta ER \cdot (FD_{h,-1} + FD_{h,-1}^W), \tag{64}$$

with $FD_h = FD_h^W = 0$ for $h = A, I$.

7.1.7 Private Investment

The determinants of private investment in Turkey have been the subject of a large literature, going back to Chibber and van Wijnbergen (1992), and including more recently studies by Guncavdi, Bleaney, and McKay (1998, 1999) and Erden (2002). Chibber and van Wijnbergen (1992), in a study over the period 1970–86, found that private investment in Turkey depends positively on the rate of capacity utilization (which captures aggregate demand pressures) and the ratio of private sector credit to GNP, and negatively on the real effective cost of borrowing and non-infrastructure public investment (which captures crowding out effects associated with public spending). Guncavdi, Bleaney, and McKay (1998) developed an error-correction model in which private investment depends in the long run on output and the relative cost of capital (as measured by the ratio of the cost of credit to the wage rate), but can be influenced in the short run by the availability of bank credit. Focusing on the period 1963–92, they found that, following the financial liberalization program implemented in the early 1980s, private investment in Turkey became less sensitive to bank credit and somewhat more sensitive to the cost of capital. By contrast, Erden (2002), in a study over the period 1968–98, found that both credit availability and uncertainty over the cost of credit (rather than its level) affect private investment, the first positively, and the second negatively.[17] In a study covering the period 1968–94, Guncavdi, Bleaney, and McKay (1999) found that financial liberalization (as measured by a dummy coefficient for the post-1980 period) appears to have had an adverse effect on investment by raising the relative cost of capital, and a positive effect by reducing credit constraints. They also find evidence of a strong accelerator effect (in both the short and the long run) and overall public investment appears to have a significant, negative effect on private capital formation.

The specification of the determinants of private investment in our model dwells on these results. As noted earlier, only firms in the private formal urban sector invest in physical capital; their desired rate of capital accumulation is assumed to depend on several factors. The first is the public capital stock in infrastructure (in proportion of the urban labor force), which has a positive impact, through its complementarity effect.[18] The second is the growth rate of real GDP, which captures the conventional accelerator effect. The third is the expected real cost of borrowing from domestic

---

[17]Neither one of these two studies accounts for the impact of public investment, as in Chibber and van Wijnbergen (1992). In addition, both studies use deposit rates to measure the cost of credit – a debatable assumption, as discussed subsequently.

[18]See Agénor and Montiel (1999) and Agénor (2004b, Chapter 2) for a detailed discussion of this effect and a review of the empirical evidence in general.

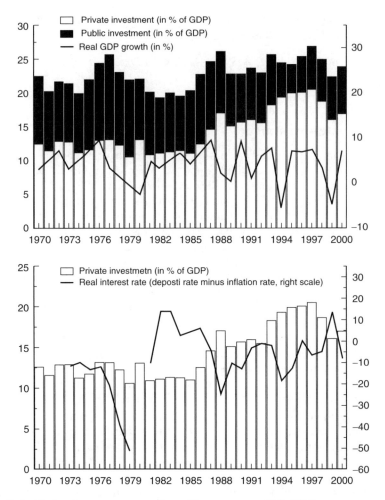

Figure 7.4   Turkey: investment, growth, and interest rates, 1970–2000.

banks, which has a negative effect. Figure 7.4 illustrates well the positive correlation between changes in private investment and real output growth (the accelerator effect), as well as the tendency for private capital formation to evolve in opposite direction to movements in real interest rates.[19]

We do not account explicitly for the quantity of credit, in addition to its cost, in our specification of the investment function, for two reasons. First, the evidence provided by Guncavdi, Bleaney, and McKay (1999), as well as others, suggests that the impact

---

[19]In Figure 3 the deposit rate is used instead of the lending rate, because we do not have sufficiently long time series on the latter variable. This is far from being a good proxy for the cost of credit, for reasons that we discuss later on.

of credit constraints on investment is less significant nowadays than was the case in the early 1980s, following financial reforms; at the same time, the (expected) cost of credit appears to have become a more important consideration for firms.[20] Second, even in the context of the recent crisis, there is no strong evidence that the fall in credit to private sector firms (at least the bigger ones) resulted from a credit crunch, that is, a supply-induced contraction in lending; on the contrary, a recent study by the World Bank (2003) suggests that demand-side factors (high interest rates, low economic activity) were largely to blame. In fact, as discussed later, we assume that the supply of bank loans to private sector firms is perfectly elastic at the prevailing interest rate, and that only formal sector households are subject to credit rationing.

Formally, the desired level of investment, Z_P^d, is given by

$$\frac{PK \cdot Z_P^d}{NGDP_{-1}} = \left(\frac{K_{INF}}{U_{URB}^s + S}\right)^{\sigma_{KI}} \left(1 + \frac{\Delta RGDP_{-1}}{RGDP_{-2}}\right)^{\sigma_{AC}} \left(\frac{1 + IL}{1 + EINFL}\right)^{-\sigma_{IL}}. \quad (65)$$

NGDP is nominal GDP at market prices, defined as the sum of value added and indirect taxes on goods and services (including tariff revenue):

$$NGDP = \sum_i PV_i V_i + INDTAX,$$

or equivalently, as the sum of expenditure and net exports:

$$NGDP = \sum_i PC_i(C_i + G_i + Z_P^i) + Z_G + ER(wpe_i E_i - wpm_i M_i). \quad (66)$$

Real GDP, *RGDP*, is defined as, using base-period prices:

$$RGDP = \sum_i PC_{i,0}(C_i + G_i + Z_P^i) + Z_G + ER_0(wpe_{i,0} E_i - wpm_{i,0} M_i), \quad (67)$$

where $Z_P^i = 0$ for $i = A, I$, $G_i = 0$ for $i = I$, and $E_i = 0$ for $i = I, G$.

Actual investment adjusts to its desired level through a partial adjustment mechanism:

$$\Delta\left(\frac{PK \cdot Z_P}{NGDP_{-1}}\right) = \lambda_{PINV}\left(\frac{PK \cdot Z_P^d}{NGDP_{-1}} - \frac{PK_{-1} \cdot Z_{P,-1}}{NGDP_{-2}}\right),$$

where $0 < \lambda_{PINV} < 1$.

The private capital stock depends on the flow level of investment and the depreciation rate of capital from the previous period, $0 < \delta_P < 1$:

$$K_P = K_{P,-1}(1 - \delta_P) + Z_{P-1}. \quad (68)$$

---

[20] It should be noted that Sancak (2002) did not find any evidence that financial liberalization led to a relaxation of the borrowing constraints faced by Turkish firms in the 1980s and 1990s. However, the methodology that he used to test for structural breaks is rather weak.

7.1.8   Asset Allocation and the Credit Market

We consider in turn the determination of the portfolio structure of each category of households, the demand for credit by firms, and the behavior of commercial banks. The balance sheets of all agents (including the central bank and the consolidated public sector) are summarized in Table 7.1.

Households

Households' financial wealth is allocated to five categories of assets: domestic money (cash holdings, which bear no interest), H_h, domestic currency-denominated bank deposits held at home, DD_h, foreign currency-denominated deposits held domestically, FD_h, foreign currency-denominated deposits held abroad, FD_h^W, and holdings of government bonds, GB_h.

By allowing households to hold foreign-currency denominated deposits in the domestic banking system, we therefore account for the high level of dollarized liabilities of the Turkish financial system. Indeed, as shown in Figure 7.1, such deposits continue to account for a sizable share of total bank deposits in Turkey.[21]

Given liabilities of DL_h, net financial wealth, WT_h, is defined as

$$WT_h = H_h + ER(FD_h + FD_h^W) + DD_h + GB_h - DL_h. \tag{69}$$

As noted earlier, rural and informal sector households hold no foreign-currency deposits, banks lend only to urban formal sector households (in addition to formal sector firms), and only profit earners hold government bonds. Thus, in the above equation, $FD_h = FD_h^W = 0$ for $h = A, I$, $DL_h = 0$ for $h \neq F$, and $GB_h = 0$ for $h \neq E$.

The demand function for currency by each household h is taken to be positively related to consumption of that group (to capture a transactions motive), CON_h, and negatively to expected inflation, $EINFL$, and the interest rate on domestic-currency deposits, ID. In addition, for formal sector households and profit earners, it also depends negatively on the rate of return on foreign-currency denominated assets, defined as a weighted average of the interest rates on foreign-currency deposits held at home and abroad, $1 + IDF$ and $1 + IF_{RF}^W$, with both rates adjusted for expected depreciation, $1 + EDEPR$:[22]

$$H_h^d = \frac{CON_h^{\theta_{CON}^h} EINFL^{-\theta_{EINFL}^h}(1 + ID)^{-\theta_{DD}^h}}{\{[(1 + IDF)(1 + EDEPR)]^{\kappa_{FD}^h}[(1 + IF_{RF}^W)(1 + EDEPR)]^{1-\kappa_{FD}^h}\}^{\theta_{IF}^h}},$$

---

[21] See Civcir (2002) for a discussion of dollarization in Turkey. Note that our specification of dollarization on the *asset* side of banks' balance sheets accounts only for foreign-currency denominated loans to firms, not households.

[22] Note that in equation (70), as well as in (74), (75), and (76), it is the *risk-free* world interest rate (which is the relevant measure of the rate of return for lenders) that appears.

Table 7.1 Turkey: Financial Balance Sheets (in domestic-currency terms, at current prices)

Households

Assets	Liabilities
Cash holdings (H)	Borrowing from Banks (DL_F)
Dom. bank dep. ($DD + ER \cdot FD$)	Net financial wealth (WT)
Foreign bank deposits ($ER \cdot FD^W$)	
Government bonds (GB_E)	

Firms

Assets	Liabilities
Private capital Stock ($PK \cdot K_P$)	Dom. borr. ($DL_P + ER \cdot DLF_P$)
	Foreign borrowing ($ER \cdot FL_P$)
	Net worth (NW_P)

Commercial Banks

Assets	Liabilities
Government bonds (GB_B^T)	Dom. bank dep. ($DD + ER \cdot FD$)
Loans to firms ($DL_P + ER \cdot DLF_P$)	Foreign borrowing ($ER \cdot FL_B$)
Loans to households (DL_F)	Borr. from central bank (DL^B)
Reserve requirements (RR)	Net worth (NW^B)

Central Bank

Assets	Liabilities
Loans to commercial banks (DL^B)	Cash in circulation (H)
Foreign reserves ($ER \cdot FF$)	Reserve requirements (RR)
Government bonds (GB_{CB})	Net worth (NW_{CB})

Government

Assets	Liabilities
Education Capital ($PK \cdot K_{EDU}$)	Government bonds (GB)
Infrastructure capital ($PK \cdot K_{INF}$)	Foreign borrowing ($ER \cdot FL_G$)
	Net worth (NW^G)

Consolidated Public Sector

Assets	Liabilities
Loans to commercial banks (DL^{BC})	Cash in circulation (H)
Foreign reserves ($ER \cdot FF$)	Reserve requirements (RR)
Education capital ($PK \cdot K_{EDU}$)	Government bonds (GB)
Infrastructure capital ($PK \cdot K_{INF}$)	Foreign borrowing ($ER \cdot FL_G$)
	Net worth (NW^{PS})

or equivalently

$$H_h^d = \frac{CON_h^{\theta_{CON}^b} EINFL^{-\theta_{EINFL}^b}(1+ID)^{-\theta_{DD}^b}}{\{(1+EDEPR)(1+IDF)^{\kappa_{FD}^b}(1+IF_{RF}^W)^{1-\kappa_{FD}^b}\}^{\theta_{IF}^b}}, \tag{70}$$

where $\theta_{IF}^b = 0$ for $b = A, I$. The coefficient κ_{FD}^b is the relative weight attached to the domestic interest rate on foreign-currency deposits held at home in the overall measure of the rate of return on foreign-currency denominated assets. It is calculated as the relative share of these deposits in the previous period:

$$\kappa_{FD}^b = \frac{FD_{b,-1}}{FD_{b,-1} + FD_{b,-1}^W}, \quad b = F, E. \tag{71}$$

The total demand for cash is thus

$$H^d = \sum_b H_b^d. \tag{72}$$

To determine the allocation of bank deposits, we must distinguish between rural and urban informal sector households, on the one hand, and formal sector households and profit earners, on the other. For the first group, which holds no foreign-currency deposits, no government bonds, and does not borrow from banks, the demand for domestic-currency deposits can be obtained from the wealth equation (69), given that (64) determines WT_b and (70) determines the demand for currency:

$$DD_b^d = WT_b - H_b^d, \quad b = A, I. \tag{73}$$

For formal sector households and profit earners, we assume that portfolio choices follow a two-step process similar to the one described in Agénor and Khan (1996). First, households determine the allocation between domestic- and total foreign-currency denominated deposits (held either at home or abroad). Second, they decide how to allocate total foreign-currency denominated deposits between deposits in the domestic banking system and deposits abroad.

Formally, in the first stage formal sector households and profit earners determine the ratio $DD_b/ER(FD_b + FD_b^W)$ as a function of the interest rate on domestic-currency deposits, on the one hand, and the overall rate of return on foreign-currency denominated assets, defined again as a weighted average of the rates of return on foreign-currency deposits held at home and abroad:

$$\frac{DD_b}{ER(FD_b + FD_b^W)} = \left\{ \frac{(1 + ID)(1 + EDEPR)^{-1}}{(1 + IDF)^{\kappa_{FD}^b}(1 + IF_{RF}^W)^{1-\kappa_{FD}^b}} \right\}^{\theta_{DD}^b}, \tag{74}$$

where $b = F, E$ and κ_{FD}^b is as defined earlier.[23]

In the second stage, the allocation of foreign-currency denominated deposits between home and abroad is given by

$$\frac{FD_b}{FD_b^W} = \left(\frac{1 + IDF}{1 + IF_{RF}^W} \right)^{\theta_{FD}^b}, \quad b = F, E, \tag{75}$$

which does not depend on exchange rate expectations.

---

[23] For profit earners, both the demand for cash (equation (70)) and the relative demand for domestic-currency deposits (equation (74)) could also be specified as negatively related to the expected rate of return on government bonds.

The second-stage portfolio decision is generally non-trivial because households may not be indifferent as to the location of their deposits as a result, for instance, of high transactions costs associated with shifting funds across borders, or a perceived risk of confiscation – which could take for instance the form of a forced conversion of foreign-currency deposits held in domestic banks into assets denominated in domestic currency. If formal sector households and profit earners were indifferent as to the location of their foreign-currency deposits, FD_h and FD_h^W would be perfect substitutes. In that case $\theta_{FD}^h \to \infty$ and, in the absence of capital controls, the following interest rate parity condition would hold exactly:

$$1 + IDF = 1 + IF_{RF}^W.$$

This condition implies that the interest rate on foreign-currency denominated deposits at home cannot deviate from the world risk-free interest rate. In general, however, we will assume that foreign-currency deposits at home and abroad are imperfect substitutes, and that (as discussed later) IDF is set domestically by commercial banks.

The demand for government bonds by profit earners, GB_E^d, measured as a proportion of interest-bearing wealth, depends on rates of returns on all interest-bearing assets:

$$\frac{GB_E^d}{WT_E - H_E} = \frac{(1 + EIB)^{\theta_{GB}^E}(1 + ID)^{-\theta_{DD}^E}}{[(1 + EDEPR)(1 + IDF)^{\kappa_{FD}^E}(1 + IF_{RF}^W)^{1-\kappa_{FD}^E}]^{\theta_{FD}^E}}, \qquad (76)$$

where κ_{FD}^E is defined in (71) and EIB is the *expected* rate of return on government bonds.

Note that, given (64), (70), (74), (75), and (76), the budget constraint (69) can be used to determine residually the demand for one of the four interest-bearing assets by profit earners – for instance the demand for domestic-currency bank deposits, in a manner similar to equation (73) for rural and informal sector households:

$$DD_E = WT_E - H_E - ER(FD_E + FD_E^W) - GB_E.$$

Similarly, for formal sector households,

$$DD_F = WT_F - H_F - ER(FD_F + FD_F^W) + DL_F.$$

Firms

Domestic firms borrow both domestically (in domestic and foreign currencies) and abroad not only to finance their working capital needs, as discussed earlier, but also to finance their investment plans. Borrowing on world capital markets, FL_P, is treated as exogenous. Taking into account retained earnings, the investment financing constraint requires that

$$PK \cdot Z_P = (1 - shp_P^F - shp_P^E)YF_P + \Delta DL_P^T + ER \cdot \Delta FL_P, \qquad (77)$$

where DL_P^T represents firms' total domestic borrowing from commercial banks.

Equation (77) can be solved for DL_P^T, that is, total demand for bank loans:

$$DL_P^T = DL_{P,-1}^T + PK \cdot Z_P - (1 - shp_P^F - shp_P^E)YF_P - ER \cdot \Delta FL_P. \qquad (78)$$

Commercial Banks

The balance sheet of commercial banks shows, on the asset side, loans to formal sector households and private formal sector firms for investment purposes, $DL_F + DL_P^T$, holdings of government bonds, GB_B^T, and reserve requirements at the central bank, RR. On the liability side, it accounts for domestic- and foreign-currency deposits by the public, $\sum_h (DD_h + ER \cdot FD_h)$, borrowing from the central bank, DL_B, and foreign loans (measured in domestic-currency terms), $ER \cdot FL_B$. With NW_B denoting commercial banks' net worth, their balance sheet can be written as

$$DL_F + DL_P^T + GB_B^T + RR - NW_B = \sum_h (DD_h + ER \cdot FD_h) + DL_B + ER \cdot FL_B.$$

$$(79)$$

Reserve requirements are levied at the same proportional rate on both domestic- and foreign-currency denominated deposits:

$$RR = rreq \sum_h (DD_h + ER \cdot FD_h), \qquad (80)$$

where $0 < rreq < 1$ is the (effective) reserve requirement rate. For simplicity, banks are assumed to hold no excess liquid reserves.

Firms' total domestic borrowing from commercial banks is defined as

$$DL_P^T = DL_P + ER \cdot DLF_P,$$

which implies, using (78),

$$DL_P = DL_P^T - ER \cdot DLF_P. \qquad (81)$$

Foreign-currency loans to domestic firms are assumed to remain constant relative to banks' foreign-currency liabilities, which consist of foreign borrowing and foreign-currency deposits from households:

$$ER \cdot DLF_P = \phi_{DL}^P \left(ER \cdot FL_B + \sum_h ER \cdot FD_h \right), \quad \phi_{DL}^P > 0. \qquad (82)$$

As in Chapter 6, commercial banks' holdings of government bonds, GB_B^T, consist of two components:

$$GB_B^T = GB_B^p + GB_B^d, \qquad (83)$$

where GB_B^p is direct placement of bonds by the government and GB_B^d is additional (market-related) commercial banks' demand for bonds. Direct bond placement with commercial banks is given as a constant share of the total outstanding stock of government bonds, GB^s:[24]

$$GB_B^p = \phi_{GB}^{B,p} \cdot GB^s, \quad \phi_{GB}^{B,p} > 0. \tag{84}$$

The additional demand for government bonds by commercial banks (as a ratio of net wealth) is positively related to the interest rate on these bonds and negatively to their opportunity cost, that is, the lending rate:

$$\frac{GB_B^d}{NW_B} = \phi_{GB}^{B,d} \left(\frac{1 + EIB}{1 + IL} \right)^{\theta_{GB}^B}, \quad \phi_{GB}^{B,d} > 0, \tag{85}$$

where EIB is again the *expected* rate of return on government bonds. We assume that due to existing banking regulations, domestic banks cannot choose to allocate freely a fraction of their wealth to holdings of foreign bonds; as a result, we exclude the rate of return on foreign-currency assets from (85).

The demand for foreign loans by commercial banks depends on the cost of domestic funding from households and the central bank, in addition to the (premium-inclusive) cost of foreign borrowing. Given the arbitrage conditions described later (equations (89) and (91)), this demand function can be specified as a function only of the official interest rate, IR, and the world interest rate (inclusive of the external risk premium), IF^W, adjusted for expected depreciation:

$$\frac{ER \cdot FL_B}{NW_B} = \phi_{FL}^B \left\{ \frac{1 + IR}{(1 + IF^W)(1 + EDEPR)} \right\}^{\theta_{FL}^B}, \quad \phi_{FL}^B > 0. \tag{86}$$

This equation implies that if domestic and foreign borrowing are perfect substitutes (that is, $\theta_{FL}^B \to \infty$), then the central bank's refinancing rate cannot deviate from the premium-inclusive, and expectations-adjusted, world interest rate:

$$1 + IR = (1 + IF^W)(1 + EDEPR).$$

As indicated earlier, banks' net income is distributed in proportion shp_B^E to profit earners. Commercial banks' net worth therefore evolves over time according to

$$\Delta NW_B = (1 - shp_B^E)PROF_B - \Delta ER \left(\sum_h FD_{h,-1} + FL_{B,-1} - DL_{F,-1} \right), \tag{87}$$

where the first term on the right-hand side represents retained earnings by commercial banks and the second term represents capital losses (gains) associated with nominal exchange rate depreciations (appreciations).

Lending by commercial banks to formal sector households, DL_F, is assumed exogenous. This is consistent with the recent evidence suggesting that in Turkey households – and to some extent small businesses – appear to be significantly affected

---

[24]This placement rule can be thought of as accounting for the bonds held by public banks, which are not explicitly modeled.

by supply-side constraints on the credit market (see World Bank (2003)). By contrast, lending to firms is taken to be demand determined, as shown in equation (78). At the same time, banks have access to an infinitely elastic supply of loans by the central bank at the prevailing official interest rate. They therefore borrow whatever residual liquidity they need, given their domestic deposit base and foreign borrowing. DL_B is thus determined residually from the balance sheet constraint (79), that is, using (80):

$$DL_B = DL_F + DL_P^T + GB_B^T - (1 - rreq) \sum_h (DD_h + ER \cdot FD_h)$$

$$- ER \cdot FL_B - NW_B.$$

$$(88)$$

Interest Rates and Risk Premia

Banks set both deposit and lending interest rates. The deposit rate on domestic currency-denominated deposits, ID, is set equal to the cost of funds provided by the central bank, IR:

$$1 + ID = 1 + IR. \qquad (89)$$

This specification implies that banks are indifferent as to the source of their domestic-currency funds – or, equivalently, they view domestic-currency deposits and loans from the central bank as perfect substitutes (at the margin).[25] The evidence suggests indeed that, in recent years, the deposit rate, the money market rate (the rate at which banks borrow from each other) and the three-month repurchase rate (which can be viewed as the policy rate, IR) have shown an increasing degree of synchronization. We therefore view the "pricing" (or arbitrage) condition (89) as a reasonable approximation.

The interest rate on foreign-currency deposits at home is set on the basis of the (premium-inclusive) marginal cost of borrowing on world capital markets:

$$1 + IDF = 1 + IF^W. \qquad (90)$$

In turn, IF^W depends on the world risk-free interest rate, IF_{RF}^W, and an external risk premium, *EXTPR*:

$$1 + IF^W = (1 + IF_{RF}^W)(1 + EXTPR). \qquad (91)$$

Combining equations (75), (90), and (91) implies that the allocation of foreign-currency deposits between home and abroad by formal sector households and profit

---

[25] Alternatively, it could be assumed that there is imperfect substitution between borrowed reserves and deposits. The deposit rate could then be specified as a positive function of both the cost of borrowing from the central bank and variables such as the expected inflation rate.

earners depends only on the external risk premium:[26]

$$\frac{FD_h}{FD_h^W} = (1 + EXTPR)^{\theta_{FD}^h}, \quad h = F, E.$$

The external risk premium consists of two components: an exogenous element, denoted *CONTAG*, which captures idiosyncratic changes in "sentiment" on world capital markets (including contagion effects, as discussed in Agénor (2005*j*)), and an endogenous component, which captures the perceived degree of country risk and depends on the ratio of the economy's total foreign debt to exports:

$$EXTPR = CONTAG + \frac{\kappa_{ERP}}{2} \left(\frac{\sum_{i=P,B,G} FL_i}{\sum_{i=A,P} wpe_i E_i} \right)^2, \tag{92}$$

where $\kappa_{ERP} > 0$ and the quadratic form is used to capture the idea that the external risk premium is a convex function of the debt-to-export ratio.[27]

The interest rate on domestic-currency loans, *IL*, is set as a premium over the marginal cost of funds. Given the arbitrage conditions (89) and (90), this cost is simply a weighted average of the cost of borrowing from the central bank, *IR* (or, equivalently, the deposit rate), and borrowing on world capital markets, IF^W. Taking into account as well the (implicit) cost of holding reserve requirements, the lending rate is thus determined by

$$1 + IL = \frac{\{(1 + IR)^{\kappa_{DL}^B}[(1 + IF^W)(1 + EDEPR)]^{1-\kappa_{DL}^B}\}}{(1 + DOMPR)^{-1}(1 - rreq)}, \tag{93}$$

where $0 < \kappa_{DL}^B < 1$ denotes the relative share of domestic-currency borrowing by banks in the previous period,

$$\kappa_{DL}^B = \frac{\sum_h DD_{h,-1} + DL_{B,-1}}{\sum_h DD_{h,-1} + DL_{B,-1} + ER_{-1}(\sum_h FD_{h,-1} + FL_{B,-1})},$$

and *DOMPR* is the domestic risk premium, which is inversely related to the ratio of firms' assets over their liabilities:

$$DOMPR = \left[\frac{\delta_c PK_{-1} K_{P-1}}{DL_{P,-1} + ER_{-1}(DLF_{P,-1} + FL_{P,-1})} \right]^{-\kappa_{DRP}}, \tag{94}$$

where $\kappa_{DRP} > 0$ and $0 < \delta_c \leq 1$.

---

[26] Note the importance of distinguishing between the premium-inclusive world interest rate faced by domestic borrowers, IF^W, on the basis of which banks set the interest rate on foreign-currency deposits held domestically, and the risk-free rate faced by lenders, IF_{RF}^W, which affects the demand for deposits held abroad by households. In the absence of a risk premium, both rates would be equal and, given the pricing condition (90), equation (75) would imply that the ratio FD_h/FD_h^W is constant over time.

[27] In line with the results of Fiess (2003) for several middle-income Latin American countries, the country risk premium could also be made a function of the domestic public debt to GDP ratio. This would provide an additional channel through which fiscal consolidation may affect the economy.

As discussed in Chapters 5 and 6, the risk premium charged by banks reflects the perceived risk of default on their loans to domestic firms. The link between the premium and firms' net worth has been much emphasized in the recent literature on real-financial sector linkages. Bernanke, Gertler, and Gilchrist (2000), and Gertler, Gilchrist, and Natalucci (2003), in particular, emphasized the impact of collateralizable wealth on bank pricing decisions.[28] The higher the value of firms' physical assets (which measures "pledgeable" collateral), $PK \cdot K_P$, or an "effective" fraction δ_c of that amount, relative to both domestic and foreign financial liabilities, $DL_P + ER \cdot (DLF_P + FL_P)$, the higher the proportion of total lending that banks can recoup in the event of default. This reduces the risk premium and the cost of borrowing.

This specification has important implications for understanding the interactions between the real and financial sides in the model. A large nominal exchange rate depreciation (that is, a rise in ER), would reduce firms' net worth, thereby raising the cost of capital and leading to a contraction of private investment. In turn, this would exert contractionary pressures. The extent to which output contracts would depend, in a general equilibrium setting, on the elasticity of the demand for loans. In the model, the demand for loans is residually determined to finance investment expenditures (see equation (78)), whose desired level depends on both the growth rate of output and the real lending rate (see equation (65)). The direct effect of a rise in the lending rate resulting from lower net worth would reduce desired investment and the demand for domestic loans, thereby offsetting at least to some extent the impact of a currency depreciation on firms' financial liabilities (which operates through $ER \cdot (DLF_P + FL_P)$), by reducing DL_P and DLF_P.

In addition, if households are net creditors in foreign currency (as is the case here), the depreciation could have a positive effect on private spending (through its impact on disposable income), thereby stimulating output. In general, therefore, the extent to which a currency depreciation is contractionary through its effect on the risk premium depends not only on the elasticity of the premium with respect to net worth but also the sensitivity of investment to the lending rate and the magnitude of wealth effects on consumption.

Changes in the risk premium may explain why, in practice, spreads between the loan and deposit rates may fluctuate significantly over time.[29] In fact, there is some evidence suggesting that the bank lending spread tends to follow a counter-cyclical

---

[28] Collateralizable wealth (or the net present value of firms' profits) could also act as a quantity constraint on bank borrowing, as for instance in the models of Krishnamurthy (2003), which extends the analysis of Kiyotaki and Moore (1997) and Xie and Yuen (2003). In both settings, shocks to credit-constrained firms are amplified through changes in collateral values and transmitted to output. See, however, Cordoba and Ripoll (2004) for a dissenting view on the ability of collateral constraints to generate output amplification.

[29] Other factors that affect the behavior of lending-deposit spreads include, of course, operating costs (which we abstract from), taxation, changes in banks' degree of risk aversion, and changes in market structure and the degree of competition. Indeed, in Turkey banks and borrowers are subject to a variety of taxes – the banking and insurance transaction tax, the foreign exchange transaction tax, and a tax levy on checks, among others. In addition, depositors must pay up to 20 percent in withholding tax on interest income. Spreads tend to be larger for loans in Turkish lira, as opposed to foreign currency. Nevertheless, we abstract from these other considerations.

pattern in Turkey. As noted in the previous chaper, this behavior is consistent with the view that, in downswings, the value of borrowers' collateral tends to fall – as a result of a fall in asset prices in general, and in our case more specifically a drop in the price of capital goods.[30] With the perceived risk of default increasing, and the value of "seizable" collateral falling, banks may charge a higher premium, as hypothesized in (94).

Banks are indifferent between lending in domestic or foreign currency. Thus, the interest rate on foreign-currency denominated loans, ILF, is determined from the arbitrage condition

$$(1 + ILF)(1 + EDEPR) = 1 + IL. \tag{95}$$

7.1.9 Public Sector

The public sector in our framework consists of the central bank and the government. We specify each agent's budget constraint (in stock and flow terms for the central bank) and account for transfers between them. We also discuss the determination of official interest rates, as well as the composition of public investment.

Central Bank

The balance sheet of the central bank consists of, on the asset side, loans to commercial banks, DL_B, foreign reserves, changes in which are taken as exogenous (possibly reflecting central bank intervention aimed at managing the exchange rate), and government bonds, GB_{CB}. Liabilities consist of the monetary base, MB. With NW_{CB} denoting the central bank's net worth, we have

$$DL_B + ER \cdot FF + GB_{CB} - NW_{CB} = MB. \tag{96}$$

The monetary base is the sum of currency in circulation, H^s, and required reserves, RR:

$$MB = H^s + RR. \tag{97}$$

Assuming no operating costs, net profits of the central bank, $PROF_{CB}$, are given by the sum of interest receipts on loans to commercial banks, and interest receipts on holdings of foreign assets and government bonds:

$$PROF_{CB} = IR \cdot DL_{B,-1} + IF_{RF}^W ER \cdot FF + IB \cdot GB_{CB,-1}. \tag{98}$$

A fraction shp_G of the central bank's profits are transferred to the government. Thus, the central bank's net worth evolves over time according to:

$$NW_{CB} = NW_{CB,-1} + (1 - shp_G)PROF_{CB} + \Delta ER \cdot FF_{-1}, \tag{99}$$

where the last term represents valuation effects. Thus, exchange rate changes that affect the domestic-currency value of the central bank's stock of foreign reserves do

---

[30]Note that the spread could also be made a direct function of the level of economic activity (or the output gap), as for instance in Atta-Mensah and Dib (2003).

not affect the monetary base; these capital gains and losses are instead absorbed via changes in the central bank's net worth. Taking first differences of (96) and using (99), the monetary base changes according to

$$\Delta MB = \Delta DL_B + ER \cdot \Delta FF + \Delta GB_{CB} - (1 - shp_G) PROF_{CB}, \qquad (100)$$

where the last term is zero if all central bank profits are transferred to the government $(shp_G = 1)$.

As noted earlier, the supply of liquidity to commercial banks by the central bank is taken to be perfectly elastic at the prevailing official interest rate, which is itself treated as predetermined. Alternatively, we could endogenize the official interest rate by specifying a monetary policy reaction function that would relate it to, say, the output gap, and deviations of inflation from a target value, as in Taylor-type rules (see Svensson (2003)). Experiments with feedback rules of this type would be particularly important for Turkey, given the expected move to a (flexible) inflation targeting framework in the near future.

Government Budget

The government primary balance, *PRBAL*, can be defined as

$$PRBAL = TXREV + PROF_G + shp_G PROF_{CB} - W_{SG} S_G^E - TRH - PG \cdot G - PC_P Z_G, \qquad (101)$$

where *TXREV* represents total tax revenues, $PROF_G$ profits by the government from sales of the public good (defined in (55)), $shp_G PROF_{CB}$ the share of central bank profits transferred to the government, $W_{SG} S_G^E$ salaries of teachers in public education, *TRH* government transfers to households, and *G* real government consumption of goods and services. Public investment, Z_G, is valued at the sales price of the composite private formal sector good, PC_P, because it is assumed to consist of expenditure on the private formal composite good only.

The overall fiscal balance, *OVBAL*, is defined as

$$OVBAL = PRBAL - IF_G^W \cdot ER \cdot FL_{G,-1} - IB \cdot GB_{-1}, \qquad (102)$$

where the last two terms account for interest payments on foreign loans (at an exogenous rate IF_G^W) and payments on government bonds held by commercial banks, the central bank, and profit earners – the stock of which is denoted GB:[31]

$$GB^s = GB_B^T + GB_{CB} + GB_E. \qquad (103)$$

Total tax revenues consist of direct taxes, *DIRTAX*, indirect taxes on goods and services, *INDTAX*, as well as payroll taxes on employers in the formal private sector and in public production, and social security contributions by employees in the

---

[31] Note that nonresidents are assumed not to hold domestic government bonds, in line with the evidence for Turkey, which suggests that such holdings are relatively small. This component – which would alter not only (103) but also the balance-of-payments equilibrium condition (108) – can be easily added.

private sector:[32]

$$TXREV = DIRTAX + INDTAX + sstax_U \sum_{j=P,G} W_{Uj} U_j$$

$$+ sstax_S \sum_{j=P,G} W_{Sj} S_j + \sum_{j=U,S} paytax_j (W_{jG} j_G + W_{jP} j_P).$$

Direct income taxes are levied on households (except those in the informal sector) and private formal sector firms:

$$DIRTAX = \sum_{h=A,F,E} inctax_h YH_h + ftax_P PROF_P.$$

Indirect taxes consist of revenue from import tariffs, taxes on gross production (at the rate $protax_i$), and taxes on domestic sales (at the rate $saltax_i$):

$$INDTAX = ER \sum_{i=A,P} wpm_i tm_i M_i + \sum_{i \neq I} protax_i PX_i X_i + \sum_{i=A,P} saltax_i PQ_i Q_i. \tag{104}$$

Public investment consists of investment in infrastructure (roads, power plants, hospitals, and so on), I_{INF}, and investment in education (school buildings, libraries, and so on, I_{EDU}, which are both considered given in real terms:

$$Z_G = I_{INF} + I_{EDU}. \tag{105}$$

Accumulation of each type of capital evolves according to

$$K_i = (1 - \delta_i)K_{i,-1} + I_{i,-1}, \quad i = INF, EDU, \tag{106}$$

where $0 < \delta_i < 1$ is a depreciation rate.

The closure rule of the model specifies a fixed growth path for government bond issuing and foreign borrowing. With no central bank financing, and exogenous foreign borrowing (in foreign-currency terms), the government budget deficit, $-OVBAL$, is therefore given from "below the line":

$$-OVBAL = ER \cdot \Delta FL_G + \Delta GB^s. \tag{107}$$

Given the path of the overall fiscal balance set by (107), equation (102) is solved for the primary balance, $PRBAL$, and (101) residually for the level of transfers to households, TRH.

7.1.10   The Balance of Payments and the Exchange Rate

Because foreign reserves are constant, the balance-of-payments constraint implies that any current account imbalance must be compensated by a net flow of foreign

---

[32] Although payroll taxes incurred in the production of public services appear in the definition of total tax revenues, they have no effect on the primary balance because (as shown in (55)) they are netted out of profits transferred to the government.

capital, given by the sum of changes in households' holdings of foreign-currency denominated deposits abroad, $\sum_h \Delta FD_h^W$, changes in foreign loans made to the government, ΔFL_G, and to private firms, ΔFL_P (both taken to be exogenous), changes in loans to domestic banks, ΔFL_B, minus the change in official reserves (also assumed to be exogenous), ΔFF, all measured in foreign-currency terms:

$$0 = \sum_{i=A,P} (wpe_i E_i - wpm_i M_i) + IF_{RF}^W \sum_{h=F,E} FD_{h,-1}^W + REMIT + IF_{RF}^W FF$$

$$- IF^W \sum_{h=P,B} FL_{j,-1} - IF_G^W FL_{G,-1} - \sum_{h=F,E} \Delta FD_h^W + \sum_{j=G,P,B} \Delta FL_j - \Delta FF,$$

(108)

where *REMIT* is the flow of remittances, defined as in Chapter 4 by

$$REMIT = \kappa_{REM} W_F FORL_{-1}, \quad 0 < \kappa_{REM} < 1,$$

with W_F denoting again the foreign wage (measured in foreign-currency terms), *FORL* the number of Turkish nationals working abroad, and κ_{REM} the share of wages being remitted. In turn, *FORL* is given by

$$FORL = (1 - \delta_{IMIG})FORL_{-1} + IMIG,$$ (109)

where $0 < \delta_{IMIG} < 1$ is the rate of "attrition" of the stock of migrants and *IMIG* is determined by equation (39). Equation (108) determines implicitly the equilibrium (nominal) exchange rate.

7.1.11   Currency and Bond Market Equilibrium

With equation (100) determining changes in the monetary base, *MB*, the supply of domestic currency can be derived from equation (97):

$$H^s = MB - RR.$$ (110)

Equality between the supply and demand for cash requires that, using (72):

$$H^s = H^d = \sum_h H_h^d.$$ (111)

The equilibrium condition of the market for government bonds, which can be solved for the expected interest rate *EIB*, is given as

$$GB = GB_E^d + GB_B^T + GB_{CB},$$ (112)

or, using (76), as well as (83), (84) and (85):

$$(1 - \phi_{GB}^{B,p})GB = NW_B \phi_{GB}^{B,d} \left(\frac{1 + EIB}{1 + IL} \right)^{\theta_{GB}^B} + GB_{CB}$$

$$+ \frac{(WT_E - H_E)(1 + EIB)^{\theta_{GB}^E}(1 + ID)^{-\theta_{DD}^E}}{[(1 + EDEPR)(1 + IDF)^{\kappa_{FD}^E}(1 + IF_{RF}^W)^{1-\kappa_{FD}^E}]^{\theta_{FD}^E}}.$$ (113)

This equation can be solved for the expected bond rate, *EIB*.

7.1.12 Price Determination

Value added prices, PV_i, are given by adjusting gross prices, PX_i, for production taxes and the cost of intermediate inputs:

$$PV_i = V_i^{-1} \left\{ PX_i(1 - protax_i) - \sum_j a_{ji} PC_j \right\} X_i, \qquad (114)$$

where $protax_I = 0$ because informal sector output is not taxed.

The world prices of imported and exported goods, wpe_i and wpm_i, are taken to be exogenously given. The domestic currency price of these goods is obtained by adjusting the world price by the nominal exchange rate, with import prices also adjusted by the tariff rate, tm:

$$PE_i = wpe_i ER, \quad i = A, P, \qquad (115)$$

$$PM_i = wpm_i(1 + tm_i)ER, \quad i = A, P. \qquad (116)$$

Gross output prices of the rural and urban private goods, PX_A and PX_P, are derived from the expenditure identity:

$$PX_i = \frac{PD_i D_i + PE_i E_i}{X_i}, \quad i = A, P. \qquad (117)$$

For the informal and public sectors (both of which do not export and produce a good that does not compete with imports), the price of gross output is equal to the domestic price, PD_i, only:

$$PX_i = PD_i, \quad i = I, G. \qquad (118)$$

For the rural sector and formal private urban production, the composite price is determined accordingly by the expenditure identity:[33]

$$PQ_i = \frac{PD_i D_i + PM_i M_i}{Q_i}, \quad i = A, P. \qquad (119)$$

Prices of the composite inputs J_1 and J_2 are derived in similar fashion, as a result of the linear homogeneity of the nested CES production functions imposed in the production of private formal urban goods:

$$PJ_1 = J_1^{-1}\{PROF_P + (1 + IL_{-1})(1 + paytax_S)W_{SP}S_P\}, \qquad (120)$$

$$PJ_2 = J_2^{-1}\{PJ_1 \cdot J_1 + (1 + IL_{-1})(1 + paytax_U)W_{UP}U_P\}, \qquad (121)$$

where $PROF_P$, as defined earlier, denotes profits of private firms in the urban formal sector.

---

[33] In principle, the cost functions derived from first-order conditions for the CET and CES aggregation functions (3), (11), and (41) could be used to determine PX and PQ prices in these two sectors. However, because CES and CET functions are linearly homogeneous, the cost functions can be replaced with the accounting identities shown in equations (117) and (119); the first-order conditions are incorporated in the export supply and import demand functions, (40) and (42).

The price of capital is defined as a geometric weighted average of the sales prices of the goods for which there is investment demand, namely, the public good and the private formal urban good (see equation (51)):

$$PK = \prod_{i=G,P} PC_i^{zz_i},$$ (122)

where $PC_i = PD_i$ for $i = G$.

The price of government spending, PG, is defined in similar fashion (see equation (49)):

$$PG = \prod_{i=A,G,P} PC_i^{gg_i}.$$ (123)

Markets for informal goods and government services clear continuously; equilibrium conditions are thus given by

$$Q_I^s = Q_I^d, \quad Q_G^s = Q_G^d.$$

These conditions are used to determine PD_I and PD_G.

As in Karadag and Westaway (1999), the value added tax is modeled as an *ad valorem* tax on purchases of final goods.[34] Specifically, the sales price for the rural and formal private sector goods, PC_i, differs from the composite price as a result of a sales tax, levied at the rate $0 < saltax_i < 1$:

$$PC_i = (1 + saltax_i)PQ_i, \quad i = A, P.$$

The consumption price index for the rural and urban sectors are given by

$$P_{RUR} = \prod_i PC_i^{wr_i}, \quad P_{URB} = \prod_i PC_i^{wu_i},$$ (124)

where $0 < wr_i, wu_i < 1$ are the relative weights of good i in each index. These weights sum to unity ($\sum_i wr_i = \sum_i wu_i = 1$) and are fixed according to the share of each of these goods in rural and urban consumption in the base period. Finally, the aggregate price level, CPI, is defined as a weighted average of rural and urban prices:

$$CPI = P_{RUR}^{wcp} \cdot P_{URB}^{1-wcp},$$ (125)

where $0 < wcp < 1$ is the relative share of spending by rural households in total consumption. The inflation rate is simply

$$INFL = \Delta CPI / CPI_{-1}.$$ (126)

---

[34]Indeed, in Turkish fiscal accounts, what is referred to as the "value added tax" is actually an *ad valorem* sales tax. We therefore chose to model it as applying to composite good prices, instead of value added prices.

7.1.13   Default Risk, Credibility, and Expectations

Our analysis of default risk dwells on the presumption that, faced with an unsustainable fiscal deficit, a government can either take fiscal measures to increase revenue, or be tempted to default at some point in the future – either through monetization or outright repudiation. In practice, governments are often tempted to resort to monetization as deficits and public debt rise because of constraints in the ability to adjust taxes; the increase in tax rates or in the tax base necessary to balance the budget may be large and politically unfeasible. The inflation tax may be an easier option, because it is the accumulation of debt that leads to a perverse increase in interest payments. In addition, there are no explicit costs associated with collecting the inflation tax, whereas with "conventional" taxes collection costs may be a convex function of the amount of revenue raised. In the Turkish case, however, we also view outright debt repudiation as a source of concern by asset holders. Expectations concerning the possibility of default will therefore affect their current behavior.

Specifically, we assume that the demand for government bonds is affected by the probability that the government will opt for (partial) default, in the form of either outright repudiation or monetization to finance its deficits. [35] Private investors assign a nonzero probability to default in the current period. The *expected* rate of return will reflect this probability, and they will demand compensation in the form of a higher nominal interest rate on government bonds. Thus, the expected rate of return on government bonds, *EIB*, can be defined as

$$EIB = (1 - PDEF)IB, \tag{127}$$

where *PDEF* is the subjective probability of default, which is supposed to depend (with a one-period lag) on the current debt-to-tax revenues ratio:[36]

$$PDEF = 1 - \exp\left[-\alpha_0 \left(\frac{GB_{-1}}{TAXREV_{-1}}\right)\right]. \tag{128}$$

This specification shows that, when debt is zero, the probability of default is also zero; by contrast, as the stock of debt (relative to tax revenues) increases without bounds, the perceived risk of default approaches unity. Put differently, the larger the stock of debt is in relation to the capacity to repay, the higher the perceived risk of default.[37]

---

[35] In principle, as noted by Masson (1985), changes in the perceived risk of default will also affect the marginal rate of substitution across periods, and thus saving. In the present setting, however, intertemporal considerations by households are not directly captured, and thus we ignore this effect.

[36] Note that using GDP as a scale variable instead of tax revenue in the probability of default would not be appropriate here, because neither agriculture nor the informal sector are subject to taxation. Thus, an increase in GDP resulting from higher output from either one of those sectors would not signal a greater capacity to repay.

[37] In principle, the government could meet its debt obligations by cutting spending (or selling assets) instead of raising taxes. Our view, however, is that (given the large share of spending allocated to wages and interest payments) most of the adjustment to cover obligations in case of default would have to come from higher tax revenues.

The view underlying our specification in (128) is that tax revenues are constrained by some upper bound, whereas the real value of the outstanding debt (and of the debt service) can be significantly reduced by a surprise increase in the rate of inflation.[38] The outcome of a postponement of action on the deficit would then eventually translate into a steadily increasing interest rate on government bonds, as a result of two factors. First, demand for these bonds depends on the expected rate of return, which is the product of the probability of repayment times the interest rate, as shown in equation (127). For a given probability of default, a continued increase in the supply of bonds will require an increase in interest rates, to induce investors to hold them. This can be seen by combining the solution to condition (113) and equation (127), to write the actual, equilibrium interest rate on government bonds as

$$IB = \frac{\Lambda(GB, ...)}{1 - PDEF}, \qquad (129)$$

where $\Lambda(\cdot)$ is a functional form that depends positively on GB and the dots represent the other determinants of the demand for government bonds by domestic banks and profit earners. An increase in the supply of bonds GB, fueled by an increase in the government deficit, would indeed raise the equilibrium bond rate, everything else equal.

Second, an increase in the stock of public debt will lead (with a one-period lag) to a rise in the perceived probability of default by investors, which will also tend to lead to higher interest rates on government bonds. As can be inferred from the previous equation, an increase in $PDEF$ would indeed raise the equilibrium bond rate. The rise in interest rates would in turn worsen the overall deficit of the government – making the adoption of corrective fiscal policies inevitable. Higher interest rates therefore make an unsustainable fiscal policy more unsustainable, hastening the need for policy reforms.

To model credibility, we assume that the expected rate of inflation (which affects directly the demand for domestic currency, private investment, saving rates, and wage formation in the private formal sector), is given as a weighted average of the perceived (or explicitly announced) inflation target of the central bank, $INFL^{TARG}$, and the one-period lagged inflation rate:

$$EINFL = CREDIB \cdot INFL^{TARG} + (1 - CREDIB)INFL_{-1}, \qquad (130)$$

where $INFL$ is defined in (126) and $0 < CREDIB < 1$ is our measure of credibility, defined as

$$CREDIB = 1 - PDEF. \qquad (131)$$

Credibility in our framework depends therefore only on fiscal policy; the stance or effectiveness of monetary policy (as measured, for instance, by deviations between actual and target inflation rates) plays no role.[39] Full credibility ($CREDIB = 1$) occurs

---

[38] See Spaventa (1987) for a detailed discussion of the view that governments typically face a limit to the tax burden that they can impose on their citizens – notably because of adverse effects on incentives and income distribution.

[39] In Ozatay (2000) and Civcir (2002), credibility is measured by the average maturity of new domestic non-indexed public debt issues. However, maturity is treated as an exogenous variable, instead of being

only if the probability of default *PDEF* is zero. An increase in the probability of default lowers credibility and leads agents to reduce the weight attached to the inflation target in forming expectations (thereby imparting greater persistence to inflation), because default is associated with a perceived increase in the risk of monetization and thus higher future inflation. In a sense, therefore, inflation expectations depend essentially on the fiscal stance – in line with the empirical results of Celasun, Gelos, and Prati (2004), based on survey data for Turkey. Although they do not provide a formal characterization of their argument, they note (p. 494) that "A credible fiscal consolidation is probably the key to reducing inflation, because inflation expectations will decline only if the public perceives that the need to monetize fiscal deficits or inflate away the debt stock has come to an end."[40]

The expected nominal depreciation rate, *EDEPR*, which affects portfolio decisions and the pricing rules of commercial banks, is defined as a weighted average of its past value and *expected* changes in the real exchange rate, measured as the difference between expected domestic inflation (given in (130)) and foreign inflation, *FINFL*, with a one-period lag:

$$EDEPR = \chi EDEPR_{-1} + (1 - \chi)(EINFL - FINFL_{-1}), \qquad (132)$$

where $0 < \chi < 1$. Thus, when domestic inflation is expected to exceed foreign inflation, that is, when the real exchange rate is expected to appreciate, agents will also expect the nominal exchange rate to depreciate, to prevent a loss in competitiveness.[41]

Note that in the model exogenous changes in the probability of default lead in general to an inverse correlation between credibility and the government bond rate. An increase in *PDEF*, for instance, raises directly the bond rate, as implied by (129). At the same time, it also reduces credibility, as implied by (131), thereby raising expected inflation, as can be inferred from (130), as long as $INFL_{-1} > INFL^{TARG}$. In turn, higher expected inflation raises the expected rate of depreciation of the nominal exchange rate, as implied by (132). From (76), and the equilibrium condition (113), the rise in *EDEPR* lowers the demand for government bonds by households. With a fixed supply of bonds, this requires an offsetting increase in *EIB*, that is, a rise in

---

(inversely) related to the debt-to-GDP ratio, as one would expect. For other ways of modeling credibility involving forward-looking expectations in stochastic models, see Laxton, Ricketts, and Rose (1994), Huh and Lansing (2000), Isard, Laxton, and Eliasson (2001), and Erceg and Levin (2003). For econometric studies, see Ruge-Murcia (1995) and Agénor and Taylor (1992).

[40]They also found that inflation expectations appear to be forward-looking, rather than backward-looking. However, this result is not consistent with those obtained by Agénor and Bayraktar (2002), who found that forward- and backward-looking components have similar weights in expectations.

[41]Alternatively, it could be assumed that expectations are rational (or, more precisely, model consistent), so that the expected depreciation rate is equal to the one-period ahead "actual" rate, as derived from the model itself. However, as noted in the previous chapter, this is a lot more involved from a computational standpoint (see Dixon et al. (2005)). Other options, as suggested to us by Peter Montiel, would be to make the expected future exchange rate a function of the current spot rate (with some elasticity parameter linking the two, with perhaps a "shift" term to capture exogenous changes in exchange rate expectations), or to make the expected future exchange rate proportional to the model's steady-state solution for the exchange rate, with the factor of proportionality representing the perceived rate at which the exchange rate converges to its steady-state value.

IB itself (as implied by (127)), which compounds the initial effect of the increase in *PDEF* on the actual bond rate.

7.2   Calibration and Solution

The Appendix to thic chapter provides a brief review of the structure of the financial SAM that underlies the model, our calibration procedure, and the parameter values (estimated and non-estimated) that we use in the behavioral equations. A more detailed description of the data and adjustment procedures used to construct the SAM is provided in Jensen and Yeldan (2004). Essentially, the calibration of the model was done by building a Financial Social Accounting Matrix (FSAM). The FSAM itself was built in two steps: *a*) construction of a MacroSAM; and *b*) disaggregation into a MicroSAM. The construction of the MacroSAM was split into a real MacroSAM and a financial MacroSAM. The link between the two types of MacroSAMs was made through the savings–investment balance account.

The solution of the model is performed with GAMS. When solving the model, the equilibrium condition (111) is dropped from the system as a result of Walras' law – if all other markets but the money market are in continuous equilibrium, then the money market must be in continuous equilibrium as well. That this is indeed the case is checked automatically when solving the model.

7.3   Policy Experiments

In this section, we report two sets of experiments. The first aims to analyze the real and financial effects of a disinflation program taking the form of a permanent increase in the official interest rate. The second set relates to fiscal adjustment and considers two scenarios: an increase in the VAT rate and an increase in the tax rate on income of profit earners. The public sector closure rule implies that transfers to households adjust to clear the public sector budget.[42] In both cases we focus on the impact of these policies on the sustainability of domestic public debt and the behavior of the labor market. We refer to effects occurring in the first two years as the "short run," those occurring between the third and fifth years as the "medium run," and those occurring between the seventh and the tenth year as the "long run."

As noted earlier, the growth path for domestic bond financing is exogenously specified in the baseline solution.[43] The bond market also includes a placement rule whereby the government places a predetermined fraction of the outstanding stock of

---

[42] Given this closure rule, the simulation results would be significantly affected if we were to assume that in the probability of default it is taxes net of transfers that matter, instead of taxes *per se*. However, doing so would implicitly amount to assuming that transfers would not be cut to redeem the debt in case of default.

[43] Note that, because GDP changes across experiments, the debt-to-GDP ratio will also change, despite the fact that the growth rate of the stock of public debt is constant.

bonds with commercial banks. The remaining share of outstanding bonds are allocated among commercial banks and profit earners according to their respective portfolio-balance equations. As can be inferred from (113) and (129), it is this secondary allocation of bond holdings that determines (together with the supply of bonds, the probability of default, and interest rates on alternative assets) the equilibrium bond rate. The two fiscal experiments are carried out using a nonneutral public sector closure. Thus, given that the overall balance is fixed by (107), the tax adjustment affects the size of the primary balance (as implied by (102)) and transfers to households (as inferred from (101)). In turn, transfers affect households' disposable income, private spending, and tax revenue. As a result of this closure rule, in each experiment deviations of the probability of default from its baseline value will reflect essentially changes in tax revenues, which are themselves closely correlated with activity in the formal sector (given that the rural and informal sectors are essentially untaxed).

7.3.1   Increase in Official Interest Rates

We first consider a permanent, 5 percentage point increase in the official interest rate, *IR*. Results are presented in Tables 7.2 and 7.3.

The inflation rate is reduced significantly in the short run by almost 3.8 percent, and remains below its baserun value until period 6. The medium-run maximum reduction in the price level (in both rural and urban areas) is around 9 percent while the long-run reduction is around 5.5 percent. The general reduction in the level of prices is the consequence of changes in factor costs and the relative demand and supply of goods and services. Indeed, the increase in the official rate raises the lending rate, which in turn exerts two types of direct effects: first, it leads to a reduction in formal sector wages through an increase in the cost of working capital; second, it leads to a strong decline in investment demand for formal sector goods.

The reduction in formal sector wages leads to a fall in real disposable income for the formal sector household. Because formal sector households have a relatively high consumption share of formal sector goods, the relative demand for formal sector goods tends to decline. In this way, the reduction in formal sector wages tends to be self-reinforcing. At the same time, the reduction in formal sector disposable income is exacerbated by the strong increase in the bond rate, despite a concomitant increase in deposit rate. The increase in the bond rate leads to higher interest payments by the government on its debt and (as a result of the public sector budget closure) a decline in transfers to households. The reduction in household transfers affects mostly the formal sector household and profit earners, because they are the main beneficiaries of public transfers. But the reduction in income is more pronounced for formal sector households, because they are affected adversely not only by the reduction in transfers, but also by the increase in the cost of borrowing.

Indeed, because formal sector households (which are the only ones borrowing from banks) are net debtors in the initial scenario, their net borrowing costs increase, despite the fact that the increase in the deposit rate (which matches the increase in the official rate) cushions the impact of the higher lending rate. Overall, real disposable income of formal sector households decline by around 12 percent in the medium run (see

Table 7.2 Turkey: simulation results. Permanent, 5-percentage point increase in the official interest rate. (Percentage deviations from baseline, unless otherwise indicated)

	Periods									
	1	2	3	4	5	6	7	8	9	10
Real Sector										
Total resources	-3.51	-6.06	-7.57	-8.67	-9.43	-9.56	-8.85	-7.58	-6.44	-5.94
Gross domestic product	-3.48	-5.85	-7.33	-8.47	-9.28	-9.42	-8.71	-7.45	-6.33	-5.88
Imports of goods and NFS	-3.61	-6.74	-8.41	-9.36	-9.95	-10.01	-9.31	-8.02	-6.76	-6.12
Total expenditure	-3.51	-6.06	-7.57	-8.67	-9.43	-9.56	-8.85	-7.58	-6.44	-5.94
Total consumption	-3.46	-5.25	-6.39	-7.40	-8.15	-8.24	-7.49	-6.29	-5.30	-4.99
Private consumption	-3.46	-5.24	-6.34	-7.32	-8.04	-8.12	-7.37	-6.18	-5.19	-4.87
Public consumption	-3.44	-5.35	-6.67	-7.87	-8.76	-8.91	-8.13	-6.85	-5.80	-5.50
Total investment	-4.08	-9.44	-12.06	-13.15	-13.68	-13.65	-12.73	-11.10	-9.51	-8.70
Private investment	-4.29	-10.89	-14.32	-15.61	-16.18	-16.17	-15.25	-13.52	-11.81	-10.99
Public investment	-3.46	-6.03	-7.57	-8.66	-9.37	-9.45	-8.68	-7.33	-6.08	-5.49
Exports of goods and NFS	-3.15	-5.64	-7.73	-9.27	-10.23	-10.50	-9.92	-8.64	-7.24	-6.35
External Sector (% of GDP)[1]										
Current account	0.15	0.35	0.24	0.09	-0.01	-0.07	-0.11	-0.11	-0.07	0.00
Exports of goods and NFS	0.10	0.06	-0.11	-0.22	-0.26	-0.29	-0.32	-0.32	-0.24	-0.13
Imports of goods and NFS	-0.04	-0.28	-0.34	-0.29	-0.22	-0.19	-0.20	-0.19	-0.14	-0.08
Labor Remittances	0.01	-0.01	-0.03	-0.03	-0.03	-0.03	-0.03	-0.02	0.00	0.02
Factor services	0.00	0.01	0.04	0.05	0.06	0.05	0.05	0.04	0.04	0.03
Capital account	-0.15	-0.35	-0.24	-0.09	0.01	0.07	0.11	0.11	0.07	0.03
Private borrowing	0.00	0.00	0.00	0.00	0.00	0.00	0.00	0.00	0.00	0.00
Commercial bank borrowing	-0.08	-0.09	-0.02	0.00	0.00	0.09	0.02	-0.03	-0.06	-0.07
Public borrowing	0.00	0.00	0.00	0.00	0.00	0.00	0.00	0.00	0.00	0.00
Household deposits abroad	0.08	0.26	0.22	0.17	0.10	0.01	-0.09	-0.14	-0.13	-0.06

Government Sector (% of GDP)[1]

Total revenue	0.35	0.23	0.27	0.37	0.42	0.36	0.24	0.15	0.14	0.21
Direct taxes	0.36	0.36	0.43	0.51	0.53	0.46	0.35	0.25	0.22	0.25
Indirect taxes	−0.01	−0.12	−0.16	−0.15	−0.12	−0.11	−0.11	−0.11	−0.08	−0.04
Total expenditure	0.70	0.99	1.40	1.82	2.07	2.02	1.71	1.35	1.14	1.14
Consumption	0.00	0.06	0.09	0.09	0.08	0.08	0.10	0.11	0.10	0.08
Investment	0.00	−0.01	−0.02	−0.02	−0.01	0.00	0.00	0.01	0.03	0.04
Transfers to households	−1.17	−2.32	−3.72	−4.81	−5.24	−4.97	−4.25	−3.44	−2.84	−2.56
Domestic interest payments	1.86	3.27	5.06	6.56	7.24	6.92	5.87	4.68	3.86	3.58
Foreign interest payments	0.00	0.00	−0.01	−0.01	−0.01	−0.01	−0.01	−0.01	0.00	0.01
Total financing	0.35	0.76	1.13	1.45	1.65	1.66	1.47	1.20	1.00	0.94
Foreign borrowing	0.00	0.00	0.00	0.00	0.00	0.00	0.00	0.00	0.00	0.00
Bond financing	0.35	0.76	1.13	1.45	1.65	1.66	1.47	1.20	1.00	0.94
Labor Market										
Nominal wages										
Rural sector	−3.45	−5.23	−6.52	−7.76	−8.72	−8.93	−8.24	−7.06	−6.10	−5.79
Informal sector	−3.37	−3.88	−4.78	−6.18	−7.39	−7.60	−6.69	−5.40	−4.78	−5.24
Private formal sector										
Unskilled	−3.55	−6.84	−8.57	−9.56	−10.12	−10.10	−9.25	−7.78	−6.39	−5.68
Skilled	−3.15	−6.40	−8.16	−9.14	−9.71	−9.79	−9.14	−7.82	−6.41	−5.54
Public sector										
Unskilled	−3.45	−5.62	−7.02	−8.17	−9.00	−9.12	−8.34	−7.03	−5.91	−5.50
Skilled	−3.45	−5.62	−7.02	−8.17	−9.00	−9.12	−8.34	−7.03	−5.91	−5.50
Employment										
Rural sector	0.00	0.00	0.04	0.10	0.16	0.22	0.26	0.30	0.33	0.35
Informal sector	0.00	0.00	−0.04	−0.11	−0.17	−0.22	−0.26	−0.28	−0.29	−0.29
Private formal sector										
Unskilled	0.05	−0.08	−0.36	−0.40	−0.34	−0.41	−0.59	−0.73	−0.68	−0.50
Skilled	−0.17	−0.25	−0.40	−0.49	−0.54	−0.58	−0.62	−0.66	−0.71	−0.78
Public sector										
Unskilled	0.00	0.00	0.00	0.00	0.00	0.00	0.00	0.00	0.00	0.00
Skilled	0.00	0.00	0.00	0.00	0.00	0.00	0.00	0.00	0.00	0.00

Table 7.2 Continued

					Periods					
	1	2	3	4	5	6	7	8	9	10
Labor supply (urban formal)										
Unskilled	0.00	0.00	−0.04	−0.11	−0.19	−0.26	−0.33	−0.39	−0.45	−0.49
Skilled	0.00	0.00	0.00	0.00	0.00	0.00	0.00	0.00	0.00	0.00
Unemployment rate[1]										
Unskilled	−0.04	0.06	0.24	0.20	0.10	0.08	0.15	0.19	0.12	−0.03
Skilled	0.09	0.13	0.19	0.22	0.23	0.23	0.23	0.24	0.24	0.24
Real wage ratios[1]										
Expected urban-rural	0.00	−0.13	−2.55	−3.02	−2.46	−1.81	−1.46	−1.28	−0.92	−0.31
Expected formal-informal	0.00	−0.47	−8.07	−9.16	−7.57	−5.83	−5.28	−5.63	−5.47	−3.80
Expected international-urban	0.00	0.52	1.97	1.71	0.84	0.20	−0.20	−0.45	−0.53	−0.35
Migration[1]										
Rural-urban (% of urban unskilled labor supply)	0.00	0.00	−0.03	−0.05	−0.05	−0.04	−0.03	−0.03	−0.02	−0.01
Formal-informal (% of urban formal unskilled labor supply)	0.00	0.00	−0.04	−0.07	−0.08	−0.07	−0.07	−0.06	−0.06	−0.04
International-Urban (% of urban unskilled labor supply)	0.00	0.00	0.01	0.02	0.02	0.01	0.01	0.00	0.00	0.00
Financial Sector										
Deposit rate	5.00	5.00	5.00	5.00	5.00	5.00	5.00	5.00	5.00	5.00
Deposit rate (Foreign Currency)	−0.02	−0.04	−0.04	−0.01	0.04	0.08	0.10	0.10	0.09	0.07
Lending rate	4.79	4.74	4.70	4.64	4.57	4.50	4.47	4.48	4.52	4.57
Lending rate (Foreign Currency)	4.18	4.28	4.34	4.33	4.25	4.12	3.95	3.76	3.61	3.54
Bond rate	6.17	7.65	9.48	10.71	11.07	10.60	9.47	8.06	6.88	6.29
Credibility	0.00	−0.81	−1.87	−2.67	−3.16	−3.41	−3.39	−3.07	−2.54	−2.07

Domestic premium	0.00	−0.02	−0.04	−0.06	−0.08	−0.09	−0.11	−0.11	−0.09	−0.08
External premium	−0.02	−0.04	−0.04	−0.01	0.03	0.07	0.10	0.10	0.09	0.07
Probability of default	0.00	0.81	1.87	2.67	3.16	3.41	3.39	3.07	2.54	2.07

Memorandum items

GDP at market prices[2]	−0.03	−0.07	−0.10	−0.12	−0.14	−0.17	−0.21	−0.24	−0.27	−0.29
Value added at factor cost[2]	−0.01	−0.02	−0.07	−0.10	−0.13	−0.15	−0.19	−0.22	−0.23	−0.24
Value added in rural sector[2]	0.00	0.00	0.02	0.05	0.08	0.11	0.13	0.15	0.17	0.18
Value added in urban informal sector[2]	0.00	0.00	−0.01	−0.02	−0.04	−0.05	−0.05	−0.06	−0.06	−0.06
Value added in urban formal sector[2]	−0.02	−0.06	−0.18	−0.28	−0.36	−0.45	−0.56	−0.66	−0.73	−0.78
Private Consumption[2]	−0.01	0.36	0.66	0.86	0.97	1.01	0.96	0.83	0.69	0.58
Private Investment[2]	−0.85	−4.78	−6.78	−7.16	−7.15	−7.11	−6.88	−6.41	−5.94	−5.82
Disposable income[2]	0.99	1.59	1.91	2.16	2.33	2.31	2.09	1.81	1.65	1.71
Nominal exchange rate[1]	−3.30	−5.98	−7.80	−9.04	−9.80	−9.91	−9.19	−7.81	−6.41	−5.59
real exchange rate[1]	0.22	0.33	0.02	−0.24	−0.36	−0.44	−0.49	−0.45	−0.31	−0.13
Inflation rate[1]	−3.78	−2.48	−1.76	−1.60	−1.25	−0.20	1.23	2.04	1.67	0.57
Ratio of debt to GDP	1.23	2.66	3.96	5.07	5.79	5.82	5.16	4.22	3.50	3.28
Ratio of tax revenues to government domestic debt[1]	−2.92	−4.21	−4.44	−4.54	−4.71	−4.86	−4.76	−4.32	−3.73	−3.35
Ratio of foreign currency deposits in total bank deposits[1]	−0.52	−0.57	−0.60	−0.59	−0.56	−0.50	−0.44	−0.38	−0.33	−0.32
Ratio of foreign currency loans in total bank loans[1]	−1.34	−1.36	−1.05	−0.23	0.79	1.54	1.71	1.39	0.93	0.59
Ratio of government primary surplus to GDP	1.50	2.51	3.93	5.11	5.59	5.26	4.40	3.48	2.86	2.64
Ratio of Interest payments to tax revenue	6.47	12.32	19.84	25.69	27.84	26.12	21.80	17.03	13.63	12.19

[1] Absolute deviations from baseline. [2] In real terms.

Table 7.3 Turkey: prices and structural indicators. Permanent, 5-percentage point increase in the official interest rate. (Percentage deviations from baseline, unless otherwise indicated)

					Periods					
	1	2	3	4	5	6	7	8	9	10
Consumer Prices and the Real Exchange Rate[1]										
Rural CPI	−3.44	−5.37	−6.68	−7.87	−8.77	−8.91	−8.14	−6.85	−5.81	−5.50
Urban CPI	−3.45	−5.62	−7.02	−8.17	−9.00	−9.12	−8.34	−7.03	−5.91	−5.50
Real exchange rate	0.22	0.33	0.02	−0.24	−0.36	−0.44	−0.49	−0.45	−0.31	−0.13
Value Added Prices[1]										
Rural	−3.45	−5.23	−6.50	−7.71	−8.63	−8.81	−8.10	−6.90	−5.92	−5.60
Urban private informal	−3.37	−3.89	−4.81	−6.26	−7.51	−7.76	−6.88	−5.61	−5.00	−5.46
Urban private formal	−3.50	−6.85	−8.71	−9.65	−10.11	−10.06	−9.27	−7.83	−6.35	−5.46
Urban public	−3.45	−5.62	−7.02	−8.17	−9.00	−9.12	−8.34	−7.03	−5.91	−5.50
Real Disposable Income[1]										
Rural households	0.31	0.70	1.40	1.91	2.12	2.07	1.88	1.65	1.47	1.40
Urban households	−0.12	0.29	0.46	0.54	0.62	0.69	0.70	0.61	0.45	0.30
Informal	0.35	1.70	2.16	1.97	1.61	1.45	1.50	1.45	1.04	0.35
Formal	−1.34	−3.95	−7.49	−10.66	−12.10	−11.50	−9.64	−7.57	−6.00	−5.17
Capitalists and rentiers	0.84	3.03	5.72	8.23	9.84	10.15	9.17	7.61	6.39	5.99
Real Private Consumption[1]										
Rural households	1.38	2.23	2.82	3.15	3.20	2.98	2.58	2.19	1.99	2.03
Urban households	0.84	1.47	1.73	1.93	2.07	2.08	1.90	1.64	1.44	1.40
Informal	0.73	2.20	2.63	2.39	1.99	1.79	1.79	1.70	1.29	0.62
Formal	−0.93	−3.38	−6.98	−10.23	−11.72	−11.18	−9.39	−7.39	−5.82	−4.95
Capitalists and rentiers	3.11	5.71	8.38	10.79	12.30	12.46	11.28	9.54	8.28	7.98

Production Structure

Size of informal sector (% of total output)	0.00	0.01	0.02	0.03	0.04	0.04	0.05	0.06	0.07	0.07
Size of rural sector (% of total output)	0.00	0.01	0.02	0.03	0.04	0.06	0.07	0.08	0.09	0.10

Composition of Employment

Employment in rural sector (% of total employment)	0.00	0.01	0.04	0.07	0.09	0.11	0.14	0.16	0.16	0.16
Employment in informal sector (% of total employment)	0.00	0.01	0.01	−0.01	−0.03	−0.04	−0.05	−0.05	−0.05	−0.06
Employment in informal sector (% of urban employment)	0.01	0.03	0.05	0.04	0.03	0.02	0.03	0.03	0.03	0.02
Employment in public sector (% of total employment)	0.00	0.00	0.00	0.00	0.00	0.00	0.00	0.00	0.00	0.00
Employment in public sector (% of urban employment)	0.00	0.00	0.00	0.00	0.00	0.00	0.01	0.01	0.01	0.01

Private Expenditures

Consumption (% of GDP)	0.01	0.45	0.76	0.90	0.98	1.02	1.02	0.95	0.82	0.71
Consumption (% of total consumption)	0.00	0.01	0.04	0.07	0.10	0.11	0.11	0.10	0.09	0.10
Investment (% of GDP)	−0.16	−0.84	−1.04	−1.03	−1.00	−1.00	−0.98	−0.92	−0.83	−0.76
Investment (% of total investment)	−0.16	−1.12	−1.71	−1.83	−1.83	−1.83	−1.78	−1.66	−1.52	−1.46

Public Expenditures

Consumption (% of GDP)	0.00	0.06	0.09	0.09	0.08	0.08	0.10	0.11	0.10	0.08
Investment (% of GDP)	0.00	−0.01	−0.02	−0.02	−0.01	0.00	0.00	0.01	0.03	0.04
Infrastructure (% of public investment)	0.00	0.00	0.00	0.00	0.00	0.00	0.00	0.00	0.00	0.00
Education (% of public investment)	0.00	0.00	0.00	0.00	0.00	0.00	0.00	0.00	0.00	0.00
Public sector wage bill (% of public expenditure)	0.70	1.69	3.52	5.62	6.65	6.10	4.79	3.61	2.86	2.56

External Sector

Rural sector exports (% of total exports)	0.00	−0.06	−0.07	−0.06	−0.04	−0.02	−0.01	0.01	0.04	0.08
Imports of nonrural sector goods (% of total imports)	−0.01	−0.06	−0.07	−0.06	−0.05	−0.05	−0.05	−0.05	−0.04	−0.03
External debt (% of GDP)	−0.13	−0.51	−0.76	−0.84	−0.83	−0.77	−0.67	−0.57	−0.49	−0.46
Degree of openness (total trade in % of GDP)	0.06	−0.22	−0.45	−0.50	−0.47	−0.48	−0.52	−0.50	−0.38	−0.21

[1] Percentage deviations from baseline.

Table 7.3, period 5) and 5 percent in the long run (see Table 7.3, period 10). In contrast, profit earners (who do not borrow directly from banks) benefit relatively strongly from increasing interest receipts on their deposits held with commercial banks and from government bond holdings. Real disposable income of this group of households increase by around 10 percent in the medium run and 6 percent in the long run (see, again, Table 7.3).

The bond rate increases strongly until period 5. Most of the upward pressure on the bond rate results from the fact that the increase in deposit rates tends to reduce the demand for bonds by profit earners; the net worth of commercial banks remain low through the medium run (making them therefore reluctant to increase bond holdings above direct placement holdings), and central bank holdings are exogenous.

Given that the supply of bonds does not change across experiments, the bond rate must increase to maintain market equilibrium and maintain bond holdings of profit earners around baserun levels.[44] The impact on the bond rate reaches a maximum of 11 percentage points in period 5, after which increases in the net worth of commercial banks start to kick in. The bond rate therefore increases less strongly after that period, by about 6 percentage points in the long run.

Banks' net worth is negatively affected by the increasing cost of central bank funding. However, it is positively affected by the increase in the bond and lending rates. The lending rate on domestic-currency loans increases by 4.8 percent in the short run and 4.5 percent in the medium run. This reflects the countering effects of *a*) the initial increase in the official rate of 5 percent; and *b*) the subsequent reductions in the expected rate of depreciation of the nominal exchange rate and a slight fall in the domestic premium. Declining expectations of nominal depreciation follow from a general decline in actual exchange rate depreciation. This affects the cost of funding through foreign-currency deposits and therefore lowers lending rates. The domestic premium also declines slightly due to the exchange rate appreciation, which lowers the domestic-currency value of firms' foreign liabilities and therefore increases the value of their net collateral–debt ratio.

The nominal exchange rate appreciates by around 10 percent in the medium run, and 6 percent in the long run. The growth path of the nominal exchange rate closely resembles the growth path of the domestic price level, and this is reflected in a relatively stable real exchange rate. Indeed, the real exchange rate depreciates by about 0.3 percent in the short run and appreciates by about 0.5 percent in the medium run, before settling down to a real appreciation of only 0.1 percent in the long run. Movements in the real exchange rate are mirrored in the trade balance and the current account, which improves in the short run but deteriorates slightly in the medium and long run.

As noted earlier, the increase in lending rates induced by the hike in official interest rates affects the real economy through two main channels: *a*) reduced investment demand; and *b*) increased costs of working capital. The first channel directly reduces demand for private formal sector investment goods. Combined with the reduction in

---

[44]This is so despite the fact that savings by profit earners tend to increase as a result of the rise in deposit rates – an increase that tends to raises total financial wealth over time (as implied by (64)) and thus to increase the demand for bonds (as implied by (76)).

formal sector disposable income and consumption, this leads to a sharp reduction in demand for private formal sector goods compared to other sectors of the economy. In addition, the medium and long run impact of lower investment (or more accurately, the reduction in the stock of private physical capital that it entails) is to lower production capacity and reduce the marginal product of other production factors (most notably skilled labor) in the private formal sector. Value added in the urban formal sector is therefore particularly affected and declines by 0.8 percent in the long run. The urban informal sector also experiences a small decline in value added of less than 0.1 percent in the long run, whereas value added in the rural sector expands by 0.2 percent. These developments are mainly due to relative price effects and the reduced outflow of workers from rural to urban areas. Overall, GDP declines by 0.3 percent in the long run.

The decline in real GDP is the outcome of the decline in private investment demand dominating the real increase in consumption. Over time, private investment declines strongly not only as a result of the increasing lending rate but also because of the negative accelerator effect emanating from the decline in GDP itself. In contrast, private consumption increases due to the income effect (alluded to above) of the increase in the deposit and bond rates, particularly on the disposable income of profit earners. Combined with a decline in relative formal sector prices, this leads to a sharp increase in real consumption of that category of households. The increase in overall real household consumption is moderated by the decline in disposable income and consumption by the formal sector household, for the reasons discussed earlier.

Wages in the labor market generally mirror changes in the overall price level. Fully indexed public sector wages move (downward) with the urban formal sector consumer price index. In addition, lower public sector wages (through their signaling effect), together with higher lending rates, higher (skilled) unemployment, and declining private sector investment, combine to lower relative wages in the formal private sector. The decline in formal sector wages spills over into declines in rural and informal sector wages as well. The former fall by more, implying that the expected wage differential between the formal and informal urban sectors drops by about 8 percentage points in the medium run (periods 4 and 5 in Table 7.2) and by about 4 percentage points in the long run, whereas the wage differential between the rural and urban sectors is narrowed by 3 percentage points in the medium run and 0.3 percentage point in the long run. Movements in these wage differentials lead to reduced migration of labor between sectors, and account for the increase in employment and value added in the rural sector, and the drop in both variables in the informal sector.

The external premium faced by domestic banks (as shown in (92)) fluctuates essentially with changes in exports. The initial exchange rate depreciation increases exports. The fall in the ratio of foreign debt (which does not change across simulations) to exports therefore lowers the external premium in the short run. The subsequent exchange rate appreciation and associated reduction in exports means, however, that the external premium increases in the long run. This leads to a higher interest rate on foreign-currency deposits held domestically (as implied by (90) and (91)), as well as higher rates on domestic- and foreign-currency loans by domestic banks (as implied by (91), (93), and (95)). In principle, the effect of interest rates on foreign-currency deposits and loans could be significant. For instance, the increase in interest rates on foreign-currency loans raises interest payments for firms in the private formal sector (which reduces income distributed to profit earners and thus dampens the increase in that group's consumption expenditure); at the same time, it raises banks' profits and thus income received by profit earners. However, because these effects tend to offset each other, and because the quantity of domestic loans denominated in foreign currency is relatively small, the net quantitative impact is not large.

The probability of government default increases due to the reduction in nominal tax revenues and the resulting increase in the debt-to-tax revenues ratio.[45] This increase in the default probability is matched by a similar decline in credibility, due to increased expectations of monetization or outright default. As a result, the bond rate tends to rise (compounding the demand effects discussed earlier) and expectations of inflation tend to increase. Over time, the rise in expected inflation tends to mitigate the positive impact of the increase in deposit rates on households' savings rates (see equation (62)). For private investment, by contrast, the rise in expected inflation tends to reduce the initial magnitude of the increase in the real lending rate, thereby dampening over time the adverse effect of a higher cost of borrowing on private capital formation.

Finally, it can be noticed that the government primary surplus-to-GDP ratio increases both in the short and the long run. The increase reaches a maximum of 5.6 percentage points over the reference path (Table 7.2, period 5), reflecting a sharp decline in government transfers to households. These transfers are squeezed due to the strong increase in the bond interest payments resulting from our assumption that bond financing is maintained at baserun levels, implying that (with exogenous foreign borrowing in foreign-currency terms) the government deficit is given from "below the line."

It is worth noting that the magnitude of the long-run decline in GDP would of course be smaller if, as a result of a Taylor-type rule, the authorities were to lower interest rates in response to lower inflation. It is also interesting to note that this experiment, a disinflation attempt based on a rise in official interest rates, leads to a rise in the probability of default (essentially because the increase in interest rates has a contractionary effect, which translates into lower tax revenues), and an initial real depreciation (see Table 7.3). These results are consistent with those derived by Blanchard (2004) in a very different setting, characterized by a direct link between the probability of default, capital flows, and movements in the exchange rate.

Nevertheless, our experiment carries a similar note of caution: in an inflation targeting framework (in which interest rates are used to achieve a specific level of inflation), an initial inflationary shock can have perverse effects. An increase in real interest rates to "choke off" inflationary pressures can lead to a real depreciation, and thus higher inflation, which may lead in turn to further increases in interest rates. In our experiment, fiscal policy is also an important potential tool to reduce inflation: by issuing less domestic debt and reducing the debt-to-tax ratio, the government would mitigate the increase in the probability of default, which would in turn dampen the rise in the bond rate. This would reduce pressure on cutting the primary deficit through

---

[45] Note that in Table 7.2 the ratio of total tax revenues to GDP increases throughout the simulation period. This is because, although both variables fall, the reduction in GDP exceeds that of tax revenues.

a reduction in transfers, thereby dampening the adverse effect on activity and tax revenues.

7.3.2 Fiscal Adjustment

As noted earlier, we discuss two types of fiscal adjustment policies: an increase in the VAT rate and a rise in the tax rate on income of profit earners.

Increase in the VAT Rate

We first consider fiscal adjustment in the form of a permanent, 2.5 percentage point increase in the value added tax, which (as noted earlier) applies solely to private formal sector goods. Results are presented in Tables 7.4 and 7.5.

The increase in the tax rate raises both the level and the growth rate of prices. Overall inflation rises by about 3.6 percent in the short and medium run (see Table 7.4, period 4). The inflationary impact becomes negative after period 6, before returning to slightly positive values in the long run. In level terms, prices (in both urban and rural areas) increase by about 15 percent above their baserun value in the long run. This general increase is driven by changes in relative demand and supply of goods and services. First, the tax hike leads directly to an increase in the price of the private formal sector good. This tends to lower demand for that good, lowering production and increasing unemployment (particularly among the unskilled) in the formal sector. At the same time, the increase in government revenues is transferred back to households, due to the public sector closure rule; this tends to stimulate consumption spending across all categories of goods and to put further upward pressure on prices.

Furthermore, the bond rate declines markedly, thereby lowering interest payments and borrowing needs by the government, and reinforcing the increase in demand through higher household transfers (which increase by about 3.4 percent of GDP in the long run). Reduced investment demand for formal sector goods pulls in the other direction. Investment is negatively affected by increasing lending rates and the "reverse" accelerator effect associated with a decline in the growth rate of GDP. However, improved credibility (through its effect on inflation expectations and the real lending rate, as discussed later) reduces the impact of this effect in the medium and long run.

The bond rate declines by less than 1 percentage point on impact and reaches a maximum reduction of 8 percentage points in the medium run (see Table 7.4, period 5). In the long run, it declines by about 6 percentage points. This decline results essentially from the increase in the *nominal* disposable income of profit earners. While these households experience a strong drop in *real* disposable income due to falling commercial bank profits (see Table 7.5), the impact of inflation on nominal income, and thus savings and wealth, is such that the nominal demand for bond holdings increases. With the supply of bonds exogenously fixed, the increase in demand tends to lower bond rates. The smaller long-run decline in the bond rate is due to movements in the net worth of commercial banks. Indeed, the declining bond rate exerts over time a self-correcting feedback effect through lower commercial banks' profits and net

Table 7.4 Turkey: simulation results. Permanent, 2.5-percentage point increase in the value added tax rate. (Percentage deviations from baseline, unless otherwise indicated)

	Periods									
	1	2	3	4	5	6	7	8	9	10
Real Sector										
Total resources	2.49	5.76	8.81	11.65	13.95	15.04	14.68	13.52	12.68	12.89
Gross domestic product	3.19	6.43	9.51	12.46	14.84	15.96	15.59	14.45	13.65	13.92
Imports of goods and NFS	0.25	3.49	6.40	8.90	10.93	11.94	11.63	10.47	9.53	9.58
Total expenditure	2.49	5.76	8.81	11.65	13.95	15.04	14.68	13.52	12.68	12.89
Total consumption	3.90	6.97	9.80	12.62	14.92	15.97	15.64	14.66	14.11	14.60
Private consumption	3.93	6.98	9.77	12.54	14.80	15.83	15.49	14.53	13.98	14.44
Public consumption	3.69	6.93	10.00	13.11	15.64	16.79	16.40	15.32	14.74	15.29
Total investment	0.74	4.97	8.63	11.53	13.77	14.79	14.14	12.42	11.00	10.90
Private investment	-0.11	4.33	8.19	11.06	13.24	14.18	13.30	11.18	9.31	8.86
Public investment	3.21	6.46	9.53	12.37	14.68	15.81	15.49	14.35	13.52	13.75
Exports of goods and NFS	0.35	2.93	5.83	8.52	10.77	12.03	11.88	10.73	9.59	9.33
External Sector (% of GDP)[1]										
Current account	-0.01	-0.19	-0.15	-0.06	0.03	0.10	0.16	0.16	0.12	0.04
Exports of goods and NFS	-0.80	-0.92	-0.88	-0.88	-0.87	-0.82	-0.78	-0.80	-0.90	-1.03
Imports of goods and NFS	-0.89	-0.83	-0.83	-0.92	-1.00	-1.03	-1.03	-1.06	-1.12	-1.19
Labor Remittances	-0.13	-0.14	-0.13	-0.14	-0.14	-0.14	-0.14	-0.15	-0.17	-0.21
Factor services	0.04	0.04	0.03	0.03	0.03	0.04	0.05	0.06	0.07	0.09
Capital account	0.01	0.19	0.15	0.06	-0.03	-0.10	-0.16	-0.16	-0.12	-0.04
Private borrowing	0.00	0.00	0.00	0.00	0.00	0.00	0.00	0.00	0.00	0.00
Commercial bank borrowing	0.00	0.02	-0.04	-0.10	-0.13	-0.11	-0.05	0.00	0.02	0.02
Public borrowing	-0.01	-0.01	-0.01	-0.01	-0.01	-0.01	-0.01	-0.01	-0.01	-0.02
Household deposits abroad	-0.01	-0.18	-0.20	-0.17	-0.12	-0.02	0.09	0.15	0.13	0.04

Government Sector (% of GDP)[1]

Total revenue	1.58	1.38	1.19	0.99	0.90	0.96	1.09	1.18	1.19	1.14
Direct taxes	−0.60	−0.71	−0.83	−0.97	−1.04	−1.00	−0.91	−0.84	−0.83	−0.86
Indirect taxes	2.18	2.09	2.02	1.96	1.94	1.96	2.00	2.02	2.01	2.00
Total expenditure	1.27	0.63	−0.06	−0.75	−1.20	−1.25	−1.01	−0.72	−0.60	−0.70
Consumption	0.05	0.06	0.06	0.08	0.10	0.10	0.11	0.12	0.16	0.21
Investment	0.00	0.00	0.00	−0.01	−0.01	−0.01	−0.01	−0.01	−0.01	−0.01
Transfers to households	1.69	2.23	3.09	3.99	4.54	4.57	4.22	3.75	3.43	3.38
Domestic interest payments	−0.43	−1.61	−3.17	−4.77	−5.77	−5.87	−5.28	−4.53	−4.11	−4.20
Foreign interest payments	−0.04	−0.04	−0.04	−0.05	−0.05	−0.05	−0.05	−0.06	−0.07	−0.08
Total financing	−0.31	−0.75	−1.25	−1.74	−2.10	−2.21	−2.10	−1.90	−1.79	−1.85
Foreign borrowing	−0.01	−0.01	−0.01	−0.01	−0.01	−0.01	−0.01	−0.01	−0.01	−0.02
Bond financing	−0.30	−0.74	−1.24	−1.74	−2.09	−2.20	−2.08	−1.89	−1.78	−1.83
Labor Market										
Nominal wages										
Rural sector	3.32	6.26	8.94	11.61	13.69	14.44	13.78	12.50	11.67	11.90
Informal sector	5.14	8.58	12.03	16.20	19.73	21.40	21.26	20.72	21.22	23.24
Private formal sector										
Unskilled	−1.35	2.06	5.23	8.00	10.27	11.45	11.21	10.10	9.25	9.47
Skilled	−2.46	0.16	2.61	4.71	6.52	7.61	7.54	6.58	5.70	5.72
Public sector										
Unskilled	3.49	6.74	9.81	12.82	15.28	16.41	16.05	14.94	14.25	14.68
Skilled	3.49	6.74	9.81	12.82	15.28	16.41	16.05	14.94	14.25	14.68
Employment										
Rural sector	0.00	0.13	0.30	0.48	0.64	0.80	0.93	1.05	1.15	1.23
Informal sector	0.00	−0.16	−0.37	−0.59	−0.80	−0.99	−1.15	−1.29	−1.40	−1.49
Private formal sector										
Unskilled	−2.12	−2.72	−3.18	−3.66	−3.97	−4.01	−3.90	−3.85	−4.00	−4.28
Skilled	−0.29	−0.23	−0.13	−0.07	−0.04	−0.04	−0.07	−0.12	−0.17	−0.23
Public sector										
Unskilled	0.00	0.00	0.00	0.00	0.00	0.00	0.00	0.00	0.00	0.00
Skilled	0.00	0.00	0.00	0.00	0.00	0.00	0.00	0.00	0.00	0.00

Continued

Table 7.4 Continued

	Periods									
	1	2	3	4	5	6	7	8	9	10
Labor supply (urban formal)										
Unskilled	0.00	-0.10	-0.26	-0.45	-0.67	-0.90	-1.14	-1.36	-1.58	-1.80
Skilled	0.00	0.00	0.00	0.00	0.00	0.00	0.00	0.00	0.00	0.00
Unemployment rate[1]										
Unskilled	1.75	2.05	2.18	2.29	2.28	2.07	1.78	1.55	1.46	1.47
Skilled	0.16	0.11	0.06	0.03	0.02	0.02	0.03	0.04	0.06	0.07
Real wage ratios[1]										
Expected urban-rural	0.00	-10.67	-8.42	-6.60	-5.84	-5.21	-4.39	-3.64	-3.24	-3.10
Expected formal-informal	0.00	-26.74	-21.70	-18.81	-19.59	-20.62	-20.62	-20.38	-21.39	-24.03
Expected international-urban	0.00	8.07	7.07	6.13	5.37	4.66	4.06	3.57	3.01	2.20
Migration[1]										
Rural-urban (% of urban unskilled labor supply)	0.00	-0.11	-0.14	-0.14	-0.13	-0.11	-0.09	-0.07	-0.05	-0.04
Formal-informal (% of urban formal unskilled labor supply)	0.00	-0.10	-0.16	-0.19	-0.21	-0.23	-0.23	-0.23	-0.22	-0.21
International-Urban (% of urban unskilled labor supply)	0.00	0.04	0.06	0.07	0.07	0.07	0.07	0.07	0.06	0.05
Financial Sector										
Deposit rate	0.00	0.00	0.00	0.00	0.00	0.00	0.00	0.00	0.00	0.00
Deposit rate (Foreign Currency)	0.01	0.03	0.03	0.02	-0.01	-0.04	-0.06	-0.06	-0.05	-0.02
Lending rate	0.00	0.05	0.12	0.20	0.27	0.32	0.34	0.33	0.30	0.29
Lending rate (Foreign Currency)	0.00	-0.06	-0.09	-0.08	-0.03	0.08	0.26	0.47	0.66	0.80
Bond rate	-0.75	-2.94	-4.99	-6.89	-8.10	-8.42	-7.90	-7.02	-6.39	-6.39
Credibility	0.00	1.94	3.09	4.21	5.11	5.71	5.90	5.68	5.23	4.89
Domestic premium	0.00	0.02	0.06	0.11	0.17	0.22	0.26	0.29	0.31	0.33

External premium	0.01	0.03	0.03	0.02	−0.01	−0.04	−0.06	−0.06	−0.04	−0.02
Probability of default	0.00	−1.94	−3.09	−4.21	−5.11	−5.71	−5.90	−5.68	−5.23	−4.89

Memorandum items

GDP at market prices[2]	−0.15	−0.18	−0.21	−0.24	−0.25	−0.25	−0.24	−0.23	−0.24	−0.25
Value added at factor cost[2]	−0.14	−0.18	−0.19	−0.21	−0.22	−0.21	−0.20	−0.19	−0.20	−0.22
Value added in rural sector[2]	0.00	0.06	0.15	0.24	0.32	0.40	0.47	0.53	0.59	0.64
Value added in urban informal sector[2]	0.00	−0.03	−0.08	−0.12	−0.17	−0.21	−0.24	−0.27	−0.30	−0.31
Value added in urban formal sector[2]	−0.34	−0.46	−0.53	−0.60	−0.65	−0.66	−0.66	−0.68	−0.73	−0.82
Private Consumption[2]	0.40	0.22	−0.02	−0.21	−0.34	−0.40	−0.35	−0.21	−0.07	0.02
Private Investment[2]	−2.97	−1.77	−0.99	−0.80	−0.80	−0.96	−1.48	−2.33	−3.15	−3.61
Disposable income[2]	0.29	−0.20	−0.58	−0.93	−1.16	−1.16	−0.95	−0.69	−0.59	−0.71
Nominal exchange rate[1]	0.71	3.64	6.63	9.33	11.56	12.75	12.53	11.38	10.37	10.34
real exchange rate[1]	−0.50	−0.79	−0.75	−0.68	−0.58	−0.42	−0.29	−0.27	−0.37	−0.52
Inflation rate[1]	3.88	3.56	3.48	3.55	2.97	1.40	−0.46	−1.36	−0.82	0.55
Ratio of debt to GDP	−1.05	−2.59	−4.35	−6.07	−7.32	−7.70	−7.30	−6.61	−6.22	−6.41
Ratio of tax revenues to government domestic debt[1]	7.71	8.04	8.37	8.93	9.77	10.58	10.99	10.91	10.67	10.72
Ratio of foreign currency deposits in total bank deposits[1]	0.01	0.05	0.05	0.01	−0.06	−0.16	−0.28	−0.38	−0.46	−0.50
Ratio of foreign currency loans in total bank loans[1]	−0.64	−1.74	−3.52	−5.84	−8.19	−9.82	−10.48	−10.53	−10.53	−10.90
Ratio of government primary surplus to GDP	−0.13	−0.86	−1.91	−3.02	−3.67	−3.66	−3.18	−2.63	−2.32	−2.35
Ratio of Interest payments to tax revenue	−3.03	−8.02	−14.73	−21.05	−24.52	−24.33	−21.53	−18.26	−16.24	−16.13

[1] Absolute deviations from baseline. [2] In real terms.

Table 7.5 Turkey: prices and structural indicators. Permanent, 2.5-percentage point increase in the value added tax rate. (Percentage deviations from baseline, unless otherwise indicated)

	Periods									
	1	2	3	4	5	6	7	8	9	10
Consumer Prices and the Real Exchange Rate[1]										
Rural CPI	3.67	6.92	10.00	13.12	15.65	16.80	16.40	15.32	14.73	15.27
Urban CPI	3.49	6.74	9.81	12.82	15.28	16.41	16.05	14.94	14.25	14.68
Real exchange rate	-0.50	-0.79	-0.75	-0.68	-0.58	-0.42	-0.29	-0.27	-0.37	-0.52
Value Added Prices[1]										
Rural	3.32	6.35	9.14	11.93	14.13	14.99	14.40	13.18	12.41	12.69
Urban private informal	5.14	8.45	11.71	15.66	18.99	20.46	20.17	19.51	19.89	21.80
Urban private formal	-2.82	0.13	2.89	5.22	7.18	8.31	8.18	7.16	6.24	6.28
Urban public	3.49	6.74	9.81	12.82	15.28	16.41	16.05	14.94	14.25	14.68
Real Disposable Income[1]										
Rural households	-0.59	-0.61	-0.94	-1.33	-1.64	-1.83	-1.93	-1.96	-1.99	-2.06
Urban households	0.76	0.52	0.29	0.17	0.09	0.08	0.18	0.38	0.61	0.77
Informal	1.37	1.39	1.53	2.20	2.81	3.06	3.15	3.48	4.24	5.28
Formal	0.91	2.16	4.38	6.77	8.24	8.25	7.20	5.88	4.92	4.65
Capitalists and rentiers	-0.41	-2.89	-5.75	-8.64	-10.61	-11.18	-10.51	-9.39	-8.74	-8.97
Real Private Consumption[1]										
Rural households	-0.59	-0.92	-1.25	-1.54	-1.73	-1.74	-1.61	-1.47	-1.46	-1.63
Urban households	0.67	0.16	-0.22	-0.52	-0.69	-0.63	-0.36	-0.03	0.20	0.23
Informal	1.37	1.32	1.46	2.15	2.79	3.08	3.22	3.59	4.36	5.38
Formal	0.91	2.02	4.23	6.66	8.19	8.30	7.38	6.16	5.22	4.89
Capitalists and rentiers	-0.41	-3.11	-5.97	-8.79	-10.67	-11.11	-10.27	-9.02	-8.33	-8.64
Production Structure										
Size of informal sector (% of total output)	0.05	0.05	0.05	0.04	0.04	0.03	0.01	0.01	0.01	0.01
Size of rural sector (% of total output)	0.03	0.05	0.07	0.09	0.11	0.13	0.14	0.15	0.17	0.18

Composition of Employment

Employment in rural sector (% of total employment)	0.09	0.17	0.25	0.33	0.41	0.47	0.51	0.55	0.59	0.63
Employment in informal sector (% of total employment)	0.08	0.05	−0.01	−0.07	−0.12	−0.18	−0.22	−0.26	−0.28	−0.28
Employment in informal sector (% of urban employment)	0.22	0.22	0.20	0.17	0.14	0.09	0.03	−0.01	−0.03	−0.03
Employment in public sector (% of total employment)	0.00	0.00	0.00	0.00	0.00	0.00	0.00	0.00	0.00	0.01
Employment in public sector (% of urban employment)	0.00	0.01	0.01	0.01	0.02	0.02	0.02	0.02	0.03	0.03

Private Expenditures

Consumption (% of GDP)	0.48	0.35	0.17	0.06	−0.03	−0.08	−0.06	0.05	0.19	0.30
Consumption (% of total consumption)	0.02	0.01	−0.02	−0.06	−0.09	−0.11	−0.11	−0.10	−0.10	−0.11
Investment (% of GDP)	−0.61	−0.31	−0.17	−0.16	−0.18	−0.21	−0.27	−0.40	−0.54	−0.63
Investment (% of total investment)	−0.62	−0.43	−0.27	−0.27	−0.29	−0.33	−0.45	−0.67	−0.91	−1.07

Public Expenditures

Consumption (% of GDP)	0.05	0.06	0.06	0.08	0.10	0.10	0.11	0.12	0.16	0.21
Investment (% of GDP)	0.00	0.00	0.00	−0.01	−0.01	−0.01	−0.01	−0.01	−0.01	−0.01
Infrastructure (% of public investment)	0.00	0.00	0.00	0.00	0.00	0.00	0.00	0.00	0.00	0.00
Education (% of public investment)	0.00	0.00	0.00	0.00	0.00	0.00	0.00	0.00	0.00	0.00
Public sector wage bill (% of public expenditure)	−0.94	−1.35	−2.23	−3.29	−3.94	−3.90	−3.44	−2.93	−2.61	−2.56

External Sector

Rural sector exports (% of total exports)	−0.13	−0.11	−0.09	−0.09	−0.09	−0.08	−0.07	−0.07	−0.08	−0.08
Imports of nonrural sector goods (% of total imports)	−0.11	−0.10	−0.11	−0.12	−0.13	−0.13	−0.12	−0.12	−0.13	−0.13
External debt (% of GDP)	−0.26	−0.08	0.07	0.12	0.09	0.00	−0.15	−0.32	−0.47	−0.55
Degree of openness (total trade in % of GDP)	−1.69	−1.75	−1.72	−1.80	−1.87	−1.85	−1.81	−1.86	−2.02	−2.21

[1] Percentage deviations from baseline.

worth. This lowers the overall demand for bonds and creates pressure for a (partial) long-run correction in the drop in the bond rate.

Banks' net worth is also affected by a slight increase in the interest rate on domestic-currency loans, of the order of 0.3 percentage point in the long run. This increase follows mainly from a rise in the domestic premium, which results in turn from actual exchange rate depreciation: by increasing the domestic-currency value of foreign-currency loans, the nominal depreciation reduces the net value of firms' collateral. At the same time, expectations of exchange rate depreciation remain relatively unchanged. The reason is that the higher actual rate of exchange rate depreciation is mitigated by lower expected inflation in the long run, due to improved credibility and declining inflation in the long run. In turn, credibility improves because increasing (nominal) tax revenues lower the debt-to-tax ratio, thereby lowering the probability of default. In turn, the reduction in the probability of default (that is, the credibility gain) tends to lower the actual bond rate, thereby contributing to the decline discussed earlier.

The nominal exchange rate depreciates by about 12 percent in the medium run and 10 percent in the long run. The growth path of the nominal exchange rate resembles the growth path of the domestic price level, but less so than in the case of an increase in the official interest rate. Accordingly, the real exchange rate tends to appreciate, remaining around 0.5 percent below the baserun level in the long run. Nevertheless, both the trade balance and the current account tend to improve in the long run. This occurs both because of the decline in real total consumption induced by the fall in disposable income (which reduces overall spending on the composite private formal sector good) and because the relative price of private formal sector goods declines strongly – in spite of the increase in the tax rate. Combined with strong nominal depreciation, this leads to a decline in the relative demand for imports of the private good and (despite an appreciation of the "overall" real exchange rate) a slight improvement in the current account in the long run.

The combination of an increasing lending rate and tax-induced increases in the price of formal sector investment goods leads to a strong reduction in investment demand initially. In the short run, increased expectations of inflation due to high actual inflation reduce the cost of borrowing, which tends to mitigate the fall in investment demand over the medium run. However, improved credibility and declining actual inflation lead to lower expected inflation in the long run, pushing the real cost of borrowing back up. The increase in the (expected) real lending rate, combined with a negative accelerator effect, tend to reduce real private investment again, by 3.6 percent in the long run. Over time, lower levels of investment lead to lower production capacity and a reduction in the marginal product of other production factors in the private formal sector. The general decline in demand for formal sector goods therefore leads to a sharp long-run reduction in unskilled employment, of about 4.3 percent, whereas skilled employment drops by about 0.2 percent. As a consequence, value added in the urban formal sector declines by 0.8 percent in the long run. Urban informal sector value added also declines by 0.3 percent, whereas value added in the rural sector improves by about 0.6 percent in the long run. Increasing value added in the rural sector and reduced value added in the urban informal sector result mainly from lower migration of workers from rural to urban areas, itself reflecting movements in wage differentials. Overall, GDP declines by 0.3 percent in the long run.

The decline in real GDP mainly reflects the diverging growth paths of components of aggregate demand. While private investment demand declines strongly at first, recovers somewhat, and starts declining again, real private consumption remains relatively unchanged in the long run; it experiences an initial short-run expansion of 0.4 percent, followed by a medium-run contraction of the same magnitude. These movements reflect the behavior of the real disposable income of profit earners, which declines strongly by 11 percent in the medium run and by 9 percent in the long run. In turn, as noted earlier, the declining income of profit earners is mainly due to the sharp drop in interest income from bond holdings.

Over time, declining real investment tends to reduce the capital stock in the private formal sector – and therefore the demand for skilled labor, given the high degree of complementarity between these factors. Combined with reduced demand for formal sector goods, this leads to a reduction in skilled employment, but only by a moderate amount in the long run (0.2 percent). In contrast, the long-run reduction in unskilled employment amounts to 4.3 percent, indicating that bargained wages for unskilled workers are increasing too fast. Partly because of the marked increase in formal sector unemployment, the wage differential between formal and informal sector declines strongly. This (together with a reduction in the probability of finding a job in the private formal sector) implies that migration toward the formal sector is reversed in the long run. Nevertheless, the reduced level of formal sector migration cannot fully compensate for reduced employment in that sector. Unskilled open unemployment therefore increases by 1.4 percent in the long run. By contrast, skilled unemployment increases by a much smaller proportion (0.1 percent) at the same horizon.

Finally, the results indicate that the hike in the tax rate leads to a sharp increase (by 11 percent) in the ratio of tax revenues to domestic debt in the long run. This is partly due to the direct impact of an increased VAT rate, but mostly due to the impact of higher prices on tax revenues. Combined with the strong decline in the bond rate, this leads to a significant long-run reduction in the interest payments-to-tax revenue ratio. Furthermore, the reduced interest payments implies that there is less need for a government primary surplus. Accordingly, the reduction in interest payments leads to increased household transfers (and thus higher spending, as noted earlier) and a long-run reduction in the primary surplus of around 2.4 percent of GDP.

Increase in the Tax Rate on Profit Earners

We next consider a permanent, 5 percentage point increase in the tax rate on income of profit earners. Results are reported in Tables 7.6 and 7.7.

The main impact of the tax increase is to lower real disposable income of profit earners (by about 3.2–3.8 percent in the short and long run) and to increase real disposable income of other urban sector households. It also leads to an in increase in government revenues amounting to 1 percent of GDP in the short to medium run, and 1.2 percent of GDP in the long run.

As a result of our public budget closure rule (which, again, keeps the supply of bonds fixed and treats foreign borrowing as exogenous), the increase in government

Table 7.6 Turkey: simulation results. Permanent, 5-percentage point increase in income tax rate on profit earners. (Percentage deviations from baseline, unless otherwise indicated)

	Periods									
	1	2	3	4	5	6	7	8	9	10
Real Sector										
Total resources	0.78	1.69	2.28	2.64	2.74	2.45	1.78	0.96	0.35	0.11
Gross domestic product	0.94	1.84	2.43	2.81	2.92	2.62	1.93	1.11	0.49	0.25
Imports of goods and NFS	0.27	1.19	1.78	2.07	2.13	1.87	1.26	0.48	-0.12	-0.35
Total expenditure	0.78	1.69	2.28	2.64	2.74	2.45	1.78	0.96	0.35	0.11
Total consumption	1.27	2.08	2.55	2.88	2.97	2.65	1.97	1.19	0.63	0.43
Private consumption	1.22	2.03	2.50	2.82	2.89	2.57	1.89	1.12	0.57	0.36
Public consumption	1.57	2.39	2.91	3.30	3.43	3.10	2.36	1.51	0.92	0.71
Total investment	0.17	1.45	2.29	2.59	2.57	2.19	1.39	0.42	-0.32	-0.57
Private investment	-0.02	1.39	2.35	2.62	2.53	2.08	1.19	0.10	-0.74	-1.04
Public investment	0.73	1.60	2.18	2.53	2.64	2.37	1.72	0.92	0.31	0.08
Exports of goods and NFS	0.07	0.76	1.43	1.87	2.10	1.98	1.47	0.72	0.06	-0.25
External Sector (% of GDP)[1]										
Current account	-0.07	-0.14	-0.12	-0.07	-0.03	0.01	0.03	0.03	0.01	-0.01
Exports of goods and NFS	-0.25	-0.30	-0.26	-0.23	-0.20	-0.15	-0.11	-0.10	-0.11	-0.13
Imports of goods and NFS	-0.21	-0.19	-0.19	-0.21	-0.23	-0.22	-0.20	-0.19	-0.19	-0.19
Labor Remittances	-0.04	-0.04	-0.04	-0.04	-0.04	-0.04	-0.03	-0.03	-0.04	-0.04
Factor services	0.01	0.01	0.00	-0.01	-0.02	-0.02	-0.02	-0.03	-0.03	-0.03
Capital account	0.07	0.14	0.12	0.07	0.03	-0.01	-0.03	-0.03	-0.01	0.01
Private borrowing	0.00	0.00	0.00	0.00	0.00	0.00	0.00	0.00	0.00	0.00
Commercial bank borrowing	0.00	0.02	0.01	-0.01	-0.02	-0.01	0.01	0.02	0.03	0.02
Public borrowing	0.00	0.00	0.00	0.00	0.00	0.00	0.00	0.00	0.00	0.00
Household deposits abroad	-0.07	-0.12	-0.11	-0.08	-0.05	0.00	0.04	0.05	0.04	0.01

Government Sector (% of GDP)[1]

Total revenue	0.89	0.95	1.03	1.08	1.11	1.14	1.17	1.19	1.21	1.23
Direct taxes	1.01	1.06	1.14	1.19	1.23	1.25	1.27	1.29	1.30	1.33
Indirect taxes	−0.12	−0.11	−0.11	−0.12	−0.12	−0.11	−0.10	−0.09	−0.09	−0.09
Total expenditure	0.80	0.73	0.69	0.65	0.65	0.73	0.88	1.03	1.13	1.19
Consumption	0.07	0.06	0.06	0.06	0.07	0.07	0.06	0.06	0.07	0.08
Investment	−0.01	−0.02	−0.02	−0.02	−0.02	−0.02	−0.02	−0.02	−0.02	−0.02
Transfers to households	0.70	0.82	1.05	1.27	1.34	1.22	0.99	0.75	0.59	0.53
Domestic interest payments	0.06	−0.13	−0.39	−0.65	−0.73	−0.53	−0.15	0.24	0.50	0.61
Foreign interest payments	−0.01	−0.01	−0.01	−0.01	−0.01	−0.01	−0.01	−0.01	−0.01	−0.01
Total financing	−0.09	−0.22	−0.34	−0.43	−0.46	−0.41	−0.29	−0.17	−0.07	−0.04
Foreign borrowing	0.00	0.00	0.00	0.00	0.00	0.00	0.00	0.00	0.00	0.00
Bond financing	−0.09	−0.22	−0.34	−0.43	−0.46	−0.41	−0.29	−0.16	−0.07	−0.04
Labor Market										
Nominal wages										
Rural sector	1.42	2.21	2.66	2.98	3.04	2.67	1.92	1.08	0.48	0.26
Informal sector	3.78	4.39	4.72	5.24	5.48	5.07	4.17	3.27	2.75	2.66
Private formal sector										
Unskilled	0.16	1.12	1.78	2.13	2.25	2.02	1.40	0.61	0.02	−0.18
Skilled	−0.14	0.62	1.17	1.43	1.52	1.36	0.87	0.17	−0.41	−0.63
Public sector										
Unskilled	1.22	2.08	2.63	3.01	3.13	2.82	2.11	1.28	0.68	0.46
Skilled	1.22	2.08	2.63	3.01	3.13	2.82	2.11	1.28	0.68	0.46
Employment										
Rural sector	0.00	0.03	0.07	0.11	0.15	0.17	0.20	0.21	0.22	0.23
Informal sector	0.00	−0.02	−0.05	−0.06	−0.06	−0.06	−0.04	−0.01	0.03	0.08
Private formal sector										
Unskilled	−0.46	−0.62	−0.67	−0.74	−0.76	−0.69	−0.58	−0.51	−0.51	−0.55
Skilled	−0.04	−0.02	0.02	0.03	0.04	0.04	0.03	0.02	0.00	−0.01
Public sector										
Unskilled	0.00	0.00	0.00	0.00	0.00	0.00	0.00	0.00	0.00	0.00
Skilled	0.00	0.00	0.00	0.00	0.00	0.00	0.00	0.00	0.00	0.00

Continued

Table 7.6 Continued

		Periods								
	1	2	3	4	5	6	7	8	9	10
Labor supply (urban formal)										
Unskilled	0.00	-0.05	-0.12	-0.19	-0.27	-0.34	-0.41	-0.47	-0.53	-0.57
Skilled	0.00	0.00	0.00	0.00	0.00	0.00	0.00	0.00	0.00	0.00
Unemployment rate[1]										
Unskilled	0.38	0.44	0.41	0.38	0.33	0.22	0.08	-0.01	-0.05	-0.06
Skilled	0.02	0.01	-0.01	-0.02	-0.02	-0.02	-0.01	-0.01	0.00	0.00
Real wage ratios[1]										
Expected urban-rural	0.00	-2.70	-2.01	-1.36	-1.13	-0.93	-0.63	-0.33	-0.18	-0.12
Expected formal-informal	0.00	-12.90	-9.44	-7.12	-6.80	-6.65	-6.04	-5.29	-4.99	-5.23
Expected international-urban	0.00	0.65	0.19	-0.14	-0.29	-0.40	-0.50	-0.58	-0.70	-0.90
Migration[1]										
Rural-urban (% of urban unskilled labor supply)	0.00	-0.03	-0.03	-0.03	-0.03	-0.02	-0.01	-0.01	0.00	0.00
Formal-informal (% of urban formal unskilled labor supply)	0.00	-0.05	-0.07	-0.07	-0.08	-0.07	-0.07	-0.06	-0.05	-0.04
International-Urban (% of urban unskilled labor supply)	0.00	0.00	0.00	0.00	0.00	0.00	0.00	0.00	-0.01	-0.01
Financial Sector										
Deposit rate	0.00	0.00	0.00	0.00	0.00	0.00	0.00	0.00	0.00	0.00
Deposit rate (Foreign Currency)	0.01	0.02	0.02	0.02	0.01	0.01	0.01	0.01	0.02	0.04
Lending rate	0.00	0.01	0.03	0.05	0.05	0.05	0.03	0.00	-0.03	-0.06
Lending rate (Foreign Currency)	0.00	-0.03	-0.03	-0.02	0.01	0.07	0.14	0.21	0.26	0.28
Bond rate	0.59	0.34	0.08	-0.18	-0.22	0.06	0.59	1.17	1.59	1.76
Credibility	0.00	0.90	1.41	1.87	2.15	2.23	2.11	1.84	1.52	1.30
Domestic premium	0.00	0.00	0.01	0.02	0.03	0.04	0.04	0.03	0.02	0.01

External premium	0.01	0.01	0.02	0.02	0.01	0.01	0.01	0.01	0.02	0.03
Probability of default	0.00	−0.90	−1.41	−1.87	−2.15	−2.23	−2.11	−1.84	−1.52	−1.30
Memorandum items										
GDP at market prices[2]	−0.02	−0.02	−0.02	−0.03	−0.02	−0.02	−0.01	0.00	0.00	0.00
Value added at factor cost[2]	−0.03	−0.03	−0.03	−0.03	−0.02	−0.01	0.00	0.00	0.01	0.00
Value added in rural sector[2]	0.00	0.02	0.04	0.06	0.07	0.09	0.10	0.11	0.11	0.12
Value added in urban informal sector[2]	0.00	0.00	−0.01	−0.01	−0.01	−0.01	−0.01	0.00	0.01	0.02
Value added in urban formal sector[2]	−0.07	−0.09	−0.09	−0.09	−0.09	−0.08	−0.06	−0.05	−0.06	−0.08
Private Consumption[2]	0.01	−0.04	−0.12	−0.17	−0.20	−0.20	−0.16	−0.11	−0.05	−0.02
Private Investment[2]	−0.30	0.23	0.57	0.51	0.32	0.11	−0.16	−0.48	−0.72	−0.79
Disposable income[2]	−0.36	−0.49	−0.56	−0.62	−0.64	−0.58	−0.46	−0.34	−0.28	−0.30
Nominal exchange rate[1]	0.23	1.03	1.67	2.06	2.21	2.03	1.46	0.69	0.06	−0.20
real exchange rate[1]	−0.31	−0.40	−0.35	−0.27	−0.19	−0.10	−0.02	0.01	−0.01	−0.05
Inflation rate[1]	1.43	0.95	0.64	0.48	0.16	−0.43	−1.01	−1.17	−0.84	−0.30
Ratio of debt to GDP	−0.32	−0.77	−1.19	−1.50	−1.61	−1.43	−1.02	−0.57	−0.25	−0.13
Ratio of tax revenues to government domestic debt[1]	3.45	3.49	3.49	3.49	3.50	3.43	3.21	2.87	2.57	2.44
Ratio of foreign currency deposits in total bank deposits[1]	−0.06	−0.09	−0.12	−0.16	−0.20	−0.25	−0.29	−0.33	−0.34	−0.34
Ratio of foreign currency loans in total bank loans[1]	−0.25	−0.56	−1.00	−1.51	−1.96	−2.12	−1.96	−1.61	−1.27	−1.03
Ratio of government primary surplus to GDP	0.16	0.10	−0.05	−0.22	−0.26	−0.12	0.15	0.40	0.58	0.65
Ratio of Interest payments to tax revenue	−0.66	−2.01	−3.95	−5.65	−6.10	−5.14	−3.38	−1.69	−0.62	−0.28

[1] Absolute deviations from baseline. [2] In real terms.

Table 7.7 Turkey: prices and structural indicators. Permanent, 5-percentage point increase in income tax rate on profit earners. (Percentage deviations from baseline, unless otherwise indicated)

	Periods									
	1	2	3	4	5	6	7	8	9	10
Consumer Prices and the Real Exchange Rate[1]										
Rural CPI	1.53	2.38	2.90	3.30	3.43	3.10	2.35	1.51	0.91	0.69
Urban CPI	1.22	2.08	2.63	3.01	3.13	2.82	2.11	1.28	0.68	0.46
Real exchange rate	−0.31	−0.40	−0.35	−0.27	−0.19	−0.10	−0.02	0.01	−0.01	−0.05
Value Added Prices[1]										
Rural	1.42	2.23	2.70	3.05	3.13	2.78	2.03	1.20	0.61	0.39
Urban private informal	3.78	4.37	4.68	5.19	5.42	5.03	4.14	3.26	2.78	2.72
Urban private formal	−0.17	0.67	1.29	1.58	1.67	1.49	0.96	0.23	−0.36	−0.58
Urban public	1.22	2.08	2.63	3.01	3.13	2.82	2.11	1.28	0.68	0.46
Real Disposable Income[1]										
Rural households	−0.22	−0.19	−0.27	−0.37	−0.43	−0.43	−0.39	−0.34	−0.29	−0.25
Urban households	0.16	0.05	−0.05	−0.09	−0.10	−0.10	−0.06	0.01	0.07	0.11
Informal	2.01	1.82	1.67	1.80	1.92	1.88	1.77	1.74	1.85	2.00
Formal	0.89	1.27	1.98	2.66	2.92	2.66	2.10	1.53	1.15	1.02
Capitalists and rentiers	−3.87	−4.32	−4.81	−5.32	−5.52	−5.27	−4.63	−3.91	−3.41	−3.22
Real Private Consumption[1]										
Rural households	−0.22	−0.31	−0.35	−0.38	−0.37	−0.30	−0.20	−0.10	−0.06	−0.07
Urban households	−0.15	−0.34	−0.45	−0.50	−0.51	−0.44	−0.31	−0.18	−0.10	−0.09
Informal	2.01	1.80	1.65	1.80	1.93	1.91	1.81	1.80	1.90	2.04
Formal	0.89	1.21	1.95	2.66	2.95	2.73	2.20	1.66	1.27	1.11
Capitalists and rentiers	−3.87	−4.40	−4.86	−5.32	−5.48	−5.17	−4.47	−3.72	−3.23	−3.08
Production Structure										
Size of informal sector (% of total output)	0.01	0.01	0.01	0.01	0.01	0.00	0.00	0.00	0.00	0.01
Size of Rural sector (% of total output)	0.01	0.01	0.01	0.02	0.02	0.02	0.02	0.02	0.02	0.02

Composition of Employment

Employment in rural sector (% of total employment)	0.02	0.04	0.05	0.06	0.07	0.07	0.07	0.07	0.07	0.07
Employment in informal sector (% of total employment)	0.02	0.01	0.00	0.00	-0.01	-0.01	-0.01	-0.01	0.00	0.01
Employment in informal sector (% of urban employment)	0.05	0.05	0.05	0.05	0.05	0.04	0.03	0.04	0.05	0.06
Employment in public sector (% of total employment)	0.00	0.00	0.00	0.00	0.00	0.00	0.00	0.00	0.00	0.00
Employment in public sector (% of urban employment)	0.00	0.00	0.00	0.00	0.00	0.00	0.00	0.00	0.00	0.00

Private Expenditures

Consumption (% of GDP)	0.18	0.13	0.05	0.01	-0.02	-0.03	-0.03	0.01	0.05	0.07
Consumption (% of total consumption)	-0.04	-0.04	-0.05	-0.06	-0.07	-0.07	-0.06	-0.06	-0.05	-0.05
Investment (% of GDP)	-0.18	-0.07	-0.01	-0.02	-0.05	-0.07	-0.10	-0.14	-0.17	-0.18
Investment (% of total investment)	-0.14	-0.04	0.04	0.02	-0.03	-0.07	-0.12	-0.19	-0.25	-0.28

Public Expenditures

Consumption (% of GDP)	0.07	0.06	0.06	0.06	0.07	0.07	0.06	0.06	0.07	0.08
Investment (% of GDP)	-0.01	-0.02	-0.02	-0.02	-0.02	-0.02	-0.02	-0.02	-0.02	-0.02
Infrastructure (% of public investment)	0.00	0.00	0.00	0.00	0.00	0.00	0.00	0.00	0.00	0.00
Education (% of public investment)	0.00	0.00	0.00	0.00	0.00	0.00	0.00	0.00	0.00	0.00
Public sector wage bill (% of public expenditure)	-0.39	-0.52	-0.82	-1.17	-1.33	-1.21	-0.95	-0.71	-0.57	-0.53

External Sector

Rural exports (% of total exports)	-0.05	-0.05	-0.04	-0.04	-0.04	-0.04	-0.03	-0.03	-0.03	-0.03
Imports of nonrural sector goods (% of total imports)	-0.04	-0.03	-0.03	-0.04	-0.04	-0.03	-0.03	-0.03	-0.03	-0.03
External debt (% of GDP)	-0.01	0.13	0.24	0.31	0.34	0.35	0.33	0.31	0.30	0.32
Degree of openness (total trade in % of GDP)	-0.46	-0.49	-0.44	-0.44	-0.42	-0.37	-0.31	-0.28	-0.30	-0.32

[1] Percentage deviations from baseline.

revenue translates into higher transfers to households. Given the initial distribution of these transfers, they go mainly toward urban formal households and profit earners. Nevertheless, urban informal households are initially the main beneficiaries of the increased transfers, with their real disposable income rising by 2.0 percent in the short run, compared to 0.9 percent for urban formal households and −0.2 percent for rural households. The strong relative increase in informal sector income is due to *a*) increasing demand for informal sector goods and production input (labor); and *b*) the fact that informal sector households are not subject to direct tax payments. Profit earners have relatively low consumption shares in informal sector goods. The redistribution of household income therefore increases demand for informal sector goods by a relatively large amount. In turn, this raises informal sector output, labor demand, and wages, thereby leading to higher real disposable income.

In the medium run (period 5), formal sector households enjoy a relatively strong increase in real disposable income (2.9 percent) compared to urban informal households (1.9 percent). The income of profit earners is relatively high in the medium run, and tax-induced redistribution toward formal sector households is therefore relatively high. In the long run, the initial pattern re-establishes itself: urban informal households gain the most (about 2 percent) compared to urban formal households (1 percent) and rural households (−0.3 percent).

Inflation is high in the short run but declines toward zero in the medium run. Rural and urban price levels reach a maximum increase of 3.1–3.4 percent (see Table 7.7, period 5). In subsequent periods, inflation turns negative and price levels return gradually to values close to their baserun levels. Price movements are driven by the increase in sectoral demand (relative to supply) for goods and services and tend to be reflected in movements of the nominal exchange rate. The real exchange rate appreciates somewhat in the short and medium run, but remains virtually unchanged in the long run. The initial exchange rate appreciation worsens the current account slightly in the short run. In the longer run, however, there is no discernible impact on external balance.

Similar to price levels, nominal wage levels reach a maximum increase in the medium run. High wage increases of around 5.5 percent are experienced by informal sector workers. In comparison, private formal skilled and unskilled workers benefit from smaller increases, of the order of 1.5 and 2.3 percent respectively. In the long run, the informal sector wage level increases by 2.7 percent whereas formal sector wages (both skilled and unskilled) decline. This decline is due to a combined switch in consumption and investment demand away from formal sector goods. The fall in unskilled wages in the formal private sector is somewhat mitigated in the medium and long run as a result of an increase in the reservation wage due to increasing public sector wages (private formal unskilled workers benefit from a high public sector leadership effect on their wages), and subsequently due to declining unskilled unemployment.

The long-run decline in unskilled unemployment (following an increase in the short and medium run) results mainly from a reduction in the supply of unskilled labor to the formal sector. The reason is that the increase in the informal sector wage relative to the private formal unskilled wage lowers the expected wage differential between the formal and informal sectors. This reduces migration into the formal sector (and thus the number of unskilled job seekers in that sector) and gradually eliminates the increase in unemployment that occurred during the short and medium run. As for rural–urban migration, the expected wage differential between urban and rural areas gets smaller, because of the decline in relative formal sector wages (and in spite of the increase in informal sector wages). The subsequent "reverse" migration from urban to rural areas implies that informal sector employment contracts slightly in the medium run; it also expands in the long run, when migration out of urban areas tapers off. Labor movements imply that rural employment continuously expands during the simulation horizon.

Unskilled employment in the urban formal sector declines both in the short and the long run, as a result of declining demand for formal sector goods. Skilled employment also declines (marginally) in the short run, but increases (marginally) in the medium term due to increasing investment and capital accumulation. As noted earlier, skilled workers benefit from the complementarity between physical capital accumulation and skilled labor employment. But because the increases in real private investment recorded between periods 2 and 6 are subsequently reversed (see below), this complementarity effect is muted. Skilled employment remain essentially unchanged in the long run.

Overall, the redistributive policy of increasing taxation of profit earners leaves real GDP unchanged in the long run. Migration increases employment and real value added in rural areas by a small amount (0.1 percent). By contrast, reduced demand for formal sector goods leads to reduced relative formal sector wages, reduced formal sector migration, and lower value added in the formal sector (−0.1percent). The net effect of increased migration to rural areas and reduced formal sector migration means that value added in the informal sector remains virtually unchanged in the long run.

Real investment declines on impact due to the accelerator effect. During the following periods (and until period 6), real investment expands because increasing inflationary expectations reduce the expected cost of borrowing for investment purposes. By the same token, real investment declines in the long run as expected inflation and the expected cost of borrowing drop. Real consumption falls in line with disposable income, whereas overall disposable income itself declines due to increasing consumer prices.

Regarding the financial sector, the interest rate on domestic-currency loans increases marginally in the medium run, and declines slightly in the long run. The medium-run increase follows from small increases in domestic and external risk premia, whereas the long-run decline follows from improved credibility, which spills over into declining expectations of inflation and exchange rate depreciation – thereby lowering the expected cost of funds. Improved credibility is the mirror image of a declining probability of default, which itself follows directly from the increase in tax revenues. The reduction in the probability of default puts downward pressure on the actual bond rate. Overall, however, the bond rate increases in both the short and the long run, as a result of a decline in the demand for bonds by profit earners, induced by lower disposable income, lower savings, and thus lower wealth accumulation over time for that category of households. In between, during the medium run, the bond rate declines slightly because of a wealth-induced increase in demand for government bonds by commercial banks. Nominal exchange rate depreciation increases the net worth of commercial banks in the medium run, and this indeed stimulates their demand for bonds.

Public finance indicators show that tax revenues expand significantly as a proportion of domestic debt throughout the adjustment period, reaching 2.4 percent in the long run. The increase in government resources implies that interest payments as a proportion of tax revenues decline strongly during the medium term. However, the subsequent increase in the bond rate implies that the interest payments–tax revenue ratio returns to a value close to its baserun level in the long run. Due to the model closure rule (flexible household transfers balancing the public sector budget), the primary budget surplus naturally reflects additional financing needs. Accordingly, the primary budget balance follows movements in the bond rate: as a proportion of GDP, the primary surplus deteriorates in the medium term, and improves (by about 0.7 percentage points) in the long run.

Finally, in evaluating the fiscal effects of a tax increase on profit earners, it should be kept in mind that the model does not account for the possibility that higher tax rates may increase incentives for tax evasion (thereby reducing the increase in the "effective" tax rate) and/or reduce incentives to participate in the labor force (which would affect output growth in the medium and long run). Both effects may lead to lower increases in tax revenues than those indicated by our simulation results. At the same time, however, there is limited evidence that participation rates are highly sensitive to tax rates in Turkey.

7.4   Concluding Remarks

The purpose of this chapter has been to analyze the effects of monetary and fiscal adjustment on public debt sustainability and the behavior of wages and unemployment in Turkey. The IMMPA framework on which the analysis is based captures a number of important structural characteristics of the Turkish economy, such as rural–urban migration, a large urban informal sector, bilateral bargaining in the formal sector, dollarization of the banking system (on both asset and liability sides), as well as the interactions between credibility, default risk on government debt, and inflation expectations. Accounting for default risk on public debt is indeed a key feature of the model, despite its deterministic nature. Our basic assumption is that if the government must engage in large-scale borrowing to meet its debt service payments and finance its budget deficit, investors will be unwilling to accumulate public bonds indefinitely. We endogenized investors' behavior by assuming that there is a non-zero perceived probability of default that depends on the debt-to-tax revenue ratio. The higher the perceived risk of default is, the lower will be the degree of credibility of the fiscal stance. Lower credibility, in turn, translates into greater inflation persistence and upward pressure on interest rates on government bonds. Thus, an unsustainable fiscal policy may force the government to adjust, as a result of growing pressure on borrowing costs.

Various simulations were performed. Specifically, we conducted two sets of experiments: a restrictive monetary policy taking the form of a permanent increase in official interest rates, and fiscal adjustment, taking the form of an increase in the VAT rate and an increase in the tax rate on income of profit earners. The results highlighted the importance of accounting for general equilibrium effects in interest rate determination, as well as the link between default risk and credibility in understanding the real and financial effects of adjustment policies. In addition, they also indicated the importance of a broad range of fiscal measures for putting domestic public debt on a sustainable path. These results are consistent with those of several other recent studies of the Turkish economy. For instance, Voyvoda and Yeldan (2003), using an overlapping-generations framework, found that whether the primary surplus target of 6.5 percent of GDP embedded in the May 2001 program is sustainable depended heavily on the vulnerability of the Turkish economy to adverse growth shocks. In addition, the debt-to-GDP ratio was likely to fall only gradually. They called for further fiscal reform to ensure a speedier fall in that ratio – and therefore allow domestic risk premia (or default probabilities) to fall and interest rates to come down, as in our framework.

As one would naturally expect in a model of this type, our simulation results depend very much on the type of closure rule that we adopted for the government budget. Instead of assuming that the supply of bonds follows an exogenous path and that any residual budget gap is "closed" through an adjustment in transfers to households – a plausible adjustment scenario for a country where the recent crisis has led to a dramatic drop in real wages and a sharp increase in poverty – we could have assumed for instance that the supply of domestic bonds (or foreign borrowing) is endogenous, with an adjustment rule involving either a change in government spending on goods and services produced in the formal sector, or a change in the VAT tax rate, when the ratio of domestic (or foreign) debt to tax revenues reaches a particular level. Such threshold rules are attractive from an empirical standpoint to the extent that they describe quite well the way policymakers tend to respond to excessive growth in their liabilities. Intuitively, the implications for our model are quite clear: by allowing the debt-to-tax ratio to fluctuate a lot more, the probability of default would also fluctuate more, thereby implying a larger effect of default risk (or, equivalently here, credibility) on the actual bond rate. In turn, fluctuations in the bond rate would imply larger effects of any given shock on the financial sector and the real economy.

In addition to the policies considered in this chapter, the model can be used to analyze the fiscal and labor market effects of a wide range of shocks. For instance, the model could be used to study the impact of various interest rate rules on output, inflation, and unemployment, or alternative fiscal rules aimed at limiting discretion in spending and ensuring public debt sustainability in the long run (see, for instance, Perry (2003) and Wyplosz (2002)). An analysis of the performance of alternative interest rate rules – which could capitalize on some of the results of Berument and Malatyali (2001), Berument and Tasci (2004), and Elekdag (2003) – would be particularly desirable, given Turkey's planned transition to inflation targeting. The response of Turkey's economy to various types of external shocks (such as contagion effects, autonomous changes in sentiment on world capital markets, or terms-of-trade disturbances) could also be analyzed in the model.

On the labor market side, an important experiment would be to examine the impact of a cut in payroll taxation. Employer-paid social security contributions averaged about 36 percent of total labor costs during 1996–2000; it has been argued that these high social security taxes create strong disincentives to job creation. More generally, many observers have called for a thorough overhaul of Turkey's social insurance system. A key issue in this context is how to shift the main pillar of unemployment protection from the severance payment system to the unemployment insurance scheme established in June 2000, and the extent to which this shift will promote labor adjustment in response to changing economic conditions.[46] The model could also be used to analyze the macroeconomic effects of a reduction in employment of unskilled workers in government. This last simulation is quite important because some observers have argued that continued fiscal adjustment in Turkey may require a sustained retrenchment in public sector employment, given a public sector wage bill that accounted for about a quarter of central government expenditure in recent years.[47]

Finally, although already quite complex, the IMMPA framework presented in this chapter can be extended or modified in various directions. We assumed that the market for bank credit was imperfectly competitive. Alternatively, it could be assumed that the banking system is oligopolistic, as for instance in Beenstock et al. (2003). This type of market structure could lead to higher, and more rigid, bank lending spreads. Second, workers' reservation wage could be made a function of severance payments, as for instance in the specification of the wage target of trade unions discussed in Chapter 3. This would allow the model to address an important issue for the Turkish labor market (see Tunali (2003)): the wage and employment effects of a reduction in firing costs. Finally, we did not model the stock market. Although the existing evidence suggests that the stock market does not play a significant financial role in Turkey at the present time, its importance may increase in the future – and so will, therefore, its potential effects on private investment and portfolio allocation.

Appendix:
Calibration and Parameter Values

The calibration of our IMMPA model for Turkey was carried out using *a*) a 1996 Financial Social Accounting Matrix (FSAM); *b*) an auxiliary data set; and *c*) a set of noncalibrated parameters. A summary description of each of these sources of information is provided in this appendix. A complete description of the creation of the 1996 Turkey FSAM and the auxiliary data set, as well as the derivation of noncalibrated parameter estimates, can be found in Jensen and Yeldan (2004).

The main data sources for the creation of the FSAM include the website of the Turkish State Planning Organization (SPO), http://www.dpt.gov.tr, and various publications by the State Institute of Statistics (SIS) and the Central Bank of Turkey

---

[46] Social security could be modeled along the lines of Agénor, Nabli, Yousef, and Jensen (2004).

[47] During the period 1999–2001, public sector employment increased by 5 percent, whereas private employment fell by 6 percent.

(CBT). The FSAM itself was built in two steps: *a*) construction of a MacroSAM; and *b*) disaggregation into a MicroSAM. The construction of the MacroSAM was split into a real MacroSAM and a financial MacroSAM. The link between the two types of MacroSAMs was made through the savings–investment balance account. Accordingly, this account was forced to be identical in the two SAMs. In the following, the construction and key characteristics of the real and financial MacroSAMs are described. The more disaggregated characteristics are presented in the publication mentioned above.

The real MacroSAM was built around final demand and cost components of GDP data from the SIS. SIS publications were generally preferred as the main data source for the input–output part of the MacroSAM, because they allowed for better correspondence with other data sources. Intermediate consumption, however, was derived from the 1996 Turkey input–output table.

SPO data were used as the main source for public sector budget data, whereas the CBT publications were used as the main source for the current account of the balance of payments. Data regarding commercial banks and the Central Bank of Turkey were mainly obtained from the SIS publications. The balanced real MacroSAM is presented in Table A7.1.

The real MacroSAM indicates that foreign trade (as measured by the sum of exports and imports of goods and services) makes up around 50 percent of GDP, implying that Turkey is a fairly open economy. Exports make up around 13 percent of total production, while imports make up around 13 percent of absorption. The large current account deficit, which amounts in the MacroSAM to about 5 percent of GDP, indicates that absorption is significantly larger than production. Accordingly, the trade balance deficit amounts to more than 20 percent of export earnings.

Looking at savings rates, the data indicate that domestic firms save around 20 percent of their disposable income whereas households save around 14 percent of their disposable income. In comparison, the government primary surplus amounts to 3.4 percent of GDP. Finally, it can be noticed that interest payments by the public sector amount to around 39 percent of tax revenues, indicating that the public sector is running an unsustainable overall budget deficit of 6.9 percent of GDP.

The financial MacroSAM was built around the savings and investment aggregates from the real MacroSAM. Accordingly, the correspondence between the savings–investment balance accounts of the two SAMs were ensured by construction. The main data sources used in the construction of the financial MacroSAM, as noted earlier, were CBT and SIS publications. SIS publications were used to obtain information about public sector financial flows as well as private sector borrowing in foreign currency. The remaining data in the financial MacroSAM were derived from CBT publications. The balanced financial MacroSAM is presented in Table A7.2.

The financial MacroSAM shows that government bond issuing was around 7.1 percent of GDP. This is slightly higher than the overall financing need of 6.9 percent, reflecting the fact that the Turkish government reduced foreign borrowing slightly in 1996. The increase in bond holdings of commercial banks accounts for around 90 percent of the total increase in government bonds. Profit earners and the CBT hold the remaining 10 percent of newly issued bonds.

Table A7.1 Turkey: real 1996 MacroSAM (in billions of Turkish liras)

	Activities	Commodities	Labor Factor	Capital Factor	Households	Domestic Banks
Activities		25,276,448			10,543,236	
Commodities	11,752,353					
Labor Factor	4,993,374					
Capital Factor	7,734,324					
Households			4,616,421	5,789,799		1,898,905
Domestic Banks	46,811			375,181	598,218	
Central Bank						2,904
Government	749,586	951,298	673,670	864,225	301,420	94,032
Private Investment				1,419,097	1,669,534	64,358
Public Investment						
Rest of the World		4,110,584		173,507		72,853
Total Expenditures	**25,276,448**	**30,338,330**	**5,290,091**	**8,621,809**	**13,112,408**	**2,133,051**

Continued

Table A7.1 Continued

	Central Bank	Government	Private	Public Investment	ROW Investment	Total Receipts
Activities						25,276,448
Commodities		1,170,126	2,893,335	796,975	3,182,305	30,338,330
Labor Factor		296,717				5,290,091
Capital Factor		599,936			287,550	8,621,809
Households		464,618		55,279	287,387	13,112,408
Domestic Banks	2,914			1,109,926		2,133,051
Central Bank				150,574	30,021	183,500
Government	180,586			−997,648	737,995	3,814,817
Private Investment	0					2,893,335
Public Investment		1,283,420				1,283,420
Rest of the World				168,314		4,525,258
Total Expenditures	183,500	3,814,817	2,893,335	1,283,420	4,525,258	

Table A7.2 Turkey: financial 1996 MacroSAM (in billions of Turkish liras)

	HOUSEHOLDS	CAPITAL	GOVERNMENT	DOMESTIC BANKS	REST OF THE WORLD	CENTRAL BANKS	PRIVATE INVESTMENT	TOTAL
HOUSEHOLDS			8,851	1,878,328	70,816	129,559		2,087,554
CAPITAL							2,893,335	2,893,335
GOVERNMENT								0
DOMESTIC BANKS	418,020	1,341,625	922,757			218,150		2,900,552
REST OF THE WORLD		132,613	−29,564	955,982	250,220			1,059,031
CENTRAL BANK			95,604	1,885				347,709
PRIVATE INVESTMENT	1,669,534	1,419,097	−997,648	64,358	737,995			2,893,335
TOTAL	2,087,554	2,893,335	0	2,900,552	1,059,031	347,709	2,893,335	

Money issuing, including lending to commercial banks, stood at 2.4 percent of GDP. This is a relatively small number, but it reflects the fact that inflation was high in 1996. Money issuing would therefore represent a substantially higher proportion of lagged GDP, reflecting significant use of the inflation tax in 1996.

Foreign exchange reserves increased by around 6.1 percent of imports. Again, the current import number is inflated by strong depreciation of the exchange rate in 1996. The change in foreign exchange reserves would therefore be significant when compared to lagged imports, indicating that significant exchange reserve accumulation took place in 1996.

Households increased borrowing from commercial banks by around 2.9 percent of GDP or 25 percent of household savings. In comparison, firms increased their borrowing by around 9.3 percent of GDP or 95 percent of firms' savings. This pattern indicates that commercial banks mainly invest their funds in *a*) loans to firms for investment purposes; and b) government bonds. Finally, it may be noticed that commercial banks mainly funds themselves out of domestic deposits. The share of deposits in total additional funding was around 65 percent in 1996.

The auxiliary data set includes mainly level data and interest rates that could not be directly derived from the 1996 Turkey FSAM. The Turkish economy was characterized by much instability over the 1996–2003 period. The base year of 1996 was a relatively normal year, but it was still characterized by very high inflation and underlying volatility.

Accordingly, it does not make much sense to use 1995–6 financial stock data to derive implicit interest rates, or to use 1995–6 interest rates to derive implicit data on financial stocks. Instead, initial and lagged values for interest rates, inflation rates and depreciation rates were chosen (in close correspondence with country experts) so as to match 2003 values and to give rise to reasonable stock numbers. In sum, auxiliary data on financial stocks were derived by applying the chosen interest rates to the interest payments recorded in the FSAM.

The auxiliary data for the labor market indicate that unskilled labor is overwhelmingly employed in the rural and informal sectors. Specifically, 49 percent of the unskilled employed workers are working in the rural sector while 39 percent are working in the urban informal sector. In comparison, 11 percent of unskilled employed are working in the urban private formal sector while only 1 percent is initially employed in the public sector. Skilled employment is more of an urban public sector phenomenon. Indeed, the data indicate that 62 percent of employed skilled workers are working in the urban private formal sector whereas 38 percent of the total are working in the urban public sector. Initial rates of open unemployment among workers in the urban formal sector can be derived from estimates of sectoral labor supply. Initial unemployment rates are estimated to be 11 percent among unskilled workers and 15 percent among skilled workers.

Initial levels of the private formal sector capital stock, as well as public capital stocks of infrastructure and education capital, were derived from a combination of initial data and sensitivity analyses. Depreciation rates were estimated to be 2.1 percent for public sector infrastructure capital and 3.4 percent for public sector education capital and private formal sector capital.

Growth rates of rural and urban labor stocks were estimated to be respectively 0.1 percent and 2.3 percent. The reason why the rural labor supply growth rate is so low is because of the relatively high level of migration of families from rural to urban areas. While fertility levels remain relatively high in rural compared to urban areas, migration of families bring children into urban areas before they reach the age for entering the labor market.

The relatively high levels of migration between segments of the Turkish labor market is evident from the data as well. Estimates indicate that yearly migration from rural to urban areas amounts to around 2.5 percent of the rural labor force. In comparison, overseas migration amounts to around 1.5 percent of the urban labor force, while migration between the informal and formal labor market segments amounts to around 0.9 percent of the informal sector labor force. Accordingly, migration plays a very important role for labor market developments in Turkey. In addition, the yearly number of unskilled workers receiving education to achieve skilled status, is estimated to be around 1.7 percent of the urban labor force.

The initial inflation rate was set at around 30 percent while the initial depreciation rate of the nominal exchange rate was set at around 10 percent. The initial expected depreciation rate was also set at 10 percent. In addition, the levels of bond holdings of profit earners, commercial banks, and the CBT, were set so as to imply an initial bond rate of about 16 percent (consistent with the interest payments on government bonds given in the FSAM). The initial bond rate was allowed to be relatively low so as to achieve a sensible balance between the financial stocks and flows. Accordingly, these initial levels allowed for a public debt stock of around 66 percent of GDP. Nevertheless, inflation and exchange rate depreciation were allowed to increase to levels around 30–40 percent (and the bond rate around 45–50 percent) as part of the baserun solution underlying the simulations reported in this chapter. In addition, the level of household deposits with commercial banks, as well as commercial bank borrowing from the CBT, were set so as to allow for a deposit rate/official rate of 25 percent and a foreign-currency deposit rate of about 10 percent. In addition, the stock of money holdings by households were set so as to allow for a reserve requirement ratio of around 5 percent.

Levels of household and firm loan stocks with commercial banks were subsequently set so as to allow for a lending rate around 35 percent. Given the levels of domestic deposit rates and expected depreciation, as well as the reserve requirement ratio and the lending rate, a domestic premium of about 3 percent was derived. Again, the initial level of the domestic premium was set at a relatively low level in order to allow for a sensible balance between financial stocks and flows. Nevertheless, the domestic premium was allowed to increase to levels of 5–8 percent as part of the baserun solution underlying the simulations reported in the text.

The probability of default was initially set at 50 percent, but was allowed to decline to levels around 30–40 percent over the baserun. The mirror image of the decline in the probability of default was that credibility was allowed to increase from an initial level of 50 percent to around 60–70 percent over the baserun period. This also meant that expected inflation was allowed to decline slightly from an initial level of about 18 percent over the baserun. The expected depreciation rate was subsequently allowed to increase gradually from an initial level of around 10 percent (as noted above) to levels slightly below expected inflation over the baserun. Foreign inflation was set at an exogenous rate of 2 percent per year.

Most of the noncalibrated parameters were estimated from time-series data. The relative wage elasticity of rural–urban migration was estimated to be 0.019 whereas the relative wage elasticity of overseas migration was estimated to be 0.012. The partial adjustment (weighting) parameters were estimated to be respectively 0.56 and 0.28. Subsequently, the wage elasticity and partial adjustment speed of informal-formal sector migration were set at intermediate levels of 0.016 and 0.40. The rate of decline in the number of Turkish workers abroad was set at 1 percent per year, whereas the share of remittances in foreign workers' wage income was set at 10 percent. In addition, the substitution elasticity between teachers and education capital in the CES skills upgrading function (that is, the education production function) was set at a low value of 0.3.

In the money demand specification, the domestic currency interest rate elasticity was set at the commonly estimated value of -0.21 for all households, except for profit earners where the elasticity was set at the estimated value of -0.91. The foreign currency interest rate elasticity was set at the commonly estimated value of -0.63. Finally, the disposable income elasticity of money demand was set at the commonly estimated value of 0.42 for all households.

In the demand equation for foreign currency deposits, the foreign currency interest rate elasticity was set at the commonly estimated value of 0.37 for the formal sector household and profit earners (the only two categories of households in the model in possession of foreign exchange deposits). In the demand equation for government bonds by profit earners, the foreign currency interest rate elasticity was set at the estimated value of -0.37, and the domestic currency interest rate elasticity at the estimated value of -0.91 (similar to the money demand elasticity given earlier). In addition, the bond rate elasticity was set at a level of 2.0, above the estimated level of 1.2, at the suggestion of country experts.

Turning to the private wage specifications, parameters measuring worker's bargaining strength were set at the same estimated level of 0.63. The public sector wage "leadership" elasticities were set at estimated levels of respectively 0.75 and 0.06 for the unskilled and skilled wage specifications; the expected urban price elasticities were set at estimated levels of respectively 0.32 and 0.26 for the unskilled and skilled wage specifications; and the unemployment elasticities were set at estimated levels of respectively 0.23 and 0.25 for the unskilled and skilled wage specifications. Finally, the minimum wage elasticity was set at an estimated level of 0.47 for the unskilled wage specification. The plausibility of parameter values was assessed through sensitivity analysis.

Production elasticities were not immediately available but we relied to some extent on existing CGE applications for Turkey. The share of land in rural production was assumed to be 0.3, leaving a production share of 0.7 for unskilled labor (assuming that no capital is used in agricultural production). Similarly, it was assumed that there are moderate substitution possibilities between public sector infrastructure investment and unskilled rural labor, through the adoption of an elasticity of substitution of 0.75. The elasticity of transformation between domestic market and export of domestic production was taken to be at a middle level, that is, 1.0. In addition, it was assumed as a starting point that there are constant returns to scale in urban informal sector production.

Looking at urban private formal production, the top-level CES substitution elasticity between public infrastructure capital and composite primary production factors was assumed to be a moderate 0.75. At the second level, CES substitution possibilities between formal urban unskilled labor and the composite factor consisting of skilled labor and private physical capital was assumed to be higher at 1.2. Finally, the bottom-nest CES substitution elasticity between skilled labor and the private capital stock was assumed to be 0.4, reflecting little substitution possibilities at this level (as suggested by the evidence). Finally, public sector composite labor was assumed to be moderately substitutable to public infrastructure capital in the top-level public production nest, whereas substitution possibilities between unskilled and skilled public employees was assumed to be moderately high at 1.2.

Parameter estimates for the private investment equation were taken in part from the studies cited in the text. The elasticity with respect to real GDP growth (which captures the accelerator effect) was set at 1.5 and the real lending rate elasticity was set at the relatively high value of −2.5. However, for the infrastructure elasticity of investment demand, we found no reliable estimate in the literature. We chose to set it to a relatively low value, 0.1. Given that we did not consider changes in public investment in infrastructure, this particular choice has little effect on the simulation results. The partial adjustment rate of actual to desired investment was set at an estimated value of 0.63.

The relative interest rate elasticity of commercial banks' foreign borrowing was set at an estimated value of 0.46, whereas the elasticity of commercial banks' demand for government bonds with respect to the expected bond rate was set at the estimated value of 0.46. The elasticity of the banks' domestic risk premium with respect to the collateral ratio could not be estimated due to a lack of time series data. The elasticity was chosen to be 0.2, in order to avoid very large (and potentially destabilizing) amplification effects. Similarly, the partial adjustment coefficient of the expected rate of depreciation was chosen to be 0.9 at the request of country experts. Finally, the direct placement ratio of government bonds with commercial banks was set at 0.9, reflecting the placement ratio of newly issued bonds observed in the 1996 Turkey FSAM.

Chapter 8

Linking Representative Household Models with Household Surveys for Poverty Analysis: A Comparison of Alternative Methodologies

Pierre-Richard Agénor, Derek H. C. Chen, and Michael Grimm

As described in previous chapters, IMMPA models are typically based on a parsimonious production structure. They also distinguish between a fairly small number of representative households. For instance, in Mini-IMMPA there are five categories of households, consisting of workers in the rural sector, workers in the urban informal economy, urban unskilled workers in the formal sector, urban skilled workers in the formal sector, and capitalist-rentiers (see Chapter 3). In the Turkey application, there are only four categories (see Chapter 7).

The methodology used in IMMPA for poverty and distributional analysis, as discussed in Chapter 5, involves as a first step classifying data from a household survey into the categories of households contained in the structural component of the model. Following a policy or exogenous shock, real growth rates in per capita consumption and income for all categories of households are obtained from the structural component, up to the end of the simulation horizon. These growth rates are applied separately to income and consumption expenditure for each household in the survey, thus giving a new vector of absolute income and consumption levels for each individual in each category or group of households. Poverty and income distribution indicators are then calculated with these new data, after updating the initial poverty lines (using the price indexes generated by the structural component of the model), to reflect changes in the price of the consumption basket and purchasing power of income. Because changes in within-group distribution are ignored, these indicators reflect essentially changes across groups. But while appealing from a practical point of view, this approach is open to the criticism that it does not account for heterogeneity among agents within groups and introduces only in a partial manner the relevant changes that occur at the macro level as a result of shocks (most importantly, changes in employment) to the micro component of the analysis.

This chapter is essentially methodological in nature. Its goal is to compare three approaches aimed at linking micro and macro levels to analyze the poverty and distributional effects of policy and exogenous shocks in applied general equilibrium models. The first approach is the one followed in most of the IMMPA applications described earlier, and consists of introducing group-specific changes in income and consumption in a household income survey and computing postshock poverty and distributional indicators on the basis of the "adjusted" household data. The second approach extends the first in the sense that it not only incorporates changes in income and consumption occurring at the macro level in the household survey, but it also accounts for changes in the employment structure predicted by the macro component. This is done by modifying the weight given to each household in the survey. The third approach, which was pioneered by Adelman and Robinson (1978) and Dervis, de Mel,o and Robinson (1982), and revived more recently by Decaluwé, Dumont, and Savard (1999), and Decaluwé, Patry, Savard, and Thorbecke (1999), imposes a fixed, parametrically estimated distribution of income within each group and assumes that shocks shift the mean of these distributions without, however, modifying their shape. Poverty indicators are then computed based on these distributions. To illustrate and compare these three approaches we use the Mini-IMMPA framework developed in Chapter 3.

The chapter is organized as follows. Section 8.1 provides a brief discussion of the standard "Representative Household Groups" (RHG) framework. Section 8.2 presents the three alternative approaches to micro–macro linkages that we compare. Section 8.3 outlines the structure of Mini-IMMPA, the RHG framework that we use for our comparisons. Section 8.4 presents the simulation results of various policy-induced shocks on income distribution and poverty, and uses them to compare the three approaches presented in section 8.2. The last section summarizes our results and suggests further extensions of our analysis.

8.1   Macro-RHG Models and Poverty Analysis

Macroeconomic models that have been recently developed to quantify poverty reduction strategies typically distinguish between several broad categories of agents such as households, firms, the government, sometimes the central bank and commercial banks, and the rest of the world.[1] On the production side, there is

---

[1] See the references in the Introduction to this volume.

often a distinction between the rural and urban sectors, with further disaggregation within each sector. Households are generally disaggregated into several so-called "representative household groups" or RHGs, according to their education level (unskilled, semi-skilled, and skilled, for instance), their location (rural and urban), and their sector of employment (manufacturing or services). By distinguishing between rural and urban sectors and by accounting for migration dynamics, some models also allow the user to study separately the evolution of poverty in urban and rural areas and its relation with output and employment fluctuations across sectors.

In this type of model, referred to as "Macro-RHG model" in what follows, the distributional and poverty effects of shocks (exogenous or policy induced) are generally based on the association between group-specific mean incomes and the state of poverty. For instance, if the mean income of workers in the rural tradable goods sector is below the poverty line, all workers in this sector are considered poor. Likewise, inequality indicators in this framework are based only on the distance between group-specific means. Therefore, within-group heterogeneity (that is, dispersion around group means) is completely ignored.

However, a common observation is that the contribution of within-group income inequality to overall income inequality can be much more important than that of between-group inequality, even if households are disaggregated in relatively small groups and part of the intra-group inequality can be attributed to measurement errors and idiosyncratic, transitory elements of income. If, for instance, Ivorian households are classified into 10 groups according to sector of activity and educational attainment of the household head, more than 80 percent of the variance of household income per capita is within groups. Likewise, in the case of Indonesia a similar classification into 10 groups leaves 74 percent of the total variance unexplained. Or, if we separate Malagasy households into 14 even groups, we still find 76 percent of the total variance within groups.[2] Furthermore, inequality changes within groups may be at least as important as changes between groups. Because, by definition, Macro-RHG models do not account for intra-group heterogeneity, they cannot provide much insight in the analysis of the impact of government policy or exogenous shocks on income distribution.

8.2 Linking Income Survey Data with Macro-RHG Models

In what follows we present three approaches to linking Macro-RHG models with information from a Household Income Survey, such as an Integrated Survey (IS) or Living Standard Measurement Survey (LSMS). The first two approaches are what we call "micro-accounting" approaches. This term refers to a special kind of micro-simulation models that work directly with all the observations gathered in a household

---

[2]These estimates are derived from computations by the authors, based on household surveys of the respective countries.

survey, but do not take explicitly into account the behavior of agents at the micro level. Under the third approach, the Macro-RHG model supplies the household module with group-specific changes in mean income. The household survey provides additional information on income dispersion in each group, which is assumed fixed across different simulations.

8.2.1   A Simple Micro-Accounting Method

Macro-RHG models can be relatively easily connected with a household income survey to compute poverty and inequality indicators over a sample of actual households and not only over group-specific means as in the standard Macro-RHG framework. The advantage of this method is that now a uniform intra-group distribution is not assumed but instead use is made of the distribution observed for the sample of actual households. In general this method follows five steps (see Chapter 5):[3]

- Classify the available sample into the categories of households distinguished by the macro model (using information on the main source of income of the household head, for instance).
- Retain from the macro model nominal growth rates in per capita consumption or disposable income induced by a shock for all categories of households.
- Apply these growth rates separately to the per capita disposable income or consumption expenditure of each household in the household survey. This provides absolute income or consumption expenditure levels following the shock.
- Adjust poverty lines (expressed in monetary units) using changes in consumer prices given by the macro model (possibly separately for the rural and urban sectors, or even separately for each household group). Then, using the new absolute nominal levels of income and consumption for each group, calculate standard income distribution measures such as the headcount index, the poverty gap, and the Gini coefficient.
- Compare the postshock poverty and income distribution indicators with the baseline values to assess the impact of the shock on the poor.

To measure poverty we use the Foster, Greer, and Thorbecke's (FGT) poverty measure P_α (see Foster, Greer and Thorbecke (1984)):

$$P_{\alpha t} = \frac{1}{N} \sum_{y_{it}=0}^{z_t} \left(\frac{z_t - y_{it}}{z_t} \right)^\alpha, \tag{1}$$

where α is a poverty-aversion parameter, N the total number of households in the survey, y_{it} household i's income or consumption in period t, and z_t the poverty line in period t. The case $\alpha = 0$ yields the headcount ratio, that is, the percentage of poor households. The case $\alpha = 1$ yields the poverty gap index, that is, the average distance

---

[3]A similar method is followed by Löfgren, Robinson, and El-Said (2002), and Coady and Harris (2001).

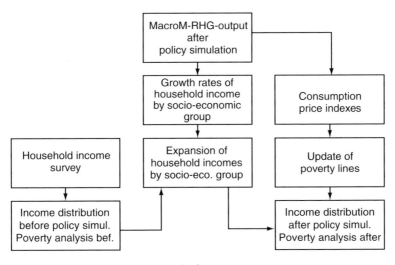

Figure 8.1   Simple micro-accounting method.

between income and the poverty line (where for nonpoor households this distance is set to zero) as a fraction of the poverty line. These measures can be calculated for each household category j, as well as for the total population.

To measure inequality we use the Gini coefficient and the Theil index.[4] The Gini coefficient is given by:

$$G_t = 1 + \frac{1}{N} - \frac{2}{\bar{y}_t N^2} \sum_{i=1}^{N} (N - i + 1) y_{it}, \qquad (2)$$

where households are ranked in ascending order of y_{it}, and $\bar{y}_t$ is mean household income or consumption in period t.

The Theil index is given by:

$$T_t = \sum_{i=1}^{N} \frac{1}{N} \frac{y_{it}}{\bar{y}_t} \ln \left(\frac{y_{it}}{\bar{y}_t} \right). \qquad (3)$$

Figure 8.1 summarizes the whole procedure, where each step is represented by a box. This approach to micro–macro linkage is "top-down" as there are no feedback effects from the household survey to the Macro-RHG model, that is, market equilibria are entirely simulated on the macro-side without accounting for any further heterogeneity in behavior within groups.

This method is not entirely satisfactory to the extent that per capita consumption and income in the household sample are adjusted to the corresponding levels in the macro model, but the employment structure is not. This implies that labor market

---

[4]For details on these indicators, see for instance Cowell (1999). Whereas the Gini coefficient is most sensitive to income differences around the middle (or, more precisely, the mode) of the distribution, the Theil index is most sensitive to income differences at the top of the distribution.

mobility affects poverty and income distribution only through relative income changes induced by, among other things, changes in the employment structure at the macro level. When the changes are transmitted to the household survey, it is thus assumed that each individual remains in his or her initial sector of activity. If the Macro-RHG model is dynamic, the same problem arises for other dimensions of the population structure; the urban–rural distribution (and possibly the age structure) may change in the macro component, but these changes are not taken into account when the link with the household survey is established. Furthermore, as noted earlier, the application of group-specific, instead of household-specific, real growth rates of consumption or income assumes that the intra-group distribution of consumption and disposable income remains constant after a shock.

To set up the procedure described above, we use instead of an actual household income and expenditure survey a "fictitious" one that we built as follows.

First, we produced a sample of 5,000 observations, where the share of each household category (five in our case, see below) corresponds exactly to that in our macro model.[5] We considered each observation to represent one household.

Second, using a random number generator and a log-normal distribution, we drew values for disposable income and consumption expenditure for each household. We imposed as parameters for each group the initial values for average disposable income and average consumption expenditure (as specified for the numerical solution of the macro model) as mean and standard deviation, except for skilled workers in the formal urban sector and for capitalists and rentiers, for which we imposed a standard deviation equal to 0.8 times the mean.[6]

Third, we set (somewhat arbitrarily) the income poverty line for the rural sector such that the percentage of poor households in the rural sector is 50 percent. We then assumed the poverty line in urban areas to be 15 percent higher. Rural and urban poverty lines for consumption expenditure were calculated in the same way. This procedure produced an economy-wide income-based headcount index of 38.6 percent and an economy-wide consumption-based headcount index of 41.1 percent. For simplicity, we assumed that poverty lines remain constant in real terms for the whole horizon of the simulation period.

8.2.2   An Extension with Reweighting Techniques

Adding changes in the employment structure to the household survey, we combine now the micro-accounting method described above with reweighting techniques.[7] The employment variable accounts in our illustrative example for three dimensions of the population structure: residence (rural or urban), sector of employment (rural,

---

[5]More specifically, the shares are 28.1 percent workers in the agricultural sector (rural), 45.3 percent workers in the informal urban sector, 13.7 percent unskilled workers in the formal urban sector, 9.9 percent skilled workers in the formal urban sector, and 3.0 percent capitalists and rentiers.

[6]This is done to limit the number of skilled workers in the formal urban sector and capitalists and rentiers who have less income and consumption expenditure than workers in the informal urban sector, or unskilled workers in the formal urban sector.

[7]The method that we describe can be extended, of course, to account for other changes in the population structure as well; see Allie and Murphy (2000).

urban informal, or urban formal), and educational attainment (skilled or unskilled). It is intuitively clear that large changes in the employment structure may have strong effects on income distribution. Whereas in the first approach we have to assume that (the sum of) within-group inequality remains constant over time, in this approach it will change to the extent that population and income shares of each group change over time.

In our approach reweighting is done through special statistical procedures that alter the distribution of desired characteristics X_i (the linkage variables) of the population by adjusting the weight attached to each of the N households indexed with i.[8] In general, the problem is to find an n-vector $\mathbf{w'}$ of adjustment factors optimizing an objective function $Z(\mathbf{w'}, \mathbf{w})$ – a function evaluating the distance between the new adjustment factors w_i' to be computed, and the available factors w_i – satisfying a certain number m of restrictions summarized in the form $\mathbf{Xw'} = \mathbf{r}$:

$$\text{Min } Z(\mathbf{w'}, \mathbf{w}), \tag{4}$$

$$\text{such that} \quad \mathbf{X_{(m,n)}w'_{(n)}} = \mathbf{r_{(m)}}. \tag{5}$$

This adjustment problem is a simultaneous one, where for even a quite large number of characteristics, just one single weighting factor has to be computed for each household, which after summing up consistently fulfills all hierarchical restrictions simultaneously (see Merz (1994)). These statistical procedures preserve the joint distribution of the other characteristics. Put differently, instead of estimating econometric models to run simulations, reweighting (or "static ageing") takes macro aggregates and then adjusts the underlying distribution to produce projections of the population distribution over time (or before and after a shock). The underlying characteristics are held constant, while the weights given to different parts of the sample are changed.

It is important to note, however, that reweighting assumes that the characteristics within a weighted group do not change over time. Therefore, if large changes occur in a variable that was not included in the macro weights, errors may arise. For instance, a weighting scheme where weights are applied according to whether a family has children or not would overestimate the number of children if the fertility rate fell as a result of a reduction in the number of large families rather than a smaller number of families with children.

Given that at this stage we want to reweight only with respect to changes in the employment structure without imposing any additional constraints, the procedure is relatively straightforward, because we have only one condition in the minimization problem. The procedure is summarized in Figure 8.2. We use the same artificial household survey as in the first approach. In a real country case the procedure may be extended to account for other changes in the population structure as well, coming either directly from the Macro-RHG model (as for instance the population growth rate) or taken from external sources such as the United Nations' demographic projections. Appendix A points out some of these issues and shows also how

---

[8]On reweighting techniques in general, see for instance Landt et al. (1994).

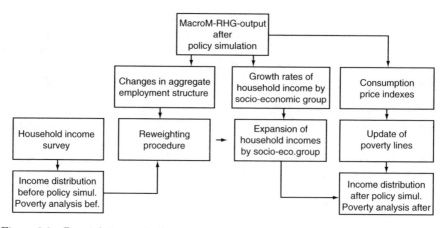

Figure 8.2   Reweighting method.

reweighting procedures could be used to achieve consistency between a Macro-RHG model and real household survey data in the base year.

Under the reweighting procedure, we calculate the household group-specific FGT poverty measures as before, but when calculating it for the urban population and the total population we now account for changes in the employment structure with respect to the initial period. The FGT poverty measures are now calculated with the formulas

$$P_{\alpha t} = \frac{\sum_j P_{\alpha jt} w_{jt}}{\sum_j w_{jt}}, \tag{6}$$

where the index j stands for household categories and w_{jt} for their respective share in the total population in period t. In the micro-accounting method presented earlier, the implicit assumption was that the coefficients w_{jt} remain constant over time.

Likewise, we can calculate the inequality measures by weighing each household with its group and period-specific weight f_{jt}, where $f_{jt} = w_{jt}/N_j$ with w_{jt} is the share of group j in the population at period t and N_j the size of group j in the initial period. In period $t = 0$, f_{j0} is thus equal to $1/N$ for each household.

8.2.3   The Use of Distribution Functions

Methodology

The third approach uses specific parametric distributions to describe the dispersion of income within each group. The parameters of these distributions are generally estimated using real household survey data. We use again our fictitious sample of household incomes and consumption expenditure.

In contrast to the two approaches presented above, once the parameters are estimated, the survey data are not used anymore to evaluate the distributional effects of shocks. Following a shock, the fitted distributions are only shifted according to changes in the group-specific mean incomes, to the right (increase in income or consumption) or to the left (decrease in income or consumption), without modifying the shape of these distributions.

The poverty indicators are also computed using the estimated shape parameters without relying, once again, on the household survey data. The overall distribution of income is generated empirically by summing the separate within-group distributions and is then used to generate overall, economy-wide measures of poverty and inequality.

It is important to note that in this approach and in the two former approaches changes in income are not distributed in the same way within groups. Whereas in the first two, we suppose usually that the *relative* increase is uniform over the whole distribution (that is, the absolute change is proportional to the initial income), in the distribution function approach the *absolute* increase is assumed to be uniform over the whole distribution (that is, the relative increase is the higher the lower the initial income). Nevertheless, with the distribution function approach we also assume that intra-group inequality remains unaffected by a shock to income or consumption levels, as in the other two approaches.

As in Decaluwé, Patry, Savard, and Thorbecke (1999) and Decaluwé, Dumont, and Savard (1999), we use Beta distribution functions to describe the within-group distributions. Of course, it would be more logical to use the log-normal distributions from which our artificial data are drawn, but in a real country case the assumption of Beta distributions may be more convenient, because of their higher degree of flexibility.[9]

The Beta density distribution is a continuous function taking values between 0 and 1. It is defined as[10]

$$I(x; \beta_1, \beta_2) = \frac{1}{B(\beta_1, \beta_2)} x^{\beta_1 - 1} (1 - x)^{\beta_2 - 1}, \tag{7}$$

where $B(\beta_1, \beta_2)$ is the beta function with the formula:

$$B(\beta_1, \beta_2) = \int_0^1 x^{\beta_1 - 1} (1 - x)^{\beta_2 - 1} dx. \tag{8}$$

The parameters β_1 and β_2 are positive. To normalize a given variable, say, income y_i, to values between 0 and 1, we impose the transformation

$$x_i = \frac{y_i - mn}{mx - mn}, \tag{9}$$

where mn and mx are the minimum and maximum values, respectively, of the distribution of y_i.

---

[9] Boccanfuso, Decaluwé, and Savard (2002) compared six alternative functional forms to model within-group distributions. They concluded that no single form is uniformly appropriate in all cases or groups of households. However, the authors end up advocating, especially when detailed disaggregation is required, flexible forms (such as the Beta function), which allows, for instance, distributions to be very negatively skewed.

[10] See the description in "A Thesaurus of Mathematics," University of Cambridge, at http://www.thesaurus.maths.org.

The parameters β_1 and β_2 have the following moments estimators:[11]

$$\hat{\beta}_1 = \bar{x}\left(\frac{\bar{x}(1-\bar{x})}{s^2} - 1\right), \quad \hat{\beta}_2 = (1-\bar{x})\left(\frac{\bar{x}(1-\bar{x})}{s^2} - 1\right), \tag{10}$$

where $\bar{x}$ stands for the sample mean and s^2 represents the sample variance.

The FGT poverty measures expressed in terms of the Beta density distribution function given in equation (7) become:

$$P_{\alpha jt} = \int_0^{z'_{tj}} \left(\frac{z'_{tj} - x}{z'_{tj}}\right)^\alpha I(x; \hat{\beta}_{1j}\hat{\beta}_{2j})dx, \tag{11}$$

where z'_{tj} is the group and period-specific normalized poverty line, defined as $z'_{tj} = (z_{tj} - mn_j)/(mx_j - mn_j)$. Thus, equation (11) allows us to compare the poverty levels obtained in the postsimulation case with those prevailing in the presimulation case. To calculate the poverty measures for the urban or the total population at time t, we can either weigh the group-specific poverty measures of equation (11) by their initial population shares, w_{j0}, or by their population shares at t, w_{jt}, as in equation (6).

Given that the household survey data are discarded once the shape parameters are estimated, and given that the distribution function approach assumes implicitly that intra-group inequality does not change following a shock, we limit now the measurement of inequality to between-group inequality. The Theil index allows an exact decomposition of total inequality between within- and between-group inequality.[12] Between-group inequality, T_{Bt}, can be calculated as:

$$T_{Bt} = \sum_j s_{jt} \ln\left(\frac{\bar{y}_{jt}}{\bar{y}_t}\right). \tag{12}$$

Therefore, between-group inequality depends only on s_{jt}, the share of total income held by group j, $\bar{y}_{jt}$, the mean income in group j, and $\bar{y}_t$, the overall mean of income. Of course, to estimate changes in overall inequality, one may measure intra-group inequality with the survey that is used to estimate the shape parameters in the first place, and then add this measure in each period to between-group inequality. Figure 8.3 summarizes the simulation procedure when using the Beta distribution method.

Estimation Results and Goodness of Fit

Table B8.1 in Appendix B presents the estimated shape parameters of the Beta density distribution function for both disposable income and consumption expenditure, using our fictitious household survey. Initial experiments indicated that the estimation

---

[11] See the internet website "Scientific Resources: Statistics–Econometrics–Forecasting," at http://www.xycoon.com/index.htm. Alternatively, one can estimate the parameters with Maximum Likelihood techniques.

[12] See for instance Shorrocks (1984), Deaton (1997), and Cowell (1999).

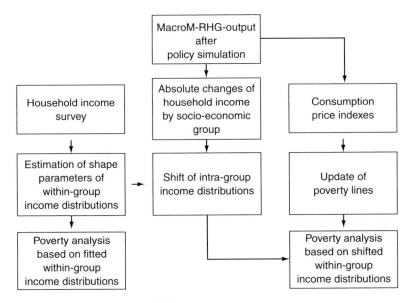

Figure 8.3 Beta distribution method.

results were very sensitive to outliers. To increase the goodness of fit of our estimates, we eliminated for each group the five highest and five lowest values of the distribution.[13]

Table B8.2 in Appendix B compares the "observed" values for the poverty measures P_0 and P_1 for income and consumption with the predicted values using both sets of estimated shape parameters, that is, with and without dropping the extreme values (as defined above). Figures B8.1 and B8.2 show the corresponding "observed" and "fitted" (after dropping extreme values) cumulative distribution functions.

From Table B8.2 it can be seen that if we correct the data for outliers the fit is quite acceptable for P_0 – at least for households in the rural sector and households in the informal urban sector. However, for the other three groups, the deviations are significant. One explanation for this outcome is that the population size is smaller for these groups, and thus the estimated shape parameters are less reliable. The poverty gap ratio is much more difficult to fit. Here the predicted indicators lie more than 40 percent above the observed values. It is interesting to see that in our case the predictions of the Beta distributions lead always to an overestimation of P_0 and P_1 (except for capitalists and rentiers), compared to the indicators that are directly measured from the survey data. Figures B8.1 and B8.2 show that the quality of the prediction depends also strongly on where the poverty line is drawn. The fitted curve crosses the observed curve for the first time around a cumulated population of 40 to 50 percent. If the poverty line is close to this intersection, than the prediction of P_1 would be of course quite good.

---

[13] Of course more powerful and reliable methods to detect and eliminate outliers exist (see, for instance, Deaton (1997)). These methods should be used in a real country application, when detailed information on socioeconomic characteristics of the households is available.

8.3   The Macro-RHG Framework

Mini-IMMPA is described at length in Chapter 3. Although Mini-IMMPA focuses only on the real side (unlike the complete IMMPA framework described in Chapter 5), it offers a more detailed treatment of the labor market, accounting for features such as employment subsidies and job security provisions. Given its focus on the real side, the building blocks of the structural component of Mini-IMMPA consist of the production side, employment, the demand side, external trade, sectoral and aggregate prices, income formation, consumption and savings, private investment, and the public sector. As noted earlier, households are defined according to the skills composition of the workforce and the sector of employment. There is one rural household, comprising all workers employed in the rural sector. In the urban sector there are two types of unskilled households, those working in the informal sector and those employed in the formal sector. The fourth type of households consists of skilled workers employed in the formal urban economy, in both the private and public sectors. Finally, there are capitalist-rentiers whose income comes mostly from firms' earnings in the urban private sector. The following description of the model is kept quite short.

8.3.1   Production and the Labor Market

The basic distinction on the production side is that between rural and urban sectors. In the rural economy firms produce one good, which is sold domestically or exported. The urban economy consists of both formal and informal components. The informal economy produces nontraded services. The formal urban economy is separated between production of a private good, and a nontraded public good.

For all activities the production technology is represented by value added functions and fixed (Leontief) intermediate input coefficients. With the exception of the public sector, the value added functions are represented by sets of nested constant elasticity of substitution functions and Cobb-Douglas functions. The rural sector uses land (assumed to be in fixed supply), unskilled labor, and the economy-wide stock of public physical capital. Production exhibits decreasing returns to scale with respect to the two latter inputs. Value added in the informal sector requires only unskilled labor and is subject to decreasing returns to scale. Urban private formal production uses as inputs both skilled and unskilled labor, as well as private and public physical capital. Skilled labor and private physical capital are assumed to have a higher degree of complementarity than private physical capital and unskilled labor. Furthermore, it is assumed that public capital is subject to congestion effects, that is, the positive externality associated with public capital decreases as its usage by the urban population increases. Value added in the public sector is measured from the government wage bill. Employment levels of skilled and unskilled workers in that sector are treated as predetermined variables. Firms in the rural and the private formal sector allocate their output to exports or the domestic market according to a production possibility frontier, defined by a constant elasticity of transformation function. Assuming imperfect substitutability, the ratio between exports and domestic sales depends on the relative prices of exported and domestic goods and the elasticity of substitution between these goods.

The demand for labor in the rural sector is derived from first-order conditions for profit maximization. Labor demand is related positively to the level of net output and negatively to the product wage (the nominal wage deflated by the net output price). The nominal wage in the rural sector adjusts to clear the labor market. The supply of labor in the rural sector is predetermined at any given point in time, but grows over time at the exogenous population growth rate, net of worker migration to urban areas. In the Harris-Todaro tradition, the incentives to migrate are taken to depend negatively on the ratio of the average expected wage in rural areas relative to the wage prevailing in urban areas. Unskilled workers in the urban economy may be employed either in the private formal sector, in which case they are paid a minimum wage, or they can enter the informal economy and receive the average income in that sector. Potential migrants are uncertain as to which type of job they will be able to get, and therefore weigh wages in each sector by the probability of finding a job in that sector.

Both the government and private firms in the formal and informal urban sectors use unskilled labor in production. The public sector is assumed to hire an exogenous level of unskilled workers at a fixed nominal wage, whereas the demand for unskilled labor by the formal private sector is determined by firms' profit maximization subject to the given minimum wage. In order to avoid corner solutions, the wage paid to unskilled labor in the formal urban sector is assumed to be systematically greater than the wage earned in the informal sector. Consequently, unskilled workers in the urban area will always seek employment in the private formal sector first, given the assumption of complete job turnover in each period. The informal labor market clears continuously; in addition, mobility of the unskilled labor force between the formal and the informal sectors is taken to be imperfect, and determined by expectations on income opportunities formed on the basis of prevailing conditions in the labor market.[14]

The supply of unskilled labor in the urban sector grows as a result of "natural" urban population growth (given that individuals are born unskilled) and migration of unskilled labor from the rural economy, as discussed earlier. Moreover, some urban unskilled workers acquire skills and leave the unskilled labor force to increase the supply of qualified labor in the formal economy. Skilled workers who cannot find employment in the formal sector do not work in the informal economy – perhaps as a result of either a high reservation wage or "adverse signaling" considerations. The acquisition of skills by unskilled workers takes place through an education technology operated by the public sector. Specifically, the flow of unskilled workers who become skilled is taken to be a CES function of the "effective" number of teachers in the public sector and the government stock of capital in education.

For the purpose of the experiments reported in this chapter, wages for skilled labor in the private sector are assumed to be determined on the basis of the "monopoly union" framework, where a centralized labor union maximizes a utility function that depends on deviations of both employment and the consumption wage from their target levels, subject to the firm's labor demand schedule (see Chapters 1 and 3). The union's target real wage is assumed to be related positively to skilled wages in the public

---

[14]See Chapter 1 for a discussion of the rationale for doing so.

sector (as a result of a "signaling" effect) and negatively to the skilled unemployment rate, and the real firing cost per skilled worker. The higher the firing cost, the greater the incentive for the union to reduce its wage demands, in order to encourage firms to hire. Both the minimum wage and nominal wages in the public sector are taken to be fully indexed on the urban consumption price index.

8.3.2   Composition of Demand and Prices

As noted above, both the informal and public sector goods are nontradables, and both markets clear continuously. In each sector, total supply is thus equal to gross production. Rural and private formal urban goods, by contrast, compete with imported goods. For the rural, public, and informal sector goods, aggregate demand consists of intermediate consumption and private demand for final consumption. Aggregate demand for the private formal good consists of intermediate consumption, final consumption by households and the public sector, and investment.

Other current government spending on goods and public investment expenditure are spent only on the private formal sector good. Each category of households determines final consumption for each type of good so as to maximize a Stone-Geary utility function. Total private investment consists of purchases of urban private sector goods. In standard fashion, the ratio of imports to both categories of domestic goods depends on the relative prices of these goods and the elasticity of substitution between these goods, given the assumption of imperfect substitutability.

The world prices of imported and exported goods are exogenously given. The domestic currency price of these goods is obtained by adjusting the world price by the exchange rate, with import prices also adjusted by the tariff rate. Prices of domestic sales in the rural and urban private sectors adjust to equilibrate supply and demand. For the informal and public sectors, where production does not compete with imports, the domestic market price is equal to the gross output price. The consumption price index is constructed separately for rural households and urban (skilled and unskilled) households. They are computed as the weighted average of price changes over all consumed goods, where the weights reflect the composition of spending by each group in the base period.

8.3.3   Profits and Income

Firms' profits are defined as revenue minus total labor costs. Profits of urban private sector firms account for both working capital costs and salaries paid to both categories of workers, as well as payroll taxes on unskilled employment and firing costs for both categories of workers. Household income is based on the return to labor (salaries), distributed profits, and government transfers. Households in both the rural sector and the informal urban economy own the firms in which they are employed.

Urban formal sector households receive no profits because skilled and unskilled workers in that sector do not own the production units in which they are employed. Firms in the private urban sector pay income taxes, and interest on their foreign borrowing. A portion of their net profits are retained for the purpose of financing investment; the remainder is transferred to capitalists and rentiers. Each category of households saves a fixed fraction of its disposable income and allocates the rest to consumption.

8.3.4   Investment–Savings Balance

Capital accumulation occurs only in the urban private sector. The desired capital stock by firms in the private urban sector is determined so as to equate the after-tax rate of return on capital, plus capital gains due to changes in the price of capital and minus depreciation, to the opportunity cost of investment, which (assuming the absence of "effective" restrictions to capital mobility) is taken to be the world interest rate. Actual investment in each period is determined by a partial adjustment process and is given as a function of the ratio between the desired capital stock and last period's capital stock.

The aggregate identity between savings and investment is specified as follows. Total gross investment in physical capital measured in nominal terms is financed by firms' after-tax retained earnings, total after-tax household savings, "primary" government savings (that is, before investment), and foreign borrowing by firms and the government (equivalently, net foreign savings). In the simulations reported in this chapter, the aggregate investment–savings identity is solved residually for total private investment.

8.3.5   Public Sector and the Balance of Payments

Government expenditures consist of current outlays and investment, with the latter consisting of investment in infrastructure, education, and health. Public capital in infrastructure and health combine to produce the stock of government capital, which affects the production process in the private sector.

All value added in the production of public goods is distributed as wages. The government fiscal balance is thus defined as total tax revenues minus the wage bill on school teachers, government transfers to households, total employment subsidies to firms in the private formal sector, other current expenditures on goods and services, investment spending, and interest payments on loans from abroad. Total tax revenues consist of revenues generated by import tariffs, sales taxes, income taxes, and payroll taxes.

The external constraint implies that any current account surplus (or deficit) must be compensated by a net outflow (or inflow) of foreign capital, given by the sum of changes in net foreign borrowing by the government and private firms.

8.4   Comparing Policy Shocks with Alternative Linkages

To compare the performance of the three alternative approaches to micro–macro linkages discussed above, the growth, employment and poverty effects of two types of labor market policies are examined in this section: a cut in the minimum wage and an increase in the employment subsidy on unskilled labor. Both experiments relate to critical policy issues in developing countries (see Chapters 1, 3, and 4). As an indicator of living standards, we consider in what follows only disposable income per capita.

8.4.1   Reduction in the Minimum Wage

The simulation results associated with a permanent, 7 percent reduction in the minimum wage are illustrated in Tables 8.1 and 8.2 for the first 10 periods after the shock.[15] This time period is referred to below as the "adjustment period." Table 8.1 provides data on the most important macroeconomic indicators, the government budget balance, and the labor market. Table 8.2 presents data on consumer prices, disposable income for each household group, and poverty and distributional indicators for the income variable, all in absolute deviations from the baseline solution.

The experiment assumes that the government borrows domestically to finance its deficit – implying therefore (as discussed earlier) an offsetting adjustment in the investment of private firms, in order to maintain the aggregate balance between savings and investment. We first comment on the general results of this simulation and then compare more specifically the effects on poverty and inequality, as measured by the three different methods.

The impact effect of the reduction in the minimum wage is an increase in the demand for unskilled labor in the private sector of almost 3.4 percent in the first year and approximately 7 to 9 percent in the following years. The increase in demand is met by the existing pool of unskilled workers seeking employment in the urban sector. As a result, the unskilled unemployment rate drops significantly, by 2.2 percentage points in the first year and by more than 8 percentage points in the following years, which reduces unemployment for this segment of workers to almost zero.

The cut in the minimum wage, by reducing the relative cost of unskilled labor, leads to substitution among production factors not only on impact but also over time. Because unskilled labor has a relatively high elasticity of substitution with respect to the composite factor consisting of skilled labor and physical capital, the lower cost of that category of labor gives private firms in the formal sector an incentive to substitute away from both factors. In turn, the fall in the demand for skilled labor puts downward pressure on skilled wages, which drop by 5.2 percent in the first period. On impact, labor supply is fixed in the rural sector and the informal economy, so the level of employment does not change in either sector – and neither does the level of activity (real value added in both sectors is constant). The rise in real disposable income (by 2.1 percent in the rural sector and 4 percent in the informal sector) and real consumption of rural and informal sector households leads to higher value added prices and higher wages in both sectors. But value added prices go up by slightly more than wages in the second and subsequent periods, implying a fall in the product wage in both sectors and a rise in employment.

---

[15]This reduction means that the minimum wage decreases from 1.23 times the poverty line to 1.14 times the poverty line.

Table 8.1 Mini-IMMPA: simulation results. 7-percent cut in unskilled labor minimum wage. (Percentage deviations from baseline, unless otherwise indicated)

					Periods					
	1	2	3	4	5	6	7	8	9	10
Macroeconomic Indicators										
GDP at market prices	−0.1	0.5	0.3	0.3	0.2	0.1	0.1	0.0	−0.1	−0.1
Value added at factor cost	0.2	0.7	0.5	0.4	0.4	0.3	0.2	0.2	0.1	0.1
Value added in rural sector	0.0	0.2	0.4	0.6	0.8	1.0	1.1	1.3	1.4	1.5
Value added in urban informal sector	0.0	0.7	0.4	0.3	0.1	0.0	−0.1	−0.2	−0.3	−0.4
Value added in urban formal sector	0.5	1.0	0.7	0.6	0.5	0.3	0.2	0.1	0.0	−0.1
Private consumption	0.5	0.9	0.8	0.8	0.7	0.7	0.7	0.6	0.6	0.6
Private investment	−10.7	−5.9	−7.2	−7.1	−7.2	−7.3	−7.4	−7.5	−7.5	−7.5
Disposable income	0.4	0.8	0.7	0.7	0.7	0.6	0.6	0.6	0.6	0.5
Government Accounts (% of GDP)[1]										
Total revenue	−0.7	−0.5	−0.5	−0.5	−0.5	−0.5	−0.4	−0.4	−0.4	−0.4
Direct taxes	−0.2	−0.1	−0.1	−0.1	−0.1	−0.1	−0.1	−0.1	−0.1	−0.1
Indirect taxes	−0.5	−0.3	−0.4	−0.4	−0.4	−0.3	−0.3	−0.3	−0.3	−0.3
Total expenditure	−0.1	−0.3	−0.2	−0.2	−0.1	−0.1	−0.1	−0.1	0.0	0.0
Consumption	0.0	−0.1	0.0	0.0	0.0	0.0	0.0	0.0	0.0	0.0
Investment	−0.1	−0.1	−0.1	−0.1	−0.1	−0.1	−0.1	−0.1	−0.1	0.0
Transfers to households	0.0	0.0	0.0	0.0	0.0	0.0	0.0	0.0	0.0	0.0
Foreign interest payments	0.0	0.0	0.0	0.0	0.0	0.0	0.0	0.0	0.0	0.0
Total financing	0.5	0.2	0.3	0.3	0.3	0.3	0.4	0.4	0.4	0.4
Foreign financing	0.0	0.0	0.0	0.0	0.0	0.0	0.0	0.0	0.0	0.0
Domestic borrowing	0.5	0.2	0.3	0.3	0.3	0.3	0.4	0.4	0.4	0.4

Continued

Table 8.1 Continued

		Periods								
	1	2	3	4	5	6	7	8	9	10
Labor Market										
Nominal wages										
Agricultural sector	3.7	3.9	2.3	1.3	0.3	-0.6	-1.4	-2.2	-2.9	-3.5
Informal sector	5.4	3.1	3.9	4.0	4.2	4.3	4.4	4.5	4.6	4.7
Private formal sector										
Unskilled	-7.0	-7.0	-7.0	-7.0	-7.0	-7.0	-7.0	-7.0	-7.0	-7.0
Skilled	-5.2	-3.8	-4.3	-4.3	-4.4	-4.5	-4.6	-4.7	-4.8	-4.8
Public sector										
Unskilled	0.0	0.0	0.0	0.0	0.0	0.0	0.0	0.0	0.0	0.0
Skilled	0.1	0.1	0.1	0.1	0.1	0.1	0.1	0.1	0.1	0.1
Employment										
Agricultural sector	0.0	0.3	0.6	0.8	1.0	1.2	1.4	1.6	1.7	1.8
Informal sector	0.0	0.9	0.5	0.3	0.2	0.0	-0.1	-0.2	-0.3	-0.4
Private formal sector										
Unskilled	3.4	7.6	7.0	7.5	7.8	8.1	8.4	8.8	9.1	9.4
Skilled	-0.5	-0.3	-0.4	-0.4	-0.4	-0.4	-0.4	-0.4	-0.4	-0.4
Public sector										
Unskilled	0.0	0.0	0.0	0.0	0.0	0.0	0.0	0.0	0.0	0.0
Skilled	0.0	0.0	0.0	0.0	0.0	0.0	0.0	0.0	0.0	0.0

Labor supply (urban formal sector)										
Unskilled	0.0	-3.6	-2.9	-3.0	-3.0	-2.9	-2.8	-2.7	-2.5	-2.4
Skilled	0.0	0.0	0.0	0.0	0.0	0.0	0.0	0.0	0.0	0.0
Unemployment rate (urban formal sector)[1]										
Unskilled	-2.2	-8.6	-7.4	-7.9	-8.0	-8.2	-8.3	-8.4	-8.4	-8.5
Skilled	0.2	0.2	0.2	0.2	0.2	0.2	0.2	0.2	0.2	0.2
Real wage differentials[1]										
Expected urban–rural (% of rural wage)	0.0	-12.7	-14.7	-12.5	-11.3	-10.0	-8.9	-7.9	-6.9	-6.0
Expected formal-informal (% of informal wage)	0.0	-9.5	2.1	-0.5	0.2	0.2	0.3	0.3	0.4	0.4
Migration[1]										
Rural-urban (% of urban labor supply)	0.0	-0.1	-0.1	-0.1	-0.1	-0.1	-0.1	-0.1	-0.1	0.0
Formal-informal (% of formal urban labor supply)	0.0	-3.6	0.8	-0.2	0.1	0.1	0.1	0.1	0.1	0.2

[1] Absolute deviations from baseline. [2] In real terms.

Table 8.2 Mini-IMMPA: price, poverty and distributional indicators. 7-percent cut in unskilled labor minimum wage. (Percentage deviations from baseline, unless otherwise indicated)

					Periods					
	1	2	3	4	5	6	7	8	9	10
Consumer Prices										
Rural CPI	1.31	1.09	0.94	0.79	0.65	0.52	0.40	0.28	0.18	0.08
Urban CPI	0.74	0.54	0.55	0.51	0.48	0.45	0.42	0.39	0.36	0.34
Cumulative Growth of Real Disposable Income[1]										
Rural households	2.08	2.76	1.77	1.20	0.60	0.07	−0.43	−0.89	−1.31	−1.69
Urban households	0.01	0.35	0.43	0.56	0.66	0.76	0.86	0.94	1.03	1.10
Informal	4.03	2.98	3.37	3.42	3.50	3.55	3.59	3.61	3.61	3.61
Formal unskilled	−2.55	−0.36	−0.65	−0.38	−0.23	−0.04	0.14	0.32	0.49	0.67
Formal skilled	−2.55	−1.90	−2.12	−2.15	−2.21	−2.26	−2.31	−2.35	−2.39	−2.43
Capitalists and rentiers	−6.09	−3.81	−3.88	−3.43	−3.08	−2.71	−2.34	−1.98	−1.62	−1.26
Household Shares										
Rural households	0.00	0.07	0.15	0.22	0.29	0.34	0.39	0.44	0.47	0.51
Urban households	0.00	−0.07	−0.15	−0.22	−0.29	−0.34	−0.39	−0.44	−0.47	−0.51
Informal	0.00	0.39	0.21	0.16	0.08	0.01	−0.05	−0.11	−0.17	−0.22
Formal unskilled	0.00	−0.47	−0.36	−0.38	−0.37	−0.36	−0.34	−0.32	−0.30	−0.28
Formal skilled	0.00	0.00	0.00	0.00	0.00	0.00	0.00	0.00	0.00	0.00
Capitalists and rentiers	0.00	0.00	0.00	0.00	0.00	0.00	0.00	0.00	0.00	0.00
Poverty and Distributional Indicators (Income-based)										
Poverty Line[1]										
Rural	1.31	1.09	0.94	0.79	0.65	0.52	0.40	0.28	0.18	0.08
Urban	0.75	0.55	0.55	0.51	0.48	0.45	0.42	0.39	0.37	0.34

Micro-accounting approach with and without reweighting

Poverty Headcount

Rural households	−1.14	−1.14	−0.64	−0.28	0.21	0.64	1.14	1.42	1.49	1.71
Urban households (without reweighting)	−1.34	−0.92	−1.17	−1.17	−1.28	−1.34	−1.34	−1.25	−1.22	−1.28
Urban households (with reweighting)	−1.34	−0.84	−1.14	−1.14	−1.26	−1.32	−1.32	−1.23	−1.22	−1.29
Informal	−2.61	−1.55	−1.86	−1.94	−1.99	−2.08	−2.12	−2.17	−2.17	−2.12
Formal unskilled	0.58	−0.88	−0.44	−0.44	−0.58	−0.73	−0.73	−0.73	−0.58	−0.58
Formal skilled	1.01	1.21	0.20	0.60	0.20	0.60	0.81	1.81	1.61	1.01
Capitalists and rentiers	1.33	1.33	1.33	1.33	1.33	0.67	0.67	0.00	0.67	0.67
Economy (without reweighting)	−1.28	−0.98	−1.02	−0.92	−0.86	−0.78	−0.64	−0.50	−0.46	−0.44
Economy (with reweighting)	−1.29	−0.92	−0.98	−0.87	−0.81	−0.72	−0.58	−0.42	−0.39	−0.37

Poverty Gap

Rural households	−0.60	−0.71	−0.35	−0.11	0.12	0.34	0.54	0.72	0.88	1.03
Urban households (without reweighting)	−0.59	−0.50	−0.58	−0.62	−0.66	−0.69	−0.72	−0.74	−0.75	−0.77
Urban households (with reweighting)	−0.60	−0.47	−0.57	−0.60	−0.65	−0.68	−0.71	−0.73	−0.75	−0.77
Informal	−1.15	−0.64	−0.84	−0.87	−0.93	−0.97	−1.01	−1.05	−1.07	−1.09
Formal unskilled	0.54	−0.61	−0.41	−0.49	−0.51	−0.54	−0.55	−0.57	−0.58	−0.58
Formal skilled	0.14	0.12	0.15	0.15	0.16	0.16	0.18	0.19	0.22	0.24
Capitalists and rentiers	0.23	0.14	0.14	0.11	0.10	0.08	0.07	0.06	0.05	0.04
Economy (without reweighting)	−0.59	−0.56	−0.52	−0.48	−0.44	−0.40	−0.36	−0.33	−0.29	−0.26
Economy (with reweighting)	−0.60	−0.53	−0.50	−0.45	−0.41	−0.37	−0.34	−0.30	−0.26	−0.23

Continued

Table 8.2 Continued

					Periods					
	1	2	3	4	5	6	7	8	9	10
Overall Inequality										
Gini-coefficient (without reweighting)	−0.0074	−0.0053	−0.0052	−0.0046	−0.0041	−0.0036	−0.0031	−0.0026	−0.0022	−0.0018
Gini-coefficient (with reweighting)	−0.0075	−0.0053	−0.0051	−0.0045	−0.0040	−0.0035	−0.0031	−0.0026	−0.0022	−0.0018
Theil-index (without reweighting)	−0.0153	−0.0116	−0.0111	−0.0099	−0.0089	−0.0079	−0.0069	−0.0059	−0.0050	−0.0041
Theil-index (with reweighting)	−0.0155	−0.0113	−0.0109	−0.0097	−0.0087	−0.0076	−0.0066	−0.0057	−0.0048	−0.0039
Beta-distribution approach with and without reweighting										
Poverty Headcount										
Rural households	−1.18	−1.36	−0.72	−0.30	0.12	0.50	0.84	1.16	1.44	1.70
Urban households (without reweighting)	−0.87	−0.97	−1.10	−1.22	−1.30	−1.37	−1.42	−1.46	−1.49	−1.51
Urban households (with reweighting)	−0.88	−0.88	−1.05	−1.17	−1.25	−1.32	−1.37	−1.42	−1.45	−1.48
Informal	−2.41	−1.31	−1.71	−1.77	−1.87	−1.95	−2.02	−2.07	−2.11	−2.15
Formal unskilled	1.33	−1.91	−1.29	−1.53	−1.57	−1.62	−1.66	−1.68	−1.69	−1.69
Formal skilled	1.70	1.22	1.30	1.27	1.25	1.24	1.22	1.20	1.19	1.17
Capitalists and rentiers	3.82	1.37	1.09	0.19	0.00	0.00	0.00	0.00	0.00	0.00
Economy (without reweighting)	−0.96	−1.08	−0.99	−0.96	−0.90	−0.84	−0.78	−0.72	−0.66	−0.61
Economy (with reweighting)	−0.96	−1.01	−0.94	−0.90	−0.84	−0.78	−0.72	−0.66	−0.60	−0.54

Poverty Gap										
Rural households	−0.76	−0.87	−0.46	−0.19	0.08	0.32	0.54	0.75	0.93	1.09
Urban households (without reweighting)	−0.60	−0.62	−0.71	−0.78	−0.83	−0.87	−0.90	−0.92	−0.94	−0.96
Urban households (with reweighting)	−0.61	−0.57	−0.68	−0.74	−0.80	−0.84	−0.87	−0.90	−0.92	−0.94
Informal	−1.52	−0.83	−1.08	−1.12	−1.18	−1.23	−1.28	−1.31	−1.34	−1.36
Formal unskilled	0.79	−1.13	−0.77	−0.91	−0.93	−0.97	−0.99	−1.00	−1.01	−1.01
Formal skilled	0.91	0.66	0.71	0.69	0.68	0.68	0.67	0.66	0.66	0.65
Capitalists and rentiers	1.99	0.71	0.57	0.10	0.00	0.00	0.00	0.00	0.00	0.00
Economy (without reweighting)	−0.64	−0.69	−0.64	−0.61	−0.57	−0.53	−0.45	−0.45	−0.42	−0.38
Economy (with reweighting)	−0.65	−0.65	−0.61	−0.58	−0.54	−0.49	−0.45	−0.41	−0.38	−0.34
Between-group Inequality										
Theil-index (without reweighting)	−0.0173	−0.0127	−0.0124	−0.0111	−0.0100	−0.0089	−0.0078	−0.0068	−0.0058	−0.0048
Theil-index (with reweighting)	−0.0174	−0.0127	−0.0124	−0.0110	−0.0099	−0.0088	−0.0078	−0.0068	−0.0058	−0.0048

[1] Percentage deviations from baseline. [2] Gini Coefficients and Theil Indices measure between-group inequality.

Over time, changes in wage differentials affect both rural–urban and formal–informal migration flows, and therefore the supply of labor in the various production sectors. The expected unskilled wage in the formal economy is constant on impact. Despite the increase in unskilled employment in the private sector in the first period (and thus the increase in the probability of finding a job), the fall in the minimum wage is such that the urban expected wage falls. Moreover, because rural sector wages rise, the expected urban–rural wage differential (measured in proportion of the rural wage) falls by more than 12 percentage points in the second period, with this differential narrowing over time. As a result, the inflow of unskilled workers into the formal sector (measured in proportion of the total formal urban labor supply) falls by about 3.6 percent in period 2. This drop becomes progressively less significant, given the increased probability of finding a job in the formal sector. Although the nominal wage in the informal sector increases (by 3.1 percent in period 2, 3.9 percent in period 3, and by almost 5 percent in period 10), the product wage falls, to absorb the increase in labor supply in that sector. In turn, this increase in the informal sector wage, coupled with the reduction in the minimum wage, leads in period 2 to a sharp fall in the expected formal–informal wage differential, which tends to reduce the supply of unskilled labor in the formal private sector (by 3.6 percent in period 2, and about 2.5 percent at the end of the adjustment period), that is, the number of workers willing to queue for employment in the urban private sector. This, coupled with the sustained effect of the cut in the minimum wage on labor demand, explains the large effect on unemployment.

Although the behavior of nominal wages in the rural sector reflects essentially changes in value added prices on impact, over time it is also affected by changes in labor demand and migration flows – just like the informal sector wage. After an initial increase in nominal wages, lower migration flows to urban areas begin to put downward pressure on rural wages, which end up falling (in nominal terms) by 2.9 percent in period 9 and 3.5 percent in the last period. As also indicated earlier, the reduction in the cost of unskilled labor induces a substitution away from skilled labor, which brings a sustained fall in skilled wages in nominal terms (by about 4.8 percent after 10 periods). However, the overall effect on labor demand is not large; skilled employment in the private formal sector falls in the long run by only about 0.4 percent. And because the supply of skilled labor remains roughly constant throughout (public investment in education and the number of school teachers are held constant at their baseline values), the skilled unemployment rate rises by only 0.2 percentage points. The reason for the small effect on skilled employment is that the direct substitution effect associated with the reduction in the minimum wage is offset by a fall in the skilled wage, resulting from general equilibrium effects.

The effect on aggregate output (or real GDP) is slightly positive in the periods following the shock, at about 0.3 percent, and close to zero over the rest of the adjustment period. Changes in real output (as measured by real value added) are also positive in the urban informal sector and the urban formal sector in the periods after the shock, but slightly negative at the end of the simulation horizon. In contrast, in the rural sector, changes in real output are positive throughout the simulation period and actually tend to grow slightly over time, as a result of the gradual fall in rural sector wages.

On the fiscal side, total revenue falls by about 0.4 percentage points as a share of GDP during the adjustment period, mostly as a result of indirect taxes changing at a slower pace than nominal GDP. Given that public investment remains essentially constant, the closure rule requires private investment to fall (by about 7.5 percent) to maintain aggregate balance between investment and savings. There is therefore a significant "crowding out" effect. In addition, profits of private firms suffer from lower disposable income of skilled workers, capitalists and rentiers.

Despite relatively large changes in disposable income, overall poverty indicators change only slightly during the adjustment period. This is, of course, related to the fact that the aggregate growth and income effects of the shock are fairly limited and involve essentially a reallocation of resources across sectors. However, there are significant differences among household groups. The proportion of poor households in rural areas increases by 1.7 percentage points, whereas the poverty gap (the average distance between income and the poverty line as fraction of the poverty line) rises by 1 percentage point. Although disposable income of capitalists and rentiers drops significantly, and the incidence of poverty increases by 0.7 percentage point toward the end of the adjustment period, the poverty gap changes only in the short run, but is almost unaffected in the long run. For unskilled workers, both measures of poverty indicate an improvement in the longer run, especially for those workers involved in the informal sector. However, for unskilled workers in the formal sector, poverty increases on impact – by about 0.8 percentage point, suing the poverty gap measure. There is therefore a potential *short-run trade-off* emerging between unemployment and poverty:[16] although the reduction in the minimum wage lowers open unskilled unemployment in the formal sector, it also increases poverty for that category of households. For skilled workers in the formal sector, poverty tends to increase slightly, in both the short and the long run by approximately 1.2 percentage points (using the headcount index).

Overall, therefore, poverty increases in rural areas and decreases in urban areas, resulting in a slight decrease in poverty at the economy-wide level. Changes in the income-based Gini coefficient indicate that income distribution is affected only modestly by a cut in the minimum wage; the degree of inequality falls by only a small amount in the long run. This effect is directly related to the sharp reduction in disposable income experienced by skilled workers and capitalists and rentiers, relative to other household groups.

Let us now examine in more detail the differences concerning the impact on poverty and inequality as measured by the three approaches to micro–macro linkages presented in the previous section. With the simple micro-accounting method (in which changes in disposable income are fed into the household survey without taking into account changes in the employment structure and thus in the size of relative groups), poverty is overestimated on impact compared to the more elaborate approach based on reweighting techniques, but as we can see from Table 8.2 this differences becomes smaller over the adjustment period. This holds regardless of whether we look at the headcount ratio or the poverty gap. The difference represents between 0.10 and

---

[16]See Agénor (2004*d*) for a more detailed discussion of unemployment–poverty trade-offs.

490   *Chapter 8*

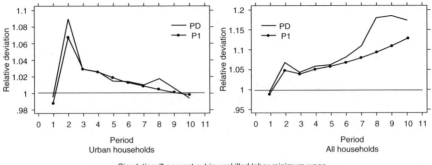

Figure 8.4 Comparison of the poverty impact measured by the simple micro-accounting method relative to that measured by the micro-accounting method combinded with reweighting techniques (ratio of absolute deviations from baseline).

0.25 percentage points, which may not seem that large; however, it is equivalent to up to 20 percent of the total change in poverty relative to the initial period. In terms of absolute deviations from the baseline, the discrepancy is smaller, because the baseline projection is affected by a bias in the same direction, but, likewise, in relative terms, it is not negligible.

Figure 8.4 traces the absolute deviations from the baseline measured by the simple micro-accounting method relative to the absolute deviations from the baseline measured by the micro-accounting method combined with reweighting techniques, for both P_0 and P_1. For urban households, as well as all households put together, the change is overestimated over the entire adjustment period. The difference amounts to up to 9 percent for urban households (with a peak in the second period) and to almost up to 20 percent for all households together (with a peak at the end of the adjustment period). However, for urban households the discrepancy is almost zero in period 10. The pattern of differences with P_0 and P_1 is very similar. The decrease in inequality is also overestimated if changes in the employment structure are not taken into account. Again, in absolute terms the difference is not large, but given the small change in inequality, the relative difference is.

One reason why we do not observe even more pronounced differences between the two methods is due to the fact that the employment structure is not affected very much by the cut in the minimum wage. Therefore, in this case, it does not appear to matter much whether we reweigh or not to account for changes in the employment structure.

However, this results from the fact that the labor market structure and the parameters that we impose on Mini-IMMPA imply a fairly strong degree of segmentation between the different components of the labor market, with only limited mobility between them. The degree of mobility from rural to urban areas, and from the urban informal sector to the formal sector, responds only to a limited extent to changes in relative wages, and the speed at which skills are acquired by unskilled workers are driven by public investment in education infrastructure and the number of teachers, neither one of which changes during the adjustment period. Were we to use higher elasticities of migration flows to relative wages, or were we to account for the impact of changes in relative wages on the decision to acquire skills (as in the full IMMPA prototype for low-income countries described in Chapter 5), the model would yield much larger changes in the composition of employment and the differences between the first and second approaches to micro–macro linkages would be much larger.

As outlined in section 8.3, the Beta distribution approach poses problems if we are interested in calculating exact levels of poverty. As indicated earlier, there are significant differences between the poverty level in the base year predicted by the Beta distribution approach and the actual, survey-based measure. If we compare now the micro-accounting framework with the Beta distribution approach, we can see from Table 8.2 that the latter indicates always the same direction of changes in P_0 and P_1 as the micro-accounting framework. When aggregating the predicted group-specific distributions (as discussed in section 8.3), reweighting by changes in the population shares matters, as before. However, we can also see that the Beta distribution approach overestimates systematically (except for capitalists and rentiers) changes in the FGT indicators.

Figure 8.5 shows again the relative differences with respect to the micro-accounting framework combined with reweighting techniques. For workers in the rural sector, the discrepancy fluctuates and is between plus–minus 50 percent, but lower in the beginning and at the end of the adjustment period. For workers in the urban informal sector, the indicated change for P_1 lies systematically between 25 to 30 percent above, whereas for unskilled workers the difference is between 100 to 250 percent for P_0 and nearly 100 percent for P_1 above. For skilled workers in the urban sector, the deviations are equivalent to up to 6 times the change indicated by the micro-accounting plus reweighting method, but they are small for P_0 in the beginning, in the middle and at the end of the adjustment period.

In addition, the Beta distribution approach appears to induce a bias concerning poverty differentials between groups. Skilled workers seem to have almost the same headcount ratio and poverty gap as unskilled workers, which is not the case if we use the micro-accounting approach. For a stronger shock (or possibly other shocks), the Beta distribution approach may even induce a different ranking of household groups.

With the Beta distribution approach, as noted earlier, we can only measure changes in between-group inequality. Between-group inequality amounts in our artificial survey to approximately 25 percent of total inequality, but given that we expand incomes for each household with group-specific growth rates, total within-group inequality changes only slightly and insofar as we change the weights given to each within-group distribution. The change computed by the Beta distribution method is slightly higher than that computed by the micro-accounting method, but both operate in the same direction.

8.4.2 Increase in Employment Subsidies

The simulation results associated with a permanent doubling of the nominal employment subsidy on unskilled labor (that is, an increase in the subsidy rate from

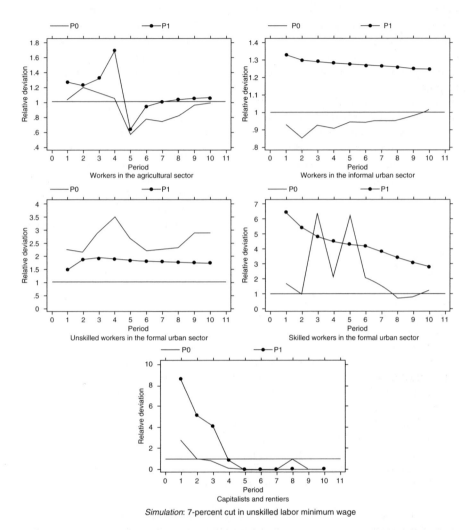

Figure 8.5   Comparison of the poverty impact measured by the the BETA distribution method relative to that measured by the micro-accounting method combined with reweighting techniques (ratio of absolute deviations from baseline).

5 to 10 percentage points of the nominal minimum wage) are illustrated in Tables 8.3 and 8.4 for the first 10 periods after the shock, as before. This subsidy is paid on a per worker basis. We assume that the government changes nothing else in the tax and transfer system, implying therefore an offsetting adjustment in the investment of private firms, in order to maintain the aggregate balance between savings and investment. Again, we first comment on the general results of this simulation and then compare more specifically the effects on poverty and inequality as they are measured by the three different methods.

Table 8.3 Mini-IMMPA: simulation results. Doubling (from 5 to 10 percent of the minimum wage) in employment subsidy. (Percentage deviations from baseline, unless otherwise indicated)

					Periods					
	1	2	3	4	5	6	7	8	9	10
Macroeconomic Indicators										
GDP at market prices	−0.1	0.0	−0.1	−0.1	−0.2	−0.2	−0.2	−0.3	−0.3	−0.3
Value added at factor cost	0.0	0.1	0.0	0.0	−0.1	−0.1	−0.1	−0.2	−0.2	−0.3
Value added in rural sector	0.0	0.0	0.0	0.1	0.1	0.1	0.1	0.1	0.1	0.1
Value added in urban informal sector	0.0	0.2	0.0	0.0	−0.1	−0.1	−0.2	−0.2	−0.2	−0.3
Value added in urban formal sector	0.1	0.1	0.0	−0.1	−0.2	−0.2	−0.3	−0.4	−0.4	−0.5
Private consumption	0.4	0.5	0.4	0.4	0.3	0.3	0.2	0.2	0.2	0.2
Private investment	−6.0	−4.5	−4.8	−4.6	−4.5	−4.4	−4.4	−4.3	−4.2	−4.1
Disposable income	0.3	0.4	0.3	0.3	0.3	0.2	0.2	0.2	0.2	0.1
Government Accounts (% of GDP)[1]										
Total revenue	−0.5	−0.4	−0.4	−0.4	−0.4	−0.3	−0.3	−0.3	−0.3	−0.3
Direct taxes	−0.1	−0.1	−0.1	0.0	0.0	0.0	0.0	0.0	0.0	0.0
Indirect taxes	−0.4	−0.3	−0.3	−0.3	−0.3	−0.3	−0.3	−0.3	−0.3	−0.3
Total expenditure	0.0	−0.1	0.0	0.0	0.0	0.0	0.0	0.0	0.1	0.1
Consumption	0.0	0.0	0.0	0.0	0.0	0.0	0.0	0.0	0.0	0.0
Investment	−0.1	0.0	0.0	0.0	0.0	0.0	0.0	0.0	0.0	0.0
Transfers to households	0.0	0.0	0.0	0.0	0.0	0.0	0.0	0.0	0.0	0.0
Foreign interest payments	0.0	0.0	0.0	0.0	0.0	0.0	0.0	0.0	0.0	0.0
Total financing	0.4	0.3	0.4	0.4	0.4	0.4	0.4	0.4	0.4	0.4
Foreign financing	0.0	0.0	0.0	0.0	0.0	0.0	0.0	0.0	0.0	0.0
Domestic borrowing	0.4	0.3	0.4	0.4	0.4	0.4	0.4	0.4	0.4	0.4

Continued

Table 8.3 Continued

					Periods					
	1	2	3	4	5	6	7	8	9	10
Labor Market										
Nominal wages										
Agricultural sector	1.6	1.6	1.1	0.8	0.5	0.3	0.1	-0.1	-0.2	-0.4
Informal sector	2.5	1.8	1.9	1.8	1.7	1.7	1.6	1.5	1.5	1.4
Private formal sector										
Unskilled	0.0	0.0	0.0	0.0	0.0	0.0	0.0	0.0	0.0	0.0
Skilled	-2.5	-2.1	-2.3	-2.3	-2.4	-2.4	-2.5	-2.5	-2.5	-2.5
Public sector										
Unskilled	0.0	0.0	0.0	0.0	0.0	0.0	0.0	0.0	0.0	0.0
Skilled	0.1	0.0	0.0	0.0	0.0	0.0	0.0	0.0	0.0	0.0
Employment										
Agricultural sector	0.0	0.0	0.1	0.1	0.1	0.1	0.1	0.1	0.1	0.1
Informal sector	0.0	0.2	0.1	0.0	-0.1	-0.1	-0.2	-0.2	-0.3	-0.3
Private formal sector										
Unskilled	0.5	1.9	1.9	2.2	2.4	2.7	2.9	3.1	3.3	3.5
Skilled	-0.2	-0.2	-0.2	-0.2	-0.2	-0.2	-0.2	-0.2	-0.2	-0.2
Public sector										
Unskilled	0.0	0.0	0.0	0.0	0.0	0.0	0.0	0.0	0.0	0.0
Skilled	0.0	0.0	0.0	0.0	0.0	0.0	0.0	0.0	0.0	0.0

Labor supply (urban formal sector)										
Unskilled	0.0	-0.8	-0.3	-0.1	0.1	0.3	0.5	0.7	1.0	1.2
Skilled	0.0	0.0	0.0	0.0	0.0	0.0	0.0	0.0	0.0	0.0
Unemployment rate (urban formal sector)[1]										
Unskilled	-0.4	-2.0	-1.5	-1.6	-1.5	-1.5	-1.4	-1.3	-1.3	-1.2
Skilled	0.1	0.1	0.1	0.1	0.1	0.1	0.1	0.1	0.1	0.1
Real wage differentials[1]										
Expected urban–rural (% of rural wage)	0.0	-1.4	-1.6	-1.0	-0.6	-0.3	0.0	0.3	0.5	0.7
Expected formal-informal (% of informal wage)	0.0	-2.1	1.2	0.5	0.6	0.6	0.6	0.6	0.6	0.5
Migration[1]										
Rural-urban (% of urban labor supply)	0.0	0.0	0.0	0.0	0.0	0.0	0.0	0.0	0.0	0.0
Formal-informal (% of formal urban labor supply)	0.0	-0.8	0.5	0.2	0.2	0.2	0.2	0.2	0.2	0.2

[1] Absolute deviations from baseline. [2] In real terms.

Table 8.4 Mini-IMMPA: price, poverty, and distributional indicators. Doubling (from 5 to 10 percent of the minimum wage) in employment subsidy. (Percentage deviations from baseline, unless otherwise indicated)

	Periods									
	1	2	3	4	5	6	7	8	9	10
Consumer Prices										
Rural CPI	0.59	0.50	0.44	0.38	0.32	0.27	0.22	0.18	0.15	0.12
Urban CPI	0.34	0.27	0.25	0.23	0.21	0.19	0.17	0.15	0.14	0.12
Cumulative Growth of Real Disposable Income[1]										
Rural households	0.88	0.99	0.66	0.46	0.26	0.09	−0.06	−0.19	−0.30	−0.40
Urban households	0.19	0.26	0.26	0.27	0.27	0.28	0.28	0.28	0.28	0.27
Informal	1.91	1.48	1.48	1.37	1.28	1.20	1.11	1.02	0.94	0.86
Formal unskilled	0.03	0.78	0.80	0.98	1.11	1.25	1.38	1.50	1.62	1.73
Formal skilled	−1.22	−1.05	−1.13	−1.15	−1.17	−1.19	−1.21	−1.23	−1.24	−1.25
Capitalists and rentiers	−2.92	−2.14	−2.05	−1.81	−1.62	−1.42	−1.24	−1.07	−0.91	−0.75
Household Shares										
Rural households	0.00	0.01	0.02	0.02	0.03	0.03	0.03	0.02	0.02	0.02
Urban households	0.00	−0.01	−0.02	−0.02	−0.03	−0.03	−0.03	−0.02	−0.02	−0.02
Informal	0.00	0.09	0.02	0.00	−0.04	−0.06	−0.09	−0.11	−0.13	−0.15
Formal unskilled	0.00	−0.10	−0.04	−0.02	0.01	0.04	0.06	0.09	0.11	0.13
Formal skilled	0.00	0.00	0.00	0.00	0.00	0.00	0.00	0.00	0.00	0.00
Capitalists and rentiers	0.00	0.00	0.00	0.00	0.00	0.00	0.00	0.00	0.00	0.00
Poverty and Distributional Indicators (Income-based)										
Poverty Line[1]										
Rural	0.59	0.50	0.44	0.38	0.32	0.27	0.22	0.18	0.15	0.12
Urban	0.34	0.27	0.26	0.23	0.21	0.19	0.17	0.15	0.14	0.12

Micro-accounting approach with and without reweighting

Poverty Headcount

Rural households	-0.50	-0.50	-0.28	-0.21	-0.14	0.00	0.14	0.21	0.21	0.21
Urban households (without reweighting)	-0.70	-0.45	-0.47	-0.39	-0.42	-0.47	-0.47	-0.25	-0.25	-0.17
Urban households (with reweighting)	-0.70	-0.42	-0.47	-0.39	-0.42	-0.48	-0.49	-0.26	-0.26	-0.18
Informal	-1.24	-0.75	-0.80	-0.75	-0.71	-0.66	-0.66	-0.62	-0.57	-0.44
Formal unskilled	0.00	-0.44	-0.15	0.00	-0.15	-0.29	-0.29	0.00	-0.15	-0.15
Formal skilled	0.20	0.60	0.20	0.40	0.20	0.00	0.00	1.01	0.81	0.81
Capitalists and rentiers	1.33	0.67	0.67	0.67	0.67	0.00	0.00	0.00	0.67	0.67
Economy (without reweighting)	-0.64	-0.46	-0.42	-0.34	-0.34	-0.34	-0.30	-0.12	-0.12	-0.06
Economy (with reweighting)	-0.64	-0.44	-0.41	-0.34	-0.34	-0.34	-0.31	-0.12	-0.12	-0.07

Poverty Gap

Rural households	-0.26	-0.28	-0.17	-0.11	-0.05	0.00	0.04	0.08	0.11	0.14
Urban households (without reweighting)	-0.34	-0.28	-0.29	-0.28	-0.27	-0.26	-0.25	-0.24	-0.23	-0.21
Urban households (with reweighting)	-0.34	-0.28	-0.29	-0.28	-0.27	-0.26	-0.25	-0.24	-0.23	-0.22
Informal	-0.56	-0.38	-0.42	-0.40	-0.40	-0.38	-0.37	-0.36	-0.35	-0.34
Formal unskilled	0.01	-0.29	-0.20	-0.20	-0.19	-0.17	-0.15	-0.14	-0.12	-0.10
Formal skilled	0.06	0.06	0.08	0.08	0.08	0.08	0.09	0.10	0.11	0.12
Capitalists and rentiers	0.10	0.07	0.06	0.05	0.04	0.04	0.03	0.03	0.02	0.02
Economy (without reweighting)	-0.31	-0.28	-0.26	-0.23	-0.21	-0.19	-0.17	-0.15	-0.13	-0.12
Economy (with reweighting)	-0.31	-0.28	-0.25	-0.23	-0.21	-0.19	-0.17	-0.15	-0.14	-0.12

Overall Inequality

Gini-coefficient (without reweighting)	-0.0036	-0.0028	-0.0027	-0.0024	-0.0022	-0.0019	-0.0017	-0.0016	-0.0014	-0.0012
Gini-coefficient (with reweighting)	-0.0036	-0.0028	-0.0027	-0.0024	-0.0022	-0.0020	-0.0018	-0.0016	-0.0015	-0.0013
Theil-index (without reweighting)	-0.0076	-0.0062	-0.0058	-0.0052	-0.0047	-0.0042	-0.0037	-0.0033	-0.0029	-0.0026
Theil-index (with reweighting)	-0.0077	-0.0061	-0.0058	-0.0052	-0.0048	-0.0043	-0.0039	-0.0035	-0.0031	-0.0028

Continued

Table 8.4 Continued

	Periods									
	1	2	3	4	5	6	7	8	9	10
Beta-distribution approach with and without reweighting										
Poverty Headcount										
Rural households	−0.50	−0.53	−0.35	−0.24	−0.13	−0.03	0.05	0.11	0.17	0.22
Urban households (without reweighting)	−0.56	−0.55	−0.54	−0.52	−0.50	−0.48	−0.45	−0.42	−0.40	−0.37
Urban households (with reweighting)	−0.56	−0.53	−0.53	−0.51	−0.49	−0.47	−0.45	−0.42	−0.40	−0.38
Informal	−1.12	−0.76	−0.82	−0.79	−0.77	−0.74	−0.72	−0.69	−0.66	−0.63
Formal unskilled	−0.05	−0.88	−0.63	−0.63	−0.56	−0.51	−0.46	−0.41	−0.36	−0.30
Formal skilled	0.82	0.67	0.69	0.68	0.67	0.66	0.65	0.63	0.62	0.61
Capitalists and rentiers	0.82	0.00	0.00	0.00	0.00	0.00	0.00	0.00	0.00	0.00
Economy (without reweighting)	−0.55	−0.55	−0.49	−0.44	−0.39	−0.35	−0.31	−0.27	−0.24	−0.21
Economy (with reweighting)	−0.54	−0.53	−0.48	−0.43	−0.39	−0.35	−0.31	−0.27	−0.24	−0.21
Poverty Gap										
Rural households	−0.32	−0.34	−0.22	−0.15	−0.08	−0.02	0.03	0.07	0.11	0.14
Urban households (without reweighting)	−0.37	−0.35	−0.35	−0.33	−0.32	−0.31	−0.29	−0.27	−0.26	−0.24
Urban households (with reweighting)	−0.37	−0.34	−0.34	−0.33	−0.32	−0.30	−0.29	−0.28	−0.26	−0.25
Informal	−0.71	−0.48	−0.52	−0.50	−0.49	−0.47	−0.46	−0.44	−0.42	−0.40
Formal unskilled	−0.03	−0.52	−0.37	−0.37	−0.34	−0.31	−0.28	−0.24	−0.21	−0.18
Formal skilled	0.44	0.36	0.38	0.37	0.36	0.36	0.35	0.35	0.34	0.34
Capitalists and rentiers	0.43	0.00	0.00	0.00	0.00	0.00	0.00	0.00	0.00	0.00
Economy (without reweighting)	−0.36	−0.35	−0.31	−0.28	−0.25	−0.23	−0.20	−0.18	−0.15	−0.13
Economy (with reweighting)	−0.36	−0.34	−0.31	−0.28	−0.25	−0.22	−0.20	−0.18	−0.16	−0.14
Between-group Inequality										
Theil-index (without reweighting)	−0.0085	−0.0068	−0.0064	−0.0058	−0.0052	−0.0047	−0.0042	−0.0038	−0.0033	−0.0029
Theil-index (with reweighting)	−0.0086	−0.0068	−0.0065	−0.0058	−0.0053	−0.0048	−0.0043	−0.0039	−0.0035	−0.0031

[1] Percentage deviations from baseline. [2] Gini Coefficients and Theil Indices measure between-group inequality.

The impact effect of an increase in the employment subsidy is qualitatively similar to a cut in the minimum wage: by reducing the effective cost of unskilled labor, it tends to increase immediately the demand for that category of labor – in the present case by 0.5 percent in the first year, and by about 2.6 percent on average during the adjustment period. The unskilled unemployment rate drops by 0.4 percentage points in the first year and 2.0 percentage points in the second year, and then remains at about 1.2 to 1.6 percentage points below baseline until the end of the simulation horizon.

The reduction in the "effective" cost of unskilled labor leads firms in the private formal urban sector to substitute away (as before) from skilled labor and physical capital, leading to a reduction in skilled wages by about 2.5 percent in nominal terms and a reduction in the price of value added in the private formal sector. In the present case, the skilled nominal wage falls by more than the price of value added in the private formal sector, implying a fall in the product wage, which stimulates the demand for that category of labor. Thus, the adverse impact of the substitution effect induced by the reduction in the cost of unskilled labor on the demand for skilled labor is dampened. Overall, skilled employment falls by about 0.2 percent on impact and in the longer run, bringing with it a concomitant increase in the skilled unemployment rate.

The (expected) urban–rural wage differential (expressed in percentage of the rural wage) drops by 1.4 and 1.6 percentage points in the first and second period after the shock, then decreases to zero in period 7, eventually turning positive. It rises by 0.7 percentage points by the end of the adjustment period. The expected formal–informal wage differential (expressed in percentage of the informal wage) decreases also in the first period after the shock by 2.1 percentage points and then adjusts to plus 0.6 percentage points in the medium and longer run. This evolution is qualitatively similar to the one described in the previous experiment, although the magnitude of the initial effects are not as large. The reason is that the increase in unskilled employment raises the probability of finding a job in the private sector, thereby increasing the expected formal sector wage. As a result, there is an increase in the supply of unskilled job seekers in the formal economy by slightly more than 1 percent in the longer run, which therefore mitigates the initial reduction in unemployment. However, because of the increase in the informal sector wage (itself due to the reduction in labor supply in the informal economy), the expected formal–informal wage differential increases only slightly – thereby mitigating the incentives to seek employment in the formal sector.

The overall effect on aggregate real output is, again, fairly small. The government budget is of course significantly affected, with indirect tax revenue falling by about 0.3 percentage points of GDP. As with the reduction in the minimum wage, private investment decreases significantly. This is again due to lower profits resulting from lower disposable income of skilled workers, as well as capitalists and rentiers, and the crowding-out effect associated with the higher government deficit.

In the short run, the drop in poverty of rural households and unskilled households in the urban informal and formal sectors is quite significant. In the longer run, however, poverty decreases only slightly for urban informal and formal unskilled workers, and it even increases in the rural sector (despite the small increase in the level of employment) as well as for skilled workers, and capitalist and rentiers. These effects are qualitatively

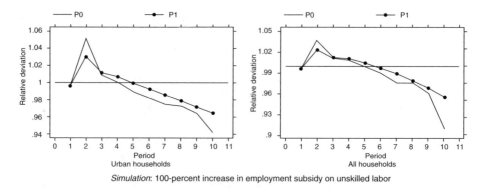

Figure 8.6   Comparison of the poverty impact measured by the simple micro-accounting method relative to that measured by the micro-accounting method combinded with reweighting techniques (ratio of absolute deviations from baseline).

very similar to those observed for the cut in the minimum wage, but much smaller in magnitude. As with the previous experiment, income inequality decreases, but by less than before. At the end of the adjustment period, the difference with respect to the baseline is even close to zero.

To what extent do these results depend on the method used to link the micro with the macro level? As before, the simple micro-accounting method overstates P_0 and P_1 with respect to the second method, which combines micro-accounting with reweighting (see Table 8.4). Again, because changes in the employment structure following the shock are small, the absolute differences are also small, lying between 0.12 and 0.25 percentage points. In relative terms, however, this corresponds to differences of between 15 to almost 100 percent of the total change occurring between periods 1 and 10. Figure 8.6 shows, as before, absolute deviations from the baseline measured by the simple micro-accounting method, relative to the absolute deviations from the baseline measured by the micro-accounting method combined with reweighting techniques.

For both poverty indicators, P_0 and P_1, and for urban households and all households together, the change with respect to the baseline is overestimated in the short run (by approximately 5 percent) and underestimated in the long run (also by approximately 5 percent). If the household survey is not reweighted, the decrease in inequality is slightly underestimated; the difference between the two approaches is again very small in absolute terms but large in relative terms.

If we now compare the micro-accounting framework with the Beta distribution approach, our results again show that the latter indicates always the same direction of change in P_0 and P_1 as the former (except for P_1 in period 1 for unskilled workers in the urban formal sector). Figure 8.7 shows that for workers in the rural sector, the Beta distribution approach indicates for P_0 and P_1 in the short term a much higher change, and then in the medium term a much lower change, with respect to the baseline. However, at the end of the adjustment period both methods lead almost to the same change. For unskilled workers in the urban informal sector, changes in P_0

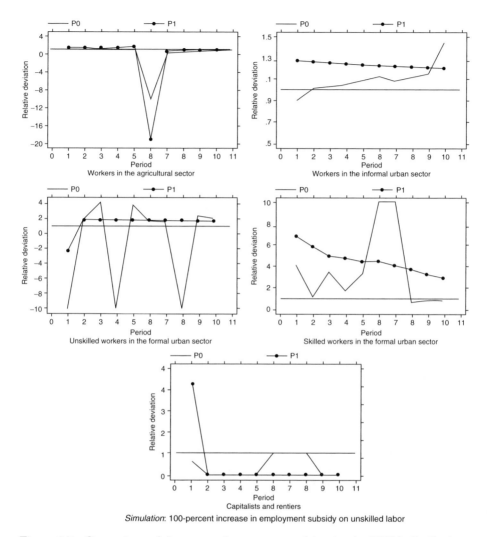

Figure 8.7   Comparison of the poverty impact measured by the the BETA distribution method relative to that measured by the micro-accounting method combined with reweighting techniques (ratio of absolute deviations from baseline).

and P_1 are overestimated, for P_0 in the long run by more than 30 percent, and for P_1 by 20 to 30 percent throughout the adjustment period. For unskilled workers in the urban formal sector, the change of P_0 fluctuates around the change indicated by the micro-accounting framework and amounts in some periods to more than 300 percent of the latter. The indicated direction of the change of P_1 is on impact even the opposite of that indicated by the micro-accounting method; it goes afterward in the correct direction, but it overestimates continuously by almost 100 percent. For skilled workers in the urban formal sector, changes in both poverty indicators as measured by the Beta distribution method are more than 2 to 10 times higher than those measured by the micro-accounting method, but the deviations decrease over time. For capitalists and rentiers, the micro-accounting method shows a slight increase of P_0 and P_1, except through periods 6 to 8, the Beta distribution approach shows no change at all after the second period.

In sum, both experiments lead to qualitatively similar results. A low impact on aggregate output, an increase of rural poverty and a decrease of urban poverty. In rural areas the increase in labor supply, resulting from lower incentives to migrate to urban areas, puts pressure on wages. In urban areas lower unemployment leads to less poverty. Both policies result in a slight reduction in poverty at the economy-wide level. These changes are captured in a similar way by the three methods that we compared – but only in a qualitative sense, not in a quantitative manner.

8.5   Conclusions

The purpose of this chapter was to compare three approaches to model linkages between a macroeconomic model with representative households and micro household income data to evaluate the distributional and poverty effects of poverty reduction strategies and other exogenous shocks. The three methods were evaluated by performing a set of simulations with the Mini-IMMPA framework described in Chapter 3, and two typical labor market policies: a cut in the minimum wage and an increase in employment subsidies for unskilled labor. The results of these simulations were discussed and the three methods compared.

The distributional and poverty effects indicated by the three approaches did not prove to be fundamentally different. They differed neither in the direction of the effects nor in the ranking of the household categories with respect to poverty. However, from both a conceptual and practical point of view, it is tempting to view the micro-accounting method combined with reweighting for changes in the employment structure as constituting the most appealing method among the three, despite the fact that it has its own shortcomings. The reason is that the simple micro-accounting method ignores changes in the employment structure, whereas the distribution approach relies on approximate, instead of real, income distributions and depends therefore on the quality of the corresponding estimates of the shape parameters.

Indeed, our results indicate that the two other methods, and especially the Beta distribution approach, induce significant differences concerning the *magnitude* of poverty changes. In addition, as noted earlier, the distribution approach may not be appropriate if one is interested in the exact level of poverty and not only in changes relative to the baseline. Of course, the problem of predicting the initial levels might partly be due to the fact that we try to model with Beta distributions artificial household data generated by log-normal distributions in the first place. The Beta distribution approach might work better with real household data. However, the nonparametric method, that is, the extended micro-accounting framework, can readily be used with actual survey data. Given the performance of standard micro-computers and statistical software nowadays, there is really no need to use the distribution approach, except perhaps for very large household surveys. However, economists who advocate this approach suggest using it if the sample of households is small, because then the fitted distribution is smooth even if the observed one is not. The smoothing thus avoids, so goes the argument, the possibility that small shifts in the income distribution would lead to huge changes in the poverty measure. The problem with this argument is that the estimated distribution parameters, as Table B8.2 indicates, are not very reliable if they are estimated over a small sample of households (compare the observed and fitted poverty measures for the group of skilled workers in the formal urban sector and of capitalist-rentiers). Therefore the parametric approach runs the risk of producing biased results.

The potential errors when using the simple micro-accounting framework or the distribution framework are of course much more important if policies with strong effects on the employment structure and the group-specific income levels are analyzed. For instance, if the minimum wage was reduced by 50 percent in our model, then the employment structure would change dramatically. The share of rural workers would be divided by two, the share of informal workers would increase by 25 percent and the share of formal unskilled workers would double. Poverty indicators calculated by both methods would differ by more than 10 percentage points, whether these changes are taken into account or not. Other policies that form part of poverty reduction strategies, such as changes in the composition of public investment for instance, might in the long run also be connected with important variations in the composition of employment. Alternatively, as noted earlier, changes in the employment structure would be a lot larger than those obtained in our experiments if migration flows responded more rapidly and significantly to changes in relative wages.

As mentioned above, the micro-accounting framework combined with reweighting for changes in the employment structure also has shortcomings. First, one might think, especially when conducting dynamic analyses, of extending this framework by reweighting for changes in other dimensions of the population structure (for instance, age structure, household size, or gender) as well. This issue will be addressed in future work. Then, a further step in taking into account individual and household heterogeneity and to allow the intra-group distributions to vary explicitly would imply reliance on a micro-simulation model that accounts for labor supply decisions and earnings at the level of the household, or better, the individual. The difference with the reweighting approach is that then we would not change the weights of individuals, but we would shift them from one sector to another using behavioral functions econometrically estimated.[17]

---

[17] Examples in the field of poverty analysis include Cogneau (2001), Cogneau and Robilliard (2001), Cockburn (2002), Robilliard, Bourguignon, and Robinson (2002), Bourguignon, Robilliard, and Robinson (2002), Grimm (2005), and Cogneau and Grimm (2002). In general, the application of micro-simulation techniques to developing countries is rather new and raises a number of specific problems, as discussed by Cogneau, Grimm, and Robilliard (2003).

However, the drawback of this type of modeling is that the use of a microeconomic model of income generation needs for econometric estimation as well as simulation a powerful software package (beside the software usually used to solve Macro-RHG models) and may therefore be more difficult to standardize. By contrast, the micro-accounting framework combined with reweighting for changes in the employment structure preserves a high degree of user-friendliness, which may help its eventual adoption by researchers and policy advisers in an environment where skills and resources are scarce.

Appendix A
Reweighting when Using Real Survey Data

In a specific country application it might be necessary, as a first step, to ensure consistency between the Macro-RHG model and the household survey data in the base year.[18] Computed macro aggregates, such as household production, income, or consumption, from household survey data almost never match published national accounts data even though sample weights are designed to represent the national population. In particular, it is possible that the composition of employment, output, and the inter-group income distribution generated by the Macro-RHG model and the household survey are different.

Many reasons are offered to explain this mismatch. On the household survey side, there may be sampling errors due to inadequate survey design and/or measurement errors, because it is difficult to get accurate responses from households concerning economic variables. On the national accounts side, while supply-side information on output and income for some sectors is based on high-quality survey or census data for agriculture and industry, information for subsistence farmers and informal producers is harder to obtain and usually of lower quality. However, there are also good reasons why household data and national accounts data for some variables do not match. For instance, consumption in national accounts is typically determined as a residual and is thus contaminated by errors and omissions elsewhere in the accounts. In practice, researchers often end up treating one source or the other as the "correct" or "most reliable" one – despite the fact that it is likely that both sources of information are subject to errors.

Another issue when working with real household data is that it may be important to account for, besides changes in the employment structure (which includes region of residence, education, and sector of activity), other policy target variables as well. Most poverty profiles show that age of the household head, sex of the household head, as well as household size, are very important variables in this respect. Changes in the population structure are of course particularly important when the Macro-RHG model is dynamic. The information about these additional changes may come either

---

[18] See Robilliard and Robinson (1999), for instance, who reconcile a Malagasy household survey and national accounts data.

directly from the Macro-RHG model or taken from external sources such as the United Nations' demographic projections for age structure.

In this case, if the reweighting procedure includes more than one dimension of the population structure and if constraints are put on the moments of some variables then this procedure becomes slightly more difficult. In general, reweighting can be done in two ways: either by the simple matching of matrices constructed for the reference data and the data that have to be adjusted (see for instance Landt et al. (1994)) or by the explicit use of minimum distance functions, which calculate weights such that they match certain criteria with respect to the distance between the initial and the adjusted distribution of weights (see for instance Merz (1994)).

Appendix B
Estimated Shape Parameters and Fitted Poverty Measures with Beta Distribution Functions

Table B8.1 Parameters for the beta density distribution function; moments estimates

	RU	UI	UU	US	KAP
Household Consumption Expenditure Per Capita					
\bar{y}	0.080	0.097	0.122	0.229	0.306
min(y)	0.006	0.008	0.013	0.035	0.076
max(y)	0.454	0.680	0.699	1.089	0.932
\bar{x}	0.164	0.132	0.159	0.184	0.269
s^2	0.025	0.018	0.024	0.024	0.047
\hat{\beta_1}	0.739	0.731	0.710	0.944	0.855
\hat{\beta_2}	3.768	4.799	3.759	4.192	2.323
Disposable Household Income Per Capita					
\bar{c}	0.089	0.111	0.134	0.280	0.426
min(c)	0.007	0.009	0.012	0.045	0.071
max(c)	0.625	0.880	0.612	1.228	1.175
\bar{x}	0.134	0.117	0.203	0.199	0.321
s^2	0.017	0.013	0.032	0.028	0.058
\hat{\beta_1}	0.753	0.818	0.820	0.936	0.880
\hat{\beta_2}	4.881	6.188	3.230	3.776	1.858
Sample size	1397	2253	674	486	140

Notes: "RU" stands for workers in the agricultural sector (rural), "UI" for workers in the informal urban sector, "UU" for unskilled workers in the formal urban sector, "US" for skilled workers in the formal urban sector, and "KAP" for capitalist-rentiers.

Table B8.2 Observed and fitted poverty measures using the estimated shape parameters of the beta distribution, without (nco) and with correction of outliers (co)

	Headcount ratio			Gap ratio		
	Obs.	Fit. (nco)	Fit. (co)	Obs.	Fit. (nco)	Fit. (co)
Disposable Household Income Per Capita						
RU	50.04	50.90	49.09	20.57	30.90	29.20
UI	43.35	51.59	45.66	17.41	31.69	26.57
UU	32.16	37.89	36.48	13.03	21.39	20.62
US	4.44	14.88	9.60	1.15	7.50	4.99
KAP	3.33	4.66	0.00	0.40	2.44	0.00
Household Consumption Expenditure Per Capita						
RU	50.11	50.82	49.38	20.77	29.72	29.66
UI	46.40	48.40	48.32	19.31	28.34	29.01
UU	37.72	47.45	40.31	13.89	29.83	24.32
US	8.27	18.73	12.93	2.02	9.58	6.65
KAP	2.00	8.59	0.00	0.45	4.41	0.00

Notes: "RU" stands for workers in the agricultural sector (rural), "UI" for workers in the informal urban sector, "UU" for unskilled workers in the formal urban sector, "US" for skilled workers in the formal urban sector, and "KAP" for capitalist-rentiers.

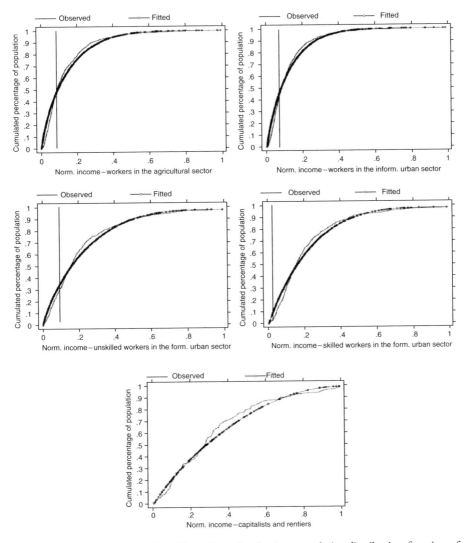

Figure B8.1 Observed and fitted by a Beta-distribution cumulative distribution function of normalized disposable income for each category of household (the vertical line corresponds to the normalized poverty line).

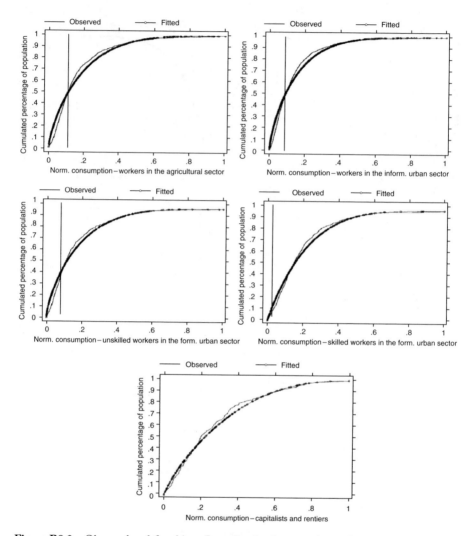

Figure B8.2 Observed and fitted by a Beta-distribution cumulative distribution function of normalized consumption for each category of household (the vertical line corresponds to the normalized poverty line).

Chapter 9

Some Research Perspectives

Pierre-Richard Agénor, Alejandro Izquierdo, and Henning Tarp Jensen

Many fruitful lessons on the impact of adjustment policies on unemployment and poverty have emerged from existing IMMPA studies – particularly with respect to labor market reforms, tax reform, and disinflation policies based on high interest rates. Some of these lessons have been reviewed in preceding chapters; others were discussed in companion papers. For instance, Agénor, Nabli, Yousef, and Jensen (2004) developed a prototype labor-exporting country model for the Middle East and North Africa based on Mini-IMMPA. Drawing on their analysis of the growth and employment effects of labor market reforms, they concluded that, in assessing the impact of these reforms, it is critical to account not only for direct (partial equilibrium) effects but also for dynamic general equilibrium effects.

A case in point is a subsidy to unskilled employment in the private formal sector to reduce unemployment. A partial equilibrium analysis reveals that, by lowering the relative cost of unskilled labor, a subsidy leads to an increase in the demand for that category of labor, which may be particularly significant if wages are fixed (as a result of, say, a binding minimum wage). As long as the increase in labor demand does not prompt greater participation in the labor force (that is, if unskilled labor supply is fairly inelastic), unskilled unemployment will fall unambiguously. However, the increase in subsidies must be financed, and this can occur in a variety of ways. If the government chooses to let its fiscal deficit increase and borrow from the rest of the economy, large crowding-out effects can lead to a fall in private investment (as in the Morocco model discussed in Chapter 4), thereby slowing the economy's growth rate and restraining the expansion of demand for all categories of labor over time. Thus, the longer-run effect of the policy on unskilled labor may be either nil or negative. Similarly, an increase in, say, taxes on profit earners and rentiers to keep the deficit constant may also restrain private capital formation (by reducing the expected net rate of return) and have an adverse effect on employment in the medium and the long run. A reduction in payroll taxes aimed at stimulating the demand for unskilled labor could have similar effects, depending on how the government chooses to adjust its spending pattern and other tax instruments.

A number of additional issues can be discussed in the context of existing IMMPA models or in slight extensions of them. Some of these issues have been discussed in the previous chapters, so we will not repeat them here. Instead, this chapter provides some further suggestions on issues to address; it constitutes therefore an agenda for further research – albeit a very partial one, which reflects our own interests and involvement in policy analysis. Specifically, we consider possible extensions in the following areas: labor market structure and policies, the macroeconomics of foreign aid, public investment allocation and growth, and methods for linking macroeconomic models and household surveys. We conclude with an emphasis on data collection and econometric estimation of key behavioral parameters.[1]

9.1   Labor Market Structure and Policies

Although a number of labor market policies were studied in the previous chapters, a number of other policies can be addressed, either in Mini-IMMPA or a full-blown IMMPA model. One option is to examine the wage and employment effects of a reduction in union bargaining power. To the extent that this translates into lower wages for skilled workers, this may have a positive effect on the labor market; at the same time, however, the reduction in the skilled–unskilled wage differential may affect incentives to acquire skills. Another option is to analyze the impact of changes in firing costs. As noted by Lindbeck and Snower (2001), firing costs can increase a union's bargaining power, and help to explain excessive real wages and resultant involuntary unemployment. Yet another option would be to study the impact of a reduction in public unskilled employment in the production of government services, coupled with a deficit-neutral increase in subsidies to unskilled employment in the private formal sector.[2]

Regarding the structure of the labor market, existing models could be extended in several directions. First, to the extent that part of the job market problem is a shortage of skilled workers (or an excess supply of unskilled labor), subsidies to skills acquisition and/or on-the-job training could be accounted for. Second, as discussed in Chapter 1, labor taxation and labor market regulations may encourage firms to go informal.[3] This is captured only indirectly in present versions of IMMPA. To the extent that changes in tax rates have a direct effect on the propensity to go informal,

---

[1] Another important issue, not discussed in detail here, is related to the need to account for home consumption in agriculture and marketing margins; see Arndt, Jensen, and Tarp (2000). We also leave aside issues associated with the solution and calibration of IMMPA models.

[2] Some of these shocks are analyzed by Agénor, Nabli, Yousef, and Jensen (2004), as noted earlier.

[3] Kugler (2000) developed a model in which job security regulations provide incentives for high turnover firms to operate in the informal sector. See also Schneider and Enste (2000) for a more general discussion.

an inverted U-shape curve between taxation and growth may emerge, depending on the use of tax revenues. Suppose, for instance, that revenues are used to finance higher spending on infrastructure. An increase in income taxes may well have a positive effect on growth initially (by stimulating private production), but a negative effect afterward, as further increases tend to drive activity underground and reduce overall revenue. Third, the model could be extended to consider the impact of the introduction of social insurance on savings, labor supply, and unemployment.[4]

9.2 Macroeconomic Effects of Foreign Aid

In recent years, the macroeconomic effects of foreign aid have been the subject of renewed attention, particularly in the context of low-income countries. Studies of the effects of foreign aid have focused, in particular, on the impact of external assistance on domestic savings, the government budget and fiscal policy, the real exchange rate, the rate of economic growth, and more recently poverty and the incentives for reform in the recipient country. Fiscal response models for instance have been used to examine the impact of aid on taxes and government expenditure, that is, the degree of fungibility of aid (see Franco-Rodriguez (2000), McGillivray (2000), and McGillivray and Ouattara (2003)). Some of these studies have shown that an increase in aid may lead to a decline in public savings through lower tax revenues, as governments reduce their tax collection effort. Others found that shortfalls in aid – depending on its composition – tend on the contrary to translate into shortfalls in domestic revenue (Gupta et al. (2003)), despite the fact that aid appears to be more volatile than domestic revenues (Bulir and Hamann (2003, 2005)).

Another line of research has focused on the Dutch disease effects of foreign assistance. The argument, essentially, is that if aid is (at least partially) spent on nontraded goods, it may put upward pressure on domestic prices and lead to a real exchange rate appreciation. In turn, the real appreciation may induce a reallocation of labor toward the nontraded goods sector, thereby raising real wages in terms of the price of tradables. The resulting deterioration in competitiveness may lead to a decline in export performance and an adverse effect on growth. It has also been argued, however, that if there is learning by doing (that is, endogenous productivity gains) and learning spillovers between production sectors, or if aid has a direct effect on public investment in infrastructure, then the longer-run effect on the real exchange rate may be ambiguous (see Torvik (2001) and Adam and Bevan (2003)).

Yet another area of research in recent years has been the empirical link between aid and growth. In a contribution that led to much subsequent controversy, Burnside and Dollar (2000) argued that foreign aid is effective in enhancing growth of GDP per capita only in countries with good fiscal, monetary, and trade policies. Indeed, using cross-country regressions for 56 developing countries over the period 1970-93, they found that aid has no impact on the rate of economic growth in countries with poor

---

[4]See Karni (1999) for a thorough discussion of issues associated with the design of unemployment benefit schemes.

macroeconomic policies. In a recent update of their initial study, based on data for the 1990s, Burnside and Dollar (2004) argued that the evidence continues to corroborate their main conclusion – that the positive effect of aid on growth is conditional on having "good" institutions.

However, a number of studies have questioned the robustness of the dependence of the aid-growth link on the policy regime. Guillaumont and Chauvet (2001) and Chauvet and Guillaumont (2003) found that although the marginal effect of aid on growth appears to depend on policies, as suggested by Burnside and Dollar, policies themselves depend on aid, whereas aid effectiveness depends also on the degree of economic vulnerability (measured as a function of long-term changes in the terms of trade and export instability) and domestic political instability. Dalgaard and Hansen (2001) found that the Burnside-Dollar results are very fragile. Five observations, which are excluded in Burnside and Dollar's "preferred" regressions, have a critical influence on the parameter of interest. They argued that aid appears to spur growth unconditionally (that is, regardless of whether policies are "good" or "bad") but with decreasing marginal returns – perhaps as a result of gradually binding constraints on absorptive capacity. Hansen and Tarp (2001) found similar results. In addition, they found that when physical investment and human capital are controlled for, aid has no direct effect on growth but only an indirect one, through its impact on capital formation. Easterly, Levine, and Roodman (2003), using a specification similar to Burnside and Dollar but with an extended sample, found that the interaction term between aid and policies was also insignificant. Moreover, Easterly (2003) and Roodman (2003) found that even in the same sample as Burnside and Dollar (2000), the result was not robust to alternative (and equally plausible) definitions of aid, policies, and long-run growth.

An important issue for IMMPA applications to low-income countries is to capture the links between foreign aid, the level and composition of public investment, growth, and poverty. An important step in that direction was taken by Agénor, Bayraktar, and El Aynaoui (2005), and Agénor, Bayraktar, Pinto Moreira, and El Aynaoui (2005). Their model focuses on the fiscal and supply-side effects of aid, as well as the stock and flow effects of public investment, while accounting at the same time for potential congestion effects associated with the use of public services. As in IMMPA applications, the heart of the model is a production function that accounts explicitly for the effect of public capital (in health and infrastructure) on output and the marginal productivity of private production inputs. Public capital in education also plays a role in the production process, because "raw" labor must be turned into educated labor to become productive. The domestic (composite) good is imperfectly substitutable with the foreign good. By accounting for changes in relative prices, the model allows therefore the user to analyze potential Dutch disease effects associated with aid flows (as discussed earlier), in both the short and the long run.

The model also captures explicitly the link between aid and public investment, and the possible adverse effects of large inflows of foreign aid on fiscal accounts (as emphasized in fiscal response models). Moreover, it accounts for the fact that aid may finance initial investments (whether in education, health, or infrastructure) but then saddle governments with recurrent costs into the medium term that are not supported by donor assistance. Accounting explicitly for recurrent spending shows that higher investment does put pressure on the budget by increasing future recurrent expenditure; lack of maintenance expenditure could also increase the speed at which capital depreciates. Thus, as discussed in a more formal context by Agénor (2005*i*), a genuine trade-off may exist between increasing expenditure on new capital and spending more, to maintain the efficiency of the existing capital stock.

However, the model referred to in the foregoing discussion has only one domestic production sector and only one (aggregate) household. This precludes an analysis of issues associated with intersectoral reallocation of resources and income redistribution. Thus, an important avenue for applying IMMPA to low-income countries is to account for foreign aid, as well as recurrent spending. The latter extension would indeed help to stress the fact that there may be a trade-off between the quantity and quality of public capital. For instance, noninterest current expenditure could be disaggregated to isolate explicitly maintenance expenditure associated with health, education, and infrastructure – all of which modeled as a function of the rate of depreciation of each capital stock.

9.3 Public Investment, Growth, and Congestion Costs

Public investment can affect growth through a variety of channels (see Agénor (2004*b*, Chapter 12)). First, public investment (particularly in infrastructure) may increase private capital formation and thus the overall rate of accumulation of physical capital. Second, public investment may affect output growth by influencing the rate of productivity growth, independently of its effect on factor accumulation. Physical capital may enhance the productivity of (skilled) human capital if there is, as is often the case in practice, a high degree of complementarity between these factors. Similarly, public capital in infrastructure may make the existing stock of private capital more productive, if there is sufficient complementarity between the services produced by both stocks of capital. Third, an increase in public investment outlays may lead to higher private investment (as argued earlier), through a complementarity effect.

But public investment may also displace private capital formation, and therefore reduce the economy's capacity to sustain a higher level of output. Such crowding-out effects may occur if increases in public investment are financed through higher taxes (which may reduce the net rate of return on private investment, and therefore the incentive to invest) or by borrowing on domestic financial markets, thereby driving up domestic interest rates and the cost of capital, or leading to greater rationing in the quantity of credit allocated to the private sector.

Various empirical studies have shown that public investment, particularly in infrastructure, plays indeed an important role in developing countries. According to the World Bank (1994), services associated with the use of infrastructure account for roughly 7–9 percent of GDP in low- and middle-income countries, whereas investment in infrastructure represents about 20 percent of total domestic investment and between 40 and 60 percent of public investment. Physical infrastructure is thus an important input in the production process of the private sector, affecting both productivity and efficiency. In a more formal study, Loayza, Fajnzylber, and Calderón (2004) found that public infrastructure (measured by the number of telephone lines per capita) has a positive and significant effect on growth in Latin America and the Caribbean. The evidence of a robust and substantial effect of the share of total domestic investment in output on steady-state growth provided by Bond, Leblebicioglu, and Schiantarelli (2004) is also consistent with the view that public investment plays an important role (either directly or indirectly, through private investment) in the growth process.

An issue that has attracted much interest in recent years relates to the optimal allocation of public investment in a growth context. Some recent contributions have focused on the allocation between education, infrastructure, and health in an endogenous growth framework (see Agénor (2005*b*, 2005*c*, and 2005*d*)). In all of these models, private decisions to acquire skills are abstracted from and education is instead assumed to be a public good. The provision of various types of public services is simultaneously accounted for, in order to study potential trade-offs associated with the allocation of public spending. In Agénor (2005*b*), for instance, growth depends on government provision of both education and infrastructure services. As a result, the optimal allocation of tax revenue can be examined, given the effect of public infrastructure and education services on the marginal productivity of private capital.

However, we need to understand better interactions between components of public capital in order to determine optimal allocation rules. For instance, a significant body of research has shown that food intake and health are important factors in determining the quantity and quality of human capital (see Galor and Meyer (2002)). Healthier and well-fed children tend to do better in school, and healthier workers perform their tasks better. Thus, increasing the health of individuals may increase the effectiveness of education. At the same time, increasing education can also improve health. This suggests that escaping from a poverty trap through a "big push" (as discussed in Chapter 2) may require not only a large increase in public investment in infrastructure, but also an increase in investment in education and health.

This point is worth stressing. In models emphasizing the role of public investment in infrastructure (such as Agénor and Aizenman (2005)), the ability of a "big push" to lift a country from a poverty and low-growth trap depends on how the increase in public capital formation is financed. If financing occurs through a cut in unproductive spending, an increase in foreign aid, or debt cancellation, this may be a very effective instrument – despite the possibility that, with an aid-financed increase in public investment, Dutch disease effects, and adverse effects of aid on tax effort, may be important in the short run (see Agénor, Bayraktar, and El Aynaoui (2005)). By contrast, if the increase in investment in infrastructure is financed by a reduction in other types of productive government spending, such as on education or health, then higher public spending on roads, telecommunications, and the like, may not allow the government to break the cycle of stagnation, because the lack of qualified and healthy workers may continue to act as a constraint. Thus, in designing a program aimed at helping countries escape a poverty trap, accounting for policy complementarities are also important.

An important issue also in IMMPA models is the existence and magnitude of congestion costs, which imply that the productivity gains associated with a greater stock of public capital may diminish over time because the services produced by this stock are overused. This is a particularly acute problem for some types of public infrastructure, such as roads, which tend to get overcrowded due to the lack of alternatives. But it may also be the case for health and education services. According to World Bank estimates, in 1999, the pupil–teacher ratio in primary schooling (a common indicator of the quality of education) was 16.9 for high-income countries, but only 21.4 in middle-income countries and 38.9 in low-income countries. In the same year, the ratio was 41.5 in South Asia and 46.7 in Sub-Saharan Africa. Although some initial results regarding the impact of congestion costs in education on the optimal allocation rule for public investment have recently been derived (see Agénor (2005*b*, 2005*c*)), more research is needed. Moreover, the specifications that are typically used in IMMPA models can be improved upon – by modeling, for instance, mixed public–private education systems and interactions between public and private investment in learning technology. Accounting explicitly for recurrent spending would also help to stress the fact that there may be a trade-off between the quantity and quality of public capital, as noted earlier.

9.4   Linking Macro Models and Surveys

As noted in Chapters 5 and 8, in the basic IMMPA approach to linking macro models and household surveys described earlier, changes in within-group distribution are ignored, and poverty and distributional indicators reflect essentially changes across groups. As also indicated in those chapters, while appealing from a practical point of view, this approach is open to the criticism that it does not account for heterogeneity among agents within groups and introduces only in a partial manner the relevant changes that occur at the macro level as a result of shocks (most importantly, changes in employment) to the micro component of the analysis. More generally, the assumption that within-group rank ordering of households and individuals are unchanged and unaffected by policy shocks implies that workers are withdrawn from the sector of origin in a representative manner (leaving the distribution of income there unchanged) and that, as they move from one sector to another, they assume immediately the income distribution characteristics of the sector of destination (in particular, the variance of income in that sector is assumed to apply to all new entrants).[5] Thus, some workers may be poor not because of their personal characteristics, but rather because of the economic circumstances that characterize their sector of employment.

At the same time, however, the nature of the practical gains entailed by dropping the assumption of a stable within-group distribution and accounting fully for heterogeneity at the micro level remain a matter of debate. In Chapter 8 we compared

---

[5] As noted in Chapter 5, it also implies that resource transfers between households in any given group are ignored. During difficult times, such transfers may be quite significant.

three approaches aimed at linking macro models and household surveys to analyze the poverty and distributional effects of policy shocks. The first approach is the one followed in most IMMPA applications described earlier, which was referred to as the "micro-accounting method." The second approach extends the first in the sense that it not only incorporates changes in income and consumption occurring at the macro level in the household survey, but also accounts for changes in the employment structure predicted by the macro component. This is done by modifying the weight given to each household in the survey. This approach was referred to as the "micro-accounting method with reweighting." The third approach, referred to as the "distribution approach," imposes a fixed, parametrically estimated distribution of income within each group and assumes that shocks shift the mean of these distributions without, however, modifying their shape. Poverty and distributional indicators are then computed on the basis of these distributions.

The numerical simulations reported in the previous chapter showed that although the distributional and poverty effects indicated by the three approaches differ in quantitative terms, they differ neither in the direction of the effects nor in the ranking of the household categories with respect to poverty. They also suggested that the micro-accounting method combined with reweighting for changes in the employment structure is the most appealing method among the three, despite the fact that it has its own shortcomings. The reason is that the simple micro-accounting method ignores changes in the employment structure, whereas the distribution approach relies on approximate, instead of real, income distributions and depends therefore on the quality of the corresponding estimates of the shape parameters.

Before drawing firm conclusions, however, more experiments along the line of those conducted in Chapter 8 would be desirable. It is also important to perform comparisons with methodologies that allow for changes in the within-household group distribution, and to move away from the unidirectional link between macro models and household surveys, and thereby account for reverse effects of changes in the poverty rate on behavioral parameters.[6] In that regard, a key feedback effect may be related to the impact of poverty and unemployment rates on precautionary savings.

To conclude, we would like to emphasize the importance of careful data collection (particularly on financial flows) and adequate econometric research to estimate key behavioral relationships and provide reliable parameters for calibration purposes. For instance, assessing whether private investment is responsive to the debt-to-tax ratio matters a great deal in assessing the incentive effects of debt reduction; and determining whether the stock of public capital in infrastructure has a large complementarity effect on private investment is crucial to calculate the growth implications of alternative investment allocation strategies by the public sector. Likewise, estimating the parameters of the rural–urban migration function (and whether factors other than income differentials matter), as well as the skills acquisition

---

[6]Jensen and Tarp (2005), for instance, solve a static CGE model for the entire distribution of income and consumption among a representative set of almost 6,000 households.

function, is essential to assess the medium- and long-term effects of policy shocks on poverty, income distribution, and the labor market. Finally, assessing the sensitivity of the finance premium to the ratio of borrowers' net worth to the amount lent is also critical to gauge interactions between the real and financial sectors and spillover effects of financial shocks. This is an area on which future IMMPA developers will need to expend much energy and effort.

References

Acemoglu, Daron, and Robert Shimer, "Efficient Unemployment Insurance," *Journal of Political Economy*, 107 (October 1999), 893–928.

Adam, Christopher, and David Bevan, "Costs and Benefits of Incorporating Asset Markets into CGE Models: Evidence and Design Issues," Working Paper No. 202, Institute of Economics and Statistics, University of Oxford (October 1998).

——, "Aid, Public Expenditure and Dutch Disease," Working Paper No. 2003-02, Centre for the Study of African Economies, Oxford University (February 2003).

Addison, John T., and Paulino Teixeira, "The Economics of Employment Protection," IZA Working Paper No. 381 (October 2001).

——, "What have we Learned about the Employment Effects of Severance Pay? Further Iterations on Lazear et al.," IZA Working Paper No. 943 (November 2003).

Adelman, Irma and Sherman Robinson, *Income Distribution Policy in Developing Countries: A case Study of Korea*, Stanford University Press (Stanford, Cal.: 1978).

Afanasieff, Tarsila S., Priscilla M. Lhacer, and Marcio I. Nakane, "The Determinants of Bank Interest Spreads in Brazil," Working Paper No. 46, Central Bank of Brazil (August 2002).

Agell, Jonas, and Kjell E. Lommerud, "Minimum Wages and the Incentives for Skill Formation," *Journal of Public Economics*, 64 (April 1997), 25–40.

Agénor, Pierre-Richard, "The Labor Market and Economic Adjustment," *IMF Staff Papers*, 43 (June 1996), 261–335.

Agénor, Pierre-Richard, "Wage Contracts, Capital Mobility, and Macroeconomic Policy," *Journal of Macroeconomics*, 20 (December 1998), 1–25.

——, "Employment Effects of Stabilization Policies," *European Journal of Political Economy*, 14 (November 2001), 853–75.

——, "Business Cycles, Economic Crises, and the Poor: Testing for Asymmetric Effects," *Journal of Policy Reform*, 5 (October 2002a), 145–60.

——, "Monetary Policy under Flexible Exchange Rates: An Introduction to Inflation Targeting," in *A Decade of Inflation Targeting in the World*, ed. by Norman Loayza and Raimundo Soto, Central Bank of Chile (Santiago: 2002b).

——, "Does Globalization Hurt the Poor?," *Journal of International Economics and Economic Policy*, 1 (March 2004a), 1–31.

——, *The Economics of Adjustment and Growth*, 2nd. ed., Harvard University Press (Boston, Mass: 2004b).

——, "Macroeconomic Adjustment and the Poor: Analytical Issues and Cross-Country Evidence," *Journal of Economic Surveys*, 18 (September 2004c), 351–409.

Agénor, Pierre-Richard, "Unemployment-Poverty Trade-offs," in *Labor Markets and Institutions*, ed. by Jorge E. Restrepo and Andrea Tokman, Central Bank of Chile (Santiago: 2004*d*).

——, "Fiscal Adjustment and Labor Market Dynamics in an Open Economy," *Journal of Development Economics*, 76 (February 2005*a*), 97–125.

——, "Infrastructure, Public Education and Growth with Congestion Costs," Working Paper No. 47, Centre for Growth and Business Cycle Research, University of Manchester (January 2005*b*).

——, "The Macroeconomics of Poverty Reduction," *Manchester School of Social and Economic Studies*, 73 (July 2005*c*), 369–434.

——, "Fiscal Policy and Endogenous Growth with Public Infrastructure," Working Paper No. 59, Centre for Growth and Business Cycle Research, University of Manchester (September 2005*d*).

——, "Health and Infrastructure in Models of Endogenous Growth," Working Paper No. 62, Centre for Growth and Business Cycle Research, University of Manchester (September 2005*e*).

——, "External Shocks and the Urban Poor," unpublished, University of Manchester (September 2005*f*).

——, "Optimal Taxation and Growth with Productive Public Goods," work in progress, University of Manchester (September 2005*g*).

——, "Escaping from Poverty Traps," work in progress, University of Manchester (September 2005*h*).

——, "Infrastructure Investment and Maintenance Expenditure: Optimal Allocation Rules in a Growing Economy," Working Paper No. 62, Centre for Growth and Business Cycle Research, University of Manchester (September 2005*i*).

——, "Market Sentiment and Macroeconomic Fluctuations under Pegged Exchange Rates," unpublished, University of Manchester (October 2005*j*). Forthcoming, *Economica*.

Agénor, Pierre-Richard, and Joshua Aizenman, "Trade Liberalization and Unemployment," *Journal of International Trade and Economic Development*, 5 (September 1996), 265–86.

——, "Technological Change, Relative Wages, and Unemployment," *European Economic Review*, 41 (February 1997), 187–205.

——, "Contagion and Volatility with Imperfect Credit Markets," *IMF Staff Papers*, 45 (June 1998), 207–35.

——, "Macroeconomic Adjustment with Segmented Labor Markets," *Journal of Development Economics*, 58 (April 1999*a*), 277–96.

——, "Volatility and the Welfare Costs of Financial Market Integration," in *The Asian Financial Crisis: Causes, Contagion and Consequences*, ed. by Pierre-Richard Agénor, Marcus Miller, David Vines, and Axel Weber (Cambridge University Press: 1999*b*).

——, "Savings and the Terms of Trade under Borrowing Constraints," *Journal of International Economics*, 63 (July 2004), 324–45.

——, "Public Capital and the Big Push," work in progress, University of Manchester (October 2005).

Agénor, Pierre-Richard, and Nihal Bayraktar, "Contracting Models of the Phillips Curve: Empirical Estimates for Middle-Income Countries," Policy Research Working Paper No. 3139, World Bank (September 2003).

Agénor, Pierre-Richard, Nihal Bayraktar, and Karim El Aynaoui, "Roads out of Poverty? Assessing the Links between Aid, Public Investment, Growth, and Poverty Reduction," unpublished, World Bank (November 2005).

Agénor, Pierre-Richard, Nihal Bayraktar, Emmanuel Pinto Moreira, and Karim El Aynaoui, "Achieving the Millennium Development Goals in Sub-Saharan Africa: A Macroeconomic Monitoring Framework," Policy Research Working Paper No. 3750, World Bank (October 2005).

Agénor, Pierre-Richard, Nadeem Ul Haque, and Peter J. Montiel, "Macroeconomic Effects of Anticipated Devaluations with Informal Financial Markets," *Journal of Development Economics*, 42 (October 1993), 133–53.

Agénor, Pierre-Richard, and Mohsin S. Khan, "Foreign Currency Deposits and the Demand for Money in Developing Countries," *Journal of Development Economics*, 50 (June 1996), 101–18.

Agénor, Pierre-Richard, C. John McDermott, and Eswar Prasad, "Macroeconomic Fluctuations in Developing Countries: Some Stylized Facts," *World Bank Economic Review*, 14 (May 2000), 251–86.

Agénor, Pierre-Richard, C. John McDermott, and E. Murat Ucer, "Fiscal Imbalances, Capital Inflows, and the Real Exchange Rate: Evidence for Turkey," *European Economic Review*, 41 (April 1997), 819–25.

Agénor, Pierre-Richard, and Peter J. Montiel, *Development Macroeconomics*, Princeton University Press, 2nd ed. (Princeton, NJ: 1999).

Agénor, Pierre-Richard, Mustapha K. Nabli, Tarik Yousef, and Henning T. Jensen, "Labor Market Reforms, Growth, and Unemployment in Labor-Exporting Countries in the Middle East and North Africa," Policy Research Working Paper No. 3328, World Bank (June 2004).

Agénor, Pierre-Richard, and Julio A. Santaella, "Efficiency Wages, Disinflation, and Labor Mobility," *Journal of Economic Dynamics and Control*, 22 (February 1998), 267–91.

Agénor, Pierre-Richard, and Mark P. Taylor, "Testing for Credibility Effects," *IMF Staff Papers*, 39 (September 1992), 545–71.

Aghion, Philippe, Eva Caroli, and Cecilia García-Peñalosa, "Inequality and Growth: The Perspective of the New Growth Theories," *Journal of Economic Literature*, 37 (December 1999), 1615–60.

Ahmed, Habib, and Stephen M. Miller, "Crowding-Out and Crowding-In Effects of the Components of Government Expenditure," *Contemporary Economic Policy*, 18 (January 2000), 124–33.

Aitchinson, J., and J. A. Brown, *The Lognormal Distribution*, Cambridge University Press (Cambridge: 1957).

Akinbobola, T., and M. Saibu, "Income Inequality, Unemployment, and Poverty in Nigeria: A Vector Autoregressive Approach," *Journal of Policy Reform*, 7 (September 2004), 175–83.

Alatas, Vivi, and Lisa Cameron, "The Impact of Minimum Wages on Employment in a Low-Income Country: An Evaluation using the Difference-in-Differences Approach," Policy Research Working Paper No. 2985, World Bank (March 2003).

Alderman, Harold, and Christina H. Paxson, "Do the Poor Insure? A Synthesis of the Literature on Risk and Consumption in Developing Countries," in *Economics in a Changing World*, ed. by Edmar Bacha, Macmillan (London: 1994).

Allie, Emile, and Brian Murphy, "Static Database Aging of Income Distributions in Canada," in *Microsimulation in Government Policy and Forecasting*, ed. by A. Gupta and V. Kapur, North Holland (Amsterdam: 2000).

Amano, Masanori, "On the Harris-Todaro Model with Intersectoral Migration of Labour," *Economica*, 50 (August 1983), 311–23.

Amaral, Pedro S., and Erwan Quintin, "The Implications of Capital–Skill Complementarity in Economies with Large Informal Sectors," unpublished, Southern Methodist University (February 2003).

Anand, Ritu, and Sweder van Wijnbergen, "Inflation and the Financing of Government Expenditure: An Introductory Analysis with an Application to Turkey," *World Bank Economic Review*, 3 (March 1989), 17–38.

Arango, Carlos A., and Angelica Pachón, "Minimum Wages in Colombia: Holding the Middle with a Bite on the Poor," unpublished, Central Bank of Colombia (February 2004).

Arestoff, Florence, and Christophe Hurlin, "The Productivity of Public Capital in Developing Countries," unpublished, University of Orléans (March 2005).

Arndt, Channing, Henning Tarp Jensen, and Finn Tarp, "Structural Characteristics of the Economy of Mozambique: A SAM-based Analysis," *Review of Development Economics*, 4 (October 2000), 292–306.

Atkinson, Anthony B., and John Micklewright, "Unemployment Compensation and Labor Market Transitions: A Critical Review," *Journal of Economic Literature*, 29 (December 1991), 1679–727.

Atta-Mensah, Joseph, and Ali Dib, "Bank Lending, Credit Shocks, and the Transmission of Canadian Monetary Policy," Working Paper 2003-9, Bank of Canada (April 2003).

Azam, Jean-Paul, "The Labor Market in Morocco," Report No. 8, CERDI (August 1995).

Azariadis, Costas, "The Theory of Poverty Traps: What Have we learned?," unpublished, Department of Economics, University of California at Berkeley (July 2001).

Azariadis, Costas, and Allan H. Drazen, "Thresholds in Economic Development," *Quarterly Journal of Economics*, 105 (May 1990), 501–25.

Azariadis, Costas, and John Stachurski, "Poverty Traps," forthcoming in *Handbook of Economic Growth*, ed. by Philippe Aghion and Steven Durlauf, North Holland (Amsterdam: 2004).

Banerjee, Abhijit V., and Esther Duflo, "Inequality and Growth: What can the Data Say?," *Journal of Economic Growth*, 8 (September 2003), 267–99.

Banerjee, Biswajit, and Gabriella A. Bucci, "On-the-Job Search in a Developing Country: An Analysis Based on Indian Data on Migrants," *Economic Development and Cultural Change*, 43 (April 1995), 565–83.

Bardhan, Pranab, "Efficiency, Equity and Poverty Alleviation: Policy Issues in Less Developed Countries," *Economic Journal*, 106 (September 1996), 1344–56.

Barro, Robert J., "Government Spending in a Simple Model of Endogenous Growth," *Journal of Political Economy*, 98 (October 1990), s103–s125.

——, "Inequality and Growth in a Panel of Countries," *Journal of Economic Growth*, 5 (March 2000), 5–30.

Barro, Robert J., and Gary S. Becker, "Fertility Choice in a Model of Economic Growth," *Econometrica*, 57 (March 1989), 481–501.

Bean, Charles, "European Unemployment: A Survey," *Journal of Economic Literature*, 32 (June 1994), 573–619.

Becker, Gary S., Kevin M. Murphy, and Robert Tamura, "Human Capital, Fertility, and Economic Growth," *Journal of Political Economy*, 98 (October 1990), s12–s37.

Beenstock, Michael, Eddy Azoulay, Akiva Offenbacher, and Olga Sulla, "A Macroeconometric Model with Oligopolistic Banks: Monetary Control, Inflation and Growth in Israel," *Economic Modelling*, 20 (May 2003), 455–86.

Belaisch, Agnès, "Do Brazilian Banks Compete?," Working Paper No. 03/113, International Monetary Fund (May 2003*a*).

——, "Exchange Rate Pass-Through in Brazil," Working Paper No. 03/141, International Monetary Fund (July 2003*b*).

Belghazi, Saad, "Le marché du travail : Atout ou contrainte pour le développement du secteur privé," unpublished (January 1998).

Bell, Linda A., "The Impact of Minimum Wages in Mexico and Colombia," *Journal of Labor Economics*, 15 (July 1997), s102–s135.

Bencivenga, Valerie R., and Bruce D. Smith, "Unemployment, Migration, and Growth," *Journal of Political Economy*, Vol. 105 (June 1997), 582–608.

Benhayoun, Gilbert, Steven Bazen, Yvette Lazzeri, Eric Moustier, and P. Guillaumet, "Le salaire minimum au Maroc," unpublished, Ministère de l'Emploi, de la Formation Professionnelle, du Développement Social et de la Solidarité (July 2001).

Bernal, Raquel, and Mauricio Cárdenas, "Determinants of Labor Demand in Colombia: 1976–1996," Working Paper No. 10077, National Bureau of Economic Research (November 2003).

Bernanke, Ben S., Mark Gertler, and Simon Gilchrist, "The Financial Accelerator in a Quantitative Business Cycle Framework," in *Handbook of Macroeconomics*, ed. by John B. Taylor and Mark Woodford, North Holland (Amsterdam: 2000).

Bertola, Guiseppe, "Job Security, Employment and Wages," *European Economic Review*, 34 (June 1990), 851–79.

Berument, Hakan, and Kamuran Malatyali, "Determinants of Interest Rates in Turkey," *Russian and East European Finance and Trade*, 37 (January 2001), 5–16.

Berument, Hakan, and Hakan Tasci, "Monetary Policy Rules in Practice: Evidence from Turkey," *International Journal of Finance and Economics*, 9 (January 2004), 33–38.

Besley, Timothy, and Robin Burgess, "Can Labor Regulation Hinder Economic Performance? Evidence from India," *Quarterly Journal of Economics*, 119 (February 2004), 91–134.

Betcherman, G., A. Luinstra, and M. Ogawa, "Labor Market Regulation: International Experience in Promoting Employment and Social Protection," Social Protection Working Paper No. 0128, the World Bank (November 2001).

Bevilaqua, Afonso S., and Marcio G. Garcia, "Debt Management in Brazil: Evaluation of the Real Plan and Challenges ahead," *International Journal of Finance and Economics*, 7 (January 2002), 15–35.

Bhalla, Surjit S., "Poor Results and Poorer Policy: A Comparative Analysis of Estimates of Global Inequality and Poverty," *CESifo Economic Studies*, 50 (March 2004), 85–132.

Bhattacharya, Amar, Peter J. Montiel, and Sunil Sharma, "Private Capital Inflows to Sub-Saharan Africa: An Overview of Trends and Determinants," in *External Finance for Low-Income Countries*, ed. by Zubair Iqbal and Ravi Kanbur, the World Bank (Washington DC: 1997).

Bhattacharya, Prabir, "Rural–Urban Migration in Economic Development," *Journal of Economic Surveys*, 7 (September 1993), 243–81.

Bigsten, Arne, and Susan Horton, "Labour Markets in Sub-Saharan Africa," unpublished, Gothenburg University (May 1998).

Blackwood, D. L., and R. G. Lynch, "The Measurement of Inequality and Poverty: A Policy Maker's Guide to the Literature," *World Development*, 22 (April 1994), 567–78.

Blanchard, Olivier J., "Fiscal Dominance and Inflation Targeting: Lessons from Brazil," Working Paper No. 10389, National Bureau of Economic Research (March 2004).

Blanchard, Olivier-Jean, and Francesco Giavazzi, "Macroeconomic Effects of Regulation and Deregulation in Goods and Labor Markets," *Quarterly Journal of Economics*, 118 (August 2003), 879–907.

Bleaney, Michael, and Akira Nishiyama, "Income Inequality and Growth: Does the Relationship Vary with the Income Level?," *Economics Letters*, 84 (September 2004), 349–55.

Bliss, Chistopher, and Nicholas H. Stern, "Productivity, Wages, and Nutrition, I: the Theory," *Journal of Development Economics*, 5 (December 1978), 331–62.

Blunch, Niels-Hugo, Sudharshan Canagarajah, and Dhushyanth Raju, "The Informal Sector Revisited: A Synthesis across Space and Time," unpublished, World Bank (July 2001).

Blunch, Niels-Hugo, and Dorte Verner, "Asymmetries in the Union Wage Premium in Ghana," *World Bank Economic Review*, 18 (June 2004), 237–52.

Boal, William M., and Michael R. Ransom, "Monopsony in the Labor Market," *Journal of Economic Literature*, 35 (March 1997), 86–112.

Boccanfuso, Dorothé, Bernard Decaluwé, and Luc Savard, "Poverty, Income Distribution and CGE Modeling: Does the Functional Form of Distribution Matter?" unpublished, CREFA, Université Laval (March 2002).

Bodart, Vincent, and Jean Le Dem, "Labor Market Representation in Quantitative Macroeconomic Models for Developing Countries: An Application to Côte d'Ivoire," *IMF Staff Papers*, 43 (June 1996), 419–51.

Bogdanski, Joel, Alexandre A. Tombini, Sérgio R. Werlang, "Implementing Inflation Targeting in Brazil," unpublished, Banco Central do Brasil (January 2000).

Boldrin, Michele, "Dynamic Externalities, Multiple Equilibria, and Growth," *Journal of Economic Theory*, 58 (December 1992), 198–218.

Bond, Steven, Asli Leblebicioglu, and Fabio Schiantarelli, "Capital Accumulation and Growth: A New Look at the Empirical Evidence," unpublished, Boston College (May 2004).

Booth, Alison L., *The Economics of the Trade Union*, Cambridge University Press (Cambridge: 1995).

——, "An Analysis of Firing Costs and their Implications for Unemployment Policy," in *Unemployment Policy: Government Options for the Labor Market*, ed. by Dennis Snower and Gillermo de la Dehesa, Cambridge University Press (Cambridge: 1997).

Booth, Alison L., and Monojit Chatterji, "Unions and Efficient Training," *Economic Journal*, 108 (March 1998), 328–43.

Botero, Juan C., Simeon Djankov, Rafael La Porta, Florencio Lopez-de-Silane, and Andrei Shleifer, "The Regulation of Labor," *Quarterly Journal of Economics*, 119 (November 2004), 1339–82.

Bourguignon, François, William H. Branson, and Jaime de Melo, "Adjustment and Income Distribution," *Journal of Development Economics*, 38 (January 1992), 17–39.

Bourguignon, François, Jaime de Melo, and Akiko Suwa, "Modeling the Effects of Adjustment Programs on Income Distribution," *World Development*, 19 (November 1991), 1527–44.

Bourguignon, François, Anne-Sophie Robilliard, and Sherman Robinson, "Representative versus Real Households in the Macroeconomic Modeling of Inequality," unpublished, World Bank (2002).

Braun, Juan, and Norman Loayza, "Taxation, Public Services, and the Informal Sector in a Model of Endogenous Growth," Policy Research Working Paper No. 1334, World Bank (August 1994).

Brecher, Richard A., "An Efficiency Wage Model with Explicit Monitoring: Unemployment and Welfare in an Open Economy," *Journal of International Economics*, 32 (February 1992), 179–91.

Breen, Richard, and Cecilia García-Peñalosa, "Income Inequality and Macroeconomic Volatility: An Empirical Investigation," *Review of Development Economics*, 9 (August 2005), 380–98.

Bulir, Ales, "Income Inequality: Does Inflation Matter?," *IMF Staff Papers*, 48 (December 2001), 139–59.

Bulir, Ales, and Javier Hamann, "Aid Volatility: An Empirical Assessment," *IMF Staff Papers*, 50 (March 2003), 64–89.

Bulir, Ales, and Javier Hamann, "Volatility of Development Aid: From the Frying Pan into the Fire?," unpublished, International Monetary Fund (February 2005).

Bulow, Jeremy I., and Lawrence H. Summers, "A Theory of Dual Labor Markets with an Application to Industrial Policy, Discrimination, and Keynesian Unemployment," *Journal of Labor Economics*, 4 (July 1986), 376–414.

Bulutay, Tuncer, "Employment, Unemployment and Wages in Turkey," International Labour Office (Ankara: 1995).

Burnside, Craig, and David Dollar, "Aid, Policies, and Growth," *American Economic Review*, 90 (September 2000), 847–68.

——, "Aid, Policies, and Growth: Revisiting the Evidence," Policy Research Working Paper No. 3251, the World Bank (March 2004).

Cahuc, Pierre, and Philippe Michel, "Minimum Wage, Unemployment and Growth," *European Economic Review*, 40 (August 1996), 1463–82.

Cahuc, Pierre, and André Zylberberg, *Labor Economics*, MIT Press Cambridge (Mass.: 2004).

Calmfors, Lars, "Centralization of Wage Bargaining and Macroeconomic Performance," Working Paper No 536, Institute for International Economics, Stockholm University (April 1993).

Calvo, Guillermo, "Urban Unemployment and Wage Determination in LDCs: Trade Unions in the Harris-Todaro Model," *International Economic Review*, 19 (February 1978), 65–81.

Campbell, Carl, and J. Michael Orszag, "A Model of the Wage Curve," *Economics Letters*, 59 (April 1998), 119–25.

Canova, Fabio, "Testing for Convergence Clubs in Income Per Capita: A Predictive Density Approach," *International Economic Review*, 45 (February 2004), 49–78.

Carmichael, Jeffrey, Jerome Fahrer, and John Hawkins, "Some Macroeconomic Implications of of Wage Indexation: A Survey," in *Inflation and Unemployment*, ed. by Victor E. Argy and John W. Neville, Allen and Unwin (London: 1985).

Castelló, Amparo, and Rafael Doménech, "Human Capital Inequality and Economic Growth: Some New Evidence," *Economic Journal*, 112 (March 2002), c187–c200.

Castro-Leal, Florencia, Julia Dayton, Lionel Demery, and Kalpana Mehra, "Public Social Spending in Africa: Do the Poor Benefit?," *World Bank Research Observer*, 14 (February 1999), 49–72.

Celasun, Oya, R. Gaston Gelos, and Alessandro Prati, "Would 'Cold Turkey' Work in Turkey?," *IMF Staff Papers*, 51 (September 2004), 493–509.

Centre Marocain de Conjoncture, "Etude sur l'estimation de la boucle des prix-salaires," unpublished, Ministère de l'Emploi, de la Formation Professionnelle, du Développement Social et de la Solidarité (July 2001).

Charmes, Jacques, "A Critical Review of Concepts, Definitions and Studies in the Informal Sector," in *The Informal Sector Revisited*, ed. by David Turnham, Bernard Salom, and Antoine Schwartz, Development Centre, OECD (Paris: 1990).

Chauvet, Lisa, and Patrick Guillaumont, "Aid and Growth Revisited: Policy, Economic Vulnerability and Political Vulnerability," Working Paper No. 2003-23, CERDI (October 2003).

Chen, Derek, Hippolyte Fofack, Henning Jensen, Alejandro Izquierdo, and Daouda Sembene, "IMMPA: Operational Manual," unpublished, the World Bank (November 2001).

Chen, Shaohua, and Martin Ravallion, "How Have the World's Poorest Fared since the Early 1980s?," *World Bank Research Observer*, 19 (Fall 2004), 141–69.

Cherkaoui Mouna, Mohamed Douidich, and Abdelkhalek Touhami, "Returns to Human Capital in Morocco," unpublished, Arab Planing Institute (November 2002).

Chibber, Ajay, and Swever van Wijnbergen, "Public Policy and Private Investment in Turkey," in *Reviving Private Investment in Developing Countries*, ed. by Ajay Chhibber, Mansoor Dailami, and Nemat Shafik, North Holland (Amsterdam: 1992).

Civcir, Irfan, "Dollarization and its Long-Run Determinants in Turkey," unpublished, Ankara University (May 2002).

Clemens, Michael, and Steven Radelet, "Absorptive Capacity: How Much Is Too Much," in *Challenging Foreign Aid: A Policymaker's Guide to the Millennium Challenge Account*, ed. by Steven Radelet, Center for Global Development (Washington DC: 2003).

Clements, Benedict, Rina Bhattacharya, and Toan Q. Nguyen, "External Debt, Public Investment, and Growth in Low-Income Countries," Working Paper No. 03/249 (December 2003).

CNJA, "Enquête Auprès des Jeunes," Collections Enquêtes, Rabat (1995).

Coady, David P., and Rebecca L. Harris, "A Regional General Equilibrium Analysis of the Welfare Impact of Cash Transfers: An Analysis of *Progresa* in Mexico," TMD Division WP No. 76, IFPRI, Washington D.C. (2001).

Cockburn, John, "Trade Liberalisation and Poverty in Nepal: A Computable General Equilibrium Micro Simulation Analysis," CSAE Working Paper No. 2002-11, University of Oxford (June 2002).

Coe, David T., and Dennis J. Snower, "Policy Complementarities: The Case for Fundamental Labor Market Reform," *IMF Staff Papers*, 44 (March 1997), 1–35.

Cogneau, Denis, "Formation du revenu, segmentation et discrimination sur le marché du travail d'une ville en développement: Antananarivo fin de siècle," Working Paper DT/2001/18, DIAL (2001).

Cogneau, Denis, and Michael Grimm, "AIDS and Income Distribution in Africa: A Micro-simulation Study for Côte d'Ivoire," Working Paper DT/2002/15, DIAL (2002).

Cogneau, Denis, Michael Grimm, and Anne-Sophie Robilliard, "Evaluating poverty Reduction Policies—The Contribution of Micro-Simulation Techniques," in Jean-Pierre Cling, Mireille Razafindrakato, and Francois Roubaud (eds.), *New International Poverty Reduction Strategies*, Routledge Books (London: 2003).

Cogneau, Denis, and Anne-Sophie Robilliard, "Croissance, distribution et pauvreté: Un modèle de micro simulation en équilibre général appliqué à Madagascar," Working Paper DT/2001/19, DIAL (2001).

Cogneau, Denis, and George Tapinos, "Libre-échange, réparitition du revenu et migrations au Maroc," *Revue d'Economie du Développement*, 2 (March 1995), 27–52.

Corden, W. Max, and Richard Findlay, "Urban Unemployment, Intersectoral Capital Mobility and Development Policy," *Economica*, 42 (February 1975), 59–78.

Cordoba, Juan-Carlos, and Marla Ripoll, "Credit Cycles Redux," *International Economic Review*, 45 (November 2004), 1011–46.

Coulombe, Serge, Jean-François Tremblay, and Sylvie Marchand, "Literacy Scores, Human Capital and Growth across 14 OECD Countries," Statistics Canada (June 2004).

Cowell, Frank A., "Measuring inequality," in Anthony B. Atkinson, and François Bourguignon (eds.), *Handbook of Income Distribution*, North Holland (Amsterdam: 1999).

Cox Edwards, Alejandra, "Labor Market Regulations in Latin America: Overview," in *Labor Markets in Latin America*, ed. by Sebastian Edwards and Nora C. Lustig, Brookings Institution (Washington DC: 1997).

Creedy, John, and Ian McDonald, "Models of Trade Union Behavior: A Synthesis," *Economic Record*, 67 (December 1991), 346–59.

Cubitt, Robin P., and Shaun P. H. Heap, "Minimum Wage Legislation, Investment and Human Capital," *Scottish Journal of Political Economy*, 46 (May 1999), 135–57.

Cukierman, Alex, and Francesco Lippi, "Central Bank Independence, Centralization of Wage Bargaining, Inflation and Unemployment: Theory and Evidence," *European Economic Review*, 43 (June 1999), 1395–1434.

Currie, Janet, and Ann Harrison, "Sharing the Costs: The Impact of Trade Reform on Capital and Labor in Morocco," *Journal of Labor Economics*, 15 (July 1997), s44–s71.

Dabalen, Andrew, "Alternative Views of the Labor Market in Sub-Saharan Africa: A Review," unpublished, the World Bank (June 2000).

Da Fonseca, Manuel A. R., "Macroeconomic Analysis: Analysis of Brazil's Macroeconomic Trends," in *Structure and Structural Change in the Brazilian Economy*, ed. by Joaquim J. M. Guilhoto and Geoffrey J. D. Hewings, Ashgate Publishing (Brookfield, Vermont: 2001).

Dalgaard, Carl-Johan, and Henrik Hansen, "On Aid, Growth, and Good Policies," *Journal of Development Studies*, 37 (August 2001), 17–41.

Dalgaard, Carl-Johan, Henrik Hansen, and Finn Tarp, "On The Empirics of Foreign Aid and Growth," *Economic Journal*, 114 (June 2004), 191–216.

Dasgupta, Partha, and Debraj Ray, "Inequality as a Determinant of Malnutrition and Unemployment: Theory," *Economic Journal*, 96 (December 1986), 1011–34.

Davidson, Carl, Lawrence Martin, and Steven Matusz, "Trade and Search Generated Unemployment," *Journal of International Economics*, 48 (August 1999), 271–99.

Deaton, Angus, *The Analysis of Household Surveys*, Johns Hopkins University Press (Baltimore, Md.: 1997).

——, "Counting the World's Poor: Problems and Possible Solutions," *World Bank Research Observer*, 16 (November 2001), 125–48.

——, "Measuring Poverty in a Growing World (or Measuring Growth in a Poor World)," *Review of Economics and Statistics*, 87 (February 2005), 1–19.

Deaton, Angus, and John Muellbauer, *Economics and Consumer Behavior*, Cambridge University Press (Cambridge: 1980).

Decaluwé, Bernard, Jean-Christophe Dumont, and Luc Savard, "Measuring Poverty and Inequality in a Computable General Equilibrium Model," Working Paper No. 99-20, Université Laval (September 1999).

Decaluwé, Bernard, and Fabien Nsengiyumva, "Policy Impact under Credit Rationing: A Real and Financial CGE for Rwanda," *Journal of African Economies*, 3 (October 1994), 263–308.

Decaluwé, Bernard, A. Patry, Luc Savard, and Erik Thorbecke, "Poverty Analysis within a General Equilibrium Framework," Working Paper No. 99-09, African Economic Research Consortium (June 1999).

DeFina, Robert H., "The Impact of Unemployment on Alternative Poverty Rates," *Review of Income and Wealth*, 50 (March 2004), 69–86.

De Fraja, Gianni, "Minimum Wage Legislation, Productivity and Employment," *Economica*, 66 (November 1999), 473–88.

De Gregorio, José, "Borrowing Constraints, Human Capital Accumulation, and Growth," *Journal of Monetary Economics*, 37 (February 1996), 49–72.

Deininger, Klaus, and Pedro Olinto, "Asset Distribution, Inequality, and Growth," Policy Research Working Paper No. 2375, World Bank (June 2000).

Delaine, Ghislaine, et al., "The Social Dimensions of Adjustment Integrated Survey: A Survey to Measure Poverty an Understand the Effects of Policy Change on Households," SDA Working Paper No. 14, the World Bank (Washington DC: 1992).

Dellas, Harris, "Unemployment Insurance Benefits and Human Capital Accumulation," *European Economic Review*, 41 (April 1997), 517–24.

Demery, Lionel, and Tony Addison, "Impact of Macroeconomic Adjustment on Poverty in the Presence of Wage Rigidities," *Journal of Development Economics*, 40 (April 1993), 331–48.

Dercon, Stefan, "Income Risk, Coping Strategies, and Safety Nets," *World Bank Research Observer*, 17 (Fall 2002), 141–66.

Dervis, Kemal, Jaime De Melo, and Sherman Robinson, *General Equilibrium Models for Development Policy*, Cambridge University Press (Cambridge: 1982).

De Santis, Roberto A., "The Impact of a Customs Union with the EU on Turkey's Welfare, Employment and Income Distribution: An AGE Model with Alternative Labour Market Structures," *Journal of Economic Integration*, 15 (June 2000), 195–238.

Dessy, Sylvain, and Stéphane Pallage, "Taxes, Inequality and the Size of the Informal Sector," *Journal of Development Economics*, 70 (February 2003), 225–33.

Devarajan, Shantayanan, Hafez Ghanem, and Karen Thierfelder, "Labor Market Regulations, Trade Liberalization and the Distribution of Income in Bangladesh," *Journal of Policy Reform*, 3 (March 1999), 1–28.

Devarajan, Shanta, Hafez Ghanem, and Karen Thierfelder, "Economic Reforms and Labor Unions: A General-Equilibrium Analysis Applied to Bangladesh and Indonesia," *World Bank Economic Review*, 11 (January 1997), 145–70.

Devarajan, Shantayanan, Delfin S. Go, Jeffrey D. Lewis, Sherman Robinson, and Pekka Sinko, "Simple General Equilibrium Modeling," in *Applied Methods for Trade Policy Analysis*, ed. by Joseph F. Francois and Kenneth A. Reinhert, Cambridge University Press (Cambridge: 1997).

Dewatripont, Mathias, and Gilles Michel, "On Closure Rules, Homogeneity, and Dynamics in Applied General Equilibrium Models," *Journal of Development Economics*, 26 (June 1987), 65–76.

Diao, Xinshen, Terry L. Roe, and A. Erinç Yeldan, "Fiscal Debt Management, Accumulation and Transitional Dynamics in a CGE Model for Turkey," *Canadian Journal of Development Studies*, 19 (June 1998), 343–75.

Dixon, Peter B., K. R. Pearson, Mark R. Picton, and Maureen T. Rimmer, "Rational Expectations for Large CGE Models: A Practical Algorithm and a Policy Application," *Economic Modelling*, 22 (December 2005), 1001–19.

Djajic, Slobodan, "Human Capital, Minimum Wage and Unemployment: A Harris-Todaro Model of a Developed Open Economy," *Economica*, 52 (November 1985), 491–508.

Djajic, Slobodan, Sajal Lahiri, and Pascalis Raimondos-Moller, "Foreign Aid, Domestic Investment and Welfare," *Economic Journal*, 109 (October 1999), 698–707.

Domingues, Edson, "Dimensão Regional e Setorial da Integração Brasileira na Área de Livre Comércio das Américas," unpublished Ph.D. dissertation, University of Sao Paulo (May 2002).

Dornbusch, Rudiger, Federico Sturzenegger, and Holger Wolf, "Extreme Inflation: Dynamics and Stabilization," *Brookings Papers on Economic Activity*, No. 2 (1990), 1–84.

Dorosh, Paul A., and David E. Sahn, "A General Equilibrium Analysis of the Effect of Macroeconomic Adjustment on Poverty in Africa," *Journal of Policy Modeling*, 22 (November 2000), 753–76.

Downes, Andrew S., Nlandu Mamingi, and Rose-Marie B. Antoine, "Labor Market Regulation and Employment in the Caribbean," unpublished, Inter-American Development Bank (June 2003).

Drèze, Jacques, Edmond Malinvaud, and others, "Growth and Employment: The Scope of a European Initiative," *European Economic Review*, 38 (April 1994), 489–504.

Duclos, Jean-Yves, "Poverty and Equity: Theory and Estimation," unpublished, Université Laval (January 2002).

Durlauf, Stephen N., and Paul A. Johnson, "Multiple Regimes and Cross-Country Behaviour," *Journal of Applied Econometrics*, 10 (October 1995), 365–84.

Durlauf, Stephen N., and Danny T. Quah, "The New Empirics of Economic Growth," in *Handbook of Macroeconomics*, ed. by John Taylor and Michael Woodford, Elsevier (Amsterdam: 1999).

Duryea, Suzanne, Olga Lucia Jaramillo, and Carmen Pagés-Serra, "Latin American Labor Markets in the 1990s: Deciphering the Decade," Working Paper No. 486, Inter-American Development Bank (May 2003).

Duryea, Suzanne, and Miguel Székely, "Labor Markets in Latin America: A Look at the Supply Side," *Emerging Markets Review*, 1 (December 2000), 199–228.

Dynan, Karen E., Jonathan Skinner, and Stephen P. Zeldes, "Do the Rich Save More?," *Journal of Political Economy*, 112 (April 2004), 397–444.

Easterly, William, "Portfolio Effects in a CGE Model: Devaluation in a Dollarized Economy," in *Socially Relevant Policy Analysis*, ed. by Lance Taylor, MIT Press (Cambridge, Mass.: 1990).

——, "Can Foreign Aid Buy Growth?," Journal of Economic Perspectives, 17 (Summer 2003), 23–48.

Easterly, William, Ross Levine, and David Roodman, "New Data, New Doubts: Revisiting Aid, Policies, and Growth," Working Paper No. 26, Center for Global Development (June 2003).

El Aynaoui, Karim J. P., "Poverty and the Segmented Urban Labor Market in Morocco: A New Approach," unpublished, Ph.D Dissertation, University of Bordeaux (June 1998).

Elbadawi, Ibrahim A., Benno J. Ndulu, and Njuguna Ndungu, "Debt Overhang and Economic Growth in Sub-Saharan Africa," in *External Finance for Low-Income Countries*, ed. By Zubair Iqbal and Ravi Kanbur, International Monetary Fund (Washington DC: 1997).

Elekdag, Selim, "Exchange Rates and Monetary Policy in Turkey," unpublished, Johns Hopkins University (September 2003).

Emini, Christian A., and Hippolyte Fofack, "A Financial Social Accounting Matrix for the Integrated Macroeconomic Model for Poverty Analysis: Application to Cameroon with a Fixed-Price Multiplier Analysis," Policy Research Working Paper No. 3219, World Bank (2004).

Erceg, Christopher J., and Andrew T. Levin, "Imperfect Credibility and Inflation Persistence," *Journal of Monetary Economics*, 50 (May 2003) 915–944.

Erden, Lutfi, "The Effects of Financial Markets on Private Capital Formation: An Empirical Analysis of Turkish Data over 1968–1998," unpublished, Mersin University (March 2002).

Esfahani, Hadi S., and Djavad Salehi-Isfahani, "Effort Observability and Worker Productivity: Towards an Explanation of Economic Dualism," *Economic Journal*, 99 (September 1989), 818–36.

Faini, Riccardo, and Jaime de Melo, "Trade Liberalization, Employment and Migration: Some Simulation Results for Morocco," Centre for Economic Policy Research, Discussion Paper No. 1198 (August 1995).

Fallon, Peter R., and Robert E. B. Lucas, "Job Security Regulations and the Dynamic Demand for Industrial Labor in India and Zimbabwe," *Journal of Development Economics*, 40 (April 1993), 241–75.

——, "The Impact of Financial Crises on Labor Markets, Household Incomes, and Poverty: A Review of Evidence," *World Bank Research Observer*, 17 (Spring 2002), 21–45.

Fargeix, André, and Elisabeth Sadoulet, "A Financial Computable General Equilibrium Model for the Analysis of Stabilization Programs," in *Applied General Equilibrium and Economic Development: Present Achievements and Future Trends*, ed. by Jean Mercenier and T. N. Srinivasan, University of Michigan Press (Ann Arbor, Michigan: 1994).

Fields, Gary S., "On-the-Job Search in a Labor Market Model: Ex Ante Choices and Ex Post Outcomes," *Journal of Development Economics*, 30 (January 1989), 159–78.

Fields, Gary S., "Labor Market Modelling and the Urban Informal Sector: Theory and Evidence," in *The Informal Sector Revisited*, ed. by D. Turnham, B. Salom, and A. Schwarz, eds., OECD Development Centre (Paris: 1990).

——, "A Welfare Economic Analysis of Labor Market Policies in the Harris-Todaro Model," *Journal of Development Economics*, 76 (February 2005), 127–46.

Fiess, Norbert M., "Capital Flows, Country Risk, and Contagion," Policy Research Working Paper No. 2943, World Bank (January 2003).

Fiess, Norbert M., and Dorte Verner, "The Dynamics of Poverty and its Determinants: The Case of the Northeast of Brazil and its States," Policy Research Working Paper No. 3259, World Bank (April 2004).

Fischer, Stanley, "Real Balances, the Exchange Rate, and Indexation: Real Variables in Disinflation," *Quarterly Journal of Economics*, 103 (February 1988), 27–49.

Flanagan, Robert J., "Macroeconomic Performance and Collective Bargaining: An International Perspective," *Journal of Economic Literature*, 38 (September 1999), 1150–75.

Fofack, Hippolyte, "Combining Light Monitoring Surveys with Integrated Surveys to Improve Targeting for Poverty Reduction: The Case of Ghana," *The World Bank Economic Review*, 14 (January 2000), 1–25.

Foguel, Miguel, Lauro Ramos, and Francisco Carneiro, "The Impact of the Minimum Wage on the Labor Market, Poverty and Fiscal Budget in Brazil," unpublished, Instituto de Pesquisa Economica Aplicada (October 2001).

Fortin, Bernard, Nicolas Marceau, and Luc Savard, "Taxation, Wage Controls and the Informal Sector," *Journal of Public Economics*, 66 (November 1997), 293–312.

Foster James, Joel Greer, and Erik Thorbecke, "A Class of Decomposable Poverty Measures," *Econometrica*, 52 (September 1984), 761–6.

Foster, James E., and Miguel Székely, "Is Economic Growth Good for the Poor? Tracking Low Incomes using General Means," Working Paper No. 453, Inter-American Development Bank (June 2001).

Franco-Rodriguez, Susana, "Recent Advances in Fiscal Response Models with an Application to Costa Rica," *Journal of International Development*, 12 (April 2000), 429–42.

Fukushima, Yoshihiko, "Active Labour Market Programmes and Unemployment in a Dual Labour Market," unpublished, Stockholm University (September 1998).

Funkhauser, Edward, "Mobility and Labor Market Segmentation: The Urban Labor Market in El Salvador," *Economic Development and Cultural Change*, 46 (October 1997), 123–53.

Galor, Oded, and David Meyer, "Food for Thought: Basic Needs and Persistent Educational Inequality," unpublished, Pan American Health Organization (August 2002).

Galor, Oded, and Joseph Zeira, "Income Distribution and Macroeconomics," *Review of Economic Studies*, 60 (January 1993), 35–52.

Gavin, Michael, "Labor Market Rigidities and Unemployment: The Case of Severance Costs," International Finance Discussion Paper No. 184, Federal Reserve Board (June 1986).

Gelb, Alan, J. B. Knight, and Richard H. Sabot, "Public Sector Employment, Rent Seeking and Economic Growth," *Economic Journal*, 101 (September 1991), 1186–99.

Gertler, Mark, Simon Gilchrist, and Fabio M. Natalucci, "External Constraints on Monetary Policy and the Financial Accelerator," Working Paper No. 10128, National Bureau of Economic Research (December 2003).

Ghatak, Subrata, Paul Levine, and Stephen W. Price, "Migration Theories and Evidence: An Assessment," *Journal of Economic Surveys*, Vol. 10 (June 1996), 159–98.

Ghura, Dhaneshwar, and Barry Goodwin, "Determinants of Private Investment: A Cross-Regional Empirical Investigation," *Applied Economics*, 32 (November 2000), 1819–29.

Giambiagi, Fabio, and Marcio Ronci, "Fiscal Policy and Debt Sustainability: Cardoso's Brazil, 1995–2002," Working Paper No. 04/156, International Monetary Fund (August 2004).

Gong, Xiaodong, Arthur van Soest, and Elizabeth Villagomez, "Mobility in the Urban Labor Market: A Panel Data Analysis," *Economic Development and Cultural Change*, 53 (October 2004), 1–36.

Gottfries, Nils, and Barry McCormick, "Discrimination and Open Unemployment in a Segmented Labour Market," *European Economic Review*, 39 (January 1995), 1–15.

Greene, William H., *Econometric Analysis*, 4th ed., Prentice Hall (Upper Saddle River, NJ: 2000).

Gregg, Paul, and Alan Manning, "Labour Market Regulation and Unemployment," in *Unemployment Policy: Government Options for the Labor Market*, ed. by Dennis Snower and Guillermo de la Dehesa, Cambridge University Press (Cambridge: 1997).

Grimm, Michael, "Educational Policies and Poverty Reduction in Côte d'Ivoire," *Journal of Policy Modeling*, 27 (March 2005), 231–47.

Grosh, Margaret, and Paul Glewwe, eds., *Designing Household Survey Questionnaires: Lessons from Ten Years of LSMS Experience for Developing Countries*, Oxford University Press (Oxford: 2000).

Groth, Charlotta, and Asa Johansson, "Bargaining Structure and Nominal Wage Flexibility," *European Economic Review*, 48 (December 2004), 1349–66.

Guilhoto, Joaquim, "Um Modelo Computável de Equilíbrio Geral para Planejamento e Análise de Políticas Agrícolas (PAPA) na Economia Brasileira," unpublished PhD. thesis, ESALQ/USP (August 1995).

Guillaumont, Patrick, and Lisa Chauvet, "Aid and Performance: A Re-assessment," *Journal of Development Studies*, 37 (August 2001), 66–92.

Gunaydin, Emek, "Analysing the Sustainability of Fiscal Deficits in Turkey," unpublished, Undersecretariat of the Treasury, Ankara (September 2003).

Guncavdi, Oner, Michael Bleaney, and Andrew McKay, "Financial Liberalisation and Private Investment: Evidence from Turkey," *Journal of Development Economics*, 57 (December 1998), 443–55.

——, "The Response of Private Investment to Structural Adjustment: A Case Study of Turkey," *Journal of International Development*, 11 (March 1999), 221–39.

Gupta, Sanjeev, Benedict Clements, Alexander Pivovasrky, and Erwin R. Tiongson, "Foreign Aid and Revenue Response: Does the Composition of Aid Matter?," Working Paper No. 03/176, International Monetary Fund (September 2003).

Haddad, Eduardo, Reynaldo Fernandes, Edson Domingues, Fernando Perobelli, and Luiz Afonso, "Notes on the Brazilian IMMPA SAM," unpublished, University of Sao Paulo (August 2003).

Hamermesh, David, *Labor Demand*, Princeton University Press (Princeton, NJ: 1993).

Hansen, Henrik, and Finn Tarp, "Aid and Growth Regressions," *Journal of Development Economics*, 64 (April 2001), 547–70.

Harris, John, and Michael P. Todaro, "Migration, Unemployment and Development: A Two-Sector Analysis," *American Economic Review*, 60 (March 1970), 126–43.

Heckman, James J., and Carmen Pagés, "The Cost of Job Security Regulation: Evidence from Latin American Labor Markets," *Journal of the Latin American and Caribbean Economic Association*, 1 (Fall 2000), 109–54.

Helpman, Elhanan, "Voluntary Debt Reduction: Incentives and Welfare," *IMF Staff Papers*, 36 (September 1989), 580–611.

Hendricks, Lutz, "Equipment Investment and Growth in Developing Countries," *Journal of Development Economics*, 61 (April 2000), 335–64.

Hillier, Brian, and Tim Worrall, "Asymmetric Information, Investment Finance and Real Business Cycles," in *The New Macroeconomics: Imperfect Markets and Policy Effectiveness*, ed. by Huw D. Dixon and Neil Rankin, Cambridge University Press (Cambridge: 1995).

Hirata, Helena, and John Humphrey, "Workers' Response to Job Loss: Female and Male Industrial Workers in Brazil," *World Development*, 19 (June 1991), 671–82.

Hoddinot, John, "Wages and Unemployment in an Urban African Labour Market," *Economic Journal*, 106 (November 1996), 1610–26.

Hoff, Karla, "Beyond Rosenstein-Rodan: The Modern Theory of Underdevelopment Traps," unpublished, World Bank (April 2000).

Hogan, Vincent, "Wage Aspirations and Unemployment Persistence," *Journal of Monetary Economics*, 51 (November 2004), 1623–43.

Hollister, Robinson Jr., and Markus Goldstein, *Reforming Labor Markets in the Near East*, ICS Press (San Francisco, Cal.: 1994).

Hopenhayn, Hugo and Juan Pablo Nicolini, "Optimal Unemployment Insurance," *Journal of Political Economy*, 105 (April 1997), 412–38.

Hopenhayn, Hugo and Richard Rogerson, "Job Turnover and Policy Evaluation: A General Equilibrium Analysis," *Journal of Political Economy*, 101 (October 1993), 915–38.

Huang, Chien-Chieh, Derek Laing, and Ping Wang, "Crime and Poverty: A Search-Theoretic Approach," *International Economic Review*, 45 (August 2004), 909–38.

Huh, Chan G., and Kevin J. Lansing, "Expectations, Credibility, and Disinflation in a Small Macroeconomic Model," *Journal of Economics and Business*, 52 (January 2000), 51–86.

Husain, Aasim M., "Domestic Taxes and the External Debt Laffer Curve," *Economica*, 64 (August 1997), 519–25.

Ihrig, Jane, and Karine S. Moe, "Tax Policies and Informal Employment: The Asian Experience," unpublished, Board of Governors of the Federal Reserve System (November 2000).

——, "Lurking in the Shadows: The Informal Sector and Government Policy," *Journal of Development Economics*, 73 (April 2004), 541–57.

Ilkkaracan, Ipek, and Raziye Selim, "The Role of Unemployment in Wage Determination: Further Evidence on the Wage Curve for Turkey," Working Paper No. 2002-11, Center for Economic Policy Analysis, New School University (August 2002).

Inter-American Development Bank, *Good Jobs Wanted: Labor Markets in Latin America*, IADB Publications (Washington DC: 2003).

International Labor Organization, *Global Employment Trends*, International Labor Office (Geneva: 2003).

——, *World Employment Report 2004–05*, International Labor Office (Geneva: 2005).

International Monetary Fund, *IMF Macroeconomic Research on Low-Income Countries*, International Monetary Fund (Washington DC: 2003).

Iradian, Garbis, "Inequality, Poverty, and Growth: Cross-country Evidence," Working Paper No. 05/28, International Monetary Fund (February 2005).

Isard, Peter, Douglas Laxton, and Ann-Charlotte Eliasson, "Inflation Targeting with NAIRU Uncertainty and Endogenous Policy Credibility," *Journal of Economic Dynamics and Control*, 25 (January 2001), 115–48.

Islam, Nazrul, "What Have we Learnt from the Convergence Debate?," *Journal of Economic Surveys*, 17 (July 2003), 309–62.

Iyoha, Milton A., "An Econometric Analysis of External Debt and Economic Growth in Sub-Saharan African Countries," in *External Debt and Capital Flight in Sub-Saharan Africa*, ed. by S. Ibi Ajayi and Mohsin Khan, International Monetary Fund (Washington DC: 2000).

Izquierdo, Alejandro, "Credit Constraints and the Asymmetric Behavior of Asset Prices and Output under External Shocks," doctoral dissertation, University of Maryland, unpublished (November 2000).

Jalan, Jyotsna, and Martin Ravallion, "Geographic Poverty Traps? A Micro Model of Consumption Growth in Rural China," *Journal of Applied Econometrics*, 17 (August 2002), 329–46.

Jensen, Henning Tarp, and Finn Tarp, "Trade Liberalization and Spatial Inequality: A Methodological Innovation in a Vietnamese Perspective," *Review of Development Economics*, 9 (February 2005), 69–86.

Jensen, Henning Tarp, and A. Erinç Yeldan, "Notes on the Social Accounting Matrix Underlying IMMPA-Turkey," unpublished, World Bank (June 2004).

Jimenez, Emmanuel, "Human and Physical Infrastructure: Public Investment and Pricing Policies in Developing Countries," in *Handbook of Development Economics*, ed. by Jere Behrman and T. N. Srinivasan, Vol. 3B, North Holland (Amsterdam: 1995).

Johnson, Simon, Daniel Kaufman, and Zoido-Lobaton, "Regulatory Discretion and the Unofficial Economy," *American Economic Review*, 88 (May 1998), 387–92.

Jones, Stephen R., "Minimum Wage Legislation in a Dual labor Market," *European Economic Review*, 31 (August 1987), 1229–46.

Jung, Hong-Sang, and Erik Thorbecke, "The Impact of Public Education Expenditure on Human Capital, Growth, and Poverty in Tanzania and Zambia: A General Equilibrium Approach," *Journal of Policy Modeling*, 25 (November 2003), 701–25.

Kakwani, Nanak, and Ernesto M. Pernia, "What is Pro-Poor Growth?," *Asian Development Review*, 18 (March 2000), 1–16.

Kaldor, Nicholas, "A Model of Economic Growth," *Economic Journal*, 57 (December 1957), 591–624.

Kanbur, Ravi, "Structural Adjustment, Macroeconomic Adjustment and Poverty: A Methodology for Analysis," *World Development*, 15 (December 1987), 1515–26.

Kannappan, Subbiah, "Urban Employment and the Labor Market in Developing Nations," *Economic Development and Cultural Change*, 33 (July 1985), 699–730.

Karadag, Metin, and Tony Westaway, "A SAM Based Computable General Equilibrium Tax Model of the Turkish Economy," Economic Research Paper No. 99/18, Loughborough University (October 1999).

Karni, Edi, "Optimal Unemployment Insurance: A Guide to the Literature," Social Protection Discussion Paper No. 9906, the World Bank (January 1999).

Khan, Mohsin S., and Nadeem U. Haque, "Foreign Borrowing and Capital Flight: A Formal Analysis," *IMF Staff Papers*, 32 (December 1985), 606–28.

King, Ian, and Linda Welling, "Search, Unemployment and Growth," *Journal of Monetary Economics*, 35 (June 1995), 499–507.

Kirman, Alan P., "Whom or What Does the Representative Individual Represent?," *Journal of Economic Perspectives*, 6 (March 1992), 117–36.

Kiyotaki, Nobuhiro, and John Moore, "Credit Cycles," *Journal of Political Economy*, 105 (April 1997), 211–48.

Klasen, Stephan, "In Search of the Holy Grail: How to Achieve Pro-Poor Growth?," unpublished, Department of Economics, University of Munich (March 2003).

Knowles, Stephen, "Inequality and Economic Growth: The Empirical Relationship Reconsidered in the Light of Comparable Data," WIDER Discussion Paper No. 2001/128 (November 2001).

Konan, Denise E., and Keith E. Maskus, "Joint Trade Liberalization and Tax Reform in a Small Open Economy: The Case of Egypt," *Journal of Development Economics*, 61 (April 2000), 365–92.

Kraay, Aart, "When is Growth Pro-Poor? Evidence from a Panel of Countries," Policy Research Working Paper No. 3225, World Bank (February 2004).

Kremer, Michael, and Daniel Chen, "Income-Distribution Dynamics with Endogenous Fertility," *American Economic Review*, 89 (May 1999), 155–60.

Krishnamurthy, Arvin, "Collateral Constraints and the Amplification Mechanism," *Journal of Economic Theory*, 111 (August 2003), 277–292.

Kristensen, Nicolai, and Dorte Verner, "Labor Market Distortions in Côte d'Ivoire: Analyses of Employer–Employee Data from the Manufacturing Sector," Policy Research Working Paper No. 3771, World Bank (November 2005).

Krugman, Paul, "Financing vs. Forgiving a Debt Overhang," *Journal of Development Economics*, 29 (November 1988), 253–68.

Kugler, Adriana D., "The Effect of Job Security Regulations on Labor Market Flexibility: Evidence from the Colombian Labor Market Reform," Working Paper No. 10215, National Bureau of Economic Research (January 2004).

Kugler, Adriana D., and Gilles Saint-Paul, "Hiring and Firing Costs, Adverse Selection and the Persistence of Uemployment," Discussion Paper No. 2410, Centre for Economic Policy Research (March 2000).

Landt John, Ann Harding, Richard Percival, and Krys Sadkowsky, "Reweighting a Base Population for a Microsimulation Model," Discussion Paper No. 3, National Centre for Social and Economic Modelling, University of Canberra (1994).

Laxton, Douglas, Nicholas Ricketts, and David Rose, "Uncertainty, Learning and Policy Credibility," in *Economic Behavior and Policy Choice under Price Stability*, Bank of Canada (Ottawa: 1994).

Lewis, Jeffrey D., "Financial Repression and Liberalization in a General Equilibrium Model with Financial Markets," *Journal of Policy Modeling*, 14 (April 1992), 135–66.

Lewis, W. Arthur, "Economic Development with Unlimited Supplies of Labor," *The Manchester School*, 22 (March 1954), 139–91.

Li, Hongyi, and Heng-fu Zou, "Income Inequality is not Harmful for Growth: Theory and Evidence," *Review of Development Economics*, 2 (September 1998), 318–34.

Lim, Cheng Hoon, and Laura Papi, "An Econometric Analysis of the Determinants of Inflation in Turkey," Working Paper No. 97/170, International Monetary Fund (December 1997).

Lindauer, David D., "Labor Market Reforms and the Poor," unpublished, the World Bank (October 1999).

Lindbeck, Assar, and Dennis J. Snower, "Insiders Versus Outsiders," *Journal of Economic Perspectives*, 15 (Winter 2001), 165–88.

Litchfield, Julie A., "Inequality: Methods and Tools," the World Bank (March 1999).

Loayza, Norman V., "Labor Regulations and the Informal Economy," Policy Research Working Paper No. 1335, World Bank (August 1994).

——, "The Economics of the Informal Sector: A Simple Model and Some Empirical Evidence from Latin America," Carnegie-Rochester Conference Series on Public Policy, Vol. 45 (June 1996).

Loayza, Norman, Pablo Fajnzylber, and César Calderón, "Economic Growth in Latin America and the Caribbean: Stylized Facts, Explanations, and Forecasts," Working Paper No. 265, Central Bank of Chile (June 2004).

Loayza, Norman V., Klaus Schmidt-Hebbel, and Luis Servén, "What Drives Saving across the World?," in *The Economics of Saving and Growth*, ed. by Klaus Schmidt-Hebbel and Luis Servén, Cambridge University Press (Cambridge: 1999).

Löfgren, Hans, "Trade Reform and the Poor in Morocco: A Rural–Urban General Equilibrium Analysis of Reduced Protection," TMD Discussion Paper No. 38, International Food Policy Research Institute (January 1999).

Löfgren, Hans, "External Shocks and Domestic Poverty Alleviation: Simulations with a CGE Model of Malawi," TMD Discussion Paper No. 71, International Food Policy Research Institute (February 2001).

Löfgren, Hans, Sherman Robinson, and M. El-Said, "Poverty and Inequality Analysis in a General Equilibrium Framework: The Representative Household Approach," unpublished, the World Bank (June 2002).

Lopez, R., and Maurice Schiff, "Migration and the Skill Composition of the Labor Force: The Impact of Trade Liberalization in LDCs," *Canadian Journal of Economics*, 31 (May 1998), 318–36.

Lucas, Robert E. B., "Internal Migration in Developing Countries," in *Handbook of Population and Family Economics*, ed. by Mark Rosenzweig and Oded Stark, Vol. 1B, Elsevier (Amsterdam: 1997).

Lustig, Nora, and Darryl McLeod, "Minimum Wages and Poverty in Developing Countries: Some Empirical Evidence," in *Labor Markets in Latin America*, ed. by Sebastian Edwards and Nora C. Lustig, Brookings Institution (Washington DC: 1997).

Maechler, Andrea, and David W. Roland-Host, "Empirical Specifications for a General Equilibrium Analysis of Labor Market Policies and Adjustments," Technical Paper No. 106, OECD (May 1995).

——, "Labor Market Structure and Conduct," in *Applied Methods for Trade Policy Analysis*, ed. by Joseph F. Francois and Kenneth A. Reinert, Cambridge University Press (Cambridge: 1997).

Marti, Christopher, "Efficiency Wages: Combining the Shirking and Turnover Cost Models," *Economics Letters*, 57 (December 1997), 327–30.

Masson, Paul R., "The Sustainability of Fiscal Deficits," *IMF Staff Papers*, 32 (December 1985), 577–605.

——, "Migration, Human Capital, and Poverty in a Dual-Economy of a Developing Country," Working Paper No. 01/128, International Monetary Fund (September 2001).

Mazumdar, Dipak, "Segmented Labor Markets in LDCs," *American Economic Review*, 73 (May 1983), 254–59.

McDonald, Ian M., and Robert M. Solow, "Wages and Employment in a Segmented Labor Market," *Quarterly Journal of Economics*, 100 (November 1985), 1115–41.

McGillivray, Mark, "Aid and Public Sector Behavior in Developing Countries," *Review of Development Economics*, 4 (June 2000), 156–63.

McGillivray, Mark, and Bazoumana Ouattara, "Aid, Debt Burden and Government Fiscal Behaviour: A New Model Applied to Côte d'Ivoire," WIDER Discussion Paper No. 2003/33 (April 2003).

McKenzie, David J., "How do Households Cope with Aggregate Shocks? Evidence from the Mexican Peso Crisis," *World Development*, 31 (July 2003), 1179–99.

Melo, G. M., and W. Rodrigues, "Determinantes do Investimento Privado no Brasil: 1970–1995," Working Paper No. 604, Instituto de Pesquisa Economica Aplicada (March 1998).

Merz, Joachim, "Microdata Adjustment by the Minimum Information Loss Principle," FFB Discussion Paper No. 10, University of Lüneburg, Lüneburg (1994).

Minella, André, Paulo S. de Freitas, Ilan Goldfajn, and Marcelo K. Muinhos, "Inflation Targeting in Brazil: Constructing Credibility under Exchange Rate Volatility," *Journal of International Money and Finance*, 22 (December 2003), 1015–40.

Moene, Karl O., Michael Wallerstein, and Michael Hoel,"Bargaining Structure and Economic Performance," in *Trade Union Behavior, Pay Bargaining and Economic Performance*, ed. by Robert Flanagan, Karl O. Moene, and Michael Wallerstein, Oxford University Press (Oxford: 1993).

Montenegro, Claudio E., and Carmen Pagés, "Who Benefits from Labor Market Regulations? Chile 1960–1998," in *Labor Markets and Institutions*, ed. by Jorge E. Restrepo and Andrea Tokman R., Central Bank of Chile (Santiago: 2004).

Montmarquette, Claude, Fouzi Mourji, and A. Garni, "L'insertion des diplômés de la formation professionnelle dans le marché du travail Marocain: Une application des modèles de durée," *Région et Développement*, No. 3 (1996), 37–57.

Morrisson, Christian, *Ajustement et equité au Maroc*, Paris, Centre de Développement, OECD (1991).

Mortensen, Dale, and Christopher Pissarides, "New Developments in Models of Search in the Labor Market," in *Handbook in Labor Economics*, ed. by Orley Ashenfelter and David Card, North Holland (Amsterdam: 1999).

Mosley, Paul, John Hudson, and Arjan Verschoor, "Aid, Poverty Reduction and the 'New Conditionality'," *Economic Journal*, 114 (June 2004), 217–43.

Mouime, Mohamed, "Salaire d'efficience et alignement des salaires sur les prix," Document de Travail No. 66, Ministère de l'économie et des Finances, Direction de la Politique Economique Générale (July 2001).

Nas, Tevfik F., and Mark J. Perry, "Turkish Inflation and Real Output Growth: 1963–2000," in *Inflation and Disinflation in Turkey*, ed. by Aykut Kibritcioglu, Libby Rittenberg, and Faruk Selcuk, Ashgate Publishing Co. (Aldershot: 2002).

Nelson, Joan, "Organized Labor, Politics, and Labor Market Flexibility in Developing Countries," in *Labor Markets in an Era of Adjustment*, Vol. I, ed. by Susan Horton, Ravi Kanbur, and Dipak Mazumdar, World Bank (Washington, DC: 1994).

Nicoló, Gianni de, Patrick Honohan, and Alain Ize, "Dollarization of Bank Deposits: Causes and Consequences," *Journal of Banking and Finance*, 29 (July 2005), 1697–727.

Nurkse, Ragnar, *Problems of Capital Formation in Underdeveloped Countries*, Oxford University Press (Oxford: 1953).

O'Connell, Lesley, "Collective Bargaining Systems in Six Latin American Countries: Degrees of Autonomy and Decentralization," Working Paper No. 399, Inter-American Development Bank (June 1999).

OECD, *Economic Surveys: Turkey 1996*, OECD (Paris: 1996).

Ogaki, Masao, and Andrew Atkeson, "Rate of Time Preference, Intertemporal Elasticity of Subsitution, and Level of Wealth," *Review of Economics and Statistics*, 79 (November 1997), 564–72.

Onaran, Ozlem, "Measuring Wage Flexibility: The Case of Turkey before and after Structural Adjustment," *Applied Economics*, 34 (April 2002), 767–81.

Ozatay, Fatih, "A Quarterly Macroeconometric Model for a Highly Inflationary and Indebted Country: Turkey," *Economic Modelling*, 17 (January 2000), 1–11.

Ozcan, Kivilcim M., Asli Gunay, and Seda Ertac, "Determinants of Private Savings Behaviour in Turkey," *Applied Economics*, 35 (August 2003), 1405–16.

Paes de Barros, Ricardo, and Carlos Henrique Corseuil, "The Impact of Regulations on Brazilian Labor Performance," Working Paper No. R-427, Inter-American Development Bank (October 2001).

Pallage, Stéphane, and Michel A. Robe, "On the Welfare Cost of Economic Fluctuations in Developing Countries," *International Economic Review*, 44 (May 2003), 677–98.

Panagides, Alexis, and Harry A. Patrinos, "Union–Nonunion Wage Differentials in the Developing World: A Case Study of Mexico," Policy Research Working Paper No 1269, the World Bank (March 1994).

Park, Young-Bum, "Union–Nonunion Wage Differentials in the Korean Manufacturing Sector," *International Economic Journal*, 5 (Winter 1991), 79–91.

Parkin, Vincent, *Chronic Inflation in an Industrializing Economy: The Brazilian Experience*, Cambridge University Press (Cambridge: 1991).

Pattillo, Catherine, Hélène Poirson, and Luca Ricci, "External Debt and Growth," Working Paper No. 02/69, International Monetary Fund (April 2002).

Pencavel, John, "The Legal Framework for Collective Bargaining in Developing Countries," in *Labor Markets in Latin America*, ed. by Sebastian Edwards and Nora C. Lustig, Brookings Institution (Washington DC: 1997).

Perotti, Roberto, "Political Equilibrium, Income Distribution, and Growth," *Review of Economic Studies*, 60 (October 1993), 755–76.

Perry, Guillermo, "Can Fiscal Rules Help Reduce Macroeconomic Volatility in the Latin America and the Caribbean Region?," Policy Research Working Paper No. 3080, World Bank (June 2003).

Phelps, Edmund S., *Structural Slumps*, Harvard University Press (Cambridge, Mass.: 1994).

Pisauro, Giuseppe, "The Effect of Taxes on Labour in Efficiency Wage Models," *Journal of Public Economics*, 46 (December 1991), 329–45.

Prasad, Eswar, "What Determines the Reservation Wages of Unemployed Workers? New Evidence from German Micro Data," Working Paper No. 03/4, International Monetary Fund (January 2003).

Pritchett, Lant, "Mind your P's and Q's. The Cost of Public Investment is not the Value of Capital," Policy Research Working Paper No. 1660, World Bank (October 1996).

Quibria, Muhammad G., "Migration, Trade Unions, and the Informal Sector: A Note on Calvo," *International Economic Review*, 29 (August 1988), 557–63.

Rama, Martín, "Do Labor Market Policies and Institutions Matter? The Adjustment Experience in Latin America and the Caribbean," unpublished, World Bank (June 1995).

Ravallion, Martin, *Poverty Comparisons*, Harwood Academic Press (Chur: 1994).

——, "Measuring Aggregate Welfare in Developing Countries: How Well Do National Accounts and Surveys Agree?," unpublished, the World Bank (May 2000).

——, "Pro-Poor Growth: A Primer," Policy Research Working Paper No. 3242, World Bank (March 2004).

Robilliard, Anne-Sophie, François Bourguignon, and Sherman Robinson, "Crisis and Income Distribution: A Micro-Macro Model for Indonesia," unpublished, DIAL and IFPRI, Washington DC (2002).

Robilliard, Anne-Sophie, and Sherman Robinson, "Reconciling Household Surveys and National Accounts Data using Cross-Entropy Estimation," TMD Division Working Paper 50, IFPRI, Washington D.C. (1999).

Robinson, Sherman, "Macroeconomics, Financial Variables, and Computable General Equilibrium Models," *World Development*, 19 (November 1991), 1509–25.

Robinson, Sherman, Mary E. Burfisher, Raul Hinojosa-Ojeda, and Karen E. Thierfeldfer, "Agricultural Policies and Migration in a U.S.-Mexico Free Trade Area: A Computable General Equilibrium Analysis," *Journal of Policy Modeling*, 15 (November 1993), 673–701.

Robinson, Sherman, Antonio Yùnez-Naude, Raùl Hinojosa-Ojeda, Jeffrey D. Lewis, and Shantayanan Devarajan, "From Stylized to Applied Models: Building Multisector CGE Models for Policy Analysis," *North American Journal of Economics and Finance*, 10 (March 1999) 5–38.

Rodrik, Dani, "What Drives Public Employment in Developing Countries?," *Review of Development Economics*, 4 (October 2000), 229–43.

Rogerson, Richard, Robert Shimer, and Randall Wright, "Search-Theoretic Models of the Labor Market: A Survey," Working Paper No. 10655, National Bureau of Economic Research (August 2004).

Romer, Paul, "Poverty and Macroeconomic Activity," *Economic Review* (Federal Reserve Bank of Kansas, Mars 2000), 1–13.

Roodman, David, "The Anarchy of Numbers: Aid, Development, and Cross-Country Empirics," Working Paper No. 32, Center for Global Development (September 2003).

Rosensweig, Jeffrey, and Lance Taylor, "Devaluation, Capital Flows, and Crowding-Out: A CGE Model with Portfolio Choice for Thailand," in *Socially Relevant Policy Analysis*, ed. by Lance Taylor, MIT Press (Cambridge, Mass.: 1990).

Rosenzweig, Mark, "Labour Markets in Low-Income Countries," in Hollis Chenery, and T. N. Srinivasan, eds., *Handbook of Development Economics*, Vol. I, North Holland (Amsterdam: 1988).

Ruge-Murcia, Francisco J., "Credibility and Changes in Policy Regime," *Journal of Political Economy*, 103 (February 1995), 176–208.

Rutherford, Thomas F., E. Rustrom, and David Tarr, "L'accord de libre-échange entre le Maroc et la CEE : Une évaluation quantitative," *Revue d'Economie du Développement*, 1 (March 1994), 97–133.

Saavedra, Jaime, "Labor Markets during the 1990s," in *After the Washington Consensus: Restarting Growth and Reform in Latin America*, ed. by Pedro-Pablo Kuczynski and John Williamson, Institute of International Economics (Washington DC: 2003).

Sachs, Jeffrey, "The Debt Overhang of Developing Countries," in *Debt, Stabilization and Development*, ed. by Guillermo A. Calvo et al., Blackwell Publishing (Oxford: 1989).

Sahn, David E., and Stephen D. Younger, "Growth and Poverty Reduction in Sub-Saharan Africa: Macroeconomic Adjustment and Beyond," *Journal of African Economies*, 13 (July 2004), 66–95.

Said, Mona, "Public Sector Employment and Labor Markets in Arab Countries: Recent Developments and Policy Implications," in *Labor and Human Capital in the Middle East*, ed. by Djavad Salehi-Ishfahani, Ithaca Press (Reading, UK: 2001).

Saint-Paul, Gilles, "The Political Economy of Employment Protection," *Journal of Political Economy*, 110 (June 2002), 672–704.

Salman, Ferhan, "Balancing Turkey's Intertemporal Budget Gap," unpublished, Boston University (July 2003).

Sancak, Cemile, "Financial Liberalization and Real Investment: Evidence from Turkish Firms," Working Paper No. 02/100, International Monetary Fund (June 2002).

Sanchez-Robles, B., "Infrastructure Investment and Growth: Some Empirical Evidence," *Contemporary Economic Policy*, 16 (January 1998), 98–108.

Sanz, Ismael, and Francisco J. Velázquez, "The Composition of Public Expenditure and Growth: Different Models of Government Expenditure Distribution by Functions," unpublished, University of Madrid (August 2001).

Sarte, Pierre-Daniel, "Informality and Rent-Seeking Bureaucracies in a Model of Long-Run Growth," *Journal of Monetary Economics*, 46 (August 2000), 173–97.

Schaffner, Julie A., "Premiums to Employment in Larger Establishments: Evidence from Peru," *Journal of Development Economics*, 55 (February 1998), 81–113.

Schmidt-Hebbel, Klaus, and Tobias Muller, "Private Investment under Macroeconomic Adjustment in Morocco," in *Reviving Private Investment in Developing Countries*, ed. by Ajay Chhibber, Mansoor Dailami, and Nemat Shafik, North Holland (Amsterdam: 1992).

Schmidt-Sorensen, Jan B., "The Equilibrium-Wage Elasticity in Efficiency-Wage Models," *Economic Letters*, 32 (April 1990), 365–69.

Schneider, Friedrich, "Shadow Economies around the World: What Do We Really Know?," *European Journal of Political Economy*, 21 (September 2005), 598–642.

Schneider, Friedrich, and Dominik Enste, "Shadow Economies: Size, Causes, and Consequences," *Journal of Economic Literature*, 38 (March 2000), 77–114.

Schneider, Martin, and Aaron Tornell, "Balance Sheet Effects, Bailout Guarantees, and Financial Crises," *Review of Economic Studies*, 71 (July 2004), 883–913.

Servén, Luis, "Uncertainty, Instability, and Irreversible Investment: Theory, Evidence, and Lessons for Africa," PRE Working Paper No. 1722, the World Bank (February 1997).

Servén, Luis, "Macroeconomic Uncertainty and Private Investment in Developing Countries," PRE Working Paper No. 2035, the World Bank (December 1998).

Shapiro, Carl, and Joseph E. Stiglitz, "Equilibrium Unemployment as a Worker Discipline Device," *American Economic Review*, 74 (June 1984), 433–44.

Shorrocks, Anthony F., "Inequality Decomposition by Population Subgroup," *Econometrica*, 52 (September 1984), 1369–85.

Simonsen, Mario Henrique, "Indexation: Current Theory and the Brazilian Experience," in *Inflation, Debt, and Indexation*, ed. by Rudiger Dornbusch and Mario Henrique Simonsen, MIT Press (Cambridge, Mass.: 1983).

Soto, Claudio, "Unemployment and Consumption in Chile," Working Paper No. 258, Central Bank of Chile (May 2004).

Spaventa, Luigi, "The Growth of Public Debt," *IMF Staff Papers*, 34 (June 1987), 374–99.

Stark, Oded, *The Migration of Labor*, Blackwell Publishing (Oxford: 1991).

Stevenson, Gail, "How Public Sector Pay and Employment Affect Labor Markets," PRE Working Paper No. 944, the World Bank (August 1992).

Stiglitz, Joseph E., "Alternative Theories of Wage Determination and Unemployment in LDCs: The Labor Turnover Model," *Quarterly Journal of Economics*, 98 (May 1974), 194–227.

——, "Alternative Theories of Wage Determination and Unemployment: The Efficiency Wage Model," in *The Theory and Experience of Economic Development*, ed. by Mark Gersovitz et al., Allen and Unwin (London: 1982).

Stokey, Nancy L., "Free Trade, Factor Returns, and Factor Accumulation," *Journal of Economic Growth*, 1 (June 1996), 421–49.

Strand, Jon, "The Decline or Expansion of Unions: A Bargaining Model with Heterogeneous Labor," *European Journal of Political Economy*, 19 (June 2003), 317–40.

——, "Wage Bargaining versus Efficiency Wages: A Synthesis," *Bulletin of Economic Research*, 55 (January 2003), 1–20.

Svensson, Lars E. O., "What is Wrong with Taylor Rules? Using Judgment in Monetary Policy through Targeting Rules," *Journal of Economic Literature*, 41 (June 2003), 426–77.

Tansel, Aysit, "Wage Earners, Self Employed and Gender in the Informal Sector in Turkey," unpublished, Middle East Technical University (November 2000).

Tanzi, Vito, and Howell H. Zee, "Fiscal Policy and Long-Run Growth," *IMF Staff Papers*, 44 (June 1997), 179–209.

Taylor, Lance, *Structuralist Macroeconomics*, Basic Books (New York: 1983).

Taymaz, Erol, and Sule Ozler, "Labor Markets," unpublished presentation, Ankara (March 2003).

Thierfelder, Karen E., and Clinton R. Shiells, "Trade and Labor Market Behavior," in *Applied Methods for Trade Policy Analysis*, ed. by Joseph F. Francois and Kenneth A. Reinert, Cambridge University Press (Cambridge: 1997).

Thissen, Mark, "Financial CGE Models: Two Decades of Research," unpublished (June 1999).

——, *Building Financial CGE Models: Data, Parameters, and the Role of Expectations*, University of Groningen (Groningen: 2000).

Thissen, Mark, and Robert Lensink, "Macroeconomic Effects of a Currency Devaluation in Egypt: An Analysis with a Computable General Equilibrium Model with Financial Markets and Forward-Looking Expectations," *Journal of Policy Modeling*, 23 (May 2001), 411–19.

Thorbecke, Erik, in collaboration with B. Kim, Daniel Roland-Holst, and D. Berrian, "A Computable General Equilibrium Model Integrating Real and Financial Transactions," in *Adjustment and Equity in Indonesia*, ed. Erik Thorbecke, OECD Development Centre (Paris: 1992).

Tirole, Jean, "A Theory of Collective Reputations (with Applications to the Persistence of Corruption and to Firm Quality)," *Review of Economic Studies*, 63 (January 1996), 1–22.

Tornell, Aaron, and Frank Westermann, "Credit Market Imperfections in Middle-Income Countries," Working Paper No. 9737, National Bureau of Economic Research (May 2003).

Torvik, Ragnar, "Learning by Doing and the Dutch Disease," *European Economic Review*, 45 (February 2001), 285–306.

Touhami, Abdelkhalek, "Construction d'une matrice de comptabilité sociale de l'économie Marocaine : Base comptable du modèle IMMPA," unpublished monograph, INSEA (January 2003).

Townsend, Robert M., "Optimal Contracts and Competitive Markets with Costly State Verification," *Journal of Economic Theory*, 21 (October 1979), 265–93.

Tunali, Insan, "Background Study on Labour Market and Employment in Turkey," European training Foundation, Torino (June 2003).

Uctum, Merih, and Michael Wickens, "Debt and Deficit Ceilings, and Sustainability of Fiscal Policies: An Intertemporal Analysis," *Oxford Bulletin of Economics and Statistics*, 62 (May 2000), 197–222.

United Nations, *Escaping the Poverty Trap*, The Least Developed Countries Report 2002, United Nations Conference on Trade and Development (New York: 2002).

van Gompel, J., "Stabilization with Wage Indexation and Exchange Rate Flexibility," *Journal of Economic Surveys*, 8 (September 1994), 251–81.

van Wijnbergen, Sweder, "Stagflationary Effects of Monetary Stabilization Policies," *Journal of Development Economics*, 10 (April 1982), 133–69.

Velenchik, Ann D., "Cash Seeking Behavior and Migration: A Place-to-Place Migration Function for Côte d'Ivoire," *Journal of African Economies*, 2 (December 1993), 329–47.

——, "Government Intervention, Efficiency Wages, and the Employer Size Wage Effect in Zimbabwe," *Journal of Development Economics*, 53 (August 1997), 305–38.

Voyvoda, Ebru, and A. Erinç Yeldan, "Managing Turkish Debt: An OLG Investigation of the IMF's Fiscal Programming Model for Turkey," unpublished, Bilkent University (June 2003).

Wang, Eric C., "Public Infrastructure and Economic Growth: A New Approach Applied to East Asian Economies," *Journal of Policy Modeling*, 24 (August 2002), 411–35.

Wasmer, Etienne, and Philippe Weil, "The Macroeconomics of Labour and Credit Market Imperfections," *American Economic Review*, 94 (September 2004), 944–63.

Webber, Don J., "Policies to Stimulate Growth: Should we Invest in Health or Education?," *Applied Economics*, 34 (September 2002), 1633–43.

Weiss, Andrew, "Job Queues and Layoffs in Labor Markets with Flexible Wages," *Journal of Political Economy*, 88 (June 1980), 526–38.

——, *Efficiency Wages*, Oxford University Press (Oxford: 1991).

Winters, L. Alan, Neil McCulloch, and Andrew McKay, "Trade Liberalization and Poverty: The Evidence So Far," *Journal of Economic Literature*, 42 (March 2004), 72–115.

World Bank, *Investing in Infrastructure*, World Development Report 1994, Oxford University Press (New York: 1994).

——, *Workers in An Integrating World*, World Development Report (Washington, DC: 1995).

——, "Kingdom of Morocco: Public Expenditure Review," draft, Social and Economic Development Group (MNSED), Middle East and North Africa, Washington, DC (December 2002).

——, *Turkey Country Economic Memorandum: Towards Macroeconomic Stability and Sustained Growth*, 3 Volumes, the World Bank (May 2003).

——, *Unlocking the Employment Potential in the Middle East and North Africa: Towards a New Social Contract*, World Bank (Washington DC: 2004).

——, *Millennium Development Goals: From Consensus to Momentum*, Global Monitoring Report 2005, World Bank (Washington DC: 2005).

Wyplosz, Charles, "Fiscal Discipline in Emerging Market Countries: How to Go About It?," unpublished, Graduate Institute for International Studies, Geneva (May 2002).

Xie, Danyang, and Chi-Wa Yuen, "A Dynamic General Equilibrium Framework of Investment with Financing Constraints," *IMF Staff Papers*, 50 (July 2003), 274–90.

Yamada, Gustavo, "Urban Informal Employment and Self-Employment in Developing Countries: Theory and Evidence," *Economic Development and Cultural Change*, 44 (January 1996), 289–314.

Yeldan, A. Erinç, "Financial Liberalization and Fiscal Repression in Turkey: Policy Analysis in a CGE Model With Financial Markets," *Journal of Policy Modeling*, 19 (February 1997), 79–117.

——, "On Structural Sources of the 1994 Turkish Crisis: A CGE Modelling Analysis," *International Review of Applied Economics*, 12 (September 1998), 397–414.

Yilmaz, Akyüz, and Korkut Boratav, "The Making of the Turkish Financial Crisis," *World Development*, 31 (September 2003), 1549–66.

Young, Eric R., "Unemployment Insurance and Capital Accumulation," *Journal of Monetary Economics*, 51 (November 2004), 1683–710.

Zeufack, Albert G., "Structure de propriété et comportement d'investissement en environnement incertain," *Revue d'Economie du Développement*, 5 (March 1997), 29–59.